The first person to invent a car that runs on water…

… may be sitting right in your classroom! Every one of your students has the potential to make a difference. And realizing that potential starts right here, in your course.

When students succeed in your course—when they stay on-task and make the breakthrough that turns confusion into confidence—they are empowered to realize the possibilities for greatness that lie within each of them. We know your goal is to create an environment where students reach their full potential and experience the exhilaration of academic success that will last them a lifetime. *WileyPLUS* can help you reach that goal.

Wiley**PLUS** is an online suite of resources—including the complete text—that will help your students:

- come to class better prepared for your lectures
- get immediate feedback and context-sensitive help on assignments and quizzes
- track their progress throughout the course

"I just wanted to say how much this program helped me in studying… I was able to actually see my mistakes and correct them. … I really think that other students should have the chance to use *WileyPLUS*."

Ashlee Krisko, *Oakland University*

www.wiley.com/college/wileyplus

WILEY **PLUS**

80% of students surveyed said it improved their understanding of the material.*

FOR INSTRUCTORS

WileyPLUS is built around the activities you perform in your class each day. With WileyPLUS y

Prepare & Present
Create outstanding class presentations using a wealth of resources such as PowerPoint™ slides, image galleries, interactive simulations, and more. You can even add materials you have created yourself.

Create Assignments
Automate the assigning and grading of homework or quizzes by using the provided question banks, or by writing your own.

Track Student Progress
Keep track of your students' and analyze individual and ov results.

Now Available with WebCT and Blac

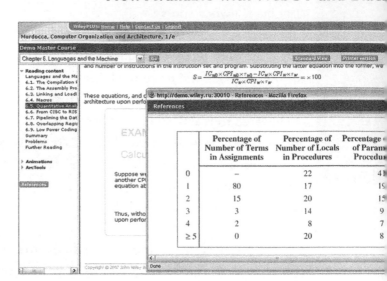

"It has been a great help, and I believe it has helped me to achieve a better grade."

Michael Morris,
Columbia Basin College

FOR STUDENTS

You have the potential to make a difference!

WileyPLUS is a powerful online system packed with features to help you make the most of your potential and get the best grade you can!

With WileyPLUS you get:

- A complete online version of your text and other study resources.
- Problem-solving help, instant grading, and feedback on your homework and quizzes.
- The ability to track your pr and grades throughout the

For more information on what *WileyPLUS* can do to help you and your students reach their potential, please visit www.wiley.com/college/*wileyplus*.

76% of students surveyed said it made them better prepared for tests.*

*Based on a survey of 972 student users of *WileyPLUS*

COMPUTER ARCHITECTURE
AND ORGANIZATION:
AN INTEGRATED APPROACH

1807
⊛WILEY
2007

BICENTENNIAL
BICENTENNIAL
BICENTENNIAL
BICENTENNIAL

THE WILEY BICENTENNIAL—KNOWLEDGE FOR GENERATIONS

*E*ach generation has its unique needs and aspirations. When Charles Wiley first opened his small printing shop in lower Manhattan in 1807, it was a generation of boundless potential searching for an identity. And we were there, helping to define a new American literary tradition. Over half a century later, in the midst of the Second Industrial Revolution, it was a generation focused on building the future. Once again, we were there, supplying the critical scientific, technical, and engineering knowledge that helped frame the world. Throughout the 20th Century, and into the new millennium, nations began to reach out beyond their own borders and a new international community was born. Wiley was there, expanding its operations around the world to enable a global exchange of ideas, opinions, and know-how.

For 200 years, Wiley has been an integral part of each generation's journey, enabling the flow of information and understanding necessary to meet their needs and fulfill their aspirations. Today, bold new technologies are changing the way we live and learn. Wiley will be there, providing you the must-have knowledge you need to imagine new worlds, new possibilities, and new opportunities.

Generations come and go, but you can always count on Wiley to provide you the knowledge you need, when and where you need it!

WILLIAM J. PESCE
PRESIDENT AND CHIEF EXECUTIVE OFFICER

PETER BOOTH WILEY
CHAIRMAN OF THE BOARD

COMPUTER ARCHITECTURE AND ORGANIZATION: AN INTEGRATED APPROACH

MILES J. MURDOCCA
Internet Institute USA

VINCENT P. HEURING
University of Colorado

John Wiley & Sons, Inc.

EXECUTIVE PUBLISHER	Don Fowley
ASSOCIATE PUBLISHER	Dan Sayre
SENIOR ACQUISITIONS EDITOR	Catherine Fields Shultz
PROJECT EDITOR	Gladys Soto
EDITORIAL ASSISTANT	Chelsee Pengal
SENIOR PRODUCTION EDITOR	Ken Santor
COVER DESIGNER	Hope Miller
COVER PHOTO	© Jook Leung
BICENTENNIAL LOGO DESIGN	Richard J. Pacifico

This book was set in Framemaker by Preparé, Inc.
The cover was printed by Phoenix Color.

This book is printed on acid free paper. ∞

ISBN-13   978-0-471-73388-1

10 9 8 7 6 5 4 3 2 1

For Ellen, Alexandra, and Nicole
and
For Gretchen

Wiley Series in Electrical and Computer Engineering

PREFACE

Welcome to *Computer Architecture and Organization: An Integrated Approach*. Our goal in writing this book is to expose the inner workings of the modern digital computer at a level that demystifies what goes on inside the machine. The only prerequisite to *Computer Architecture and Organization* is a working knowledge of a high-level programming language. The breadth of material has been chosen to cover topics normally found in a first course in computer architecture or computer organization. The breadth and depth of coverage have also been steered to place the beginning student on a solid track for continuing studies in computer-related disciplines.

In preparation for further studies, this book is consistent with the most recent IEEE/ACM Computing Curricula in Computer Science:

http://www.computer.org/education/cc2001/final/cc2001.pdf

and provides complete coverage of the GRE Subject Area test in Computer Science for computer architecture:

http://www.gre.org/subjtest.html

In creating a computer architecture textbook, the choices of topics fall into place fairly naturally, and it is the organizational issues that bring important features to fruition. Some of the features that receive the greatest attention in *Computer Architecture and Organization* include the instruction set architecture (ISA), the coverage of network-related topics, the programming methodology, and a voluminous use of case studies, examples, and exercises. Networking in particular has emerged as a significant aspect of computer architecture, and is treated as a continuing thread throughout the book.

The Instruction Set Architecture

A textbook that covers assembly language programming needs to deal with the issue of which ISA to use: either one of the many commercial architectures, or a simplified teaching architecture. The choice of ISA impacts the instructor's delivery of the material; the instructor may want an ISA that matches a local platform used for student assembly language programming assignments. To complicate matters, the local platform may change from semester to semester: yesterday the MIPS, today the SPARC or ARM, and tomorrow something else. We opted for having it both ways by adopting a subset of a real-world processor (the SPARC) for an instructional ISA, called "A RISC Computer" (ARC), which is carried through the mainstream of the book, and complementing it with platform-independent software tools that simulate the ARC ISA.

Case Studies, Examples, and Exercises

Every chapter contains case studies that introduce the student to "real world" examples of topics covered. A case study can place a topic in perspective and, in the authors' opinion, lends an air of reality and interest to the material.

There has been a historical competition for market share between the Intel and Motorola processor lines, with notable developments along the way. Each chapter has a boxed feature covering a different aspect of the competition, keyed to the chapter content.

We incorporated as many examples and exercises as we practically could, covering the most significant points in the text. In addition, there is a wealth of additional problems with solutions posted on the book Website at: `www.wiley.com/college/murdocca`.

■ COVERAGE OF TOPICS

Our presentation views a computer as an integrated system. The subtitle for the book, "An Integrated Approach," reflects the high-level threads that tie the material together. Each topic is covered in the context of the entire machine of which it is a part, and with a perspective as to how the implementation affects behavior. For example, the finite precision of binary numbers is brought to bear in observing how many 1s can be added to a floating-point number before the error in the representation exceeds 1. As another example, subroutine linkage is covered with the expectation that the reader may someday be faced with writing C, Java, or assembly language programs that make calls to code in other high-level languages.

As yet another example of the integrated approach, a networking thread is woven throughout the chapters. At appropriate places throughout the text, network considerations are exposed and are placed in context with respect to the topic under discussion. Error detection and correction are covered in the context of networking, with the expectation that the reader may tackle networking applications in which bit errors and data packet losses are commonplace.

Computer architecture has an impact on many of the ordinary things that computer professionals do, and taking an integrated approach addresses the great diversity of areas in which a computer professional should be educated. This emphasis reflects a transition that is taking place in many computer-related undergraduate curricula. As computer architectures become more complex they must be treated at greater levels of abstraction, and in some ways they also become more technology dependent, which places a focus on the lower levels as well. For this reason, the major portion of the text deals with a high-level look at computer architecture, while the appendix and case studies cover lower-level, technology-dependent aspects.

The Chapters

Chapter 1: Introduction This chapter lays the groundwork for the rest of the book. It begins with a brief history of the digital computer, and then discusses the computer system at various levels of abstraction. The conventional von Neumann model of a digital computer is introduced, followed by the System Bus Model, followed by a topical exploration of a typical computer. An emphasis is placed on the network as an integral part of the computer system.

Chapter 2: Data Representation covers basic data representation, beginning with unsigned binary numbers, and progressing to one's and two's complement, signed magnitude, and excess representations of signed numbers. The representation of floating-point numbers is covered, including the IEEE 754 floating-point standard. The chapter concludes with a discussion of the ASCII, EBCDIC, and Unicode character codes.

Chapter 3: Arithmetic covers computer arithmetic and advanced data representations. Fixed-point addition, subtraction, multiplication, and division are covered for signed and unsigned integers. Floating-point arithmetic is also covered. High-performance methods such as carry-lookahead addition, array multiplication, and division by functional iteration are covered. A short discussion of residue arithmetic introduces an unconventional high-performance approach.

A networking example is covered in which one's complement addition is applied to the calculation of checksums in packet headers.

Chapter 4: The Instruction Set Architecture introduces the basic architectural components involved in program execution. Machine language and the fetch-execute cycle are covered. The organization of a central processing unit is detailed, and the role of the system bus in interconnecting the arithmetic/logic unit, registers, memory, input and output units, and the control unit are discussed.

Assembly language programming is covered in the context of the instructional ARC (A RISC Computer), which is loosely based on the commercial SPARC architecture. The instruction names, instruction formats, data formats, and the assembly language syntax for the commercial SPARC are retained in the ARC, but a number of simplifications have been made. Only the most important instructions for the examples and problems used in the book are discussed, and only a 32-bit unsigned integer data type is allowed initially (but is expanded to byte and halfword operations in Appendix B and the supporting ARC-Tools). This subset makes it possible to work with real-world code while maintaining sufficient simplicity for short classroom presentations. Instruction formats and addressing modes are covered. Subroutine linkage is explored in a number of styles, with a detailed discussion of parameter passing using a stack. A case study covers the Java Virtual Machine (JVM).

This chapter also covers procedural programming with the expectation that the student may have learned object-oriented programming (OOP) as the primary method of high-level language programming. While OOP is very important for high-level languages, procedural programming is important for efficiency and expression when it comes to exploiting architecture-specific features such as for embedded systems and for device driver development.

Chapter 5: Datapath and Control provides a step-by-step analysis of the datapath and control unit. Two methods of control are discussed: microprogrammed and hardwired. The instructor may adopt one method and omit the other, or cover both methods as time permits. The example microprogrammed and hardwired control units implement the ARC instruction set.

Chapter 6: Languages and the Machine connects the programmer's view of a computer system with the architecture of the underlying machine. System software issues are covered with the goal of making the low-level machine visible to a programmer. The chapter starts with an explanation of the compilation process, first covering the steps involved in compilation, and then focusing on code generation. The assembly process is described for a two-pass assembler, and examples are given of generating symbol tables. Linking, loading, and macros are also covered.

Computer professionals should understand how low-level architecture details impact efficiency. Efficiency at all levels has gained in importance, because the high-level programming tools that simplify the programmer's job can unfortunately mask low-level details that influence the efficiency of an application.

Chapter 6 covers a number of topics that expose significant aspects of hardware and programming efficiency:

- pipelining;
- exploiting architecture-specific features that are not generally available in high-level languages (such as instruction reordering);
- optimizing code for low power applications.

The latter part of the chapter covers the motivation for reduced instruction set computer (RISC) processors, and the architectural implications of RISC. A case study makes RISC features visible to the programmer in a step-by-step analysis of a C compiler-generated ARC program, with explanations of the stack frame usage, register usage, and pipelining.

Chapter 7: Memory covers computer memory beginning with the organization of a basic random access memory, and moving to advanced concepts such as cache and virtual memory. The traditional direct, associative, and set-associative cache-mapping schemes are covered, along with multilevel caches. Issues such as overlays, replacement policies, segmentation, fragmentation, and the translation lookaside buffer are also discussed.

Chapter 8: Input, Output, and Devices covers bus communication and bus access methods. Bus-to-bus bridging is described. The chapter covers various input/output (I/O) devices in common use such as keyboards, mice, tablets, printers, and displays. Current I/O directions have moved away from parallel communication and toward high-speed serial communication, such as USB, Firewire, and wireless. Some inside-the-box interconnection approaches make use of switching fabrics, which is a new direction for workstation/laptop architectures that has migrated from server architectures. The outside-the-box connectivity offers ports to which many devices can be simultaneously connected, which is a departure from the traditional fixed, special-purpose ports that would be reserved for a printer, mouse, keyboard, etc.

Magnetic and optical storage technologies such as rotating magnetic disks and redundant arrays of inexpensive disks (RAID) technology, magnetic tape and optical disks are covered. Case studies cover a graphics processing unit and how viruses infect a machine.

Chapter 9: Communication covers network architectures, focusing on both local-area networks and wide-area networks. The emphasis is on network component architecture rather than network protocols (which could fill volumes), with just enough discussions of protocols to highlight key features of network architecture. The TCP/IP protocol suite is introduced in the context of the Internet. Error detection and correction are covered. The chapter covers an important emerging application of networking: the storage area network (SAN), in which a distributed network of storage devices improves access times and provides fault tolerance. The chapter concludes with a case study of a router network architecture, highlighting the internal components that give it the characteristics of a conventional computer.

Chapter 10: Advanced Computer Architecture covers advanced architectural features that have either emerged or taken new forms in recent years. The chapter covers parallel and distributed architectures, interconnection networks used in parallel and distributed processing, and performance metrics. The chapter covers multiple instruction issue machines, and very large instruction word (VLIW) machines. Application-specific integrated circuits (ASICs) and field programmable gate arrays (FPGAs) are also covered. The chapter concludes with a few unconventional architectural approaches.

Appendix A: Digital Logic covers combinational logic and sequential logic, and provides a foundation for understanding the logical makeup of components discussed in the rest of the book. Appendix A begins with a description of truth tables, Boolean algebra, and logic equations. The synthesis of combinational logic circuits is described, and a number of examples are explored. Medium-scale integration (MSI) components such as multiplexers and decoders are discussed, and examples of synthesizing circuits using MSI components are explored.

Synchronous logic is also covered in Appendix A, starting with an introduction to timing issues that relate to flip-flops. The synthesis of synchronous logic circuits is covered with respect to state transition diagrams, state tables, and synchronous logic designs.

Finally, methods are covered for the reduction of combinational and sequential logic. Minimization is covered using algebraic reduction, Karnaugh maps, and the Quine-McCluskey method for single and multiple functions. State reduction is also covered.

Appendix B: Using ARCTools covers the ARCTools suite of tools, which includes an assembler and a simulator for the ARC ISA used throughout the book. See below for more on ARCTools.

Chapter Ordering

The order of chapters is created so that the chapters can be taught in numerical order, but an instructor can modify the ordering to suit a particular curriculum and syllabus. Figure P-1 shows prerequisite relationships among the chapters. Special considerations regarding chapter sequencing are detailed below.

Chapter 2 (Data Representation) should be covered prior to Chapter 3 (Arithmetic), which has the greatest need for it. Appendix A (Digital Logic) can be omitted if digital logic is covered earlier in the curriculum, but if the material is not covered, then the structure of some components (such as an arithmetic logic unit or a register) will remain a mystery in later chapters if Appendix A is not covered before Chapter 3.

Chapter 4 (The Instruction Set Architecture) appears in the early half of the book for two reasons: (1) it introduces the student to the workings of a computer at a fairly high level, which allows a top-down approach to the study of computer architecture; and (2) it is important to get started on assembly language programming early if hands-on

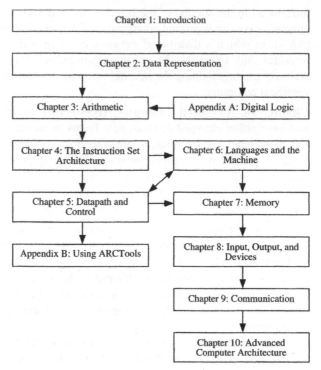

Figure P-1
Preequisite relationships among chapters.

programming is part of the course. Appendix B (Using ARCTools) supports the ARC ISA that is introduced in this chapter.

Chapter 5 (Datapath and Control) is designed to flow naturally after Chapter 4, although Chapter 5 can be delayed until after Chapter 6 (Languages and the Machine) so that all of the assembly language topics are covered together. The chapters were written to support either order.

The remaining chapters are intended to appear in numerical order but the instructor is encouraged to modify the order to suit the needs of the course. For example, the material in Chapter 10 (Advanced Computer Architecture) typically appears in higher-level architecture courses, and should therefore be covered only as time permits, after the material in the earlier chapters is covered.

■ THE COMPANION WEB SITE

A companion Web site

www.wiley.com/college/murdocca

pairs with this textbook. The companion Web site contains a wealth of supporting material such as the ARCTools software, Powerpoint slides, practice problems with solutions, and errata. Solutions for all of the problems in the book are available from the publisher for textbook adopters.

Software Tools

We provide the ARCTools assembler and simulator for the ARC subset of the SPARC instruction set. Written as Java applications for easy portability for Windows, Unix, Mac OS X, and other platforms, these tools are available via download from the companion Web site. The tools support the examples used in the book, and have several new features including support for input and output, halfword and byte data types, and several new instructions.

Slides

All of the figures and tables in *Computer Architecture and Organization* are available as Powerpoint slides and also in Adobe Acrobat format. The slides can be downloaded from the companion Web site.

Animations

Several interactive animations have been developed that support various course topics. An animation covering cache memory visibly exposes the behavior of a cache as it fills. Other animations cover number representation, arithmetic, input/output handshaking and more.

Practice Problems and Solutions

The problems and solutions (available from Wiley for instructors who adopt the book) have been fully class tested. The problems are numerous enough to serve as exam and quiz problems, and to also serve as practice problems for review sessions at the instructor's discretion. There are additional problems and solutions posted on the companion Web site that mirror the textbook problems. The student is encouraged to make use of this valuable resource.

■ IF YOU FIND AN ERROR

In spite of the best of the best efforts of the authors, editors, reviewers, and class testers, this book undoubtedly contains errors. If you find one, check online at the authors' companion Web site http://iiusatech.com/murdocca/CAO to see if it has been catalogued. You can report errors to caobugs@iiusatech.com. Please mention the chapter number where the error occurs in the Subject: header line.

■ CREDITS AND ACKNOWLEDGMENTS

We did not create this book entirely on our own, and we gratefully acknowledge the support of many people for their influence in the preparation of the book and on our thinking in general. We first wish to thank our Executive/Acquisitions Editors, William Zobrist and

Catherine Schultz, who had the foresight and vision to guide this book and its supporting materials through to completion. Saul Levy, Donald Smith, Vidyadhar Phalke, Ajay Bakre, Jinsong Huang, and Srimat Chakradhar helped test the material in courses at Rutgers, and provided some of the text, problems, and valuable explanations. Brian Davison and Shridhar Venkatanarisam worked on an early version of the solutions and provided many helpful comments. Irving Rabinowitz provided a number of problem sets. Ulrich Kremer was an important influence on the low power discussions. Ann Yasuhara provided text on Turing's contributions to computer science. Hilary Kahn provided several helpful details and corrections for the University of Manchester machine and other historically significant projects. William Waite provided a number of the assembly language examples.

The reviewers, whose names we do not know, are gratefully acknowledged for their help in steering the project. Ann Root did a superb job on the initial development of the supporting ARCTools suite, which was further developed and enhanced into its current form by Michael Wilson. Jeania Kimbrough contributed Web resources and encouragement throughout the project. Daniel Desormeaux and Arif Rahman did a great job of capturing the key elements in coding the animations. The Rutgers University and University of Colorado student populations provided important proving grounds for the material, and we are grateful for their patience and recommendations while the book was under development.

I (MJM) was encouraged by my parents Dolores and Nicholas Murdocca, my sister MaryBeth, and my brother Mark. My wife Ellen and my daughters Alexandra and Nicole have been an endless source of encouragement and inspiration. I do not think I could have found the energy for such an undertaking without all of their support.

I (VPH) wish to acknowledge the support of my wife Gretchen, who was exceedingly patient and encouraging throughout the process of writing this book.

There are surely other people and institutions who have contributed to this book, either directly or indirectly, whose names we have inadvertently omitted. To those people and institutions we offer our tacit appreciation and apologize for having omitted explicit recognition here.

Miles J. Murdocca
Internet Institute USA
murdocca@iiusatech.com

Vincent P. Heuring
University of Colorado at Boulder
heuring@colorado.edu

CONTENTS

CHAPTER 1

INTRODUCTION

Computer architecture deals with the functional behavior of a computer system as viewed by a programmer. This view includes aspects such as the sizes of data types (e.g. 32 binary digits represent an integer) and the types of operations that are supported (like addition, subtraction, and subroutine calls). *Computer organization* deals with structural relationships that may not be visible to the programmer, such as interfaces to peripheral devices, the clock frequency, and the technology used for the memory. This textbook deals with both architecture and organization, with the term "architecture" referring broadly to both architecture and organization.

There is a concept of *levels* in computer architecture. The basic idea is that there are many levels, or views, at which a computer can be considered, from the highest level, where the user is running programs, to the lowest level, consisting of transistors and wires. Between the highest and lowest levels are a number of intermediate levels. The purpose of stratifying computer architecture into levels is that it helps manage the complexity of computers by considering each level on its own, without getting distracted by details of the other levels.

Before we discuss those levels, we will present a brief history of computing in order to gain a perspective on how it all came about. The history of computing is rich with personalities, events, and advances, and there is enough to write volumes on the subject. For the purpose of introduction, the next section covers just a few of the more celebrated architectural advances (like the development of mechanical calculating devices) as opposed to mathematical advances (such as the adoption of zero in Chinese mathematics, ca. 800 A.D.).

1.1 A BRIEF HISTORY OF COMPUTING

Even before recorded history, humans have used objects to represent information. As far back as 25,000–30,000 B.C., counting, or "tallying", was done by making notches in objects such as bones. A wolf bone (Figure 1-1) found in Czechoslovakia in 1937 dating back to this era, which corresponds to the appearance of Cro-Magnon man, shows 55 cuts in two series of groups of five in which a notch of double length separates the first 25 from the rest.

People naturally count with their fingers, thus the use of groups of fives in the wolf bone, and the rise of the base 10 number system. As civilization progressed, other methods of tallying were developed such as **tally sticks** which were used in England as recently as the 1800s, and knots in cords, pebbles in bags, beads on a wire, etc.

Figure 1-1
Wolf radius bone ca. 25,000–30,000 B.C. showing 55 cuts in groups of five, suggesting a
rudimentary form of multiplication or division. (Source: *Illustrated London News*, October 2, 1937.)

A tally stick (Figure 1-2) is a form of a receipt, and can be traded or sold much as loan
portfolios are bought and sold today. Cuts are made indicating the amount of money paid.
The stick is then split lengthwise with the larger piece going to the payee and the smaller
piece being kept by the payer. No two sticks split exactly the same way, and so this
method of bookkeeping provides protection from forgeries.

With the invention of the abacus in Babylonia (ca. 3000 B.C.) came the widespread use
of a **weighted position code**, in which digits (abacus columns) have increasing significance
as we move to the left. The modern wire and bead abacus was developed around 1300 A.D.
(Figure 1-3), in which each column has two **Heaven** beads on the top and five **Earth** beads
on the bottom, with the Heaven and Earth beads separated by the **Bar**. Each of the two
Heaven beads are worth five Earth beads, and a single column can take on a value from 0
to 9, with an additional six values (10 to 15) used for intermediate calculations.

Figure 1-3 shows the representation of 39,017 on the abacus. Each column corresponds to a digit in the number. In order to represent 0, all five Earth beads in a column are

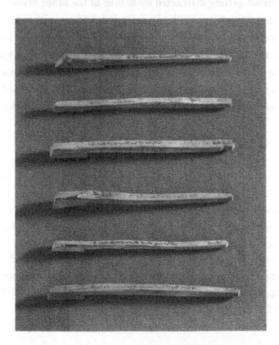

Figure 1-2
Original wooden tally sticks from
Westminster, England,
ca. 1250–1275 A.D.
© SSPL/The ImageWorks.

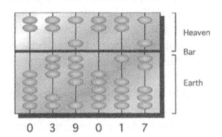

Figure 1-3
Representation of 39,017 on a Chinese abacus.

Figure 1-4
Victorian Swiss cylinder music box, dated 1862. (Source: http://www.liveauctioneers.com/auctions/ebay/497199.html.)

lowered away from the Bar, and the two Heaven beads are raised away from the Bar. In order to represent 1, 2, 3, or 4, the corresponding number of Earth beads are raised. For 5, 6, 7, 8, or 9, one Heaven bead is lowered and zero, one, two, three, or four Earth beads are raised, respectively. The additional bead combinations that represent 10–15 are used for carries when adding and for borrows when subtracting. The abacus is effective as a counting/calculating device and is still used in commerce in some regions.

Mechanical devices for controlling complex operations have been in existence since at least the 1500s, when rotating pegged cylinders were used in music boxes much as they are today (Figure 1-4). Machines that perform calculations, as opposed to simply repeating a predetermined melody, came in the next century.

Blaise Pascal (1623–1662) developed a mechanical calculator to help in his father's tax work. The Pascal calculator **Pascaline** contains eight dials that connect to a drum (Figure 1-5), with an innovative linkage that causes a dial to rotate one notch when a carry is

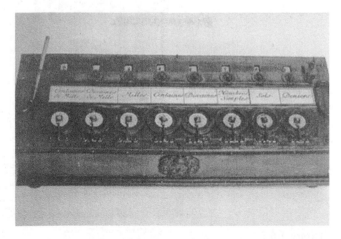

Figure 1-5
Pascal's calculating machine. (Reproduced from an IBM Archives photograph.)

produced from a dial in a lower position. A window is placed over the dial to allow its position to be observed, much like the odometer in a car except that the dials are positioned horizontally, like a rotary telephone dial. Some of Pascal's adding machines, which he started to build in 1642, still exist today. It would not be until the 1800s, however, until someone would put the concepts of mechanical control and mechanical calculation together into a machine that we recognize today as having the basic parts of a digital computer. That person was Charles Babbage.

Charles Babbage (1791–1871) is sometimes referred to as the grandfather of the computer, rather than the father of the computer, because he never built a practical version of the machines he designed. Babbage lived in England at a time when mathematical tables were used in navigation and scientific work. The tables were computed manually, and as a result, they contained numerous errors. Frustrated by the inaccuracies, Babbage set out to create a machine that would compute tables by simply setting and turning gears. The machine he designed would even produce a plate to be used by a printer, thus eliminating errors that might be introduced by a typesetter.

Figure 1-6 shows a portion of Babbage's Difference Engine No. 1, which was assembled by his chief engineer Joseph Clement in 1832. This portion represents one seventh of the machine, which was never completed.

Babbage's machines had a means for reading input data, storing data, performing calculations, producing output data, and automatically controlling the operation of the machine. These are basic functions that are found in nearly every modern computer. Babbage created a small prototype of his Difference Engine (Figure 1-6), which evaluates polynomials using the method of finite differences. The success of the difference engine concept gained him government support for the much larger Analytical Engine. This more

Figure 1-6
Working portion of Babbage's Difference Engine No. 1, which is the first known automatic calculator. © SSPL/The ImageWorks.

Figure 1-7
The Jacquard pattern weaving loom (ca. 1804). (Source: by Joseph-Marie Jacquard,
http://www.deutsches-museum.de/ausstell/meister/e_web.htm.)

sophisticated machine had a mechanism for branching (making decisions) and a means for programming, using punched cards in the manner of the Jacquard pattern-weaving loom (Figure 1-7), in which a hole in a punched card determines whether a vertical **weft** thread is raised or lowered on each pass of the harness that passes the horizontal **gut** thread. Complex patterns are created by raising selected weft threads on each pass of the harness.

The Analytical Engine was designed, but was never built by Babbage because the mechanical tolerances required by the design could not be met with the technology of the day. A version of Babbage's Difference Engine No. 2 was actually built by the Science Museum in London in 1991, and can still be viewed today.

It took over a century, until the start of World War II, before the next major thrust in computing was initiated. In England, German U-boat submarines were inflicting heavy damage on Allied shipping. The U-boats received communications from their bases in Germany using an encryption code, which was implemented by a machine made by Siemens AG known as Enigma (Figure 1-8).

The process of encrypting information had been known for a long time, and even the United States president Thomas Jefferson (1743–1826) designed a forerunner of Enigma, though he did not construct the machine. The process of decoding encrypted data was a much harder task. It was this problem that prompted the efforts of Alan Turing (1912–1954) and other scientists in England in creating codebreaking machines. During World War II, Turing was the leading cryptographer in England and was among those who changed cryptography from a subject for people who deciphered ancient languages to a subject for mathematicians. It is at Bletchley Park, England that Turing developed the "Bombe," which could break Enigma enciphered messages.

Figure 1-8
Siemens Halkse T-52 Sturgeon (Enigma) cipher machine. (Source: Photo and copy courtesy John Alexander, G7GCK Leicester, England. See http://www.jproc.ca/crypto/sturg.html.)

The Colossus (Figure 1-9) was a successful codebreaking machine that came out of Bletchley Park, It was based on a concept developed by Max Newman (1897–1984) and designed and constructed by Tommy Flowers (1905–1998). Its purpose was to break the Lorenz encoding. Vacuum tubes in the Colossus store the contents of a paper tape that is fed into the machine, and computations take place among the vacuum tubes and a second tape that is fed into the machine. Programming is performed with plugboards.

Figure 1-9
The Colossus (ca. 1944). (Source: http://www.turing.org.uk/turing/scrapbook/electronic.html.)

Figure 1-10
The ENIAC. Time & Life Pictures/Getty Images.

Around the same time as Turing's efforts on the Bombe, J. Presper Eckert and John Mauchly set out to create a machine that could be used to compute tables of ballistic trajectories for the U.S. Army. The result of the Eckert-Mauchly effort was the Electronic Numerical Integrator And Computer (ENIAC). The ENIAC (Figure 1-10) consists of 18,000 vacuum tubes, which make up the computing section of the machine. Programming and data entry are performed by setting switches and changing cables. There is no concept of a stored program, and there is no central memory unit, but these are not serious limitations because all that the ENIAC needed to do was to compute ballistic trajectories. Even though it did not become operational until 1946, after World War II was over, it was considered quite a success, and was used for nine years.

After the success of ENIAC, Eckert and Mauchly, who were at the Moore School at the University of Pennsylvania, were joined by John von Neumann (1903–1957), who was at the Institute for Advanced Study at Princeton. Together, they worked on the design of a stored program computer called the EDVAC. A conflict developed, however, and the Pennsylvania and Princeton groups split. The concept of a stored program computer thrived, however, and construction of a stored program computer loosely based on the EDVAC ideas, the EDSAC, was started by Maurice Wilkes, of Cambridge University, in 1947. The EDSAC became operational in May, 1949, and the EDVAC did not become operational in 1951.

The first working demonstration of a stored program computer, however, was designed and developed by FC Williams (1911–1977) and Tom Kilbum (1921–2001) at the University of Manchester. This was the Small Scale Experimental Machine (known as the "Baby") on June 21, 1948. Enhancements to the Baby led to the Manchester Mark 1, which became fully operational in October, 1949. The Manchester Mark 1 is notable for the demonstration of a number of innovations, such as a magnetic drum for auxiliary storage.

Two significant developments propelled computing technology beyond the World War II era computers in the years to come: **transistors** and **integrated circuits**. The transistor, invented in 1947 by William Bradford Shockley, John Bardeen, and Walter Houser

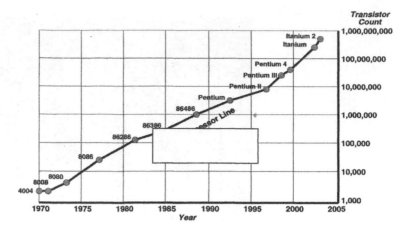

Figure 1-11
Moore's Law. (Source: http://www.intel.com/research/mooreslaw.htm.)

Brittain at AT&T Bell Labs, is a so-called **solid state device** (because it is based on solid state physics, which deals with crystals) that replaced the bulkier vacuum tubes that would burn out periodically. The transistor allowed denser circuits running at lower powers and greater reliability, and at much less expense. The transistor at the time was a discrete device, which means that it was packaged as a single component.

Building on the success of the transistor, the development of the integrated circuit almost simultaneously at Texas Instruments by Jack Kilby (1958) and at Fairchild Semi-conductor by Robert Noyce (1959) used a photolithographic process to fabricate multiple devices (like transistors, resistors, and capacitors) on the same crystal in a single packaged component. Further advances led to the development of the Intel 4004 microprocessor in 1971, which contained thousands of devices in a single packaged component.

Through continuing innovations, transistor density has doubled roughly every 18 months, as described by Moore's law, attributed to Intel founder Gordon Moore who reported on the trend in 1965. While this doubling cannot continue forever, it is expected to continue through the first decade of 2000 (Figure 1-11). Figure 1-12 shows a top-level view of a **very large scale integrated (VLSI)** circuit. Areas are marked showing the cache memories (I-cache, Data cache, L2/L3 areas, TLB), which are covered in later chapters, floating point unit (FPU), instruction logic, processor cores C0 and C1, System (Bus) Interface Unit (SIU), which matches cache line lengths with the width of the bus (covered later in the book), memory control unit (MCU), and other areas. Interestingly, the instruction logic and processor cores, which are the heart of a processor, account for less than half of the area. Most of the area is devoted to memory. Approximately 70% of an integrated circuit is made up of wires, some of which are visible in the metallization layer on the top, while the rest is made up primarily of switching devices such as transistors and storage elements.

Even with all of the technological advances in computing over the years, the basic principles have not changed greatly. Some of the most basic principles are covered in the next few sections, starting with the **von Neumann model.** Despite the simplicity of these

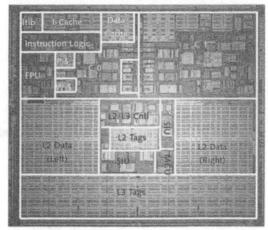

Figure 1-12
Die photo of Ultrasparc IV+, 295 million transistors, 19.7 mm × 17.0 mm. (Source: "Best Servers of 2004", Kevin Krewell, 1/18/05, Microprocessor, www.MPRonline.com, Reed Electronics Group, ref: h10018.www1.hp.com/.)

underlying principles, a great deal of complexity comes with the sophistication of computer design. This complexity is managed by treating computer architecture in abstraction levels, which we explore toward the end of the chapter. Finally we cover a modern digital computer, in which we can see these principles at work in a typical computer.

■ 1.2 THE VON NEUMANN MODEL

Conventional digital computers have a common form that is attributed to John von Neumann (1903–1957), although historians agree that others, notably the ENIAC team leaders J. Presper Eckert and John William Mauchly at the University of Pennsylvania, share in the development of the model. The **von Neumann model** consists of five major components as illustrated in Figure 1-13. The Input Unit provides instructions and data to the system, which are subsequently stored in the Memory Unit. The instructions and data are processed by the Arithmetic and Logic Unit (ALU) under the direction of the Control Unit. The results are sent to the Output Unit. The ALU and control unit are frequently referred to collectively as the Central Processing Unit (CPU). Most commercial computers can be decomposed into these five basic units.

The execution of a **stored program** is the most important aspect of the von Neumann model. A program is stored in the computer's memory along with the data to be processed. Although we now take this for granted, prior to the development of the stored-program computer, programs were stored on external media, such as plugboards or punched cards or tape. In the stored-program computer the program can be manipulated as if it is data. This gave rise to compilers and operating systems, and makes possible the great versatility of the modern computer as we know it today.

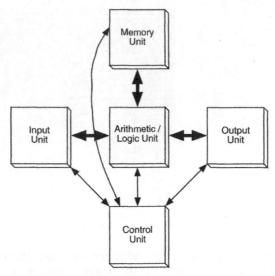

Figure 1-13
The von Neumann model of a digital computer. Thick arrows represent data paths. Thin arrows represent control paths.

■ 1.3 THE SYSTEM BUS MODEL

Although the von Neumann model prevails in modern computers, it has been streamlined. Figure 1-14 shows the system bus model of a computer system. This model decomposes a computer system into three subunits: CPU, Memory, and Input/Output (I/O). This refinement of the von Neumann model combines the ALU and the control unit into one functional unit, the CPU. The input and output units are also combined into a single I/O unit.

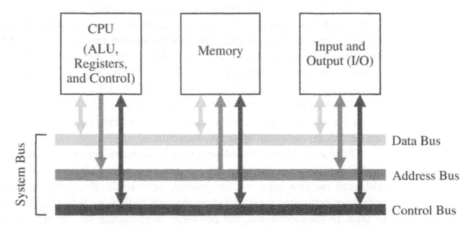

Figure 1-14
The system bus model of a computer system.

Most important to the system bus model, communication among the components is implemented by means of a shared pathway called the **system bus**, which is made up of the **data bus** (which carries the information being transmitted), the **address bus** (which identifies where the information is originating or is being sent), and the **control bus** (which describes aspects of how the information is being sent, and in what manner). There is also a **power bus** for electrical power to the components, which is not shown (but its presence is understood). Some architectures may also have a separate **I/O bus** in which slower input and output traffic is separated from the faster system bus traffic, as is the typical configuration these days.

Physically, buses are made up of collections of wires that are grouped by function. A 64-bit data bus has 64 individual wires, each of which carries one bit of data (as opposed to address or control information). In this sense, the system bus is actually a group of individual buses classified by function.

The data bus moves data among the system components. Some systems have separate data buses for moving information to and from the CPU, in which case there is a data-in bus and a data-out bus. More often a single data bus moves data in either direction, although never both directions at the same time.

If the bus is to be shared among communicating entities, then the entities must have distinguished identities: *addresses*. In some computers all addresses are assumed to be memory addresses whether they are in fact part of the computer's memory or are actually I/O devices, while in others I/O devices have separate I/O addresses. (This topic of I/O addresses is covered in more detail in Chapter 8.)

A memory address identifies a memory location where data is stored, similar to the way a postal address identifies the location where a recipient receives and sends mail. During a memory read or write operation the address bus contains the address of the memory location where the data is to be read or written. Note that the terms "read" and "write" are with respect to the CPU: the CPU *reads* data from memory and *writes* data into memory. If data is to be read from memory then the data bus contains the value read from that address in memory. If the data is to be written into the memory then the data bus contains the data value to be written into the memory.

The control bus is somewhat more complex, and we defer discussion of this bus to later chapters. For now the control bus can be thought of as coordinating access to the data bus and to the address bus, and directing data to specific components.

■ 1.4 LEVELS OF MACHINES

As with any complex system, a computer can be viewed from a number of perspectives, or **levels,** from the highest "user" level to the lowest, transistor level. Each of these levels represents an abstraction of the computer. Perhaps one of the reasons for the enormous success of the digital computer is the extent to which these levels of abstraction are separate or independent from one another. This is readily seen: a user who runs a word-processing program needs to know nothing about its programming. Likewise a programmer need not be concerned with the transistor structure inside the computer.

1.4.1 Upward Compatibility

One interesting way that the separation of levels has been exploited is in the development of upwardly compatible machines. The invention of the transistor led to a rapid development of computer hardware, and with this development came a problem of compatibility. Computer users wanted to take advantage of the newest and fastest machines, but each new computer model had a new architecture, and the old software would not run on the new hardware. The hardware/software compatibility problem became so serious that users often delayed purchasing a new machine because of the cost of rewriting the software to run on the new hardware. When a new computer was purchased, it would often sit unavailable to the target users for months while the old software and data sets were converted to the new systems.

In a successful gamble that pitted compatibility against performance, IBM pioneered the concept of a "family of machines" with its 360 series. More capable machines in the same family could run programs written for less capable machines without modifications to those programs, thus achieving upward compatibility. Upward compatibility allows a user to upgrade to a faster, more capable machine without rewriting the software that runs on the less capable model.

1.4.2 The Levels

Figure 1-15 shows seven levels in computer architecture, from the user level down to the transistor level. These are arguably fewer or more levels depending on perspective, but these levels have clear delineations that we will use in the remainder of the text. As we progress from the top level downward, the levels become less abstract and more of the internal structure of the computer shows through. We discuss these levels below.

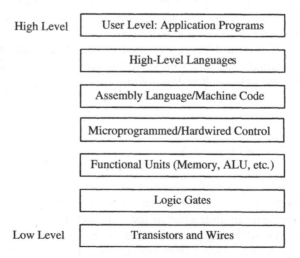

Figure 1-15
Levels of machines in the computer hierarchy.

User Level

We are most familiar with the user or application-program level of the computer. At this level, the user interacts with the computer by running programs such as word processors, spreadsheet programs, or games. Here the user sees the computer through the programs that run on it, and little (if any) of its internal or lower-level structure is visible.

High-Level Language Level

Anyone who has programmed a computer in a high-level language such as C, Java, Pascal, or Fortran has interacted with the computer at this level. Here, a programmer sees only the language, and none of the low-level details of the machine. At this level the programmer sees the data types and instructions of the high-level language, but needs no knowledge of how those data types are actually implemented in the machine. It is the role of the compiler to map data types and instructions from the high-level language to the actual computer hardware. Programs written in a high-level language can be recompiled for various machines that will (hopefully) run the same and provide the same results regardless of the machine on which they are compiled and executed. We can say that programs are compatible across machine types if written in a high-level language, and this kind of compatibility is referred to as **source code compatibility**.

Assembly Language/Machine Code Level

As pointed out above, the high-level language level really has little to do with the machine on which the high-level language is translated (compiled). The compiler translates the source code into the actual machine instructions, sometimes referred to as **machine language** or **machine code**. High-level languages "cater" to the programmer by providing a certain set of presumably well-thought-out language constructs and data types. Machine languages look "downward" in the hierarchy, and thus cater to the needs of the lower-level aspects of the machine design. As a result, machine languages deal with hardware issues such as registers (storage elements) and the transfer of data between them. In fact, many machine instructions can be described in terms of the register transfers that they effect. The collection of machine instructions for a given machine is referred to as the **instruction set** of that machine.

Of course, the actual machine code is just a collection of 1s and 0s, sometimes referred to as machine binary code or just **binary code**. As we might imagine, programming with 1s and 0s is tedious and error prone. As a result, one of the first computer programs written was the **assembler**, which translates ordinary language mnemonics such as MOVE Data, Acc, into their corresponding machine language in 1s and 0s. This language, whose constructs bear a one-to-one relationship to machine language, is known as **assembly language**.

As a result of the separation of levels, it is possible to have many different machines that differ in the lower-level implementation but have the same instruction set, or subsets or supersets of that instruction set. This allowed IBM to design a product line such as the IBM 360 series with guaranteed upward compatibility of machine code. Machine code running on the 360 Model 35 would run unchanged on the 360 Model 50, should the customer wish to upgrade to the more powerful machine. This kind of compatibility is known as "binary compatibility," because the binary code will run unchanged on the various family members. This feature was responsible in large part for the great success of the IBM 360 series of computers.

Intel Corporation has stressed binary compatibility in its family members. In this case, binaries written for the original member of a family, such as the 8086, will run unchanged on all subsequent family members, such as the 80186, 80286, 80386, 80486, 80586 (known as the Pentium, or P5), 80686 (Pentium Pro, or P6), and Itanium (IA-64) processor (although Intel built an 80x86 decoder into the IA-64 because the IA-64's EPIC instruction set is not backwardly compatible with the 80x86 precursors). Of course this does not address the fact that there are other computers that present different instruction sets to the users, which also makes it difficult to port an installed base of software from one family of computers to another.

The Control Level

It is the control unit that effects the register transfers described above. It does so by means of control signals that transfer the data from register to register, possibly through a logic circuit that transforms it in some way. The control unit interprets the machine instructions one by one, causing the specified register transfer or other action to occur.

How it does this is of no concern to the assembly language programmer. The Intel 80x86 family of processors presents the same behavioral view to an assembly language programmer regardless of which processor in the family is considered. This is because each future member of the family is designed to execute the original 8086 instructions in addition to any new instructions implemented for that particular family member.

As Figure 1-15 indicates, there is more than one way of implementing the control unit. Probably the most popular way at the present time is by "hardwiring" the control unit. This means that the control signals that effect the register transfers are generated from a block of digital logic components. Hardwired control units have the advantages of speed and component count, but until recently were exceedingly difficult to design and modify. (We will study this technique more fully in Chapter 5.)

A somewhat slower but simpler approach is to implement the instructions as a **microprogram**. A microprogram is actually a small program written in an even lower-level language and implemented in the hardware, whose job is to interpret the machine-language instructions. This microprogram is referred to as **firmware** because it spans both hardware and software. Firmware is executed by a microcontroller, which executes the actual microinstructions. (We will also explore microprogramming in Chapter 5.)

Functional Unit Level

The register transfers and other operations implemented by the control unit move data in and out of "functional units," so-called because they perform some function that is important to the operation of the computer. Functional units include internal CPU registers, the ALU, and the computer's main memory.

Logic Gates, Transistors, and Wires

The lowest levels at which any semblance of the computer's higher-level functioning is visible is at the logic gate and transistor levels. It is from logic gates that the functional units are built, and from transistors that logic gates are built. The logic gates implement the lowest-level logical operations upon which the computer's functioning depends. At the very lowest level, a computer consists of electrical components such as transistors and wires, which make up the logic gates, but at this level the functioning of the computer is lost in details of voltage, current, signal propagation delays, quantum effects, and other low-level issues.

Interactions Between Levels

The distinctions within levels and between levels are frequently blurred. For instance, a new computer architecture may contain floating-point instructions in a full-blown implementation, but a minimal implementation may have only enough hardware for integer instructions. The floating-point instructions can be **trapped**[1] prior to execution and replaced with a sequence of machine language instructions that imitate or **emulate** the floating-point instructions using the existing integer instructions. This is the case for microprocessors that use optional floating-point coprocessors. Those without floating-point coprocessors emulate the floating-point instructions by a series of floating-point routines that are implemented in the machine language of the microprocessor, and frequently stored in a **ROM**, which is a read-only memory chip. The assembly language and high-level language view for both implementations is the same except for execution speed.

It is possible to take this emulation to the extreme of emulating the entire instruction set of one computer on another computer. The software that does this is known as an **emulator**, and was used by Apple Computer to maintain binary code compatibility when they began employing Motorola PowerPC chips in place of Motorola 68000 chips, which had an entirely different instruction set.

The high-level language level and the firmware and functional unit levels can be so intermixed that it is hard to identify what operation is happening at which level. The value in stratifying a computer architecture into a hierarchy of levels is not so much for the purpose of classification, which can be difficult at times, but rather to simply give us some focus when we study these levels.

The Programmer's View—The Instruction Set Architecture

As described in the discussion of levels above, the assembly language programmer is concerned with the assembly language and functional units of the machine. This collection of instruction set and functional units is known as the **instruction set architecture** (ISA) of the machine.

The Computer Architect's View

The computer architect views the system at all levels. The architect who focuses on the design of a computer is invariably driven by performance requirements and cost constraints. Performance may be specified by the speed of program execution, the storage capacity of the machine, or a number of other parameters. Cost may be reflected in monetary terms, or in size, or weight, or power consumption. The design proposed by a computer architect must attempt to meet the performance goals while staying within the cost constraints. This usually requires trade-offs between and among the levels of the machine.

---

[1] Traps are covered in Chapter 5.

■ 1.5 A TYPICAL COMPUTER SYSTEM

Modern computers have evolved from the great behemoths of the 1950s and 1960s to the much smaller and more powerful computers that surround us today. Even with all of the great advances in computer technology that have been made in the past several decades, the five basic units of the von Neumann model are still distinguishable in modern computers.

Figure 1-16 shows a typical configuration for a desktop computer. The input unit is composed of the keyboard and mouse, through which a user enters data and commands. A video monitor comprises the output unit, which displays the output in a visual form. The ALU and the control unit are bundled into a single microprocessor that serves as the CPU. The memory unit consists of individual memory circuits and also a hard disk unit, a diskette unit, and a (compact disk–read-only memory) device.

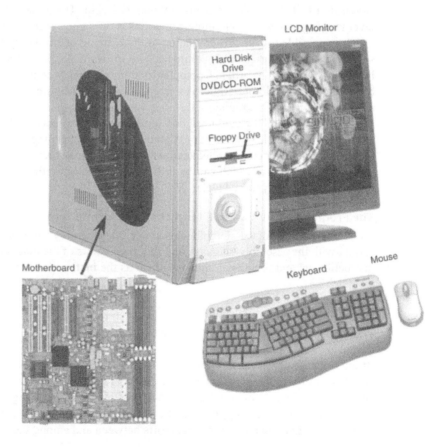

Figure 1-16
A desktop computer system. (Computer case source: www.baber.com/cases/ mpe_md14_silver.htm. Motherboard source: ftp://ftp.tyan.com/img_mobo/i_s2895.tif.)

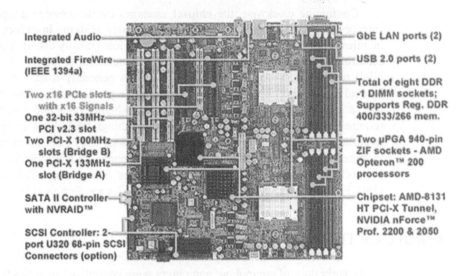

Integrated Audio

Integrated FireWire
(IEEE 1394a)

Two x16 PCIe slots
with x16 Signals
One 32-bit 33MHz
PCI v2.3 slot
Two PCI-X 100MHz
slots (Bridge B)
One PCI-X 133MHz
slot (Bridge A)

SATA II Controller
with NVRAID™

SCSI Controller: 2-
port U320 68-pin SCSI
Connectors (option)

GbE LAN ports (2)

USB 2.0 ports (2)

Total of eight DDR
-1 DIMM sockets;
Supports Reg. DDR
400/333/266 mem.

Two µPGA 940-pin
ZIF sockets - AMD
Opteron™ 200
processors

Chipset: AMD-8131
HT PCI-X Tunnel,
NVIDIA nForce™
Prof. 2200 & 2050

Figure 1-17
An AMD Opteron 200 based motherboard. Courtesy Tyan Computer Corp. (USA).

As we look deeper inside the machine, we can see that the heart of the computer is contained on a single motherboard, such as the one shown in Figure 1-17. The motherboard contains integrated circuits (ICs), plug-in expansion card slots, and the wires that interconnect the ICs and expansion card slots. Several areas of the motherboard are highlighted. Starting at the top center of the board and moving clockwise, the first highlighted area shows the integrated audio ("integrated" just means that it is part of the motherboard, not on a separate circuit card). This component supports a microphone input and a stereo speaker output.

The next component supports integrated **Firewire** (IEEE 1394a), which is a shared 400 Mb/s medium for interconnecting up to 63 peripheral devices in a daisy-chained manner, with the additional capability of supporting **isochronous** data in which real-time data must be delivered in a fixed period of time. The GbE LAN ports support 1 GB/s Ethernet network connectivity. The universal synchronous bus (USB) 2.0 ports are used similarly to Firewire, for up to 127 external peripheral devices, with data rates up to 480 Mb/s. Isochronous data is not supported with USB.

Continuing in a clockwise direction around the motherboard, the eight DDR (double data rate) DIMM (dual in-line memory module) sockets support eight memory modules. The two micro-**pin grid array** (µPGA) 940-pin **zero insertion force (ZIF)** sockets hold dual AMD Opteron 200 processors. The Opteron 200 competes with the Intel line of server/workstation processors and is instruction-set-compatible with the Intel line. It takes a great deal of force to insert or remove a 940 pin module, enough force to destroy the motherboard were it not for the use of the ZIF socket. The ZIF socket has a lever that manually opens and closes the 940 pin receptacles, thus greatly reducing the mechanical force needed to insert or remove a PGA module.

Continuing clockwise, the **chipset** manages traffic between peripheral devices, the memory, and the processors. The **small computer systems interface** (SCSI) controller handles parallel bus interfaces for peripheral devices (mostly disks). The **serial advanced technology attachment** (SATA) II controller handles serial (bit by bit, as opposed to parallel) transfer rates starting at 150 Mb/s and is generally used for external disks now instead of the older SCSI technology. Although a parallel connection may seem better, in fact, a serial connection can more easily run at higher rates and generates less heat and requires less area and thinner cables: all good things for today's computers. Finally, the **peripheral component interconnect** (PCI) sockets hold external circuit boards that are mounted orthogonal to the motherboard. PCI boards are used for disk controllers, video controllers, and several other types of interfaces. The use of PCI is being displaced by USB, Firewire, and SATA. All of these technologies are discussed further in later chapters.

■ 1.6 ROLE OF THE NETWORK

In the early days of computing, computers were centralized facilities that contained most of the resources used by the populations they serviced. Data was transferred between computers via media (punched paper cards, paper tapes, magnetic tapes, and magnetic disks), hand-carried by an operator.

As computers became more numerous and less expensive, costs shifted away from hardware and more toward labor, and it became economical to link computers directly so that resources could be shared. This is what networking is about, which we explore at a high level in Chapter 9. Networking has grown so much in importance that it is a dominant consideration in the architecture of many computers, which is why we give it special attention in this book.

In this chapter, we take a component-level view of networking, in which each network component contains its own computer architecture in a so-called **embedded system**, a topic we cover later in the book. Figure 1-18 shows an end-to-end network involving data and voice (computers and telephones). All network components have some form of computer architecture, and despite their specialized functions, they all take the form of the von Neumann model. These components are referred to as embedded systems because the computer is embedded in the component and is configured to work on a specific task, rather than being used for general-purpose computing.

The devices shown in the figure include computers, telephones, hubs, switches, routers, firewalls, multiplexers, transmission equipment, encryption devices, line drivers, and private branch exchanges (PBXs). Understanding each of these components may seem daunting at first, but each component has a well defined purpose that can be more easily understood when placed in the context of the overall system. The personal computer generates a stream of bits that the router forwards to its destination based on an address in the bit stream. The switch helps prevent bit streams from multiple computers from colliding. An optional encryption device adds protection from eavesdropping and must be paired with a decryption device on the receiving end. The firewall protects undesirable network traffic from each side from getting across to the other side. The voice phone switch converts analog telephone signals into digitized bit streams and provides call routing.

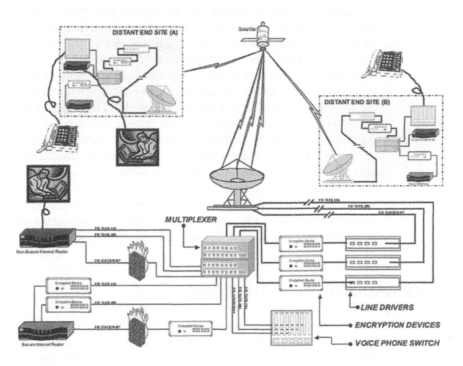

Figure 1-18
End-to-end communication over a network. Highlighted architectural components include
computers, hubs, switches, routers, firewalls, multiplexers, and phone switches. (Source: MSG
Scott Bramwell.)

The voice and data streams are merged onto **trunk** lines by the multiplexer, where
outbound data is encrypted, and the signals are reformatted for transmission over long distances with **line drivers**. The bit streams are then sent to a satellite or other transmission
medium, where the signals go through a reverse process on their way to their destination.
In the chapters that follow, we will focus on a number of these devices as we explore the
architectures of network components.

For most of the book, we will look primarily at the components closest to the personal
computer. Looking again at the motherboard in Figure 1-17, we see that several networks
are supported: Ethernet, Firewire, USB, and to a degree SCSI and SATA can be thought of
as networks. Although each if these networks extends the computer by allowing other
devices to be connected to it, only the Ethernet extends the system to other computers; the
other networks extend the machine in various ways, but they use media that has endpoints.
The Ethernet connects to other network devices that connect to other network devices,
which connect to other network devices, ad infinitum. That is not to say that an Ethernet or
some other network could not be added as a device on Firewire, USB, etc., but only the
Ethernet supports routing beyond its own local cable.

Something that all of the long-range networks share is that communication takes place in a bit-serial manner. If 32 bits need to be transferred from one location to another, those bits line up behind each other and are transferred one bit at a time, like cars traveling on a one-lane road. This is partly because the time-of-flight communication delays are a significant component of overall end-to-end delays; if more capacity is needed, additional serial lines can simply be added rather than making a wider link. This is also because of the difficulty of lining up so many bits in parallel at high speeds over large distances.

In terms of computer architecture, the network connection can be viewed as just another peripheral device, with details that are specific to transferring data. While this view may be true in the abstract, it hides a great deal of computer architecture that exists outside of the computer. Given the great importance of networking these days, we will cover the architecture of some of the more significant network components. We will not cover details of network protocols; the subject is so broad and deep that there are countless books and courses covering these topics. Our primary interest here is to understand what is special about the architecture of these network devices, and how all of these components work together.

■ 1.7 ORGANIZATION OF THE BOOK

We explore the inner workings of computers in the chapters that follow. Chapter 2 covers the representation of data, which provides background for all of the chapters that follow. Chapter 3 covers methods for implementing computer arithmetic. Chapters 4 and 6 cover the instruction set architecture, which serves as a vehicle for understanding how the components of a computer interact. Chapter 5 ties the earlier chapters together in the design and analysis of a control unit for the instruction set architecture. Chapter 7 covers the organization of memory units and memory-management techniques. Chapter 8 covers input, output, and communication. Chapter 9 covers communication and advanced aspects of single-CPU systems (which might have more than one processing core). Chapter 10 covers advanced aspects of multiple-CPU systems, such as parallel and distributed architectures. In Appendix A, we look into the design of digital logic circuits, which are the building blocks for the basic components of a computer. Appendix B covers the ARC-Tools software that supports the assembly language used throughout the book.

■ 1.8 CASE STUDY: WHAT HAPPENED TO SUPERCOMPUTERS?

The Manchester University Mark 1 computer (Figure 1-19), which is based on the Manchester Baby (the left side of the figure), successfully demonstrated the integration of a number of emerging technologies. Experimental first-of-a-kind computers like the Manchester Baby and Manchester Mark 1 serve important roles in furthering knowledge, and although costs are always a consideration, the lessons learned get the most attention. Supercomputers, on the other hand, are often first-of-a-kind machines too but are much more sensitive to costs. The costs of a supercomputer compared to the work accomplished (the "price to performance ratio") can price a supercomputer line out of existence. It is just this issue that we investigate here.

Figure 1-19
The Manchester University Mark 1, showing the Manchester Baby portion which was made operational on 21 June 1948. (Source: The University of Manchester, www.computer50.org/mark1/ip-mm1.mark1.html.) (Not to be confused with the Harvard Mark I, donated to Harvard University by International Business Machines in August, 1944.) Reprinted with permission from the School of Computer Science, The University of Manchester.

[The following contribution comes from Web page www.paralogos.com/DeadSuper created by Kevin D. Kissell at kevink@acm.org. Kissell's Web site lists dozens of supercomputing projects that have fallen by the wayside. One of the primary reasons for the near-extinction of supercomputers is that ordinary, everyday computers achieve a significant fraction of supercomputing power at a price that the common person can afford. The price-to-performance ratio for personal computers is very favorable due to low costs achieved through mass market sales. Supercomputers enjoy no such mass markets and continue to suffer very high price-to-performance ratios.

Following Kissell's contribution is an excerpt from an Electrical Engineering Times *article that highlights the enormous investment in everyday microprocessor development, which helps maintain the favorable price-to-performance ratio for low-cost desktop computers.]*

The Passing of a Golden Age?

From the construction of the first programmed computers until the mid-1990s, there was always room in the computer industry for someone with a clever, if sometimes challenging, idea on how to make a more powerful machine. Computing became strategic during the Second World War, and remained so during the Cold War that followed. High-performance computing is essential to any modern nuclear weapons program, and a computer technology "race" was a logical corollary to the arms race. While powerful computers are of great value to a number of other industrial sectors, such as petroleum, chemistry, medicine, aeronautical, automotive, and civil engineering, the role of governments, and particularly the national laboratories of the US government, as catalysts and incubators for innovative computing technologies can hardly be overstated. Private industry may buy more machines, but rarely do they risk buying those with single-digit serial numbers. The passing of Soviet communism and the end of the Cold War brought us a generally safer and more prosperous world, but it removed the *raison d'être* for many merchants of performance-at-any-price.

Accompanying these geopolitical changes were some technological and economic trends that spelled trouble for specialized producers of high-end computers. Microprocessors began in the 1970s as devices whose main claim to fame was that it was possible to put a stored-program computer on a single piece of silicon. Competitive pressures, and the desire to generate sales by obsoleting last year's product, made for the doubling of microprocessor computing power every 18 months, Moore's celebrated "law." Along the way, microprocessor designers borrowed almost all the tricks that designers of mainframe and numerical supercomputers had used in the past: storage hierarchies, pipelining, multiple functional units, multiprocessing, out-of-order execution, branch prediction, SIMD processing, speculative and predicated execution. By the mid-1990s, research ideas were going directly from simulation to implementation in microprocessors destined for the desktops of the masses. Nevertheless, it must be noted that most of the gains in raw performance achieved by microprocessors in the preceding decade came, not from these advanced techniques of computer architecture, but from the simple speedup of processor clocks and quantitative increase in processor resources made possible by advances in semiconductor technology. By 1998, the CPU of a high-end Windows-based personal computer was running at a higher clock rate than the top-of-the-line Cray Research supercomputer of 1994.

It is thus hardly surprising that the policy of the US national laboratories has shifted from the acquisition of systems architected from the ground up to be supercomputers to the deployment of large ensembles of mass-produced microprocessor-based systems, with the ASCI project as the flagship of this activity. As of this writing, it remains to be seen if these agglomerations will prove to be sufficiently stable and usable for production work, but the preliminary results have been at least satisfactory. The halcyon days of supercomputers based on exotic technology and innovative architecture may well be over.

[...]

Kevin D. Kissell
kevink@acm.org
February, 1998

[The following excerpt is taken from the Electronic Engineering Times, *source: tech-web.cmp.com/eet/news/98/994news/invest.html. Although dated by a few years, the ideas are as true as ever.]*

Invest or die: Intel's life on the edge

By Ron Wilson and Brian Fuller

SANTA CLARA, Calif. -- With about $600 million to pump into venture companies this year, Intel Corp. has joined the major leagues of venture-capital firms. But the unique imperative that drives the microprocessor giant to invest gives it influence disproportionate to even this large sum. For Intel, venture investments are not just a source of income; they are a vital tool in the fight to survive.

Survival might seem an odd preoccupation for the world's largest semiconductor company. But Intel, in a way all its own, lives hanging in the balance. For every new generation of CPUs, Intel must make huge investments in process development, in buildings and in fabs---an investment too huge to lose.

Gordon Moore, Intel chairman emeritus, gave scale to the wager. "An R&D fab today costs $400 million just for the building. Then you put about $1 billion of equipment in it. That gets you a quarter-micron fab for maybe 5,000 wafers per week, about the smallest practical fab. For the next generation," Moore said, "the minimum investment will be $2 billion, with maybe $3 billion to $4 billion for any sort of volume production. No other industry has such a short life on such huge investments."

Much of this money will be spent before there is a proven need for the microprocessors the fab will produce. In essence, the entire $4 billion per fab is bet on the proposition that the industry will absorb a huge number of premium-priced CPUs that are only somewhat faster than the currently available parts. If for just one generation that didn't happen---if everyone judged, say, that the Pentium II was fast enough, thank you---the results would be unthinkable.

"My nightmare is to wake up some day and not need any more computing power," Moore said.

Intel vs. Motorola: The First Microprocessors

The Intel and Motorola corporations represent two extremes in almost every aspect of their corporate lives. Intel was started by Bob Noyce and Gordon Moore in 1968 with the explicit purpose of exploiting semiconductor technology for the development of digital devices and systems. Their first product, released in 1969, was the 3001 64-bit RAM chip, followed shortly thereafter by a number of similar digital devices such as decoders and shift registers. The first microprocessor, the 4-bit 4004, was released in 1971, followed in 1972 by the first 8-bit microprocessor, the 8008. An enhanced version, the very popular 8080, was released in 1974, and can be thought of as igniting the microprocessor revolution.

As a corporate entity Motorola has been in business since 1928, originally as the Galvin Company, selling car radios under the Motorola trademark. Anticipating the importance of semiconductors to the business, Motorola established a semiconductor R&D facility in the 1940s, and was, by the early 1950s, the world's largest manufacturer of analog semiconductors. By 1960 the company had branched out into consumer electronics with the first transistorized television set, and, in 1969, had the honor of supplying the transponder used for communications during the first moon landing. Motorola was also quietly working on digital electronic devices, and released their first 8-bit microprocessor, the MC6800, in 1974.

Both microprocessors were quickly seized by hobbyists, who were solely responsible for developing and popularizing the personal computer: the January 1975 *Popular Electronics* cover article featured the Micro Instrumentation Technology Systems (MITS) Altair 8800 microcomputer kit, containing an Intel 8080, complete for $397. It had neither keyboard nor monitor, neither software nor permanent storage. It was programmed, byte by byte, by flipping 16 address switches and 8 data switches. The only output was blinking lights. They received orders for over 2000 units within the first few days of the magazine's publication. In that same month Bill Gates and Paul Allen wrote to MITS saying that they had a BASIC interpreter for the Altair. Several weeks later they begin writing it. Within a year there were several dozen microcomputers on the market, including the Southwest Technology SWTP 6800, which employed the Motorola 6800 as its microprocessor. In March 1976 Steve Wozniak and Steve Jobs developed the Apple I, which used the MOS Technology 6502, a variant of the 6800. The microcomputer revolution was on!

Summary

Computer architecture deals with those aspects of a computer that are visible to a programmer, while computer organization deals with those aspects that are at a more physical level and are not made visible to a programmer. Historically, programmers had to deal with every aspect of a computer - Babbage with mechanical gears, and ENIAC programmers with plugboard cables. As computers grew in sophistication, the concept of levels of machines became more pronounced, allowing computers to have very different internal and external behaviors while managing complexity in stratified levels. The single most significant development that makes this possible is the stored program computer, which is embodied in the von Neumann model. It is the von Neumann model that we see in most conventional computers today.

Problems

1.1 Moore's law, which is attributed to Intel founder Gordon Moore, states that computing power doubles every 18 months for the same price. An unrelated observation is that floating-point instructions are executed 100 times faster in hardware than via emulation. Using Moore's law as a guide, how long will it take for computing power to improve to the point that floating-point instructions are emulated as quickly as their (earlier) hardware counterparts?

1.2 What number is represented on the abacus below?

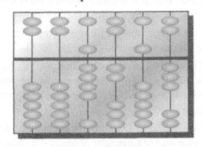

1.3 Match the terms in the list below with the components shown in the table. Not all of the terms will be used.

keyboard, mouse, floppy drive, CD-ROM/DVD drive, heat sink, memory module, monitor, battery, crystal oscillator, motherboard, Ethernet connector, USB memory device, ZIF socket, hard disk drive, integrated circuit

1.4 Refer to Figure 1-12, which is a die photo of the Ultrasparc IV+. What percentage of the die area is devoted to computing logic, after subtracting area devoted to memory and wires?

1.5 List which motherboard components in Figure 1-17 are most closely associated with the three components of the system bus model (CPU, memory, and input/output).

1.6 Consider the quote from Gordon Moore in the section preceding the Chapter Summary, "My nightmare is to wake up some day and not need any more computing power." Give three examples where present-day computing power is insufficient or too expensive to meet users' needs.

1.7 Until recently, Apple's Macintosh computers employed members of the PowerPC microprocessor for the CPU. This processor has a radically different ISA from the more common Windows-based Intel x86 machines. Yet a product named Virtual PC for Mac, developed by Connectix Corporation and later sold to Microsoft, allows Windows x86 programs to run, albeit more slowly, without change on the Macintosh PowerPC machines. Describe how this is accomplished.

Further Reading

The history of computing is riddled with interesting personalities and milestones. (Anderson, 1991) gives a short, readable account of both during the last century. (Bashe et al., 1986) give an interesting account of the IBM machines. (Bromley, 1987) chronicles Babbage's machines. (Ralston and Reilly, 2003) give short biographies of the more celebrated personalities. (Lucas et al, 1988) provides details on the celebrated wolf bone (25,000–30,000 B.C.). (IEEE, 1996) gives a concise but thorough overview of computing history up through the mid-1990s. A very readable Web-based history of computers by Michelle A. Hoyle can also be found at www.interpac.net/~eingang/Lecture/toc.html. (Swade, 1993) covers the method of finite differences as it appears in Babbage's machines and the version of the analytical difference engine created by the Science Museum in London. A readable account of tallying methods is provided in (Hays, 2005). (Dilson, 1995) details the use of the Chinese abacus. (Tanenbaum, 1999) is one of a number of texts that popularizes the notion of levels of machines. Historical details of the University of Manchester Baby and Mark 1 machines can be found at: www.computer50.org/mark1.

Anderson, Harlan, Dedication Address for the Digital Computer Laboratory at the University of Illinois, April 17, 1991, as reprinted in *IEEE Circuits and Systems: Society Newsletter*, **2**, no. 1, pp. 3–6 (March 1991).

Bashe, Charles J., Johnson, Lyle R., Palmer, John H., and Pugh, Emerson W., *IBM's Early Computers*, The MIT Press (1986).

Bromley, A. G., "The Evolution of Babbage's Calculating Engines," *Annals of the History of Computing*, **9**, pp. 113–138 (1987).

Bunt, Lucas, N. H., Jones, Phillip S., and Bedient, Jack D., *The Historical Roots of Elementary Mathematics*, Dover Publications (February 1988).

Dilson, Jesse, *The Abacus: The World's First Computer Systems*, St. Martin's Griffin (March 1995).

Hays, John, http://members.fortunecity.com/jonhays/tallying.htm, as referenced (June 28, 2005).

IEEE, "Timeline of Computing History," *IEEE Computer*, **29**, no. 10, www.computer.org/computer/timeline/timeline.pdf (October 1996), as referenced 13 March 2005.

Ralston, A., Reilly, E. D., and Hemmendinger, D., eds., *Encyclopedia of Computer Science*, 4/e, Wiley (September 2003).

Swade, Doron D., "Redeeming Charles Babbage's Mechanical Computer," *Scientific American*, pp. 86–91 (February 1993).

Tanenbaum, A., *Structured Computer Organization*, 4/e, Prentice Hall (1999).

CHAPTER 2

DATA REPRESENTATION

In the early days of computing, there were common misconceptions about computers. One misconception was that the computer was only a giant adding machine performing arithmetic operations. Computers could do much more than that, even in the early days. The other common misconception, in contradiction to the first, was that the computer could do anything. We now know that there are indeed classes of problems that even the most powerful imaginable computer finds intractable with the von Neumann model. The correct perception, of course, is somewhere between the two.

We are familiar with computer operations that are non-arithmetic: computer graphics, digital audio, even the manipulation of the computer mouse. Regardless of what kind of information is being manipulated by the computer, the information must be represented by patterns of 1s and 0s (also known as "on-off" codes). This immediately raises the question of how that information should be described or represented in the machine—this is the *data representation*, or *data encoding*. Graphical images, digital audio, or mouse clicks must all be encoded in a systematic, agreed-upon manner.

We might think of the decimal representation of information as the most natural form because we know it the best, but the use of on-off codes to represent information predated the computer by many years, in the form of Morse code.

This chapter introduces several of the simplest and most important encodings: the encoding of signed and unsigned fixed-point numbers, real numbers (referred to as *floating-point numbers* in computer jargon), and the printing characters. We shall see that in all cases there are multiple ways of encoding a given kind of data, some useful in one context, some in another. We will also take an early look at computer arithmetic for the purpose of understanding some of the encoding schemes, although we will defer details of computer arithmetic until Chapter 3.

In the process of developing a data representation for computing, a crucial issue is deciding how much storage should be devoted to each data value. For example, a computer architect may decide to treat integers as being 32 bits in size, and to implement an ALU that supports arithmetic operations on those 32-bit values that return 32-bit results. Some numbers can be too large to represent using 32 bits, however, and in other cases, the operands may fit into 32 bits, but the result of a computation will not, creating an *overflow* condition (which is described in Chapter 3). Thus we need to understand the limits imposed on the accuracy and range of numeric calculations by the finite nature of the data representations. We will investigate these limits in the next few sections.

■ 2.1 FIXED-POINT NUMBERS

In a fixed-point number system, each number has exactly the same number of digits, and the "point" is always in the same place. Examples from the decimal number system are 0.23, 5.12, and 9.11. Ordinary integers like 2 and 53 are also fixed-point numbers, in which the position of the decimal point is implied to the immediate right of the rightmost digit. There are implied 0s to the left, and so there can also be three digits for these integers: 002 and 053. In the 0.23, 5.12, and 9.11 examples, each number has three digits and the decimal point is located two places from the right. Examples from the **binary** number system (in which each digit can take on only one of the values: 0 or 1) would be 11.10, 01.10, and 00.11, where there are four binary digits and the binary point is in the middle.

An important difference between the way that we represent fixed-point numbers on paper and the way that we represent them in the computer is that when fixed-point numbers are represented in the computer *the binary point is not stored anywhere*, but only assumed to be in a certain position. One could say that the binary point exists only in the mind of the programmer.

We begin coverage of fixed-point numbers by investigating the range and precision of fixed-point numbers, using the decimal number system. We then take a look at the nature of number bases, such as decimal and binary, and how to convert between the bases. With this foundation, we then investigate several ways of representing negative fixed-point numbers, and take a look at simple arithmetic operations that can be performed on them.

2.1.1 Range and Precision in Fixed-Point Numbers

A fixed-point representation can be characterized by the **range** of expressible numbers (that is, the distance between the largest and smallest numbers) and the **precision** (the distance between two adjacent numbers on a number line.) For the fixed-point decimal examples above, using three digits and the decimal point placed two digits from the right, the range is from 0.00 to 9.99 inclusive of the endpoints, denoted as [0.00, 9.99], the precision is .01, and the **error** is 1/2 of the difference between two "adjoining" numbers, such as 5.01 and 5.02, which have a difference of .01. The error is thus .01/2 = .005. That is, we can represent any number within the range 0.00 to 9.99 to within .005 of its true or precise value.

Notice how range and precision trade off: with the decimal point on the far right, the range is [000, 999] and the precision is 1.0. With the decimal point at the far left, the range is [.000, .999] and the precision is .001.

In either case, there are only 10^3 different decimal "objects," ranging from 000 to 999 or from .000 to .999, and thus it is possible to represent only 1,000 different items, regardless of how we apportion range and precision.

There is no reason why the range must begin with 0. A 2-digit decimal number can have a range of [00,99] or a range of [–50, +49], or even a range of [–99, +0]. (The representation of negative numbers is covered more fully in Section 2.1.6.)

Range and precision are important issues in computer architecture because both are finite in the implementation of the architecture, but are infinite in the real world, and so the user must be aware of the limitations of trying to represent external information in internal form.

2.1.2 The Associative Law of Algebra Does Not Always Hold in Computers

In early mathematics, we learned the associative law of algebra:

$$a + (b + c) = (a + b) + c$$

As we will see, the associative law of algebra does not always hold for fixed-point numbers having a finite representation. Consider a 1-digit decimal fixed-point representation with the decimal point on the right, and a range of $[-9, 9]$, with $a = 7$, $b = 4$, and $c = -3$. Now $a + (b + c) = 7 + (4 + -3) = 7 + 1 = 8$. If we apply the parentheses differently, $(a + b) + c = (7 + 4) + -3 = 11 + -3$, but 11 is outside the range of our number system! We have **overflow** in an intermediate calculation, even though the correct final result would be within the number system. This is every bit as bad as if the final result is outside of the range of the number system, because the final result will be wrong if an intermediate result is wrong.

Thus we can see by the example that the associative law of algebra does not always hold for finite-length fixed-point numbers. This is an unavoidable consequence of this form of representation, and there is nothing practical to be done except to detect overflow wherever it occurs, and either terminate the computation immediately and notify the user of the condition or, having detected the overflow, repeat the computation with numbers of greater range. (The latter technique is seldom used except in critical applications.)

2.1.3 Radix Number Systems

In this section, we learn how to work with numbers having arbitrary bases, although we will focus on the bases most used in computing, such as base 2 (binary), and its close cousins base 8 (octal) and base 16 (hexadecimal).

The **base** or **radix** of a number system defines the range of possible values that a digit may have. In the base 10 (decimal) number system, one of the 10 values 0, 1, 2, 3, 4, 5, 6, 7, 8, 9 is used for each digit of a number. The most natural system for representing numbers in a computer is base 2, in which data is represented as a collection of 1s and 0s.

The general form for determining the decimal value of a number in a radix k fixed-point number system is shown below:

$$Value = \sum_{i=-m}^{n-1} b_i \cdot k^i$$

The value of the digit in position i is given by b_i. There are n digits to the left of the radix point and there are m digits to the right of the radix point. This form of a number, in which each position has an assigned weight, is referred to as a **weighted position code**. Consider evaluating $(541.25)_{10}$, in which the subscript 10 represents the base. We have $n = 3$, $m = 2$, and $k = 10$:

$$5 \times 10^2 + 4 \times 10^1 + 1 \times 10^0 + 2 \times 10^{-1} + 5 \times 10^{-2} =$$

$$(500)_{10} + (40)_{10} + (1)_{10} + (2/10)_{10} + (5/100)_{10} = (541.25)_{10}$$

Now consider the base 2 number $(1010.01)_2$ in which $n = 4$, $m = 2$, and $k = 2$:

$$1 \times 2^3 + 0 \times 2^2 + 1 \times 2^1 + 0 \times 2^0 + 0 \times 2^{-1} + 1 \times 2^{-2} =$$

$$(8)_{10} + (0)_{10} + (2)_{10} + (0)_{10} + (0/2)_{10} + (1/4)_{10} = (10.25)_{10}$$

This suggests how to convert a number from an arbitrary base into a base 10 number using the **polynomial method**. The idea is to multiply each digit by the weight assigned to its position (powers of two in this example) and then sum up the terms to arrive at the converted number. Although conversions can be made among all of the bases in this way, some bases pose special problems, as we will see in the next section.

Note that in these weighted number systems we define the bit that carries the most weight as the **most significant bit (MSB)**, and the bit that carries the least weight as the **least significant bit (LSB)**. Conventionally, the MSB is the leftmost bit and the LSB the rightmost bit.

2.1.4 Conversions Among Radices

In the previous section, we saw an example of how a base 2 number can be converted into a base 10 number. A conversion in the reverse direction is more involved. The easiest way to convert fixed-point numbers containing both integer and fractional parts is to convert each part separately. Consider converting $(23.375)_{10}$ to base 2. We begin by separating the number into its integer and fractional parts:

$$(23.375)_{10} = (23)_{10} + (.375)_{10}$$

Converting the Integer Part of a Fixed-Point Number—The Remainder Method

As suggested in the previous section, the general polynomial form for representing a binary integer is:

$$b_i \times 2^i + b_{i-1} \times 2^{i-1} + \dots + b_1 \times 2^1 + b_0 \times 2^0$$

If we divide the integer by 2, then we will obtain:

$$b_i \times 2^{i-1} + b_{i-1} \times 2^{i-2} + \dots + b_1 \times 2^0$$

with a remainder of b_0. As a result of dividing the original integer by 2, we discover the value of the first binary coefficient b_0. We can repeat this process on the remaining polynomial and determine the value of b_1. We can continue iterating the process on the remaining polynomial and thus obtain all of the b_i. This process forms the basis of the **remainder method** of converting integers between bases.

We now apply the remainder method to convert $(23)_{10}$ to base 2. As shown in Figure 2-1, the integer is initially divided by 2, which leaves a remainder of 0 or 1. For this case, 23/2 produces a quotient of 11 and a remainder of 1. The first remainder is

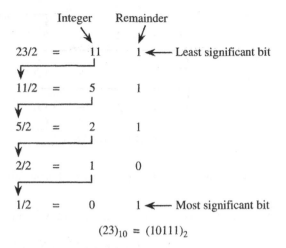

Figure 2-1
A conversion from a base 10-integer to a base 2 integer using the remainder method.

the least significant **binary** dig**it** (**bit**) of the converted number (the rightmost bit). In the next step, 11 is divided by 2, which creates a quotient of 5 and a remainder of 1. Next, 5 is divided by 2, which creates a quotient of 2 and a remainder of 1. The process continues until we are left with a quotient of 0. If we continue the process after obtaining a quotient of 0, we will only obtain 0s for the quotient and remainder, which will not change the value of the converted number. The remainders are collected into a base 2 number in the order shown in Figure 2-1 to produce the result $(23)_{10} = (10111)_2$. In general, we can convert any base 10 integer to any other base by simply dividing the integer by the base to which we are converting.

We can check the result by converting it from base 2 back to base 10 using the polynomial method:

$$(10111)_2 = 1 \times 2^4 + 0 \times 2^3 + 1 \times 2^2 + 1 \times 2^1 + 1 \times 2^0$$

$$= 16 + 0 + 4 + 2 + 1$$

$$= (23)_{10}$$

At this point, we have converted the integer portion of $(23.375)_{10}$ into base 2, and now the fractional portion needs to be converted.

Converting the Fractional Part of a Fixed-Point Number—The Multiplication Method

The conversion of the fractional portion can be accomplished by successively multiplying the fraction by 2 as described below.

A binary fraction is represented in the general form:

$$b_{-1} \times 2^{-1} + b_{-2} \times 2^{-2} + b_{-3} \times 2^{-3} + \ldots$$

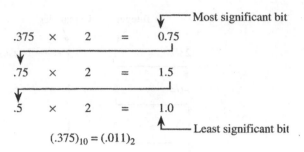

Figure 2-2
A conversion from a base 10 fraction to a base 2 fraction using the multiplication method.

If we multiply the fraction by 2, then we will obtain:

$$b_{-1} + b_{-2} \times 2^{-1} + b_{-3} \times 2^{-2} + \dots$$

We thus discover the coefficient b_{-1}. If we iterate this process on the remaining fraction, then we will obtain successive b_i. This process forms the basis of the **multiplication method** of converting fractions between bases. For the example used here (Figure 2-2), the initial fraction $(.375)_{10}$ is less than 1. If we multiply it by 2, then the resulting number will be less than 2. The digit to the left of the radix point will then be 0 or 1. This is the first digit to the right of the radix point in the converted base 2 number, as shown in the figure.

We repeat the process on the fractional portion until either we are left with a fraction of 0, at which point only trailing 0s are created by additional iterations, or we have reached the limit of precision used in our representation. The digits are collected and the result is obtained: $(.375)_{10} = (.011)_2$.

For this process, the multiplier is the same as the target base. The multiplier is 2 here, but if we wanted to make a conversion to another base, such as 3, then we would use a multiplier of 3.

We again check the result of the conversion by converting from base 2 back to base 10 using the polynomial method as shown below:

$$(.011)_2 = 0 \times 2^{-1} + 1 \times 2^{-2} + 1 \times 2^{-3} = 0 + 1/4 + 1/8 = (.375)_{10}$$

We now combine the integer and fractional portions of the number and obtain the final result:

$$(23.375)_{10} = (10111.011)_2.$$

Non-Terminating Fractions

Although this method of conversion will work among all bases, some precision can be lost in the process. For example, not all terminating base 10 fractions have a terminating base 2 form. Consider converting $(.2)_{10}$ to base 2 as shown in Figure 2-3. In the last row of the conversion, the fraction .2 reappears, and the process repeats *ad infinitum*.

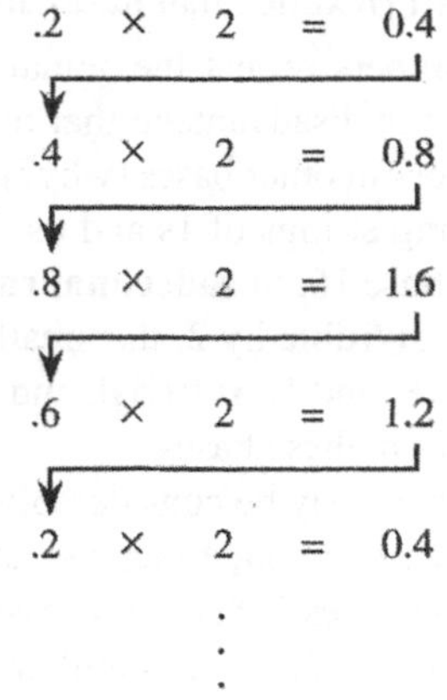

$$.2 \ \times \ 2 \ = \ 0.4$$

$$.4 \ \times \ 2 \ = \ 0.8$$

$$.8 \ \times \ 2 \ = \ 1.6$$

$$.6 \ \times \ 2 \ = \ 1.2$$

$$.2 \ \times \ 2 \ = \ 0.4$$

$$\vdots$$

Figure 2-3
A terminating base 10 fraction that does not have a terminating base 2 form.

As to why this can happen, consider that any non-repeating base 2 fraction can be represented as $i/2^k$ for some integers i and k. (Repeating fractions in base 2 cannot be so represented.) Algebraically,

$$i/2^k = i{\times}5^k/(2^k{\times}5^k) = i{\times}5^k/10^k = j/10^k$$

where j is the integer $i{\times}5^k$. The fraction is thus non-repeating in base 10. This hinges on the fact that only non-repeating fractions in base b can be represented as i/b^k for some integers i and k. The condition that must be satisfied for a non-repeating base 10 fraction to have an equivalent non-repeating base 2 fraction is:

$$i/10^k = i/(5^k{\times}2^k) = j/2^k$$

where $j = i/5^k$, and 5^k must be a factor of i. For one-digit decimal fractions, only $(.0)_{10}$ and $(.5)_{10}$ are non-repeating in base 2 (20% of the possible fractions); for two-digit decimal fractions, only $(.00)_{10}$, $(.25)_{10}$, $(.50)_{10}$, and $(.75)_{10}$ are non-repeating (4% of the possible fractions); etc. There is a link between relatively prime numbers and repeating fractions that is helpful in understanding why some terminating base 10 fractions do not have a terminating base 2 form. (Knuth, 1981) provides some insight in this area.

Binary versus Decimal Representations

While most computers use base 2 for internal representation and arithmetic, some calculators and business computers use an internal representation of base 10, and thus do not suffer from this representational problem. The motivation for using base 10 in business computers is not entirely to avoid the terminating fraction problem, however, but also to avoid the conversion processes at the input and output units, which historically have taken a significant amount of time. Nowadays, the base 2 format tends to be used for all applications. A detailed description of base 10 formats (9's complement, 10's complement, binary coded decimal) can be found on the companion Web site.

Binary, Octal, and Hexadecimal Radix Representations

While binary numbers reflect the actual internal representation used in most machines, they suffer from the disadvantage that numbers represented in base 2 tend to need more digits than numbers in other bases (why?), and it is easy to make errors when writing them because of the long strings of 1s and 0s. We mentioned earlier in the chapter that base 8, **octal radix**, and base 16, **hexadecimal radix**, are related to base 2. This is due to the three radices all being divisible by 2, the smallest one. We show below that converting among the three bases 2, 8, and 16 is trivial, and there are significant practical advantages to representing numbers in these bases.

Binary numbers may be considerably wider than their base 10 equivalents. As a notational convenience, we sometimes use larger bases than 2 that are even multiples of 2. Converting among bases 2, 8, or 16 is easier than converting to and from base 10. The values used for the base 8 digits are familiar to us as base 10 digits, but for base 16 (hexadecimal) we need six more digits than are used in base 10. The letters A, B, C, D, E, F or their lower-case equivalents are commonly used to represent the corresponding values (10, 11, 12, 13, 14, 15) in hexadecimal. The digits commonly used for bases 2, 8, 10, and 16 are summarized in Figure 2-4. In comparing the base 2 column with the base 8 and base 16 columns, we need three bits to represent each base 8 digit in binary, and we need four bits to represent each base 16 digit in binary. In general, k bits are needed to represent each digit in base 2^k, in which k is an integer, so base $2^3 = 8$ uses three bits and base $2^4 = 16$ uses four bits.

In order to convert a base 2 number into a base 8 number, we partition the base 2 number into groups of three starting from the radix point, and pad the outermost groups with 0s as needed to form triples. Then, we convert each triple to the octal equivalent. For

Binary (base 2)	Octal (base 8)	Decimal (base 10)	Hexadecimal (base 16)
0	0	0	0
1	1	1	1
10	2	2	2
11	3	3	3
100	4	4	4
101	5	5	5
110	6	6	6
111	7	7	7
1000	10	8	8
1001	11	9	9
1010	12	10	A
1011	13	11	B
1100	14	12	C
1101	15	13	D
1110	16	14	E
1111	17	15	F

Figure 2-4
Values for digits in the binary, octal, decimal, and hexadecimal number systems.

conversion from base 2 to base 16, we use groups of four. Consider converting $(10110)_2$ to base 8:

$$(10110)_2 = (010)_2 \, (110)_2 = (2)_8 \, (6)_8 = (26)_8$$

Notice that the leftmost two bits are padded with a 0 on the left in order to create a full triplet.

Now consider converting $(10110110)_2$ to base 16:

$$(10110110)_2 = (1011)_2 \, (0110)_2 = (B)_{16} \, (6)_{16} = (B6)_{16}$$

(Note that 'B' is a base 16 digit corresponding to 11_{10}. B is not a variable.)

The conversion methods can be used to convert a number from any base to any other base, but it may not be very intuitive to convert something like $(513.03)_6$ to base 7. As an aid in performing an unnatural conversion, we can convert to the more familiar base 10 form as an intermediate step, and then continue the conversion from base 10 to the target base. As a general rule, we use the polynomial method when converting *into* base 10, and we use the remainder and multiplication methods when converting *out of* base 10.

Why again would we consider using representations other than base 10? Well, base 6 and base 7 are not very common, but base 2 is the most natural form for representing digital information due to constraints on the physical implementation (see Section A.4.1) and so the base 2 representation is used throughout computing. Base 2 numbers become long rather quickly, and so base 8 and base 16 are used as a notational convenience to keep the lengths of numbers manageable, with base 16 being the more prevalent form these days.

2.1.5 An Early Look at Computer Arithmetic

We will explore computer arithmetic in detail in Chapter 3, but for the moment, we need to learn how to perform simple binary addition because it is used in representing signed binary numbers in the following section. Binary addition is performed similarly to the way we perform decimal addition by hand, as illustrated in Figure 2-5. Two binary numbers A

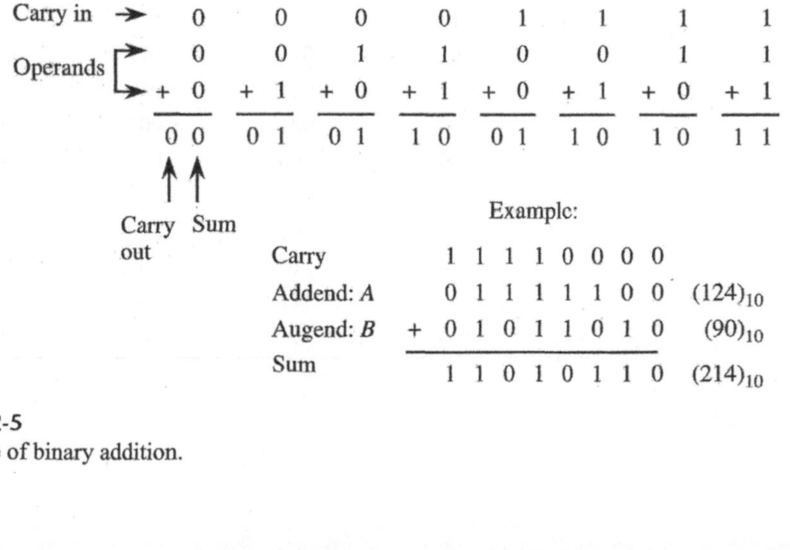

Figure 2-5
Example of binary addition.

and B are added from right to left, creating a sum and a carry in each bit position. Since the rightmost bits of A and B can each assume one of two values, four cases must be considered: $0 + 0$, $0 + 1$, $1 + 0$, and $1 + 1$, with a carry of 0, as shown in the figure. The carry into the rightmost bit position defaults to 0. For the remaining bit positions, the carry into the position can be 0 or 1, so that a total of eight input combinations must be considered, as shown in the figure.

Notice that the largest number we can represent using the eight-bit format shown in Figure 2-5 is $(11111111)_2 = (255)_{10}$ and that the smallest number that can be represented is $(00000000)_2 = (0)_{10}$. The bit patterns 11111111 and 00000000 and all of the intermediate bit patterns represent numbers on the closed interval from 0 to 255, which are all positive numbers.

Up to this point we have considered only unsigned numbers, but we need to represent signed numbers as well, in which (approximately) one half of the bit patterns is assigned to positive numbers and the other half is assigned to negative numbers. Four common representations for base 2 signed numbers are discussed in the next section.

2.1.6 Signed Fixed-Point Numbers

We have considered only the representation of unsigned fixed-point numbers. The situation is quite different in representing *signed* fixed-point numbers. There are four different ways of representing signed numbers that are commonly used: signed magnitude, one's complement, two's complement, and excess notation. We will cover each in turn, using integers for our examples. Throughout the discussion, the reader may wish to refer to Table 2.1, which shows how the various representations appear for a 3-bit number.

Table 2.1   **3-bit integer representations**

Decimal	Unsigned	Sign-Mag.	1's Comp.	2's Comp.	Excess 4
7	111	–	–	–	–
6	110	–	–	–	–
5	101	–	–	–	–
4	100	–	–	–	–
3	011	011	011	011	111
2	010	010	010	010	110
1	001	001	001	001	101
+0	000	000	000	000	100
–0	–	100	111	000	100
–1	–	101	110	111	011
–2	–	110	101	110	010
–3	–	111	100	101	001
–4	–	–	–	100	000

Signed Magnitude

The **signed magnitude** (also referred to as **sign and magnitude**) representation is most familiar to us in the base 10 number system. A plus or minus sign to the left of a number indicates whether the number is positive or negative, as in $+12_{10}$ or -12_{10}. In the binary signed magnitude representation, the leftmost bit is used for the sign, which takes on a value of 0 or 1 for '+' or '−', respectively. The remaining bits contain the absolute magnitude.

Consider representing $(+12)_{10}$ and $(-12)_{10}$ in an eight-bit format:

$$(+12)_{10} = (00001100)_2$$

$$(-12)_{10} = (10001100)_2$$

The negative number is formed by simply changing the sign bit in the positive number from 0 to 1. Notice that there are both positive and negative representations for zero: 00000000 and 10000000.

There are eight bits in this example format, and all bit patterns represent valid numbers, so there are $2^8 = 256$ possible patterns. Only $2^8 - 1 = 255$ different numbers can be represented, however, since +0 and −0 represent the same number.

We will make use of the signed magnitude representation when we look at floating-point numbers in Section 2.2.

One's Complement

The **one's complement** operation is trivial to perform: convert all of the 1s in the number to 0s, and all of the 0's to 1s. See the fourth column from the left in Table 2.1 for examples. We can observe from the table that in the **one's complement** representation the leftmost bit is 0 for positive numbers and 1 for negative numbers, as it is for the signed magnitude representation. This negation, changing 1s to 0s and changing 0s to 1s, is known as **complementing** the bits.

Consider again representing $(+12)_{10}$ and $(-12)_{10}$ in an eight-bit format, now using the one's complement representation:

$$(+12)_{10} = (00001100)_2$$

$$(-12)_{10} = (11110011)_2$$

Note again that there are representations for both +0 and −0, which are 00000000 and 11111111, respectively. As a result, there are only $2^8 - 1 = 255$ different numbers that can be represented, even though there are 2^8 different bit patterns.

The one's complement representation is not commonly used in arithmetic calculations. This is at least partly due to the difficulty in making comparisons when there are two representations for 0. There is also additional complexity involved in adding numbers, which is discussed further in Chapter 3. However, one's complement does have practical applications, such as computing **checksums** in the headers of network packets (see the Example section in Chapter 3).

Two's Complement

The two's complement is formed in a way similar to forming the one's complement: complement all of the bits in the number, but then add 1, and if that addition results in a carry-out from the most significant bit of the number, discard the carry-out. Examination of the fifth column of Table 2.1 shows that in the **two's complement** representation, the leftmost bit is again 0 for positive numbers and is 1 for negative numbers. However, this number format does not have the unfortunate characteristic of signed-magnitude and one's complement representations: it has only one representation for zero. To see that this is true, consider forming the negative of $(+0)_{10}$, which has the bit pattern:

$$(+0)_{10} = (00000000)_2$$

Forming the one's complement of $(00000000)_2$ produces $(11111111)_2$ and adding 1 to it yields $(00000000)_2$, thus $(-0)_{10} = (00000000)_2$. The carry-out of the leftmost position is discarded in two's complement addition (except when detecting an overflow condition, which is covered in Chapter 3). Since there is only one representation for 0, and since all bit patterns are valid, there are $2^8 = 256$ different numbers that can be represented.

Consider again representing $(+12)_{10}$ and $(-12)_{10}$ in an eight-bit format, this time using the two's complement representation. Starting with $(+12)_{10} = (00001100)_2$, complement or negate the number, producing $(11110011)_2$. Now add 1, producing $(11110100)_2$, and thus $(-12)_{10} = (11110100)_2$:

$$(+12)_{10} = (00001100)_2$$

$$(-12)_{10} = (11110100)_2$$

There is an equal number of positive and negative numbers provided zero is considered to be a positive number, which is reasonable because its sign bit is 0. The positive numbers start at 0, but the negative numbers start at -1, and so the magnitude of the most negative number is one greater than the magnitude of the most positive number. The positive number with the largest magnitude is $+127$, and the negative number with the largest magnitude is -128. There is thus no positive number that can be represented that corresponds to the negative of -128. If we try to form the two's complement negative of -128, then we will arrive at a negative number, as shown below:

$$(-128)_{10} = (10000000)_2$$
$$\Downarrow$$

$$
\begin{array}{r}
01111111 \\
+ \quad\quad 1 \\
\hline
(10000000)_2
\end{array}
$$

The two's complement representation of signed integers is the representation most commonly used in conventional computers, and we will use it throughout the book.

Excess Representation

In the **excess** or **biased** representation, the number is treated as unsigned, but is "shifted" in value by subtracting the bias from it. The concept is to assign the smallest numerical bit pattern, all zeros, to the negative of the bias, and assign the remaining numbers in sequence as the bit patterns increase in magnitude. A convenient way to think of an excess representation is that a number is represented as the sum of its two's complement form and another number, which is known as the "excess," or "bias." Once again, refer to Table 2.1, the rightmost column, for examples.

Consider again representing $(+12)_{10}$ and $(-12)_{10}$ in an eight-bit format but now using an excess 128 representation. An excess 128 number is formed by adding 128 to the original number, and then creating the unsigned binary version. For $(+12)_{10}$, we compute $(128 + 12 = 140)_{10}$ and produce the bit pattern $(10001100)_2$. For $(-12)_{10}$, we compute $(128 + -12 = 116)_{10}$ and produce the bit pattern $(01110100)_2$:

$$(+12)_{10} = (10001100)_2$$

$$(-12)_{10} = (01110100)_2$$

Note that there is no numerical significance to the excess value: it simply has the effect of shifting the representation of the two's complement numbers.

There is only one excess representation for 0, since the excess representation is simply a shifted version of the two's complement representation. For the previous case, the excess value is chosen to have the same bit pattern as the largest negative number, which has the effect of making the numbers appear in numerically sorted order if the numbers are viewed in an unsigned binary representation. Thus, the most negative number is $(-128)_{10} = (00000000)_2$ and the most positive number is $(+127)_{10} = (11111111)_2$. This representation simplifies making comparisons between numbers, since the bit patterns for negative numbers have numerically smaller values than the bit patterns for positive numbers. This is important for representing the exponents of floating-point numbers, in which exponents of two numbers are compared in order to make them equal for addition and subtraction. We will explore floating-point representations in the next section.

EXAMPLE 2-1 Wrapped Sequence Numbers in Networking

Most traffic over the Internet travels in chunks of bytes called **packets**, in which there is a header that describes parameters of the packet and a **payload** that is the actual data. Successive packets may take different paths on the way to their destination and arrive out of order. A correct in-order reassembly of packets can be done with the use of a **sequence number** field in the header:

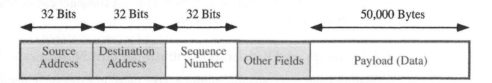

Every byte has a 32-bit numbered position in a stream of bytes that can span many packets. The sequence number identifies the first byte in the payload, and increases by X for a payload of X bytes for the next packet. As we will see, the finite representation of 32 bits for the sequence number can cause problems.

Suppose that the time needed to transmit a packet with a payload of 50,000 bytes is 500 µs (500 millionths of a second), and that a misrouted packet (which happens frequently) can survive in a network for 60 seconds. Is there a danger that two packets with the same sequence numbers will be present in the network?

First, let's figure out how much data can survive in the network in a 60-second interval, and then compare that to how much data the sequence number field can record. The amount of data that could potentially be active in a 60-second interval is:

$$60 \text{ sec } / (500 \text{ µs } / 50,000 \text{ bytes}) = 6 \text{ GB}$$

The 32-bit sequence number field can keep track of only $2^{32} = 4$ GB, which is 2 GB less than the amount of data that can be transmitted and survive in a 60-second interval, and so there is indeed a danger of two packets with the same sequence numbers coexisting for a period of time. (When the sequence number hits its highest value, it wraps around to zero.)

This is a real problem in computer networks, with a few solutions. One solution (**protection against wrapped sequence numbers—PAWS**) effectively extends the sequence number field by using an additional **timestamp** field.

■ 2.2   FLOATING-POINT NUMBERS

The fixed-point number representation, which we explored in Section 2.1, has a fixed position for the radix point, and a fixed number of digits to the left and right of the radix point. A fixed-point representation may need a great many digits in order to represent a practical range of numbers. For example, a computer that can represent a number as large as a trillion[1] maintains at least 40 bits to the left of the radix point since $2^{40} \approx 10^{12}$. If the same computer needs to represent one trillionth, then 40 bits must also be maintained to the right of the radix point, which results in a total of 80 bits per number.

In practice, much larger numbers and much smaller numbers appear during the course of computation, which places even greater demands on a computer. A great deal of hardware is required in order to store and manipulate numbers with 80 or more bits of precision, and computation proceeds more slowly for a large number of digits than for a small number of digits. Fine precision, however, is generally not needed when large numbers are used, and conversely, large numbers do not generally need to be represented when calculations are made with small numbers. A more efficient computer can be realized when only as much precision is retained as is needed.

2.2.1   Range and Precision In Floating-Point Numbers

A **floating-point** representation allows a large range of expressible numbers to be represented in a small number of digits by separating the digits used for *precision* from the dig-

---

[1] In the American number system, which is used here, a trillion = 10^{12}. In the British number system, this is a "million million," or simply a "billion." The British "milliard," or a "thousand million" is what Americans call a "billion."

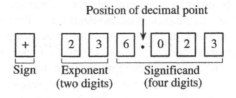

Figure 2-6
Representation of a base 10 floating-point number.

its used for *range*. The base 10 floating-point number representing Avogadro's number is shown below:

$$+6.023 \times 10^{23}$$

Here, the range is represented by a power of 10, 10^{23} in this case, and the precision is represented by the digits in the fixed-point number, 6.023 in this case. In discussing floating-point numbers, the fixed-point portion is often referred to as the **mantissa** or **significand** of the number. Thus a floating-point number can be characterized by a triple of numbers: sign, exponent, and significand.

The range is determined primarily by the number of digits in the exponent (two digits are used here) and the base to which it is raised (base 10 is used here) and the precision is determined primarily by the number of digits in the significand (four digits are used here). Thus the entire number can be represented by a sign and six digits, two for the exponent and four for the significand. Figure 2-6 shows how the triple of sign, exponent, significand, might be formatted in a computer. Notice how the digits are packed together with the sign first, followed by the exponent, followed by the significand. This ordering will turn out to be helpful in comparing two floating-point numbers. The reader should be aware that the decimal point does not need to be stored with the number as long as the decimal point is always in the same position in the significand. (This will be discussed in Section 2.2.2.)

If we need a greater range, and if we are willing to sacrifice precision, then we can use just three digits in the fraction and have three digits left for the exponent without increasing the number of digits used in the representation. An alternative method of increasing the range is to increase the base, which has the effect of increasing the precision of the smallest numbers but decreasing the precision of the largest numbers. The range/precision trade-off is a major advantage of using a floating-point representation, but the reduced precision can cause problems, sometimes leading to disaster, an example of which is described in Section 2.3.

2.2.2 Normalization and The Hidden Bit

A potential problem with representing floating-point numbers is that the same number can be represented in different ways, which makes comparisons and arithmetic operations difficult. For example, consider the numerically equivalent forms shown below:

$$3584.1 \times 10^0 = 3.5841 \times 10^3 = .35841 \times 10^4.$$

In order to avoid multiple representations for the same number, floating-point numbers are maintained in **normalized** form. That is, the radix point is shifted to the left or to the right and the exponent is adjusted accordingly until the radix point is to the left of the leftmost nonzero digit. The rightmost number above is the normalized one. Unfortunately, the number 0 cannot be represented in this scheme, so to represent 0 an exception is made. The exception to this rule is that 0 is represented as all 0s in the mantissa.

If the mantissa is represented as a binary, that is, base 2, number, and if the normalization condition is that there is a leading "1" in the normalized mantissa, then there is no need to store that "1" and in fact, most floating-point formats do *not* store it. Rather, it is "chopped off" before packing up the number for storage, and it is restored when unpacking the number into the exponent and mantissa. This results in having an additional bit of precision on the right of the number, due to removing the leftmost bit. This missing bit is referred to as the **hidden bit**, also known as a **hidden 1**. For example, if the mantissa in a given format is .11010 after normalization, then the bit pattern that is stored is 1010—the leftmost bit is truncated, or hidden. We will see that the IEEE 754 floating-point format uses a hidden bit.

2.2.3 Representing Floating-Point Numbers in the Computer—Preliminaries

Let us design a simple floating-point format to illustrate the important factors in representing floating-point numbers on the computer. Our format may at first seem to be unnecessarily complex, but each element has a purpose. We will represent the significand in signed magnitude format, with a single bit for the sign bit and three hexadecimal digits for the magnitude. The exponent will be a three-bit excess-4 number, with a radix of 16. The normalized form of the number has the hexadecimal point to the left of the three hexadecimal digits.

The bits will be packed together as follows: The sign bit is on the left, followed by the three-bit exponent, followed by the three hexadecimal digits of the significand. Neither the radix nor the hexadecimal point will be stored in the packed form.

The reason for these rather odd-seeming choices is that numbers in this format can be compared for =, ≠, ≤, and ≥ in their "packed" format, which is shown in the illustration below:

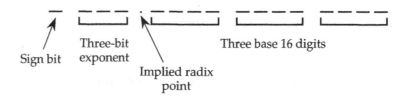

Sign bit   Three-bit exponent   Implied radix point   Three base 16 digits

Consider representing $(358)_{10}$ in this format. The first step is to convert the fixed-point number from its original base into a fixed-point number in the target base. Using the method described in Section 2.1.4, we convert the base 10 number into a base 16 number as shown below:

	Integer	**Remainder**
358/16 =	22	6
22/16 =	1	6
1/16 =	0	1

Thus $(358)_{10} = (166)_{16}$. The next step is to convert the fixed-point number into a floating-point number:

$$(166)_{16} = (166.)_{16} \times 16^0$$

Note that the form 16^0 reflects a base of 16 with an exponent of 0, and that the number 16 as it appears on the page uses a base 10 form. That is, $(16^0)_{10} = (10^0)_{16}$. This is simply a notational convenience used in describing a floating-point number.

The next step is to normalize the number:

$$(166.)_{16} \times 16^0 = (.166)_{16} \times 16^3$$

Finally, we fill in the bit fields of the number. The number is positive, and so we place a 0 in the sign bit position. The exponent is 3, but we represent it in excess 4, so the bit pattern for the exponent is computed as shown below:

$$
\begin{array}{lll}
 & 0\ 1\ 1 & (+3)_{10} \\
\text{Excess 4} & +\ 1\ 0\ 0 & (+4)_{10} \\
\hline
\text{Excess 4 exponent} & 1\ 1\ 1 &
\end{array}
$$

Alternatively, we could have simply computed $3 + 4 = 7$ in base 10, and then made the equivalent conversion $(7)_{10} = (111)_2$.

Finally, each of the base 16 digits is represented in binary as $1 = 0001$, $6 = 0110$, and $6 = 0110$. The final bit pattern is shown below:

$$
\begin{array}{ccccc}
0 & 1\ 1\ 1 & 0\ 0\ 0\ 1 & 0\ 1\ 1\ 0 & 0\ 1\ 1\ 0 \\
+ & 3 & 1 & 6 & 6 \\
\text{Sign} & \text{Exponent} & & \text{Fraction} &
\end{array}
$$

Notice again that the radix point is not explicitly represented in the bit pattern, but its presence is implied. The spaces between digits are for clarity only, and do not suggest that the bits are stored with spaces between them. The bit pattern as stored in a computer's memory would look like this:

$$0111000101100110$$

The use of an excess 4 exponent instead of a two's complement or a signed magnitude exponent simplifies addition and subtraction of floating-point numbers (which we cover in detail in Chapter 3). In order to add or subtract two normalized floating-point numbers, the smaller exponent (smaller in degree, not magnitude) must first be increased to the larger exponent (this retains the range), which also has the effect of unnormalizing the smaller number. In order to determine which exponent is larger, we only need to treat the bit patterns as unsigned numbers and then make our comparison. That is, using an excess 4 representation, the smallest exponent is -4, which is represented as 000. The largest exponent is $+3$, which is represented as 111. The remaining bit patterns for $-3, -2, -1, 0, +1$, and $+2$ fall in their respective order as 001, 010, 011, 100, 101, and 110.

Now if we are given the bit pattern shown above for $(358)_{10}$ along with a description of the floating-point representation, then we can easily determine the number. The sign bit is a 0, which means that the number is positive. The exponent in unsigned form is the number $(+7)_{10}$, but since we are using excess 4, we must subtract 4 from it, which results in an actual exponent of $(+7 - 4 = +3)_{10}$. The fraction is grouped in four-bit hexadecimal digits, which gives a fraction of $(.166)_{16}$. Putting it all together results in $(+.166 \times 16^3)_{16} = (358)_{10}$.

Now suppose that only 10 bits are allowed for the fraction in the above example, instead of the 12 bits that group evenly into fours for hexadecimal digits. How does the representation change? One approach might be to round the fraction and adjust the exponent as necessary. Another approach, which we use here, is to simply truncate the least significant bits by **chopping** and avoid making adjustments to the exponent, so that the number we actually represent is:

$$
\begin{array}{ccccc}
0 & 1\;1\;1 & .\;0\;0\;0\;1 & 0\;1\;1\;0 & 0\;1\;x\;x \\
+ & 3 & 1 & 6 & 4 \\
\text{Sign} & \text{Exponent} & & \text{Fraction} &
\end{array}
$$

If we treat the missing bits as 0s, then this bit pattern represents $(.164 \times 16^3)_{16}$. This method of truncation produces a biased error, since values of 00, 01, 10, and 11 in the missing bits are all treated as 0, and so the error is in the range from 0 to $(.003)_{16}$. The bias comes about because the error is not symmetric about 0. We will explore the bias problem further in the next section; a more thorough discussion can be found in (Hamacher et al., 2001 and Koren, 2001).

We again stress that whatever the floating-point format is, it must be known to all parties that intend to store or retrieve numbers in that format. The Institute of Electrical and Electronics Engineers (IEEE) has taken the lead in standardizing floating-point formats. The IEEE 754 floating-point format, which is in nearly universal usage, is discussed in Section 2.2.5.

2.2.4 Error in Floating-Point Representations

The fact that finite precision introduces error means that we should consider how great the error is (by "error" we mean the distance between two adjacent representable numbers) and whether it is acceptable for our application. As an example of a potential pitfall, consider representing one million in floating point, and then subtracting one million 1s from it. We may still be left with a million if the error is greater than 1.[2]

---

[2] Most computers these days will let this upper bound get at least as high as 8 million using the default precision.

In order to characterize error, range, and precision, we use the following notation:

b Base

s Number of significant *digits* (not bits) in the fraction

M Largest exponent

m Smallest exponent

The number of significant digits in the fraction is represented by s, which is different from the number of bits in the fraction if the base is anything other than 2 (for example, base 16 uses four bits for each digit). In general, if the base is 2^k where k is an integer, then k bits are needed to represent each digit. The use of a hidden 1 increases s by one bit even though it does not increase the number of representable numbers. In the previous example, there are three significant digits in the base 16 fraction and there are 12 bits that make up the three digits. There are three bits in the excess 4 exponent, which gives an exponent range of $[-2^2$ to $2^2 - 1]$. For this case, $b = 16$, $s = 3$, $M = 3$, and $m = -4$.

In the analysis of a floating-point representation, there are five characteristics that we consider: the number of representable numbers, the numbers that have the largest and smallest magnitudes (other than zero), and the sizes of the largest and smallest gaps between successive numbers.

The number of representable numbers can be determined as shown in Figure 2-7. The sign bit can take on two values, as indicated by the position marked with an encircled "A." The total number of exponents is indicated in position B. Note that not all exponent bit patterns are valid in all representations. The IEEE 754 floating-point standard, which we will study shortly, has a smallest exponent of -126 even though the eight-bit exponent can support a number as small as -128. The forbidden exponents are reserved for special numbers, such as zero and infinity.

The first digit of the fraction is considered next, which can take on any value except 0 in a normalized representation (except when a hidden 1 is used), as indicated by $(b - 1)$ at position C. The remaining digits of the fraction can take on any of the b values for the base, as indicated by b^{s-1} at position D. If a hidden 1 is used, then position C is removed and position D is replaced with b^s. Finally, there must be a representation for 0, which is accounted for in position E.

Consider now the numbers with the smallest and largest magnitudes. The number with the smallest magnitude has the smallest exponent and the smallest nonzero normalized fraction. There must be a nonzero value in the first digit, and since a 1 is the smallest value we

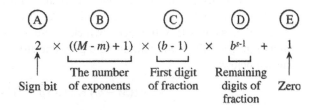

Figure 2-7
Calculation of the number of representable numbers in a floating-point representation.

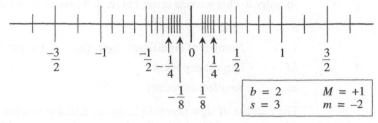

Figure 2-8
A number line showing all representable numbers in a simple floating-point format.

can place there, the smallest fraction is b^{-1}. The number with the smallest magnitude is then $b^m \cdot b^{-1} = b^{m-1}$. Similarly, the number with the largest magnitude has the largest exponent and the largest fraction (when the fraction is all 1s), which is equal to $b^M \cdot (1 - b^{-s})$.

The smallest and largest gaps are computed in a similar manner. The smallest gap occurs when the exponent is at its smallest value and the least significant bit of the fraction changes. This gap is $b^m \cdot b^{-s} = b^{m-s}$. The largest gap occurs when the exponent is at its largest value and the least significant bit of the fraction changes. This gap is $b^M \cdot b^{-s} = b^{M-s}$.

As an example, consider a floating-point representation in which there is a sign bit, a two-bit excess 2 exponent, and a three-bit normalized base 2 fraction in which the leading 1 is visible; that is, the leading 1 is not hidden. The representation of 0 is the bit pattern 000000. A number line showing all possible numbers that can be represented in this format is shown in Figure 2-8. Notice that there is a relatively large gap between 0 and the first representable number, because the normalized representation does not support bit patterns that correspond to numbers between 0 and the first representable number.

The smallest representable number occurs when the exponent and the fraction are at their smallest values. The smallest exponent is -2, and the smallest normalized fraction is $(.100)_2$. The smallest representable number is then $b^m \times b^{-1} = b^{m-1} = 2^{-2-1} = 1/8$.

Similarly, the largest representable number occurs when the exponent and the fraction are both at their largest values. The largest fraction occurs when the fraction is all 1s, which is a number that is 2^{-3} less than 1 since there are three digits in the fraction. The largest representable number is then $b^M \times (1 - b^{-s}) = 2^1 \times (1 - 2^{-3}) = 7/4$.

The smallest gap occurs when the exponent is at its smallest value and the least significant bit of the fraction changes, which is $b^m \times b^{-s} = b^{m-s} = 2^{-2-3} = 1/32$. Similarly, the largest gap occurs when the exponent is at its largest value and the least significant bit of the fraction changes, which is $b^M \times b^{-s} = b^{M-s} = 2^{1-3} = 1/4$.

The number of bit patterns that represent valid numbers is less than the number of possible bit patterns, due to normalization. As discussed earlier, the number of representable numbers consists of five parts, which take into account the sign bit, the exponents, the first significant digit, the remaining digits, and the bit pattern for 0. This is computed as shown below:

$$2 \times ((M - m) + 1) \times (b - 1) \times b^{s-1} + 1$$

$$= 2 \times ((1 - (-2)) + 1) \times (2 - 1) \times 2^{3-1} + 1$$

$$= 33 \text{ representable numbers}$$

Notice that the gaps are small for small numbers and that the gaps are large for large numbers. In fact, the relative error is approximately the same for all numbers. If we take the ratio of a large gap to a large number, and compare that to the ratio of a small gap to a small number, then the ratios are the same:

$$\text{A large gap} \longrightarrow \frac{b^{M-s}}{b^M \times (1 - b^{-s})} = \frac{b^{-s}}{1 - b^{-s}} = \frac{1}{b^s - 1}$$

and

$$\text{A small gap} \longrightarrow \frac{b^{m-s}}{b^m \times (1 - b^{-s})} = \frac{b^{-s}}{1 - b^{-s}} = \frac{1}{b^s - 1}$$

The representation for a "small number" is used here, rather than the smallest number, because the large gap between zero and the first representable number is a special case.

EXAMPLE 2-2   Floating-Point Conversion

Consider the problem of converting $(9.375 \times 10^{-2})_{10}$ to base 2 scientific notation. That is, the result should have the form $x.yy \times 2^z$. We start by converting from base 10 floating point to base 10 fixed point by moving the decimal point two positions to the left, which corresponds to the -2 exponent: .09375. We then convert from base 10 fixed point to base 2 fixed point by using the multiplication method:

$$.09375 \times 2 = 0.1875$$
$$.1875 \times 2 = 0.375$$
$$.375 \times 2 = 0.75$$
$$.75 \times 2 = 1.5$$
$$.5 \times 2 = 1.0$$

so $(.09375)_{10} = (.00011)_2$. Finally, we convert to normalized base 2 floating point: $.00011 = .00011 \times 2^0 = 1.1 \times 2^{-4}$.

■

2.2.5 The IEEE 754 Floating Point Standard

There are many ways to represent floating point numbers, a few of which we have already explored. Each representation has its own characteristics in terms of range, precision, and the number of representable numbers. In an effort to improve software portability and ensure uniform accuracy of floating-point calculations, the IEEE 754 floating-point standard for binary numbers was developed (IEEE, 1985). There are a few entrenched product lines that predate the standard that do not use it, such as the IBM/370, the DEC VAX, and the Cray line, but virtually all new architectures generally provide some level of IEEE 754 support.

The IEEE 754 standard as described below must be supported by a computer *system*, and not necessarily by the hardware entirely. That is, a mixture of hardware and software can be used while still conforming to the standard.

2.2.5.1 Formats

There are two primary formats in the IEEE 754 standard: **single-precision** and **double-precision**. Figure 2-9 summarizes the layouts of the two formats. The single-precision format occupies 32 bits, whereas the double precision format occupies 64 bits. The double-precision format is simply a wider version of the single precision format.

The sign bit is in the leftmost position and indicates a positive or negative number for a 0 or a 1, respectively. The 8-bit excess 127 (*not* 128) exponent follows, in which the bit patterns 00000000 and 11111111 are reserved for special cases, as described below. For double precision, the 11-bit exponent is represented in excess 1023, with 00000000000 and 11111111111 reserved. The 23-bit base 2 fraction follows. There is a hidden bit to the *left* of the binary point, which when taken together with the single-precision fraction form a 23 + 1 = 24-bit significand of the form 1.fff...f where the fff...f pattern represents the 23-bit fractional part that is stored. The double-precision format also uses a hidden bit to the left of the binary point, which supports a 52 + 1 = 53 bit significand. For both formats, the number is normalized unless **denormalized** numbers are supported, as described later.

There are five basic types of numbers that can be represented. Nonzero normalized numbers take the form described above. A so-called "clean zero" is represented by the reserved bit pattern 00000000 in the exponent and all 0s in the fraction. The sign bit can be 0 or 1, and so there are two representations for zero: +0 and –0.

Infinity has a representation in which the exponent contains the reserved bit pattern 11111111, the fraction contains all 0s, and the sign bit is 0 or 1. Infinity is useful in handling overflow situations or in giving a valid representation to a number (other than zero) divided by zero. If zero is divided by zero or infinity is divided by infinity, then the result is undefined. This is represented by the **NaN** (not a number) format in which the exponent contains the reserved bit pattern 11111111, the fraction is nonzero and the sign bit is 0 or 1. A NaN can also be produced by attempting to take the square root of –1.

As with all normalized representations, there is a large gap between zero and the first representable number. The denormalized, "dirty zero" representation allows numbers in this

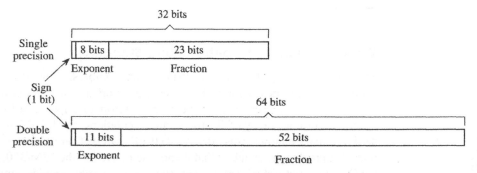

Figure 2-9
Single-precision and double-precision IEEE 754 floating-point formats.

	Value	Sign	Exponent	Fraction
		Bit Pattern		
(a)	$+1.101 \times 2^5$	0	1000 0100	101 0000 0000 0000 0000 0000
(b)	-1.01011×2^{-126}	1	0000 0001	010 1100 0000 0000 0000 0000
(c)	$+1.0 \times 2^{127}$	0	1111 1110	000 0000 0000 0000 0000 0000
(d)	$+0$	0	0000 0000	000 0000 0000 0000 0000 0000
(e)	-0	1	0000 0000	000 0000 0000 0000 0000 0000
(f)	$+\infty$	0	1111 1111	000 0000 0000 0000 0000 0000
(g)	$+2^{-128}$	0	0000 0000	010 0000 0000 0000 0000 0000
(h)	$+NaN$	0	1111 1111	011 0111 0000 0000 0000 0000
(i)	$+2^{-128}$	0	011 0111 1111	0000 0000 0000 0000 0000 0000 0000 0000 0000 0000 0000 0000 0000 0000

Figure 2-10

Examples of IEEE 754 floating-point numbers in single precision format (a–h) and double-precision format (i). Spaces are shown for clarity only: they are not part of the representation.

gap to be represented. The sign bit can be 0 or 1, the exponent contains the reserved bit pattern 00000000 which represents −126 for single precision (−1022 for double precision), and the fraction contains the actual bit pattern for the magnitude of the number. Thus, there is no hidden 1 for this format. Note that the *denormalized* representation is not an *unnormalized* representation. The key difference is that there is only one representation for each denormalized number, whereas there are infinitely many unnormalized representations.

Figure 2-10 illustrates some examples of IEEE 754 floating-point numbers. Examples (a) through (h) are in single-precision format and example (i) is in double precision format. Example (a) shows an ordinary single-precision number. Notice that the significand is 1.101, but that only the fraction (101) is explicitly represented. Example (b) uses the smallest single-precision exponent (−126) and example (c) uses the largest single precision exponent (127).

Examples (d) and (e) illustrate the two representations for zero. Example (f) illustrates the bit pattern for $+\infty$. There is also a corresponding bit pattern for $-\infty$. Example (g) shows a denormalized number. Notice that although the number itself is 2^{-128}, the smallest representable exponent is still −126. The exponent for single-precision denormalized numbers is always −126, which is represented by the bit pattern 00000000 and a nonzero fraction. The fraction represents the magnitude of the number, rather than a significand. Thus we have $+2^{-128} = +.01 \times 2^{-126}$, which is represented by the bit pattern shown in Figure 2-10g.

Example (h) shows a single-precision NaN. A NaN can be positive or negative. Finally, example (i) revisits the representation of 2^{-128} but now using double precision. The representation is for an ordinary double-precision number and so there are no special considerations here. Notice that 2^{-128} has a significand of 1.0, which is why the fraction field is all 0s.

In addition to the single-precision and double-precision formats, there are also **single-extended** and **double-extended** formats. The extended formats are not visible to the user, but they are used to retain a greater amount of internal precision during calculations to reduce the effects of roundoff errors. The extended formats increase the widths of the exponents and fractions by a number of bits that can vary depending on the implementation. For instance, the single-extended format adds at least three bits to the exponent and eight bits to the fraction. The double-extended format is typically 80 bits wide, with a 15-bit exponent and a 64-bit fraction.

2.2.5.2 Rounding

An implementation of IEEE 754 must provide at least single precision, whereas the remaining formats are optional. Further, the result of any single operation on floating-point numbers must be accurate to within half a bit in the least significant bit of the fraction. This means that some additional bits of precision may need to be retained during computation (referred to as **guard bits**), and there must be an appropriate method of rounding the intermediate result to the number of bits in the fraction.

There are four rounding modes in the IEEE 754 standard. One mode rounds toward 0, another rounds toward $+\infty$, and another rounds toward $-\infty$. The default mode rounds to the nearest representable number. Halfway cases round to the number whose low order digit is even. For example, 1.01101 rounds to 1.0110 whereas 1.01111 rounds to 1.1000.

EXAMPLE 2-3 IEEE 754 Representation

For this example, we will convert the decimal floating-point number -153.81×10^{-5} into a single-precision IEEE 754 floating-point format. As we will see, this terminating base 10 number does not terminate in base 2, and will have a roundoff issue to consider.

There are three fields in the 32-bit single-precision format that must be filled in: sign, exponent, and fraction. For the sign bit, we assign a value of 1 because -153.81×10^{-5} is a negative number. Note that the sign bit is for the number as a whole, and is unrelated to the sign bit of the exponent.

Next, we convert -153.81×10^{-5} to a fixed-point base 10 representation, and then normalize and fill in the exponent and fraction fields for the single-precision format. The conversion to fixed-point base 10 is shown below (the sign has been accounted for and so we can ignore it in this step):

$$153.81 \times 10^{-\textcircled{5}}$$

$$\Downarrow$$

$$.\ 0\ 0\ 1\ 5\ 3\ 8\ 1$$

Decimal point is moved 5
places to the left.

Now convert to base 2 (using the multiplication method, as one approach):

.00000000 01100100 11001101 00001001 0 0110...

When do we stop computing digits to the right? In single precision format, there are 23 places to the right of the leftmost 1. Scan the fraction from left to right and locate the first 1. Count 23 places to the right and keep that many bits. The remaining bits to the right (the shaded area above) can be ignored. Actually, we do need a few bits in the shaded area for proper rounding. For this example we will round toward $+\infty$, and for this case the shaded area changes the rightmost bit in the fraction to 1. The next step is to normalize, by moving the radix point to the right of the leftmost 1 (10 places to the right) and adding an exponent to correspond:

$$1.10010011001101000010011 \times 2^{-10}$$

In the final representation, the 1 to the left of the radix point is hidden and only the 23 bits to the right of the radix point are explicitly represented. The exponent is in excess 127, which for this case is -10 + 127 = 117, which in binary is: $117_{10} = 01110101_2$.

The final representation is shown below:

1   01110101   10010011001101000010011

Sign   Exponent   Fraction

Note that if we rounded to the nearest representable number, that the rightmost bit of the fraction would be 0 instead of 1. The rightmost bit of the fraction would also be 0 for the remaining two rounding methods: round toward 0, and round toward $-\infty$.

■

■ 2.3 CASE STUDY: PATRIOT MISSILE DEFENSE FAILURE CAUSED BY LOSS OF PRECISION

During the 1991–1992 Operation Desert Storm conflict between Coalition forces and Iraq, the Coalition used a military base in Dhahran, Saudi Arabia that was protected by six U.S. Patriot Missile batteries. The Patriot system was originally designed to be mobile and to operate for only a few hours in order to avoid detection.

The Patriot system tracks and intercepts certain types of objects, such as cruise missiles or Scud ballistic missiles, one of which hit a U.S. Army barracks at Dhahran on February 5, 1991, killing 28 Americans. The Patriot system failed to track and intercept the incoming Scud due to a loss of precision in converting integers to a floating-point number representation.

A radar system operates by sending out a train of electromagnetic pulses in various directions and then listening for return signals that are reflected from objects in the path of the radar beam. If an airborne object of interest such as a Scud is detected by the Patriot radar system, then the position of a **range gate** is determined (see Figure 2-11), which estimates the position of the object being tracked during the next scan. The range gate also allows information outside of its boundaries to be filtered out, which simplifies tracking. The position of the object (a Scud for this case) is confirmed if it is found within the range gate.

The prediction of where the Scud will next appear is a function of the Scud's velocity. The Scud's velocity is determined by its change in position with respect to time, and time is updated in the Patriot's internal clock in 100 ms intervals. Velocity is represented as a 24-bit floating-point number, and time is represented as a 24-bit integer, but both must be

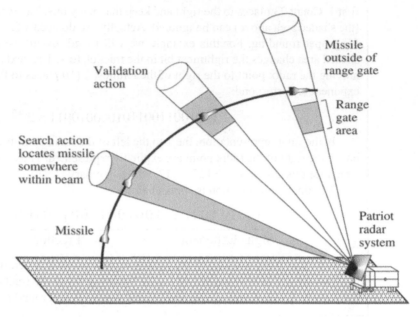

Figure 2-11
Effect of conversion error on range gate calculation.

represented as 24-bit floating-point numbers in order to predict where the Scud will next appear.

The conversion from integer time to real time results in a loss of precision that increases as the internal clock time increases. The error introduced by the conversion results in an error in the range gate calculation, which is proportional to the target's velocity and the length of time that the system is running. The cause of the Dhahran incident, after the Patriot battery had been operating continuously for over 100 hours, is that the range gate shifted by 687 m, resulting in the failed interception of a Scud.

The conversion problem was known two weeks in advance of the Dhahran incident as a result of data provided by Israel, but it took until the day after the attack for new software to arrive due to the difficulty of distributing bug fixes in a wartime environment. A solution to the problem, until a software fix could be made available, would have been to simply reboot the system every few hours, which would have the effect of resetting the internal clock. Since field personnel were not informed of how long was too long to keep a system running, which was in fact known at the time from data provided by Israel, this solution was never implemented. The lesson for us is to be very aware of the limitations of relying on calculations that use finite precision.

■ 2.4 CHARACTER CODES

Unlike real numbers, which have an infinite range, there is only a finite number of characters. An entire character set can be represented with a small number of bits per character.

Intel vs. Motorola: Floating-Point Errors

As this chapter shows, floating-point accuracy and precision are not the clear-cut matters that they are when operating with integers and fixed-point numbers. Both Intel and Motorola have had issues with errors in floating-point operations, though from opposite ends of the spectrum.

One of the most famous, or infamous, was the Pentium floating-point bug, discovered by a mathematician in 1994. It was found that with certain number combinations the Pentium would return answers with errors as far up as the third digit. An example of one of the worst was 962,306,957,033/ 11,010,046. Correct answer: 87,402.6282027341; incorrect answer: 87,399.5805831329. One of the most popular was to enter the following formula into an Excel® spreadsheet: =4195835–((4195835/3145727)*3145727. A processor without this error will return exactly 0. This flaw was widely reported; Intel's initial response was that users were very unlikely to encounter the error, and they would only replace processors for users who could demonstrate the need for high accuracy in their use of the machine. Shortly thereafter

IBM announced that they were halting the production of machines with Pentium processors, and showed that certain spreadsheet users could encounter the error much more frequently. Intel capitulated and announced that they would provide free replacements upon demand.

Motorola's "error" is that because of the large word size in their floating-point registers, variables stored there during calculation will have *too much* precision. Normally this would not be a problem, but a few programs rely on the precise definition of the IEEE floating-point standard and count on the specified normal rounding errors in their algorithms. The gnu gcc compiler has a switch, -ffloat-store, that prevents storage of floating-point numbers in registers and inhibits other options that might cause storage of floating-point values in registers instead of memory. (For the curious, the Unix "man gcc" command provides information about this compiler option.)

Three of the most common character representations, ASCII, EBCDIC, and Unicode, are described here.

2.4.1 The ASCII Character Set

The American Standard Code for Information Interchange (**ASCII**) is summarized in Figure 2-12, using hexadecimal indices. The representation for each character consists of seven bits, and all 2^7 possible bit patterns represent valid characters. The characters in positions 00–1F and position 7F are special control characters that are used for transmission, printing control, and other non-textual purposes. The remaining characters are all printable, and include letters, numbers, punctuation, and a space. The digits 0-9 appear in sequence, as do the upper- and lower-case letters[3]. This organization simplifies character manipulation. In order to change the character representation of a digit into its numerical value, we can subtract $(30)_{16}$ from it. In order to convert the ASCII character '5,' which is in position $(35)_{16}$, into the number 5, we compute $(35 - 30 = 5)_{16}$. In order to convert an upper-case letter into a lower-case letter, we add $(20)_{16}$. For example, to convert the letter

---

[3] As an aside, the character 'a' and the character 'A' are different and have different codes in the ASCII table. The small letters like 'a' are called **lower case** and the capital letters like 'A' are called **upper case**. The naming comes from the positions of the characters in a printer's typecase. The capital letters appear above the small letters, which resulted in the upper-case/lower-case naming. These days, typesetting is almost always performed electronically, but the traditional naming is still used.

00 NUL	10 DLE	20 SP	30 0	40 @	50 P	60 `	70 p
01 SOH	11 DC1	21 !	31 1	41 A	51 Q	61 a	71 q
02 STX	12 DC2	22 "	32 2	42 B	52 R	62 b	72 r
03 ETX	13 DC3	23 #	33 3	43 C	53 S	63 c	73 s
04 EOT	14 DC4	24 $	34 4	44 D	54 T	64 d	74 t
05 ENQ	15 NAK	25 %	35 5	45 E	55 U	65 e	75 u
06 ACK	16 SYN	26 &	36 6	46 F	56 V	66 f	76 v
07 BEL	17 ETB	27 '	37 7	47 G	57 W	67 g	77 w
08 BS	18 CAN	28 (	38 8	48 H	58 X	68 h	78 x
09 HT	19 EM	29)	39 9	49 I	59 Y	69 i	79 y
0A LF	1A SUB	2A *	3A :	4A J	5A Z	6A j	7A z
0B VT	1B ESC	2B +	3B ;	4B K	5B [	6B k	7B {
0C FF	1C FS	2C ,	3C <	4C L	5C \	6C l	7C |
0D CR	1D GS	2D -	3D =	4D M	5D]	6D m	7D }
0E SO	1E RS	2E .	3E >	4E N	5E ^	6E n	7E ~
0F SI	1F US	2F /	3F ?	4F O	5F _	6F o	7F DEL

NUL	Null	FF	Form feed	CAN	Cancel
SOH	Start of heading	CR	Carriage return	EM	End of medium
STX	Start of text	SO	Shift out	SUB	Substitute
ETX	End of text	SI	Shift in	ESC	Escape
EOT	End of transmission	DLE	Data link escape	FS	File separator
ENQ	Enquiry	DC1	Device control 1	GS	Group separator
ACK	Acknowledge	DC2	Device control 2	RS	Record separator
BEL	Bell	DC3	Device control 3	US	Unit separator
BS	Backspace	DC4	Device control 4	SP	Space
HT	Horizontal tab	NAK	Negative acknowledge	DEL	Delete
LF	Line feed	SYN	Synchronous idle		
VT	Vertical tab	ETB	End of transmission block		

Figure 2-12
The ASCII character code, shown with hexadecimal indices.

'H,' which is at location $(48)_{16}$ in the ASCII table, into the letter 'h,' which is at position $(68)_{16}$, we compute $(48 + 20 = 68)_{16}$.

2.4.2 The EBCDIC Character Set

A problem with the ASCII code is that only 128 characters can be represented, which is a limitation for many keyboards that have a lot of special characters in addition to upper- and lower-case letters. The Extended Binary Coded Decimal Interchange Code (**EBCDIC**) is an eight-bit code that is used extensively in IBM mainframe and midrange computers such as the AS/400. Since seven-bit ASCII characters are frequently represented in an eight-bit modified form (one character per byte), in which a 0 or a 1 is appended to the left of the seven-bit pattern, the use of EBCDIC does not place a greater demand on the storage of characters in a computer. For serial transmission, however (see Chapter 9), an eight-bit code takes more time to transmit than a seven-bit code, and for this case the wider code does make a difference.

The EBCDIC code is summarized in Figure 2-13. There are gaps in the table that can be used for application-specific characters. The fact that there are gaps in the upper- and lower-case sequences is not a major disadvantage because character manipulations can still be done as for ASCII, but using different offsets.

00	NUL	20	DS	40	SP	60	–	80		A0		C0	{	E0	\
01	SOH	21	SOS	41		61	/	81	a	A1	~	C1	A	E1	
02	STX	22	FS	42		62		82	b	A2	s	C2	B	E2	S
03	ETX	23		43		63		83	c	A3	t	C3	C	E3	T
04	PF	24	BYP	44		64		84	d	A4	u	C4	D	E4	U
05	HT	25	LF	45		65		85	e	A5	v	C5	E	E5	V
06	LC	26	ETB	46		66		86	f	A6	w	C6	F	E6	W
07	DEL	27	ESC	47		67		87	g	A7	x	C7	G	E7	X
08		28		48		68		88	h	A8	y	C8	H	E8	Y
09		29		49		69		89	i	A9	z	C9	I	E9	Z
0A	SMM	2A	SM	4A	¢	6A	'	8A		AA		CA		EA	
0B	VT	2B	CU2	4B	.	6B	,	8B		AB		CB		EB	
0C	FF	2C		4C	<	6C	%	8C		AC		CC		EC	
0D	CR	2D	ENQ	4D	(	6D	_	8D		AD		CD		ED	
0E	SO	2E	ACK	4E	+	6E	>	8E		AE		CE		EE	
0F	SI	2F	BEL	4F	|	6F	?	8F		AF		CF		EF	
10	DLE	30		50	&	70		90		B0		D0	}	F0	0
11	DC1	31		51		71		91	j	B1		D1	J	F1	1
12	DC2	32	SYN	52		72		92	k	B2		D2	K	F2	2
13	TM	33		53		73		93	l	B3		D3	L	F3	3
14	RES	34	PN	54		74		94	m	B4		D4	M	F4	4
15	NL	35	RS	55		75		95	n	B5		D5	N	F5	5
16	BS	36	UC	56		76		96	o	B6		D6	O	F6	6
17	IL	37	EOT	57		77		97	p	B7		D7	P	F7	7
18	CAN	38		58		78		98	q	B8		D8	Q	F8	8
19	EM	39		59		79		99	r	B9		D9	R	F9	9
1A	CC	3A		5A	!	7A	:	9A		BA		DA		FA	|
1B	CU1	3B	CU3	5B	$	7B	#	9B		BB		DB		FB	
1C	IFS	3C	DC4	5C	*	7C	@	9C		BC		DC		FC	
1D	IGS	3D	NAK	5D	)	7D	'	9D		BD		DD		FD	
1E	IRS	3E		5E	;	7E	=	9E		BE		DE		FE	
1F	IUS	3F	SUB	5F	¬	7F	"	9F		BF		DF		FF	

STX	Start of text	RS	Reader Stop	DC1	Device Control 1	BEL	Bell
DLE	Data Link Escape	PF	Punch Off	DC2	Device Control 2	SP	Space
BS	Backspace	DS	Digit Select	DC4	Device Control 4	IL	Idle
ACK	Acknowledge	PN	Punch On	CU1	Customer Use 1	NUL	Null
SOH	Start of Heading	SM	Set Mode	CU2	Customer Use 2		
ENQ	Enquiry	LC	Lower Case	CU3	Customer Use 3		
ESC	Escape	CC	Cursor Control	SYN	Synchronous Idle		
BYP	Bypass	CR	Carriage Return	IFS	Interchange File Separator		
CAN	Cancel	EM	End of Medium	EOT	End of Transmission		
RES	Restore	FF	Form Feed	ETB	End of Transmission Block		
SI	Shift In	TM	Tape Mark	NAK	Negative Acknowledge		
SO	Shift Out	UC	Upper Case	SMM	Start of Manual Message		
DEL	Delete	FS	Field Separator	SOS	Start of Significance		
SUB	Substitute	HT	Horizontal Tab	IGS	Interchange Group Separator		
NL	New Line	VT	Vertical Tab	IRS	Interchange Record Separator		
LF	Line Feed	UC	Upper Case	IUS	Interchange Unit Separator		

Figure 2-13
The EBCDIC character code, shown with hexadecimal indices.

2.4.3 The Unicode Character Set

The ASCII and EBCDIC codes support the historically dominant (Latin) character sets used in computers. There are many more character sets in the world, and a simple ASCII-to-language-X mapping does not work for the general case, and so a new universal character standard was developed that supports a great breadth of the world's character sets, called **Unicode**.

Unicode is an evolving standard. It changes as new character sets are introduced into it, and as existing character sets evolve and their representations are refined. In version 4.0 of the Unicode standard, there are 96,382 distinct coded characters that cover the principal written languages of the Americas, Europe, the Middle East, Africa, India, Asia, and Pacifica.

The Unicode Standard uses a 16-bit code set in which there is a one-to-one correspondence between 16-bit codes and characters. Like ASCII, there are no complex modes or escape codes. While Unicode supports many more characters than ASCII or EBCDIC, it is not the end-all standard. In fact, the 16-bit Unicode standard is a subset of the 32-bit ISO 10646 Universal Character Set (UCS-4).

Glyphs for the first 256 Unicode characters are shown in Figure 2-14, according to Unicode version 4.1. Note that the first 128 characters are the same as in ASCII.

Summary

All data in a computer is represented in terms of bits, which can be organized and interpreted as integers, fixed-point numbers, floating-point numbers, or characters. Character codes, such as ASCII, EBCDIC, and Unicode, have finite sizes and can thus be completely represented in a finite number of bits. The number of bits used for representing numbers is also finite, and as a result only a subset of the real numbers can be represented. This leads to the notions of range, precision, and error. The range for a number representation defines the largest and smallest magnitudes that can be represented, and is almost entirely determined by the base and the number of bits in the exponent for a floating-point representation. The precision is determined by the number of bits used in representing the magnitude (excluding the exponent bits in a floating-point representation). Error arises in floating-point representations because there are real numbers that fall within the gaps between adjacent representable numbers.

0000	NUL	0020	SP	0040	@	0060	`	0080	Ctrl	00A0	NBS	00C0	À	00E0	à
0001	SOH	0021	!	0041	A	0061	a	0081	Ctrl	00A1	¡	00C1	Á	00E1	á
0002	STX	0022	"	0042	B	0062	b	0082	Ctrl	00A2	¢	00C2	Â	00E2	â
0003	ETX	0023	#	0043	C	0063	c	0083	Ctrl	00A3	£	00C3	Ã	00E3	ã
0004	EOT	0024	$	0044	D	0064	d	0084	Ctrl	00A4	€	00C4	Ä	00E4	ä
0005	ENQ	0025	%	0045	E	0065	e	0085	Ctrl	00A5	¥	00C5	Å	00E5	å
0006	ACK	0026	&	0046	F	0066	f	0086	Ctrl	00A6	¦	00C6	Æ	00E6	æ
0007	BEL	0027	'	0047	G	0067	g	0087	Ctrl	00A7	§	00C7	Ç	00E7	ç
0008	BS	0028	(	0048	H	0068	h	0088	Ctrl	00A8	¨	00C8	È	00E8	è
0009	HT	0029	)	0049	I	0069	i	0089	Ctrl	00A9	©	00C9	É	00E9	é
000A	LF	002A	*	004A	J	006A	j	008A	Ctrl	00AA	ª	00CA	Ê	00EA	ê
000B	VT	002B	+	004B	K	006B	k	008B	Ctrl	00AB	«	00CB	Ë	00EB	ë
000C	FF	002C	,	004C	L	006C	l	008C	Ctrl	00AC	¬	00CC	Ì	00EC	ì
000D	CR	002D	-	004D	M	006D	m	008D	Ctrl	00AD	–	00CD	Í	00ED	í
000E	SO	002E	.	004E	N	006E	n	008E	Ctrl	00AE	®	00CE	Î	00EE	î
000F	SI	002F	/	004F	O	006F	o	008F	Ctrl	00AF	¯	00CF	Ï	00EF	ï
0010	DLE	0030	0	0050	P	0070	p	0090	Ctrl	00B0	°	00D0	Ð	00F0	¶
0011	DC1	0031	1	0051	Q	0071	q	0091	Ctrl	00B1		00D1	Ñ	00F1	ñ
0012	DC2	0032	2	0052	R	0072	r	0092	Ctrl	00B2	²	00D2	Ò	00F2	ò
0013	DC3	0033	3	0053	S	0073	s	0093	Ctrl	00B3	³	00D3	Ó	00F3	ó
0014	DC4	0034	4	0054	T	0074	t	0094	Ctrl	00B4	´	00D4	Ô	00F4	ô
0015	NAK	0035	5	0055	U	0075	u	0095	Ctrl	00B5		00D5	Õ	00F5	õ
0016	SYN	0036	6	0056	V	0076	v	0096	Ctrl	00B6	¶	00D6	Ö	00F6	ö
0017	ETB	0037	7	0057	W	0077	w	0097	Ctrl	00B7	·	00D7	×	00F7	
0018	CAN	0038	8	0058	X	0078	x	0098	Ctrl	00B8	¸	00D8	Ø	00F8	ø
0019	EM	0039	9	0059	Y	0079	y	0099	Ctrl	00B9	¹	00D9	Ù	00F9	ù
001A	SUB	003A	:	005A	Z	007A	z	009A	Ctrl	00BA	º	00DA	Ú	00FA	ú
001B	ESC	003B	;	005B	[	007B	{	009B	Ctrl	00BB	»	00DB	Û	00FB	û
001C	FS	003C	<	005C	\	007C			009C	Ctrl	00BC	1/4	00DC	Ü	00FC	þ
001D	GS	003D	=	005D	]	007D	}	009D	Ctrl	00BD	1/2	00DD	Ý	00FD	P
001E	RS	003E	>	005E	^	007E	~	009E	Ctrl	00BE	3/4	00DE	ý	00FE	ß
001F	US	003F	?	005F	_	007F	DEL	009F	Ctrl	00BF	¿	00DF	§	00FF	ÿ

NUL	Null	SOH	Start of heading	CAN	Cancel	SP	Space
STX	Start of text	EOT	End of transmission	EM	End of medium	DEL	Delete
ETX	End of text	DC1	Device control 1	SUB	Substitute	Ctrl	Control
ENQ	Enquiry	DC2	Device control 2	ESC	Escape	FF	Form feed
ACK	Acknowledge	DC3	Device control 3	FS	File separator	CR	Carriage return
BEL	Bell	DC4	Device control 4	GS	Group separator	SO	Shift out
BS	Backspace	NAK	Negative acknowledge	RS	Record separator	SI	Shift in
HT	Horizontal tab	NBS	Non-breaking space	US	Unit separator	DLE	Data link escape
LF	Line feed	ETB	End of transmission block	SYN	Synchronous idle	VT	Vertical tab

Figure 2-14
The first 256 glyphs in Unicode, shown with hexadecimal indices.

Problems

2.1 Given a signed, fixed-point representation in base 10, with three digits to the left and right of the decimal point:
a) What is the range? (Calculate the highest positive number and the lowest negative number.)
b) What is the precision? (Calculate the difference between two adjacent numbers on a number line. Remember that the error is 1/2 the precision.)

2.2 Convert the following numbers as indicated, using as few digits in the results as necessary.
a) $(47)_{10}$ to unsigned binary.
b) $(-27)_{10}$ to binary signed magnitude.
c) $(213)_{16}$ to base 10.
d) $(10110.101)_2$ to base 10.
e) $(34.625)_{10}$ to base 4.

2.3 Convert the following numbers as indicated, using as few digits in the results as necessary.
a) $(011011)_2$ to base 10.
b) $(-27)_{10}$ to excess 32 in binary.
c) $(011011)_2$ to base 16.
d) $(55.875)_{10}$ to unsigned binary.
e) $(132.2)_4$ to base 16.

2.4 Convert $.201_3$ to decimal.

2.5 Convert $(43.3)_7$ to base 8 using no more than one octal digit to the right of the radix point. Truncate any remainder by chopping excess digits. Use an ordinary unsigned octal representation.

2.6 Represent $(17.5)_{10}$ in base 3, then convert the result back to base 10. Use two digits of precision to the right of the radix point for the intermediate base 3 form.

2.7 Find the decimal equivalent of the four-bit two's complement number 1000.

2.8 Find the decimal equivalent of the four-bit one's complement number 1111.

2.9 For a given word width, are there more representable integers in one's complement, two's complement or are they the same?

2.10 Complete the following table for the 5-bit representations (including the sign bits) indicated below. Show your answers as signed base 10 integers.

	5-bit signed magnitude	5-bit excess 16
Largest number		
Most negative number		
No. of distinct numbers		

2.11 Complete the following table using base 2 scientific notation and an eight-bit floating-point representation in which there is a three-bit exponent in excess 3 notation (not excess 4), and a four-bit normalized fraction with a hidden 1. In this representation, the hidden 1 is to the left of the radix point. This means that the number 1.0101 is in normalized form, whereas .101 is not.

Base-2 scientific notation	Floating-point representation Sign	Exponent	Fraction
-1.0101×2^{-2}			
$+1.1 \times 2^{2}$			
	0	001	0000
	1	110	1111

2.12 The IBM short floating-point representation uses base 16, one sign bit, a seven-bit excess 64 exponent and a normalized 24-bit fraction.
a) What number is represented by the bit pattern shown below?

$$1 \ 0111111 \ 01110000 \ 00000000 \ 00000000$$

Show your answer in decimal. Note: the spaces are included in the number for readability only.
b) Represent $(14.3)_6$ in this notation.

2.13 For a normalized floating-point representation, keeping everything else the same:
a) decreasing the base will increase/decrease/not change the number of representable numbers.
b) increasing the number of significant digits will increase/decrease/not change the smallest representable positive number.
c) increasing the number of bits in the exponent will increase/decrease/not change the range.
d) changing the representation of the exponent from excess 64 to two's complement will increase/decrease/not change the range.

2.14 For parts (a) through (e), use a floating-point representation with a sign bit in the leftmost position, followed by a two-bit two's complement exponent, followed by a normalized three-bit fraction in base 2. Zero is represented by the bit pattern 0 0 0 0 0 0. There is no hidden '1'.
a) What decimal number is represented by the bit pattern 1 0 0 1 0 0?
b) Keeping everything else the same but changing the base to 4 will: increase/decrease/not change the smallest representable positive number.

c) What is the smallest gap between successive numbers?

d) What is the largest gap between successive numbers?

e) There are a total of six bits in this floating point representation, and there are $2^6 = 64$ unique bit patterns. How many of these bit patterns are valid?

2.15 Represent $(107.15)_{10}$ in a floating-point representation with a sign bit, a seven-bit excess 64 exponent, and a normalized 24-bit fraction in base 2. There is no hidden 1. Truncate the fraction by chopping bits as necessary (round toward zero).

2.16 For the following single-precision IEEE 754 bit patterns, show the numerical value as a base 2 significand with an exponent (e.g. 1.11×2^5).

a) 0 10000011 01100000000000000000000

b) 1 10000000 00000000000000000000000

c) 1 00000000 00000000000000000000000

d) 1 11111111 00000000000000000000000

e) 0 11111111 11010000000000000000000

f) 0 00000001 10010000000000000000000

g) 0 00000011 01101000000000000000000

2.17 Show the IEEE 754 bit patterns for the following numbers:

a) $+1.1011 \times 2^5$ (single precision)

b) $+0$ (single precision)

c) -1.00111×2^{-1} (double precision)

d) $-NaN$ (single precision)

2.18 Using the IEEE 754 single-precision format, show the value (not the bit pattern) of:

a) The largest positive representable number (note: ∞ is not a number).

b) The smallest positive nonzero number that is normalized.

c) The smallest positive nonzero number in denormalized format.

d) The smallest normalized gap.

e) The largest normalized gap.

f) The number of normalized representable numbers (including 0; note that ∞ and NaN are not numbers).

2.19 Two programmers write random number generators for normalized floating-point numbers using the same method. Programmer A's generator creates random numbers on the closed interval from 0 to 1/2, and programmer B's generator creates random numbers on the closed interval from 1/2 to 1. Programmer B's generator works correctly, but Programmer A's generator produces a skewed distribution of numbers. What could be the problem with Programmer A's approach?

2.20 A hidden 1 representation will not work for base 16. Why not?

2.21 With a hidden 1 representation, can 0 be represented if all possible bit patterns in the exponent and fraction fields are used for nonzero numbers?

2.22 Given a base 10 floating-point number (e.g. $.583 \times 10^3$), can the number be converted into the equivalent base 2 form $x \times 2^y$ by separately converting the fraction (.583) and the exponent (3) into base 2?

Further Reading

(Hamacher et al., 2001 and Koren, 2001) provide a good explanation of biased error in floating-point representations. The IEEE 754 floating-point standard is described in (IEEE, 1985). The analysis of range, error, and precision in Section 2.2 was influenced by (Forsythe, 1970). The GAO report (U.S. GAO report GAO/IMTEC-92-26) gives a very readable account of the software problem that led to the Patriot failure in Dhahran. See www.unicode.org for information on the Unicode standard.

Forsythe, G.E., "Pitfalls in Computation, or Why a Math Book Isn't Good Enough," *The American Mathematical Monthly*, **77**, no. 9, pp. 931-956 (Nov. 1970).

Hamacher, V. C., Vranesic, Z. G., and Zaky, S. G., *Computer Organization*, 5/e, McGraw Hill (2001).

IEEE, "IEEE Standard for Binary Floating Point Arithmetic," *ANSI/IEEE Standard 754-1985*. An early version also appears in *IEEE COMPUTER*, **14**, pp. 51-62 (Mar. 1981).

Knuth, D. E., *The Art of Computer Programming, vol. 2, Semi-Numerical Algorithms*, 2/e, Addison-Wesley-Longman (1981).

Koren, I., *Computer Arithmetic Algorithms*, 2/e, A. K. Peters, Ltd. (2001).

U.S. General Accounting Office report GAO/IMTEC-92-26, "Patriot Missile Defense Software Problem Led to System Failure at Dhahran, Saudi Arabia," U.S. General Accounting Office, P.O. Box 6015, Gaithersburg, Maryland, 20877 (Feb. 1992).

CHAPTER 3

ARITHMETIC

In the previous chapter we explored a few ways that numbers can be represented in a digital computer, but we only briefly touched upon arithmetic operations that can be performed on those numbers. In this chapter we cover four basic arithmetic operations: addition, subtraction, multiplication, and division. We begin by describing how these four operations can be performed on fixed-point numbers, and continue with a description of how these four operations can be performed on floating-point numbers.

Some of the largest problems, such as weather calculations, quantum-mechanical simulations, and land-use modeling, tax the abilities of even today's largest computers. Thus the topic of high-performance arithmetic is also important. We conclude the chapter with an introduction to some of the algorithms and techniques used in speeding arithmetic operations.

■ 3.1 FIXED-POINT ADDITION AND SUBTRACTION

The addition of binary numbers and the concept of overflow were briefly discussed in Chapter 2. Here, we cover addition and subtraction of both signed and unsigned fixed-point numbers in detail. Since the two's complement representation of integers is almost universal in today's computers, we will focus primarily on two's complement operations. We will briefly cover operations on one's complement numbers, however, which have a foundational significance for other areas of computing and practical applications in networking.

3.1.1 Two's Complement Addition and Subtraction

In this section, we look at the addition of signed two's complement numbers. As we explore the addition of signed numbers, we implicitly cover subtraction as well, as a result of the arithmetic principle:

$$a - b = a + (-b).$$

We can negate a number by complementing it (and adding 1, for two's complement), and so we can perform subtraction by complementing and adding. This results in a savings of hardware because it avoids the need for a separate hardware subtractor. We will cover this topic in more detail later.

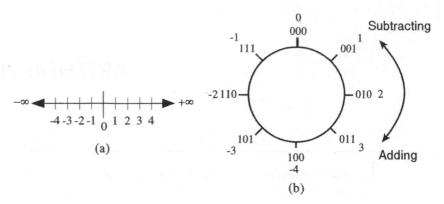

Figure 3-1
(a) Real number line and (b) number circle for 3-bit two's complement numbers.

We will need to modify the interpretation that we place on the results of addition when we add two's complement numbers. To see why this is the case, consider Figure 3-1. With addition on the real number line, numbers can be as large or as small as desired—the number line extends to $\pm\infty$, so the real number line can accommodate numbers of any size. On the other hand, computers represent data using a finite number of bits, and as a result can only store numbers within a certain range. For example, an examination of Table 2.1 shows that if we restrict the size of a number to, for example, 3 bits, there will only be eight possible two's complement values that the number can assume. In Figure 3-1 these values are arranged in a circle beginning with 000 and proceeding around the circle to 111 and then back to 000. The figure also shows the base 10 equivalents of these same numbers.

Some experimentation with the number circle shows that numbers can be added or subtracted by traversing the number circle clockwise for addition and counterclockwise for subtraction. Numbers can also be subtracted by two's complementing the subtrahend and adding. Notice that overflow can only occur for addition when the operands ("addend" and "augend") are of the same sign. Furthermore, overflow occurs if a transition is made from +3 to −4 while proceeding around the number circle when adding, or from −4 to +3 while subtracting. (Two's complement overflow is discussed in more detail later in the chapter.)

Here are two examples of 8-bit two's complement addition, first using two positive numbers:

$$
\begin{array}{ll}
00001010 & (+10)_{10} \\
+\ 00010111 & (+23)_{10} \\
\hline
00100001 & (+33)_{10}
\end{array}
$$

A positive and a negative number can be added in a similar manner:

$$
\begin{array}{ll}
00000101 & (+5)_{10} \\
+\ 11111110 & (-2)_{10} \\
\end{array}
$$

Discard carry $\rightarrow$ 1 00000011 $(+3)_{10}$

The carry produced by addition at the highest (leftmost) bit position is discarded in two's complement addition. A similar situation arises with a carry-out of the highest bit position when adding two negative numbers:

$$
\begin{array}{ll}
11111111 & (-1)_{10} \\
+\ 11111100 & (-4)_{10} \\
\end{array}
$$

Discard carry $\rightarrow$ 1 11111011 $(-5)_{10}$

The carry-out of the leftmost bit is discarded because the number system is **modular**—it "wraps around" from the largest positive number to the largest negative number, as Figure 3-1 shows.

Although an addition operation may have a (discarded) carry-out from the MSB, this does not mean that the result is erroneous. The two examples above yield correct results in spite of the fact that there is a carry-out of the MSB. The next section discusses overflow in two's complement addition in more detail.

Overflow

When two numbers are added that have large magnitudes and the same sign, an **overflow** will occur if the result is too large to fit in the number of bits used in the representation. Consider adding $(+80)_{10}$ and $(+50)_{10}$ using an eight-bit format. The result should be $(+130)_{10}$; however, as shown below, the result is $(-126)_{10}$:

$$
\begin{array}{ll}
01010000 & (+80)_{10} \\
+\ 00110010 & (+50)_{10} \\
\hline
10000010 & (-126)_{10}
\end{array}
$$

This should come as no surprise, since we know that the largest positive eight-bit two's complement number is $+(127)_{10}$, and it is therefore impossible to represent $(+130)_{10}$. Although the result 10000010_2 "looks" like 130_{10} if we think of it in unsigned form, the sign bit indicates a negative number in the signed form, which is clearly wrong.

In general, if two numbers of opposite signs are added, then an overflow cannot occur. Intuitively, this is because the magnitude of the result can be no larger than the magnitude of the larger operand. This leads us to the definition of two's complement overflow:

If the numbers being added are of the same sign and the result is of the opposite sign, then an overflow occurs and the result is incorrect. If the numbers being added are of opposite signs, then an overflow will never occur. As an alternative method of detecting overflow for addition, an overflow occurs if and only if the carry-into the sign bit differs from the carry-out of the sign bit.

If a positive number is subtracted from a negative number and the result is positive, or if a negative number is subtracted from a positive number and the result is negative, then an overflow occurs. If the numbers being subtracted are of the same sign, then an overflow will never occur.

3.1.2 Sign Extension

The leftmost bit in the four signed integer representations we have studied thus far (one's complement, two's complement, signed magnitude, excess) is assigned to the sign. What happens to the sign bit if we place a number into a larger or smaller container? For positive numbers, the conversion is trivial; all that we need to do is pad the left side with 0s:

$$\text{8-bit } +12_{10} \quad \text{becomes} \quad \text{16-bit } +12_{10}$$

$$00001100 \quad \rightarrow \quad 00000000\ 00001100$$

$$\uparrow \qquad\qquad\qquad \uparrow$$

$$\text{Sign} = \text{``+''} \qquad\qquad \text{Sign} = \text{``+''}$$

For negative numbers, we cannot simply pad the left side with 0s because that would change the value of the number:

$$\text{8-bit } -12_{10} \quad \begin{array}{l}\text{incorrectly}\\ \text{becomes}\end{array} \quad \text{16-bit } +244_{10}$$

$$11110100 \quad \rightarrow \quad 00000000\ 11110100$$

$$\uparrow \qquad\qquad\qquad \uparrow$$

$$\text{Sign} = \text{``-''} \qquad\qquad \text{Sign} = \text{``+''}$$

As it turns out, all that we need to do is copy the sign bit for as many places as there are to the left, and the number will be correctly extended, regardless of the value of the sign. This process is known as **sign extension:**

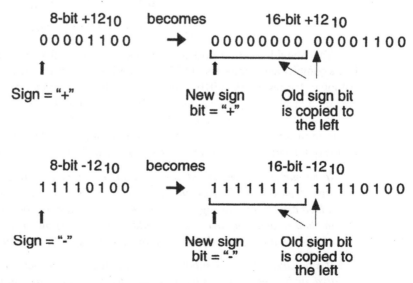

If we want to reduce the size of the word, we can simply remove bits on the left and the resulting sign will be correct, as long as the number can be represented in the remaining bits:

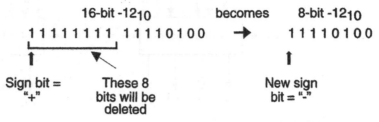

3.1.3 Hardware Implementation of Adders and Subtractors

Up until now we have focused on algorithms for addition and subtraction. Now we will take a look at implementations of simple adders and subtractors.

Ripple-Carry Addition and Ripple-Borrow Subtraction

In Appendix A, a design of a four-bit ripple-carry adder is covered. The adder is modeled after the way that we normally perform decimal addition by hand, by summing digits in one column at a time while moving from right to left. In this section, we review the **ripple-carry adder**, and then take a look at a **ripple-borrow subtractor**. We then combine the two into a single addition/subtraction unit.

Figure 3-2 shows a four-bit ripple-carry adder that is developed in Appendix A. Two binary numbers A and B are added from right to left, creating a sum and a carry at the outputs of each full adder for each bit position.

Four four-bit ripple-carry adders are cascaded in Figure 3-3 to add two 16-bit numbers. The rightmost full adder has a carry-in of 0. Although the rightmost full adder can be simplified as a result of the carry-in of 0, we will use the more general form and set c_0 to 0 in order to simplify subtraction later on.

Subtraction of binary numbers proceeds in a fashion analogous to addition. We can subtract one number from another by working in a single column at a time, subtracting digits of the **subtrahend** b_i, from the **minuend** a_i, as we move from right to left. As in

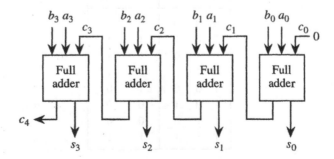

Figure 3-2
Ripple-carry adder.

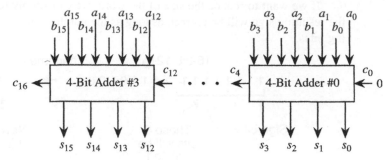

Figure 3-3
A 16-bit adder is made up of a cascade of four 4-bit ripple-carry adders.

decimal subtraction, if the subtrahend is larger than the minuend or there is a borrow from a previous digit then a borrow must be propagated to the next most significant bit. Figure 3-4 shows the truth table and a "black-box" circuit for subtraction.

Full subtractors can be cascaded to form **ripple-borrow** subtractors in the same manner that full adders are cascaded to form ripple-carry adders. Figure 3-5 illustrates a four-bit ripple-borrow subtractor that is made up of four full subtractors.

As discussed above, an alternative method of implementing subtraction is to form the two's complement negative of the subtrahend and *add* it to the minuend. The circuit that is shown in Figure 3-6 performs both addition and subtraction on four-bit two's complement numbers by allowing the b_i inputs to be complemented when subtraction is desired. An $\overline{\text{ADD}}$ /SUBTRACT control line determines which function is performed. The bar over the ADD symbol indicates the ADD operation is active when the signal is low. That is, if the control line is 0, then the a_i and b_i inputs are passed through to the adder, and the sum is generated at the s_i outputs. If the control line is 1, then the a_i inputs are passed through to the adder, but the b_i inputs are one's complemented by the XOR gates before they are passed on to the adder. In order to form the two's complement negative, we must add 1 to the one's complement negative, which is accomplished by setting the *carry_in* line (c_0)

a_i	b_i	bor_i	$diff_i$	bor_{i+1}
0	0	0	0	0
0	0	1	1	1
0	1	0	1	1
0	1	1	0	1
1	0	0	1	0
1	0	1	0	0
1	1	0	0	0
1	1	1	1	1

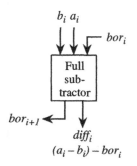

Figure 3-4
Truth table and schematic symbol for a ripple-borrow subtractor.

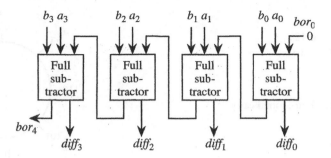

Figure 3-5
Ripple-borrow subtractor.

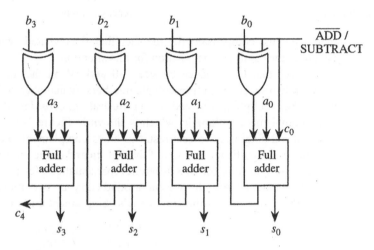

Figure 3-6
Addition/subtraction unit.

to 1 with the control input. In this way, we can share the adder hardware among both the adder and the subtractor.

3.1.4 One's Complement Addition and Subtraction

Although it is not heavily used in mainstream computing anymore, the one's complement representation was used in early computers and it is still commonly used in networking. One's complement addition is handled somewhat differently from two's complement addition: the carry-out of the leftmost position is not discarded, but is added back into the least significant position of the integer portion as shown in Figure 3-7. This is known as an **end-around carry**.

We can better visualize the reason that the end-around carry is needed by examining the three-bit one's complement number circle in Figure 3-8. Notice that the number circle has two positions for 0. When we add two numbers, if we traverse through both −0 and +0,

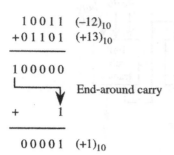

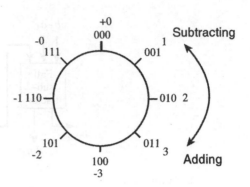

Figure 3-7
An example of one's complement addition
with an end-around carry.

Figure 3-8
Number circle for a three-bit signed one's complement
representation.

then we must compensate for the fact that 0 is visited twice. The end-around carry advances the result by one position for this situation.

Notice that the distance between -0 and $+0$ on the number circle is the distance between two successive representable numbers, which may be less than 1.0 depending on where the radix point is placed. As an illustration, consider adding $(5.5)_{10}$ and $(-1.0)_{10}$ in one's complement arithmetic, which is shown in Figure 3-9. In order to add $(+5.5)_{10}$ and $(-1.0)_{10}$ and obtain the correct result in one's complement, we add the end-around carry into the least significant position of the significand of the number as shown.

The need to look for two different representations for zero and the potential need to perform another addition for the end-around carry are two important reasons for preferring the two's complement arithmetic to one's complement arithmetic.

$$
\begin{array}{r}
0\ 1\ 0\ 1\ .\ 1 \quad (+5.5)_{10} \\
+\quad 1\ 1\ 1\ 0\ .\ 1 \quad (-1.0)_{10} \\
\hline
1\ 0\ 1\ 0\ 0\ .\ 0 \\
+\ \llcorner\!\!\longrightarrow .\ 1 \\
\hline
0\ 1\ 0\ 0\ .\ 1 \quad (+4.5)_{10}
\end{array}
$$

Figure 3-9
The end-around carry complicates addition for non-integers.

■ 3.2 FIXED-POINT MULTIPLICATION AND DIVISION

Multiplication and division of fixed-point numbers can be accomplished with addition, subtraction, and shift operations. The sections that follow describe methods for performing multiplication and division of fixed-point numbers in both unsigned and signed forms using these basic operations. We will first cover unsigned multiplication and division, and then we will cover signed multiplication and division.

$$
\begin{array}{r}
1\ \ 1\ \ 0\ \ 1 \\
\times\ 1\ \ 0\ \ 1\ \ 1 \\
\hline
1\ \ 1\ \ 0\ \ 1 \\
1\ \ 1\ \ 0\ \ 1 \\
0\ \ 0\ \ 0\ \ 0 \\
1\ \ 1\ \ 0\ \ 1 \\
\hline
1\ \ 0\ \ 0\ \ 0\ \ 1\ \ 1\ \ 1\ \ 1
\end{array}
$$

$(13)_{10}$ Multiplicand M

$(11)_{10}$ Multiplier Q

Partial products

$(143)_{10}$ Product P

Figure 3-10
Multiplication of two unsigned binary integers.

3.2.1 Unsigned Multiplication

Multiplication of unsigned binary integers is handled similarly to the way it is carried out by hand for decimal numbers. Figure 3-10 illustrates the multiplication process for two unsigned binary integers. Each bit of the multiplier determines whether or not the multiplicand, shifted left according to the position of the multiplier bit, is added into the product. When two unsigned n-bit numbers are multiplied, the result can be as large as $2n$ bits. For the example shown in Figure 3-10, the multiplication of two four-bit operands results in an eight-bit product. When two signed n-bit numbers are multiplied, the result can be only as large as $2(n-1)+1 = (2n-1)$ bits, because this is equivalent to multiplying two $(n-1)$-bit unsigned numbers and then introducing the sign bit.

A hardware implementation of integer multiplication can take a similar form to the manual method. Figure 3-11 shows a layout of a multiplication unit for four-bit numbers, in which there is a four-bit adder, a control unit, three four-bit registers, and a one-bit carry register. In order to multiply two numbers, the multiplicand is placed in the M register, the multiplier is placed in the Q register, and the A and C registers are cleared to zero. During multiplication, the rightmost bit of the multiplier determines whether the multiplicand is added into the product at each step. After the multiplicand is added into the product, the

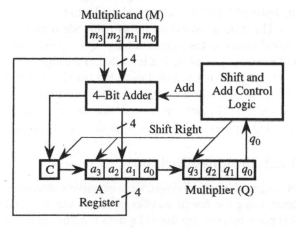

Figure 3-11
A serial multiplier.

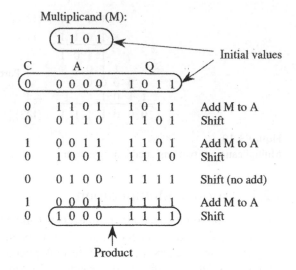

Figure 3-12
Example of multiplication using the serial multiplier.

multiplier and the A register are simultaneously shifted to the right. This has the effect of shifting the multiplicand to the left (as for the manual process) and exposing the next bit of the multiplier in position q_0.

Figure 3-12 illustrates the multiplication process. Initially, C and A are cleared, and M and Q hold the multiplicand and multiplier, respectively. The rightmost bit of Q is 1, and so the multiplier M is added into the product in the A register. The A and Q registers together make up the eight-bit product, but the A register is where the multiplicand is added. After M is added to A, the A and Q registers are shifted to the right. Since the A and Q registers are linked as a pair to form the eight-bit product, the rightmost bit of A is shifted into the leftmost bit of Q. The rightmost bit of Q is then dropped, C is shifted into the leftmost bit of A, and a 0 is shifted into C.

The process continues for as many steps as there are bits in the multiplier. On the second iteration, the rightmost bit of Q is again 1, and so the multiplicand is added to A and the C/A/Q combination is shifted to the right. On the third iteration, the rightmost bit of Q is 0 so M is not added to A, but the C/A/Q combination is still shifted to the right. Finally, on the fourth iteration, the rightmost bit of Q is again 1, and so M is added to A and the C/A/Q combination is shifted to the right. The product is now contained in the A and Q registers, in which A holds the high-order bits and Q holds the low-order bits.

3.2.2 Unsigned Division

In longhand binary division, we successively attempt to subtract the divisor from the dividend, using the fewest number of bits in the dividend as we can. Figure 3-13 illustrates this point by showing that $(11)_2$ does not "fit" in 0 or 01, but *does* fit in 011, as indicated by the pattern 001 that starts the quotient.

$$\begin{array}{r} 0\ 0\ 1\ 0\ \ \mathrm{R}1 \\ 1\ 1\ \overline{\rvert\ 0\ 1\ 1\ 1} \\ \underline{1\ 1} \\ 0\ 1 \end{array}$$

Figure 3-13
Example of base 2 division.

Computer-based division of binary integers can be handled similarly to the way that binary integer multiplication is carried out, but with the complication that the only way to tell if the dividend does not "fit" is actually to do the subtraction and test if the remainder is negative. If the remainder is negative then the subtraction must be "backed out" by adding the divisor back in, as described below.

In the division algorithm, instead of shifting the product to the right as we did for multiplication, we now shift the quotient to the left, and we subtract instead of adding. When two n-bit unsigned numbers are being divided, the result is no larger than n bits.

Figure 3-14 shows a layout of a division unit for four-bit numbers in which there is a five-bit adder, a control unit, a four-bit register for the dividend Q, and two five-bit registers for the divisor M and the remainder A. Five-bit registers are used for A and M, instead of four-bit registers as we might expect, because an extra bit is needed to indicate the sign of the intermediate result. Although this division method is for unsigned numbers, subtraction is used in the process and negative partial results sometimes arise, which extends the range from −16 through +15; thus there is a need for five bits to store intermediate results.

In order to divide two four-bit numbers, the dividend is placed in the Q register, the divisor is placed in the M register, and the A register and the high-order bit of M are cleared to zero. The leftmost bit of the A register determines whether the divisor is added

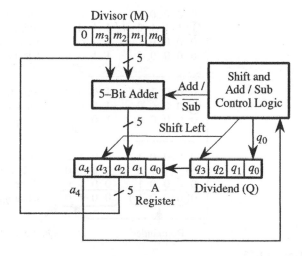

Figure 3-14
A serial divider.

back into the dividend at each step. This is necessary in order to restore the dividend when the result of subtracting the divisor is negative, as described above. This is referred to as **restoring division**, because the dividend is restored to its former value when the remainder is negative. When the result is not negative, then the least significant bit of Q is set to 1, which indicates that the divisor "fits" in the dividend at that point.

Figure 3-15 illustrates the division process. Initially, A and the high-order bit of M are cleared, and Q and the low-order bits of M are loaded with the dividend and divisor, respectively. The A and Q registers are shifted to the left as a pair and the divisor M is subtracted from A. Since the result is negative, the divisor is added back to restore the dividend, and q_0 is cleared to 0. The process repeats by shifting A and Q to the left, and by subtracting M from A. Again, the result is negative, so the dividend is restored and q_0 is cleared to 0. On the third iteration, A and Q are shifted to the left and M is again subtracted from A, but now the result of the subtraction is not negative, so q_0 is set to 1. The process continues for one final iteration, in which A and Q are shifted to the left and M is subtracted from A, which produces a negative result. The dividend is restored and q_0 is cleared to 0. The quotient is now contained in the Q register and the remainder is contained in the A register.

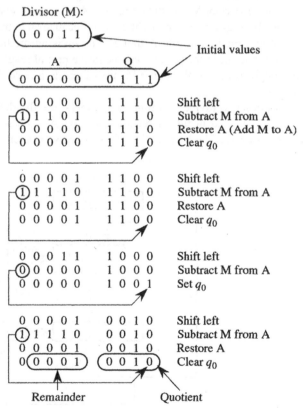

Figure 3-15
Example of division using the serial divider.

$$
\begin{array}{r}
1\ \ 1\ \ 1\ \ 1 \quad (-1)_{10} \\
\times\ 0\ \ 0\ \ 0\ \ 1 \quad (+1)_{10} \\
\hline
1\ \ 1\ \ 1\ \ 1 \\
0\ \ 0\ \ 0\ \ 0 \\
0\ \ 0\ \ 0\ \ 0 \\
0\ \ 0\ \ 0\ \ 0 \\
\hline
0\ \ 0\ \ 0\ \ 0\ \ 1\ \ 1\ \ 1\ \ 1 \quad (+15)_{10}
\end{array}
\qquad
\begin{array}{r}
1\ \ 1\ \ 1\ \ 1\ \ 1\ \ 1\ \ 1\ \ 1 \quad (-1)_{10} \\
\times\ \ \ \ \ \ \ \ \ \ \ \ \ \ 0\ \ 0\ \ 0\ \ 1 \quad (+1)_{10} \\
\hline
1\ \ 1\ \ 1\ \ 1\ \ 1\ \ 1\ \ 1\ \ 1 \\
0\ \ 0\ \ 0\ \ 0\ \ 0\ \ 0\ \ 0 \\
0\ \ 0\ \ 0\ \ 0\ \ 0\ \ 0 \\
0\ \ 0\ \ 0\ \ 0\ \ 0 \\
\hline
1\ \ 1\ \ 1\ \ 1\ \ 1\ \ 1\ \ 1\ \ 1 \quad (-1)_{10}
\end{array}
$$

(Incorrect; result should be −1)

Figure 3-16
Multiplication of signed integers.

3.2.3 Signed Multiplication and Division

If we apply the multiplication and division methods described in the previous sections to signed integers, then we will run into some trouble. Consider multiplying −1 by +1 using four-bit words, as shown on the left side of Figure 3-16. The eight-bit equivalent of +15 is produced instead of −1. What went wrong is that the sign bit did not get extended to the left of the result. This is not a problem for a positive result because the high-order bits default to 0, producing the correct sign bit 0.

A solution is shown on the right side of Figure 3-16, in which each partial product is extended to the width of the result, and only the rightmost eight bits of the result are retained. If both operands are negative, then the signs are extended for both operands, again retaining only the rightmost eight bits of the result.

Signed division is more difficult. We will not explore the methods here, but as a general technique, we can convert the operands into their positive forms, perform the division, and then convert the result into its true signed form as a final step.

◼ 3.3 FLOATING-POINT ARITHMETIC

Arithmetic operations on floating-point numbers can be carried out using the fixed-point arithmetic operations described in the previous sections, with attention given to maintaining aspects of the floating-point representation. In the sections that follow, we explore floating-point arithmetic in base 2 and base 10, keeping the requirements of the floating-point representation in mind.

3.3.1 Floating-Point Addition and Subtraction

Floating-point arithmetic differs from integer arithmetic in that exponents must be handled as well as the magnitudes of the operands, and special considerations must be given to rounding. As in ordinary base 10 arithmetic using scientific notation, the exponents of the operands must be made equal prior to addition and subtraction. The significands are then added or subtracted as appropriate, and the result is normalized.

This process of adjusting the significand and also rounding the result can lead to a loss of precision in the result. Consider the unsigned floating point addition ($.101 \times 2^3 + .111 \times 2^4$) in which the significands have three significant digits. We start by adjusting the smaller exponent to be equal to the larger exponent, and adjusting the significand accordingly. Thus we have $.101 \times 2^3 = .010 \times 2^4$, losing $.001 \times 2^3$ of precision in the process. The resulting sum, including a normalization step, is:

$$(.010 + .111) \times 2^4 = 1.001 \times 2^4 = .1001 \times 2^5$$

After rounding to three significant digits using the "round to nearest even" method in which ties that can round up or down go to the nearest even number (see Chapter 2), we obtain $.100 \times 2^5$, and we have lost another $0.0001 \times 2^5 = 0.001 \times 2^4$ in the rounding process.

Summarizing the precision losses above, we first lost $.001 \times 2^3$ of precision and then we lost $.001 \times 2^4$ of precision, which cumulatively amounts to $.001 \times 2^3 + .001 \times 2^4 = .0001 \times 2^4 + .001 \times 2^4 = .0011 \times 2^4$ of precision. This is not an entirely accurate assessment, however. If we simply added the numbers using as much precision as we needed and then applied rounding only in the final normalization step, then the calculation would go like this:

$$.101 \times 2^3 + .111 \times 2^4 =$$
$$.0101 \times 2^4 + .111 \times 2^4 =$$
$$1.0011 \times 2^4.$$

Normalizing yields $.10011 \times 2^5$, and rounding to three significant digits using the round to nearest even method yields $.101 \times 2^5$.

As to which calculation is correct, according to the IEEE 754 standard, the final result should be the same as if the maximum precision needed is used before applying the rounding method, and so the correct result is $.101 \times 2^5$. This raises the issue of how to compute the intermediate results with sufficient accuracy and without requiring too much hardware, and for this we use **guard**, **round**, and **sticky** bits.

As it turns out, it is enough to perform intermediate calculations using only two additional digits to the right, which are the guard and round bits, plus a third (sticky) bit which keeps track of any nonzero digits to the right of the round bit. IEEE 754 has four rounding modes: round to nearest even number on ties (default), round toward 0, round toward $+\infty$, and round toward $-\infty$. We will use round toward the nearest even method here. For the previous example, applying guard (g) and round (r) bits with the round toward nearest even method, we have:

$$
\begin{array}{ll}
.101 & \times 2^3 \\
+ \ .111 & \times 2^4
\end{array}
\Rightarrow
\begin{array}{ll}
.0101 & \times 2^4 \\
+ \ .111 & \times 2^4 \\
\hline
1.00110 & \times 2^4 \\
\quad gr
\end{array}
$$

Only one extra bit is needed for this intermediate result, the guard bit (g), but we also show the round bit ($r = 0$) to locate its position. As we shift the number to normalize, we set a sticky bit (s) if any of the shifted out bits are nonzero. For this case, there are no non-zero bits to the right of the r bit and so $s = 0$:

$$1.0011 \times 2^4 = 1.00110 \times 2^4$$
$$gr \searrow$$
0 is shifted
out, so $s = 0$

Now for the rounding step: simply append the sticky bit to the right of the result before rounding. There is no tie as there would be for .100100 and so we round up, otherwise we would have rounded down to the closest even number (.100):

$$.100110 \times 2^5 \cong .101 \times 2^5$$
$$grs$$

For this case, the guard, round, and sticky bits changed our previous result. Note that if r is 0 instead of 1, so that the grs combination is 100, we would have rounded down to .100 because .100 is even whereas .101 is not.

Why do floating-point numbers have such complicated formats?

We may wonder why floating-point numbers have such a complicated structure, with the mantissa being stored in signed-magnitude representation, the exponent stored in excess notation, and the sign bit separated from the rest of the magnitude by the intervening exponent field. There is a simple explanation for this structure. Consider the complexity of performing floating-point arithmetic in a computer. Before any arithmetic can be done, the number must be unpacked from the form it takes in storage. The exponent and mantissa must be extracted from the packed bit pattern before an arithmetic operation can be performed. After the arithmetic operation(s) are performed, the result must be renormalized and rounded, and then the bit patterns are repacked into the requisite format.

The virtue of a floating-point format that contains a sign bit followed by an exponent in excess notation, followed by the magnitude of the mantissa, is that two floating-point numbers can be compared for >, <, and = without unpacking. The sign bit is most important in such a comparison, and it appropriately is the MSB in the floating-point format. Next most important in comparing two numbers is the exponent, since a change of ± 1 in the exponent changes the value by a factor of 2 (for a base 2 format), whereas a change in even the MSB of the significand will change the value of the floating-point number by less than that.

In order to account for the sign bit, the signed magnitude significands are represented as integers and are converted into two's complement form. After the addition or subtraction operation takes place in two's complement, there may be a need to normalize the result and adjust the sign bit. The result is then converted back to signed magnitude form.

EXAMPLE 3-1   Floating-Point Arithmetic

For this example, we show the process of addition and subtraction with guard (g), round (r), and sticky (s) bits, maintaining four bits of precision and rounding to the nearest representable number (nearest even number for ties), for (a) $.1011 \times 2^7 + .0111 \times 2^4$, and (b) $.1011 \times 2^7 - .0111 \times 2^4$.

Addition:

$$.1011 \ \times 2^7 \qquad\qquad .1011 \quad\ \times 2^7$$
$$+\ .0111 \ \times 2^4 \quad \Rightarrow \quad +\ .0000111 \times 2^7$$
$$\overline{\qquad\qquad\qquad\qquad\qquad\qquad\ .1011111 \times 2^7}$$
$$grs$$

The nearest four-bit number is then $.1100 \times 2^7$.

Subtraction:

$$.1011 \ \times 2^7 \qquad\qquad .1011000 \times 2^7$$
$$-\ .0111 \ \times 2^4 \quad \Rightarrow \quad -\ .0000111 \times 2^7$$
$$\overline{\qquad\qquad\qquad\qquad\qquad\qquad\ .1010001 \times 2^7}$$
$$grs$$

The guard, round, and sticky bits apply in the same way for subtraction as for addition, and so the rounded result is $.1011 \times 2^7$.

3.3.2 Floating-Point Multiplication and Division

Floating-point multiplication and division are performed in a manner similar to floating-point addition and subtraction, except that the sign, exponent, and significand of the result can be computed separately. If the operands have the same sign, then the sign of the result is positive. Unlike signs produce a negative result. The exponent of the result before normalization is obtained by adding the exponents of the source operands for multiplication, or by subtracting the divisor exponent from the dividend exponent for division. The significands are multiplied or divided according to the operation, followed by normalization.

Consider using three-bit significands in performing the base 2 computation $(+.101 \times 2^2) \times (-.110 \times 2^{-3})$. The source operand signs differ, which means that the result will have a negative sign. We add exponents for multiplication, and so the exponent of the result is $2 + -3 = -1$. We multiply the significands, which produces the product $.01111$. Normalizing the product and retaining only three bits in the significand by rounding with the nearest even method produces $-.100 \times 2^{-1}$.

Now consider using three-bit significands in performing the base 2 computation $(+.110 \times 2^5) / (+.100 \times 2^4)$. The source operand signs are the same, which means that the result will have a positive sign. We subtract exponents for division, and so the exponent of the result is $5 - 4 = 1$. We divide significands, which can be done in a number of ways. If we treat the significands as unsigned integers, then we will have $110/100 = 1$ with a remainder of 10. What we really want is a contiguous set of bits representing the significand instead of a separate result and remainder, and so we can scale the dividend to the left by two positions, producing the result $11000/100 = 110$ (see the next section for another approach). We then scale the result to the right by two positions to restore the original scale factor, producing 1.1. Putting it all together, the result of dividing $(+.110 \times 2^5)$ by $(+.100 \times 2^4)$ is $(+1.10 \times 2^1)$. After normalization, the final result is $(+.110 \times 2^2)$.

Intel vs. Motorola: Floating-Point Coprocessors

By the late 1970s Moore's law had increased the number of components possible on an integrated circuit to a sufficient extent that 16-bit and larger microprocessors were possible. Thus in 1979 Intel introduced the 16-bit 8086 and Motorola introduced their 16/32-bit 68000 microprocessor. (The 68000 was referred to as 16/32-bit because although the internal registers and data paths were 32 bits wide, the original 68000 had only a 16-bit data path to memory.) Both companies knew that it was important to implement floating-point calculations in hardware in order to accommodate the needs of scientific and engineering applications, but neither had sufficient room to incorporate floating-point hardware directly on their microprocessor chips. As a result they developed the 8087 and 68881 math coprocessors, respectively. These were separately packaged devices that were intended to be tightly coupled to their respective microprocessors on the computers' motherboards, and most motherboards had sockets intended for that use. Floating-point units can speed up floating-point and other complex operations by factors of 50 to over 100.

The 8087 was the first math coprocessor to implement the new IEEE 754 floating-point standard. It was implemented with eight stack-like registers, and could handle 32-bit single-precision, 64-bit double-precision and 80-bit extended-precision data types. The 87 had instructions for the normal arithmetic functions, as well as square root, tangent, arctangent, base 2 exponentiation, and base 2 logarithms.

The 68881 coprocessor had eight 80-bit data registers, and could handle 32-bit single-precision, 64-bit double-precision and 80-bit extended-precision data types. It also has instructions for the common arithmetic operations, as well as square root, sine, cosine, tangent, arcsine, arccosine, arctangent, the hyperbolic sine, cosine, tangent, and arctangent, exponentiation and logs to the bases 2, e, and 10.

The normalization situation is easier for multiplication and division than it is for addition and subtraction. When multiplying two normalized significands, at most one shift left is needed to normalize the result. When dividing two normalized significands, at most one shift right is needed. For the round to nearest even rounding method, at most one guard bit and one round bit are thus needed.

■ 3.4 HIGH-PERFORMANCE ARITHMETIC

For many applications, the speed of arithmetic operations are the bottleneck to performance. Most supercomputers are considered "super" because they excel at performing fixed- and floating-point arithmetic. In this section we discuss a number of ways to improve the speed of addition, subtraction, multiplication, and division.

3.4.1 High-Performance Addition

The ripple-carry adder that we reviewed in Section 3.1.3 may introduce too much delay into a system. The longest path through the adder is from the inputs of the least significant full adder to the outputs of the most significant full adder. The process of summing the inputs at each bit position is relatively fast (a small two-level circuit suffices) but the carry propagation takes a long time to work its way through the circuit. In fact, the propagation time is proportional to the number of bits in the operands. This is unfortunate, since more significance in an addition translates to more time to perform the addition. In this section, we look at a method of speeding the carry propagation in what is known as a **carry lookahead adder**.

In Appendix A, reduced Boolean expressions for the sum (s_i) and carry outputs (c_{i+1}) of a full adder are created. These expressions are repeated below, with subscripts added to denote the relative position of a full adder in a ripple-carry adder:

$$s_i = \overline{a_i}\,\overline{b_i}c_i + \overline{a_i}b_i\overline{c_i} + a_i\overline{b_i}\,\overline{c_i} + a_ib_ic_i$$

$$c_{i+1} = b_ic_i + a_ic_i + a_ib_i$$

We can factor the second equation and obtain:

$$c_{i+1} = a_ib_i + (a_i + b_i)c_i$$

which can be rewritten as:

$$c_{i+1} = G_i + P_ic_i$$

where: $G_i = a_ib_i$ and $P_i = a_i + b_i$.

The G_i and P_i terms are referred to as **generate** and **propagate** functions, respectively, for the effect they have on the carry. When $G_i = 1$, a carry is generated at stage i. When $P_i = 1$, then a carry is propagated through stage i if either a_i or b_i is a 1. The G_i and P_i terms can be created in one level of logic since they only depend on an AND or an OR of the input variables, respectively.

The carries again take the most time. The carry c_1 out of stage 0 is $G_0 + P_0c_0$, and since $c_0 = 0$ for addition, we can rewrite this as $c_1 = G_0$. The carry c_2 out of stage 1 is $G_1 + P_1c_1$, and since $c_1 = G_0$, we can rewrite this as: $c_2 = G_1 + P_1G_0$. The carry c_3 out of stage 2 is $G_2 + P_2c_2$, and since $c_2 = G_1 + P_1G_0$, we can rewrite this as: $c_3 = G_2 + P_2G_1 + P_2P_1G_0$. Continuing one more time for a four-bit adder, the carry out of stage 3 is $G_3 + P_3c_3$, and since $c_3 = G_2 + P_2G_1 + P_2P_1G_0$, we can rewrite this as: $c_4 = G_3 + P_3G_2 + P_3P_2G_1 + P_3P_2P_1G_0$.

We can now create a four-bit carry lookahead adder as shown in Figure 3-17. We still have the delay through the full adders as before, but now the carry chain is broken into independent pieces that require one gate delay for G_i and P_i and two more gate delays to generate c_{i+1}. Thus, a depth of three gate delays is added, but the ripple-carry chain is removed. If we assume that each full adder introduces a gate delay of two, then a four-bit carry lookahead adder will have a maximum gate delay of five, whereas a four-bit ripple-carry adder will have a maximum gate delay of eight. The difference between the two approaches is more pronounced for wider operands. This process is limited to about eight bits of carry-lookahead, because of gate fan-in limitations (discussed in Appendix A). For additions of numbers having more than eight bits, the carry-lookahead circuits can be cascaded to compute the carry-in and carry-out of each carry-lookahead unit. (See the Example.)

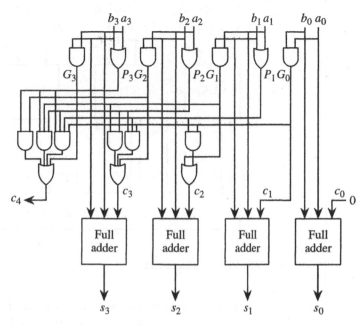

Figure 3-17
Carry-lookahead adder.

EXAMPLE 3-2   Wide-Word High-Performance Adder

A practical word width for a carry lookahead adder (CLA) is four bits, whereas a 16-bit word width is not as practical because of the large fan-ins and fan-outs needed for the internal logic. We can subdivide a 16-bit addition problem into four four-bit groups in which carry lookahead is used within the groups, and in which carry lookahead is also used among the groups. This organization is referred to as a **group carry lookahead adder** (GCLA) and is a more practical approach to extending the word width. For this example, we will compare a 16-bit CLA with a 16-bit GCLA in terms of gate delays, fan-ins, and fan-outs.

Figure 3-18 shows a 16-bit GCLA that is composed of four four-bit CLAs, with some additional logic that generates the carries between the four-bit groups. Each group behaves as an ordinary CLA, except that the least significant carry into each CLA is treated as a variable instead of as a 0, and that **group generate** (GG) and **group propagate** (GP) signals are generated. A GG signal is generated when a carry is generated somewhere within a group, and all of the more significant propagate signals are true. This means that a carry into a group will propagate all the way through the group. The corresponding equations for the least significant GG and GP signals in Figure 3-18 are:

$$GG_0 = G_3 + P_3G_2 + P_3P_2G_1 + P_3P_2P_1G_0$$

$$GP_0 = P_3P_2P_1P_0$$

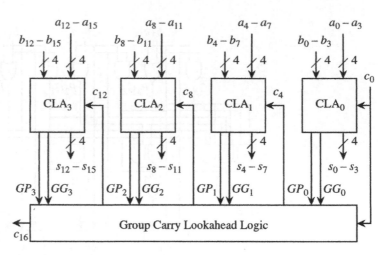

Figure 3-18
A 16-bit group carry lookahead adder.

The remaining GG and GP signals are computed similarly.

The carry into each group, except for the carry into CLA_0, is computed from the GG and GP signals. For example, c_4 is true when GG_0 is true or when GP_0 and c_0 are both true. The corresponding equation is:

$$c_4 = GG_0 + GP_0c_0.$$

Higher-order carries out of each group are computed in a similar manner:

$$c_8 = GG_1 + GP_1c_4 = GG_1 + GP_1GG_0 + GP_1GP_0c_0.$$

$$c_{12} = GG_2 + GP_2c_8 = GG_2 + GP_2GG_1 + GP_2GP_1GG_0 + GP_2GP_1GP_0c_0.$$

$$c_{16} = GG_3 + GP_3c_{12} = GG_3 + GP_3GG_2 + GP_3GP_2GG_1$$
$$+ GP_3GP_2GP_1GG_0 + GP_3GP_2GP_1GP_0c_0.$$

In terms of gate delays, a 16-bit CLA has a longest path of five gate delays to produce the most significant sum bit, as discussed in Section 3.4.1. Each of the CLAs in the 16-bit GCLA also has at least five gate delays on the longest path. The GG and GP signals are generated in three gate delays, and the carry signals out of each group are generated in two more gate delays, resulting in a total of five gate delays to generate the carry out of each group. In the highest bit position (s_{15}), five gate delays are needed to generate c_{12} and another five gate delays are needed to generate s_{15}, for a worst-case path of 10 gate delays through the 16-bit GCLA.

With regard to fan-in and fan-out, the maximum fan-in of any gate in a four-bit CLA is four (refer to Figure 3-17), and in general, the maximum fan-in of any gate in an n-bit CLA is n. Thus, the maximum fan-in of any gate in a 16-bit CLA is 16. By comparison, the maximum fan-in for a 16-bit GCLA is five (for generating c_{16}). The fan-outs for both cases are the same as the fan-ins.

In summary, the 16-bit CLA has only half of the depth of the 16-bit GCLA (five gate delays vs. 10 gate delays). The highest fan-in for a 16-bit CLA is 16, which is more than three times the highest fan-in for a 16-bit GCLA (16 *vs.* five). The highest fan-outs are the same as the highest fan-ins for each case.

3.4.2 High-Performance Multiplication

A number of methods exist for speeding the process of multiplication. Two methods are described in the sections below. The first approach gains performance by skipping over blocks of 1s, which eliminates addition steps. A parallel multiplier is described next, in which a cross product among all pairs of multiplier and multiplicand bits is formed. The result of the cross product is summed by rows to produce the final product.

The Booth Algorithm

The Booth algorithm treats positive and negative numbers uniformly. It operates on the fact that strings of 0s or 1s in the multiplier require no additions—just shifting. Additions or subtractions take place at the boundaries of the strings, where transitions take place from 0 to 1 or from 1 to 0. A string of 1s in the multiplier from bit positions with weights 2^u to 2^v can be treated as $2^{u+1} - 2^v$. For example, if the multiplier is 001110 $(+14)_{10}$, then $u = 3$ and $v = 1$, so $2^4 - 2^1 = 14$.

In a hardware implementation, the multiplier is scanned from right to left. The first transition is observed going from 0 to 1, and so 2^1 is subtracted from the initial value (0). On the next transition, from 1 to 0, 2^4 is added, which results in +14. A 0 is considered to be appended to the right side of the multiplier in order to define the situation in which a 1 is in the rightmost digit of the multiplier.

If the multiplier is recoded according to the Booth algorithm, then fewer steps may be needed in the multiplication process. Consider the multiplication example shown in Figure 3-19. The multiplier $(14)_{10}$ contains three 1s, which means that three addition operations are required for the shift/add multiplication procedure that is described in Section 3.2.1. The Booth-recoded multiplier is obtained by scanning the original multiplier from right to left, placing a −1 in the position where the first 1 in a string is

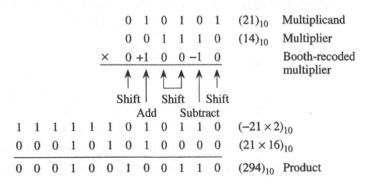

Figure 3-19
Multiplication of signed integers.

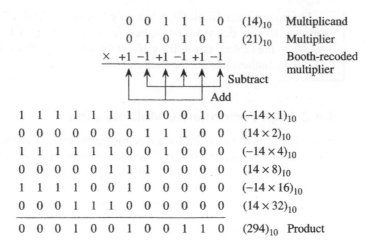

```
    0  0  1  1  1  0    (14)₁₀   Multiplicand
    0  1  0  1  0  1    (21)₁₀   Multiplier
  ×  +1 −1 +1 −1 +1 −1           Booth-recoded
                                 multiplier
```

Figure 3-20
A worst-case Booth-recoded multiplication example.

encountered and placing a +1 in the position where the next 0 is seen. The multiplier 001110 thus becomes 0 +1 0 0 −1 0. The Booth-recoded multiplier contains just two nonzero digits, +1 and −1, which means that only one addition operation and one subtraction operation are needed, and so a savings is realized for this example.

A savings is not always realized, however, and in some cases the Booth algorithm may cause more operations to take place than if it is not used at all. Consider the example shown in Figure 3-20, in which the multiplier consists of alternating 1s and 0s. This is the same example shown in Figure 3-19 but with the multiplicand and multiplier swapped. Without Booth recoding of the multiplier, three addition operations are required for the three 1s in the multiplier. The Booth-recoded multiplier, however, requires six addition and subtraction operations, which is clearly worse. We improve on this in the next section.

The Modified Booth Algorithm

One solution to this problem is to group the recoded multiplier bits in pairs, known as **bit-pair recoding** and also as the **modified Booth algorithm**. Grouping bit pairs from right to left produces three "+1,−1" pairs as shown in Figure 3-21. Since the +1 term is to the left

```
             0  0  1  1  1  0       (21)₁₀   Multiplicand
             0  1  0  1  0  1       (14)₁₀   Multiplier
          ×  +1 −1 +1 −1 +1 −1      Booth-recoded multiplier
               +1    +1    +1       Bit-pair-recoded multiplier

 0  0  0  0  0  0  0  0  1  1  1  0   (14 × 1)₁₀
 0  0  0  0  0  0  1  1  1  0  0  0   (14 × 4)₁₀
 0  0  0  0  1  1  1  0  0  0  0  0   (14 × 16)₁₀
───────────────────────────────────
 0  0  0  1  0  0  1  0  0  1  1  0   (294)₁₀   Product
```

Figure 3-21
Multiplication with bit-pair recoding of the multiplier.

Booth pair $(i + 1, i)$			Recoded bit pair (i)	Corresponding multiplier bits $(i + 1, i, i - 1)$
0	0	=	0	000 or 111
0	+1	=	+1	001
0	−1	=	−1	110
+1	0	=	+2	011
+1	+1	=	—	
+1	−1	=	+1	010
−1	0	=	−2	100
−1	+1	=	−1	101
−1	−1	=	—	

Figure 3-22
Recoded bit pairs.

of the −1 term, it has a weight that is twice as large as the weight for the −1 position. Thus, we might think of the pair as having the collective value $+2 - 1 = +1$.

In a similar manner, the pair −1,+1 is equivalent to $-2 + 1 = -1$. The pairs +1,+1 and −1,−1 cannot occur. There are a total of seven pairs that can occur, which are shown in Figure 3-22. For each case, the value of the recoded bit pair is multiplied by the multiplicand and is added to the product. In an implementation of bit-pair recoding, the Booth recoding and bit-pair recoding steps are collapsed into a single step by observing three multiplier bits at a time, as shown in the corresponding multiplier bit table.

The process of bit-pair recoding of a multiplier guarantees that in the worst case, only $w/2$ additions (or subtractions) will take place for a w-bit multiplier.

Array Multipliers

The serial method we used for multiplying two unsigned integers in Section 3.1.1 requires only a small amount of hardware, but the time required to multiply two numbers of length w grows as w^2. We can speed the multiplication process so that it completes in just $2w$ steps by implementing the manual process shown in Figure 3-10 in parallel. The general idea is to form a one-bit product between each multiplier bit and each multiplicand bit, and then sum each row of partial product elements from the top to the bottom in **systolic** (row by row) fashion.

The structure of a systolic **array multiplier** is shown in Figure 3-23. A partial product (PP) element is shown at the bottom of the figure. A multiplicand bit (m_i) and a multiplier bit (q_j) are multiplied by the AND gate, which forms a partial product at position (i, j) in the array. This partial product is added to the partial product from the previous stage (b_j) and any carry that is generated in the previous stage (a_j). The result has a width of $2w$ and appears at the bottom of the array (the high-order w bits) and at the right of the array (the low-order w bits).

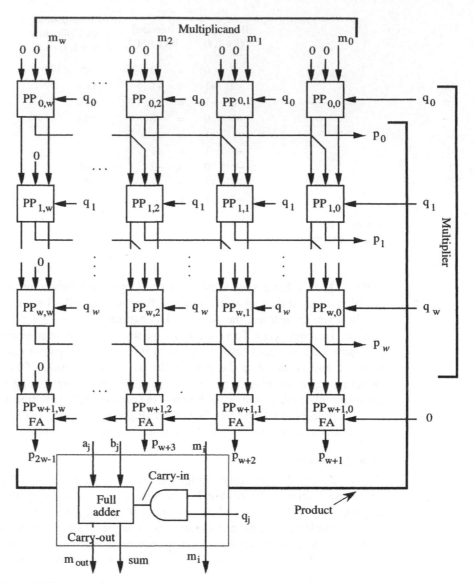

Figure 3-23
Parallel pipelined array multiplier.

3.4.3 High-Performance Division

We can extend the unsigned integer division technique of Section 3.2.2 to produce a fractional result in computing a/b. The general idea is to scale a and b to look like integers, perform the division process, and then scale the quotient to correspond to the actual result of dividing a by b.

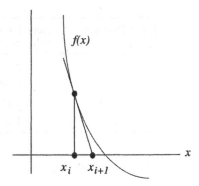

Figure 3-24
Newton's iteration for zero finding. Adapted from [Goldberg, 1990].

A faster method of division makes use of a lookup table and iteration. An iterative method of finding a root of a polynomial is called **Newton's iteration**, which is illustrated in Figure 3-24. The goal is to find where the function $f(x)$ crosses the x axis by starting with a guess x_i and then using the error between $f(x_i)$ and zero to refine the guess.

The tangent line at $f(x_i)$ can be represented by the equation:

$$y - f(x_i) = f'(x_i)(x - x_i).$$

The tangent line crosses the x axis at:

$$x_{i+1} = x_i - \frac{f(x_i)}{f'(x_i)}$$

The process repeats while $f(x)$ approaches zero.

The number of bits of precision doubles on each iteration (see [Goldberg, 1990]), and so if we are looking to obtain 32 bits of precision and we start with a single bit of precision, then five iterations are required to reach our target precision. The problem now is to cast division in the form of finding a zero for $f(x)$.

Consider the function $1/x - b$, which has a zero at $1/b$. If we start with b, then we can compute $1/b$ by iteratively applying Newton's method. Since $f'(x) = -1/x^2$, we now have:

$$x_{i+1} = x_i - \frac{1/x_i - b}{-1/x_i^2} = x_i + x_i - x_i^2 b = x_i(2 - x_i b)$$

Thus, we only need to perform multiplication and subtraction in order to perform division. Further, if our initial guess for x_0 is good enough, then we may only need to perform the iteration a few times.

Before using this method on an example, we need to consider how we will obtain our initial guess. If we are working with normalized significands, then it is relatively easy to make use of a lookup table for the first few digits. Consider computing $1/.101101$ using a 16-bit normalized base 2 significand in which the leading 1 is not hidden. The first three bits for any binary significand will be one of the patterns .100, .101, .110, or .111. These significands correspond to the base 10 numbers 1/2, 5/8, 3/4, and 7/8, respectively. The

B = First three bits of b	Actual base 10 value of 1/B	Corresponding lookup table entry
.100	2	10
.101	1 3/5	01
.110	1 1/3	01
.111	1 1/7	01

Figure 3-25
A three-bit lookup table for computing x_0.

reciprocals of these numbers are 2, 8/5, 4/3, and 8/7, respectively. We can store the binary equivalents in a lookup table, and then retrieve x_0 based on the first three bits of b.

The leading 1 in the significand does not contribute to the precision, and so the leading three bits of the significand only provide two bits of precision. Thus, the lookup table only needs two bits for each entry, as shown in Figure 3-25.

Now consider computing 1/.1011011 using this floating-point representation. We start by finding x_0 using the table shown in Figure 3-25. The first three bits of the significand b are 101, which corresponds to $x_0 = 01$. We compute $x_1 = x_0(2 - x_0 b)$ and obtain, in unsigned base 2 arithmetic, $x_1 = 01(10 - (01)(.1011011)) = 1.0100101$. Our two bits of precision have now become four bits of precision. For this example, we will retain as much intermediate precision as we can. In general, we only need to retain at most $2p$ bits of intermediate precision for a p-bit result. We iterate again, obtaining eight bits of precision:

$$x_2 = x_1(2 - x_1 b) = 1.0100101(10 - (1.0100101)(.1011011))$$

$$= 1.011001011001001011101.$$

We iterate again, obtaining our target 16 bits of precision:

$$x_3 = x_2(2 - x_2 b) = (1.011001011001001011101)(2 - (1.011001011001001011101)(.1011011))$$

$$= 1.011010000001001$$

$$= (1.40652466)_{10}.$$

The precise value is $(1.40659341)_{10}$, but our 16-bit value is as close to the precise value as it can be.

3.4.4 Residue Arithmetic

Addition, subtraction, and multiplication can all be performed in a single, carryless step using **residue arithmetic**. The residue number system is based on relatively prime integers called **moduli**. The residue of an integer with respect to a particular modulus is the least positive integer remainder of the division of the integer by the modulus. A set of possible moduli is 5, 7, 9, and 4. With these moduli, $5 \times 7 \times 9 \times 4 = 1260$ integers can be uniquely represented. A table showing the representation of the first twenty decimal integers using moduli 5, 7, 9, and 4 is shown in Figure 3-26.

Decimal	Residue 5794	Decimal	Residue 5794
0	0000	10	0312
1	1111	11	1423
2	2222	12	2530
3	3333	13	3641
4	4440	14	4052
5	0551	15	0163
6	1662	16	1270
7	2073	17	2381
8	3180	18	3402
9	4201	19	4513

Figure 3-26
Representation of the first twenty decimal integers in the residue number system for the given moduli.

Addition and multiplication in the residue number system result in valid residue numbers, provided the size of the chosen number space is large enough to contain the results. Subtraction requires each residue digit of the subtrahend to be complemented with respect to its modulus before performing addition. Addition and multiplication examples are shown in Figure 3-27. For these examples, the moduli used are 5, 7, 9, and 4. Addition is performed in parallel for each column, with no carry propagation. Multiplication is also performed in parallel for each column, independent of the other columns.

Although residue arithmetic operations can be very fast, there are a number of disadvantages to the system. Division and sign detection are difficult, and a representation for significands is also difficult. Conversions between the residue number system and weighted number systems are complex, and often require involved methods such as the **Chinese remainder theorem**. The conversion problem is important because the residue number system is not very useful without being translated to a weighted number system so that magnitude comparisons can be made. However, for integer applications in which the time spent in addition, subtraction, and multiplication outweighs the time spent in division, conversion, etc., the residue number system may be a practical approach. An important application area is matrix-vector multiplication, which is used extensively in signal processing.

$29 + 27 = 56$	
Decimal	Residue 5794
29	4121
27	2603
56	1020

$10 \times 17 = 170$	
Decimal	Residue 5794
10	0312
17	2381
170	0282

Figure 3-27
Examples of addition and multiplication in the residue number system.

EXAMPLE 3-3   One's Complement Addition Used
in Network Error Checking

Errors happen when data is transferred over a network, and we need a way to check on the receiving end if any bits have been erroneously flipped. One's complement addition is used as a simple form of error checking over the header portion of an Internet Protocol (IP) **datagram** (which is a different name for a packet).

The header is treated as a sequence of 16-bit words, padded with 0s on the right as needed for an even multiple of 16-bit words. The 16-bit words are added to form a 16-bit **checksum** word that is transmitted along with the header. The receiver performs a similar computation and compares the transmitted checksum with its own computation. If the checksums differ, then an error occurred during transmission. If the checksums agree, then either there is no error or there are multiple errors that this approach cannot detect. Higher-level mechanisms are used for dealing with errors that this method misses.

The header length can vary depending on what options are specified, but for the purpose of example, consider adding just the two 16-bit numbers $CD7A_{16}$ and 5555_{16}. The one's complement calculations are shown below:

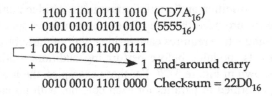

$$
\begin{array}{ll}
1100\ 1101\ 0111\ 1010 & (CD7A_{16}) \\
+\ 0101\ 0101\ 0101\ 0101 & (5555_{16}) \\
\hline
1\ 0010\ 0010\ 1100\ 1111 & \\
+\qquad\qquad\qquad\qquad 1 & \text{End-around carry} \\
\hline
0010\ 0010\ 1101\ 0000 & \text{Checksum} = 22D0_{16}
\end{array}
$$

Note that if a change is made to a portion of the header, which is a frequent occurrence when a packet passes through a router, only an incremental update needs to be made to the checksum: a full sequence of one's complement additions over all of the 16-bit words is unnecessary. However, incremental updates to the checksum can play havoc with error checking because there are two representations for 0 in one's complement: 00000000 00000000 and 11111111 11111111. Both representations must be considered in the error-checking algorithms, which is a drawback to this approach. Nevertheless, this approach is in pervasive use today. ■

Summary

Computer arithmetic can be carried out as we normally carry out decimal arithmetic by hand, while taking the base into account. A two's complement representation is normally used for integers, whereas signed magnitude is normally used for significands due to the difficulty of manipulating positive and negative significands in a uniform manner.

Performance can be improved by skipping over 1s in the Booth and bit-pair recoding techniques. An alternative method of improving performance is to use carryless addition, such as in residue arithmetic. Although carryless addition may be the fastest approach in terms of time complexity and circuit complexity, the more common weighted position codes are normally used in practice in order to simplify comparisons and the representation of significands.

Problems

3.1 Show the results of adding the following pairs of five-bit (i.e. one sign bit and four data bits) two's complement numbers and indicate whether or not overflow occurs for each case:

$$
\begin{array}{r} 1\,0\,1\,1\,0 \\ +\,1\,0\,1\,1\,1 \\ \hline \end{array}
\qquad
\begin{array}{r} 1\,1\,1\,1\,0 \\ +\,1\,1\,1\,0\,1 \\ \hline \end{array}
\qquad
\begin{array}{r} 1\,1\,1\,1\,1 \\ +\,0\,1\,1\,1\,1 \\ \hline \end{array}
$$

3.2 One way to determine that overflow has occurred when adding two numbers is to detect that the result of adding two positive numbers is negative, or that the result of adding two negative numbers is positive. The overflow rules are different for subtraction: there is overflow if the result of subtracting a negative number from a positive number is negative or the result of subtracting a positive number from a negative number is positive.

Subtract the numbers shown below and determine whether or not an overflow has occurred. Do not form the two's complement of the subtrahend and add: perform the subtraction bit by bit, showing the borrows generated at each position:

$$
\begin{array}{r} 0\ 1\ 0\ 1 \\ -\ 0\ 1\ 1\ 0 \\ \hline \end{array}
$$

3.3 Add the following two's complement and one's complement binary numbers as indicated. For each case, indicate if there is overflow.

Two's complement	One's complement
1 0 1 1.1 0 1	1 0 1 1.1 0 1
+ 0 1 1 1.0 1 1	+ 0 1 1 1.0 1 1

3.4 Show the process of serial unsigned multiplication for 1010 (multiplicand) multiplied by 0101 (multiplier). Use the form shown in Figure 3-12.

3.5 Show the process of serial unsigned multiplication for 11.1 (multiplicand) multiplied by 01.1 (multiplier) by treating the operands as integers. The result should be 101.01.

3.6 Show the process of serial unsigned division for 1010 divided by 0101. Use the form shown in Figure 3-15.

3.7 Show the process of serial unsigned division for 1010 divided by 0100, but instead of generating a remainder, compute the significand by continuing the process. That is, the result should be 10.1_2.

3.8 Using the approach shown in this chapter, compute $.100 \times 2^3 + .111 \times 2^6$ with three bits of precision and rounding to the nearest number (nearest even number for a tie).

3.9 Using the approach shown in this chapter, compute $(.101 \times 2^3) \times (.101 \times 2^6)$ with three bits of precision and rounding to the nearest number (nearest even number for a tie).

3.10 The equation used in Section 3.4.1 for c_4 in a carry lookahead adder assumes that c_0 is 0 for addition. If we perform subtraction by using the addition/subtraction unit shown in Figure 3-6, then $c_0 = 1$. Rewrite the equation for c_4 when $c_0 = 1$.

3.11 The 16-bit adder shown below uses a ripple carry among four-bit carry lookahead adders.

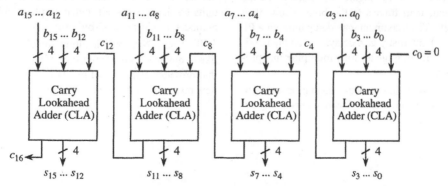

(a) What is the longest gate delay through this adder?

(b) What is the shortest gate delay through this adder, from any input to any output?

(c) What is the gate delay for s_{12}?

3.12 Use the Booth algorithm (not bit-pair recoding) to multiply 010011 (multiplicand) by 011011 (multiplier).

3.13 Use bit-pair recoding to multiply 010011 (multiplicand) by 011011 (multiplier).

3.14 Compute the maximum gate delay through a 32-bit carry lookahead adder.

3.15 What is the maximum number of inputs for any logic gate in a 32-bit carry lookahead adder, using the scheme described in this chapter?

3.16 In a **carry-select adder** a carry is propagated from one adder stage to the next, similar to but not exactly the same as a carry lookahead adder. As with many other adders, the carry out of a carry-select adder stage is either 0 or 1. In a carry-select adder, two sums are computed in parallel for each adder stage: one sum assumes a carry-in of 0, and the other sum assumes a carry-in of 1. The actual carry-in selects which of the two sums to use (with a MUX, for example). The basic layout is shown below for an eight-bit carry-select adder:

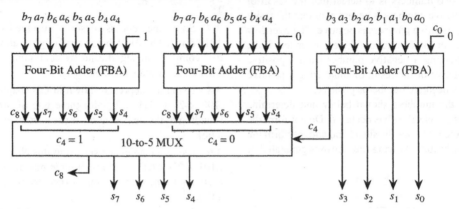

Assume that each four-bit adder (FBA) unit uses carry lookahead internally. Compare the number of gate delays needed to add two eight-bit numbers using FBA units in a carry-select configuration vs. using FBA units in which the carry is rippled from one FBA to the next.
(a) Draw a diagram of a functionally equivalent eight-bit carry lookahead configuration using the FBAs shown above.
(b) Show the number of gate delays for each adder configuration, by both the eight-bit carry-select adder shown above and the adder designed in part (a) above.

3.17 The path with the maximum gate delay through the array multiplier shown in Figure 3-23 starts in the top right PP element, then travels to the bottom row, then across to the left. The maximum gate delay through a PP element is three. How many gate delays are on the maximum gate delay path through an array multiplier that produces a p-bit result?

3.18 Given multiplication units that each produce a 16-bit unsigned product on two unsigned eight-bit inputs,

and 16-bit adders that produce a 16-bit sum and a carry-out on two 16-bit inputs and a carry-in, connect these units so that the overall unit multiplies 16-bit unsigned numbers, producing a 32-bit result.

3.19 Using Newton's iteration for division, we would like to obtain 32 bits of precision. If we use a lookup table that provides eight bits of precision for the initial guess, how many iterations need to be applied?

Further Reading

(Goldberg, 1995) is a concise but thorough source of numerous aspects of computer arithmetic. (Hamacher et al., 2001) provides a classic treatment of integer arithmetic. (Flynn, 1970) gives an early treatment of division by zero finding. (Garner, 1959) gives a complete description of the residue number system, whereas (Koren, 2001) gives a more tutorial treatment of the subject. (Huang and Goodman, 1979) describes how a memory-based residue processor can be constructed. Koren (2001) also provides additional details on cascading carry lookahead units. A classic reference on network protocols is (Stevens, 1994), which also covers the one's complement example used in this chapter.

Flynn, M. J., "On division by functional iteration," *IEEE Trans. Comp.*, **C-19**, no. 8, pp. 702-706 (Aug. 1970).

Garner, H. L., "The Residue Number System," *IRE Transactions on Electronic Computers*, **8**, pp. 140-147 (Jun. 1959).

Goldberg, D., "Computer Arithmetic," in Patterson, D. A. and Hennessy, J. L., *Computer Architecture: A Quantitative Approach*, 2/e, Morgan Kaufmann (1995).

Hamacher, V. C., Vranesic, Z. G., and Zaky, S. G., *Computer Organization*, 5/e, McGraw Hill (2001).

Huang, A. and Goodman, J. W., "Number Theoretic Processors, Optical and Electronic," *SPIE Optical Processing Systems*, **185**, pp. 28-35 (1979).

Koren, I., *Computer Arithmetic Algorithms*, 2/e, A. K. Peters, Ltd. (2001).

Stevens, W. Richard, *TCP/IP Illustrated, Volume 1: The Protocols*, Addison-Wesley, pp. 36-37 (1994).

CHAPTER 4

THE INSTRUCTION
SET ARCHITECTURE

In this chapter we tackle a central topic in computer architecture: the language understood by the computer's hardware, referred to as its *machine language*. The machine language is usually discussed in terms of its *assembly language*, which is functionally equivalent to the corresponding machine language except that the assembly language uses more intuitive names such as Move, Add, and Jump instead of the actual binary words of the language. (Programmers find constructs such as "Add r0, r1, r2" more easily understood than 01101011 10101101.)

We begin by describing the instruction set architecture (ISA) view of the machine and its operations. The ISA is sometimes referred to as the programmer's model of the machine, because it contains all the information that an assembly language programmer needs to write programs for that machine architecture. It consists of all of the instructions that the machine supports, along with a description of all the programmer-accessible registers. The ISA view corresponds to the Assembly Language/Machine Code level described in Figure 1-15. It is between the High-Level Language view, where little or none of the machine hardware is visible or of concern, and the Control level, where machine instructions are interpreted as register transfer actions, at the Functional Unit level.

In order to describe the nature of assembly language and assembly language programming, we choose as a model architecture the *ARC* machine, which is a simplification of the commercial SPARC architecture common in Sun computers.

We illustrate the utility of the various instruction classes with practical examples of assembly language programming, and we conclude with a Case Study of the Java bytecodes as an example of a common, portable assembly language that can be implemented using the native language of another machine.

■ 4.1 HARDWARE COMPONENTS OF THE INSTRUCTION SET ARCHITECTURE

The ISA of a computer presents the assembly language programmer with a view of the machine that includes all of the programmer-accessible hardware and the instructions that manipulate data within the hardware. In this section we look at the hardware components as viewed by the assembly language programmer. We begin with a discussion of the system as a whole: the CPU interacting with its internal (main) memory and performing input and output with the outside world.

4.1.1 The System Bus Model Revisited

Figure 4-1 revisits the system bus model that was introduced in Chapter 1.

The purpose of a bus is to reduce the number of interconnections between the CPU and its subsystems. Rather than have separate communication paths between memory and each I/O device, the CPU is interconnected with its memory and I/O systems via a shared **system bus**. In more complex systems there may be separate buses between the CPU and memory and CPU and I/O.

Not all of the components are connected to the system bus in the same way. The CPU generates addresses that are placed onto the address bus, and the memory receives addresses from the address bus. The memory never generates addresses, and the CPU never receives addresses, and so there are no corresponding connections in those directions.

In a typical scenario, a user writes a high-level program that a compiler translates into assembly language. An assembler then translates the assembly language program into machine code, which is stored on a disk. Prior to execution, the machine code program is loaded from the disk into the main memory by an operating system.

During program execution, each instruction is brought into the CPU from the memory, one instruction at a time, along with any data that is needed to execute the instruction. The output of the program is placed on a device such as a video display, disk, or printer. All of these operations are orchestrated by the control unit, which we will explore in detail in Chapter 6. Communication among the three components (CPU, Memory, and I/O) is handled with buses.

An important consideration is that the instructions are executed inside of the CPU, even though all of the instructions and data are initially stored in the memory. This means that instructions and data must be loaded from the memory into the CPU registers, and results must be stored back to the memory from the CPU registers.

4.1.2 Memory

Computer memory consists of a collection of consecutively numbered (addressed) cells, each one of which normally holds one **byte**. A byte is a collection of eight bits (sometimes

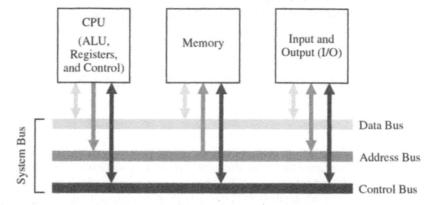

Figure 4-1
The system bus model of a computer system.

Bit	$\boxed{0}$
Nibble	$\boxed{0110}$
Byte	$\boxed{10110000}$
16-bit word (halfword)	$\boxed{11001001\ 01000110}$
32-bit word	$\boxed{10110100\ 00110101\ 10011001\ 01011000}$
64-bit word (double)	$\boxed{\begin{array}{llll} 01011000 & 01010101 & 10110000 & 11110011 \\ 11001110 & 11101110 & 01111000 & 00110101 \end{array}}$
128-bit word (quad)	$\boxed{\begin{array}{llll} 01011000 & 01010101 & 10110000 & 11110011 \\ 11001110 & 11101110 & 01111000 & 00110101 \\ 00001011 & 10100110 & 11110010 & 11100110 \\ 10100100 & 01000100 & 10100101 & 01010001 \end{array}}$

Figure 4-2

Common sizes for data types.

referred to by those in the communications community as an **octet**). Each cell has an address, referred to as a **memory location**. A **nibble**, or **nybble** as it is sometimes spelled, refers to a collection of four adjacent bits. The meanings of the terms "bit," "byte," and "nibble" are generally agreed upon regardless of the specifics of an architecture, but the meaning of **word** depends upon the particular processor. Typical word sizes are 16, 32, 64, and 128 bits, with the 32-bit word size being the common form for ordinary computers these days and the 64-bit word growing in popularity. In this text, words will be assumed to be 32 bits wide unless otherwise specified. A comparison of these data types is shown in Figure 4-2.

In a byte-addressable machine, the smallest object that can be referenced in memory is the byte; however, there are usually instructions that read and write multi-byte words. Multi-byte words are stored as a sequence of bytes, addressed by the byte of the word that has the lowest address. Most machines today have instructions that can access bytes, half-words, words, and double-words.

When multi-byte words are used, there are two choices about the order in which the bytes are stored in memory: most significant byte at lowest address, referred to as **big-endian**, or least significant byte stored at lowest address, referred to as **little-endian**. (The term "endian" comes from the issue of whether eggs should be broken on the big or little end, which caused a war between bickering politicians in Jonathan Swift's *Gulliver's Travels*.) Examples of big- and little-endian formats for a 4-byte, 32-bit word appear in Figure 4-3.

The bytes in a multi-byte word are stored at consecutive addresses, as shown in Figure 4-3. In a byte-addressable memory each byte is accessed by its specific **address**. By universal convention, the four-byte word is *always* accessed by referencing the address of the byte with the lowest address, x in Figure 4-3, regardless of whether it is big-endian or little-endian. Since addresses are counted in sequence beginning with zero, the lowest address is 0, and the highest address is one less than the size of the memory. The highest address for a 2^{32} byte memory is $2^{32}-1$.

Figure 4-4 shows the **memory map** of ARC, the example architecture that we will describe and use in this chapter. A memory map is just a drawing that shows how various segments of memory are allocated. This memory has a 32-bit **address space**, which means

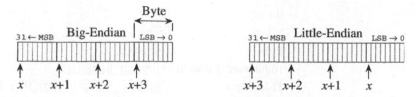

Word address is x for both big-endian and little-endian formats.

Figure 4-3
Big-endian and little-endian formats.

that a program can access a byte of memory anywhere in the range from 0 to $2^{32} - 1$. The address space for our example architecture is divided into distinct regions that are used for the operating system, input and output (I/O), user programs, and the system stack. The memory map differs from one implementation to another, which is partly why programs compiled for the same type of processor may not be compatible across systems.

The lower $2^{11} = 2048$ addresses of the memory map are reserved for use by the operating system. The user space is where a user's assembled program is loaded, and can grow during operation from location 2048 until it meets up with the system stack. The system stack starts at location $2^{31} - 4$ and grows toward lower addresses. The portion of the address space between 2^{31} and $2^{32} - 1$ is reserved for I/O devices. The memory map is thus not entirely composed of real memory, and in fact there may be large gaps where neither real memory nor I/O devices exist. Since I/O devices are treated like memory locations,

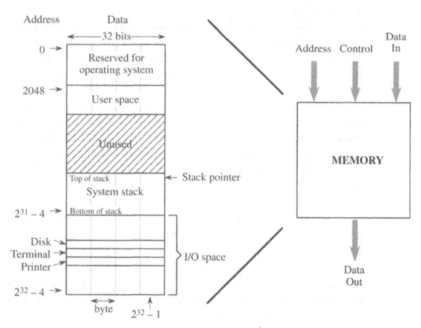

Figure 4-4
A memory map for the example ARC architecture (not drawn to scale).

ordinary memory read and write commands can be used for reading and writing devices. This is referred to as **memory-mapped I/O**.

It is important to keep the distinction clear between what is an address and what is data. An address in this example memory is 32 bits wide, and a word happens also to be 32 bits wide, but they are not the same thing. An address is a pointer to a memory location that holds data. Table 4.1 illustrates both the distinction between an address and the data that is stored there, and the fact that ARC/SPARC is a big-endian machine. The table shows four bytes stored at consecutive addresses 00001000 to 00001003. Thus the byte address 0x00001003 contains the byte 0xDD. Since this is a big-endian machine (the big end is stored at the lowest address) the *word* stored at address 0x00001000 is 0xAABBCCDD. Note that all addresses are *byte* addresses regardless of whether a given byte is part of a larger data object such as a halfword or word. Also note that the memory has no knowledge of whether the byte is part of a larger data object.

The computer's memory can be thought of as an array of bytes, halfwords, or words. We will occasionally refer to memory in this way: MB[xxxx], MH[xxxx], or M[xxxx] to refer to the byte, the halfword, or the word located at address xxxx. So in Table 4.1 MB[1003] is 0xDD, and MH[1000] is 0xAABB.

Table 4.1 **Example of ARC/SPARC Memory Layout**

Hex. Address	Hex. Value
...	...
00001003	DD
00001002	CC
00001001	BB
00001000	AA
...	...

In this chapter we assume that the computer's memory is organized in a single address space, sometimes referred to as a **flat address space**. The term **address space** refers to the numerical range of memory addresses to which the CPU can refer. In Chapter 7 (Memory), we will see that there are other ways that memory can be organized, but for now, we assume that memory as seen by the CPU has a single range of addresses. What decides the size of that range? It is the size of a memory address that the CPU can place on the address bus during read and write operations. A memory address that is n bits wide can specify one of 2^n items. This memory could be referred to as having an n-bit address space, or equivalently as having a (2^n) byte address space. For example, a machine having a 32-bit address space will have a maximum capacity of 2^{32} (4 GB) of memory. The memory addresses will range from 0 to 2^{32}- 1, which is 0 to 4,294,967,295 decimal, or in the easier-to-manipulate **hexadecimal** format, from 0x00000000 to 0xFFFFFFFF. (The '0x' indicates a hexadecimal number in C and many other languages.)

Many if not most modern processor architectures, ARC and SPARC included, have what is referred to as **hard-alignment** constraints on the addresses of multi-byte words. Hard alignment means that two-byte halfwords have to be stored with their memory addresses aligned on even-byte boundaries, and four-byte words have to be aligned on even-word boundaries. In other words, half words must have addresses that are even, i.e. ending in zero; words must have addresses that are multiples of 4, ending in 00. The "hard" in hard alignment means that an attempt to access an unaligned memory object causes the program to abort execution or to execute some "fixup" routine. Other architectures, in particular the Intel x86 family, impose **soft-alignment** constraints. Soft alignment means that unaligned memory objects are permitted, but fetching them from memory may require more time than fetching aligned objects. The assembler directive .align is used to align a machine instruction on the proper boundary. It is discussed later in this chapter. Alignment issues in general are discussed further in Section 8.4.3.

4.1.3 The CPU

Now that we are familiar with the basic components of the system bus and memory, we are ready to explore the internals of the CPU. At a minimum, the CPU consists of a **data section** that contains registers and an ALU, and a **control section** that interprets instructions and effects register transfers, as illustrated in Figure 4-5. The data section is also referred to as the **datapath**.

The control unit of a computer is responsible for executing the program instructions, which are stored in the main memory. (Here we will assume that the machine code is interpreted by the control unit one instruction at a time, though in Chapter 10 we shall see that many modern processors can process several instructions simultaneously.) There are two registers that form the interface between the control unit and the data unit, known as the **program counter** (PC)[1] and the **instruction register** (IR). The PC contains the address of the instruction being executed. The instruction that is pointed to by the PC is fetched from the memory, and is stored in the IR where it is interpreted. The steps that the control unit carries out in executing a program are:

1. Fetch the next instruction to be executed from memory.

2. Decode the opcode.

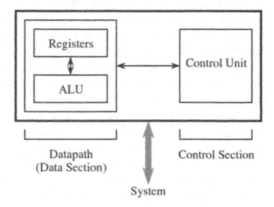

Figure 4-5
High-level view of a CPU.

---

[1] In Intel processors the program counter is called the **instruction pointer**, IP.

3. Read operand(s) from main memory, if any.

4. Execute the instruction and store results, if any.

5. Go to step 1.

This is known as the **fetch-execute cycle**. *Fetching* just means retrieving the object from memory. Each instruction contains a code, the *opcode* (short for operation code), that specifies exactly what the instruction is to do. After the instruction is fetched from memory the control unit *decodes* it and performs the specified action.

The control unit is responsible for coordinating these different units in the execution of a computer program. It can be thought of as a form of a "computer within a computer" in the sense that it makes decisions as to how the rest of the machine behaves. We will treat the control unit in detail in Chapter 6.

The datapath is made up of a collection of registers known as the **register file**, the arithmetic and logic unit (ALU), and perhaps other registers. An example datapath is shown in Figure 4-6. The figure depicts the datapath of an example processor we will use in the remainder of the chapter.

The register file in the figure can be thought of as a small, fast memory, separate from the system memory, that is used for temporary storage during computation. Typical sizes for a register file range from a few to a few thousand registers. Like the system memory, each register in the register file is assigned an address in sequence starting from zero. These register "addresses" are much smaller than main memory addresses: a register file containing 32 registers would have only a five-bit address, for example. The major difference between the register file and the system memory is that the register file is contained within the CPU and is therefore much faster. An instruction that operates on data from the register file can often run tens or hundreds of times faster than the same instruction that

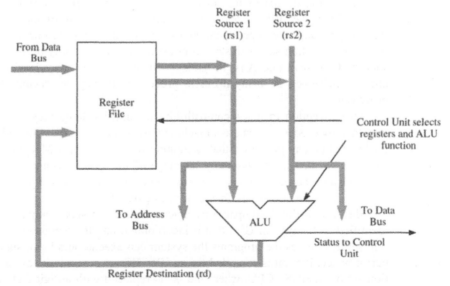

Figure 4-6
An example datapath.

operates on data in memory. For this reason, register-intensive programs are faster than the equivalent memory-intensive programs, even if it takes more register operations to do the same tasks than would be required with the operands located in memory.

Notice that there are several busses *inside* the datapath of Figure 4-6. Three buses connect the datapath to the system bus. This allows data to be transferred to and from main memory and the register file. Three additional buses connect the register file to the ALU. These buses allow two operands to be fetched from the register file simultaneously, which are operated on by the ALU, with the results returned to the register file.

The ALU implements a variety of binary (two-operand) and unary (one-operand) operations. Examples include add, and, not, or, and multiply. Operations and operands to be used during the operations are selected by the Control Unit according to which instruction is being executed. The two source operands are fetched from the register file onto buses labeled "Register Source 1 (rs1)" and "Register Source 2 (rs2)." The output from the ALU is placed on the bus labeled "Register Destination (rd)," where the results are conveyed back to the register file. In most systems these connections also include a path to the System Bus so that memory and devices can be accessed. This is shown as the three connections labeled "From Data Bus," "To Data Bus," and "To Address Bus."

The Instruction Set

The **instruction set** is the collection of instructions that a processor can execute, and in effect, it defines the processor. All instructions can be classified by the kinds of operations they implement. **Data movement** instructions move data back and forth between the CPU and memory or the I/O system. **Arithmetic and logic instructions** perform arithmetic or logical operations on data. **Control instructions** transfer control from one section of the program to another.

Although all instruction sets implement the three classes of instructions described above, specific details of the instruction sets for each processor type differ from one another. They may differ in the sizes of instructions, the kinds of operations they allow, the types of operands they operate on, and the types of results they provide. This incompatibility in instruction sets is in stark contrast to the compatibility of higher-level languages such as C, Pascal, and Ada. Programs written in these higher-level languages can run almost unchanged on many different processors if they are **recompiled** for the target processor.

One exception to this incompatibility of machine languages is programs compiled into Java bytecodes, which are a machine language for a **virtual machine**. They will run unchanged on any processor that is running the Java Virtual Machine. The Java Virtual Machine, written in the assembly language of the target machine, intercepts each Java bytecode and executes it as if it were running on a Java hardware ("real") machine. See the Case Study at the end of this chapter for more details.

Because of this incompatibility among instruction sets, computer systems are often identified by the type of CPU that is incorporated into the computer system. The instruction set determines the programs the system can execute and has a significant impact on performance. Programs compiled for an IBM PC (or compatible) system use the instruction set of an 80x86 CPU, where the 'x' is replaced with a digit that corresponds to the version, such as 80586, more commonly referred to as a Pentium processor. These programs will not run on a Sun Microsystems SPARC computer or an IBM RS6000 computer, since the Sun uses the SPARC processor and IBM machines execute the instruction set of the IBM Power CPU. This does not mean that all computer systems that use the same CPU can execute the same programs, however, because of differences in operating systems and I/O conventions.

We will cover a subset of the SPARC instruction set in detail later in Section 4.2.

Software for generating machine-language programs

A **compiler** is a computer program that transforms programs written in a high-level language such as C, Pascal, or Fortran into machine language. Compilers for the same high-level language generally have the same "front end," the part that recognizes statements in the high-level language. They will have different "back ends," however, one for each target processor. The compiler's back end is responsible for generating assembly language or machine code for a specific target processor. On the other hand, the same program, compiled by different C compilers for the *same* machine can produce different compiled programs for the same source code, as we will see.

In the process of compiling a program (referred to as the **translation process**), a high-level source program is transformed into **assembly language**, and the assembly language is then translated into machine code for the target machine by an **assembler**. These translations take place at **compile time** and **assembly time**, respectively. The resulting object program can be linked with other object programs at **link time**. After linking the separately assembled programs together, the linker attaches a fragment of operating system code to the end of the linked module. The purpose of this code fragment is to transfer control back to the operating system when the program has completed execution. The resulting program, sometimes referred to as a **load module**, is usually stored on a disk, loaded into main memory at **load time**, and executed by the CPU at **run time**. In modern desktop operating systems such as Microsoft Windows or the Mac OS, program loading and running can be initiated by the user double-clicking on an application icon.

Although most code is written in high-level languages, programmers may use assembly language for programs or fragments of programs that are time- or space-critical. In addition, compilers may not be available for some special-purpose processors, or their compilers may be inadequate to express the special operations that are required. In these cases, also, the programmer may need to resort to programming in assembly language.

High-level languages allow us to ignore the target computer architecture during coding. At the machine-language level, however, the underlying architecture is the primary consideration. A program written in a high-level language like C, Pascal, or Fortran may look the same and execute correctly after compilation on several different computer systems. The object code that the compiler produces for each machine, however, will be very different for each computer system, even if the systems use the same instruction set, because of differences in operating systems.

Having discussed the system bus, main memory, and the CPU, we are now in a position to examine details of a model instruction set, the ARC.

Intel vs. Motorola: The 16- and 16/32-Bit Instruction Set Architectures

In the previous chapter we saw that Intel and Motorola both released 16-bit (Intel) and 16/32-bit (Motorola) architectures in the late 1970s. Once again their philosophies were diametrically opposed. Intel demanded of its architects that the new 16-bit processor be upwardly **source-code compatible** with the 8080. Source-code compatibility meant that 8080 source code would run on the new 8086 merely by being recompiled on an 8086 compiler. While this was greatly appreciated by those developers who had a large amount of "legacy" 8080 code, it placed severe constraints on the designers of the new 16-bit machine. The register structure had to have similarities to its older eight-bit ancestor, and, more constraining, the processor had to be capable of handling the old 16-bit addresses. The registers in the 8080, and in fact in all eight-bit microprocessors, each had its own purpose and its own name. This concept was extended to the '86, whose 16-bit processing registers were named AX, BX, CX, and DX, and could be divided into twice as many eight-bit registers, in deference to the fact that the 8080 had eight-bit data registers. These registers were special-purpose in the sense that each one could be used for only one kind of operation. For example, only AX and DX could be used for arithmetic operations. The new processor also had four additional special-purpose registers for

memory addressing: SI, DI, BP, and SP. In order to accommodate addresses greater than 16 bits in size, the processor also had four 20-bit segment registers, the least-significant four bits of which were set to zero. A 20-bit memory address was formed by adding one of the 16-bit address register to one of the 20-bit segment registers, yielding a 20-bit physical memory address. Thus the processor could directly address only one megabyte of memory. The instruction set and addressing modes were also severely hampered by the compatibility constraint.

Motorola took the opposite approach of doing a "clean sheet of paper" design. While this eliminated the possibility of upward compatibility, it freed them from the constraints Intel placed on their architects. The results were a much more regular and general-purpose register structure, instruction set, and addressing modes. Simply put, the machine had 32-bit internal data paths, eight general-purpose 32-bit data registers, eight general-purpose 32-bit address registers, and 16 addressing modes that were common to most instructions. The processor was capable of generating 32-bit addresses in a "flat" 32-bit memory space. (The original 68000 only had 24 address pins, however, and thus could address only 16 MB of memory.)

■ 4.2 ARC, A RISC COMPUTER

In the remainder of this chapter, we will study a model architecture that is based on the commercial Scalable Processor Architecture (**SPARC**) processor that was developed at Sun Microsystems in the mid-1980s. The SPARC has become a popular architecture since its introduction, partly due to its "open" nature: the full definition of the SPARC architecture is made readily available to the public (SPARC, 1992). In this chapter, we will look at just a subset of the SPARC, which we call "A RISC Computer" (**ARC**). "RISC" is yet another acronym, for **reduced instruction set computer**, which is discussed in Chapter 6. For now, consider the RISC style as having simpler instructions that do less but can be executed faster. The ARC has most of the important features of the SPARC architecture, but without some of the more complex features that are present in a commercial processor.

We now describe the ARC ISA: first the memory, then the programmer-accessible CPU registers, and finally the instruction set.

4.2.1 ARC Memory

The ARC is a 32-bit machine with byte-addressable memory: it can manipulate 32-bit data types, but all data is stored in memory as bytes, and the address of a 32-bit word is the address of its byte that has the lowest address. As described in Figure 4-4, the ARC has a 32-bit address space, in which our example architecture is divided into distinct regions devoted to operating system code, user program code, the system stack (used to store temporary data), and input and output, (I/O).

These memory regions are detailed as follows:

- The lowest $2^{11} = 2048$ addresses of the memory map are reserved for use by the operating system.

- The user space is where a user's assembled program is loaded, and can grow during operation from location 2048 until it meets up with the system stack.

- The system stack starts at location $2^{31} - 4$ and grows "downward" toward lower addresses. The reason for this organization of programs growing upward in memory and the system stack growing downward can be seen in Figure 4-4: it accommodates both large programs with small stacks and small programs with large stacks.

- The portion of the address space located at the top of memory, between 2^{31} and $2^{32} - 1$, is reserved for I/O devices. Each device has a collection of one or more memory addresses where its data is stored, which is referred to as "memory-mapped I/O."

The ARC has several data types (byte, halfword, integer, etc.), but for now we will consider only the 32-bit integer data type. Each integer is stored in memory as a collection of four bytes. ARC is a **big-endian** architecture: the highest-order byte of a word or halfword is stored at the lowest address. The largest possible byte address in the ARC is $2^{32} - 1$, so the address of the highest word in the memory map is three bytes lower than this, or $2^{32} - 4$. As mentioned above, the ARC architecture imposes hard alignment constraints.

4.2.2 ARC Registers

Figure 4-7 shows the programmer-accessible registers:

- ARC has 32 32-bit registers, labeled `%r0` - `%r31`, of which 31 are general-purpose and one, `%r0`, always contains the value 0. Registers `%r14` and `%r15` have additional uses as a **stack pointer** (`%sp`) and a **link register**, respectively, as described later.

- The 32-bit **program counter** (PC), labeled `%pc`, contains the address of the instruction being executed.

- The 32-bit **Processor Status Register** (PSR), labeled `%psr`, contains information about the state of the processor, including information about the results of previous arithmetic operations. The "arithmetic flags" in the PSR are called the **condition codes**. They specify whether a specified arithmetic operation resulted in a zero value (z), a negative value (n), a carry-out from the 32-bit ALU (c), and an overflow (v). The v bit is set when the results of the arithmetic operation are too large to be handled by the ALU. Specific details of which flags are set under which circumstances will

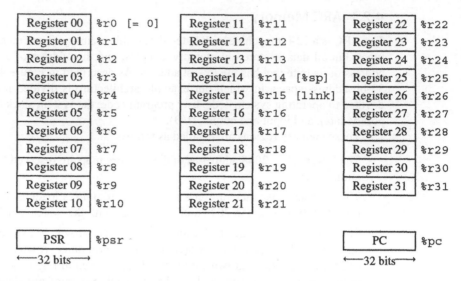

Figure 4-7
User-visible registers in the ARC.

vary from processor to processor, and the programmer must check the processor manual for specific details.

The PSR also has several bit fields to support **traps**. Traps provide a mechanism for external or internal events to interrupt normal processing. They are actions the processor takes when it changes the instruction flow in response to the presence of an exception, an interrupt, or a trap instruction in the program stream. There are no standard definitions for the terms "exception" or "interrupt." We will adopt the SPARC conventions of defining an **exception** as a condition that makes it impossible for the processor to continue executing the current instruction stream without software intervention, and an **interrupt** as a request for service by an external device. In support of the trap mechanism, the PSR contains the et, Traps Enabled bit, and the four-bit field PIL, Processor Interrupt Level field, which will be discussed later.

There are several additional features of the ARC ISA:

- All instructions are one word (32 bits) in size.
- The ARC is a **load-store** machine: the only way an instruction can access operands in memory is through the load and store instructions. All arithmetic operations operate on values that are contained in registers, and the results are placed in a register. There are approximately 200 instructions in the SPARC instruction set, upon which the ARC instruction set is based. The ARC processor implements only a small subset of them.
- The ARC and SPARC are *two's complement* machines, as are nearly all general-purpose computers. This means that arithmetic operations such as add and sub (subtract) treat their operands as two's complement numbers.

The next section delves into the syntax of ARC assembly language instructions. Unless otherwise stated, the ARC and SPARC instruction syntax and behaviors are identical.

4.2.3 ARC Assembly Language Format

Each assembly language has its own syntax, and they vary widely according to the particular machine type. Furthermore, even within a given machine's assembly language each instruction class often has different syntaxes. We will begin with a short excursion into the three classes of instructions: arithmetic and logic, memory access, and transfer of control, which should be familiar from higher-level language studies.

The ARC Arithmetic and Logic Instructions

Figure 4-8 shows the assembly language syntax for the ARC arithmetic and logic instructions, in particular the add instruction. The instruction labeled lab_1 shows the contents of two registers, %r1 and %r2, being added and the results stored in a third, %r3. The instruction labeled lab_2 shows a register, %r1, being added to the constant 12, and the results being stored in %r3. The lab_3 instruction, addcc, performs the same operation as the instruction above it, lab_2, but in addition it sets the condition codes, z, n, c, and v, according to whether the add instruction generates a result that is zero, negative, has a carry-out from its MSB, or overflowed its register, respectively. As the figure indicates, the second source operand may be either a register or a constant. These constants are called **immediate** constants because they are actually embedded or carried along in the 32-bit instruction.

The comment field describes, in **register transfer language (RTL)**, what the instruction actually does: add two registers or a register and a constant, and store the result in a destination register. The left-pointing arrow, ←, is the **assignment operator** in RTL. As a shorthand way of describing instructions whose second operand can either be in a register or an immediate constant we will use the notation

    add rs1, reg_or_imm, rd

where *rs1* denotes the first operand, in source register rs1, *reg_or_imm* denotes the second operand, which may be in a register or an immediate constant, and *rd* is the destination register. For these classes of instructions, immediate constants are limited to 13 bits, denoted as *simm13*, and are taken to two's complement numbers. Thus the range of the immediate constant is -4196 to +4195. *Immediate constants are sign-extended to 32 bits before being used in any operation.*

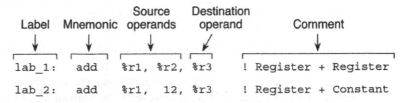

Figure 4-8
Syntax for ARC (and SPARC) arithmetic and logic instructions.

The meaning of "**sign extended**" is that the leftmost bit of the 13-bit field (the sign bit) is copied to the left into the remaining bits that make up a 32-bit integer, before adding it to rs1 in this case. This ensures that a two's complement negative number remains negative (and a two's complement positive number remains positive). For instance, $(-13)_{10} = (1111111110011)_2$, and after sign extension to a 32-bit integer, we have $(11111111111111111111111111110011)_2$, which is still equivalent to $(-13)_{10}$.

The ARC ALU instructions consist of six fields: an optional label field, an opcode field, two fields specifying the source operands, a field specifying the destination operand, and an optional comment field. A label may consist of any combination of alphabetic or numeric characters, underscores (_), dollar signs ($), or dots (.), as long as the first character is not a digit. *The programmer should avoid using leading underscores and dots (.), as they convey a special meaning to the assembler.*

A label must be followed by a colon. The language is sensitive to case, and so a distinction is made between upper- and lower-case letters. The language is "free format" in the sense that any field can begin in any column, but the relative left-to-right ordering must be maintained. Registers are denoted by a beginning percent sign, "%." Operands are separated by commas, the source operands are on the left, and the destination operand always appears in the rightmost position in the operand field; that is, the flow from operands to results is left to right. (Instruction sets for other machine architectures may use the opposite convention: operand flow right to left. Consult the particular programmer's manual for details.)

Numbers in the ARC assembly language are interpreted as base 10 unless preceded by "0x," which denotes a hexadecimal number. The comment field follows the operand field, begins with an exclamation mark '!' and terminates at the end of the line.

The examples shown in Figure 4-8 are representative of all of the arithmetic and logic instructions of the ARC instruction set, which we shall describe in Section 4.2.4 below.

Once again we emphasize that register %r0 is special. When used as an operand in an instruction it returns the value 0. When it occurs as the destination operand, the result is discarded. This behavior may seem odd, but it allows instructions to do double duty, as we shall show later.

The ARC Load and Store Instructions

Figure 4-9 shows the ARC load and store instruction syntax and behavior. The ld instruction loads words *from* memory into the specified register, and the st instruction stores words *into* memory from the specified register. There are also similar instructions to load signed and unsigned bytes, ldsb, and ldub, and halfwords, ldsh, and lduh, and to store bytes and halfwords, stb and sth, respectively. The load signed byte and halfword instructions sign-extend the byte or halfword to 32 bits, in a manner similar to that shown in the discussion of sign extension on page 106.

Notice that the memory address from which the operand should be fetched is set in brackets, as in [%r1], [%r1+%r2], and [%r1-122]. The brackets are a reminder that the value in the brackets is a memory address, and once again the left-pointing arrow, ←, denotes assignment, and M[xxxx] represents the word stored at memory location xxxx.

Notice also that addresses can be formed from a simple register, as in the instructions at lab_3 and lab_6, or from the sum of two registers, as in lab_4 and lab_7, or from the sum of a register and a constant, as in lab_5 and lab_7. Not shown, but implied, is

| | | Source | Destination | |
| Label | Mnemonic | operand | operand | Comment |

```
lab_3:    ld    [%r1],    %r3     ! %r3 ← M[%r1]

lab_4:    ld    [%r1+%r2],%r3     ! %r3 ← M[%r1+%r2]

lab_5:    ld    [%r1-122],%r3     ! %r3 ← M[%r1-122]

lab_6:    st    %r3,    [%r1]     ! M[%r1]      ← %r3

lab_7:    st    %r3,[%r1+%r2]     ! M[%r1+%r2] ← %r3

lab_8:    st    %r3,[%r1-122]     ! M[%r1-122] ← %r3
```

Figure 4-9
Syntax of ARC Load and Store Instructions.

that the address may be a constant. Why? [Hint: think %r0.] **Address arithmetic**, such as [%r3-122], is needed to support various higher-level language constructs such as arrays and structs.

The notation that describes the load and store instructions is:

```
ld [address], rd     and
st rd, [address]
```

where *address* is *rs1* + *rs2*, or *rs1* + *simm13*, and *rd* is the destination address for *ld*, and is the source register for *st*. Once again we remind the student that *simm13* is a two's complement number *that is sign-extended to 32 bits before being used in the operation*.

Figure 4-10 shows a simple program fragment using our ld, st, and add instructions. This fragment is equivalent to the C statement

```
z = x + y;
```

Since ARC is a load-store machine, the code must first fetch the x and y operands from memory using ld instructions, then perform the addition, and then store the result back into z using an st instruction.

```
ld        [x],      %r1

ld        [y],      %r2

add       %r1,      %r2,      %r3

st        %r3       [z]
```

Figure 4-10
Simple example: add two numbers.

The ARC Control Transfer Instructions

Figure 4-11 shows just a few of the control transfer instructions in the ARC instruction set. The instructions shown are called **branch instructions**. They are used to unconditionally

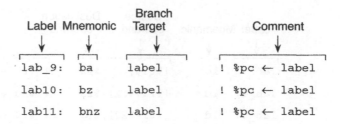

Figure 4-11
ARC transfer of control sequence.

or conditionally transfer control, or branch, to another part of the program. A moment's reflection will show that the way to transfer control to another part of the program is to load the PC, %pc, with the address of the instruction where program execution is to continue. The branch may be unconditional, that is, branch always, **ba**, or conditional based on whether some condition is true or false. The unconditional branch, ba, would be equivalent to the much-maligned goto instruction that is part of many programming languages. The instruction labelled lab_9 does a *branch always* to label, where label is some label within the program.

Conditional branches such as the ones labeled lab10 and lab11 branch only under certain conditions, as determined by the particular branch instruction and the state of one or more of the four flags in the Processor Status Register, z, n, c, and v. See the discussion below Figure 4-7 for information on the flags in the PSR. The **bz** instruction labelled lab10 is the "branch if zero" instruction. It branches only if the result of the previous instruction is equal to zero. It operates by testing the z flag and branching only if z=1, meaning TRUE. The **bnz** instruction tests the z flag and branches if z=0, or FALSE. This is the paradigm used in most modern microprocessor instruction sets: use an instruction to set the flags and then use a branch instruction to test whether the condition is true or false.

The notation describing the branch instructions is

```
bcc        label
```

where *cc* is one of the branch conditions, such as always (a), or zero (z), or not zero (nz). The address to which the program branches, label, is $\%PC + (4 \times \text{sign\_ext}(simm22))$, where sign_ext denotes sign-extending *simm22* to 32 bits. Why multiply by 4? Because ARC and SPARC have hard-alignment constraints. This means that instructions must be aligned on four-byte boundaries, which in turn means that the LSBs of all instructions must be 00. Thus multiplying by four (or, equivalently, shifting left by two bits), serves double duty: it ensures that the branch target will be a valid address, and it extends the range of the branch target by a factor of 4.

As an example, consider the absolute value function, abs:

$$\text{abs}(x) := \text{if } (x < 0) \text{ then } x = -x;$$

An ARC fragment to implement this would be as shown in Figure 4-12. The second instruction, subcc, negates the number in %r1, one might say as a "guess," and sets the condition codes. If the result of the subtraction is less than zero, it means that the original

```
abs:      ld        [x],      %r1

          subcc     %r0,      %r1,      %r1

          bl        over

          st        %r1,      [x]

over:     . . .
```

Figure 4-12
ARC fragment that computes the absolute value.

number was greater than or equal to zero, and so x should be left as it is. Thus the next instruction, bl, branch on less than zero, branches around the code to negate the operand, to the label over, if the result is less than zero. Otherwise the program "falls through" the branch instruction to the st, store, instruction, which stores the now positive number back into memory location x. The label over represents the continuation of the program.

There are several other kinds of control transfer instructions that we will cover under *Control Instructions* on page 112.

4.2.4 The ARC instruction set

The ARC instruction set consists of more than 35 most commonly used instructions. A subset of 17 of the more common instructions is shown in Figure 4-13. Each instruction is represented by a **mnemonic**, a name that represents the instruction.

	Mnemonic	Meaning
Memory	ld	Load a register from memory
	st	Store a register into memory
	sethi	Load the 22 most significant bits of a register
Logic	andcc	Bitwise logical AND
	orcc	Bitwise logical OR
	orncc	Bitwise logical NOR
	srl	Shift right (logical)
Arithmetic	addcc	Add
	call	Call subroutine
	jmpl	Jump and link (return from subroutine call)
	be	Branch if equal
Control	bneg	Branch if negative
	bcs	Branch on carry
	bvs	Branch on overflow
	ba	Branch always

Figure 4-13
A subset of the instruction set for the ARC ISA.

Data Movement Instructions

The first two instructions, **ld** (load) and **st** (store), are discussed above.

The **sethi** instruction, pronounced, "set hi," sets the 22 most significant bits (MSBs) of a register with a 22-bit constant contained within the instruction. It is commonly used for constructing an arbitrary 32-bit constant in a register, in conjunction with another instruction that sets the low-order 10 bits of the register. It is necessary because in the ARC all instructions are exactly one 32-bit word long, and it is therefore impossible to place a 32-bit immediate constant into a register in one instruction. The syntax is

```
sethi simm22, rdst
```

which means rdst ← simm22 | 0000000000. The vertical bar | denotes concatenation.

Figure 4-14 shows how sethi, in conjunction with or, can be used to load the 32-bit constant 0xAABBCCDD into register %r2. The most significant 22 bits can be found by converting the constant to binary: 0xAABBCCDD = 1010 1010 1011 1011 1100 1100 1101 1101. The most significant 22 bits are 10 1010 1010 1110 1111 0011, or 0x2AAEF3. The least significant 10 bits are 0x0DD, which are or'd into %r2 after the sethi instruction, with the result placed back into %r2:

```
sethi   0x2AAEF3,   %r2

or      %r2,        0xDD,   %r2
```

Figure 4-14
Placing a 32-bit constant in a register.

The Arithmetic and Logic Instructions

Although the shift instructions are considered to be part of the arithmetic and logic class, we will discuss them separately in the next section, as they differ somewhat from the arithmetic and other logic instructions in the way they are treated in the SPARC and ARC instruction sets.

As the discussion of Figure 4-8 points out, in all the arithmetic and logic instructions one of the two source operands must be in a register. The other may either be in a register or it may be a 13-bit two's complement constant, *simm13*, contained in the instruction, which is sign-extended to 32 bits before it is used. The result is stored in a register.

The **and** and **or** instructions perform a bit-by-bit logical AND and OR, respectively, on their operands.[2] The **orcc** instruction performs the same logical OR of its operands, but in addition it sets the condition code bits. The "cc" version of these instructions specifies that after performing the specified operation, the condition code bits in the PSR are updated to reflect the results of the operation.

The **add** and **addcc** instructions perform a 32-bit two's complement addition on their operands; the latter instruction also sets the condition codes.

All of these arithmetic and logic instructions have the same syntax as the figure shows, repeated here for emphasis:

```
add rs1, reg_or_imm, rd
```

---

[2] Bitwise logic operations are discussed in detail in Section A.4.

Setting the Condition Codes

The ARC (and SPARC) processors adopt a simple rule for setting the condition code bits in the PSR: only the arithmetic and logic instructions can set the condition codes by appending cc to the instruction. The condition code bits are set as follows when cc is specified as part of an arithmetic or logic instruction:

The zero, z, bit is set if the result of the arithmetic or logic operation is zero.

The negative bit, n, is set if, after the arithmetic or logic operation is performed, the MSB, bit 31, of the result is a 1, indicating that the result is a negative two's complement number.

The carry bit, c, is set if there is a carry out of bit 31, the MSB, when the add operation is performed, or if there is a borrow into bit 31 after a subtraction.

The overflow bit, v, is set if the result of the operation could not be correctly represented as a 32-bit number.

The Shift Instructions

The shift instructions shift the contents of the source register right or left by zero to 31 bit positions and store the shifted result in the destination register, rd. The **srl** (shift right *logical*) instruction shifts a register to the right, and copies zeros into the leftmost bit(s). The **sra** (shift right *arithmetic*) instruction (not shown) shifts the original register contents to the right, placing copies of the MSB of the original register into the newly created vacant bit(s) in the left side of the register. This results in sign-extending the number, thus preserving its arithmetic sign. Not shown, the **sll** (shift left logical) behaves as expected. The number of bit positions to shift the source is referred to as the **shift count**. The shift count is a five-bit unsigned number, which can be in a register or an immediate value stored in the instructions. The notation is

```
sll rs1, reg_or_shcnt, rd
```

where *reg_or_shcnt* operates in an analogous way to *reg_or_imm*, except that only the five LSBs are used if the shift count is in a register, and *shcnt* is a five-bit unsigned integer. The shift instructions *cannot* affect the condition codes. That is, instructions such as srlcc are not part of the instruction set.

Let us exercise our use of the arithmetic logic and shift instructions by extracting the exponent part of a floating point number originally in %r2 into %r3. Figure 4-15 shows the program fragment. Register %r2 is first shifted right by nine bit positions, and the result is stored in %r3. This places the sign bit and the exponent field into the least significant nine bits of %r3. Finally we and the **mask**, 0xFF, into %r3, clearing the sign bit.

```
srl    %r2,    23,     %r3

and    %r3,    0xFF,   %r3
```

Figure 4-15
Extracting the exponent from a 32-bit floating-point number.

Control Instructions

The **call** and **jmpl** instructions in Figure 4-13 form a pair that are used in calling and returning from a subroutine, respectively. jmpl is also used to transfer control to another part of the program. The notations are

```
call label
jmpl address, rd
```

where label is any word address in memory and as with the load and store instructions, *address* is formed from *rs1 + rs2*, or *rs1 + simm13*. The jmpl instruction copies %pc into *rd* prior to transferring control to *address*. jmpl can be thought of fancifully as the "Hansel and Gretel" instruction, since, as Hansel placed pebbles on the ground to find his way back home, the call instruction places the current value of the PC in register rd, so a later jmpl instruction can return to the starting address by jmpl %rd+4. Four is added to %rd because that is the address of the next instruction after the original jmpl instruction.

The **be**, **bneg**, **bcs**, **bcc**, and **bz** instructions are **conditional branch** instructions. They are called conditional because they test one or more of the condition code bits in the PSR, and branch if the bits indicate the condition is met. They are used in implementing high-level constructs such as if-then-else and do-while. The conditions specified in these instructions are *equal*, *negative*, *carry set*, *carry clear*, and *zero*, respectively. As discussed, the **ba** instruction causes an unconditional branch to the target address, and can be used to implement the high-level goto instruction. Detailed descriptions of these instructions and examples of their usages are given in the sections that follow.

The final instruction in the figure is **ta**, "trap always." When invoked in a program, trap instructions interrupt the normal flow of the program to perform some requested service. For example, traps can place calls to the operating system requesting some sort of system service. That service could be a request to print a string of characters, read from the disk, or request some other activity. We will use the ta instruction to transfer control back to the operating system when our program has completed.

4.2.5 ARC Instruction Formats

As we mentioned above, the assembly language instructions must be translated, or encoded, one by one into machine language. Normally this is done by the assembler, but it is important that the process be understood. The ARC (and SPARC) **instruction formats** define how the various bit fields of an instruction are laid out by the assembler, and how they are interpreted by the ARC control unit. The ARC architecture has just a few instruction formats. The four formats are: **SETHI** and **Branch**, **Call**, **Arithmetic**, and **Memory**, as shown in Figure 4-16. (Note that these four instruction formats are defined by the bit pattern of the first two MSBs, and thus do not directly correspond to the four instruction classifications shown in Figure 4-13.)

The instruction formats use the two MSBs, the op field, as a sort of primary definition of what the operation is, and additional bit fields, op2, op3, and cond, in the rest of the instruction word completely define the instruction. The meaning of *rs1*, *rs3*, *rd*, *simm13*, etc., are as previously defined.

The SETHI and Branch formats both contain 00 in the op field, and so they can be considered together as the SETHI/Branch format. Whether it is a SETHI or Branch format

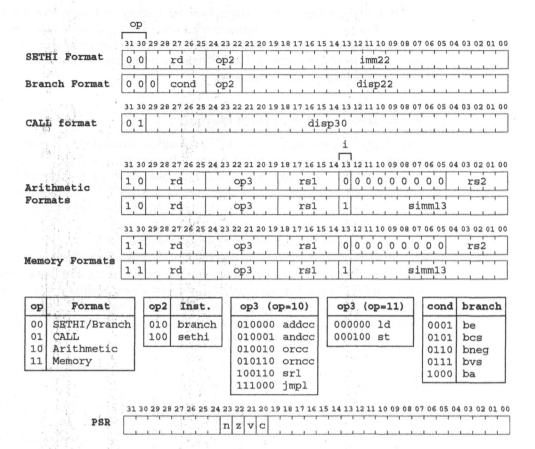

Figure 4-16
Instruction formats and PSR format for the ARC.

is determined by the bit pattern in the op2 opcode field (010 = Branch; 100 = SETHI). Bit 29 in the Branch format always contains a zero. The five-bit rd field identifies the target register for the SETHI operation.

The cond field identifies the type of branch, based on the condition code bits (n, z, v, and c) in the PSR, as indicated at the bottom of Figure 4-16. There are 16 different branch conditions.

The CALL format contains only two fields: the op field, which contains the bit pattern 01, and the disp30 field, which contains a 30-bit displacement that is used in calculating the address of the called routine. Analogous to the shifting left of simm22 to compute branch labels, disp30 is shifted left by two bits to form the 32-bit target address of the CALL instruction. This allows the CALL to reach any address in the ARC 32-bit address space.

The Arithmetic (op = 10) instructions need two source operands and a destination operand. The first operand is always in a register, *rs1*. The second operand is in *rs2* when i = 0, and is *simm13* sign extended when i = 1. The result is stored in *rd*.

Both memory (op = 11) formats form the memory address from rs1 + rs2 when i = 0, and from *rs1* + simm13 sign extended when i = 1. The various flavors of the ld instruction place the result fetched from memory into *rd*. The various st instructions store the operand in *rd* into memory. The op3 opcode field identifies the instruction according to the op3 tables shown in Figure 4-16.

4.2.6 SPARC and ARC Data Formats

The SPARC supports eight different data formats, as illustrated in Figure 4-17. The data formats are grouped into three types: integer, floating point, and tagged. Integer sizes are byte (eight bits), halfword (16 bits), word (32 bits), and **doubleword** (64 bits). Floating point sizes can be single word (32 bits), double word (64 bits) and **quadword** (128 bits). These correspond to the IEEE 754-1985 standard for floating point numbers. The SPARC has a set of floating-point instructions that conform to the IEEE 754-1985 standard (see Chapter 2). These instructions can be found in (SPARC, 1992).

The SPARC also supports the **tagged** word (32 bits, in which the two least significant bits form a **tag** and the most significant 30 bits form the value), **doubleword** (64 bits), and **quadword** (128 bits). The tagged word uses the two least significant bits to indicate **overflow**, in which the result of a computation cannot be stored in the allocated 30 bits of the 32-bit word. *Of these data formats, ARC supports loads and stores of integer bytes, halfwords, and words, signed and unsigned.*

4.2.7 ARC Instruction Descriptions

Now that we know the instruction formats, we can create detailed descriptions of the 17 instructions listed in Figure 4-13, plus some additional, commonly used instructions given below. The translation to object code is provided as a reference, and is described in detail in Chapter 5. In the descriptions below, a reference to the *contents* of a memory location (for ld and st) is indicated by square brackets, as in "ld [x], %r1," which copies the word at memory location x into %r1. A reference to the *address* of a memory location is specified directly, without brackets, as in "call sub_r," which makes a call to subroutine at memory location sub_r. Only ld and st can access memory, therefore only ld and st use brackets. Registers are always referred to in terms of their contents, and never in terms of an address, and so there is no need to enclose references to registers in brackets.

Data Movement Instructions: Load, Store, and Sethi

The load and store instructions access memory, whereas the sethi instruction places an immediate constant, contained in the instruction, into a register.

Instruction: ld (op3 = 00000)

Description: Load a register from main memory. As we described earlier in the chapter, the address is computed from two components, *rs1* + *rs2*, or *rs1* + *simm13* (sign extended). The resulting memory address must be aligned on a word boundary (that is, the address must be evenly divisible by 4). It is possible to omit either one of the two components in the pairs above by replacing the missing component with %r0,

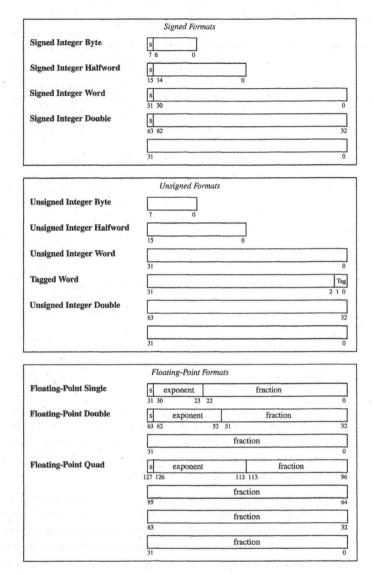

Figure 4-17
ARC data formats.

which, you will recall, is always 0. Table 4.2 shows the four possibilities for forming the address using this "%r0 trick":

Meaning: Copy the contents of memory location *address* into register %r1.

The encoding of examples (a) and (b) is shown in Tables 4.3 and 4.4, below, for x = simm13 = 2064.

In examples (c) and (d) the programmer was able to omit the %r0 that replaces the missing address component because the assembler assumed the task of inserting it. When the assembler replaces a more complicated instruction with a simpler one that

Table 4.2   Load instruction syntax and meaning

Example	Programmer writes:	Assembler inserts	Meaning
a)	ld [%r5 + x], %r1	ld [%r5 + x], %r1	%r1 ← M[%r5 + x]
b)	ld [%r2 + %r4], %r1	ld [%r2 + %r4], %r1	%r1 ← M[%r2 + %r4]
c)	ld [x], %r1	ld [%r0 + x], %r1	%r1 ← M[x]
d)	ld [%r3], %r1	ld [%r3+ %r0], %r1	%r1 ← M[%r3]

Table 4.3   Example (a): `ld [%r5 + x], %r1`

Field Name:	op	rd	op3 (ld)	rs1	i	simm13
Field Size (bits):	2	5	6	5	1	13
Field ID:		%r1	000000	%r5	1	2064
Object code:	11	00001	000000	00101	1	0100000010000

Table 4.4   Example (b): `ld [%r2 + %r4], %r1`

Field Name:	op	rd	op3 (ld)	rs1	i	00000000	rs2
Field Size (bits):	2	5	6	5	1	8	5
Field ID:		%r1	000000	%r2	0	00000000	%r4
Object code:	11	00001	000000	00010	0	00000000	00100

has the same meaning, the replacement instruction is called a **synthetic instruction**. It is synthetic because it does not actually exist in the instruction set, but is *synthesized* from an existing instruction by the assembler. We shall see more examples of synthetic instructions farther along in the chapter and in Appendix B.

Instruction: st (op3 = 000001)

Description: Store a register into main memory. As with ld, the address is computed from two components, *rs1 + rs2, or rs1 + simm13*, sign extended. The memory address must be aligned on a word boundary (that is, the address must be evenly divisible by 4). Once again synthetic instructions are inserted by the assembler when an address component is missing. The rd field of this instruction is used for the source register.

Example usage: st %r1, [%r5 + x]

Meaning: Copy the contents of register %r1 into memory location [%r5 + x].
The encoding of st %r1, [%r5 + x] is shown in Table 4.5 for x = simm13 = 2064.

Table 4.5   Encoding st %r1, [%r5 + x]

Ex.	Field Name:	op	rd	op3 (st)	rs1	i	simm13
	Field Size:	2	5	6	5	1	13
a)	Object code:	11	00001	000100	00101	1	0100000010000

Notice that the encoding of the load and store instructions `ldsb`, `ldsh`, `ldub`, `lduh`, `ld`, and `stb`, `sth`, and `st` differ *only* in the six-bit `op 3` (`op=11`) field, as described in Figure 4-16.

Instruction: `sethi` (`op2 = 100`)

Description: Set the high 22 bits with *simm22*, and zero the low 10 bits of a register. If the operand is 0 and the register is %r0, then the instruction behaves as a **no-op (NOP)**, which means that no operation takes place.

Example usage: `sethi 0x304F15, %r1`

Meaning: Set the high 22 bits of `%r1` to $(304F15)_{16}$, and set the low 10 bits to zero. The encoding of this instruction is shown in Table 4.6.

Table 4.6 Encoding `sethi 0x304F15, %r1`

Field Name:	op	rd	op2	imm22
Field Size:	2	5	3	22
Field ID:	2	%r1	100	0x304F15
Object code:	00	00001	100	1100000100111100010101

Logical Instructions: and, andn, or, orn, xor, xnor, and the Related cc Equivalents

An examination of Figure 4-16 shows that all the logical instructions are encoded exactly the same as one another except for the `op3` field, which specifies the logical operation to perform, and the `i` field, which specifies `rs2` (`i=0`) or `simm13` (`i=1`). Encoding the op3 field is even more regular in that the only difference between the non-cc form and the cc form is the presence of a 0 or a 1 in the second-most-significant bit of the field.

Since the encoding is so much alike for these instructions, we will take this opportunity to introduce some additional logic instruction definitions that were not shown in Figure 4-13.

Instruction: `and` (`op3 = 000001`), `andcc` (`op3 = 010001`)

Description: Bitwise AND the source operands into the destination operand. If `andcc`, set the condition codes according to the result.

Example usage: a) `and %r1, 0xAAB, %r3`
b) `andcc %r3, %r2, %r5`

Meaning: Logically AND `%r1` and `%r2` and place the result in `%r3`. If `andcc`, set the condition codes according to the result. Tables 4.7 and 4.8 show the encoding of examples (a) and (b) above:

The following ALU instructions are encoded exactly as the AND example above, except for the op3 field.

Instruction: `andn` (`op3 = 000101`), `andncc` (`op3 = 010101`)

Description: And Not. Bitwise `and` rs1 with the not of rs2, and store the result into the destination register. If `andncc`, set the condition codes according to the result.

Table 4.7 **Encoding** and %r1, 0xAAB, %r3

Ex.	Field Name:	op	rd	op3 (and)	rs1	i	simm13
	Field Size:	2	5	6	5	1	13
	Field ID:		%r3	and	%r1	1	0xAABB
a)	Object code:	10	00011	000000	00001	1	101010101011

Table 4.8 **Encoding** and %r3, %r2, %r5

Ex.	Field Name:	op	rd	op3 (andcc)	rs1	i	00000000	rs2
	Field Size:	2	5	6	5	1	8	5
	Field ID:		%r5	andcc	%r3	1	00000000	%r2
b)	Object code:	10	00101	010000	00011	0	00000000	00010

The formal definition of this operation is rdst ← (rs1 • $\overline{\text{rs2\_or\_simm13}}$). *Simm13* is sign-extended.

Example usage: andn %r1, 1, %r1

Meaning: Clear the least significant bit of %r1 to 0.

Object code: 10 00001 000101 00001 1 0000000000001

Instruction: or (op3 = 000010), orcc (op3 = 010010)

Description: Bitwise OR the source operands into the destination operand. If orcc, set the condition codes according to the result.

Example usage: orcc %r1, 1, %r1

Meaning: Set the least significant bit of %r1 to 1.

Object code: 10 00001 010010 00001 1 0000000000001

Instruction: orn (op3 = 000110), and orncc (op3 = 010110)

Description: "Or Not." Bitwise OR rs1 with the NOT of the second operand. If orncc, set the condition codes. The formal definition for this operation is rdst ← (rs1 + $\overline{\text{rs2\_or\_simm13}}$).

Instruction: xor (op3 = 000011), xorcc (op3 = 010011)

Description: Exclusive OR. Bitwise XOR the source operands into the destination operand. If xorcc, set the condition codes according to the result. The formal definition for this operation is rdst ← (rs1 ⊕ rs2_or_simm13).

Instruction: xnor (op3 = 000111), and xnorcc (op3 = 010111)

Description: Exclusive NOR. Bitwise XNOR the source operands into the destination operand. If xnorcc, set the condition codes according to the result. The formal definition for this function is rdst ← $\overline{(\text{rs1} ⊕ \text{rs2\_or\_simm13})}$.

Both XOR and XNOR have the same syntax and behavior as the other logic functions.

The Shift Instructions: srl, sra, and sll

The shift instructions encode exactly as the logical instructions with the exception that *simm13* is replaced by *simm5*, a five-bit positive integer representing the shift count from 0 to 31 bit positions. No cc variations are possible with the shift instructions.

Instruction: srl (op3 = 100110)

Description: Shift right logical. Shift a register to the right by $0 - 31$ bits. The vacant bit positions in the left side of the shifted register are filled with 0s.

Example usage: srl %r1, 3, %r2

Meaning: Shift %r1 right by three bits and store in %r2. Zeros are copied into the three most significant bits of %r2.

Object code: 1000010 100110 0000110000000000011

Instruction: sra (op3 = 100111)

Description: Shift right arithmetic. Shift a register to the right by $0 - 31$ bits and sign extend. The bit positions in the left side of the shifted register are filled with copies of the MSB of the original operand.

Example usage: sra %r1, 3, %r2

Meaning: Shift %r1 right by three bits and store in %r2. Zeros are copied into the three most significant bits of %r2.

Object code: 10 00010 100111 00001 1 0000000000011

Instruction: sll (op3 = 100101)

Description: Shift left logical. Shift a register to the right by $0 - 31$ bits. The vacant bit positions in the left side of the shifted register are filled with 0's.

Example usage: srl %r1, 3, %r2

Meaning: Shift %r1 right by three bits and store in %r2. Zeros are copied into the three least significant bits of %r2.

Object code: 10 00010 100101 00001 1 0000000000011

Arithmetic instructions: add and sub

Instruction: add (op3 = 000000), and addcc (op3 = 010000)

Description: Add the source operands into the destination operand using two's complement arithmetic. If addcc, the condition codes are set according to the result.

Example usage: addcc %r1, 5, %r1

Meaning: Add 5 to %r1.

Object code: 10 00001 010000 00001 1 0000000000101

Instruction: sub (op3 = 000100), and subcc (op3 = 010100)

Description: Subtract rs2 from rs1 using 2's complement arithmetic, and place the result into the destination register. If subcc, the condition codes are set according to the result.

Example usage: subcc %r1, 5, %r1

Meaning: Add 5 to %r1.

Object code: 10 00001 010100 00001 1 0000000000101

The Control Instructions: call, jmpl, and branches

Instruction: call

Description: Call a subroutine and store the address of the current instruction (the address of the call itself) in %r15, which effects a "call and link" operation. In the assembled code, the disp30 field in the CALL format will contain a 30-bit *word* displacement from the address of the call instruction. The address of the call target is computed by shifting disp30 left by two bits, converting it to a byte address that conforms to a word boundary because the resulting address ends in 00. Note that disp30 can be negative.

Example usage: call sub_r

Meaning: Call a subroutine that begins at location sub_r. For the object code shown below, sub_r is 25 words (100 bytes) farther in memory than the call instruction.

Object code: 01 000000000000000000000000011001

Instruction: jmpl

Description: Jump and link. Jump to a new address and store the address of the current instruction (where the jmpl instruction is located) in the destination register. jmpl is also used to return *from* a subroutine. By convention the linkage register is %r15.

Example usage jumping to subroutine: jmpl %r1 + 28, %r15

Meaning: Store the current value of the PC in %r15 for later return, then transfer control to the instruction at address computed from %r1 + 28.

Object code: 10 1111 111000 00001 1 0000000000100

Example usage returning from a subroutine: jmpl %r15 + 4, %r0

Meaning: Return from subroutine. The value of the PC for the call instruction was previously saved, by convention, in %r15, and so the return address should be computed for the instruction that follows the call, at %r15 + 4. The current address is discarded in %r0.

Object code: 10 00000 111000 11111 1 0000000000100

Instruction: be

Description: If the z condition code is 1, then branch to the address computed by adding $4 \times disp22$ in the Branch instruction format to the address of the current instruction. If the z condition code is 0, then control is transferred to the instruction that follows be.

Example usage: be label

Meaning: Branch to label if the z condition code is 1. For the object code shown below, label is five words (20 bytes) farther in memory than the be instruction.

Object code: 00 0 0001 010 000000000000000000000101
The encoding of this instruction is shown in Table 4.9.

Table 4.9 **Encoding of be label**

Field Name:	op	0	cond	op2	imm22
Field Size:	2	1	5	3	22
Field ID:	op		equal	br	Branch target/4
Object code:	00	0	0001	010	000000000000000000000101

The rest of the branch instructions are encoded and used in exactly the same way using the appropriate cond encoding. Table 4.10 shows the encoding for all 16 branches, along with information about which of the condition code flags are tested on each branch. Notice that some of the branches assume that the operands being tested are unsigned. The comparisons "less than," "less than or equal," "greater than," and "greater than or equal," must test different condition codes depending upon whether the programmer is treating the operands as signed or unsigned.

Table 4.10 **Branch on condition codes**

Opcode	cond	Operation	Flags tested
ba	1000	Branch Always	1
bn	0000	Branch Never	0
bne	1001	Branch on Not Equal	**not** Z
be	0001	Branch on Equal	Z
bg	1010	Branch on Greater	**not** (Z **or** (N **xor** V))
ble	0010	Branch on Less or Equal	Z **or** (N **xor** V)
bge	1011	Branch on Greater or Equal	**not** (N **xor** V)
bl	0011	Branch on Less	N **xor** V
bgu	1100	Branch on Greater Unsigned	**not** (C **or** Z)
bleu	0100	Branch on Less or Equal Unsigned	C **or** Z
bcc	1101	Branch on Carry Clear (Greater than or Equal, Unsigned)	**not** C
bcs	0101	Branch on Carry Set (Less than, Unsigned)	C
bpos	1110	Branch on Positive	**not** N
bneg	0110	Branch on Negative	N
bvc	1111	Branch on Overflow Clear	**not** V
bvs	0111	Branch on Overflow Set	V

Control Instructions: Software Traps

Software **traps** provide a mechanism for a user program to invoke the services of the operating system, such as reading or writing information from the file system or from some external device, or, in our case, returning control to the operating system. Traps are similar to subroutine calls, except that they provide protection from rogue or malicious programs because they place the system in **supervisor mode** where they can execute privileged instructions to handle I/O and other processes. Privileged instructions can only be executed by the operating system or a trusted user.

The syntax for the trap instruction is

ta *software_trap_number*

where software_trap_number is an unsigned integer from 0 to 127, contained in the least significant seven bits of reg_or_imm. Figure 4-18a shows the formats for software trap instruction. From left to right, op = 10, bit 29 is undefined, bits 28..25, cond, specify the trap condition, bits 24..19, op3, specify the trap instruction, and the remainder of the instructions, *reg_or_simm*, specify the trap number. In this case, ta, trap always, cond = always, 1000, but as the table implies, it is possible to branch on any of the 16 conditions, a **conditional trap**. For example, tvs 12 means execute trap 12 if the V (overflow) bit is set.

Trap type 0, as in ta 0, is a call to the operating system for some kind of system service. The particular kind of system service is specified by an integer stored in %r1 prior to the ta 0 instruction.

When there is occasion to return from a trap routine to the main program, the return is via the rett, return from trap, instruction, whose formats are shown in Figure 4-18c. The syntax of the rett instruction is

rett [*address*]

where once again address is *rs1 + rs2, or rs1 + simm13*. See (8) below for a description of the execution of the rett instruction.

The **trap address**, the address where the trap routine starts, is constructed in the **Trap Base Register**, **TBR**, Figure 4-18c, by copying the seven-bit software trap number into the lower seven bits of tt, the trap type, field of the TBR. The eighth bit of the tt field, which is bit 11 of the TBR, is set to 1. Thus software trap types range from 128 (10000000) to 255 (11111111). The upper 20 bits of the TBR, which form the base of the **trap table**, are set by and can be read by two privileged instructions normally executed by the operating system. Take note of the fact that since the four LSBs in the

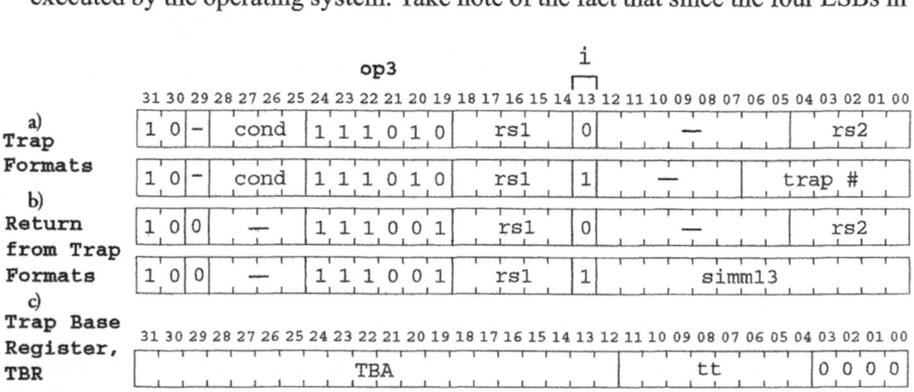

Figure 4-18
Software trap formats and the Trap Base Register.

TBR are zeros, a new trap routine begins every $2^4/2^2$ or four instructions. Thus one of the four will probably be a branch to the actual trap routine.

The following is the sequence of events that take place upon execution of a trap:

1) A trap instruction is encountered.

2) If and only if the et bit is set in the PSR, then:

3) the et bit is cleared,

4) the processor is put into the supervisor state if not already there,

5) `%r16 ← PC` and `%r18 ← PSR`, saving the current state,

6) the TBR is constructed as described above, from the trap number.

7) PC ← TBR, thus starting execution of the trap routine.

8) At the end of the trap routine the rett, return from trap instruction, is executed: rett %r16, which sets the et bit to 1 and transfers control to the instruction immediately after the just-executed trap instruction. If the et bit is set when rett executes, execution is terminated with an illegal_instruction error.

Instruction: ta

Description: Trap always. Transfer control to a software trap routine.

Example usage: `or %r0, 1, %r1` !put exit code in %r1
             `ta 0`   !and execute trap

Meaning: If the et bit is set then the PC is stored in %r16, and the PSR is stored in %r18. the Trap Base Register, TBR, is updated with the trap type, tt, a number between 0 and 127 (0 in this case), the et bit is cleared, and control is transferred to the contents of the TBR.

Syntax: The trap instruction syntax is tcc *reg_or_simm*.

Instruction: rett

Description: Return from trap.

Example usage: rett %r16+4

Meaning: If the et bit is clear, it is set, and control is transferred to %r16 + 4, the address of the instruction immediately following the trap instruction previously executed. the PSR is stored in %r18. If the et bit is set when rett executes, execution is terminated and an illegal_instruction error message is printed on the console.

Syntax: The trap instruction syntax is tcc *reg_or_simm*.

■ 4.3 PSEUDO-OPERATIONS

In addition to the ARC instructions that are supported by the architecture, there are also **pseudo-operations** (pseudo-ops) that are not opcodes at all, but rather instructions to the assembler to perform some action at assembly time. A list of pseudo-ops and examples of their usages are shown in Figure 4-19. Note that unlike processor opcodes, which are specific to a given machine, the kind and nature of the pseudo-ops are specific to a given *assembler*, because they are executed by the assembler itself.

Pseudo-Op	Usage	Meaning
.equ	X .equ #10	Treat symbol X as $(10)_{16}$
.begin	.begin	Start assembling
.end	.end	Stop assembling
.org	.org 2048	Change location counter to 2048
.dwb	.dwb 25	Reserve a block of 25 words
.global	.global Y	Y is used in another module
.extern	.extern Z	Z is defined in another module
.macro	.macro M a, b, ...	Define macro M with formal parameters a, b, ...
.endmacro	.endmacro	End of macro definition
.if	.if <cond>	Assemble if <cond> is true
.endif	.endif	End of .if construct
.align	.align 4	Round location counter up to even multiple of 4.

Figure 4-19
Pseudo-ops for the ARC assembly language.

The .equ pseudo-op instructs the assembler to *equate* a value or a character string with a symbol, so that the symbol can be used throughout a program as if the value or string were written in its place. The .begin and .end pseudo-ops tell the assembler when to start and stop assembling. Any statements that appear before .begin or after .end are ignored. A single program may have more than one .begin/.end pair, but there must be a .end for every .begin, and there must be at least one .begin. The use of .begin and .end is helpful in making portions of the program invisible to the assembler during debugging.

The .org (origin) pseudo-op causes the next instruction to be assembled at the specified memory location (location 2048 in Figure 4-19). The .dwb (define word block) pseudo-op reserves a block of four-byte words, typically for an array. The **location counter** (which keeps track of which instruction is being assembled by the assembler) is moved ahead of the block according to the number of words specified by the argument to .dwb multiplied by 4.

The .global and .extern pseudo-ops deal with names of variables and addresses that are defined in one assembly code module and are used in another. The .global pseudo-op makes a label available for use in other modules. The .extern pseudo-op identifies a label that is used in the local module and is defined in another module (which should be marked with a .global in that module). We will see how .global and .extern are used when linking and loading are covered in the next chapter. The .macro, .endmacro, .if, and .endif pseudo-ops are also covered in the next chapter.

The .align pseudo-op is used to ensure that SPARC alignment constraints are met. If the location counter isn't currently on such a boundary, it rounds it up to the next alignment boundary, where

```
((location_counter mod boundary)==0);
```

The **mod**, modulo, operator is the remainder after division. The argument to .align can generally be any power of 2.

4.4 SYNTHETIC INSTRUCTIONS

As we mentioned earlier, many assemblers will accept synthetic instructions that are converted to actual machine-language instructions during assembly. Figure 4-20 shows some commonly used synthetic instructions. We should stress that synthetic instructions are single instructions that replace single instructions. When several instructions are substituted for a single instruction, the group of instructions is referred to as a **macro**. Macros are discussed in detail in Chapter 5.

Synthetic Instruction	Instruction Generated	Comment
not *rs1*, *rd*	xnor *rs1*, %r0, *rd*	1's complement
neg *rs1*, *rd*	sub %r0, *rs1*, *rd*	2's complement
inc *rd*	add *rd*, 1, *rd*	increment by 1
dec *rd*	sub *rd*, 1, *rd*	decrement by 1
clr *rd*	and *rd*, %r0, *rd*	clear a register
cmp *rs1, reg_or_imm*	subcc *rs1, reg_or_imm*, %r0	compare, set ccs
tst *rs1*	orcc %r0, *rs1*, %r0	test
mov *reg_or_imm, rd*	or %r0, *reg_or_imm, rd*	Move a value
set value, *rd*	or %r0, value, *rd*	|value| < 4096

Figure 4-20
Synthetic ARC instructions.

4.5 EXAMPLES OF ASSEMBLY LANGUAGE PROGRAMS

The process of writing an assembly language program is similar to the process of writing a high-level program, except that many of the details that are abstracted away in high-level programs are made explicit in assembly language programs. In this section, we take a look at two examples of ARC assembly language programs.

Program: Add Two Integers

In Section 4.2.3 we showed an example of adding two integers. This program has the additional code and pseudo-code to allow it to run as an independent program. It adds the integers 15 and 9. One possible coding is shown in Figure 4-21. The program begins and ends with a .begin/.end pair. The .org pseudo-op instructs the assembler to begin assembling code starting at address 2048. The operands 15 and 9 are stored in variables x and y, respectively. We can only add numbers that are stored in registers in the ARC (because only ld and st can access main memory), and so the program begins by loading registers %r1 and %r2 with x and y. The addcc instruction adds %r1 and %r2 and places the result

```
! This programs adds two numbers
        .begin
        .org 2048
prog1:  ld      [x], %r1        ! Load x into %r1
        ld      [y], %r2        ! Load y into %r2
        addcc   %r1, %r2, %r3   ! %r3 ← %r1 + %r2
        st      %r3, [z]        ! Store %r3 into z
        jmpl    %r15 + 4, %r0   ! Return
x:      15
y:      9
z:      0
        .end
```

Figure 4-21

An ARC assembly language program that adds two integers.

in %r3. The st instruction then stores %r3 in memory location z. The jmpl instruction causes a return to the calling program, whereas a ta 0 instruction with the exit code, 1, in %r1, would cause a return to the operating system. The variables x, y, and z are stored in memory following the program, and are initialized to the values 15, 9, and 0 when the program is loaded into memory.

This program would not run correctly on the SPARC (although it would run correctly on the ARC). The ld, st, and jmpl instructions all take at least two instruction cycles to complete, and since SPARC begins a new instruction at each clock tick, these instructions need to be followed by an instruction that does not rely on their results. This property of launching a new instruction before the previous one has completed is called **pipelining**, and is covered in more detail in Chapters 6 and 10.

Program: Sum an Array of Integers

Now consider a more complex program that sums an array of integers. One possible coding is shown in Figure 4-22. As in the previous example, the program begins and ends with a .begin/.end pair. The .org pseudo-op instructs the assembler to begin assembling the program starting at location 2048. A pseudo-operand is created for the symbol a_start, which is assigned a value of 3000.

The program begins by loading the length of array a, which is given in bytes, into %r1. The program then loads the starting address of array a into %r2 and clears %r3, which will hold the partial sum. Register %r3 is cleared by ANDing it with %r0, which always holds the value 0. Register %r0 can be ANDed with any register, for that matter, and the result will still be zero.

The label loop begins a loop that adds successive elements of array a into the partial sum (%r3) on each iteration. The loop starts by checking if the number of remaining array elements to sum (%r1) is zero. It does this by ANDing %r1 with itself, which has the side effect of setting the condition codes. We are interested in the z flag, which will be set to 1 if %r1 = 0. The remaining flags (n, v, and c) are set accordingly. The value of z is tested by making use of the be instruction. If there are no remaining array elements to sum, then the program branches to done, which returns to the calling routine via the jmpl instruc-

```
! This program sums LENGTH numbers
! Register usage:        %r1 — Length of array a
!                        %r2 — Starting address of array a
!                        %r3 — The partial sum
!                        %r4 — Pointer into array a
!                        %r5 — Holds an element of a
            .begin           ! Start assembling
            .org  2048       ! Start program at 2048
a_start     .equ  3000       ! Address of array a
            ld    [length], %r1 ! %r1 ← length of array a
            ld    [address],%r2 ! %r2 ← address of a
            andcc %r3, %r0, %r3 ! %r3 ← 0
loop:       andcc %r1, %r1, %r0 ! Test # remaining elements
            be    done       ! Finished when length=0
            addcc %r1, −4, %r1 ! Decrement array length
            addcc %r1, %r2, %r4 ! Address of next element
            ld    %r4, %r5   ! %r5 ← Memory[%r4]
            addcc %r3, %r5, %r3 ! Sum new element into r3
            ba    loop       ! Repeat loop.

done:       jmpl  %r15 + 4, %r0 ! Return to calling routine
                             ! Note: use ta 0 instead when
                             !   exiting back to ARCTools

length:          20          ! 5 numbers (20 bytes) in a
address:         a_start
            .org  a_start    ! Start of array a
a:               25          ! length/4 values follow
                −10
                 33
                 −5
                  7
            .end             ! Stop assembling
```

Figure 4-22

An ARC program that sums five integers.

tion (but `ta  0` would be used if the routine returns to the top level of the ARCTools control program).

If the loop is not exited after the test for $\%r1 = 0$, then $\%r1$ is decremented by the width of a word in bytes (4) by adding −4. The starting address of array a (which is stored in $\%r2$) and the index into a ($\%r1$) are added into $\%r4$, which then points to a new element of a. The element pointed to by $\%r4$ is then loaded into $\%r5$, which is added into the partial sum ($\%r3$). The top of the loop is then revisited as a result of the "ba loop" statement. The variable length is stored after the instructions. The .org pseudo-op specifies that the five elements of array a are to be assembled beginning at location 3000.

Notice that there are three instructions for computing the address of the next array element, given the address of the top element in $\%r2$, and the length of the array in bytes in $\%r1$:

```
addcc %r1, -4, %r1   ! Point to next element to be added
addcc %r1, %r2, %r4  ! Add it to the base of the array
ld %r4, %r5          ! Load the next element into %r5.
```

This technique of computing the address of a data value as the sum of a base plus an index is so frequently used that the ARC and most other assembly languages have special "addressing modes" to accomplish it. In the case of ARC, the ld instruction address is computed as the sum of two registers or a register plus a 13-bit constant. Recall that register %r0 always contains the value zero, so by specifying %r0, which is being done implicitly in the ld line above, we are wasting an opportunity to have the ld instruction itself perform the address calculation. A single register can hold the operand address, and we can accomplish in two instructions what takes three instructions in the example:

```
addcc %r1, -4, %r1   ! Point to next element to be added
ld %r1 + %r2, %r5    ! Load the next element into %r5.
```

Notice that we also save a register, %r4, which was used as a temporary place holder for the address.

4.5.1 Variations in Machine Architectures and Addressing

The ARC is typical of a RISC-type machine—the only access to operands in memory is by load and store instructions, all instructions are one word in size, there are only a few, simple addressing modes, and all instructions are designed to execute in a few clock cycles. As we shall discuss in Chapter 6, the RISC paradigm was developed in large part so that all instructions would fit into an execution pipeline, one after the other, in assembly-line fashion. This approach comes at the cost of more memory occupied per program, and is disadvantageous when the program's memory size, or "footprint," is important. This is the case, for example, in many embedded system applications, where the processor is embedded in another device such as a microwave oven or child's toy; execution speed may be less important than the cost of the additional RAM.

It was also not the case when memories were orders of magnitude more expensive[3] and CPUs were orders of magnitude smaller, as was the situation earlier in the computer age. When RAM costs are significant it is cost-effective to make each instruction do more, even at the cost of variable instruction sizes and execution times, and to provide more complex addressing modes. Machines with such ISAs are referred to as CISC, complicated instruction set computer, machines.

Under these earlier conditions, CPUs had only one or two registers to hold arithmetic values, and intermediate results had to be stored in memory. Machines had **three-address**, **two-address**, and **one-address** arithmetic instructions. By this we mean that an instruction could do arithmetic with three, two, or one of its operands or results in memory, as opposed to the ARC, where all arithmetic and logic operands *must* be in registers.

Let us consider how the C expression A = B*C + D might be evaluated by each of the three-, two-, and one-address instruction types. In the examples below, referring to a variable "A" actually means "the operand whose address is A." In order to calculate some per-

---

[3]In 1977, when the Apple II was introduced, 16 KB of RAM cost $600.

formance statistics for the program fragments below we will make the following assumptions:

- Addresses and data words are 16 bits—a common size in earlier machines.
- Opcodes are 8 bits in size.
- Operands and opcodes are moved to and from memory one word at a time.

We will compute both program size, in bytes, and program memory traffic with these assumptions.

Memory traffic has two components: the code itself, which must be fetched from memory to the CPU in order to be executed, and the data values—operands must be moved into the CPU in order to be operated upon, and results moved back to memory when the computation is complete. Observing these computations allows us to visualize some of the trade-offs between program size and memory traffic that the various instruction classes offer.

Three-Address Instructions

In a three-address instruction, the expression $A = B \times C + D$ might be coded as:

```
mult      B, C, A
add       D, A, A
```

which means multiply B by C and store the result at A. (The `mult` and `add` operations are generic; they are not ARC instructions.) Then, add D to A (at this point in the program, A holds the temporary result of multiplying B times C) and store the result at address A. The program size is 7×2 or 14 bytes. Memory traffic is $14 + 2 \times (2 \times 3)$ or 26 bytes.

Two-Address Instructions

In a two-address instruction, one of the operands is overwritten by the result. Here, the code for the expression $A = B \times C + D$ is:

```
load      B, A
mult      C, A
add       D, A
```

The program size is now $3 \times (1 + 2 + 2)$ or 15 bytes. Memory traffic for the program, operand fetch, and store operations is then $15 + 2 \times 3 + 2 \times 2 = 31$ bytes.

One-Address or Accumulator Instructions

A one-address instruction employs a single arithmetic register in the CPU, known as the **accumulator**. The accumulator typically holds one arithmetic operand, and also serves as the target for the result of an arithmetic operation. The one-address format is not in common use these days, but was more common in the early days of computing when registers were more expensive and frequently served multiple purposes. It serves as temporary storage for one of the operands and also for the result. The code for the expression $A = B \times C + D$ is now:

```
load      B
mult      C
```

```
add       D
store     A
```

The load instruction loads B into the accumulator, mult multiplies C by the accumulator and stores the result in the accumulator, and add does the corresponding addition. The store instruction stores the accumulator in A. The program size is now 3×4 or 12 bytes, and memory traffic is $12 + 4 \times 2$ or 20 bytes.

Comparison to ARC instructions

This example assumes that ARC has a multiply instruction and that operands are half-words. The equivalent program written using ARC instructions would then appear as:

```
ld     [B],    %r1
ld     [C],    %r2
ld     [D],    %r3
mult   %r1,    %r2,  %r4
add    %r4,    %r3,  %r5
st     %r5,    [A]
```

This program size is 6×4 or 24 bytes, compared with 16 to 18 bytes for the examples above, a 50% penalty in program size. Memory traffic is $24 + 4 \times 2$ or 32 bytes. This is a typical example of the difference between CISC and RISC program memory usage.

Special-Purpose Registers

In addition to the general-purpose registers and the accumulator described above, most modern architectures include other registers that are dedicated to specific purposes. Examples include

- Memory index registers: The Intel 80x86 Source Index (SI) and Destination Index (DI) registers. These are used to point to the beginning or end of an array in memory. Special "string" instructions transfer a byte or a word from the starting memory location pointed to by SI to the ending memory location pointed to by DI, and then increment or decrement these registers to point to the next byte or word.

- Floating-point registers: Many current-generation processors have special registers and instructions that handle floating-point numbers.

- Registers to support time and timing operations: The PowerPC 601 processor has Real-Time Clock registers that provide a high-resolution measure of real time for indicating the date and the time of day. They provide a range of approximately 135 years, with a resolution of 128 ns.

- Registers in support of the operating system: most modern processors have registers to support the memory system.

- Registers that can be accessed only by "privileged instructions," or when in "supervisor mode." In order to prevent accidental or malicious damage to the system, many processors have special instructions and registers that are unavailable to the ordinary user and application program. These instructions and registers are used only by the operating system.

4.5.2 Performance of Instruction Set Architectures

While the program size and memory usage statistics calculated above are observed out of context from the larger programs in which they would be contained, they do show that having even one temporary storage register in the CPU can have a significant effect on program performance. In fact, the Intel Pentium processor, considered among the faster of the general-purpose CPUs, has only a single accumulator, though it has a number of special-purpose registers that support it. There are many other factors that affect real-world performance of an instruction set, such as the time an instruction takes to perform its function and the speed at which the processor can run.

■ 4.6 ACCESSING DATA IN MEMORY—ADDRESSING MODES

Up to this point, we have seen four ways of computing the address of a value in memory: (1) a constant value, known at assembly time, (2) the contents of a register, (3) the sum of two registers, and (4) the sum of a register and a constant. Table 4.11 gives names to these addressing modes, and shows a few others as well. Notice that the syntax of the table differs from that of the ARC. This is a common, unfortunate feature of assembly languages: each one differs from the rest in its syntax conventions. The notation M[x] in the Meaning column assumes memory is an array, M, whose byte index is given by the address computation in brackets. There may seem to be a bewildering assortment of addressing modes, but each has its usage:

- Immediate addressing allows a reference to a constant that is known at assembly time.
- Direct addressing is used to access data items whose address is known at assembly time.
- Indirect addressing is used to access a pointer variable whose address is known at compile time. This addressing mode is seldom supported in modern processors because it requires two memory references to access the operand, making it a complicated instruction. Programmers who wish to access data in this form must use two instructions, one to access the pointer and another to access the value to which it refers. This has the beneficial side effect of exposing the complexity of the addressing mode, perhaps discouraging its use.

Table 4.11 **Addressing modes**

Addressing Mode	Syntax	Meaning
Immediate	#K	K
Direct	K	M[K]
Indirect	(K)	M[M[K]]
Register Indirect	(Rn)	M[Rn]
Register Indexed	(Rm + Rn)	M[Rm + Rn]
Register Based	(Rm + X)	M[Rm + X]
Register Based Indexed	(Rm + Rn + X)	M[Rm + Rn + X]

- Register indirect addressing is used when the address of the operand is not known until run time. Stack operands fit this description, and are accessed by register indirect addressing, often via push and pop instructions that also decrement and increment the register respectively.

- Register indexed, register based, and register based indexed addressing are used to access components of arrays such as the one in Figure 4-22, and components buried beneath the top of the stack, in a data structure known as the **stack frame**, which is discussed in the next section.

■ 4.7 SUBROUTINE LINKAGE AND STACKS

A **subroutine**, sometimes called a **function** or **procedure**, is a sequence of instructions that is invoked in a manner that makes it appear to be a single instruction in a high-level view. When a program calls a subroutine, control is passed from the program to the subroutine, which executes a sequence of instructions and then returns to the location just past where it was called. There are a number of methods for passing arguments to and from the called routine, referred to as **calling conventions**. The process of passing arguments between routines is referred to as **subroutine linkage**.

One calling convention simply places the arguments in registers. The code in Figure 4-23 shows a program that loads two arguments into %r1 and %r2, calls subroutine add_1, and then retrieves the result from %r3. Subroutine add_1 takes its operands from %r1 and %r2 and places the result in %r3 before returning via the jmpl instruction. This method is fast and simple, but it will not work if the number of arguments that are passed between the routines exceeds the number of free registers, or if subroutine calls are deeply nested.

A second calling convention creates a **data link area**. The address of the data link area is passed in a predetermined register to the called routine. Figure 4-24 shows an example of this method of subroutine linkage. The .dwb pseudo-op in the calling routine sets up a data link area that is three words long, at addresses x, x+4, and x+8. The calling

```
! Calling routine              ! Called routine
        .                      ! %r3 ← %r1 + %r2
        .
        .
        ld      [x], %r1
        ld      [y], %r2       add_1:  addcc   %r1, %r2, %r3
        call    add_1                  jmpl    %r15 + 4, %r0
        st      %r3, [z]

        .
        .
x:   53
y:   10
z:    0
```

Figure 4-23
Subroutine linkage using registers.

```
! Calling routine          | ! Called routine
      .                     | ! x[2] ← x[0] + x[1]
      .                     |
      .                     |
      st     %r1, [x]       | add_2:  ld     %r5, %r8
      st     %r2, [x+4]     |         ld     %r5 + 4, %r9
      sethi  x, %r5         |         addcc  %r8, %r9, %r10
      srl    %r5, 10, %r5   |         st     %r10, %r5 + 8
      call   add_2          |         jmpl   %r15 + 4, %r0
      ld     [x+8], %r3     |
      .                     |
      .                     |
      .                     |
! Data link area           |
x:  .dwb  3                 |
```

Figure 4-24
Subroutine linkage using a data link area.

routine loads its two arguments into x and x+4, calls subroutine add_2, and then retrieves
the result passed back from add_2 from memory location x+8. The address of data link
area x is passed to add_2 in register %r5.

Note that sethi must have a constant for its source operand, and so the assembler
recognizes the sethi construct shown for the calling routine and replaces x with its
address. The srl that follows the sethi moves the address x into the least significant 22
bits of %r5, since sethi places its operand into the leftmost 22 bits of the target register.
An alternative approach to loading the address of x into %r5 would be to use a storage
location for the address of x, and then simply apply the ld instruction to load the address
into %r5. While the latter approach is simpler, the sethi/srl approach is faster because
it does not involve a time-consuming access to the memory.

Subroutine add_2 reads its two operands from the data link area at locations %r5 and
%r5 + 4, and places its result in the data link area at location %r5 + 8 before returning.
By using a data link area, arbitrarily large blocks of data can be passed between routines
without copying more than a single register during subroutine linkage. Recursion can create a burdensome bookkeeping overhead, however, since a routine that calls itself will
need several data link areas. Data link areas have the advantage that their size can be
unlimited, but also have the disadvantage that the size of the data link area must be known
at assembly time.

A third calling convention uses a stack. The general idea is that the calling routine
pushes all of its arguments (or pointers to arguments, if the data objects are large) onto a
last-in-first-out stack. The called routine then pops the passed arguments from the stack
and pushes any return values onto the stack. The calling routine then retrieves the return
value(s) from the stack and continues execution. A register in the CPU, known as the
stack pointer, contains the address of the top of the stack. Many machines have push and
pop instructions that automatically decrement and increment the stack pointer as data
items are pushed and popped.

An advantage of using a stack is that its size grows and shrinks as needed. This supports
arbitrarily deep nesting of procedure calls without having to declare the size of the stack at
assembly time. An example of passing arguments using a stack is shown in Figure 4-25.

```
! Calling routine          ! Called routine
        .                   ! Arguments are on stack.
        .                   ! %sp[0] ← %sp[0] + %sp[4]
%sp .equ    %r14               %sp .equ    %r14
    addcc %sp, -4, %sp  add_3:  ld    %sp, %r8
    st    %r1, %sp             addcc %sp, 4, %sp
    addcc %sp, -4, %sp         ld    %sp, %r9
    st    %r2, %sp             addcc %r8, %r9, %r10
    call  add_3               st    %r10, %sp
    ld    %sp, %r3            jmpl  %r15 + 4, %r0
    addcc %sp, 4, %sp
        .
        .
```

Figure 4-25
Subroutine linkage using a stack.

Register %r14 serves as the stack pointer (%sp), which is initialized by the operating system prior to execution of the calling routine. The calling routine places its arguments (%r1 and %r2) onto the stack by decrementing the stack pointer (which moves %sp to the next free word above the stack) and by storing each argument on the new top of the stack. Subroutine add_3 is called, which pops its arguments from the stack, performs an addition operation, and then stores its return value on the top of the stack before returning. The calling routine then retrieves its argument from the top of the stack and continues execution.

For each of the calling conventions, the call instruction is used, which saves the current PC in %r15. When a subroutine finishes execution, it needs to return to the instruction that *follows* the call, which is one word (four bytes) past the saved PC. Thus, the statement "jmpl %r15 + 4, %r0" completes the return. If the called routine calls *another* routine, however, then the value of the PC that was originally saved in %r15 will be overwritten by the nested call, which means that a correct return to the original calling routine through %r15 will no longer be possible. In order to allow nested calls and returns, the current value of %r15 (which is called the **link register**) should be saved on the stack, along with any other registers that need to be restored after the return.

If a register-based calling convention is used, then the link register should be saved in one of the unused registers before a nested call is made. If a data link area is used, then there should be space reserved within it for the link register. If a stack scheme is used, then the link register should be saved on the stack. For each of the calling conventions, the link register and the local variables in the called routines should be saved before a nested call is made; otherwise, a nested call to the same routine will cause the local variables to be overwritten.

There are many variations to the basic calling conventions, but the stack-oriented approach to subroutine linkage is probably the most popular. When a stack-based calling convention is used that handles nested subroutine calls, a **stack frame** is built that contains arguments that are passed to a called routine, the return address for the calling routine, and any local variables. A sample high-level program is shown in Figure 4-26 that illustrates nested function calls. The operation that the program performs is not important,

```
Line   /* C program showing nested subroutine calls */
No.
00  main()
01  {
02      int w, z;          /* Local variables */
03      w = func_1(1,2);   /* Call subroutine func_1 */
04      z = func_2(10);    /* Call subroutine func_2 */
05  }                      /* End of main routine */

06  int func_1(x,y)        /* Compute x * x + y */
07  int x, y;          /* Parameters passed to func_1 */
08  {
09      int i, j;          /* Local variables */
10      i = x * x;
11      j = i + y;
12      return(j);     /* Return j to calling routine */
13  }

14  int func_2(a)          /* Compute a * a + a + 5 */
15  int a;                 /* Parameter passed to func_2 */
16  {
17      int m, n;          /* Local variables */
18      n = a + 5;
19      m = func_1(a,n);
20      return(m);         /* Return m to calling routine */
21  }
```

Figure 4-26

A C program illustrating nested function calls.

nor is the fact that the C programming language is used; what is important is how the sub-routine calls are implemented.

The behavior of the stack for this program is shown in Figure 4-27. The main program calls func_1 with arguments 1 and 2, and then calls func_2 with argument 10 before finishing execution. Function func_1 has two local variables i and j that are used in computing the return value j. Function func_2 has two local variables m and n that are used in creating the arguments to pass through to func_1 before returning m.

The stack pointer (%r14 by convention, which will be referred to as %sp) is initialized before the program starts executing, usually by the operating system. The compiler is responsible for implementing the calling convention, and so the compiler produces code for pushing parameters and the return address onto the stack, reserving room on the stack for local variables, and then reversing the process as routines return from their calls. The stack behavior shown in Figure 4-27 is thus produced as the result of executing compiler-generated code, but the code might just as well have been written directly in assembly language.

As the main program begins execution, the stack pointer points to the top element of the system stack (Figure 4-27a). When the main routine calls func_1 at line 03 of the program shown in Figure 4-26 with arguments 1 and 2, the arguments are pushed onto the stack, as shown in Figure 4-27b. Control is then transferred to func_1 through a call

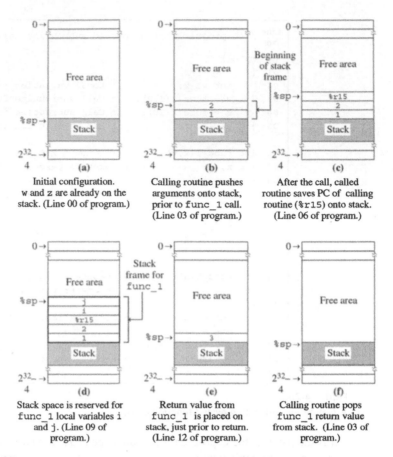

Figure 4-27
(a–f) Stack behavior during execution of the program in Figure 4-26.

instruction (not shown), and func_1 then saves the return address, which is in %r15 as a result of the call instruction, onto the stack (Figure 4-27c). Stack space is reserved for local variables i and j of func_1 (Figure 4-27d). At this point, we have a complete stack frame for the func_1 call as shown in Figure 4-27d, which is composed of the arguments passed to func_1, the return address to the main routine, and the local variables for func_1.

Just prior to func_1 returning to the calling routine, it releases the stack space for its local variables, retrieves the return address from the stack, releases the stack space for the arguments passed to it, and then pushes its return value onto the stack, as shown in Figure 4-27e. Control is then returned to the calling routine through a jmpl instruction, and the calling routine is then responsible for retrieving the returned value from the stack and decrementing the stack pointer to its position from before the call, as shown in Figure 4-27f. Routine func_2 is then executed, and the process of building a stack frame starts all over again, as shown in Figure 4-27g. Since func_2 makes a call to func_1 before it returns, there will be stack frames for both func_2 and func_1 on the stack at the same time, as

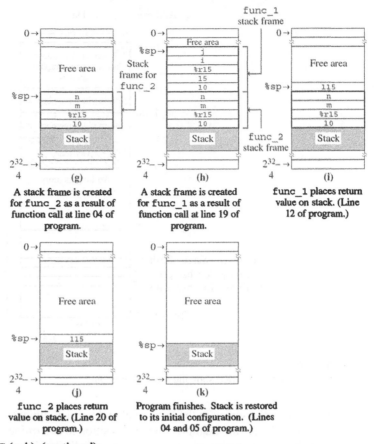

Figure 4-27 (g–k) (continued).

shown in Figure 4-27h. The process then unwinds as before, finally resulting in the stack pointer at its original position, as shown in Figure 4-27 i–k.

4.9 INPUT AND OUTPUT IN ASSEMBLY LANGUAGE

Finally, we come to ways in which an assembly language program can communicate with the outside world: input and output (I/O) activities. One way that communication between I/O devices and the rest of the machine can be handled is with special instructions and with a special I/O bus reserved for this purpose. An alternative method for interacting with I/O devices is through the use of **memory-mapped I/O**, in which devices occupy sections of the address space where no ordinary memory exists. Devices are accessed as if they were memory locations, and so there is no need for handling devices with new instructions.

As an example of memory-mapped I/O, consider again the memory map for the ARC, which is illustrated in Figure 4-28. We see a few new regions of memory, for two add-in video memory modules and for a **touchscreen**. A touchscreen comes in two forms, photonic and electrical. An illustration of the photonic version is shown in Figure 4-29. A matrix of

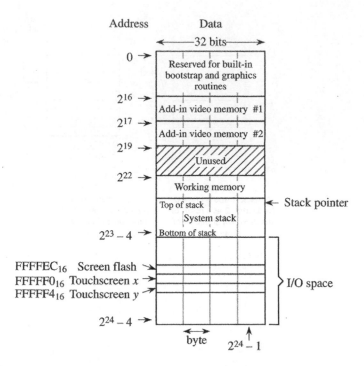

Address   Data

←——32 bits——→

0 →   Reserved for built-in
bootstrap and graphics
routines

2^{16} → Add-in video memory #1

2^{17} → Add-in video memory #2

2^{19} → Unused

2^{22} → Working memory

Top of stack   ← Stack pointer

System stack

$2^{23} - 4$ → Bottom of stack

$FFFFEC_{16}$ Screen flash →
$FFFFF0_{16}$ Touchscreen x →   } I/O space
$FFFFF4_{16}$ Touchscreen y →

$2^{24} - 4$ →

←→
byte $2^{24} - 1$

Figure 4-28
Memory map for the ARC showing memory mapping.

beams covers the screen in the horizontal and vertical dimensions. If the beams are interrupted (by a finger for example) then the position is determined by the interrupted beams. (In an alternative version of the touchscreen, the display is covered with a touch-sensitive surface. The user must make contact with the screen in order to register a selection.)

The only real memory occupies the address space between 2^{22} and $2^{23} - 1$. (Remember: $2^{23} - 4$ is the address of the leftmost byte of the highest word in the big-endian format.) The rest of the address space is occupied by other components. The address space between 0 and $2^{16} - 1$ (inclusive) contains built-in programs for the power-on bootstrap

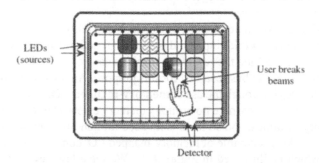

LEDs
(sources)

User breaks
beams

Detector

Figure 4-29
A user selecting an object on a touchscreen.

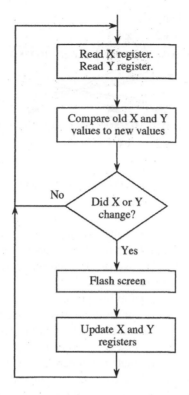

Figure 4-30
Flowchart illustrating the control structure
of a program that tracks a touchscreen.

operation and basic graphics routines. The address space between 2^{16} and $2^{19} - 1$ is used for two add-in video memory modules that we will study in Problem Figure 4.11. Note that valid information is available only when the add-in memory modules are physically inserted into the machine.

Finally, the address space between 2^{23} and $2^{24} - 1$ is used for I/O devices. For this system, the X and Y coordinates that mark the position where a user has made a selection are automatically updated in registers that are placed in the memory map. The registers are accessed by simply reading from the memory locations where these registers are located. The "screen flash" location causes the screen to flash whenever it is written.

Suppose that we would like to write a simple program that flashes the screen whenever the user changes position. The flowchart in Figure 4-30 illustrates how this might be done. The X and Y registers are first read, and are then compared with the previous X and Y values. If either position has changed, then the screen is flashed and the previous X and Y values are updated and the process repeats. If neither position has changed, then the process simply repeats. This is an example of the programmed I/O method of accessing a device. (See Problem 4.11 for a more detailed description.)

EXAMPLE 4-1 Big-/Little-Endian Formats and Network Programming

The big-endian vs. little-endian issue is sometimes ignored, with little consequence, when the application and data stay on the same machine. When a network is involved, however,

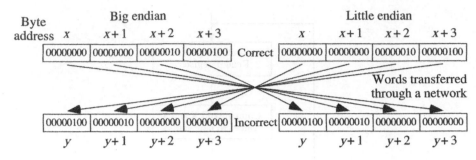

Figure 4-31
A 32-bit word is incorrectly transferred between big-endian and little-endian systems.

data may be transferred between two machines that have incompatible endianness, and then the process breaks unless something is done to address the incompatibility.

Figure 4-31 illustrates the problem in which four-byte words are transferred between big- and little-endian systems. The words are incorrectly seen in byte-reversed order on the receiving side of the transmission.

This big vs. little-endian compatibility problem may be obscured by the way that the operating system handles network connections. Every packet of data that goes onto a network contains the addresses of the source and destination machines and the **port** numbers of the sending and receiving processes, all contained in a **packet header**. The packet header has an exact byte ordering that is independent of the big-/little-endianness issue. For this reason, packets can be delivered correctly to their destination even though the data (referred to as the packet **payload**) is incorrectly received in byte-reversed order.

A simple solution is to write networking programs using endian-independent code. The Java networking classes and supporting methods correctly abstract this issue away for the programmer.

■

■ 4.9 CASE STUDY: THE JAVA VIRTUAL MACHINE ISA

Java is a high-level programming language developed by Sun Microsystems that has taken a prominent position in the programming community. A key aspect of Java is that Java binary codes are platform-independent, which means that the same compiled code can run without modification on any computer that supports the **Java Virtual Machine** (JVM). The JVM is how Java achieves its platform independence: a standard specification of the JVM is implemented in the native instruction sets of many underlying machines, and compiled Java codes can then run in any JVM environment.

Programs that are written in fully compiled languages like C, C++, and Fortran are compiled into the native code of the target architecture, and are generally not portable across platforms unless the source code is recompiled for the target machine. Interpreted languages, like Perl, Tcl, AppleScript, and shell script, are largely platform independent, but can execute 100 to 200 times slower than a fully compiled language. Java programs are compiled into an intermediate form known as **bytecodes**, which execute on the order

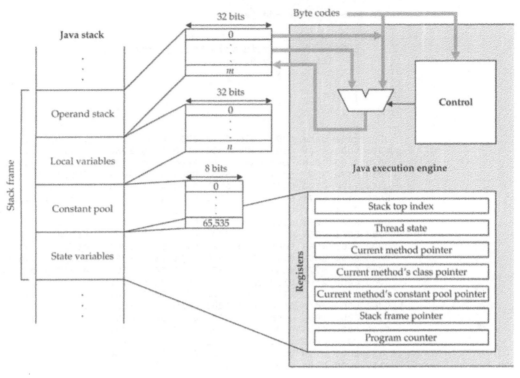

Figure 4-32
Architecture of the Java virtual machine.

of 10 times more slowly than fully compiled languages, but the cross-platform compatibility and other language features make Java a favorable programming language for many applications.

A high-level view of the JVM architecture is shown in Figure 4-32. The JVM is a stack-based machine, which means that the operands are pushed and popped from a stack, instead of being transferred among general-purpose registers. There are, however, a number of special-purpose registers, and also a number of local variables that serve the function of general-purpose registers in a "real" (non-virtual) architecture. The Java Execution Engine takes compiled Java bytecodes at its input and interprets the bytecodes in a software implementation of the JVM, or executes the bytecodes directly in a hardware implementation of the JVM.

Figure 4-33 shows a Java implementation of the SPARC program we studied in Figure 4-21. The figure shows both the Java source program and the bytecodes into which it has been compiled. The bytecode file is known as a Java **class file** (which is what a compiled Java program is called).

Only a small number of bytes in a class file actually contain instructions; the rest is overhead that the file must contain in order to run on the JVM. In Figure 4-34 we have "disassembled" the bytecodes back to their higher-level format. The bytecode locations are given in hexadecimal, starting at location 0x00. The first four bytes contain the **magic number** 0xcafebabe which identifies the program as a compiled Java class file. The

```
// This is file add.java

public class add {
    public static void main(String args[]) {
        int x=15, y=9, z=0;
        z = x + y;
        }
    }
```

```
0000 cafe babe 0003 002d 0012 0700 0e07 0010      ...............
0010 0a00 0200 040c 0007 0005 0100 0328 2956      ...............()V
0020 0100 1628 5b4c 6a61 7661 2f6c 616e 672f      ...([Ljava/lang/
0030 5374 7269 6e67 3b29 5601 0006 3c69 6e69      String;)V...<ini
0040 743e 0100 0443 6f64 6501 000d 436f 6e73      t>...Code...Cons
0050 7461 6e74 5661 6c75 6501 000a 4578 6365      tantValue...Exce
0060 7074 696f 6e73 0100 0f4c 696e 654e 756d      ptions...LineNum
0070 6265 7254 6162 6c65 0100 0e4c 6f63 616c      berTable...Local
0080 5661 7269 6162 6c65 7301 000a 536f 7572      Variables...Sour
0090 6365 4669 6c65 0100 0361 6464 0100 0861      ceFile...add...a
00a0 6464 2e6a 6176 6101 0010 6a61 7661 2f6c      dd.java...java/l
00b0 616e 672f 4f62 6a65 6374 0100 046d 6169      ang/Object...mai
00c0 6e00 2100 0100 0200 0000 0000 0200 0900      n...............
00d0 1100 0600 0100 0800 0000 2d00 0200 0400      ...........-.....
00e0 0000 0d10 0f3c 1009 3d03 3e1b 1c60 3eb1      .....<..=.>..`>.
00f0 0000 0001 000b 0000 000e 0003 0000 0004      ................
0100 0008 0006 000c 0002 0001 0007 0005 0001      ................
0110 0008 0000 001d 0001 0001 0000 0005 2ab7      ............*.
0120 0003 b100 0000 0100 0b00 0000 0600 0100      ................
0130 0000 0100 0100 0d00 0000 0200 0f00          ..............
```

Figure 4-33
Java program and compiled class file.

major version and minor version numbers refer to the Java runtime system for which the program is compiled. The number of entries in the **constant pool** follows, which is actually 17 in this example: the first entry (constant pool location 0) is always reserved for the JVM, and is not included in the class file, although indexing into the constant pool starts at location 0 as if it were explicitly represented. The constant pool contains the names of **methods** (functions), attributes, and other information used by the runtime system.

The remainder of the file is mostly composed of the constant pool and executable Java instructions. We will not cover all details of the Java class file here. The reader is referred to (Meyer & Downing, 1997) for a full description of the Java class file format.

The actual code that corresponds to the Java source program, which simply adds the constants 15 and 9 and returns the result (24) to the calling routine on the stack, appears in locations 0x00e3 - 0x00ef. Figure 4-35 shows how that portion of the bytecode is interpreted. The program pushes the constants 15 and 9 onto the stack, using local variables 0 and 1 as intermediaries, and invokes the iadd instruction that pops the top two stack elements, adds them, and places the result on the top of the stack. The program then returns.

A cursory glance at the code shows some of the reasons why the JVM runs 10 times slower than native code. Notice that the program stores the arguments in local variables 1 and 2 and then transfers them to the Java stack before adding them. This transfer would be viewed as redundant by native code compilers for other languages, and would be eliminated.

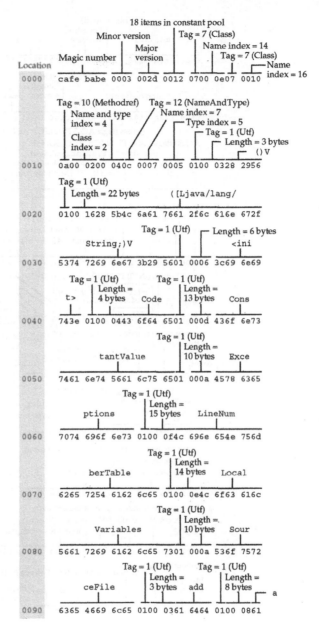

Figure 4-34
A Java class file.

Given this example alone, there is probably considerable room for speed improvements from the 10× slower execution time of today's JVMs. Other improvements may also come in the form of **just-in-time** (JIT) compilers. Rather than interpreting the JVM bytecodes one by one into the target machine code each time they are encountered, JIT compilers take

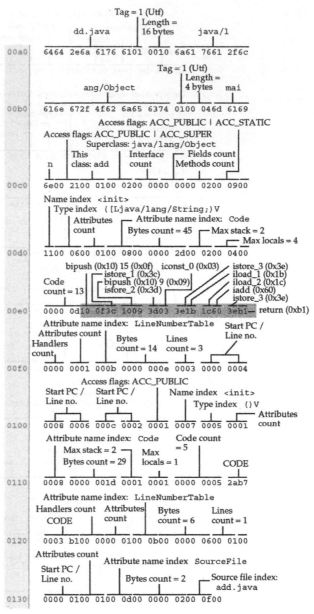

Figure 4-34
A Java class file (continued).

advantage of the fact that most programs spend most of their time in loops and other iterative routines. As the JIT encounters each line of code for the first time, it compiles it into native code and stores it away in memory for possible later use. The next time that code is executed, it is the native, compiled form that is executed rather than the bytecodes.

Location	Code	Mnemonic	Meaning
0x00e3	0x10	bipush	Push next byte onto stack
0x00e4	0x0f	15	Argument to bipush
0x00e5	0x3c	istore_1	Pop stack to local variable 1
0x00e6	0x10	bipush	Push next byte onto stack
0x00e7	0x09	9	Argument to bipush
0x00e8	0x3d	istore_2	Pop stack to local variable 2
0x00e9	0x03	iconst_0	Push 0 onto stack
0x00ea	0x3e	istore_3	Pop stack to local variable 3
0x00eb	0x1b	iload_1	Push local variable 1 onto stack
0x00ec	0x1c	iload_2	Push local variable 2 onto stack
0x00ed	0x60	iadd	Add top two stack elements
0x00ee	0x3e	istore_3	Pop stack to local variable 3
0x00ef	0xb1	return	Return

Figure 4-35

Disassembled version of the code that implements the Java program in Figure 4-33.

Summary

In this chapter, we introduced the ARC ISA and studied some general properties of ISAs. In the design of an instruction set, a balance must be struck between system performance and the characteristics of the technology in which the processor is implemented. Interaction between the CPU and the memory is a key consideration.

When a memory access is made, the way in which the address is calculated is called the memory addressing mode. We examined the sequence of computations that can be combined to make up an addressing mode. We also looked at some specific cases that are commonly identified by name.

We also looked at several parts of a computer system that play a role in the execution of a program. We learned that programs are made up of sequences of instructions, which are taken from the instruction set of the CPU. In Chapter 6, we will study how these sequences of instructions are translated into object code.

Problems

4.1 A memory has 2^{24} addressable locations. What is the smallest width in bits that the address can be while still being able to address all 2^{24} locations?

4.2 In Table 4.1, what is the value of the halfword stored at address 0x00001002?

4.3 What are the lowest and highest addresses in a 2^{20} byte memory in which a four-byte word is the smallest addressable unit?

4.4 Make a table indicating which of the instructions addcc, andcc, orcc, and the synthetic instruction not, can set the z, n, c, and v flags to 1.

4.5   At the end of Section 4.2.3 there is a description of how the address of a branch target is computed: %PC + (4 × sign_ext(*simm22*)).

(a) What is the range of the branch target relative to the PC, in bytes?

(b) What is the range in words?

4.6   ARC provides instructions to load both signed and unsigned bytes and halfwords, but only instructions to store bytes and halfwords without providing for signed or unsigned values. Is this reasonable?

4.7   Encode the following ARC instructions in binary. Show the identity of the individual bit fields, and then the entire instruction word in hexadecimal notation. Assume label_d is 64 bytes ahead of the instruction in which it is referenced, and label_b is 0xFFFFFFFC.

```
a)   sethi 0xABCD, %r12      b)   call label_b
c)   orcc %r15, 255, %r22    d)   be label_d
e)   st %r25, [%r9 + 128]    f)   srl %r8, 31, %r9
```

4.8   Which of the following ARC instructions are legal, and if not, why not? Assume l_b is 0xFFFB.

```
a)   sethi 0xABCDEF, %r12    b)   call l_b
c)   or %r15, 0x1FFF, %r22   d)   be -4
e)   st %r25, [%r9 + 128]    f)   srl %r8, 32, %r9
```

4.9   Suppose you wished to write the instruction be lbl, where lbl was beyond the range of the branch instruction. Give a two-instruction fragment that would accomplish this action.

4.10   Shift instructions cannot set the condition codes. Suppose you had a need to do an sll %r1, %r2, %r3 and then branch to Tgt if the result is negative. Provide a three-instruction fragment that accomplishes this.

4.11   The memory map for the ARC is shown in Figure 4-28.

(a) How much memory (in bytes) is available for each of the add-in video memory modules? (Give your answer as powers of two or sums of powers of two, e.g. 2^{10}.)

(b) When a finger is drawn across the touchscreen, the horizontal (x) and vertical (y) positions of the joystick are updated in registers that are accessed at locations $(FFFFF0)_{16}$ and $(FFFFF4)_{16}$, respectively. When the number '1' is written to the register at memory location $(FFFFEC)_{16}$, the screen flashes and then location $(FFFFEC)_{16}$ is automatically cleared to zero by the hardware (the software does not have to clear it). Write an ARC program that flashes the screen every time the user's position changes. Use the skeleton program shown below.

```
        .begin
        ld      [x], %r7        ! %r7 and %r8 now point to the
        ld      [y], %r8        ! touchscreen x and y locations
        ld      [flash], %r9    ! %r9 points to flash location
loop:   ld      %r7, %r1        ! Load current touchscreen
        ld      %r8, %r2        ! position in %r1=x and %r2=y
        ld      [old_x], %r3    ! Load old touchscreen
        ld      [old_y], %r4    ! position in %r3=x and %r4=y
        orncc   %r0, %r3, %r3   ! Form 1's complement of old_x
        addcc   %r3, 1, %r3     ! Form 2's complement of old_x
        addcc   %r1, %r3, %r3   ! %r3 <- x - old_x
        be      x_not_moved     ! Branch if x did not change
        ba      moved           ! x changed, so no need to check y
x_not_moved:                    ! Your code starts here, about four lines.

                <- YOUR CODE GOES HERE

        ! This portion of the code is entered only if
        ! touchscreen cursor is moved.
```

```
            ! Flash screen; store new x, y values; repeat.
moved:      orcc    %r0, 1, %r5     ! Place 1 in %r5
            st      %r5, %r9        ! Store 1 in flash register
            st      %r1, [old_x]    ! Update old joystick position
            st      %r2, [old_y]    !   with current position
            ba      loop            ! Repeat
flash:      #FFFFEC                 ! Location of flash register
x:          #FFFFF0                 ! Location of touchscreen x register
y:          #FFFFF4                 ! Location of touchscreen y register
old_x:      0                       ! Previous x position
old_y:      0                       ! Previous y position
            .end
```

4.12 Write an ARC subroutine that performs a swap operation on the 32-bit operands x = 25 and y = 50, which are stored in memory. Use as few registers as you can.

4.13 A section of ARC assembly code is shown below. What does it do? Express your answer in terms of the actions it goes through. Does it add up numbers, or clear something out? Does it simulate a **for** loop, a **while** loop, or something else? Assume that a and b are memory locations that are defined elsewhere in the code.

```
Y:      ld      [k], %r1
        addcc   %r1, -4, %r1
        st      %r1, [k]
        bneg    X
        ld      [a], %r1, %r2
        ld      [b], %r1, %r3
        addcc   %r2, %r3, %r4
        st      %r4, %r1, [c]
        ba      Y
X:      jmpl    %r15 + 4, %r0
k:      40
```

4.14 A pocket pager contains a small processor with 2^7 eight-bit words of memory. The ISA has four registers: R0, R1, R2, and R3. The instruction set is shown in Figure 4-36, as well as the bit patterns that correspond to each register, the instruction format, and the **modes**, which determine if the operand is a register (mode bit = 0) or the operand is a memory location (mode bit = 1). Either or both of the operands can be registers, but both operands cannot be memory locations. If the source or destination is a memory location, then the corresponding source or destination field in the instruction is not used, since the address field is used instead.

(a) Write a program using object code (not assembly code) that swaps the contents of registers R0 and R1. You are free to use the other registers as necessary, but do not use memory. Use no more than four lines of code (fewer lines are possible). Place 0s in any positions where the value does not matter.

(b) Write a program using object code that swaps the contents of memory locations 12 and 13. As in part (a), you are free to use the other registers as necessary, but do not use other memory locations. Place 0s in any positions where the value does not matter.

4.15 An ARC program calls the subroutine foo, passing it three arguments, a, b, and c. The subroutine has two local variables, m and n. Show the position of the stack pointer and the contents of the relevant stack elements for a stack-based calling convention at the points in the program shown below. Note that subroutine foo does not return anything.

(1) just before executing the call at label x;
(2) when the stack frame for foo is completed;
(3) just before executing the ld at label z (i.e., when the calling routine resumes).

Use the stack notation shown in Figure 4-27.

```
        ! Push the arguments a, b, and c
x:      call    foo
z:      ld      %r1, %r2
        .
        .
        .

foo:    ! Subroutine starts here
        .
        .
        .
y:      jmpl    %r15 + 4, %r0
```

INSTRUCTION FORMAT

MODE BIT PATTERNS

Mode	Bit Pattern
Register	0
Direct	1

REGISTER BIT PATTERNS

Register	Bit Pattern
R0	00
R1	01
R2	10
R3	11

INSTRUCTION SET

Mnemonic	Opcode	Meaning
LOAD	000	Dst ← Src or Memory
STORE	001	Dst or Memory ← Src
ADD	010	Dst ← Src + Dst
AND	011	Dst ← AND(Src, Dst)
BZERO	100	Branch if Src = 0
JUMP	101	Unconditional jump
COMP	110	Dst ← Complement of Src
RSHIFT	111	Dst ← Src shifted right 1 bit

Note: Dst = Destination register
Src = Source register

Figure 4-36
A pocket pager ISA.

4.16 Why does sethi only load the high 22 bits of a register? It would be more useful if sethi loaded all 32 bits of a register. What is the problem with having sethi load all 32 bits?

4.17 Which of the three subroutine linkage conventions covered in this chapter (registers, data link area, stack) is used in Figure 4-22?

4.18 A program compiled for a SPARC ISA writes the 32-bit unsigned integer 0xABCDEF01 to a file, and reads it back correctly. The same program compiled for a Pentium ISA also works correctly. However, when the file is transferred between machines, the program incorrectly reads the integer from the file as 0x01EFCDAB. What is going wrong?

4.19 Refer to Figure 4-34. Show the Java assembly language instructions for the code shown in locations 0x011e - 0x0122. Use the syntax format shown in locations 0x00e3 - 0x0ef of that same figure. You will need to make use of the following Java instructions:

invokespecial n (opcode 0xb7) – Invoke a method with index n into the constant pool. Note that n is a 16-bit (two-byte) index that follows the invokespecial opcode.

aload_0 (opcode 0x2a) – Push local variable 0 onto the stack.

4.20 Is the JVM a little-endian or big-endian machine? Hint: Examine the first line of the bytecode program in Figure 4-33.

4.21 Write an ARC program that implements the bytecode program shown in Figure 4-35. Assume that, analogous to the code in the figure, the arguments are passed on a stack and that the return value is placed on the top of the stack.

4.22 A JVM is implemented directly in hardware. How many memory references are generated when the program of Figure 4-35 executes? Compute only the number of references for both instructions and data, not the number of bytes transferred.

4.23 Can a Java bytecode program ever run as fast as a program written in the native language of the processor? Defend your answer in one or two paragraphs.

4.24 (a) Write three-address, two-address, and one-address programs to compute the function A = (B-C) × (D-E). Assume eight-bit opcodes, 16-bit operands and addresses, and that data is moved to and from memory in 16-bit chunks. (Also assume that the opcode must be transferred from

memory by itself.) Your code should not overwrite any of the operands. Use any temporary registers needed.
(b) Compute the size of your program in bytes.
(c) Compute the memory traffic your program will generate at execution time, including instruction fetches.

4.25 Repeat Exercise 4.24 above, using ARC assembly language. Note that the subtract mnemonic is `subcc` and that the multiplication mnemonic is `smul`.

Further Reading

The material in this chapter is for the most part a collection of the historical experience gained in fifty years of stored program computer designs. Although each generation of computer systems is typically identified by a specific hardware technology, there have also been historically important instruction set architectures. In the first-generation systems of the 1950s, such as Von Neumann's EDVAC, Eckert and Mauchly's UNIVAC and the IBM 701, programming was performed by hand in machine language. Although simple, these instruction set architectures defined the fundamental concepts surrounding opcodes and operands.

The concept of an instruction set architecture as an identifiable entity can be traced to the designers of the IBM S/360 in the 1960s. The VAX architecture for Digital Equipment Corporation can also trace its roots to this period when its minicomputers, the PDP-4 and PDP-8, were being developed. Both the 360 and VAX are two-address architectures. Significant one-address architectures include the Intel 8080, which is the predecessor to the modern 80x86, and its contemporary at that time, the Zilog Z-80. As a zero-address architecture, the Burroughs B5000 is also of historical significance.

There are a host of references that cover the various machine languages in existence, too many to enumerate here, and so we mention only a few of the more celebrated cases. The machine languages of Babbage's machines are covered in (Bromley, 1987). The machine language of the early Institute for Advanced Study (IAS) computer is covered in (Stallings, 1996). The IBM 360 machine language is covered in (Struble, 1975). The machine language of the 68000 can be found in (Gill, 1987) and the machine language of the SPARC can be found in (SPARC, 1992). A full description of the JVM and the Java class file format can be found in (Meyer & Downing, 1997).

Bromley, A. G., "The Evolution of Babbage's Calculating Engines," *Annals of the History of Computing*, **9**, pp. 113-138 (1987).

Gill, A., Corwin, E. and Logar, A., *Assembly Language Programming for the 68000*, Prentice-Hall (1987).

Meyer, J. and Downing, T., *Java Virtual Machine*, O'Reilly & Associates (1997).

SPARC International, Inc., *The SPARC Architecture Manual: Version 8*, Prentice Hall (1992).

Stallings, W., *Computer Organization and Architecture*, 4/e, Prentice Hall (1996).

Struble, G. W., *Assembler Language Programming: The IBM System/360 and 370*, 2/e, Addison-Wesley (1975).

CHAPTER 5

DATAPATH AND CONTROL

In the earlier chapters, we examined the computer at the application level, the high-level language level, and the assembly language level (as shown in Figure 1-15.) In Chapter 4 we introduced the concept of an ISA: an instruction set that effects operations on registers and memory. In this chapter, we explore the part of the machine that is responsible for implementing these operations: the control unit of the CPU. In this context, we view the machine at the microarchitecture level (the microprogrammed/hardwired control level in Figure 1-15). The microarchitecture consists of the control unit and the programmer-visible registers, functional units such as the ALU, and any additional registers that may be required by the control unit.

A given ISA may be implemented with different microarchitectures. For example, the Intel Pentium ISA has been implemented in different ways, all of which support the same ISA. Not only Intel, but a number of competitors such as AMD and Cyrix have implemented Pentium ISAs. A certain microarchitecture might stress high instruction execution speed, while another stresses low power consumption and another, low processor cost. Being able to modify the microarchitecture while keeping the ISA unchanged means that processor vendors can take advantage of new IC and memory technology while affording the user upward compatibility for their software investment. Programs run unchanged on different processors as long as the processors implement the same ISA, regardless of the underlying microarchitectures.

In this chapter we examine two polarizingly different microarchitecture approaches, microprogrammed control units and hardwired control units, by showing how a subset of the ARC processor can be implemented using these two design techniques.

■ 5.1 BASICS OF THE MICROARCHITECTURE

The functionality of the microarchitecture centers around the fetch-execute cycle, which is in some sense the "heart" of the machine. As discussed in Chapter 4, the steps involved in the fetch-execute cycle are:

1. Fetch the next instruction to be executed from memory.
2. Decode the opcode.
3. Read operand(s) from main memory or registers, if any.
4. Execute the instruction and store results (referred to as *writeback*).
5. Go to Step 1.

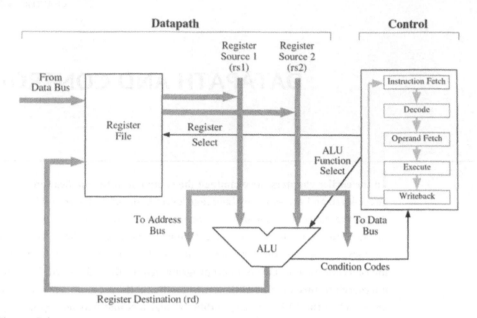

Figure 5-1
High-level view of a microarchitecture.

It is the microarchitecture that is responsible for making these steps happen. The microarchitecture fetches the next instruction to be executed, determines which instruction it is, fetches the operands, executes the instruction, stores the results, and then repeats.

The microarchitecture consists of a **data section**, which contains registers and an ALU, and a **control section**, as illustrated in Figure 5-1. The data section is also referred to as the **datapath**. Microprogrammed control uses a a special-purpose **microprogram**, not visible to the user, to implement operations on the registers and on other parts of the machine. Often, the microprogram contains many program steps that collectively implement a single ISA-level instruction. **Hardwired** control units adopt the view that the steps to be taken to implement an operation comprise states in a finite state machine, and the design proceeds using conventional digital design methods (such as the methods covered in Appendix A). In either case, the datapath remains largely unchanged, although there may be minor differences to support the differing forms of control. In designing the ARC control unit, the microprogrammed approach will be explored first, and then the hardwired approach; for both cases the datapath will remain the same.

■ 5.2 THE DATAPATH

In this section, we consider the datapath and its associated control signals. The instruction subset that we will concentrate on and the instruction format for this ARC subset are shown in Figure 5-2. There are 15 instructions that are grouped into four formats according to the leftmost two bits of the coded instruction. The processor status register %psr is also shown.

Mnemonic	Meaning
ld	Load a register from memory
st	Store a register into memory
sethi	Load the 22 most significant bits of a register
andcc	Bitwise logical AND
orcc	Bitwise logical OR
orncc	Bitwise logical NOR
srl	Shift right (logical)
addcc	Add
call	Call subroutine
jmpl	Jump and link (return from subroutine call)
be	Branch if equal
bneg	Branch if negative
bcs	Branch on carry
bvs	Branch on overflow
ba	Branch always

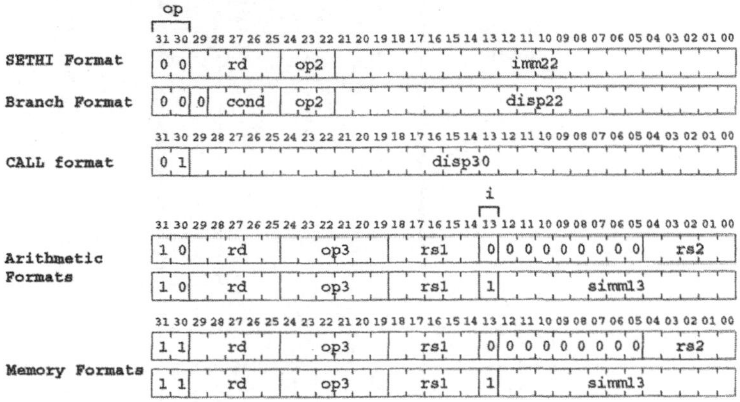

op

31 30 29 28 27 26 25 24 23 22 21 20 19 18 17 16 15 14 13 12 11 10 09 08 07 06 05 04 03 02 01 00

SETHI Format | 0 0 | rd | op2 | imm22

Branch Format | 0 0 0 | cond | op2 | disp22

31 30 29 28 27 26 25 24 23 22 21 20 19 18 17 16 15 14 13 12 11 10 09 08 07 06 05 04 03 02 01 00

CALL format | 0 1 | disp30

i

31 30 29 28 27 26 25 24 23 22 21 20 19 18 17 16 15 14 13 12 11 10 09 08 07 06 05 04 03 02 01 00

Arithmetic Formats
| 1 0 | rd | op3 | rs1 | 0 0 0 0 0 0 0 0 0 | rs2
| 1 0 | rd | op3 | rs1 | 1 | simm13

31 30 29 28 27 26 25 24 23 22 21 20 19 18 17 16 15 14 13 12 11 10 09 08 07 06 05 04 03 02 01 00

Memory Formats
| 1 1 | rd | op3 | rs1 | 0 0 0 0 0 0 0 0 0 | rs2
| 1 1 | rd | op3 | rs1 | 1 | simm13

op	Format	op2	Inst.	op3 (op=10)		op3 (op=11)		cond	branch
00	SETHI/Branch	010	branch	010000	addcc	000000	ld	0001	be
01	CALL	100	sethi	010001	andcc	000100	st	0101	bcs
10	Arithmetic			010010	orcc			0110	bneg
11	Memory			010110	orncc			0111	bvs
				100110	srl			1000	ba
				111000	jmpl				

31 30 29 28 27 26 25 24 23 22 21 20 19 18 17 16 15 14 13 12 11 10 09 08 07 06 05 04 03 02 01 00

PSR | n z v c | pil | e t

Figure 5-2

Instruction subset and instruction formats for the ARC.

5.2.1 Datapath Overview

A datapath for the ARC is illustrated in Figure 5-3. The datapath contains 32 user-visible data registers (%r0 – %r31), the program counter (%pc), the instruction register (%ir), the ALU, four temporary registers not visible at the ISA level (%temp0 – %temp3), and the connections among these components. The number adjacent to a diagonal slash on some of the lines is a simplification that indicates the number of separate wires that are represented by the corresponding single line.

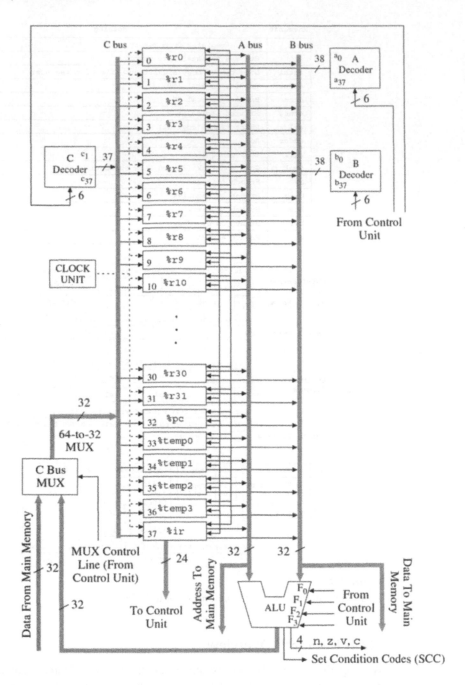

Figure 5-3
The datapath of the ARC.

Registers %r0 – %r31 are directly accessible by a user. Register %r0 always contains the value 0, and cannot be changed. The %pc register is the program counter, which keeps track of the next instruction to be read from the main memory. The user has direct access to %pc only through the call and jmpl instructions. The temporary registers %temp0 – %temp3 are used in interpreting the ARC instruction set, and are not visible to the user. The %ir register holds the current instruction that is being executed. It is not visible to the user.

The ALU

The ALU performs one of 16 operations on the A and B buses according to the table shown in Figure 5-4. For every ALU operation, the 32-bit result is placed on the C bus, unless it is blocked by the C bus MUX when a word of memory is placed onto the C bus instead.

The ANDCC and AND operations perform a bit-by-bit logical AND of corresponding bits on the A and B buses. Note that only operations that end with "CC" affect the condition codes, and so ANDCC affects the condition codes whereas AND does not. (There are times when we wish to execute arithmetic and logic instructions without disturbing the condition codes.) The ORCC and OR operations perform a bit-by-bit logical OR of corresponding bits on the A and B buses. The ORNCC and ORN operations perform a bit-by-bit logical $A + \overline{B}$ of corresponding bits on the A and B buses. The ADDCC and ADD operations carry out addition using two's complement arithmetic on the A and B buses.

The SRL (shift right logical) operation shifts the contents of the A bus to the right by the amount specified on the B bus (from 0 to 31 bits). Zeros are copied into the leftmost

F_3 F_2 F_1 F_0	Operation	Changes Condition Codes
0 0 0 0	ANDCC (A, B)	yes
0 0 0 1	ORCC (A, B)	yes
0 0 1 0	ORNCC(A, B)	yes
0 0 1 1	ADDCC (A, B)	yes
0 1 0 0	SRL (A, B)	no
0 1 0 1	AND (A, B)	no
0 1 1 0	OR (A, B)	no
0 1 1 1	ORN(A, B)	no
1 0 0 0	ADD (A, B)	no
1 0 0 1	LSHIFT2 (A)	no
1 0 1 0	LSHIFT10 (A)	no
1 0 1 1	SIMM13 (A)	no
1 1 0 0	SEXT13 (A)	no
1 1 0 1	INC (A)	no
1 1 1 0	INCPC (A)	no
1 1 1 1	RSHIFT5 (A)	no

Figure 5-4
ARC ALU operations.

bits of the shifted result, and the rightmost bits of the result are discarded. LSHIFT2 and LSHIFT10 shift the contents of the A bus to the left by two and 10 bits, respectively. Zeros are copied into the rightmost bits.

SIMM13 retrieves the least significant 13 bits of the A bus, and places zeros in the 19 most significant bits. SEXT13 performs a sign extension of the 13 least significant bits on the A bus to form a 32-bit word. That is, if the leftmost bit of the 13 bit group is 1, then 1s are copied into the 19 most significant bits of the result; otherwise, 0s are copied into the 19 most significant bits of the result. The INC operation increments the value on the A bus by 1 and the INCPC operation increments the value on the A bus by four, which is used in incrementing the PC register by one word (four bytes). INCPC can be used on any register placed on the A bus.

The RSHIFT5 operation shifts the operand on the A bus to the right by five bits, copying the leftmost bit (the sign bit) into the five new bits on the left. This has the effect of performing a five-bit sign extension. When applied three times in succession to a 32-bit instruction, this operation also has the effect of placing the leftmost bit of the COND field in the branch format (refer to Figure 5-2) into the position of bit 13. This operation is useful in decoding the branch instructions, as we will see later in the chapter. The sign extension for this case is inconsequential.

Every arithmetic and logic operation can be implemented with just these ALU operations. As an example, a subtraction operation can be implemented by forming the two's complement negative of the subtrahend (making use of the ORN operation and adding 1 to it with INC) and then performing addition on the operands. A shift to the left by one bit can be performed by adding a number to itself. A "do-nothing" operation, which is frequently needed for simply passing data through the ALU without changing it, can be implemented by logically ANDing an operand with itself and discarding the result in %r0. A logical XOR can be implemented with the AND, OR, and ORN operations, making use of DeMorgan's theorem (see Problem 5.5).

The ALU generates the c, n, z, and v condition codes which are true for a carry, negative, zero, or overflow result, respectively. The condition codes are changed only for the operations indicated in Figure 5-4. A signal (SCC) is also generated that tells the %psr register when to update the condition codes.

The ALU can be implemented in a number of ways. For the sake of simplicity, let us consider using a **lookup table** (LUT) approach. The ALU has two 32-bit data inputs A and B, a 32-bit data output C, a four-bit control input F, a four-bit condition code output (N, V, C, Z), and a signal (SCC) that sets the flags in the %psr register. We can decompose the ALU into a cascade of 32 LUTs that implement the arithmetic and logic functions, followed by a **barrel shifter** that implements the shifts. A block diagram is shown in Figure 5-5.

The barrel shifter shifts the input word by an arbitrary amount (from 0 to 31 bits) according to the settings of the control inputs. The barrel shifter performs shifts in levels, in which a different bit of the shift amount (SA) input is observed at each level. A partial gate-level layout for the barrel shifter is shown in Figure 5-6. Starting at the bottom of the circuit, we can see that the outputs of the bottom stage will be the same as the inputs to that stage if the SA_0 bit is 0. If the SA_0 bit is 1, then each output position will take on the value of its immediate left or right neighbor, according to the direction of the shift, which

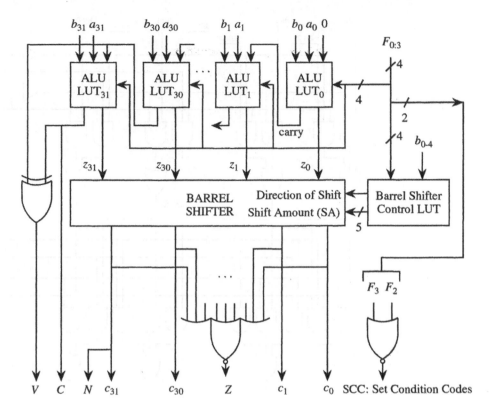

Figure 5-5
Block diagram of the 32-bit ALU.

is indicated by the shift right input. At the next higher level, the method is applied again, except that the SA_1 bit is observed and the amount of the shift is doubled. The process continues until bit SA_4 is observed at the highest level. Zeros are copied into positions that have no corresponding inputs. With this structure, an arbitrary shift from 0 to 31 bits to the left or the right can be implemented.

Each of the 32 ALU LUTs is implemented (almost) identically, using the same lookup table entries, except for changes in certain positions such as for the INC and INCPC operations (see Problem 5.20). The first few entries for each LUT are shown in Figure 5-7. The barrel shifter control LUT is constructed in a similar manner, but with different LUT entries.

The condition code bits n, z, v, and c are implemented directly. The n and c bits are taken directly from the c_{31} output of the barrel shifter and the carry-out position of ALU LUT_{31}, respectively. The z bit is computed as the NOR over the barrel shifter outputs. The z bit is 1 only if all of the barrel shifter outputs are 0. The v (overflow) bit is set if the carry-into the most significant position is different than the carry-out of the most significant position, which is implemented with an XOR gate.

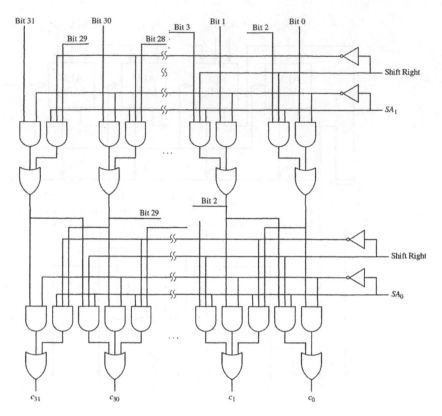

Figure 5-6
Gate-level layout of barrel shifter.

Only the operations that end in "CC" should set the condition codes, and so a signal is generated that informs the condition codes to change, as indicated by the label "SCC: Set Condition Codes." This signal is true when both F_3 and F_2 are false.

The Registers

All of the registers are composed of *falling-edge-triggered* D flip-flops (see Appendix A). This means that the outputs of the flip-flops do not change until the clock makes a transition from high to low (the *falling edge* of the clock). The registers all take a similar form, and so we will only look at the design of register %r1. All of the datapath registers are 32 bits wide, and so 32 flip-flops are used for the design of %r1, which is illustrated in Figure 5-8.

The CLK input to register %r1 is ANDed with the select line (c_1) from the C decoder. This ensures that %r1 only changes when the control section instructs it to change. The data inputs to %r1 are taken directly from the corresponding lines of the C bus. The outputs are written to the corresponding lines of the A and B buses through tri-state buffers, which are "electrically disconnected" unless their enable inputs are set to 1. The outputs of the buffers are enabled onto the A and B buses by the a_1 and b_1 outputs of the A and B decoders, respectively. If neither a_1 nor b_1 are high (meaning they are equal to 1), then the

	F_3 F_2 F_1 F_0	Carry In	a_i b_i	z_i	Carry Out
ANDCC	0 0 0 0	0	0 0	0	0
	0 0 0 0	0	0 1	0	0
	0 0 0 0	0	1 0	0	0
	0 0 0 0	0	1 1	1	0
	0 0 0 0	1	0 0	0	0
	0 0 0 0	1	0 1	0	0
	0 0 0 0	1	1 0	0	0
	0 0 0 0	1	1 1	1	0
ORCC	0 0 0 1	0	0 0	0	0
	0 0 0 1	0	0 1	1	0
	0 0 0 1	0	1 0	1	0
	0 0 0 1	0	1 1	1	0
	0 0 0 1	1	0 0	0	0
	0 0 0 1	1	0 1	1	0
		.		.	.
		.		.	.
		.		.	.

Figure 5-7
Truth table for most of the ALU LUTs.

outputs of $\%r1$ are electrically disconnected from both the A and B buses since the tri-state buffers are disabled.

The remaining registers take a similar form, with a few exceptions. Register $\%r0$ always contains a 0, which cannot be changed. Register $\%r0$ thus has no inputs from the C bus nor any inputs from the C decoder, and does not need flip-flops (see Problem 5.11). The $\%ir$ register has additional outputs that correspond to the rd, rs1, rs2, op, op2, op3, and bit-13 fields of an instruction, as illustrated in Figure 5-9. These outputs are used by the control section in interpreting an instruction, as we will see in Section 5.3.2. The

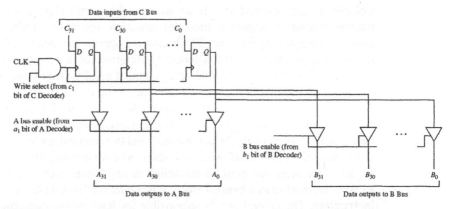

Figure 5-8
Design of register $\%r1$.

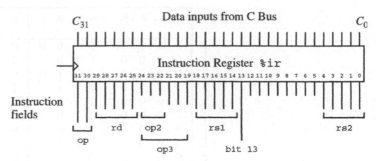

Figure 5-9
Outputs to control unit from register %ir.

program counter can only contain values that are evenly divisible by 4, and so the right-most two bits in %pc can be hardwired to 0.

The A, B, and C decoders shown in Figure 5-3 simplify register selection. The six-bit inputs to the decoders select a single register for each of the A, B, and C buses. There are $2^6 = 64$ possible outputs from the decoders, but there are only 38 data registers. The index shown to the left of each register (in base 10) in Figure 5-3 indicates the value that must be applied to a decoder input to select the corresponding register. The 0 output of the C decoder is not used because %r0 cannot be written. Indices that are greater than 37 do not correspond to any registers, and are free to be used when no registers are to be connected to a bus.

■ 5.3 THE CONTROL SECTION—MICROPROGRAMMED

The control section carries out the process: instruction fetch → decode → operand fetch → execute → writeback. There are two general approaches to implementing a control unit: microprogrammed and hardwired. In a microprogrammed approach, a small "processor within a processor" implements the control function. In a hardwired approach, the control unit is implemented as a finite state machine with flip-flops and logic gates. The microprogrammed approach manages complex operations more easily, and allows changes through programming. The hardwired approach is smaller, faster, works well for streamlined architectures, and is generally preferred for newer processors.

We will look at both the microprogrammed and hardwired approaches for the ARC, starting with the microprogrammed approach. The two approaches are interchangeable, and these sections have been written so that they can be read in either order.

The entire microprogrammed ARC microarchitecture is shown in Figure 5-10. The figure shows the datapath, the control unit, and the connections between them. At the heart of the control unit is a 2048-word × 41-bit read-only memory (ROM) that contains values for all of the lines that must be controlled to implement each user-level instruction. The ROM is referred to as a **control store** in this context. Each 41-bit word is called a **micro-instruction**. The control unit is responsible for fetching microinstructions and executing them, in much the same way as user-level ARC macroinstructions are fetched and

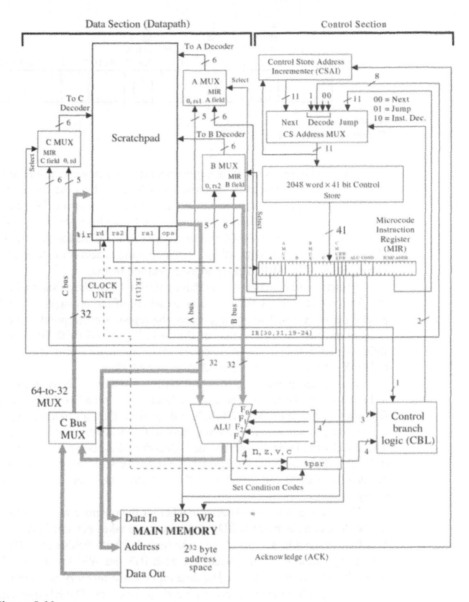

Figure 5-10

The microarchitecture of the ARC.

executed. This microinstruction execution is controlled by the microprogram instruction register (MIR), the processor status register (%psr), and a mechanism for determining the next microinstruction to be executed: the control branch logic (CBL) unit and the control store (CS) address MUX. A separate PC for the microprogram is not needed to store the address of the next microinstruction, because it is recomputed on every clock cycle and therefore does not need to be stored for future cycles.

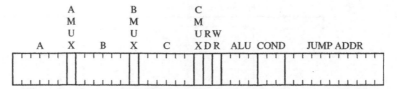

Figure 5-11
The microword format.

When the microarchitecture begins operation (at power-on time, for example), a reset circuit (not shown) places the microword at location 0 in the control store into the MIR and executes it. From that point onward, a microword is selected for execution from either the next, the decode, or the jump inputs to the CS address MUX, according to the settings in the COND field of the MIR and the output of the CBL logic. After each microword is placed in the MIR, the datapath performs operations according to the settings in the individual fields of the MIR. This process is detailed below.

A microword contains 41 bits that comprise 11 fields, as shown in Figure 5-11. Starting from the left, the A field determines which of the registers in the datapath are to be placed on the A bus. The bit patterns for the registers correspond to the binary representations of the base 10 register indices shown in Figure 5-3 (000000 – 100101). The AMUX field selects whether the A decoder takes its input from the A field of the MIR (AMUX = 0) or from the rs1 field of %ir (AMUX = 1).

In a similar manner, the B field determines which of the registers in the datapath are to be placed on the B bus. The BMUX field selects whether the B decoder takes its input from the B field of the MIR (BMUX = 0) or from the rs2 field of %ir (BMUX = 1). The C field determines which of the registers in the datapath is to be written from the C bus. The CMUX field selects whether the C decoder takes its input from the C field of the MIR (CMUX = 0) or from the rd field of %ir (CMUX = 1). Since %r0 cannot be changed, the bit pattern 000000 can be used in the C field when none of these registers are to be changed.

The RD and WR lines determine whether the memory will be read or written, respectively. A read takes place if RD = 1, and a write takes place if WR = 1. Both the RD and WR fields cannot be set to 1 at the same time, but both fields can be 0 if neither a read nor a write operation is to take place. For both RD and WR, the address for the memory is taken directly from the A bus. The data input to the memory is taken from the B bus, and the data output from the memory is placed on the C bus. The RD line controls the 64-to-32 C bus MUX, which determines whether the C bus is loaded from the memory (RD = 1) or from the ALU (RD = 0).

The ALU field determines which of the ALU operations is performed according to the settings shown in Figure 5-4. All 16 possible ALU field bit patterns correspond to valid ALU operations. This means that there is no way to "turn the ALU off" when it is not needed, such as during a read or write to memory. For this situation, an ALU operation should be selected that has no unwanted side effects. For example, ANDCC changes the condition codes and would not be appropriate, whereas the AND operation does not affect the condition codes and would therefore be appropriate.

C_2 C_1 C_0	Operation
0 0 0	Use NEXT ADDR
0 0 1	Use JUMP ADDR if $n = 1$
0 1 0	Use JUMP ADDR if $z = 1$
0 1 1	Use JUMP ADDR if $v = 1$
1 0 0	Use JUMP ADDR if $c = 1$
1 0 1	Use JUMP ADDR if IR[13] $= 1$
1 1 0	Use JUMP ADDR
1 1 1	DECODE

Figure 5-12
Settings for the COND field of the microword.

The COND (conditional jump) field instructs the **microcontroller** (which is another name for the heart of the microcoded control section) to take the next microword either from the next control store location, or from the location in the JUMP ADDR field of the MIR, or from the opcode bits of the instruction in %ir. The COND field is interpreted according to the table shown in Figure 5-12. If the COND field is 000, then no jump is taken, and the next input to the CS address MUX is used. The next input to the CS Address MUX is computed by the control store address incrementer (CSAI) shown in Figure 5-10, which increments the current output of the CS address MUX by 1. If the COND field is 001, 010, 011, 100, or 101, then a conditional jump is taken to the control store location in the JUMP ADDR field, according to the value of the n, z, v, or c flags, or bit 13 of %ir, respectively. The syntax "IR[13]" means "bit 13 of the instruction register %ir." If the COND field is 110, then an unconditional jump is taken.

The bit pattern 111 is used in the COND field when an instruction is being decoded. When the COND field is 111, then the next control store location that is copied into the MIR is taken from neither the next input to the CS address MUX nor the jump input, but from a combination of 11 bits created by appending 1 to the left of bits 30 and 31 of %ir and appending 00 to the right of bits 19-24 of %ir. This DECODE address format is shown in Figure 5-13. The purpose of using this addressing scheme is to allow an instruction to be decoded in a single step, by branching to a different location according to the settings in the op, op2, and op3 fields of an instruction.

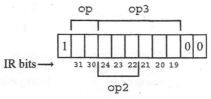

Figure 5-13
DECODE format for a microinstruction address.

Finally, the JUMP ADDR field appears in the rightmost 11 bits of the microword format. There are 2^{11} microwords in the control store, and so 11 bits are needed in the JUMP ADDR field in order to jump to any microstore location.

5.3.1 Timing

The microarchitecture operates on a two-phase clock cycle, in which the master sections of all of the registers change on the rising edge of the clock and the slave sections change on the falling edge of the clock, as shown in Figure 5-14. All of the registers use falling-edge-triggered master/slave D flip-flops except for %r0, which does not need flip-flops. On the falling edge of the clock, data stored in the master sections of the registers are clocked into the slave sections. This makes the data available for operations involving the ALU. While the clock is low, the ALU, CBL, and MUX functions are performed, which settle in time for the rising edge of the clock. On the rising edge of the clock, the new values of the registers are written into the master sections. The registers settle while the clock is high, and the process then repeats.

5.3.2 Developing the Microprogram

In a microprogrammed architecture, instructions are interpreted by the microprogram in the control store. The microprogram is often referred to as **firmware** because it bridges the gap between the hardware and the software. The microarchitecture shown in Figure 5-10 needs firmware in order to execute ARC instructions, and one possible coding is described in this section.

A portion of a microprogram that implements the fetch-execute cycle for the ARC is shown in Figure 5-15. In the control store, each microstatement is stored in coded form (1s and 0s) in a single microword. For simplicity, the **microassembly language** shown in Figure 5-15 is loosely defined here, and we will leave out labels, pseudo-ops, etc., that we would normally associate with a full-featured assembly language. Translation to the 41-bit format used in the microstore is not difficult to perform by hand for a small microprogram, and is frequently performed manually in practice (as we will do here) rather than creating a suite of software tools for such a small program.

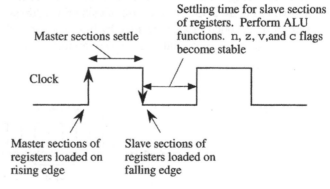

Figure 5-14
Timing relationships for the registers.

Address	Operation Statements	Comment
0:	R[ir] ← AND(R[pc],R[pc]); READ;	/ Read an ARC instruction from main memory
1:	DECODE;	/ 256-way jump according to opcode
	/ sethi	
1152:	R[rd] ← LSHIFT10(ir); GOTO 2047;	/ Copy imm22 field to target register
	/ call	
1280:	R[15] ← AND(R[pc],R[pc]);	/ Save %pc in %r15
1281:	R[temp0] ← ADD(R[ir],R[ir]);	/ Shift disp30 field left
1282:	R[temp0] ← ADD(R[temp0],R[temp0]);	/ Shift again
1283:	R[pc] ← ADD(R[pc],R[temp0]);	/ Jump to subroutine
	GOTO 0;	
	/ addcc	
1600:	IF R[IR[13]] THEN GOTO 1602;	/ Is second source operand immediate?
1601:	R[rd] ← ADDCC(R[rs1],R[rs2]);	/ Perform ADDCC on register sources
	GOTO 2047;	
1602:	R[temp0] ← SEXT13(R[ir]);	/ Get sign extended simm13 field
1603:	R[rd] ← ADDCC(R[rs1],R[temp0]);	/ Perform ADDCC on register/simm13
	GOTO 2047;	/ sources
	/ andcc	
1604:	IF R[IR[13]] THEN GOTO 1606;	/ Is second source operand immediate?
1605:	R[rd] ← ANDCC(R[rs1],R[rs2]);	/ Perform ANDCC on register sources
	GOTO 2047;	
1606:	R[temp0] ← SIMM13(R[ir]);	/ Get simm13 field
1607:	R[rd] ← ANDCC(R[rs1],R[temp0]);	/ Perform ANDCC on register/simm13
	GOTO 2047;	/ sources
	/ orcc	
1608:	IF R[IR[13]] THEN GOTO 1610;	/ Is second source operand immediate?
1609:	R[rd] ← ORCC(R[rs1],R[rs2]);	/ Perform ORCC on register sources
	GOTO 2047;	
1610:	R[temp0] ← SIMM13(R[ir]);	/ Get simm13 field
1611:	R[rd] ← ORCC(R[rs1],R[temp0]);	/ Perform ORCC on register/simm13 sources
	GOTO 2047;	
	/ orncc	
1624:	IF R[IR[13]] THEN GOTO 1626;	/ Is second source operand immediate?
1625:	R[rd] ← ORNCC(R[rs1],R[rs2]);	/ Perform ORNCC on register sources
	GOTO 2047;	
1626:	R[temp0] ← SIMM13(R[ir]);	/ Get simm13 field
1627:	R[rd] ← ORNCC(R[rs1],R[temp0]);	/ Perform ORNCC on register/simm13
	GOTO 2047;	/ sources
	/ srl	
1688:	IF R[IR[13]] THEN GOTO 1690;	/ Is second source operand immediate?
1689:	R[rd] ← SRL(R[rs1],R[rs2]);	/ Perform SRL on register sources
	GOTO 2047;	
1690:	R[temp0] ← SIMM13(R[ir]);	/ Get simm13 field
1691:	R[rd] ← SRL(R[rs1],R[temp0]);	/ Perform SRL on register/simm13 sources
	GOTO 2047;	
	/ jmpl	
1760:	IF R[IR[13]] THEN GOTO 1762;	/ Is second source operand immediate?
1761:	R[pc] ← ADD(R[rs1],R[rs2]);	/ Perform ADD on register sources
	GOTO 0;	

Figure 5-15

Partial microprogram for the ARC. Microwords are shown in logical sequence (not numerical sequence).

Although our microassembly language is indeed an assembly language, it is not the same kind of assembly language as the ARC that we studied in Chapter 4. The ARC assembly language is visible to the user, and is used for coding general-purpose programs. Our microassembly language is used for coding firmware and is not visible to the user. The sole purpose of the firmware is to interpret a user-visible instruction set. A change to the instruction set involves changes to the firmware, whereas a change in user-level software has no influence on the firmware.

Each statement in the microprogram shown in Figure 5-15 is preceded by a decimal number that indicates the address of the corresponding microword in the 2048-word

```
1762: R[temp0] ← SEXT13(R[ir]);              / Get  sign extended simm13 field
1763: R[pc] ← ADD(R[rs1],R[temp0]);          / Perform ADD on register/simm13 sources
      GOTO 0;
      / ld
1792: R[temp0] ← ADD(R[rs1],R[rs2]);         / Compute source address
      IF R[IR[13]] THEN GOTO 1794;
1793: R[rd] ← AND(R[temp0],R[temp0]);        / Place source address on A bus
      READ; GOTO 2047;
1794: R[temp0] ← SEXT13(R[ir]);              / Get  simm13 field for source address
1795: R[temp0] ← ADD(R[rs1],R[temp0]);       / Compute source address
      GOTO 1793;
      / st
1808: R[temp0] ← ADD(R[rs1],R[rs2]);         / Compute destination address
      IF R[IR[13]] THEN GOTO 1810;
1809: R[ir] ← RSHIFT5(R[ir]); GOTO 40;       / Move rd field into position of rs2 field
  40: R[ir] ← RSHIFT5(R[ir]);                / by shifting to the right by 25 bits.
  41: R[ir] ← RSHIFT5(R[ir]);
  42: R[ir] ← RSHIFT5(R[ir]);
  43: R[ir] ← RSHIFT5(R[ir]);
  44: R[0] ← AND(R[temp0], R[rs2]);          / Place destination address on A bus and
      WRITE; GOTO 2047;                      /   place operand  on B bus
1810: R[temp0] ← SEXT13(R[ir]);              / Get  simm13 field for destination address
1811: R[temp0] ← ADD(R[rs1],R[temp0]);       / Compute destination address
      GOTO 1809;
      / Branch instructions: ba, be, bcs, bvs, bneg
1088: GOTO 2;                                / Decoding tree for branches
   2: R[temp0] ← LSHIFT10(R[ir]);            / Sign extend the 22 LSB's of %temp0
   3: R[temp0] ← RSHIFT5(R[temp0]);          / by shifting left 10 bits, then right 10
   4: R[temp0] ← RSHIFT5(R[temp0]);          / bits. RSHIFT5 does sign extension.
   5: R[ir] ← RSHIFT5(R[ir]);                / Move COND field to IR[13] by
   6: R[ir] ← RSHIFT5(R[ir]);                / applying RSHIFT5 three times. (The
   7: R[ir] ← RSHIFT5(R[ir]);                / sign extension is inconsequential.)
   8: IF R[IR[13]] THEN GOTO 12;             / Is it ba?
      R[ir] ← ADD(R[ir],R[ir]);
   9: IF R[IR[13]] THEN GOTO 13;             / Is it not be?
      R[ir] ← ADD(R[ir],R[ir]);
  10: IF Z THEN GOTO 12;                     / Execute be
      R[ir] ← ADD(R[ir],R[ir]);
  11: GOTO 2047;                             / Branch for be not taken
  12: R[pc] ← ADD(R[pc],R[temp0]);           / Branch is taken
      GOTO 0;
  13: IF R[IR[13]] THEN GOTO 16;             / Is it bcs?
      R[ir] ← ADD(R[ir],R[ir]);
  14: IF C THEN GOTO 12;                     / Execute bcs
  15: GOTO 2047;                             / Branch for bcs not taken
  16: IF R[IR[13]] THEN GOTO 19;             / Is it bvs?
  17: IF N THEN GOTO 12;                     / Execute bneg
  18: GOTO 2047;                             / Branch for bneg  not taken
  19: IF V THEN GOTO 12;                     / Execute bvs
  20: GOTO 2047;                             / Branch for bvs not taken
2047: R[pc] ← INCPC(R[pc]); GOTO 0;          / Increment %pc and start over
```

Figure 5-15
(continued)

control store. The address is followed by a colon. The operation statements follow the address, and are terminated by semicolons. An optional comment follows the operation field and begins with a slash '/.' The comment terminates at the end of the line. More than one operation is allowed per line, as long as all of the operations can be performed in a single clock cycle. The ALU operations come from Figure 5-4, and there are a few others, as we will see. Note that the 65 statements are shown in logical sequence, rather than in numerical sequence.

Before the microprogram begins execution, the PC is set up with the starting address of a program that has been loaded into the main memory. This may happen as the result of an initialization sequence when the computer is powered on, or may be done by the operating system during the normal course of operation.

The first task in the execution of a user-level program is to bring the instruction pointed to by the PC from the main memory into the IR. Recall from Figure 5-10 that the address lines to main memory are taken from the A bus. In line 0, the PC is loaded onto the A bus, and a Read operation is initiated to memory. The notation "R[x]" means "register x," in which x is replaced with one of the registers in the datapath, and so "R[1]" means "register %r1," "R[ir]" means "register %ir," and "R[rs1]" means the register that appears in the five-bit rs1 field of an instruction (refer to Figure 5-2).

The expression "AND(R[pc],R[pc])" simply performs a logical AND of %pc with itself in a literal interpretation. This operation is not very useful in a logical sense, but what we are interested in are the side effects. In order to place %pc onto the A bus, we have to choose an ALU operation that uses the A bus but does not affect the condition codes. There is a host of alternative choices that can be used, and the AND approach is arbitrarily chosen here. Note that the result of the AND operation is discarded because the C bus MUX in Figure 5-10 only allows the data output from main memory onto the C bus during a read operation.

A read operation normally takes more time to complete than the time required for one microinstruction to execute. The access time of main memory can vary depending on the memory organization, as we will see in Chapter 7. In order to take into account variations in the access times of memory, the control store address incrementer (CSAI) does not increment the address until an acknowledge (ACK) signal is sent, which indicates the memory has completed its operation.

Flow of control within the microprogram defaults to the next higher numbered statement unless a GOTO operation or a DECODE operation is encountered, and so microword 1 (line 1) is read into the MIR on the next cycle. Notice that some of the microcode statements in Figure 5-15 take up more than one line on the page, but are part of a single microinstruction. See, for example, lines 1283 and 1601.

Now that the instruction is in the IR as a result of the read operation in line 0, the next step is to decode the opcode fields. This is performed by taking a 256-way branch into the microcode as indicated by the DECODE keyword in line 1 of the microprogram. The 11-bit pattern for the branch is constructed by appending a 1 to the left of bits 30 and 31 of the IR, followed by bits 19-24 of the IR, followed by the pattern 00. After the opcode fields are decoded, execution of the microcode continues according to which of the 15 implemented ARC instructions is being interpreted.

As an example of how the decode operation works, consider the addcc instruction. According to the Arithmetic instruction format in Figure 5-2, the op field is 10 and the op3 field is 010000. If we append a 1 to the left of the op bit pattern, followed by the op3 bit pattern, followed by 00, the DECODE address is $11001000000 = (1600)_{10}$. This means that the microinstructions that interpret the addcc instruction begin at control store location 1600.

A number of DECODE addresses should never arise in practice. There is no Arithmetic instruction that corresponds to the invalid op3 field 111111, but if this situation does arise, possibly due to an errant program, then a microstore routine should be placed at the corresponding DECODE address $11011111100 = (1788)_{10}$ in order to deal with the illegal instruction. These locations are left blank in the microprogram shown in Figure 5-15.

Instructions in the SETHI/Branch and Call formats do not have op3 fields. The SETHI/Branch formats have op and op2 fields, and the Call format has only the op field. In order to maintain a simple decoding mechanism, we can create duplicate entries in the control store. Consider the SETHI format. If we follow the rule for constructing the DECODE address, then the DECODE address will have a 1 in the leftmost position, followed by 00 for the op field, followed by 100, which identifies SETHI in bit positions 19–21, followed by the bits in positions 22–24 of the IR, followed by 00, resulting in the bit pattern 100100xxx00 where xxx can take on any value, depending on the imm22 field. There are eight possible bit patterns for the xxx bits, and so we need to have duplicate SETHI codes at locations 100100**000**00, 100100**001**00, 100100**010**00, 100100**011**00, 100100**100**00, 100100**101**00, 100100**110**00, and 100100**111**00. DECODE addresses for the Branch and CALL formats are constructed in duplicate locations in a similar manner. Only the lowest addressed version of each set of duplicate codes is shown in Figure 5-15.

Although this method of decoding is fast and simple, a large amount of control-store memory is wasted. An alternative approach that wastes much less space is to modify the decoder for the control store so that all possible branch patterns for SETHI point to the same location, and the same for the Branch and Call format instructions. For our microarchitecture, we will stay with the simpler approach and pay the price of having a large control store.

Consider now how the ld instruction is interpreted. The microprogram begins at location 0, and at this point does not know that ld is the instruction that the PC points to in main memory. Line 0 of the microprogram begins the Read operation as indicated by the READ keyword, which brings an instruction into the IR from the main memory address pointed to by the PC. For this case, let us assume that the IR now contains the 32-bit pattern:

```
11  00010  000000  00101  1  0000001010000
op  rd     op3     rs1    i  simm13
```

which is a translation of the ARC assembly code: ld [%r5 + 80], %r2. Line 1 then performs a branch to control store address $(11100000000)_2 = (1792)_{10}$.

At line 1792, execution of the ld instruction begins. In line 1792, the immediate bit i is tested. For this example, i = 1, and so control is transferred to microword 1794. If instead we had i = 0, then control would pass to the next higher numbered microword, which is 1793 for this case. Line 1792 adds the registers in the rs1 and rs2 fields of the instruction, in anticipation of a non-immediate form of ld, but this only makes sense if i = 0, which it is not for this example. The result that is stored in %temp0 is thus discarded when control is transferred to microword 1794, but this introduces no time penalty and does not produce any unwanted side effects (ADD does not change the condition codes).

In microword 1794, the simm13 field is extracted (using sign extension, as indicated by the SEXT13 operation), which is added with the register in the rs1 field in microword 1795. Control is then passed to microword 1793, which is where the READ operation takes place. Control passes to line 2047 where the PC is incremented in anticipation of reading the next instruction from main memory. Since instructions are four bytes long and must be aligned on word boundaries in memory, the PC is incremented by four. Control then returns to line 0 where the process repeats. A total of seven microinstructions are thus executed in interpreting the ld instruction. These microinstructions are repeated here:

```
   0: R[ir] ← AND(R[pc],R[pc]); READ;        / Read an ARC instruction from main memory.
   1: DECODE;                                / 256-way jump according to opcode
1792: R[temp0] ← ADD(R[rs1],R[rs2]);         / Compute source address
      IF IR[13] THEN GOTO 1794;
1794: R[temp0] ← SEXT13(R[ir]);              / Get simm13 field for source address
1795: R[temp0] ← ADD(R[rs1],R[temp0]);         Compute source address
      GOTO 1793;
1793: R[rd] ← AND(R[temp0],R[temp0]);        / Place source address on A bus
      READ; GOTO 2047;
2047: R[pc] ← INCPC(R[pc]); GOTO 0;          / Increment %pc and start over
```

The remaining instructions, except for branches, are interpreted similarly to the way ld is interpreted. Additional decoding is needed for the branch instructions because the type of branch is determined by the COND field of the branch format (bits 25 – 28), which is not used during a DECODE operation. The approach used here is to shift the COND bits into IR[13] one bit at a time, and then jump to different locations in the microcode depending on the COND bit pattern.

For branch instructions, the DECODE operation on line 2 of the microprogram transfers control to location 1088. We need more space for the branch instructions than the four-word-per-instruction allocation, so line 1088 transfers control to line 2, which is the starting address of a large section of available control store memory.

Lines 2–4 extract the 22-bit displacement for the branch by zeroing the high-order 10 bits and storing the result in %temp0. This is accomplished by shifting %ir to the left by 10 bits and storing it in %temp0, and then shifting the result back to the right by 10 bits. (Notice that sign extension is performed on the displacement, which may be negative. RSHIFT5 implements sign extension.) Lines 5–7 shift %ir to the right by 15 bits so that the most significant COND bit (IR[28]) lines up in position IR[13], which allows the Jump on IR[13]=1 operation to test each bit. Alternatively, we could shift the COND field to IR[31] one bit at a time, and use the Jump on n condition to test each bit. (Note that there is a subtle error in how the PC is updated in line 12. See Problem 5.21 for an explanation.)

Line 8 starts the branch decoding process, which is summarized in Figure 5-16. If IR[28], which is now in IR[13], is set to 1, then the instruction is ba, which is executed in line 12. Notice that control returns to line 0, rather than to line 2047, so that the PC does not get changed twice for the same instruction.

If IR[28] is zero, then %ir is shifted to the left by one bit by adding it to itself, so that IR[27] lines up in position IR[13]. Bit IR[27] is tested in line 9. If IR[27] is zero, then the be instruction is executed in line 10; otherwise %ir is shifted to the left and IR[26] is then tested in line 13. The remaining branch instructions are interpreted in a similar manner.

Microassembly Language Translation

A microassembly language microprogram must be translated into binary object code before it is stored in the control store, just as an assembly language program must be translated into a binary object form before it is stored in main memory. Each line in the ARC microprogram corresponds to exactly one word in the control store, and there are no unnumbered forward references in the microprogram, so we can assemble the ARC microprogram one line at a time in a single pass. Consider assembling line 0 of the microprogram shown in Figure 5-15:

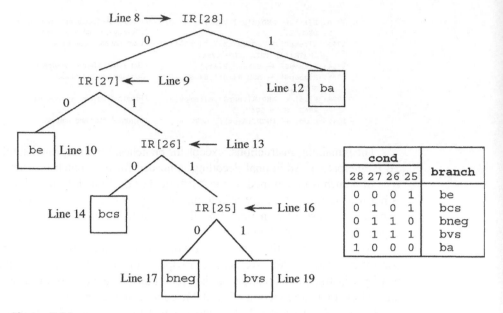

Figure 5-16
Decoding tree for branch instructions, showing corresponding microprogram lines.

```
0: R[ir] ← AND(R[pc],R[pc]); READ;
```

We can fill in the fields of the 41-bit microword as shown below:

	A M U X	B	B M U X	C	C M U X D R	'ALU	COND	JUMP ADDR

`1 0 0 0 0 0|0|1 0 0 0 0 0|0|1 0 0 1 0 1|0|1|0|0 1 0 1|0 0 0|0 0 0 0 0 0 0 0 0 0 0 0`

The PC is enabled onto both the A and B buses for the AND operation, which transfers a word through the ALU without changing it. The A and B fields have the bit pattern for the PC ($32_{10} = 100000_2$). The AMUX and BMUX fields both contain 0s, since the inputs to these MUXes are taken from the MIR. The target of the Read operation is the IR, which has a corresponding bit pattern of ($37_{10} = 100101_2$) for the C field. The CMUX field contains a 0 because the input to the CMUX is taken from the MIR. A read operation to memory takes place, and so the RD field contains a 1 and the WR field contains a 0. The ALU field contains 0101, which corresponds to the AND operation. Note that the condition codes are not affected, which would happen if ANDCC is used instead. The COND field contains 000 since control passes to the next microword, and so the bit pattern in the JUMP ADDR field does not matter. Zeros are arbitrarily placed in the JUMP ADDR field.

The second microword implements the 256-way branch. For this case, all that matters is that the bit pattern 111 appears in the COND field for the DECODE operation, and that no registers, memory, or condition codes are disturbed. The corresponding bit pattern is then:

A	A M U X	B	B M U X	C	C M U X D R	ALU	COND	JUMP ADDR
000000	0	000000	0	000000	0 0 0	0101	111	00000000000

A number of different bit patterns would also work for line 1. For example, any bit patterns can appear in the A, B, or JUMP ADDR fields when a DECODE operation takes place. The use of the zero bit patterns is an arbitrary choice. The ALU field is 0101, which is for AND and does not affect the condition codes. Any other ALU operation that does not affect the condition codes can also be used.

The remainder of the microprogram is translated in a similar manner. The translated microprogram is shown in Figure 5-17, except for gaps where duplicate branch code would appear or where "illegal instruction" code would appear.

EXAMPLE 5-1 Microcoding the `subcc` Instruction

Consider adding an instruction called `subcc` to the microcoded implementation of the ARC instruction set, which subtracts its second source operand from the first, using two's complement arithmetic. The new instruction uses the Arithmetic format and an `op3` field of 001100.

We need to modify the microprogram to add this new instruction. We start by computing the starting location of `subcc` in the control store, by appending a '1' to the left of the op field, which is 10, followed by the op3 field, which is 001100, followed by 00. This results in the bit pattern 11000110000, which corresponds to control store location $(1584)_{10}$. We can then create microassembly code that is similar to the `addcc` microassembly code at location 1600, except that the two's complement negative of the subtrahend (the second source operand) is formed before performing the addition. The subtrahend is complemented by making use of the ORN operation, and 1 is added to it by using the INC operation. The subtraction is then completed by using the code for `addcc`. A microassembly coding for `subcc` is shown below:

```
1584: R[temp0] ← SEXT13(R[ir]);               / Extract rs2 operand
      IF IR[13] THEN GOTO 1586;               / Is second source immediate?
1585: R[temp0] ← R[rs2];                       / Extract sign extended immediate operand
1586: R[temp0] ← ORN(R[0], R[temp0]);         / Form one's complement of subtrahend
1587: R[temp0] ← INC(R[temp0]); GOTO 1603;    / Form two's complement of subtrahend
```

The corresponding microcode for one possible translation is then:

	A	A M U X	B	B M U X	C	C M U X D R	ALU	COND	JUMP ADDR
1584	100101	0	000000	0	100001	0 0 0	1100	101	11000110010
1585	000000	0	000000	1	100001	0 0 0	1000	000	00000000000
1586	000000	0	100001	0	100001	0 0 0	0111	000	00000000000
1587	100001	0	000000	0	100001	0 0 0	1101	110	11001000011

■

Microstore Address	A	AMUX (X)	B	BMUX (X)	C	CMUX (X)	RD (D)	WR (R)	ALU	COND	JUMP ADDR
0	100000	0	100000	0	100101	0	1	0	0101	000	00000000000
1	000000	0	000000	0	000000	0	0	0	0101	111	00000000000
1152	100101	0	000000	0	000000	1	0	0	1010	110	11111111111
1280	100000	0	100000	0	001111	0	0	0	0101	000	00000000000
1281	100101	0	100101	0	100001	0	0	0	1000	000	00000000000
1282	100001	0	100001	0	100001	0	0	0	1000	000	00000000000
1283	100000	0	100001	0	100000	0	0	0	1000	110	00000000000
1600	000000	0	000000	0	000000	0	0	0	0101	101	11001000010
1601	000001	1	000001	1	000001	0	0	0	0011	110	11111111111
1602	100101	0	000000	0	100001	0	0	0	1100	000	00000000000
1603	000001	1	100001	0	000001	0	0	0	0011	110	11111111111
1604	000000	0	000000	0	000000	0	0	0	0101	101	11001000110
1605	000001	1	000001	1	000001	0	0	0	0000	110	11111111111
1606	100101	0	000000	0	100001	0	0	0	1011	000	00000000000
1607	000001	1	100001	0	000001	0	0	0	0000	110	11111111111
1608	000000	0	000000	0	000000	0	0	0	0101	101	11001001010
1609	000001	1	000001	1	000001	0	0	0	0011	110	11111111111
1610	100101	0	000000	0	100001	0	0	0	1011	000	00000000000
1611	000001	1	100001	0	000001	0	0	0	0011	110	11111111111
1624	000000	0	000000	0	000000	0	0	0	0101	101	11001011010
1625	000001	1	000001	1	000001	0	0	0	0010	110	11111111111
1626	100101	0	000000	0	100001	0	0	0	1011	000	00000000000
1627	000001	1	100001	0	000001	0	0	0	0010	110	11111111111
1688	000000	0	000000	0	000000	0	0	0	0101	000	11010011010
1689	000001	1	000001	1	000001	0	0	0	0100	110	11111111111
1690	100101	0	000000	0	100001	0	0	0	1011	000	00000000000
1691	000001	1	100001	0	000001	0	0	0	0100	110	11111111111
1760	000000	0	000000	0	000000	0	0	0	0101	101	11011100010
1761	000000	1	000000	1	100000	0	0	0	1000	110	00000000000
1762	100101	0	000000	0	100001	0	0	0	1100	000	00000000000
1763	000001	1	100010	0	100000	0	0	0	1000	110	00000000000
1792	000001	0	000001	1	100001	0	0	0	1000	101	11100000010

Figure 5-17
Assembled microprogram for the ARC instruction subset.

5.3.3 Traps and Interrupts

As discussed in Chapter 4, a **trap** is an automatic procedure call initiated by the hardware after an exceptional condition caused by an executing program, such as an illegal instruction, overflow, underflow, dividing by zero, etc. When a trap occurs, control is transferred to a "trap handler," which is a routine that is part of the operating system. The handler might do something like print a message and terminate the offending program. Recall that in Chapter 4 we introduced the ta (trap always) instruction, which returns control to the ARC simulator when invoked as "ta 0".

| | | A MUX | | B MUX | | C MUX | | | |
| | | A / M / U | | B / M / U | | C / M / U / R W | | | |
Addr	A	X	B	X	C	X D R	ALU	COND	JUMP ADDR
1793	100001	0	100001	0	000000	110	0101	110	1111111111
1794	100101	0	000000	0	100001	000	1100	000	0000000000
1795	000000	1	100001	0	100001	000	1000	110	1110000001
1808	000000	1	000000	1	100001	000	1000	101	1110010010
1809	100101	0	000000	0	100101	000	1111	110	0000101000
40	100101	0	000000	0	100101	000	1111	000	0000000000
41	100101	0	000000	0	100101	000	1111	000	0000000000
42	100101	0	000000	0	100101	000	1111	000	0000000000
43	100101	0	000000	0	100101	000	1111	000	0000000000
44	100001	0	000000	1	000000	001	0101	110	1111111111
1810	100101	0	000000	0	100001	000	1100	000	0000000000
1811	000000	1	100001	0	100001	000	1000	110	1110010001
1088	000000	0	000000	0	000000	000	0101	110	0000000010
2	100101	0	000000	0	100001	000	1010	000	0000000000
3	100001	0	000000	0	100001	000	1111	000	0000000000
4	100001	0	000000	0	100001	000	1111	000	0000000000
5	100101	0	000000	0	100101	000	1111	000	0000000000
6	100101	0	000000	0	100101	000	1111	000	0000000000
7	100101	0	000000	0	100101	000	1111	000	0000000000
8	100101	0	100100	0	100101	000	1000	101	0000001100
9	100101	0	100100	0	100101	000	1000	101	0000001101
10	100101	0	100100	0	100101	000	1000	010	0000001100
11	000000	0	000000	0	000000	000	0101	110	1111111111
12	100000	0	100001	0	100000	000	1000	110	0000000000
13	100101	0	100101	0	100101	000	1000	101	0000010000
14	000000	0	000000	0	000000	000	0101	100	0000001100
15	000000	0	000000	0	000000	000	0101	110	1111111111
16	000000	0	000000	0	000000	000	0101	101	0000010011
17	000000	0	000000	0	000000	000	0101	001	0000001100
18	000000	0	000000	0	000000	000	0101	110	1111111111
19	000000	0	000000	0	000000	000	0101	011	0000001100
20	000000	0	000000	0	000000	000	0101	110	1111111111
2047	100000	0	000000	0	100000	000	1110	110	0000000000

Figure 5-17
(continued.)

One way to handle traps is to modify the microcode, possibly to check the status bits. For instance, we can check the v bit to see if an overflow has occurred. The microcode can then load an address into the PC (if a trap occurs) for the starting location of the trap handler.

Normally, there is a fixed section of memory for trap handler starting addresses where only a single word is allocated for each handler. This section of memory forms a **branch table** that transfers control to the handlers, as illustrated in Figure 5-18. The reason for using a branch table is that the absolute addresses for each type of trap can be embedded in the microcode this way, while the targets of the jumps can be changed at the user level to handle traps differently.

Address	Contents	Trap Handler
	⋮	
60	JUMP TO 2000	Illegal instruction
64	JUMP TO 3000	Overflow
68	JUMP TO 3600	Underflow
72	JUMP TO 5224	Zerodivide
76	JUMP TO 4180	Disk
80	JUMP TO 5364	Printer
84	JUMP TO 5908	TTY
88	JUMP TO 6048	Timer
	⋮	

Figure 5-18
A branch table for trap handlers and interrupt service routines.

A historically common trap is for floating-point instructions, which may be **emulated** by the operating system if they are not implemented directly in hardware. Floating-point instructions have their own opcodes, but if they are not implemented by the hardware (that is, the microcode does not know about them) then they will generate an illegal instruction trap when an attempt is made to execute them. When an illegal instruction occurs, control is passed to the illegal-instruction handler, which checks to see if the trap is caused by a floating-point instruction, and, if so, then passes control to a floating-point emulation routine as appropriate for the cause of the trap. Although floating-point units are normally integrated into CPU chips these days, this method is still used when extending the instruction set for other instructions, such as graphics extensions to the ISA.

Interrupts are similar to traps, but are initiated after a hardware **exception** such as a user hitting a key on a keyboard, an incoming telephone call for a modem, a power fluctuation, an unsafe operating temperature, etc. Traps are *synchronous* with a running program, whereas interrupts are *asynchronous*. Thus, a trap will always happen at the same place in the same program running with the same data set, whereas the timing of interrupts is largely unpredictable.

When a key is pressed on an interrupt-based keyboard, the keyboard asserts an interrupt line on the bus, and the CPU then asserts an acknowledge line as soon as it is ready (this is where **bus arbitration** comes in, as covered in Chapter 8, if more than one device wants to interrupt at the same time). The keyboard then places an **interrupt vector** onto the data bus, which identifies itself to the CPU. The CPU then pushes the program counter and processor status register (where the flags are stored) onto the stack. The interrupt vector is used to index into the branch table, which lists the starting addresses of the interrupt service routines.

When a trap handler or an interrupt service routine begins execution, it saves the registers that it plans to modify on the stack, performs its task, restores the registers, and then returns from the interrupt. The process of returning from a trap is different from returning from a subroutine, since the process of entering a trap is different from a subroutine call (because the `%psr` register is also saved and restored). For the ARC, the `rett` instruction (see Chapter 4) is used for returning from a trap or interrupt. Interrupts can interrupt other interrupts, and so the first thing that an interrupt service routine might do is raise its priority (using a special **supervisor mode** instruction) so that no interrupts of lower priority are accepted.

5.3.4 Nanoprogramming

If the microstore is wide and has lots of the same words, then we can save microstore memory by placing one copy of each unique microword in a **nanostore**, and then use the microstore to index into the nanostore. For instance, in the microprogram shown in Figure 5-15, lines 1281 and 1282 are the same. Lines 3, 4, and 40-44 are the same, and there are a number of other microinstructions that recur, especially for the duplicated branch microcode and the duplicated illegal instruction microcode.

Figure 5-19a illustrates the space requirement for the original microstore ROM. There are $n = 2048$ words that are each 41 bits wide, giving an area complexity of $2048 \times 41 = 83{,}968$ bits. Suppose now that there are 100 unique microwords in the ROM (the microprogram in Figure 5-15 is only partially complete so we cannot measure the number of unique microwords directly). Figure 5-19b illustrates a configuration that uses a nanostore, in which an area savings can be realized if there are a number of bit patterns that recur in the original microcode sequence. The unique microwords (100 for this case) form a nanoprogram, which is stored in a ROM that is only 100 words deep by 41 bits wide.

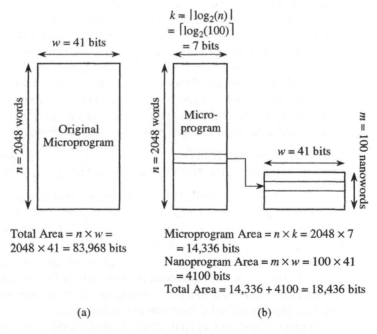

$$k = \lceil \log_2(n) \rceil$$
$$= \lceil \log_2(100) \rceil$$
$$= 7 \text{ bits}$$

$w = 41$ bits

$n = 2048$ words

Original Microprogram

Total Area $= n \times w =$
$2048 \times 41 = 83{,}968$ bits

Micro-program

$w = 41$ bits

$m = 100$ nanowords

Microprogram Area $= n \times k = 2048 \times 7$
$= 14{,}336$ bits
Nanoprogram Area $= m \times w = 100 \times 41$
$= 4100$ bits
Total Area $= 14{,}336 + 4100 = 18{,}436$ bits

(a)   (b)

Figure 5-19
(a) Microprogramming vs. (b) nanoprogramming.

The microprogram now indexes into the nanostore. The microprogram has the same number of microwords regardless of whether or not a nanostore is used, but when a nanostore is used, *pointers* into the nanostore are stored in the microstore rather than the wider 41-bit words. For this case, the microstore is now 2048 words deep by $\lceil \log_2(100) \rceil = 7$ bits wide. The area complexity using a nanostore is then $100 \times 41 + 2048 \times 7 = 18,436$ bits, which is a considerable savings in area over the original microcoded approach.

For small m and large n, where m is the length of the nanoprogram, we can realize a large savings in memory. This frees up area that can be applied in some other way, possibly to improve performance. However, instead of accessing only the microstore, we must now access the microstore first, followed by an access to the nanostore. The machine will thus run more slowly, but will fit into a smaller area.

■ 5.4 THE CONTROL SECTION—HARDWIRED

An alternative approach to a microprogrammed control unit is to use a **hardwired** approach, in which a direct implementation is created using flip-flops and logic gates, instead of using a control store and a microword selection mechanism. States in a finite state machine replace steps in the microprogram.

In order to manage the complexity of design for a hardwired approach, a **hardware description language** (HDL) is frequently used to represent the control structure. One example of an HDL is **VHDL**, which is an acronym for **VHSIC Hardware Description Language** (in which VHSIC is yet another acronym for **Very High Speed Integrated Circuit**). VHDL is used for describing an architecture at a very high level, and can be compiled into hardware designs through a process known as **silicon compilation**. For the hardwired control unit we will design here, a lower-level HDL that is sometimes referred to as a **register transfer language** (RTL) is more appropriate.

We will define a simple HDL/RTL in this section that loosely resembles Hill and Peterson's **A Hardware Programming Language** (AHPL) (Hill and Peterson, 1987). The general idea is to express a control sequence as a series of numbered statements that can then be directly translated into a hardware design. Each statement consists of a data portion and a transfer of control portion, as shown below:

```
5:   A ← ADD(B,C);                     ! Data portion
     GOTO {10 CONDITIONED ON IR[12]}.  ! Control portion
```

The statement is labelled "5," which means that it is preceded by statement 4 and is succeeded by statement 6, unless an out-of-sequence transfer of control takes place. The left arrow ($\leftarrow$) indicates a data transfer, to register A for this case. The "ADD(B,C)" construct indicates that registers B and C are sent to a combinational logic unit (CLU) that performs the addition. Comments begin with an exclamation mark (!) and terminate at the end of the line. The GOTO construct indicates a transfer of control. For this case, control is transferred to statement 10 if bit 12 of register IR is true, otherwise control is transferred to the next higher numbered statement (6 for this case).

Figure 5-20 shows an HDL description of a modulo-4 counter. The counter produces the output sequence 00, 01, 10, 11 and then repeats as long as the input line x is 0. If the input line is set to 1, then the counter returns to state 0 at the end of the next clock cycle.

```
           ⎡ MODULE: MOD_4_COUNTER.
           ⎪ INPUTS: x.
Preamble  ⎨  OUTPUTS: Z[2].
           ⎪ MEMORY:
           ⎣

           ⎡ 0: Z ← 0,0;
           ⎪    GOTO {0 CONDITIONED ON x,
           ⎪          1 CONDITIONED ON x̄}.
           ⎪ 1: Z ← 0,1;
           ⎪    GOTO {0 CONDITIONED ON x,
           ⎪          2 CONDITIONED ON x̄}.
Statements⎨  2: Z ← 1,0;
           ⎪    GOTO {0 CONDITIONED ON x,
           ⎪          3 CONDITIONED ON x̄}.
           ⎪ 3: Z ← 1,1;
           ⎪    GOTO 0.
           ⎣

           ⎡ END SEQUENCE.
Epilogue  ⎨  END MOD_4_COUNTER.
           ⎣
```

Figure 5-20
HDL sequence for a resettable modulo-4 counter.

The comma is the catenation operator, and so the statement "$Z \leftarrow 0,0;$" assigns the two-bit pattern 00 to the two-bit output Z.

The HDL sequence is composed of three sections: the *preamble*, the *numbered statements*, and the *epilogue*. The preamble names the module with the "MODULE" keyword and declares the inputs with the "INPUTS" keyword, the outputs with the "OUTPUTS" keyword, and the arity (number of signals) of both, as well as any additional storage, with the "MEMORY" keyword (none for this example). The numbered statements follow the preamble. The epilogue closes the sequence with the key phrase "END SEQUENCE." The key phrase "END MOD_4_COUNTER" closes the description of the module. Anything that appears between "END SEQUENCE" and "END MOD_4_COUNTER" occurs *continuously*, independent of the statement number. There are no such statements for this case.

In translating an HDL description into a design, the process can be decomposed into separate parts for the control section and the data section. The control section deals with how transitions are made from one statement to another. The data section deals with producing outputs and changing the values of any memory elements.

We consider the control section first. There are four numbered statements, and so we will use four flip-flops, one for each statement, as illustrated in Figure 5-21. This is referred to as a **one-hot encoding** approach, because exactly one flip-flop holds a true value at any time. Although four states can be encoded using only two flip-flops, studies have shown that the one-hot encoding approach results in approximately the same circuit area when compared with a more densely encoded approach; more importantly, the transfers from one state to the next are generally simpler and can be implemented with shallow combinational logic circuits, which means that the clock rate can be faster for a one-hot encoding approach than for a densely encoded approach.

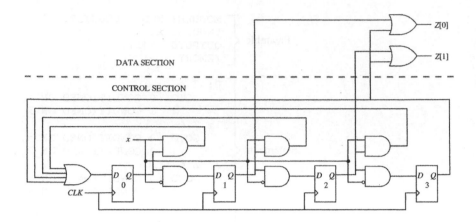

Figure 5-21
Logic design for a modulo-4 counter described in HDL.

In designing the control section, we first draw the flip-flops, apply labels as appropriate, and connect the clock inputs. The next step is to scan the numbered statements in numerical order and add logic as appropriate for the transitions. From statement 0, there are two possible transitions to statements 0 or 1, conditioned on x or its complement, respectively. The output of flip-flop 0 is thus connected to the inputs of flip-flops 0 and 1, through AND gates that take the value of the x input into account. Note that the AND gate leading into flip-flop 1 has a circle at one of its inputs, a notation that means x is complemented by an inverter before entering the AND gate.

A similar arrangement of logic gates is applied for statements 1 and 2, and no logic is needed at the output of flip-flop 3 because statement 3 returns to statement 0 unconditionally. The control section is now complete and can execute correctly on its own. No outputs are produced, however, until the data section is implemented.

We now consider the design of the data section, which is trivial for this case. Both bits of the output Z change in every statement, and so there is no need to condition the generation of an output on the state. We only need to produce the correct output values for each of the statements. The least significant bit of Z is true in statements 1 and 3, and so the outputs of the corresponding control flip-flops are ORed to produce $Z[0]$. The most significant bit of Z is true in statements 2 and 3, and so the outputs of the corresponding control flip-flops are ORed to produce $Z[1]$. The entire circuit for the mod-4 counter is now complete, as shown in Figure 5-21.

We can now use our HDL in describing the control section of the ARC microarchitecture. There is no need to design the data section, since we have already defined its form in Figure 5-10. The data section is the same for both the microcoded and hardwired approaches. As for the microcoded approach, the operations that take place for a hardwired approach are:

1. Fetch the next instruction to be executed from memory.

2. Decode the opcode.

3. Read operand(s) from main memory or registers, if any.

4. Execute the instruction and store the results.

5. Go to Step 1.

The microcode of Figure 5-15 can serve as a guide for what needs to be done. The first step is to fetch the next user-level instruction from main memory. The following HDL line describes this operation:

```
0: ir ← AND(pc, pc); Read = 1.
```

The structure of this statement is very similar to the first line of the microprogram, which may not be surprising since the same operations must be carried out on the same datapath.

Now that the instruction has been fetched, the next operation is to decode the opcode. This is where the power of a hardwired approach comes into play. Since every instruction has an op field, we can decode that field first, and then decode the op2, op3, and cond fields as appropriate for the instruction.

The next line of the control sequence decodes the op field:

```
1: GOTO {2 CONDITIONED ON IR[31]×IR[30],  ! Branch/Sethi format: op=00
         4 CONDITIONED ON IR[31]×IR[30],  ! Call format: op=01
         8 CONDITIONED ON IR[31]×IR[30],  ! Arithmetic format: op=10
        10 CONDITIONED ON IR[31]×IR[30]}. ! Memory format: op=11
```

The product symbol "×" indicates a logical AND operation. Control is thus transferred to one of the four numbered statements 2, 4, 8, or 10, depending on the bit pattern in the op field.

Figure 5-22 shows a complete HDL description of the control section. We may have to do additional decoding depending on the value of the op field. At line 4, which is for the Call format, no additional decoding is necessary. The call instruction is then implemented in statements 4-7, which are similar to the microcoded version.

In statement 2, additional decoding is performed on the op2 field, which is checked to determine if the instruction is sethi or a branch. Since there are only two possibilities, only one bit of op2 needs to be checked in line 2. Line 3 then implements sethi and line 19 implements the branch instructions.

Line 8 begins the Arithmetic format section of the code. Line 8 gets the second source operand, which can be either immediate or direct, and can be sign extended to 32 bits (for addcc) or not sign extended. Line 9 implements the Arithmetic format instructions, conditioned on the op3 field. The XNOR function returns true if its arguments are equal; otherwise it returns false, which is useful in making comparisons.

Line 10 begins the Memory format section of the code. Line 10 gets the second source operand, which can either be a register or an immediate operand. Line 11 decodes the op3 field. Since the only Memory format instructions are ld and st, only a single bit (IR[21]) needs to be observed in the op3 field. Line 12 then implements the ld instruction, and lines 13-18 implement the st instruction. Finally, line 20 increments the program counter and transfers control back to the first statement.

Now that the control sequence is defined, the next step is to design the logic for the control section. Since there are 21 statements, there are 21 flip-flops in the control section,

```
MODULE: ARC_CONTROL_UNIT.
INPUTS:
OUTPUTS: C, N, V, Z.   ! These are set by the ALU
MEMORY: R[16][32], pc[32], ir[32], temp0[32], temp1[32], temp2[32],
        temp3[32].

0: ir ← AND(pc, pc); Read ← 1;           ! Instruction fetch
   ! Decode op field
1: GOTO {2 CONDITIONED ON ir[31]×ir[30],    ! Branch/sethi format: op=00
         4 CONDITIONED ON ir[31]×ir[30],    ! Call format: op=01
         8 CONDITIONED ON ir[31]×ir[30],    ! Arithmetic format: op=10
        10 CONDITIONED ON ir[31]×ir[30]}.   ! Memory format: op=11
   ! Decode op2 field
2: GOTO 19 CONDITIONED ON ir[24].           ! Goto 19 if Branch format
3: R[rd] ← ir[imm22];                       ! sethi
   GOTO 20.
4: R[15] ← AND(pc, pc).                      ! call: save pc in register 15
5: temp0 ← ADD(ir, ir).                      ! Shift disp30 field left
6: temp0 ← ADD(ir, ir).                      ! Shift again
7: pc ← ADD(pc, temp0); GOTO 0.              ! Jump to subroutine
   ! Get second source operand into temp0 for Arithmetic format
8: temp0 ← { SEXT13(ir) CONDITIONED ON ir[13]×NOR(ir[19:22]),    ! addcc
   R[rs2] CONDITIONED ON ir[13]×NOR(ir[19:22]),                  ! addcc
   SIMM13(ir) CONDITIONED ON ir[13]×OR(ir[19:22]),  ! Remaining
   R[rs2] CONDITIONED ON ir[13]×OR(ir[19:22])}.  ! Arithmetic instructions
   ! Decode op3 field for Arithmetic format
9: R[rd] ← {
   ADDCC(R[rs1], temp0) CONDITIONED ON XNOR(IR[19:24], 010000),  ! addcc
   ANDCC(R[rs1], temp0) CONDITIONED ON XNOR(IR[19:24], 010001),  ! andcc
   ORCC(R[rs1], temp0) CONDITIONED ON XNOR(IR[19:24], 010010),   ! orcc
   ORNCC(R[rs1], temp0) CONDITIONED ON XNOR(IR[19:24], 010110),  ! orncc
   SRL(R[rs1], temp0) CONDITIONED ON XNOR(IR[19:24], 100110),    ! srl
   ADD(R[rs1], temp0) CONDITIONED ON XNOR(IR[19:24], 111000)};   ! jmpl
   GOTO 20.
   ! Get second source operand into temp0 for Memory format
10: temp0 ← {SEXT13(ir) CONDITIONED ON ir[13],
            R[rs2] CONDITIONED ON ir[13]}.
11: temp0 ← ADD(R[rs1], temp0).
   ! Decode op3 field for Memory format
   GOTO {12 CONDITIONED ON ir[21],                               ! ld
         13 CONDITIONED ON ir[21]}.                              ! st
12: R[rd] ← AND(temp0, temp0); Read ← 1; GOTO 20.
13: ir ← RSHIFT5(ir).
14: ir ← RSHIFT5(ir).
15: ir ← RSHIFT5(ir).
16: ir ← RSHIFT5(ir).
17: ir ← RSHIFT5(ir).
18: r0 ← AND(temp0, R[rs2]); Write ← 1; GOTO 20.
19: pc ← {  ! Branch instructions
    ADD(pc, temp0) CONDITIONED ON ir[28] + ir[28]×ir[27]×Z +
        ir[28]×ir[27]×ir[26]×C + ir[28]×ir[27]×ir[26]×ir[25]×N +
        ir[28]×ir[27]×ir[26]×ir[25]×V,
    INCPC(pc) CONDITIONED ON ir[28]×ir[27]×Z +
        ir[28]×ir[27]×ir[26]×C + ir[28]×ir[27]×ir[26]×ir[25]×N +
        ir[28]×ir[27]×ir[26]×ir[25]×V};
    GOTO 0.
20: pc ← INCPC(pc); GOTO 0.
END SEQUENCE.
END ARC_CONTROL_UNIT.
```

Figure 5-22
HDL description of the ARC control unit.

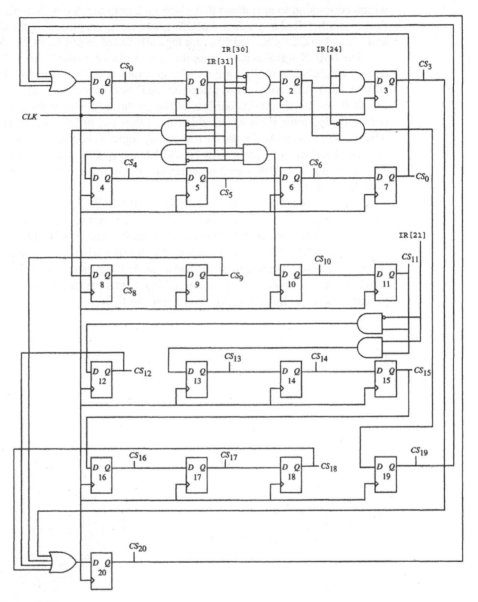

Figure 5-23
The hardwired control section of the ARC: generation of the control signals.

as shown in Figure 5-23. A control signal (CS_i) is produced for each of the 21 states, which is used in the data section of the hardwired controller.

In Figure 5-24, the data section of the hardwired controller generates the signals that control the datapath. There are 27 OR gates that correspond to the 27 signals that control the datapath. (Refer to Figure 5-10. Count the 27 signals that originate in the control section and terminate in the datapath.) The AMUX signal is set to 1 only in lines 9 and 11, which correspond to operations that place rs1 onto the A bus. Signals CS_9 and CS_{11} are thus logically ORed to produce AMUX. Likewise, rd is placed on the C bus in lines 3, 9, and 12, and so CS_3, CS_9, and CS_{12} are logically ORed to produce CMUX.

The BMUX signal is more complex. rs2 is placed on the B bus in lines 8, 10, and 18, and so CS_8, CS_{10}, and CS_{18} are used to generate BMUX as shown. However, in line 8, BMUX is set (indicating rs2 is placed on the B bus) only if IR[13] = 0 and IR[19:22] are all 0 (for the rightmost four bits of the six-bit op3 pattern for addcc: 010000). The corresponding logic is shown for this case. Likewise, in line 10, BMUX is set to 1 only when IR[13] = 0. Again, the corresponding logic is shown.

The Read signal is set in lines 10 and 12, and so CS_0 and CS_{12} are logically ORed to produce Read. The Write signal is generated only in line 18, and thus needs no logic other than the signal CS_{18}.

There are four signals that control the ALU: ALU[0], ALU[1], ALU[2], and ALU[3], which correspond to F_0, F_1, F_2, and F_3, respectively, in the ALU operation table shown in Figure 5-4. These four signals need values in each of the 20 HDL lines. In line 0, the ALU operation is AND, which corresponds to ALU[3:0] = 0101. Line 1 has no ALU operation specified, and so we can arbitrarily choose an ALU operation that has no side effects, like AND (0101). Continuing in this way, taking CONDITIONED ON statements into account produces the logic for ALU[3:0] as shown in the figure.

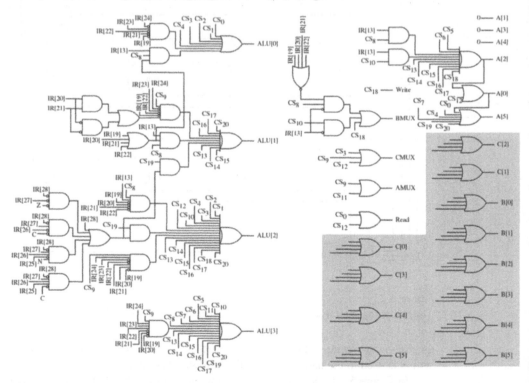

Figure 5-24
The hardwired control section of the ARC: signals from the data section of the control unit to the datapath. (Shaded areas are not detailed here.)

The control signals are sent to the datapath similarly to the way that the MIR controls the datapath in the microprogrammed approach of Figure 5-10. The hardwired and micro-controlled approaches can thus be considered interchangeable, except with varying costs. There are only 21 flip-flops in the hardwired approach, but there are 2048×41 = 83,968 flip-flops in the microprogrammed approach (although in actuality, a ROM would be used, which consumes less space because smaller storage elements than flip/flops can be used). The amount of additional combinational logic is comparable. The hardwired approach is faster in executing ARC instructions, especially in decoding the Branch format instructions, but is more difficult to change once it is committed to fabrication.

EXAMPLE 5-2   Hardwiring the `subcc` Instruction

Consider adding the `subcc` instruction from the previous example (Section 5.3.2) to the hardwired implementation of the ARC instruction set. As before, the `subcc` instruction uses the Arithmetic format and an `op3` field of 001100.

Only line 9 of the HDL code needs to be changed, by inserting the expression:

```
ADDCC (R[rs1], INC_1(temp0)) CONDITIONED ON XNOR(IR[19:24],
001100), ! subcc
```

before the line for `addcc`.

The corresponding signals that need to be modified are `ALU[3:0]`. The `INC_1` construct in the line above indicates that an adder CLU, which would be defined in another HDL module, should be created (in a hardwired control unit, there is a lot of flexibility in what can be done).

■

■ 5.5 CASE STUDY: THE VHDL HARDWARE DESCRIPTION LANGUAGE

In this section we cover a brief overview of the VHDL hardware description language. Hardware description languages like VHDL and AHPL are used for describing computer hardware, and focus primarily on logic devices and IC design. In the case of VHDL, however, designs can be specified at many different levels. For example, the control unit implemented in the previous section could be specified in VHDL.

We first cover the background that led to the development of VHDL, and then describe some of its properties. We then take a look at a VHDL specification of the majority function.

5.5.1 Background

VHDL was the result of a collaboration between the Department of Defense (DOD) and many US industries. DOD, primarily through its Defense Advanced Research Projects Agency (DARPA), realized in the late 1970s that IC design and fabrication was becoming so complex that a set of integrated design tools was needed for both design and simulation. It was felt that the tools should allow the user to specify a circuit or system from the highest or behavioral level down to the lowest levels of actual IC layout and design, and furthermore, all of these specifications should be verifiable by simulators and other rule checkers.

The first preliminary requirements definition for the language was issued by DOD in 1981, in recognition of the need for a more consistent approach to computer hardware design. The contract for the first version of the language was won by a consortium of IBM, Texas Instruments, and Intermetrics, a software engineering firm specializing in programming language design and implementation.

The consortium released a preliminary version for testing and comment in 1985. An updated version was submitted to the IEEE for standardization in 1986, the result being named IEEE 1076-1987. In 1993, a newer version, IEEE 1076-1993, was approved that addressed a number of minor problems and added several new features. The most current revision as of this writing is 1076-2000.

By almost any measure VHDL is a success, with many users both inside and outside the defense contractor community. DOD now requires that all application-specific integrated circuits (ASICs) be accompanied by their VHDL model for checking and simulation. Almost all CAD vendors now support VHDL in their toolsets.

5.5.2 What is VHDL?

In its most basic terms, VHDL is a hardware description language that can be used to describe and model digital systems. VHDL has an inherent sense of time, and can manage the progression of events through time. Unlike most procedural languages that are in common use, VHDL supports **concurrent execution**, and is **event driven**.

Concurrent execution

Concurrent execution means that unless special efforts are taken to specify sequential execution, all of the statements in a VHDL specification are executed in parallel. This is the way it should be, since when power is applied to a digital system the system runs "in parallel." That is, current flows through circuits according to the rules of physics and logic, without any inherent sense of "which came first."

Event-driven systems

VHDL deals with signals propagating through digital systems, and therefore logically and naturally supports the concept of changes in state as a function of time. Having a sense of time, it supports concepts such as "after," "until," and "wait." As an event-driven system, it begins execution by executing any initialization code and then records all changes in signal values, from $0 \rightarrow 1$ and $1 \rightarrow 0$, occurring at the inputs and outputs of components. It records these changes, or events, in a time-ordered queue known as the event queue. It examines these events and if an event has an effect upon some component, that effect is evaluated. If the effect causes further events to take place, the simulator likewise places these new events in the event queue, and the process continues until and unless there are no further events to process.

Levels of abstraction and hierarchical decomposition

As mentioned above, VHDL specifications can be written at almost any level of abstraction, from the purely algorithmic level, where behavior is specified by formal algorithms, to the logic level, where behavior is specified by Boolean expressions.

Furthermore, a VHDL specification may be composed of a hierarchy of components; that is, components may contain components that may themselves contain components. This models the physical world, where, for example, a motherboard may contain IC chips, which are composed of modules, which are in turn composed of submodules, all the way down to individual logic gates, and finally transistors.

5.5.3 A VHDL Specification of the Majority Function

Let us explore how VHDL can be used to implement a small digital component by examining several implementations of the **majority function**, which produces a 1 at its output when more than half of its inputs are 1, and otherwise produces a 0 at its output. This is a useful function for fault tolerance, in which multiple systems that perform the same operations on the same data set "vote," and if one of the systems deviates from the others, its output is effectively ignored. The majority function is discussed in detail in Appendix A. Its truth table is shown in Figures A-17 and A-18, reproduced here as Figure 5-25.

In VHDL the specification of any component such as the majority function is split into two parts, an **entity** part and an **architecture** part. These correspond roughly to the syntactic and semantic parts of a language specification: the entity part describes the interface of the component without saying anything about its internal structure. The architecture part describes the internal behavior of the component. Here is an entity specification for the three-input majority function.

Interface specification for the majority component

```
-- Interface
entity MAJORITY is
   port
       (A_IN, B_IN, C_IN : in BIT
        F_OUT            : out BIT);
   end MAJORITY;
```

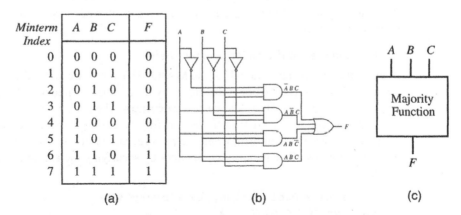

(a)   (b)   (c)

Figure 5-25

The majority function: (a) truth table; (b) AND-OR implementation; (c) black-box representation.

Keywords are shown in bold, and comments begin with "--" and end at the end of the line. Statements are separated by semicolons, ";".

The **entity** specification describes just the "black-box" input and output signals in Figure 5-25c. The **port** declaration describes the kind of signals going into and out of the entity. Port modes include **in** for signals that flow into the entity, **out** for signals that flow out of the entity, and **inout** for bidirectional signals. There are also several other special-purpose port modes.

With the interface to the majority component specified we can now model the internal functioning of the component, using the **architecture** specification.

Behavioral model for the majority component

```
-- Body
architecture LOGIC_SPEC of MAJORITY is
begin
-- compute the output using a Boolean expression
F_OUT    <= (not A_IN and B_IN and C_IN) or
            (A_IN and not B_IN and C_IN) or
            (A_IN and B_IN and not C_IN) or
            (A_IN and B_IN and C_IN) after 4 ns;
end LOGIC_SPEC;
```

This model describes the relationship between the entity declaration of MAJORITY and the architecture of MAJORITY. The names A_IN, B_IN, C_IN, and F_OUT in the architecture model must match the names used in the entity declaration.

This kind of architectural specification is referred to as a behavioral one, since it defines the input/output function by specifying an explicit transfer function. That function is a Boolean expression that implements the Boolean function shown in Figure 5-25a,b. Notice, however, that even at this level of specification we can include a time delay between inputs and outputs, using the **after** keyword. In this case, the event computing the value of F_OUT will be triggered 4 ns after a change in any of the input values.

It is also possible to specify the architecture at a level closer to the hardware by specifying logic gates instead of logic equations. This is referred to as a structural model. Here is such a specification.

Structural model for the majority component

In generating a structural model for the MAJORITY entity we will follow the gate design given in Figure 5-25b. We begin the model by describing a collection of logic operators in a special construct of VHDL known as a **package**. The package is assumed to be stored in a working library called WORK. Following the package specification we repeat the **entity** declaration, and then, using the package and entity declarations, we specify the internal workings of the majority component by specifying the architecture at a structural level.

```
-- Package declaration, in library WORK
package LOGIC_GATES is
component AND3
    port (A, B, C : in BIT; X : out BIT);
```

```
    end component;
component OR4
    port (A, B, C, D : in BIT; X : out BIT);
    end component;
component NOT1
    port (A : in BIT; X : out BIT);
    end component;

-- Interface
entity MAJORITY is
    port
        (A_IN, B_IN, C_IN : in BIT
         F_OUT           : out BIT);
end MAJORITY;

-- Body
-- Uses components declared in package LOGIC_GATES
-- in the WORK library
-- import all the components in WORK.LOGIC_GATES
use WORK.LOGIC_GATES.all
architecture LOGIC_SPEC of MAJORITY is
-- declare signals used internally in MAJORITY
signal A_BAR, B_BAR, C_BAR, I1, I2, I3, I4: BIT;
begin
-- connect the logic gates
NOT_1 : NOT1 port map (A_IN, A_BAR);
NOT_2 : NOT1 port map (B_IN, B_BAR);
NOT_3 : NOT1 port map (C_IN, C_BAR);
AND_1 : AND3 port map (A_BAR, B_IN, C_IN, I1);
AND_2 : AND3 port map (A_IN, B_BAR, C_IN, I2);
AND_3 : AND3 port map (A_IN, B_IN, C_BAR, I3);
AND_4 : AND3 port map (A_IN, B_IN, C_IN, I4);
OR_1 : OR3 port map (I1, I2, I3, I4, F_OUT);
end LOGIC_SPEC;
```

The **package** declaration supplies three gates: a three-input AND gate, AND3, a four-input OR gate, OR4, and a NOT gate, NOT1. The architectures of these gates are assumed to be declared elsewhere in the package. The **entity** declaration is unchanged, as we would expect, since it specifies MAJORITY as a "black box."

The body specification begins with a **use** clause that imports **all** of the declarations in the LOGIC_GATES package within the WORK library. The **signal** declaration declares seven BIT signals that will be used internally. These signals are used to interconnect the components within the architecture.

The instantiations of the three NOT gates follow, NOT_1, NOT_2, and NOT_3, all of which are NOT1 gates, and the mapping of their input and output signals are specified, following the **port map** keywords. Signals at the inputs and outputs of the logic gates are mapped according to the order in which they were declared within the package.

The rest of the body specification connects the NOT gates, the AND gates, and the OR gate together, as shown in Figure 5-25b.

Notice that this form of architecture specification separates the design and implementation of the logic gates from the design of the MAJORITY entity. It would be possible to have several different implementations of the logic gates in different packages and to use any one of them by merely changing the **uses** clause.

5.5.4 Nine-Value Logic System

This brief treatment of VHDL only gives a small taste of the scope and power of the language. The full language contains capabilities to specify clock signals and various timing mechanisms, sequential processes, and several different kinds of signals. There is an IEEE standard nine-value logic system, known as STD_ULOGIC, IEEE 1164-1993. It has the following logic values:

```
type STD_ULOGIC is (
    'U',    -- Uninitialized
    'X',    -- Forcing unknown
    '0',    -- Forcing 0
    '1',    -- Forcing 1
    'Z',    -- High impedance
    'W',    -- Weak unknown
    'L',    -- Weak 0
    'H',    -- Weak 1
    '-',    -- Don't care
);
```

Without getting into too much detail, these values allow the user to detect logic flaws within a design and to follow the propagation of uninitialized or weak signals through the design.

■ 5.6 CASE STUDY: WHAT HAPPENS WHEN A COMPUTER BOOTS UP?

When a computer boots up, it typically goes through two phases: power-on self-test (POST) and loading the operating system. Many integrated circuits have built-in self-test (BIST) hardware, and the POST invokes the BIST mechanisms and determines the health of the system before handing off control to the "bootstrap" mechanism that loads the operating system. The sequences described in the sections that follow will differ from one system to the next, but for the most part these steps need to happen regardless of the platform and configuration.

Power-On Self-Test (POST)

The POST outlined below is for desktop Intel-based machines but can be applied to other systems as well. Parameters such as the supervisor password, special device parameters, and disk drive search order for the operating system are generally configurable through a special keyboard sequence on bootup.

Intel vs. Motorola: Microprogramming in the 8086 and 68000

In the late 1970s, microprogramming enjoyed a significant edge over hardwiring in control unit design. Microprogramming is akin to assembly language programming, and microprogram assemblers were in common use. The microprogram design process was one of editing a microprogram, assembling it, downloading the results to an EPROM, an Erasable Programmable ROM that could be plugged into a socket, tested immediately, and bugs fixed immediately. New instructions could be added and tested with little impact on the existing control unit. Hardwiring had no such tools. VHDL and other hardware design languages were well in the future, as were programmable gate arrays. Prototyping meant building the design from existing small- and medium-scale integrated circuits such as decoders, etc., and each time the design changed, the digital logic of the control unit had to be rewired. Microprogramming was the tool of choice for control unit design; both Intel and Motorola used it in the development of their first 16-bit and16/32-bit microprocessors, respectively.

Intel used a vertical microprogram that consisted of 504 21-bit words. Fields of the microinstruction could be decoded and input to small hardwired functional units, lessening the time penalty imposed by having to access a microcontrol store. When hardware description languages and compilers became available, the x86 family was migrated to hardwired control. However even the Pentium III has an 8K × 72-bit microprogram to handle the more complex, less frequently used instructions.

Motorola used a more sophisticated two-level approach where a 10-bit field in the microinstruction could be used as a microbranch address or as input to another microcode control unit as a "nanoinstruction." The 68000 control store was appreciably larger than the 8086's partly because of the more complex instruction set but also because it used a wider word. At this period IBM was casting about for a way to regain dominance in the desktop computer market. Surprisingly, the IBM 370, which was renowned among mainframe computer users, had almost the same register set as the 68000—16 32-bit registers. This led IBM to develop a "370 on a desktop" using two Motorola 68000s re-microprogrammed to emulate the IBM 360's instruction set. Two were used because a single 68000's control store was too small to emulate the entire 370 instruction set. The result was known as the IBM PC XT/370. While the idea of a 370 on a desktop seemed appealing, buyers balked at the cost of software developed for the mainframe market.

1. The processor is tested. A **boundary scan** is done through special **JTAG** (Joint Test Action Group) pins by loading test vectors into the processor and observing the output. If the test fails then the system may stop.

2. The system ROMs are checked by performing a checksum over the ROMs.

3. The DMA controller is checked.

4. The interrupt controller is checked.

5. The system timing chip, which provides clocking for the processor and buses, is checked.

6. The video card is checked.

7. The expansion cards are initialized, and any code or data that is needed by the drivers is copied from the expansion card ROMs into memory. (Note that this code and data is not the system drivers, which are loaded in the operating system phase.)

8. RAM is counted and tested. If memory is added or removed, this is the step that figures out how much memory the system has available. There are ROM-based parameters on the RAM chips that describe the configuration of the chips, timing, and other information that are checked in this step.

9. The keyboard, mouse, and other peripherals are tested.

10. The location of the operating system (on a hard disk, CD-ROM, etc.) is determined and the operating system loader is invoked.

At this point, the hardware has been tested, and the next step is to load the operating system.

Loading the Operating System

The boot process for the operating system goes through similar steps for common platforms. Here, we cover the process for Windows XP and Red Hat Linux.

After the POST finishes, the BIOS (Basic Input/Output System) performs system checks and then looks for an operating system. This is the point at which a choice is made as to which operating system is loaded, of which there may be several. The BIOS looks for a Master Boot Record (MBR) starting at the first sector on the first hard drive, loads its contents into memory, and then passes control to it.

For Windows XP, what the BIOS finds is the NTLDR file (a historical name for the older Windows NT loader), which is copied from the hard disk (or CD-ROM or other device) into the system memory. Note that NTLDR is not the Windows XP operating system itself, but is responsible for loading the operating system.

The NTLDR program invokes a rudimentary file system to read the BOOT.INI file, which is located in the root (top level) of the main disk drive. BOOT.INI holds parameters for the available operating systems, of which one must be chosen either by the user or by default in NTLDR.

Next, NTLDR invokes the NTDETECT.COM program, which scans the I/O space, detects devices, and passes this information back to NTLDR. This information is used later in the boot process when Windows selects device drivers to load.

Finally, NTLDR loads and passes control to WIN.COM, which is the Windows operating system.

For Linux, the boot process is not all that different. After the POST finishes, the BIOS performs system checks and then looks for an operating system. For the case of Windows, as described above, what the BIOS finds is the NTLDR file that loads the Windows operating system. For the case of Linux, the BIOS will generally find the LInux LOader (LILO), or GRand Unified Bootloader (GRUB). The BIOS then passes control to either LILO or GRUB, which we will use here.

In the default Red Hat Linux configuration, GRUB uses settings in the MBR to display boot options in a menu that the operator can change at boot time. After making any boot option changes, the operator then exits the menu and GRUB hands off control to the Linux operating system, which goes through its initialization sequence before opening up login sessions for users.

There are several tasks that the operating system starts up and manages, such as device-driver loading, starting the file systems, and networking. Although different operating systems may do things differently, the same types of tasks need to take place in a similar (although not exact) sequence.

Summary

A microarchitecture consists of a datapath and a control section. The datapath contains data registers, an ALU, and the connections among them. The control section contains registers for microinstructions (for a microprogramming approach) and for condition codes, and a controller. The controller can be microprogrammed or hardwired. A microprogrammed controller interprets microinstructions by executing a microprogram that is stored in a control store. A hardwired controller is organized as a collection of flip-flops that maintains state information, and combinational logic that implements transitions among the states.

The hardwired approach is fast, and consumes a small amount of hardware in comparison with the microprogrammed approach. The microprogrammed approach is flexible, and simplifies the process of modifying the instruction set. The control store consumes a significant amount of hardware, which can be reduced to a degree through the use of nanoprogramming. Nanoprogramming adds delay to the microinstruction execution time. The choice of microprogrammed or hardwired control thus involves trade-offs: the microprogrammed approach is large and slow, but is flexible and lends itself to simple implementations, whereas the hardwired approach is small and fast, but is difficult to modify, and typically results in more complicated implementations.

Problems

5.1 Design a one-bit arithmetic logic unit (ALU) using the circuit shown in Figure 5-26 that performs bitwise addition, AND, OR, and NOT on the one-bit inputs A and B. A one-bit output Z is produced for each operation, and a carry is also produced for the case of addition. The carry is zero for AND, OR, and NOT. Design the one-bit ALU using the components shown in the diagram. Just draw the connections among the components. Do not add any logic gates, MUXes, or anything else. Note: The Full Adder takes two one-bit inputs (X and Y) and a Carry In, and produces a Sum and a Carry Out.

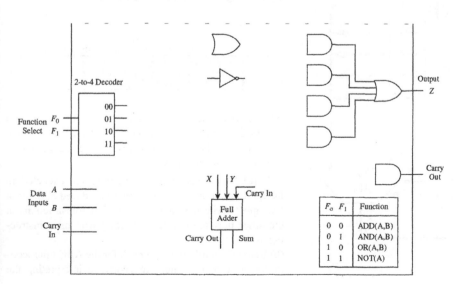

Figure 5-26
A one-bit ALU.

5.2 Design an ALU that takes two eight-bit operands X and Y and produces an eight-bit output Z. There is also a two-bit control input C in which 00 selects logical AND, 01 selects OR, 10 selects NOR, and 11 selects XOR. In designing your ALU, follow this procedure: (1) draw a block diagram of eight one-bit ALUs that each accept a single bit from X and Y and both control bits, and produce the corresponding single-bit output for Z; (2) create a truth table that describes a one-bit ALU; (3) design one of the one-bit ALUs using an 8-to-1 MUX.

5.3 Design a control unit for a simple hand-held video game in which a character on the display catches objects. Treat this as an FSM problem in which you show only the state transition diagram. Do not show a circuit. The input to the control unit is a two-bit vector in which 00 means "Move Left," 01 means "Move Right," 10 means "Do Not Move," and 11 means "Halt." The output Z is 11 if the machine is halted and is 00, 01, or 10 otherwise, corresponding to the input patterns. Once the machine is halted, it must remain in the halted state indefinitely.

5.4 In Figure 5-3, there is no line from the output of the C Decoder to %r0. Why is this the case?

5.5 Refer to the diagram in Figure 5-27. Registers 0, 1, and 2 are general-purpose registers. Register 3 is initialized to the value +1; this can be changed by the microcode, but you must make certain that it does not get changed.

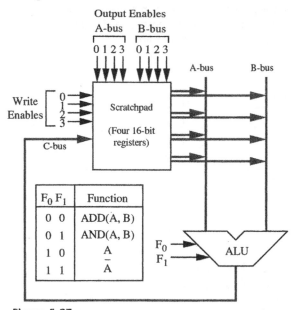

Figure 5-27
A small microarchitecture.

a) Write a control sequence that forms the two's complement difference of the contents of registers 0 and 1, leaving the result in register 0. Symbolically, this might be written as r0 ← r0 − r1. Do not change any registers except r0 and r1 (if needed). Fill in the table shown below with 0s or 1s (use 0s when the choice of 0 or 1 does not matter) as appropriate. Assume that, when no registers are selected for the A-bus or the B-bus, the bus takes on a value of 0.

Write Enables				A-bus enables				B-bus enables				F_0 F_1	Time
0	1	2	3	0	1	2	3	0	1	2	3		
													0
													1
													2

b) Write a control sequence that forms the exclusive-OR of the contents of registers 0 and 1, leaving the result in register 0. Symbolically, this might be written as r0 ← XOR(r0, r1). Use the same style of solution as for part (a).

5.6 Write the binary form for the microinstructions shown below. Use the style shown in Figure 5-17. Use the value 0 for any fields that are not needed.

```
60: R[temp0] ← ORN(R[0],R[temp0]);
    IF Z THEN GOTO 64;
61: R[rd] ← INC(R[rs1]);
```

5.7 Three binary words are shown below, each of which can be interpreted as a microinstruction. Write the mnemonic version of the binary words using the microassembly language introduced in this chapter.

A	A	B	B	C	C X D R	ALU	COND	JUMP ADDR
M		M		M				
U		U		U R W				
A	X	B	X	C	X D R	ALU	COND	JUMP ADDR
100101	0	000000	0	100001	0 0 0	1100	000	00000000000
000000	1	100001	0	100001	0 0 0	1000	110	11100000001
000000	1	000000	1	100001	0 0 0	1000	101	11100010010

5.8 Rewrite the microcode for the `call` instruction starting at line 1280 so that only three lines of microcode are used instead of four. Use the LSHIFT2 operation once instead of using ADD twice.

5.9 (a) How many microinstructions are executed in interpreting the `subcc` instruction introduced in the first Example? Write the numbers of the microinstructions in the order they are executed, starting with microinstruction 0.

(b) Using the hardwired approach for the ARC microcontroller, how many states are visited in interpreting the addcc instruction? Write the states in the order they are executed, starting with state 0.

5.10 (a) List the microinstructions that are executed in interpreting the ba instruction.
(b) List the states (Figure 5-22) that are visited in interpreting the ba instruction.

5.11 Register %r0 can be designed using only tri-state buffers. Show this design.

5.12 What bit pattern should be placed in the C field of a microword if none of the registers are to be changed?

5.13 A control unit for a machine tool is shown in Figure 5-28. You are to create the microcode for this machine. The behavior of the machine is as follows: If the Halt input A is ever set to 1, then the output of the machine stays halted forever and outputs a perpetual 1 on the X line and 0 on the V and W lines. A waiting light (output V) is enabled (set to 1) when no inputs are enabled. That is, V is lit when the A, B, and C inputs are 0, and the machine is not halted. A bell is sounded ($W=1$) on every input event ($B=1$ and/or $C=1$) except when the machine is halted. Input D and output S can be used for state information for your microcode. Use 0s for any fields that do not matter. Hint: Fill in the lower half of the table first.

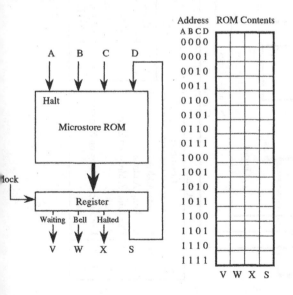

Figure 5-28
Control unit for a machine tool.

5.14 For this problem, you are to extend the ARC instruction set to include a new instruction by modifying the microprogram. The new ARC instruction to be microcoded is:

xorcc — Perform an exclusive OR on the operands, and set the condition codes accordingly. This is an Arithmetic format instruction. The op3 field is 010011.

Show the new microinstructions that will be added for xorcc.

5.15 Show a design for a four-word register stack, using 32-bit registers of the form shown below:

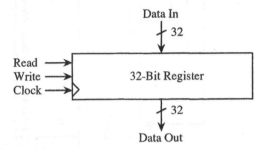

Four registers are stacked so that the output of the top register is the input to the second register, which outputs to the input of the third, which outputs to the input of the fourth. The input to the stack goes into the top register, and the output of the stack is taken from the output of the top register (*not* the bottom register). There are two additional control lines, push and pop, that cause data to be pushed onto the stack or popped off the stack, respectively, when the corresponding line is 1. If neither line is 1, or if both lines are 1, then the stack is unchanged.

5.16 In line 1792 of the ARC microprogram, the conditional GOTO appears at the end of the line, but in line 8 it appears at the beginning. Does the position of the GOTO within a microassembly line matter?

5.17 A microarchitecture is shown in Figure 5-29. The datapath has four registers and an ALU. The control section is a finite state machine in which there is a RAM and a register. For this microarchitecture, a compiler translates a high-level program directly into microcode; there is no intermediate assembly language form, and so there are no instruction fetch or decode cycles.

For this problem, you are to write the microcode that implements the instructions listed below. The microcode should be stored in locations 0, 1, 2, and 3 of the RAM. Although there are no lines that show it, assume that the n and z bits are both 0 when $C_0C_1 = 00$. That is, A_{23} and A_{22} are both 0 when there is no possible jump. Note: Each bit of the A, B, and C fields corresponds directly to a register. Thus, the pattern 1000 selects register R3, *not* register 8,

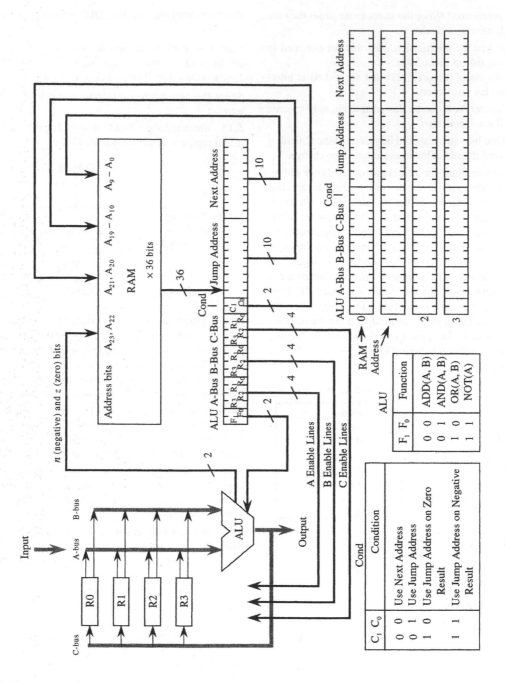

Figure 5-29
An example microarchitecture.

which does not exist. There are some complexities with respect to how branches are made in this microarchitecture, but you do not need to be concerned with how this is done in order to generate the microcode.

```
0: R1 ← ADD(R2, R3)
1: Jump if negative to (15)₁₀
2: R3 ← AND(R1, R2)
3: Jump to (20)₁₀
```

5.18 In line 2047 of the ARC microprogram shown in Figure 5-15, would the program behave differently if the "GOTO 0" portion of the instruction is deleted?

5.19 In **horizontal microprogramming**, the microwords are wide, whereas in **vertical microprogramming** the words are narrow. In general, horizontal microwords can be executed quickly, but require more space than vertical microwords, which take more time to execute. If we make the microword format shown in Figure 5-11 more horizontal by expanding the A, B, and C fields to contain a single bit for each of the 38 registers instead of a coded six-bit version, then we can eliminate the A, B, and C decoders shown in Figure 5-3. This allows the clock frequency to be increased, but also increases the space for the microstore.

(a) How wide will the new horizontal microword be?

(b) By what percentage will the microstore increase in size?

5.20 Refer to Figure 5-7. Show the ALU LUT_0 and ALU LUT_x $(x > 0)$ entries for the INC(A) operation.

5.21 On some architectures, there is special hardware that updates the PC, which takes into account the fact that the rightmost two bits are always 0. There is no special hardware presented in this chapter for updating the PC, and the branch microcode in lines 2–20 of Figure 5-15 has an error in how the PC is updated on line 12 because branch displacements are given in terms of words. Identify the error and explain how to fix it.

Further Reading

(Wilkes, 1958) is a classic reference on microprogramming. (Mudge, 1978) covers microprogramming on the DEC PDP 11/60. (Hill and Peterson, 1987) gives a tutorial treatment of the AHPL hardware description language. (Lipsett et al., 1989) and (Navabi, 1993) describe the commercial VHDL hardware description language and provide examples of its use. (Gajski, 1988) covers various aspects of silicon compilation.

Gajski, D., *Silicon Compilation*, Addison Wesley (1988).

Hill, F. J., and Peterson, G. R., *Digital Systems: Hardware Organization and Design*, 3/e, John Wiley & Sons (1987).

Lipsett, R., Schaefer, C., and Ussery, C., *VHDL: Hardware Description and Design*, Kluwer Academic Publishers (1989).

Mudge, J. Craig, *Design Decisions for the PDP11/60 Mid-Range Minicomputer*, in *Computer Engineering, A DEC View of Hardware Systems Design*, Digital Press, Bedford MA (1978).

Navabi, Z., *VHDL: Analysis and Modeling of Digital Systems*, 2/e, McGraw Hill (1997).

Wilkes, M. V., Redwick, W., and Wheeler, D., "The design of a control unit of an electronic digital computer," *Proc. IRE*, **105**, p. 21 (1958).

CHAPTER 6

LANGUAGES
AND THE MACHINE

In the last chapter we looked at the relationship among the ISA, the assembly language, and the machine language. We also saw in some detail how instructions effected register transfers and the movement of data between memory and the CPU, but we touched only briefly on the actual process of assembly and program linking and loading. In this chapter we widen our view of the relationships between computer languages and the machines on which they run.

We begin by discussing *compilation*, which is the process of translating a program written in a high-level language into a functionally equivalent program in assembly-language. Following that, we discuss the process of *assembly*, which is the translation of an assembly language program into a functionally equivalent machine-language program. We then discuss *linking*, which is the process of linking together separately assembled modules into a single program, and *loading*, which is the process of moving programs into memory and preparing them for execution. Following that, we discuss the use of assembly language *macros*, which can be thought of as akin to assembly-time procedures, with the exception that they are placed inline, or expanded, in the assembly language program at every location where they are invoked.

Following this discussion we show several ways to quantitatively estimate machine performance, and following that we treat some of the ways in which modern hardware improves performance over the simple fetch-execute model that is the basis of Chapter 4. We first discuss the differences between the *CISC* and *RISC* machine models, and how and why the RISC model arose. As we shall see, one reason the RISC model is so advantageous is that it supports the *pipelining* of instructions. We also discuss a feature unique to the SPARC family of processors, *register windows*.

■ 6.1 THE COMPILATION PROCESS

As we will see later in the chapter, the process of assembling an assembly language program into machine code is rather straightforward because there is a one-to-one mapping between assembly language statements and the equivalent machine binary codes. High-level languages, on the other hand, present a much more complex problem.

6.1.1 Steps in Compilation

Consider a simple assignment statement

```
A = B + 4;
```

The compiler is faced with a number of fairly complex tasks in converting this statement into one or more assembly language statements:

- Reducing the program text to the basic symbols of the language, for example into identifiers such as A and B, denotations such as the constant value 4, and program delimiters such as = and +. This portion of compilation is referred to as **lexical analysis**.

- Parsing the symbols to recognize the underlying program structure. In the sample statement above, for example, the **parser** must recognize the statement as being an assignment statement of the form
    Identifier "=" Expression,
  where Expression is further parsed into the form
    Identifier "+" Constant.
  Parsing is sometimes called **syntactic analysis**.

- Name analysis: associating the names A and B with particular program variables, and further associating them with particular memory locations where the variables will be located at run time.

- Type analysis: determining the types of all data items. In the case above, the variables A and B and constant 4 would be recognized as being of type int in some languages. Name and type analysis are sometimes referred to together as **semantic analysis**: determining the underlying meaning of program components.

- **Action mapping** and **code generation**: associating program statements with their appropriate assembly language sequence. In the statement above, the assembly language sequence might be as follows:

```
                    ! Simple assignment statement
ld [B], %r0, %r1    ! get variable B into a register
add %r1, 4, %r2     ! compute the value of the expr.
st %r2, %r0, [A]    ! make the assignment
```

- There are additional steps that the compiler must take such as allocating variables to registers, tracking register usage, and, should the programmer desire it, optimizing the program.

6.1.2 The Compiler Mapping Specification

When the compiler itself is being created, information about the particular ISA must be embedded into it. (Note that the ISA on which the compiler executes does not need to be the same as the ISA code that the compiler generates, a process known as **cross compilation**.) This embedding is sometimes called the **mapping specification** for the compiler. For example, the compiler writer must decide how to map variables and constants of various types into the machine's resources. This may be a function of both the machine and the high-level language. In the C language, for example, integers (ints) can be 16, 32, or some other number of bits in size, while Java specifies that all ints are 32 bits in size. The example in the previous section, if considered for the C language, maps integers to ARC 32-bit words.

The compiler writer must also take into account the features and limitations of the machine when mapping high-level language constructs to assembly language statements or statement sequences. For example, the ARC instruction set requires that all arithmetic operands must be either immediate constants or register variables. Therefore the compiler must generate code to place all variables into registers before any arithmetic instructions can be executed. This is the reason for the instruction:

```
ld [B], %r0, %r1
```

in the example above.

In this text we concentrate on the mapping of common high-level language constructs to their equivalent assembly language constructs, leaving the details of lexical and syntactic and semantic analysis to compiler texts. (Several compiler texts are described in the Further Reading section at the end of this chapter for the interested reader.)

6.1.3 How the Compiler Maps the Three Instruction Classes into Assembly Code

Now consider in detail the mapping of the three instruction classes, data movement, arithmetic, and control flow, from high-level language into assembly language. In the discussion and examples below we will use C as the example language. We choose C because of its popularity and because its syntax and semantics, while certainly high level, are still fairly close to assembly language concepts. The reader who is unfamiliar with C should not be distracted by this choice; the syntax and semantics of C are easy to understand and carry over to other high-level languages.

C Language standards and storage allocation

The C language was developed in the 1970s by Brian Kernighan and Dennis Ritchie at what was then Bell Laboratories. The first standardization of C was by the American National Standards Institute, ANSI C. It was adopted as an international standard in 1990. It may surprise some to learn that ANSI C does not specify the size of an int, only that it be a minimum of 16 bits. Most implementations of ANSI C specify that ints are 32 bits in size. The Portable Operating System Interface (POSIX) C standard, adopted internationally in 2001, was an attempt to tighten up some of the less well-defined aspects of ANSI C. It attempts to be vendor, operating system, and architecture independent. POSIX ints are 32 bits. The char character variable is an eight-bit value.

Variable storage in memory

In the example above and in most of the programming examples in this text, it has been assumed that variables can be accessed directly by their name, which is mapped to a memory location that is known at the time the program is assembled, sometimes called "assembly time." In the example above, A = B + 4, it is assumed that the variables A and B have addresses that are known when the statement is compiled. In fact, only **global variables**, known as **static variables** in C, have addresses that are known at compile time. Variables declared inside of functions or inside of blocks that are not explicitly declared as static or global only come into existence when the function or block is entered, and they disappear when the function or block is exited for the last time. These variables are called **local** or (in C), **automatic variables**. In most programs, local variables are actually much more common than global variables.

Given this ephemeral nature of local variables, a natural way of implementing them is on a last-in/first-out stack as described in Chapter 4. Variables that are stored on the stack come into existence when the stack frame is created and the function is called, and they disappear when the function is exited for the last time. While the previous chapter employed the stack pointer (%sp) to access the stack frame, it is also common to copy the contents of %sp into another register called the frame pointer %fp (also known as the base pointer) upon entry into the function, and then to use %fp to access variables on the stack frame for the duration of the function's life. This is because temporary variables may be continually pushed and popped onto and off of the stack during the lifetime of the function, resulting in a changing offset between %sp and the items on the stack frame. Using %fp means that the compiler can define a constant offset between %fp and a value stored on the stack that will remain fixed for the life of the frame.

Register-based addressing is used to access stack variables. For example, an ARC variable located on the stack at a location 12 bytes below %fp can be loaded into register %r1 by the instruction:

```
ld [%fp - 12], %r1.
```

The use of register-based addressing thus allows the address arithmetic "add the contents of %fp to -12" to be performed in a single instruction. Register-based addressing is so common that all popular instruction sets contain that addressing mode. Some instruction sets contain even more complicated addressing modes to assist in accessing complex data structures that are stored in the stack frame.

To emphasize the point, variables that are stored on the stack have memory addresses that are not known until run time. Their compile-time addresses are known as offsets from %fp. It is only at function entry time that the actual memory address of the value is known. Thus even though stack variable addresses such as [%fp-12] are much more common than global variable addresses such as A, we will assume global variables are used in the discussion below because of the greater ease in understanding the relationship between the high-level language variable name and the address as specified in assembly language. With that provision, let us now proceed to discuss three classes of program statements: data movement, arithmetic, and control flow.

6.1.4 Data movement

In addition to simple scalar variables, that is, variables that represent a single value, most programming languages provide various kinds of more complex data structures, including fixed record structures such as the C `struct` data type, which is similar to the Pascal **record**, and the array data type common in most programming languages. In this context these variables are known as **aggregates**.

Structures

An example of a C `struct` is the representation of a point in three-dimensional space having integer coordinates x, y, and z. In C this structure could be declared as:

```
struct point {
    int x;
    int y;
    int z;
}
```

An instance of this struct would be defined by the C statement

```
struct point pt;
```

Having defined point pt, the programmer can now refer to the individual components of pt by notation such as pt.x, which refers to the x component of struct pt. The compiler would lay out this structure in memory as three consecutive memory locations.

The memory address of the entire structure is taken to be the lowest or base address of the structure, so the x component would be located at address pt, the y component at address pt + 4, and the z component at address pt + 8. Thus the y component of pt would be loaded into register %r1 by the instruction

```
ld [pt + 4], %r1    ! %r1 ← y
```

Arrays

Most programming languages also allow the declaration of arrays of objects, that is, collections of identical components that can be referred to either individually or collectively. In C an array of ten integers can be defined with:

```
int A[10];
```

This definition would result in a collection of ten integers, indexed from 0 to 9.

The components of a struct must be explicitly named at programming time, for example, pt.z. References such as pt.i where i is a variable whose name is not determined until run time are not allowed. With arrays, on the other hand, the array index can be computed at run time. For example, the programmer may specify array element A[i], where i is a variable whose value is computed at run time and may assume any integer value from 0 through 9. Whereas in C the index of the first element in the array always has an index of 0, other programming languages allow more flexibility. In Pascal, for example, array declarations such as:

```
A: array [-10..10] of integer
```

are permitted. This declaration would result in an array of 21 integers with indices running from –10 to +10.

Accessing array elements presents a more complicated issue because of this need to compute the index at run time and the possibility that indices may not begin with 0. The general expression for computing the machine address of an array element at run time is given by:

$$\text{ElementAddress} = \text{BASE} + (\text{INDEX} - \text{START}) * \text{SIZE}$$

where BASE is the starting address of the array, INDEX is the index of the desired element, START is the starting index of the array, and SIZE is the size of an individual element in bytes. Thus element 5 in the Pascal array declared above would have an address of A + (5 − (−10))*4 = A + 60. In ARC assembly language, assuming BASE in %r2, INDEX in %r3, START in %r4, and SIZE = 4, the code to load an array value into memory would be given by

```
sub %r3, %r4, %r6        ! %r6 ← INDEX - START
sll %r6, 2, %r6          ! %r6 ← %r6 X 4
ld [A + %r6], %r1        ! %r1 ← array value
```

(sll is "shift left logical," which shifts %r6 two bits to the left is this example, bringing in two 0s on the right.) Note that it costs three instructions to access an array element, and more if SIZE is not a power of 2. Also note that in the C programming language, which specifies that START = 0, one machine instruction is saved for each array access. This may result in a considerable savings in scientific and engineering calculations, where heavy array references are common.

Pointers

It is a myth that pointers were designed to confuse college freshmen. Pointers are indispensable when writing programs that use data structures. A pointer is a variable whose contents are the *address* of a variable. We will translate a small C program that uses pointers into ARC assembly language to clarify how pointers work. The program below is taken from Kernighan and Ritchie's landmark book on C, referenced at the end of this chapter. The following operators are used when dealing with these matters:

```
a = b;     // Assignment. M[a] ← M[b]
a = &b;    // M[a] ← b
a = *c;    // M[a] ← M[M[c]]
```

The program fragment is:

```
int x = 1;
int y = 2;
int z[10];
int *ip;   // ip is a pointer to int.
ip = &x;   // ip now points to x.
y = *ip;   // y is now 1.
*ip = 0;   // x is now 0.
ip = &z[0]; // ip now points to z[0]
```

This program translates into ARC assembly language as follows, assuming for convenience that all addresses are less than 4096:

```
x: 1                     ! int x = 1;
y: 2                     ! int y = 2;
z: .dwb 10               ! int z[10];
ip:                      ! int ip;

                         ! ip = &x;
or %r0, x, %r1           ! %r1 ← address of x
st %r1, [ip]             ! M[ip] ← %r1, the addr of x
```

```
                       ! y = *ip;
    ld [ip], %r2       ! %r2 ← M[ip], which is addr of x
    ld [%r2], %r3      ! %r3 ← M[%r2], which is M[x]
    st %r3, [y]        ! y ← M[x], which is 1

                       ! *ip = 0;
    ld [ip], %r4       ! %r4 ← M[ip], which is addr of y
    st %r0, 0, [%r4]   ! M[%r4] ← 0, i.e. M[y] ← 0

                       ! ip = &z[0];
    or %r0, z, %r5     ! %r5 ← address of z
    st %r5, [ip]       ! M[ip] ← %r5, which is addr of z
```

This example points out one of the places where having "a few simple addressing modes" means that more instructions need to be executed to accomplish a given activity.

6.1.5 Arithmetic Instructions

Arithmetic instructions are mapped pretty much as expected according to their usage. There is a possible complication in load-store machines such as ARC and commercial RISC machines, however. Regardless of how many registers a machine has, there is always the possibility that the compiler will encounter an arithmetic expression that requires more registers than are available. In this case the compiler must temporarily store variables on the stack, a so-called "register spill." Compilers use sophisticated techniques to decide which registers are available, using a graph-theoretic technique known as register coloring, and to decide when a register is no longer needed to store a particular value, which is known as "live-dead analysis."

6.1.6 Program Control Flow

Most ISAs use unconditional and conditional branches, and the CPU arithmetic flags to implement program control flow structures. In this section we consider the mapping of the most common control flow statements.

The goto statement

The most trivial control flow statement is the goto statement, goto Label, which is simply implemented by the ba (branch always) unconditional branch:

```
    ba Label
```

The if-else statement

The C if-else statement has the syntax

```
    if (expr) stmt1 else stmt2;
```

which has the meaning, "If expr yields a value of true, execute stmt1, otherwise execute stmt2." Thus the compiler must generate code that evaluates the truth of expr, and then at runtime, the machine executes one or the other of the two statements depending upon the truth or falsity of the expression. Assume for brevity in the example below that expr is

(`%r1 == %r2`); using the `bne` (branch if not equal) instruction, the code to implement the if-else statement is:

```
          subcc %r1, %r2, %r0     ! set flags, discard result
          bne Over
          !stmt1 code
          ba End                  ! exit if-else
Over:     !stmt2 code
End:      ! ...
```

Notice that the sign of the conditional branch `bne` (branch if *not equal*) is the inverse of the expression (`%r1 == %r2`), *equals*. This is because the code falls through to the `stmt1` code if the condition is met, and must branch around this code if the condition is not met.

The `while` statement

The C `while` statement has the syntax:

```
while (expr) stmt;
```

The statement means, "Evaluate `expr`. If it is true, execute `stmt`, and repeat this process until `expr` evaluates to false." The assembly language mapping of this statement has the interesting feature that the most efficient mapping has the expression evaluation code following the statement code. Consider the C `while` statement:

```
while (%r1 == %r2) %r3 = %r3 + 1;
```

where again we use register variables to simplify the code. This statement is efficiently implemented as:

```
          ba Test
True:     add %r3, 1, %r3
Test:     subcc %r1, %r2, %r0
          be True
```

The reader can verify that placing the expression evaluation code below the statement code is more efficient than having the expression evaluation code above the statement code.

The `do-while` statement

C also has a do-while statement with the syntax:

```
do stmt while (expr);
```

This statement works like the `while` statement above except that `stmt` is always executed once prior to testing `expr`. It is implemented exactly like the `while` statement above except that the first `ba` instruction is eliminated.

The `for` statement

The C `for` statement has the syntax:

```
for (expr1; expr2; expr3) stmt;
```

The C language definition says that this statement is equivalent to:

```
expr1;
while (expr2) {
    stmt
    expr3;
}
```

Thus it is implemented exactly like the `while` statements above, with the addition of code for `expr1` and `expr3`.

■ 6.2 THE ASSEMBLY PROCESS

The process of translating an assembly language program into a machine language program is referred to as the **assembly process**. The assembly process is straightforward and rather simple, since there is a straightforward one-to-one mapping of assembly language statements to their machine language counterparts. This is in opposition to compilation, for example, in which a given high-level language statement may be translated into a number of computationally equivalent machine language statements.

While assembly is a straightforward process, it is tedious and error-prone if done by hand. In fact, the assembler was one of the first software tools developed after the invention of the digital electronic computer.

Commercial assemblers provide at least the following capabilities:

- Allow the programmer to specify the run-time location of data values and programs. (Most often, however, the programmer would not specify an absolute starting location for a program, because the program will be moved around, or relocated, by the linker and perhaps the loader, as discussed below.)

- Provide a means for the programmer to initialize data values in memory prior to program execution.

- Provide assembly-language mnemonics for all machine instructions and addressing modes, and translate valid assembly language statements into their equivalent machine language binary values.

- Permit the use of symbolic labels to represent addresses and constants.

- Provide a means for the programmer to specify the starting address of the program, if there is one. This capability is used only when writing programs for small, stand-alone systems. Programs written to run in multiprogramming environments, under the control of virtual-memory operating systems such as desktop and large computer systems, relegate the assignment of absolute addresses to the program loader and the operating system.

- Provide a degree of assemble-time arithmetic.

- Include a mechanism that allows variables to be defined in one assembly language program and used in another, separately assembled program.

```
! This program adds two numbers
        .begin
        .org 2048
main:   ld      [x], %r1          ! Load x into %r1
        ld      [y], %r2          ! Load y into %r2
        addcc   %r1, %r2, %r3     ! %r3 ← %r1 + %r2
        st      %r3, [z]          ! Store %r3 into z
        jmpl    %r15 + 4, %r0     ! Return
x:      15
y:      9
z:      0
        .end
```

Figure 6-1

A simple ARC program adds two numbers. Note that "ta 0" should be used instead of the jmpl line when returning to the ARCTools monitor.

- Provide for the expansion of **macro routines**, that is, routines that can be defined once and then instantiated as many times as needed.
- Provide the capability of specifying separate segments, or sections, to isolate code from initialized and uninitialized data, and certain other blocks of various kinds. We will discuss this in detail in Section 6.2.4.

We shall illustrate how the assembly process proceeds by "hand assembling" a simple program from ARC assembly language into ARC machine language. The program we will assemble is similar to Figure 4-21, reproduced for convenience as Figure 6-1. In assembling this program we use the ARC encoding formats shown in Figure 4-16, reproduced here as Figure 6-2. The figure shows the encoding of ARC machine language. That is, it specifies the target binary machine language of the ARC computer that the assembler must generate from the assembly language text.

6.2.1 Assembly and Two-Pass Assemblers

Most assemblers pass over the assembly language text twice, and are referred to as "two-pass assemblers." The first pass is dedicated to determining the addresses of all data items and machine instructions and selecting which machine instruction should be produced for each assembly language instruction (but not yet generating machine code).

The addresses of data items and instructions are determined by employing an assembly-time analog to the Program Counter, referred to as the **location counter.** The location counter keeps track of the address of the current instruction or data item as assembly proceeds. It is generally initialized to 0 at the start of the first pass, and is incremented by the size of each instruction. The .org pseudo operation causes the location counter to be set to the value specified by the .org statement. For example, if the assembler encounters the statement

```
.org 1000
```

it would set the location counter to 1000, and the next instruction or data item would be assembled at that address. During this pass the assembler also performs any assembly-

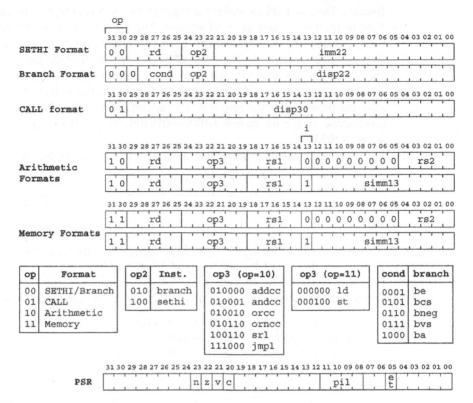

Figure 6-2

Instruction formats and PSR format for the ARC.

time arithmetic operations and inserts the definitions of all labels and constant values into a table, referred to as the **symbol table**.

The primary reason for requiring a second pass is to allow symbols to be used in the program before they are defined, which is known as **forward referencing**. After the first pass, the assembler will have identified and entered all symbols into its symbol table, and, during a second pass will generate the machine code, inserting the values of symbols which are then known.

Let us now hand assemble the program shown in Figure 6-1 into machine code. When the assembler encounters the first instruction,

```
ld      [x], %r1
```

it uses a pattern-matching process to recognize that it is a load instruction. Further pattern matching deduces that it is of the form "load *from* a memory address specified as a constant value (x in this case) plus the contents of a register (%r0 in this case) *into* a register (%r1 in this case)." This corresponds to the second Memory format shown in Figure 6-2. Examining this second Memory format, we find that the op field for this instruction (ld) is 11. The destination of this ld instruction goes in the rd field, which is 00001 for %r1 in this case. The op3 field is 000000 for ld, as shown in the op3 box below the Memory formats. The rs1 field identifies the register, %r0 in this case, that is added to the simm13 field to form the source operand address. The i bit comes next. Notice that the i bit is used to distinguish between the first Memory format (i=0) and the second (i=1). Therefore the i bit is set to 1. The simm13 field specifies the address of the label x, which appears five words after the first instruction. Since the first instruction occurs at location 2048, and since each word is composed of four bytes, the address of x is $5 \times 4 = 20$ bytes after the beginning of the program. The address of x is then $2048 + 20 = 2068$ which is represented by the bit pattern 0100000010100. This pattern fits into the signed 13-bit simm13 field.

The first line is thus assembled into the bit pattern shown below:

```
11 00001 000000 00000 1 0100000010100
└┘ └────┘ └────┘ └───┘ └┘ └──────────┘
op   rd    op3    rs1  i    simm13
```

The next instruction is similar in form, and the corresponding bit pattern is:

```
11 00010 000000 00000 1 0100000011000
└┘ └────┘ └────┘ └───┘ └┘ └──────────┘
op   rd    op3    rs1  i    simm13
```

The assembly process continues until all eight lines are assembled, as shown below:

```
ld [x], %r1          1100 0010 0000 0000 0010 1000 0001 0100
ld [y], %r2          1100 0100 0000 0000 0010 1000 0001 1000
addcc %r1,%r2,%r3    1000 0110 1000 0000 0100 0000 0000 0010
st %r3, [z]          1100 0110 0010 0000 0010 1000 0001 1100
jmpl %r15+4, %r0     1000 0001 1100 0011 1110 0000 0000 0100
15                   0000 0000 0000 0000 0000 0000 0000 1111
9                    0000 0000 0000 0000 0000 0000 0000 1001
0                    0000 0000 0000 0000 0000 0000 0000 0000
```

As a general approach, the assembly process is carried out by reading assembly language statements sequentially, from first to last, and generating machine code for each statement. As mentioned earlier, a difficulty with this approach is caused by forward referencing. Consider the program fragment shown in Figure 6-3. When the assembler sees the call statement, it does not yet know the location of sub_r since the sub_r label has not yet been seen. Thus the reference is entered into the symbol table and marked as unre-

```
            ⋮
      call  sub_r      ! Subroutine is invoked here
            ⋮
            ⋮
sub_r: st   %r1, [w]   ! Subroutine is defined here
            ⋮
            ⋮
```

Figure 6-3
An example of forward referencing.

solved. The reference is resolved when the definition of sub_r is found later in the program. The process of building a symbol table is described below.

6.2.2 Assembly and the Symbol Table

In the first pass of the two-pass assembly process, a **symbol table** is created. A symbol is either a label or a symbolic name that refers to a value used during the assembly process. The symbol table is generated in the first pass of assembly.

As an example of how a two-pass assembler operates, consider assembling the code shown earlier in Figure 4-22. Starting from the .begin statement, the assembler encounters the statement

```
.org 2048
```

This causes the assembler to set the location counter to 2048, and assembly proceeds from that address. The first statement encountered is

```
a_start    .equ    3000
```

An entry is created in the symbol table for a_start, which is given the value 3000. (Note that .equ statements do not generate any code, and thus are not assigned addresses during assembly.)

Assembly proceeds as the assembler encounters the first machine instruction:

```
ld  [length],  %r1
```

This instruction is assembled at the address specified by the location counter: 2048. The location counter is then incremented by the size of the instruction (four bytes) to 2052. Notice that when the symbol length is encountered the assembler has not seen any definition for it. An entry is created in the symbol table for length, but it is initially assigned the value "undefined," as shown by the "—" in Figure 6-4a.

The assembler then encounters the second instruction

```
ld  [address],  %r2
```

Symbol	Value
a_start	3000
length	—

(a)

Symbol	Value
a_start	3000
length	2092
address	2096
loop	2060
done	2088
a	3000

(b)

Figure 6-4
Symbol table for the ARC program shown in Figure 4-22, (a) after symbols a_start and length are seen, and (b) after completion.

It assembles this instruction at address 2052 and enters the symbol address into the symbol table, again setting its value to "undefined," since its definition has not been seen. It then increments the location counter by 4 to 2056. The andcc instruction is assembled at address 2056, and the location counter is incremented by the size of the instruction, again four bytes, to 2060. The next symbol that is seen is loop, which is entered into the symbol table with a value of 2060, the value of the location counter. The next symbol that is encountered that is not in the symbol table is done, which is also entered into the symbol table without a value, since it likewise has not yet been defined.

The first pass of assembly continues, and the unresolved symbols length, address, and done are assigned the values 2092, 2096, and 2088, respectively, as they are encountered. The label a is encountered, and is entered into the table with a value of 3000. The label done appears at location 2088 because there are 10 instructions (40 bytes) between the beginning of the program and done. Addresses for the remaining labels are computed in a similar manner. If any labels are still undefined at the end of the first pass, then an error exists in the program and the assembler will flag the undefined symbols and terminate.

After the symbol table is created, the second pass of assembly begins. The program is read a second time, starting from the .begin statement, but now object code is generated. The first statement that is encountered that causes code to be generated is ld at location 2048. The symbol table shows that the address portion of the ld instruction is $(2092)_{10}$ for the address of length, and so one word of code is generated using the Memory format as shown in Figure 6-5. The second pass continues in this manner until all of the code is

Location counter	Instruction		Object code
	.begin		
	.org	2048	
a_start	.equ	3000	
2048	ld	[length],%r1	11000010 00000000 00101000 00101100
2052	ld	[address],%r2	11000100 00000000 00101000 00110000
2056	andcc	%r3,%r0,%r3	10000110 10001000 11000000 00000000
2060 loop:	andcc	%r1,%r1,%r0	10000000 10001000 01000000 00000001
2064	be	done	00000010 10000000 00000000 00000110
2068	addcc	%r1,-4,%r1	10000010 10000000 01111111 11111100
2072	addcc	%r1,%r2,%r4	10001000 10000000 01000000 00000010
2076	ld	[%r4],%r5	11001010 00000001 00000000 00000000
2080	ba	loop	00010000 10111111 11111111 11111011
2084	addcc	%r3,%r5,%r3	10000110 10000000 11000000 00000101
2088 done:	jmpl	%r15+4,%r0	10000001 11000011 11100000 00000100
2092 length:		20	00000000 00000000 00000000 00010100
2096 address:		a_start	00000000 00000000 00001011 10111000
	.org	a_start	
3000 a:		25	00000000 00000000 00000000 00011001
3004		-10	11111111 11111111 11111111 11110110
3008		33	00000000 00000000 00000000 00100001
3012		-5	11111111 11111111 11111111 11111011
3016		7	00000000 00000000 00000000 00000111
	.end		

Figure 6-5

Output from the second pass of the assembler for the ARC program shown in Figure 4-22.

translated. The assembled program is shown in Figure 6-5. Notice that the displacements for branch addresses are given in words, rather than in bytes, because the branch instructions multiply the displacements by four.

6.2.3 Final Tasks of the Assembler

After assembly is complete the assembler must add additional information to the assembled module for the linker and loader:

- The module name and size. If the execution model involves memory segments for code, data, stack, etc., then the sizes and identities of the various segments must be specified.

- The address of the start symbol, if one is defined in the module. Most assemblers and high-level languages provide a special reserved label that the programmer can use to indicate where the program should start execution. For example, C specifies that execution will start at the function named main(). In Figure 6-1 the label "main" is a signal to the assembler that execution should start at that location.

- Information about global and external symbols. The linker will need to know the addresses of any global symbols defined in the module and exported by it, and it will likewise need to know which symbols remain undefined in the module because they are defined as global in another module.

- Information about any library routines that are referenced by the module. Some libraries contain commonly used functionality such as math or other specialized functions. We will have more to say about library usage in the sections below.

- The values of any constants that are to be loaded into memory. Some loaders expect data initialization to be specified separately from the binary code.

- Relocation information. When the linker is invoked, most of the modules that are to be linked will need to be relocated as the modules are concatenated. The whole issue of module relocation is complicated because some address references can be relocated and others cannot. We discuss relocation later, but here we note that the assembler specifies which addresses can be relocated and which others cannot.

6.2.4 Programs for Embedded vs. Virtual Memory Systems

Up until now we have been implicitly assuming that our example programs are being written for small or embedded systems where the program being written is the only program resident in the machine. In this case the programmer may well need to specify the program origin as an absolute memory location, typically by either using a .org statement if the assembler allows it, or else by using a program header file that specifies the starting and perhaps other addresses where parts of the program and data should be located. As we have alluded, when a module is being written to be run as part of a larger program on a computer with a virtual memory (VM) operating system such as Windows, Unix, or Mac OS X, the situation gets more interesting, for two reasons.

First, in these kinds of OSs the memory management unit loads each program into its own memory space, with a starting address of 0; it "lives" only in that space, and is unaware of any other programs that might be running in *their* own address space. Second, the memory management unit can assign various protection modes to each program and program **segment** (described below). For example, a segment may be marked as read only—the program cannot modify objects stored in that segment. This is ideal for the segment containing the program itself, since by general agreement programs may not modify themselves. (Why? Because self-modifying programs are virtually impossible to debug due to their changing contents as the program executes.) Other segments may be read–write.

This leads to the concept of program **segments** and **segmentation**. Depending on the operating system, there may be a number of different segmentation schemes. One of the most common standardizes on four segments: **text**, where the program itself is stored, **data**, where initialized data is stored, **bss**, block started by symbol, where uninitialized data is stored, and possibly **rodata**, where read-only data is stored. The term "bss" was coined by IBM when they were designing the software for the IBM 7094 in the 1960s. Other segmentation schemes may include stack and heap segments. The text segment may also have read-only data stored in it, typically jump tables for switch and similar statements.

The syntax for specifying the beginning and end of a segment vary. Some assemblers require the pseudo-op:

```
segment .text
```

More commonly the pseudo-ops are specified without using the segment keyword, as shown below:

```
        .text
        ...
        add %r1, %r2, %r3
        ...
        .data
a:      10
b:      20
        ...
x:      .dwb 100
        ...
```

The module may have many segments of the same kind. For example, the programmer may have several data segments inside of a single text segment. This allows the programmer to define data values close to where they are used. The assembler employs a separate location counter for each segment. When the separately assembled modules are linked, the linker collects all instances of each segment into a single segment, all texts into one segment, all datas into one segment, etc.

Module and Program Relocation

When separately assembled or compiled programs are linked together, it is difficult or impossible for the programmer to know exactly where each module will be located after linking, as they are concatenated one after the other. For this reason most addresses are specified as being **relocatable** in memory, except perhaps for addresses such as I/O addresses, which may be fixed at an absolute memory location, and equated constants. For the same reason, most assemblers will begin assembly at the default address of 0. And because modern operating systems employ a form of virtual memory, where each program resides in its own address space, the linker will also begin its starting address at 0.

In the next section we discuss relocation in more detail. Here we merely note that it is the assembler's responsibility to mark symbols as being relocatable; if not so marked, then the symbols are considered **absolute** and will not be relocated by the linker. Whether a given symbol is relocatable or not depends upon both the assembly language and the operating system's conventions. In any case, this relocation information is included in the assembled module for use by the linker and/or loader in a **relocation dictionary**. Symbols that are relocatable are often marked with an "R" after their value in the assembler's listing file.

■ 6.3 LINKING AND LOADING

Most applications of any size will have a number of separately compiled or assembled modules. These modules may be generated by different programming languages or may be present in a library provided as part of the programming language environment or operating system. Each module must provide the information described above, so that they can be linked together for loading and execution.

A **linkage editor**, or **linker**, is a software program that combines separately assembled programs (called **object modules**) into a single program, called a **load module**. The linker resolves all global-external references and relocates addresses in the separate modules. The load module can then be loaded into memory by a **loader**, which may also need to modify addresses if the program is loaded at a location that differs from the loading origin used by the linker.

When all modules including those in the library are linked together at the same time this is referred to as **static linking**. It has the advantage that all library routines are found at link time or, if not found, a link error message can be issued. Static linking has the disadvantage that code for the various library routines is redundantly stored in many executable files. Another approach is to defer linking of library routines until the program is loaded. This is referred to as **dynamic linking.** This technique has become more popular. Both Unix and Microsoft Windows operating systems employ this technique. Microsoft calls their usage **dynamic link libraries (DLLs)**. We will have more to say about dynamic linking in Section 6.3.3.

6.3.1 Linking

In combining the separately compiled or assembled modules into a load module, the linker must:

- Resolve address references that are external to modules as it links them.
- Relocate each module by combining them end-to-end as appropriate. During this relocation process many of the addresses in the module must be changed to reflect their new location.
- Specify the starting symbol of the load module.

• If the memory module includes more than one memory segment, the linker must specify the identities and contents of the various segments.

6.3.2 Resolving External References

In resolving address references the linker needs to distinguish local symbol names (used within a single source module) from global symbol names (used in more than one module). This is accomplished by making use of the .global and .extern pseudo-ops during assembly. The .global pseudo-op instructs the assembler to mark a symbol as being available to other object modules during the linking phase. The .extern pseudo-op identifies a label that is used in one module but is defined in another. A .global is thus used in the module where a symbol is defined (such as where a subroutine is located) and a .extern is used in every other module that refers to it. Note that only address labels can be global or external: it would be meaningless to mark a .equ symbol as global or external, since .equ is a pseudo-op that is used during the assembly process only, and the assembly process is completed by the time that the linking process begins.

All labels referred to in one program by another, such as subroutine names, will have a line of the form shown below in the source module:

```
.global symbol1, symbol2, ...
```

All other labels are local, which means the same label can be used in more than one source module without risking confusion since local labels are not used after the assembly process finishes. A module that refers to symbols defined in another module should declare those symbols using the form:

```
.extern symbol1, symbol2, ...
```

As an example of how .global and .extern are used, consider the two assembly code source modules shown in Figure 6-6. Each module is separately assembled into an object module, each with its own symbol table, as shown in Figure 6-7. The symbol tables have an additional field that indicates if a symbol is global or external. Program main begins at

```
! Main program                         ! Subroutine library

       .begin                                  .begin
       .org   2048                      ONE  .equ     1
       .extern sub                           .org    2048
main: ld     [x], %r2                        .global sub
       ld     [y], %r3                 sub: orncc  %r0, %r3, %r3
       call   sub                            addcc  %r3, ONE, %r3
       jmpl   %r15 + 4, %r0                   addcc  %r2, %r3, %r3
   x: 105                                     jmpl   %r15 + 4, %r0
   y: 92                                      .end
       .end
```

Figure 6-6
A program calls a subroutine that subtracts two integers.

Symbol	Value	Global/ External	Reloc- atable
sub	–	External	–
main	2048	No	Yes
x	2064	No	Yes
y	2068	No	Yes

Main Program

Symbol	Value	Global/ External	Reloc- atable
ONE	1	No	No
sub	2048	Global	Yes

Subroutine Library

Figure 6-7
Symbol tables for the assembly code source modules shown in Figure 6-6.

location 2048, and each instruction is four bytes long, so x and y are at locations 2064 and 2068, respectively. The symbol sub is marked as external as a result of the .extern pseudo-op. As part of the assembly process the assembler includes header information in the module about symbols that are global and external so that they can be resolved at link time.

Relocation

Notice in Figure 6-6 that the two programs, main and sub, both have the same starting address, 2048. Obviously they cannot both occupy that same memory address. If the two modules are assembled separately there is no way for an assembler to know about the conflicting starting addresses during the assembly phase. In order to resolve this problem, the assembler marks symbols that may have their address changed during linking as **relocatable**, as shown in the Relocatable fields of the symbol tables in Figure 6-7. The idea is that a program that is assembled at a starting address of 2048 can be loaded at address 3000 instead, for instance, as long as all references to relocatable addresses within the program are increased by $3000 - 2048 = 952$. Relocation is performed by the linker so that relocatable addresses are changed by the same amount that the loading origin is changed, but absolute or non-relocatable addresses (such as the highest possible stack address, which is $2^{31} - 4$ for 32-bit words) stay the same regardless of the loading origin.

The assembler is responsible for determining which labels are relocatable when it builds the symbol table. It has no meaning to call an external label relocatable, since the label is defined in another module, so sub has no relocatable entry in the symbol table in Figure 6-7 for program main, but it is marked as relocatable in the subroutine library. The assembler must also identify code in the object module that needs to be modified as a result of relocation. Absolute numbers, such as constants (marked by .equ, or numbers that appear in memory locations, such as the contents of x and y, which are 105 and 92, respectively), are not relocatable. Memory locations that are positioned relative to a .org statement, such as x and y (not the contents of x and y!), are generally relocatable. References to fixed locations, such as a permanently resident graphics routine that may be hardwired into the machine, are not relocatable. All of the information needed to relocate a module is stored in the relocation dictionary contained in the assembled file, and is therefore available to the linker.

6.3.3 Loading

The **loader** is a software program that places the load module into main memory. Conceptually the tasks of the loader are not difficult. It must load the various memory segments with the appropriate values and initialize certain registers, such as the stack pointer %sp, and the program counter %pc, to their initial values.

If there is only one load module executing at any time, then this model works well. In modern operating systems, however, several programs are resident in memory at any time, and there is no way that the assembler or linker can know at which address they will reside. The loader must relocate these modules at load time by adding an offset to all of the relocatable code in a module. This kind of loader is known as a **relocating loader**. The relocating loader does not simply repeat the job of the linker: the linker has to combine several object modules into a single load module, whereas the loader simply modifies relocatable addresses within a single load module so that several programs can reside in memory simultaneously. A **linking loader** performs both the linking process and the loading process: it resolves external references, relocates object modules, and loads them into memory.

The linked executable file contains header information describing where it should be loaded, starting addresses, and possibly relocation information, and entry points for any routines that should be made available externally.

Modern operating systems rely on memory management to accomplish relocation by loading a segment base register with the appropriate base to locate the code (or data) at the appropriate place in physical memory. The **memory management unit (MMU)** adds the contents of this base register to all memory references. As a result, each program can begin execution at address 0 and rely on the MMU to relocate all memory references transparently.

Dynamic link libraries

Returning to dynamic link libraries, the concept has a number of attractive features. Commonly used routines such as memory management or graphics packages need be present at only one place, the DLL library. This results in smaller program sizes because each program does not need to have its own copy of the DLL code, as would otherwise be needed. All programs share the exact same code, even while simultaneously executing.

Furthermore, the DLL can be upgraded with bug fixes or feature enhancements in just one place, and programs that use it need not be recompiled or relinked in a separate step. These same features can also become disadvantages, however, because program behavior may change in unintended ways (such as running out of memory as a result of a larger DLL). The DLL library must be present at all times, and must contain the version expected by each program. Many Windows users have seen the cryptic message, "A file is missing from the dynamic link library." Complicating the issue in the Windows implementation, there are a number of locations in the file system where DLLs are placed. The more sophisticated user may have little difficulty resolving these problems, but the naive user may be baffled.

EXAMPLE 6-1 A Programming Example

Consider the problem of adding two 64-bit numbers using the ARC assembly language. We can store the 64-bit numbers in successive words in memory and then separately add the low- and high-order words. If a carry is generated from adding the low-order words, then the carry is added into the high-order word of the result. (See Problem 6.5 for the generation of the symbol table for this example, and Problem 6.6 for the translation of the assembly code in this example to machine code.)

Figure 6-8 shows one possible coding. The 64-bit operands A and B are stored in memory in a high-endian format, in which the most significant 32 bits are stored in lower memory addresses than the least significant 32 bits. The program begins by loading the high- and low-order words of A into %r1 and %r2, respectively, and then loading the high- and low-order words of B into %r3 and %r4, respectively. Subroutine add_64 is called, which adds A and B and places the high-order word of the result in %r5 and the low order word of the result in %r6. The 64-bit result is then stored in C, and the program returns.

Subroutine add_64 starts by adding the low-order words. If a carry is not generated, then the high-order words are added and the subroutine finishes. If a carry is generated from adding the low-order words, then it must be added into the high-order word of the result. If a carry is not generated when the high-order words are added, then the carry from the low-order word of the result is simply added into the high-order word of the result and the subroutine finishes. If, however, a carry is generated when the high-order words are added, then when the carry from the low-order word is added into the high-order word, the final state of the condition codes will show that there is no carry out of the high-order word, which is incorrect.

The condition code for the carry is restored by placing a large number in %r7 and then adding it to itself. The condition codes for n, z, and v may not have correct values at this point, however. A complete solution is not detailed here, but in short, the remaining condition codes can be set to their proper values by repeating the addcc just prior to the %r7 operation, taking into account the fact that the c condition code must still be preserved.

6.4 MACROS

If a stack-based calling convention is used, then a number of registers may frequently need to be pushed and popped from the stack during calls and returns. In order to push ARC register %r15 onto the stack, we need first to decrement the stack pointer (which is in %r14) and then copy %r15 to the memory location pointed to by %r14, as shown in the code below:

```
addcc  %r14, -4, %r14  ! Decrement stack pointer
st     %r15, [%r14]    ! Push %r15 onto stack
```

A more compact notation for accomplishing this might be:

```
! Perform a 64-bit addition: C ← A + B
! Register usage: %r1 - Most significant 32 bits of A
!                 %r2 - Least significant 32 bits of A
!                 %r3 - Most significant 32 bits of B
!                 %r4 - Least significant 32 bits of B
!                 %r5 - Most significant 32 bits of C
!                 %r6 - Least significant 32 bits of C
!                 %r7 - Used for restoring carry bit
          .begin                 ! Start assembling
          .global main
          .org  2048             ! Start program at 2048
main:     ld    [A], %r1         ! Get high word of A
          ld    [A+4], %r2       ! Get low word of A
          ld    [B], %r3         ! Get high word of B
          ld    [B+4], %r4       ! Get low word of B
          call  add_64           ! Perform 64-bit addition
          st    %r5, [C]         ! Store high word of C
          st    %r6, [C+4]       ! Store low word of C
                  .
                  .
                  .
          .org  3072             ! Start add_64 at 3072
add_64:   addcc %r2, %r4, %r6 ! Add low order words
          bcs   lo_carry         ! Branch if carry set
          addcc %r1, %r3, %r5 ! Add high order words
          jmpl  %r15 + 4, %r0 ! Return to calling routine
lo_carry: addcc %r1, %r3, %r5 ! Add high order words
          bcs   hi_carry         ! Branch if carry set
          addcc %r5, 1, %r5   ! Add in carry
          jmpl  %r15, 4, %r0  ! Return to calling routine
hi_carry: addcc %r5, 1, %r5   ! Add in carry
          sethi 0x3FFFFF, %r7 ! Set up %r7 for carry
          addcc %r7, %r7, %r0 ! Generate a carry
          jmpl  %r15 + 4, %r0 ! Return to calling routine
A:                    0          ! High 32 bits of 25
                      25         ! Low 32 bits of 25
B:                    0xFFFFFFFF ! High 32 bits of -1
                      0xFFFFFFFF ! Low 32 bits of -1
C:                    0          ! High 32 bits of result
                      0          ! Low 32 bits of result
          .end                   ! Stop assembling
```

Figure 6-8
An ARC program adds two 64-bit integers.

```
push   %r15               ! Push %r15 onto stack
```

The compact form assigns a new label (push) to the sequence of statements that actually carry out the command. The push label is referred to as a **macro**, and the process of translating a macro into its assembly language equivalent is referred to as **macro expansion**.

A macro can be created through the use of a **macro definition**, as shown for push in Figure 6-9. The macro begins with a .macro pseudo-op, and terminates with a .endmacro pseudo-op. On the .macro line, the first symbol is the name of the macro (push

```
! Macro definition for 'push'
.macro     push arg1          ! Start macro definition
addcc      %r14, -4, %r14     ! Decrement stack pointer
st         arg1, [%r14]       ! Push arg1 onto stack
.endmacro                     ! End macro definition
```

Figure 6-9
A macro definition for push.

here), and the remaining symbols are command-line arguments that are used within the macro. There is only one argument for macro push, which is arg1. This corresponds to %r15 in the statement "push %r15" or to %r1 in the statement "push %r1," etc. The argument (%r15 or %r1) for each case is said to be "bound" to arg1 during the assembly process.

Additional *formal* parameters can be used, separated by commas, as in:

```
.macro name arg1, arg2, arg3, ...
```

and the macro is then invoked with the same number of *actual* parameters:

```
name %r1, %r2, %r3, ...
```

The body of the macro follows the .macro pseudo-op. Any commands can follow, including other macros, or even calls to the same macro, which results in a recursive expansion at assembly time. The parameters that appear in the .macro line can replace any text within the macro body, and so they can be used for labels, instructions, or operands.

It should be noted that during macro expansion formal parameters are replaced by actual parameters using a simple textual substitution. Thus one can invoke the push macro with either memory or register arguments:

```
push %r1
```

or

```
push foo
```

The programmer needs to be aware of this feature of macro expansion when the macro is defined, lest the expanded macro contain illegal statements.

Additional pseudo-ops are needed for recursive macro expansion. The .if and .endif pseudo-ops open and close a conditional assembly section, respectively. If the argument to .if is true (at macro expansion time) then the code that follows, up to the corresponding .endif, is assembled. If the argument to .if is false, then the code between .if and .endif is ignored by the assembler. The conditional operator for the .if pseudo-op can be any member of the set $\{<, =, >, \geq, \neq, \text{ or } \leq\}$.

Figure 6-10 shows a recursive macro definition and its expansion during the assembly process. The expanded code sums the contents of registers %r1 through %rX and places the result in %r1. The argument X is tested in the .if line. If X is greater than 2, then the macro is called again, but with the argument X - 1. If the macro recurs_add is invoked with an argument of 4, then three lines of code are generated, as shown in the bottom of the figure. The first time that recurs_add is invoked, X has a value of 4. The macro is

```
! A recursive macro definition
.macro  recurs_add X            ! Start macro definition
.if     X > 2                   ! Assemble code if X > 2
        recurs_add  X - 1       ! Recursive call
.endif                          ! End .if construct
        addcc  %r1, %rX, %r1    ! Add argument into %r1
.endmacro                       ! End macro definition

recurs_add     4                ! Invoke the macro
        Expands to:
addcc   %r1, %r2, %r1
addcc   %r1, %r3, %r1
addcc   %r1, %r4, %r1
```

Figure 6-10
A recursive macro definition and the corresponding macro expansion.

invoked again with X = 3 and X = 2, at which point the first addcc statement is generated. The second and third addcc statements are then generated as the recursion unwinds.

As mentioned earlier, for an assembler that supports macros, there must be a macro expansion phase that takes place prior to the two-pass assembly process. Macro expansion is normally performed by a **macro preprocessor** before the program is assembled. The macro expansion process may be invisible to a programmer, however, since it may be invoked by the assembler itself. Macro expansion typically requires two passes, of which the first pass records macro definitions and the second pass generates assembly language statements. The second pass of macro expansion can be very involved, however, if recursive macro definitions are supported. A more detailed description of macro expansion can be found in (Donovan, 1972).

EXAMPLE 6-2   Programming Example: Adding a Network Interface Card

In this example, we explore an example of writing code that drives a **network interface card (NIC)**. A block diagram of the NIC is shown in Figure 6-11. Data is transferred one byte at a time between the system bus and the inbound and outbound registers, which connect the outbound and inbound queues to the network. A status register keeps track of the status of incoming and outgoing data. The NIC occupies three words in the memory address space: this is an example of memory mapped I/O, in which the NIC registers can be read and written as if they are actual memory locations, although they are not. The word at location 0x10000000 is used for incoming data, of which only the lowest-numbered-byte of the word (0x80000000) is used because all data passed through the NIC is handled one byte at a time. Location 0x80000010 is used for outgoing data with the same lowest numbered byte restriction. Location 0x80000100 is the status register, in which the three most significant bits of the lowest numbered byte have the following meaning when set to 1: Bit 7—a new byte is waiting to be read in the inbound register; Bit 6—the outbound register is ready to have new data written into it; Bit 5—more data is coming into the inbound register; Bit 4—more data will be written to the outbound register.

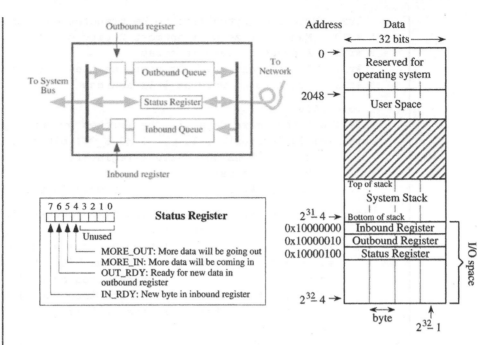

Figure 6-11
Block diagram of network interface card.

The program we will write is simplified because we will assume that we already know that data is ready to be sent or received, and because we can take full control over the CPU and the NIC without regard for other processes that may be running. In practice, an interrupt would signal the arrival of a packet of data. The operating system would transfer control to an interrupt handler, which would invoke the NIC driver, which contains code similar in function to the code here, although with more features.

Our goal is to write two subroutines named `writenic` and `readnic`, which can be placed in a dynamic link library for other programs to use.

For the `writenic` code, we are given a starting address and the length of data to be transferred in bytes in `%r8` and `%r9`, respectively. The code transfers one byte at a time in **network-byte order** (bytes are transferred in the order of their addresses, which has a side benefit of eliminating the big-/little-endian issue), checking the status register as each byte is transferred.

For the `readnic` code, we are given a starting address in `%r8` for where the data will be placed in memory. The length of data to be read is determined by the `MORE_IN` bit. During a `readnic` operation, we need to check that the `MORE_IN` bit is set, and then wait for the `IN_RDY` bit to be set before reading the next byte.

One possible coding for the `writenic` code is shown below:

```
! writenic - Write an array of bytes to a network
!  interface card (NIC)
! Register allocation:
! %r8 - Starting address of array
```

```
! %r9 - Number of bytes left to be transferred (length)
! %r10 - Mask that zeros rightmost 2 bits of 32-bit word
! %r11 - Address of byte in array
! %r12 - Address of word that contains the %r11 byte
! %r13 - Contents of word at %r12 address

        .org 2048
! Tell NIC that more data will be written by setting the
writenic: ld [status], %r10      ! MORE_OUT bit of status
        orcc %r10, MORE_OUT, %r10 ! register.
        st %r10, [status]
        ld [mask], %r10             ! Put mask in %r10

loop:   addcc %r8, %r9, %r11    ! Word align address for next
        andcc %r10, %r11, %r12  ! byte to be transferred,
        ld [%r12], %r13         ! then get the word into %r13.
        subcc %r11, %r12, %r11  ! Shift the byte to be
        be write                ! transferred by 0, 8, 16, or
        srl %r13, 8, %r13       ! 24 bits into the rightmost 8
        addcc %r11, -1, %r11    ! bits of %r13.
        be write
        srl %r13, 8, %r13
        addcc %r11, -1, %r11
        be write
        srl %r13, 8, %r13
write:  ld [status], %r12       ! Wait for OUT_RDY to be set
        andcc %r12, OUT_RDY, %r12
        be write
        st %r13, [out_reg]      ! Finally, write the byte
        addcc %r9, -1, %r9      ! Decrement length counter
        bne loop                ! Done?

        ld [status], %r12       ! Unset MORE_OUT
        andcc %r12, NOT_MORE_OUT, %r12
        st %r12, [status]
        jmpl %r15+4, %r0        ! Return to calling routine

mask: 0xFFFFFFFC
        .org 0x10000000
in_reg:                         ! in_reg is at 0x10000000
out_reg:                        ! out_reg is at 0x10000010
status:                         ! status is at 0x10000100

MORE_OUT      .equ 0x10
MORE_IN       .equ 0x20
OUT_RDY       .equ 0x40
IN_RDY        .equ 0x80
NOT_MORE_OUT  .equ 0xE0
```

The register allocation is shown in the comments at the top of the code. Six registers are used: %r8–%r13. The code can be made more efficient with fewer registers, but we will use the registers more liberally to help keep the relationships clear. The starting address of the array to be transferred is passed to writereg in %r8, along with the length of the array in %r9. A mask that is used in zeroing the rightmost two bits of a word is stored in %r10. The purpose is to form the address of a word that contains a given byte, given the byte address. Register %r11 holds the address of a byte in the array. Register %r12 holds the address of the word that contains the byte addressed in %r11. Register %r13 holds the 32-bit word at the %r12 address.

The code begins by setting the MORE_OUT bit of the status register, which tells the NIC to watch for the data we will start writing. Notice that three instructions are involved to load the contents of the status register into %r10 (which is arbitrarily chosen for this short task), set the MORE_OUT bit, and then write the result back to the status register. During this time, the operating system should not be allowed to interrupt this **critical region** of code, nor should the NIC try simultaneously to make a change to the status register. In practice, additional instructions are used to protect this region of code.

The mask 0xFFFFFFFC is loaded into %r10. We will later AND this mask with a 32-bit word to obtain a proper 32-bit word address, given a 32-bit byte address.

The main part of the code starts at loop. The address of the next byte to be transferred is computed in %r11, which is then turned into a word address in %r12. The 32-bit word that contains the 8-bit byte that we want to transfer is then loaded into %r13. The next several lines move the byte into the rightmost 8 bits of %r13.

At location write, the status register is loaded and the code **busy-waits** until the OUT_RDY bit is set by the NIC. Finally, the byte is written to the NIC with the st instruction. The length counter is decremented, and if the result is greater than 0 then the process repeats; otherwise the code "falls through," and the MORE_OUT bit is reset and the code returns to the calling routine via jmpl.

The readnic code is similar to the writenic code, but with complementary operations. Data is read from the NIC one byte at a time, into the rightmost eight bits of %r13, which is shifted left by 0, 8, 16, or 24 bits into its proper position before getting logically ORed into the corresponding word. One possible coding for readnic is shown below.

```
! readnic - Read an array of bytes from a network
! interface card (NIC)
! Register allocation:
! %r8 - Starting address where data will be placed
! %r9 - Byte index into array
! %r10 - Mask that zeros rightmost 2 bits of 32-bit word
! %r11 - Address of byte in array
! %r12 - Address of word that contains the %r11 byte
! %r13 - Holds byte to be transferred

        .org 3200
readnic: ld [mask], %r10 ! Put mask in %r10
        andcc %r0, %r0, %r9! Clear %r9
test1:ld [status], %r12! Is more data coming?
```

```
                    andcc %r12, MORE_IN, %r0
                    be done

        test2:andcc %r12, IN_RDY, %r0  ! Wait for data to be
              bne readbyte             ! ready.
              ld [status], %r12
              ba test2
        readbyte: ld [inreg], %r13     ! Read a byte from the NIC
                  addcc %r8, %r9, %r11   ! Compare byte and word
                  andcc %r10, %r11, %r12 ! addresses, and align byte
                  subcc %r11, %r12, %r11 ! to its proper word
                  be storeit             ! position.
                  srl %r13, 8, %r13
                  addcc %r11, -1, %r11
                  be storeit
                  srl %r13, 8, %r13
                  addcc %r11, -1, %r11
                  be storeit
                  srl %r13, 8, %r13

        storeit: ld [%r12], %r11       ! The new byte is ORed with
                 orcc %r11, %r13, %r11  ! the existing word.
                 st %r11, [%r12]
                 addcc %r9, 1, %r9      ! Increment byte index into
                 ba test1! array and do it again
        done: jmpl %r15+4, %r0
```

■

■ 6.5 QUANTITATIVE ANALYSES OF PROGRAM EXECUTION

Prior to the late 1970s, computer architects exploited improvements in integrated circuit technology by increasing the complexity of instructions and addressing modes, as the benefits of such improvements were thought to be obvious. It became an effective selling strategy to have more complex instructions and more complex addressing modes than a competing processor. Increases in architectural complexity catered to the belief that a significant barrier to better machine performance was the **semantic gap**—the gap between the meanings of high-level language statements and the meanings of machine-level instructions.

Unfortunately, as computer architects attempted to close the semantic gap, they sometimes made it worse. The IBM 360 architecture has the MVC (move character) instruction that copies a string of up to 256 bytes between two arbitrary locations. If the source and destination strings overlap, then the overlapped portion is copied one byte at a time. The runtime analysis that determines the degree of overlap adds a significant overhead to the execution time of the MVC instruction. Measurements show that overlaps occur only a few percent of the time and that the average string size is only eight bytes. In general, faster

Statement	Average Percent of Time
Assignment	47
If	23
Call	15
Loop	6
Goto	3
Other	7

Figure 6-12

Frequency of occurrence of instruction types for a variety of languages. The percentages do not sum to 100 due to roundoff. (Source: adapted from [Knuth, 1971].)

execution results when the MVC instruction is entirely ignored and instead its function is synthesized with simpler instructions. Although a greater number of instructions may be executed without the MVC instruction, on average, fewer clock cycles are needed to implement the copy operation without using MVC than by using it.

Long-held views began to change in 1971, when Donald Knuth published a landmark analysis of typical FORTRAN programs, showing that most of the statements are simple assignments. Later research by John Hennessy at Stanford University and David Patterson at the University of California at Berkeley confirmed that most complex instructions and addressing modes went largely unused by compilers. These researchers popularized the use of program analysis and benchmark programs to evaluate the impact of architecture upon performance.

Figure 6-12, taken from (Knuth, 1971), summarizes the frequency of occurrence of instructions in a mix of programs written in a variety of languages. Nearly half of all instructions are assignment statements. Interestingly, arithmetic and other "more powerful" operations account for only 7% of all instructions. Thus, if we want to improve the performance of a computer, our efforts would be better spent optimizing instructions that account for the greatest percentage of execution time rather than focusing on instructions that are inherently complex but rarely occur.

Related metrics are shown in Figure 6-13. From the figure, the number of terms in an assignment statement is normally just a few. The most frequent case (80%) is the simple variable assignment, $X \leftarrow Y$. There are only a few local variables in each procedure, and only a few arguments are normally passed to a procedure.

We can see from these measurements that the bulk of computer programs are very simple at the instruction level, even though more complex programs could potentially be created. This means that there may be little or no payoff in increasing the complexity of the instructions.

Discouragingly, analyses of compiled code showed that compilers usually did not take advantage of the complex instructions and addressing modes made available by computer architects eager to close the semantic gap. One important reason for this phenomenon is that it is difficult for a compiler to analyze the code in sufficient detail to locate areas where the new instructions can be used effectively, because of the great difference in

	Percentage of number of terms in assignments	Percentage of number of locals in procedures	Percentage of number of parameters in procedure calls
0	–	22	41
1	80	17	19
2	15	20	15
3	3	14	9
4	2	8	7
≥ 5	0	20	8

Figure 6-13
Percentages showing complexity of assignments and procedure calls. (Source: adapted from [Tanenbaum, 1999].)

meaning between most high-level language constructs and the expression of those constructs in assembly language. This observation, and the ever-increasing speed and capacity of integrated circuit technology, converged to bring about an evolution from complex instruction set computers (CISC) to reduced instruction set computers (RISC).

A basic tenet of current computer architecture is to make the frequent case fast, and this often means making it simple. Since the assignment statement happens so frequently, we should concentrate on making it fast (and simple as a consequence). One way to simplify assignments is to force all communication with memory into just two commands: LOAD and STORE. The LOAD/STORE model is typical of RISC architectures. We saw the LOAD/STORE concept in Chapter 4 with the `ld` and `st` instructions for the ARC.

By restricting memory accesses to LOAD/STORE instructions only, other instructions can only access data that is stored in registers. There are two consequences of this, both good and bad: (1) accesses to memory can easily be overlapped, since there are fewer side effects that would occur if different instruction types could access memory (this is good); and (2) there is a need for a large number of registers (this seems bad, but read on).

A simpler instruction set results in a simpler and typically smaller CPU, which frees up space on a microprocessor to be used for something else, like registers. Thus, the need for more registers is balanced to a degree by the newly vacant circuit area, or chip **real estate** as it is sometimes called. A key problem lies in how to manage these registers, which is discussed in Section 6.8.

6.5.1 Quantitative Performance Analysis

When we estimate machine performance, the measure that is generally most important is execution time, T. When considering the impact of some performance improvement, the effect of the improvement is usually expressed in terms of the **speedup**, S, taken as the ratio of the execution time without the improvement (T_{wo}) to the execution time with the improvement (T_w):

$$S = \frac{T_{wo}}{T_w}$$

For example, if adding a 1 MB cache module to a computer system results in lowering the execution time of some benchmark program from 12 seconds to eight seconds, then the speedup would be 12/8, = 1.5, or 50%. An equation to calculate speedup as a direct percent can be represented as:

$$S = \frac{T_{wo} - T_w}{T_w} \times 100$$

We can develop a more fine-grained equation for estimating T if we have information about the machine's clock period, τ, the number of clock cycles per instruction, CPI, and a count of the number of instructions executed by the program during its execution, IC. In this case the total execution time for the program is given by:

$$T = IC \times CPI \times \tau$$

CPI and IC can be expressed either as an average over the instruction set and total count, respectively, or summed over each kind and number of instructions in the instruction set and program. Substituting the latter equation into the former, we get:

$$S = \frac{IC_{wo} \times CPI_{wo} \times \tau_{wo} - IC_w \times CPI_w \times \tau_w}{IC_w \times CPI_w \times \tau_w} \times 100$$

These equations, and others derived from them, are useful in computing and estimating the impact of changes in instructions and architecture upon performance.

EXAMPLE 6-3 Calculating Speedup for a New Instruction Set

Suppose we wish to estimate the speedup obtained by replacing a CPU having an average CPI of 5 with another CPU having an average CPI of 3.5, with the clock period increased from 100 ns to 120 ns. The equation above becomes:

$$S = \frac{5 \times 100 - 3.5 \times 120}{3.5 \times 120} \times 100 = 19\%$$

Thus, without actually running a benchmark program we can estimate the impact of an architectural change upon performance.

∎

■ 6.6 FROM CISC TO RISC

Historically, when memory cycle times were very long and when memory prices were high, having fewer, complicated instructions held an advantage over more, simpler instructions. There came a point, however, when memory became inexpensive enough and memory hierarchies became fast and large enough that computer architects began reexamining this advantage. One technology that affected this examination was **pipelining**—that is, keeping the execution unit more or less the same, but allowing different instructions (which each require several clock cycles to execute) to use different parts of the execution unit on each clock cycle. For example, one instruction might be accessing operands in the **register file** (the set of data registers) while another is using the ALU.

We will cover pipelining in more detail in Section 6.7, but the important point to make here is that computer architects learned that CISC instructions do not fit pipelined architectures very well. For pipelining to work effectively, each instruction needs to have similarities to other instructions, at least in terms of relative instruction complexity. The reason can be viewed in analogy to an assembly line that produces different models of an automobile. For efficiency, each "station" of the assembly line should do approximately the same amount and kind of work. If the amount or kind of work done at each station is radically different for different models, then periodically the assembly line will have to "stall" to accommodate the requirements of the given model.

CISC instruction sets have the disadvantage that some instructions, such as register-to-register moves, are inherently simple, whereas others, such as the MVC instruction and others like it, are complex and take many more clock cycles to execute.

The main philosophical underpinnings of the RISC approach are:

- Prefetch instructions into an instruction queue in the CPU before they are needed. This has the effect of hiding the latency associated with the instruction fetch.

- With instruction fetch times no longer a penalty, and with cheap memory to hold a greater number of instructions, there is no real advantage to CISC instructions. All instructions should be composed of sequences of RISC instructions, even though the number of instructions needed may increase (typically by as much as 1/3 over a CISC approach).

- Moving operands between registers and memory is expensive and should be minimized.

- The RISC instruction set should be designed with pipelined architectures in mind.

- There is no requirement that CISC instructions be maintained as integrated wholes; they can be decomposed into sequences of simpler RISC instructions.

The result is that RISC architectures have characteristics that distinguish them from CISC architectures:

- All instructions are of fixed length, one machine word in size.

- All instructions perform simple operations that can be issued into the pipeline at a rate of one per clock cycle. Complex *operations* are now composed of simple *instructions* by the compiler.

- All operands must be in registers before being operated upon. There is a separate class of memory access instructions: LOAD and STORE. This is referred to as a LOAD-STORE architecture.

- Addressing modes are limited to simple ones. Complex addressing calculations are built up using sequences of simple operations.

- There should be a large number of general registers for arithmetic operations so that temporary variables can be stored in registers rather than on a stack in memory.

In the next few sections, we explore additional motivations for RISC architectures and special characteristics that make RISC architectures effective.

Intel vs. Motorola: Pentium vs. PowerPC 32-bit Architectures

The introduction of the IBM PC in 1981 lent legitimacy to the personal computer, which up to that point was viewed by many as a hobbyist toy. IBM selected the Intel 8088 microprocessor over the Motorola 68000 because it was the cheapest 16-bit microprocessor on the market at the time, even though it was crippled by an eight-bit data bus and a maximum of 1 MB of addressable memory, versus the 68000's 16-bit data bus and maximum of 16 MB of addressable memory. The design of the original PC copied that of the Apple II in many ways, including an audio cassette interface for data and program storage and a video interface that allowed it to be connected to a TV set.

Meanwhile, Apple Computer had been working on several new designs that would incorporate the Motorola 68000. Apple was pursuing designs that would incorporate a graphical user interface, or GUI, and they realized that only the 68000 had the processing power required for the advanced graphics. The original Macintosh computer was released in late 1983, to much acclaim and poor initial sales, probably due to the earlier release of the IBM PC and the perception, fostered at least partly by Apple's competitors, that the Mac was a "game machine," not suitable for serious computing. With a built-in 9″ black-and-white monitor and no capability for expansion, the reputation had some validity.

Both the IBM compatibles and the Macintosh family incorporated many incremental improvements to their microprocessors in the 1980s, culminating in the Motorola 68040 and the Intel 80486. At this point, once again, Intel and Motorola proceeded in totally different directions. Intel, certain that they could continue to make improvements to the x86 family, proceeded with development of the Pentium architecture, once again, mostly for reasons of upward binary compatibility. Apple and Motorola, convinced that the CISC architecture was a dead end, formed the AIM (Apple, IBM, Motorola) consortium, committed to creating a new RISC architecture based on the RISC IBM Power architecture.

Intel attacked the CISC bottleneck by breaking incoming CISC instructions into RISC-like "uops" that could be pipelined similarly to the way RISC instructions were pipelined. The AIM consortium developed the PowerPC, a "clean sheet of paper" RISC design, which sported 64-bit registers, simple, easy-to-decode one-word instructions, and from-the-ground-up support for virtual memory and other advanced concepts. By 1995, Apple had a new, fast, low-power microprocessor that used emulation, and so 68000 codes could run on the new PowerPC chips. Intel had an upwardly-compatible microprocessor that was also fast, but at the expense of much more power dissipation.

■ 6.7 PIPELINING THE DATAPATH

The flow of instructions through a pipeline follows the steps normally taken when an instruction is executed. In the discussion below we consider how three classes of instructions arithmetic, branch, and load-store—are executed, and then we relate this to how the instructions are pipelined.

6.7.1 Arithmetic, Branch, and Load-store Instructions

Consider the "normal" sequence of events when an **arithmetic instruction** is executed in a load-store machine:

1. Fetch the instruction from memory;

2. Decode the instruction (it is an arithmetic instruction, but the CPU has to find that out through a decode operation);

3. Fetch the operands from the register file;

4. Apply the operands to the ALU;

5. Write the result back to the register file.

There are similar patterns for other instruction classes. For **branch instructions** the sequence is:

1. Fetch the instruction from memory;

2. Decode the instruction (it is a branch instruction);

3. Fetch the components of the address from the instruction or register file;

4. Apply the components of the address to the ALU (address arithmetic);

5. Copy the resulting effective address into the PC, thus accomplishing the branch.

The sequence for **load and store instructions** is:

1. Fetch the instruction from memory;

2. Decode the instruction (it is a load or store instruction);

3. Fetch the components of the address from the instruction or register file;

4. Apply the components of the address to the ALU (address arithmetic);

5. Apply the resulting effective address to memory along with a read (load) or write (store) signal. If it is a write signal, the data item to be written must also be retrieved from the register file.

The three sequences above show a high degree of similarity in what is done at each stage: (1) instruction fetch, (2) decode, (3) operand fetch, (4) ALU operation, (5) result writeback.

Some architectures collapse phases four and five into a single fourth phase, "execute," with two subphases: ALU operation and writeback, as illustrated in Figure 6-14. The advantage of this approach is that the fifth phase, writeback, is not always needed. When it is not needed a bypass path can direct the flow of data directly to phase one of the next instruction, thus saving one clock cycle. For the sake of simplicity, in this discussion we will use a five-phase pipeline, whether or not it is actually needed.

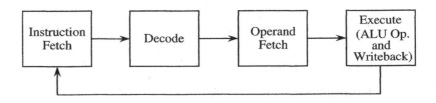

Figure 6-14
Four-stage instruction pipeline.

6.7.2 Pipelining Instructions

In practice, each CPU designer approaches the design of the pipeline from a different perspective, depending upon the particular design goals and instruction set. For example, the original SPARC implementation had only four pipeline stages, while some floating-point pipelines may have a dozen or more stages.

Each of the execution units performs a different operation in the fetch-execute cycle. After the Instruction Fetch unit finishes its task, the fetched instruction is handed off to the Decode unit. At this point, the Instruction Fetch unit can begin fetching the *next* instruction, which overlaps with the decoding of the previous instruction. When the Instruction Fetch and Decode units complete their tasks, they hand off the remaining tasks to the next units (Operand Fetch is the next unit for Decode). The flow of control continues until all units are filled.

6.7.3 Keeping the Pipeline Filled

Notice an important point: although it takes multiple steps to execute an instruction in this model, on average, one instruction can be executed per cycle as long as the pipeline stays filled. The pipeline does not stay filled, however, unless we are careful as to how instructions are ordered. We know from Figure 6-12 that approximately one in every four instructions is a branch. We cannot fetch the instruction that follows a branch until the branch completes execution. Thus, as soon as the pipeline fills, a branch is encountered, and then the pipeline has to be **flushed** by filling it with no-operations (NOPs). These NOPs are sometimes referred to as **pipeline bubbles**. A similar situation arises with the LOAD and STORE instructions. They generally require an additional clock cycle in which to access memory, which has the effect of expanding the Execute phase from one cycle to two cycles at times. The "wait" cycles are filled with NOPs.

Figure 6-15 illustrates the pipeline behavior during a memory reference and also during a branch for the ARC instruction set. The addcc instruction enters the pipeline on

	Time							
	1	2	3	4	5	6	7	8
Instruction Fetch	addcc	ld	srl	subcc	be	nop	nop	nop
Decode		addcc	ld	srl	subcc	be	nop	nop
Operand Fetch			addcc	ld	srl	subcc	be	nop
Execute				addcc	ld	srl	subcc	be
Memory Reference						ld		

Figure 6-15
Pipeline behavior during a memory reference and a branch.

```
    ┌── srl    %r3, %r5                     addcc %r1, 10, %r1
    │   addcc %r1, 10, %r1                  ld    [%r1], %r2
    │   ld    [%r1], %r2                     srl   %r3, %r5
    └─▶ nop                                  subcc %r2, %r4, %r4
        subcc %r2, %r4, %r4                  be    label
        be    label
```

(a)   (b)

Figure 6-16

SPARC code (a) with a nop inserted and (b) with srl migrated to nop position.

time step (cycle) 1. On cycle 2, the ld instruction, which references memory, enters the pipeline and addcc moves to the Decode stage. The pipeline continues filling with the srl and subcc instructions on cycles 3 and 4, respectively. On cycle 4, the addcc instruction is executed and leaves the pipeline. On cycle 5, the ld instruction reaches the Execute level, but does not finish execution because an additional cycle is needed for memory references. The ld instruction finishes execution during cycle 6.

Branch and Load Delay Slots

The ld and st instructions both require five cycles, but the remaining instructions require only four. Thus, an instruction that follows an ld or st should not use the register that is being loaded or stored. A safe approach is to insert a NOP after an ld or an st, as shown in Figure 6-16a. The extra cycle (or cycles, depending on the architecture) for a load is known as a **delayed load**, since the data from the load is not immediately available on the next cycle. A **delayed branch** is similar, as shown for the be instruction in cycles 5 through 8 of Figure 6-15. The position occupied by this NOP instruction is known as a **load delay slot** or **branch delay slot**, respectively.

It is often possible for the compiler to find a nearby instruction to fill the delay slot. In Figure 6-16a, the srl instruction can be moved to the position of the nop since its register usage does not conflict with the surrounding code and reordering instructions in this way does not affect the result. After replacing the nop line with the srl line, the code shown in Figure 6-16b is obtained. This is the code that is traced through the pipeline in Figure 6-15.

Speculative Execution of Instructions

An alternative approach to dealing with branch behavior in pipelines is simply to guess which way the branch will go and then undo any damage if the wrong path is taken. Statistically, loops are executed more often than not, and so it is usually a good guess to assume that a branch that exits a loop will not be taken. Thus, a processor can start processing the next instruction in anticipation of the direction of the branch. If the branch goes the wrong way, then the execution phase for the next instruction, and any subsequent instructions that enter the pipeline, can be stopped so that the pipeline can be flushed. This approach works well for a number of architectures, particularly those with slow cycle speeds or deep pipelines. For RISCs, however, the overhead of determining when a branch goes the wrong way and then cleaning up any side effects caused by wrong instructions entering the pipeline is generally too great. The nop instruction is normally used in RISC pipelines when something useful cannot be found to replace it.

Pipeline Hazards

Pipeline hazards are at least as problematical in keeping the pipeline filled as branch and load delays. A pipeline hazard is a situation where a result generated by an instruction is not available when it is needed by an instruction following it in the pipeline. The potential for pipeline hazards exists whenever several instructions are **in flight**, that is, in some stage of execution, at a time. Consider the program fragment in Figure 6-15. Examining Figure 6-14, we see that the `addcc` instruction updates the operand in `%r1` at the end of clock cycle 4. But the `ld` instruction following it needs its operand at the *beginning* of clock cycle 4. As with branch and load delays, one solution is to insert one or more pipeline bubbles to resolve the hazard, another is for the compiler to rearrange the code.

An optimizing compiler may be able to resolve some hazards if it "knows" the machine architecture, but this is not a good solution for several reasons. The compiler must be pessimistic about program flow, assuming that all branches take the worst possible direction, for example. The compiler can not know all of the possible architectures on which its output will run; buggy compilers could cause no end of problems.

As a result, hazards must be detected at run time, as the instruction stream enters the processor. One possible action the processor might take is to simply stall the pipeline stages behind the stage where the operand is being produced until the hazard is resolved. Another possible solution is to forward the operand directly to where it is needed rather than writing it back to the register file. A third, more radical solution is for the processor to rearrange instructions dynamically, resolving the hazard in that way. This **out-of-order execution** comes with its own set of problems, however. One of the most serious is when an instruction executing out of order generates an exception. As a result, the exception is also generated out of order.

EXAMPLE 6-4 **Analysis of Pipeline Efficiency**

In this example, we analyze the efficiency of a pipeline. A processor has a five-stage pipeline. If a branch is taken, then four cycles are needed to flush the pipeline. The branch penalty b is thus 4. The probability P_b that a particular instruction is a branch is .25. The probability P_t that the branch is taken is .5. We would like to compute the average number of cycles needed to execute an instruction, and the **execution efficiency**.

When the pipeline is filled and there are no branches, then the average number of cycles per instruction (CPI_{No_Branch}) is 1. The average number of cycles per instruction when there are branches is then:

$$CPI_{Avg} = (1 - P_b)(CPI_{No\_Branch}) + P_b[P_t(1 + b) + (1 - P_t)(CPI_{No\_Branch})]$$

$$= 1 + bP_bP_t.$$

After making substitutions, we have:

$$CPI_{Avg} = (1 - .25)(1) + .25[.5(1 + 4) + (1 - .5)(1)]$$

$$= 1.5 \text{ cycles.}$$

The execution efficiency is the ratio of the cycles per instruction when there are no branches to the cycles per instruction when there are branches. Thus we have:

$$\text{Execution efficiency} = (CPI_{No\_Branch})/(CPI_{Avg}) = 1/1.5 = 67\%$$

The processor runs at 67% of its potential speed as a result of branches, but this is still much better than the five cycles per instruction that might be needed without pipelining.

There are techniques for improving the efficiency. As stated above, we know that loops are usually executed more than once, so we can guess that a branch out of a loop will not be taken and be right most of the time. We can also run simulations on the non-loop branches, get a statistical sampling of which branches are likely to be taken, and then guess the branches accordingly. As explained above, this approach works best when the pipeline is deep or the clock rate is slow.

6.8 OVERLAPPING REGISTER WINDOWS

One modern architectural feature that has not been as widely adopted as other features (such as pipelining) is **overlapping register windows**, which to date has only been adopted by the SPARC family. This feature is based upon studies that show typical programs spend much of their time dealing with procedure call-and-return overhead, which involves passing parameters on a stack located in main memory in traditional architectures. The SPARC architecture reduces much of this overhead by employing multiple register sets that overlap. These registers are used for passing parameters between procedures, instead of using a stack in main memory.

Procedure calls may be deeply nested in an ordinary program, but for a given window of time, the nesting depth fluctuates within a narrow band. Figure 6-17 illustrates this behavior. For a nesting-depth window size of five, the window moves only 18 times for

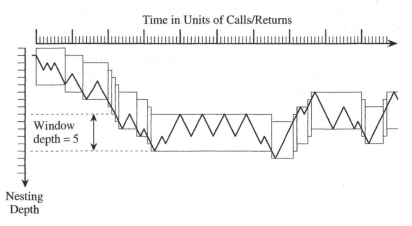

Figure 6-17

Call-return behavior as a function of nesting depth and time. (Source: adapted from [Stallings, 1996].)

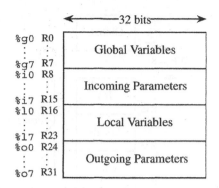

Figure 6-18
User's view of RISC I registers.

100 procedure calls. Results produced by a group at UC Berkeley (Tamir and Sequin, 1983) show that a window size of eight will shift on less than 1% of the calls or returns.

The small window size for nested calls is important for improving performance. For each procedure call, a stack frame is normally constructed in which parameters, a return address, and local variables are placed. There is thus a great deal of stack manipulation that takes place for procedure calls, but the complexity of the manipulation is not all that great. That is, stack references are highly localized within a small area.

The RISC I architecture exploits this locality by keeping the active portion of the stack in registers. Figure 6-18 shows the user's view of register usage for the RISC I. The user sees 32 registers in which each register is 32 bits wide. Registers R0–R7 are used for global variables (which are referenced as %r0–%r7 or equivalently %g0–%g7). Registers R8–R15 are used for incoming parameters and are named %r8–%r15, or equivalently %i0–%i7. Registers R16–R23 are used for local variables and are named %r16–%r23 or equivalently %l0–%l7, and registers R24–R31 are used for outgoing parameters and are named %r24–%r31, or equivalently, %o0–%o7. The eight registers within each group are enough to satisfy the bulk of call/return activity, as evidenced by the frequency distribution in Figure 6-17.

Although the user sees 32 registers, there may be several hundred registers that overlap. Figure 6-19 illustrates the concept of overlapping register windows. The global registers are detached from the others, and are continuously available as R0–R7. Registers R8–R31 make up the remaining 24 registers that the user sees, but this group of registers slides deeper into the **register file** (the entire set of registers) on each procedure call. Since the outgoing parameters for one procedure are the incoming parameters to another, these sets of registers can overlap. Registers R8-R31 are referred to as a **window**. A **current window pointer** (CWP) points to the current window and increases or decreases for calls and returns, respectively.

In the statistically rare event that there are not enough registers for the level of nesting, then main memory is used. However, main memory is used for the *lowest* numbered window, so that the new current window still uses registers. The highest register location then wraps around to the lowest, forming a **circular buffer**. As returns are made, registers

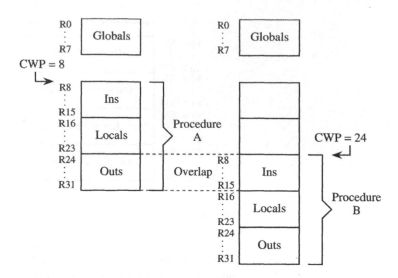

Figure 6-19
Overlapping register windows.

that were written to memory are restored to the register file. Thus, execution always takes place with registers and never directly with main memory.

EXAMPLE 6-5 Compiled Code for Overlapping Register Windows and Delayed Branches

In this section, we analyze a C compiler-produced SPARC assembly language program that exploits features of the RISC concept. We start with the C program shown in Figure 6-20, in which the main routine passes two integers to a subroutine, which returns the sum of the integers to the main routine. The code produced by a Solaris Unix C compiler using the command line

```
gcc -S file.c
```

is shown in Figure 6-21.

An explanation of the more significant aspects of the assembled code is given in Figure 6-21, which includes a number of features found only in RISC code. There are a number of new instructions and pseudo-ops introduced in this code:

.seg/.section Unix executable programs have three segments for data, text (the instructions), and the stack. The .seg pseudo-op instructs the assembler to place the code that follows into one of these three segments. Some of the segments have different protections, which is why there is a data segment and also a data1 segment. The data1 segment contains constants and should be protected from writing. The data segment is both readable and writable and is therefore not protected against reading or writing (but it is protected from being executed, as is data). Newer versions of Unix allow more text and data areas to be used for different read, write, and execute protections.

```
/* Example C program to be compiled with gcc */

#include
<stdio.h>
main ()
{
    int a, b, c;

    a = 10;
    b = 4;
    c = add_two(a, b);

    printf("c = %d\n", c);
}

int add_two(a,b)
int a, b;
{
    int result;

    result = a + b;
    return(result);
}
```

Figure 6-20
Source code for C program to be compiled with gcc.

%hi Same as ARC pseudo-op .high22.

%lo Same as ARC pseudo-op .low10.

add Same as addcc except that the condition codes are unaffected.

save Advances current window pointer and increments stack pointer to create space for local variables.

mov Same as: or %g0,register_or_immediate,destination_register. This differs from st because the destination is a register.

nop No-operation (the processor waits for one instruction cycle, while the branch finishes).

.ascii/.asciz Reserves space for an ASCII string.

set Sets a register to a value. This is a macro that expands to the sethi, %hi, and %lo constructs shown in #PROLOGUE# 1.

ret Return. Same as: jmpl %i7+8, %g0. Notice that it seems that the return should only go four bytes past the calling instruction, not eight bytes as indicated above. This is because the instruction that follows the call is a nop, inserted by the compiler to protect the integrity of the pipeline.

restore Decrements current window pointer.

b Same as ba.

.file Identifies the source file.

```
! Output produced by gcc compiler on Solaris (Sun UNIX)
! Comments added by authors.

.file    add.c  ! Identifies the source program
.section       ".rodata"      ! Read-only data for routine main
       .align 8          ! Align read-only data for routine main on an
                         ! 8-byte boundary
.LLC0
       .asciz "c = %d\n"     ! This is the read-only data
.section       "text" ! Executable code starts here
       .align 4  ! Align executable code on a 4-byte (word) boundary
       .global main
       .type   main,#function
       .proc   04
main:             ! Beginning of executable code for routine main
       !#PROLOGUE#     0
       save %sp, -128, %sp ! Create 128 byte stack frame. Advance
                          ! CWP (Current Window Pointer)
       !#PROLOGUE#     1
       mov 10, %o0  ! %o0 <- 10. Note that %o0 is the same as %r24.
! This is local variable a in main routine of C source program.
       st %o0, [%fp-20]     ! Store %o0 five words into stack frame.
       mov 4, %o0   ! %o0 <- 4. This is local variable b in main.
       st %o0, [%fp-24]    ! Store %o0 six words into stack frame.
       ld [%fp-20], %o0    ! Load %o0 and %o1 with parameters to
       ld [%fp-24], %o1    ! be passed to routine add_two.
       call add_two, 0     ! Call routine add_two
       nop     ! Pipeline flush needed after a transfer of control
       st %o0, [%fp-28]    ! Store result 67 words into stack frame.
                          ! This is local variable c in main.
       sethi %hi(.LLC0), %o1 ! This instruction and the next load
       or %o1, %lo(.LLC0), %o0 ! the 32-bit address .LLC0 into %o0
       ld [%fp-28], %o1  ! Load %o1 with parameter to pass to printf
```

Figure 6-21

gcc generated SPARC code (continued on next page).

.align Forces the code that follows onto a boundary evenly divisible by its argument.

.type Associates a label with its type.

.size Computes the size of a segment.

.ident Identifies the compiler version.

We can see the positions of the delay slots, marked with nop instructions. Despite the availability of overlapping register windows in the SPARC architecture, the unoptimized code makes no use of this feature: parameters to be passed to a routine are copied to the stack, and the called routine then retrieves these parameters from the stack. The optimizing feature of the compiler has not yet been invoked (but read on).

```
        call printf, 0
        nop     ! A nop is needed here because of the pipeline flush
                ! that follows a transfer of control.
.LL1
        ret     ! Return to calling routine (Solaris for this case)
        restore ! The complement to save. Although it follows the
                ! return, it is still in the pipeline and gets executed.
.LLfe1
        .size   main, .LLfe1-main ! Size of
        .align 4
        .global add_two
        .type   add_two, #function
        .proc 04
add_two:
        !#PROLOGUE# 0
        save %sp, -120, %sp
        !#PROLOGUE# 1
        st %i0, [%fp+68] !Same as %o0 in calling routine (variable a)
        st %i1, [%fp+72] !Same as %o1 in calling routine (variable b)
        ld [%fp+68], %o0
        ld [%fp+72], %o1
        add %o0, %o1, %o0 ! Perform the addition
        st %o0, [%fp-20]  ! Store result in stack frame
        ld [%fp-20], %i0  ! %i0 (result) is %o0 in called routine
        b .LL2
        nop
.LL2:
        ret
        restore
.LLfe2:
        .size   add_two, .LLfe2-add_two
        .ident  "GCC: (GNU) 2.5.8"
```

Figure 6-21
(continued).

Notice that the compiler does not seem to be consistent in its choice of registers for parameter passing. Prior to the call to add_two, the compiler uses %o0 and %o1 (%r24 and %r25) for parameters passed to add_two. Then, %o1 is used for the parameters passed to printf. Why did the compiler not start with %o0 again, or choose the next available register (%o2)? This is the **register assignment problem**, which has been the object of a great deal of study. We will not go into details here[1], as this is more appropriate for a course in compiler design; suffice it to say that any logically correct assignment of variables to registers will work, but that some assignments are better than others in terms of the number of registers used and the overall program execution time.

---

[1] Here are a few details, for the curious: %o0 is still in use (add_two is expecting the address of LLC0 to show up in %o0), and %o1 is no longer needed at this point, so it can be reassigned. But then, why is %o1 used in the sethi line? Would it have made sense to use %o0 instead of introducing another register into the computation? See Problem 6.17 for more on this topic.

Why are the stack frames so large? We need only three words on the stack frame for local variables a, b, and c in main. We might also need a word to store the return address, although the compiler does not seem to generate code for that. There are no parameters passed to main by the operating system, and so the stack frame that main sees should only be four words (16 bytes) in size. Thus, the line at the beginning of routine main:

```
save %sp, -128, %sp
```

should only be:

```
save %sp, -16, %sp.
```

What is all of the extra space for? There are a number of runtime situations that may need stack space. For instance, if the nesting depth is greater than the number of windows, then the stack must be used for overflow. (See Figure D-2 in [SPARC, 1992].)

If a scalar is passed from one routine to another, then everything is fine. But if a callee refers to the address of a passed aggregate, then the aggregate must be copied to the stack and referenced from there for the lifetime of the pointer (or for the lifetime of the procedure, if the pointer lifetime is not known).

Why does the return statement ret cause a return to the code that is eight bytes past the call, instead of four bytes as we have been doing it? As mentioned above, this is because there is a nop that follows call (the so-called "delay-slot instruction"). If the return went only four bytes past the call as with the ARC ISA, the code would still work fine: it would just be inefficient because an unnecessary nop would be executed.

Notice that routine labels that appear in the source code are prepended with an underscore in the assembly code, so that main, add_two, and printf in C become _main, _add_two, and _printf in gcc generated SPARC code. This means that if we want to write a C program that is linked to a gcc generated SPARC program, the C calls should be made to routines that begin with underscores. For example, if add_two is compiled into SPARC code, and we invoke it from a C main program in another file, then the C program should make a call to _add_two, and *not* add_two, even though the routine started out as add_two. Further, the C program needs to declare _add_two as external.

If the compilation for add_two is continued down to an executable file, then there is no need to treat the labels differently. The add_two routine will still be labeled _add_two, but routine main will be compiled into code that expects to see _add_two and so everything will work OK. This is not the case, however, if a gcc program makes calls to a Fortran library.

Fortran has been a commonly used language in the scientific community, and there are a number of significant Fortran libraries that are used for linear algebra, modeling and simulation, and parallel scientific applications. As programmers of language XYZ (whatever language that may be), we sometimes find ourselves wanting to write XYZ programs that make calls to Fortran routines. This is easy to do once we understand what is happening.

There are two significant issues that need to be addressed:

1. differences in routine labels;

2. differences in subroutine linkage.

In Fortran, the source code labels are prepended with two underscores in the assembly code. A C program (if C is language XYZ) that makes a call to Fortran routine `add_two` would then make a call to `__add_two`, which also must be declared as external in the C source code (and declared as global in the Fortran program).

If all of the parameters that are passed to the Fortran routines are pointers, then everything will work OK. If there are any scalars passed, then there will be trouble because C (like Java) uses call-by-value for scalars whereas Fortran uses call-by-reference. We need to "trick" the C compiler into using call-by-reference by making it explicit. Wherever a Fortran routine expects a scalar in its argument list, we use a pointer to the scalar in the C code.

As a practical consideration, the `gcc` compiler will compile Fortran programs. It knows what to do by observing the extension of the source file, which should be `.f` for Fortran.

Finally, let us take a look at how an optimizing compiler improves the code. Figure 6-22 shows the optimized code using the compiler's `-O` flag. Notice that there is not a single `nop`, `ld`, or `st` instruction. Wasted cycles devoted to `nop` instructions have been reclaimed, and memory references devoted to stack manipulation have been eliminated.

■

■ 6.9 CODING FOR LOW POWER

As transistor "feature sizes" decrease, the amount of power needed to switch the transistors correspondingly decreases. Overall power requirements should also decrease, but transistor counts continue to rise, taking advantage of the smaller feature sizes and lower per-transistor power requirements. As transistor density increases and chip sizes increase, power requirements also increase. Mobile devices that use batteries as the primary power source have increased in capability, but improvements in battery power density have not experienced the same gains. In VLSI circuits, most power is dissipated by charging and discharging capacitances, particularly for off-chip buses. Circuit components are charged and discharged when transitions are made between 0 and 1, and so if we want to reduce the demands on power, we should reduce the number of transitions. For example, a transition from 00000000 to 11111111 involves flipping eight bits from 0 to 1. If there is a different way to encode information so that fewer bit flips are needed, then power can be saved.

A sequence of eight consecutive numbers encoded as 000—111 involves 11 transitions from the starting number 000 to the last number 111. By comparison, if we use a **Gray code** sequence instead, in which exactly one bit changes between successive numbers, then we will still encode all eight numbers but with only seven transitions—a savings of $4/11 = 36\%$. The comparison is shown in Figure 6-23.

Carrying this observation through to a coding example, consider a sequence of four `ld` instructions that load four contiguous words into `%r16`—`%r19` starting at memory location 2096. The ARC sequence is shown below:

```
ld [2096], %r16
ld [2100], %r17
ld [2104], %r18
ld [2108], %r19
```

```
! Output produced by -O optimiziation for gcc compiler
.file    "add.c"
.section        ".rodata"
        .align 8
.LLC0:
        .asciz  "c = %d\n"
.section        ".text"
        .align 4
        .global main
        .type   main,#function
        .proc   04
main:
        !#PROLOGUE# 0
        save %sp,-112,%sp
        !#PROLOGUE# 1
        mov 10,%o0
        call add_two,0
        mov 4,%o1
        mov %o0,%o1
        sethi %hi(.LLC0),%o0
        call printf,0
        or %o0,%lo(.LLC0),%o0
        ret
        restore
.LLfe1:
        .size   main,.LLfe1-main
        .align 4
        .global add_two
        .type   add_two,#function
        .proc   04
add_two:
        !#PROLOGUE# 0
        !#PROLOGUE# 1
        retl
        add %o0,%o1,%o0
.LLfe2:
        .size   add_two,.LLfe2-add_two
        .ident  "GCC: (GNU) 2.7.2"
```

Figure 6-22
SPARC code generated with the -O optimization flag.

The corresponding machine code is then:

```
op   rd     op3    rs1   i  simm13         No. Transitions
                                           ARC Code       ⇓
11 10000 000000 00000 1 0100000110000   ld [2096],%r16 -
11 10001 000000 00000 1 0100000110100   ld [2100],%r17 2
11 10010 000000 00000 1 0100000111000   ld [2104],%r18 4
11 10011 000000 00000 1 0100000111100   ld [2108],%r19 4
Total:                                                  8
```

The total number of transitions is eight. However, if we can reorder the last two instructions, then the total number of transitions is reduced to six:

Normal encoding	No. of transitions	Gray code	No. of transitions
000	–	000	–
001	1	001	1
010	2	011	1
011	1	010	1
100	3	110	1
101	1	111	1
110	2	101	1
111	1	100	1
Total:	11		7

Figure 6-23

The use of a Gray code reduces the number of transitions.

```
op    rd     op3     rs1    i   simm13           No. Transitions
                                                 ARC Code      ⇓
11 10000 000000 00000 1 0100000110000   ld [2096],%r16 -
11 10001 000000 00000 1 0100000110100   ld [2100],%r17 2
11 10011 000000 00000 1 0100000111100   ld [2108],%r19 2
11 10010 000000 00000 1 0100000111000   ld [2104],%r18 2
Total:                                                 6
```

There are several other optimizations that can be made to code sequences based on choosing instructions and parameters from functionally equivalent possibilities in such a way that the number of transitions are reduced. Consider the instruction below that clears register %r9, which is taken from the earlier readnic code:

```
andcc %r0, %r0, %r9    ! Clear register %r9
```

There is a multitude of other instructions that will accomplish the same task, using different bit patterns, and with different energy consumptions depending on the number of bit transitions with respect to the surrounding code. A few alternatives are shown below:

```
orcc  %r0, %r0, %r9    ! Clear register %r9
andcc %r0, %r9, %r9    ! Clear register %r9
andcc %r8, %r0, %r9    ! Clear register %r9
```

There are several techniques for reducing power consumption in CPUs, such as dynamically scaling the voltages and frequencies to reduce the impact of processor idling, such as for L2 cache misses, recoding bus data to reduce transitions on the pins of IC packages, reducing interrupts by using static scheduling of interrupt handlers, and others. In general, however, if a program runs faster, then it consumes less energy, and reordering instructions may have the most impact on simply reducing the peak power consumed by a program. Compiling for low power will continue to be a fertile area for research as programming methodologies and architectures continue to evolve.

Summary

A high-level programming language like C or Java allows the low-level architecture of a computer to be treated as an abstraction. An assembly language program, on the other hand, takes a form that is very dependent on the underlying architecture. The instruction set architecture (ISA) is made visible to the programmer, who is responsible for handling register usage and subroutine linkage. Some of the complexity of assembly language programming is managed through the use of macros, which differ from subroutines or functions in that macros generate in-line code at assembly time, whereas subroutines are executed at run time.

A linker combines separately assembled modules into a single load module, which typically involves relocating code. A loader places the load module in memory and starts the execution of the program. The loader may also need to perform relocation if two or more load modules overlap in memory.

In practice, the details of assembly, linking, and loading are highly system-dependent and language-dependent. Some simple assemblers merely produce executable binary files, but more commonly an assembler will produce additional information so that modules can be linked together by a linker. Some systems provide linking loaders that combine the linking task with the loading task. Others separate linking from loading. Some loaders can only load a program at the address specified in the binary file, while more commonly, relocating loaders can relocate programs to a load-time-specified address. The file formats that support these processes are also operating-system dependent.

Before compilers were developed, programs were written directly in assembly language. Nowadays, assembly language is not normally used directly since compilers for high-level languages are so prevalent and also produce efficient code, but assembly language is still important for understanding aspects of computer architecture, such as how to link programs that are compiled for different calling conventions, and for exploiting extensions to architectures.

Problems

6.1   Translate the C program fragment below into ARC assembly language.

```
int i;
int series[10];
for (i = 0, i < 10, i++)
    series[i] = i;
```

6.2   Why does the text say on page 202: "This program translates into ARC assembly language as follows,

assuming for convenience that all addresses are less than 4096"?

6.3   Create a symbol table for the ARC segment shown below using a form similar to Figure 6-7. Use "U" for any symbols that are undefined.

```
x           .equ      4000
            .org      2048
            ba        main
            .org      2072
```

```
main:     sethi     x, %r2
          srl       %r2, 10, %r2
lab_4:    st        %r2, [k]
          addcc     %r1, -1, %r1
foo:      st        %r1, [k]
          andcc     %r1, %r1, %r0
          beq       lab_5
          jmpl      %r15 + 4, %r0
cons:     .dwb      3
```

6.4 Translate the following ARC code into object code. Assume that x is at location $(4096)_{10}$.

```
k .equ      1024
          .
          .
          .
          addcc     %r4, k, %r4
          ld        [%r14], %r5
          addcc     %r14, -1, %r14
          st        %r5, [x]
          .
          .
          .
```

6.5 Create a symbol table for the program shown in Figure 6-8, using a form similar to Figure 6-7.

6.6 Translate subroutine add_64 shown in Figure 6-8, including variables A, B, and C, into object code.

6.7 A **disassembler** is a software program that reads an object module and recreates the source assembly language module. Given the object code shown below, disassemble the code into ARC assembly language statements. Since there is not enough information in the object code to determine symbol names, choose symbols as you need them from the alphabet, consecutively, from 'a' to 'z.'

```
10000010 10000000 01100000 00000001
10000000 10010001 01000000 00000110
00000010 10000000 00000000 00000011
10001101 00110001 10100000 00001010
00010000 10111111 11111111 11111100
10000001 11000011 11100000 00000100
```

6.8 Given two macros push and pop as defined below, unnecessary instructions can be inserted into a program if a push immediately follows a pop. Expand the macro definitions shown below and identify the unnecessary instructions.

```
          .begin
          .macro     push      arg1
          addcc      %r14,     -4, %r14
```

```
          st         arg1,     [%r14]
          .endmacro
          .macro     pop       arg1
          ld         [%r14],   arg1
          addcc      %r14, 4, %r14
          .endmacro
! Start of program
          .org       2048
          pop        %r1
          push       %r2
          .
          .
          .
          .end
```

6.9 Write a macro called `return` that performs the function of the `jmpl` statement as it is used in Figure 6-5.

6.10 In Figure 4-24, the operand x for `sethi` is filled in by the assembler, but the statement will not work as intended if $x \geq 2^{22}$ because there are only 22 bits in the `imm22` field of the sethi format. In order to place an arbitrary 32-bit address into `%r5` at run time, we can use `sethi` for the upper 22 bits, and then use `addcc` for the lower 10 bits. For this we add two new pseudo-ops: `.high22` and `.low10`, which construct the bit patterns for the high 22 bits and the low 10 bits of the address, respectively. The construct

```
          sethi .high22(0xFFFFFFFF), %r1
```

expands to:

```
          sethi 0x3FFFFF, %r1
```

and the construct:

```
          addcc %r1, .low10(0xFFFFFFFF), %r1
```

expands to:

```
          addcc %r1, 0x3FF, %r1.
```

Rewrite the calling routine in Figure 4-24 using `.high22` and `.low10` so that it works correctly regardless of where x is placed in memory.

6.11 Assume that you have the subroutine add_64 shown in Figure 6-8 available to you. Write an ARC routine called add_128 that adds two 64-bit numbers, making use of add_64. The two 128-bit operands are stored in memory locations that begin at x and y, and the result is stored in the memory location that begins at z.

6.12 Write a macro called `subcc`, with usage similar to `addcc`, that subtracts its second source operand from the first.

6.13 Does ordinary, nonrecursive macro expansion happen at assembly time or at execution time? Does recursive macro expansion happen at assembly time or at execution time?

6.14 An assembly language programmer proposes to increase the capability of the push macro defined in Figure 6-9 by providing a second argument, arg2. The second argument would replace the addcc %r14, -4, %r14 with addcc arg2, -4, arg2. Explain what the programmer is trying to accomplish and what dangers lurk in this approach.

6.15 Rewrite the writenic code, replacing %r8— %r13 with the appropriate %g, %i, %l, and %o register naming, using the lowest numbered registers of each type as they are encountered. Simply do a %rx for %gy replacement. Do not change the instructions.

6.16 Increasing the number of cycles per instruction can sometimes improve the execution efficiency of a pipeline. If the time per cycle for the pipeline described in Section 6.7 is 20 ns, then CPI_{Avg} is 1.5×20 ns = 30 ns. Compute the execution efficiency for the same pipeline in which the pipeline depth increases from five to six and the cycle time decreases from 20 ns to 10 ns.

6.17 The SPARC code below is taken from the gcc generated code in Figure 6-21. Can %o0 be used in all three lines, instead of "wasting" %o1 in the second line?

```
    . . .
st      %o0, [%fp-28]
sethi   %hi(.LLC0), %o1
or      %o1, %lo(.LLC0), %o1
    . . .
```

6.18 Calculate the speedup that can be expected if a 200 MHz processor is replaced with a 300 MHz processor, if all other parameters remain unchanged.

6.19 What is the speedup that can be expected if the instruction set of a certain machine is changed so that the branch instruction takes one clock cycle instead of three clock cycles, if branch instructions account for 20% of all instructions executed by a certain program? Assume that other instructions average three clock cycles per instruction and that nothing else is altered by the change.

Further Reading

Compilers and compilation are treated by (Aho et al, 1985) and (Waite and Carter, 1993). There are a great many references on assembly language programming. (Donovan, 1972) is a classic reference on assemblers, linkers, and loaders. (SPARC, 1992) deals specifically with the definition of the SPARC and SPARC assembly language. Three primary characteristics of RISC architectures enumerated in Section 6.6 originated at IBM's T. J. Watson Research Center, as summarized in (Ralston et al, 2000, pp. 1510–1511). (Hennessy and Patterson, 2002) is a classic reference on much of the work that led to the RISC concept. (Stallings, 1991) is a thorough reference on RISCs. (Tamir and Sequin, 1983) show that a window size of eight will shift on less than 1% of the calls or returns. (Tanenbaum, 1999) provides a readable introduction to the RISC concept. (Knuth, 1971) is an important work that has had a significant impact on the design of ISAs.

(Hsu and Kremer, 2001) cover dynamic voltage and frequency scaling for low power. (Lekatsus, 2000) covers a low power method of reducing bit toggling on buses. (Hu, Jiménez, and Kremer, 2005) cover a methodology of combining execution-driven simulation with physical measurement for analysis of power optimizations.

Aho, A. V., Sethi, R., and Ullman, J. D., *Compilers*, Addison Wesley Longman (1985).

Donovan, J. J., *Systems Programming*, McGraw-Hill (1972).

Gill, A., Corwin, E., and Logar, A., *Assembly Language Programming for the 68000*, Prentice-Hall (1987).

Goodman, J. and Miller, K., *A Programmer's View of Computer Architecture*, Saunders College Publishing (1993).

Hennessy, J. L. and Patterson, D. A., *Computer Architecture: A Quantitative Approach*, 3/e, Morgan Kaufmann Publishers (2002).

Hsu, C. and U. Kremer, "Dynamic voltage and frequency scaling for scientific applications," in *Proceedings of the 14th Annual Workshop on Languages and Compilers for Parallel Computing* (Aug. 2001).

Hu, C., Jiménez, D. A., and Kremer, U., "Toward an evaluation infrastructure for power and energy optimizations," Workshop on High-Performance, Power-Aware Computing, Denver, CO (April 2005).

Kernighan, Brian W. and Ritchie, Dennis M, *The C Programming Language, Second Edition*, Prentice-Hall (1988).

Knuth, D. E., "An Empirical Study of FORTRAN Programs," *Software—Practice and Experience*, 1, 105–133 (1971).

Lekatsus, H., Wolf, W., and Henkel, J., "Arithmetic coding for low power embedded system design," *Data Compression Conference* (DCC '00), p. 430.

Patterson, D. A. and Hennessy, J. L., *Computer Organization and Design: The Hardware/Software Interface*, 3/e, Morgan Kaufmann Publishers (2004).

Ralston, A., Reilly, E. D., and Hemmendinger, D., eds., *Encyclopedia of Computer Science*, 4/e, Nature Publishing Group (2000).

SPARC International, Inc., *The SPARC Architecture Manual: Version 8*, Prentice Hall (1992).

Stallings, W., *Reduced Instruction Set Computers*, 3/e, IEEE Computer Society Press (1991).

Tamir, Y., and Sequin, C., "Strategies for managing the register file in RISC," *IEEE Trans. Comp.* (Nov. 1983).

Tanenbaum, A., *Structured Computer Organization*, 4/e, Prentice Hall (1999).

Waite, W. M., Carter, L. H., and Carter, L. R., *An Introduction to Compiler Construction*, Addison-Wesley Longman (1993).

CHAPTER 7

MEMORY

In the past few decades, CPU processing speed as measured by the number of instructions executed per second has doubled every 18 months for the same price. Computer memory has experienced a similar increase along a different dimension, quadrupling in size every 36 months for the same price. Memory speed, however, has only increased at a rate of less than 10% per year. Thus, while processing speed increases at the same rate that memory size increases, the gap between the speed of the processor and the speed of memory also increases.

As the gap among processor and memory speeds grows, architectural solutions help bridge the gap. A typical computer contains several types of memory, ranging from fast, expensive internal registers, to slow, inexpensive hard disks. The interplay among these different types of memory is exploited so that a computer behaves as if it has a single, large, fast memory, when in fact it contains a range of memory types that operate in a highly coordinated fashion. We begin the chapter with a high-level discussion of how these different memories are organized in what is referred to as the *memory hierarchy*.

■ 7.1 THE MEMORY HIERARCHY

Memory in a conventional digital computer is organized in a hierarchy, as illustrated in Figure 7-1. At the top of the hierarchy are registers that are matched in speed to the CPU, but tend to be large and consume a significant amount of power. There are normally only a small number of registers in a processor, on the order of a few hundred or less. At the bottom of the hierarchy are secondary and off-line storage memories such as hard magnetic disks and magnetic tapes, in which the cost per stored bit is small in terms of money and electrical power, but the access time is very long when compared with registers. Between the registers and secondary storage are a number of other forms of memory that bridge the gap between the two.

As we move up through the hierarchy, greater performance is realized, at greater costs. Table 7.1 shows some of the properties of the components of the memory hierarchy in the early 2000s for a typical desktop computer system. Access time has a number of contributing factors, and is shown in the table under favorable but typical conditions (such as accessing data in blocks rather than one word at a time). Expensive memory tends to be closer to the CPU, which shortens communication times. Notice that Typical Cost, arrived at by multiplying Cost/MB × Typical amount used (in which "MB" is a unit of megabytes), is roughly the same for each member of the hierarchy. Notice also that access times

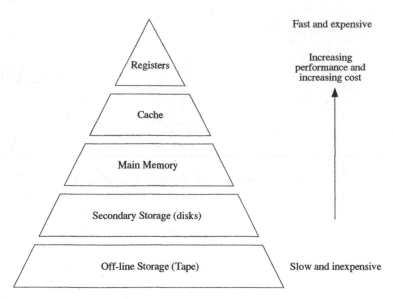

Figure 7-1
The memory hierarchy.

vary by approximately factors of 10 except for disks, which have access times 10,000 times slower than main memory. This large mismatch has an important influence on how the operating system handles the movement of blocks of data between disks and main memory, as we will see in Section 7.6.

Table 7.1 **Properties of the memory hierarchy**

Memory type	Access time	Cost/MB	Typical amount used	Typical cost
Registers	0.5 ns	High	2 KB	—
Cache	5–20 ns	$80	2 MB	$160
Main memory	40–80ns	$0.40	512 MB	$205
Disk memory	5 ms	$0.005	40 GB	$200

■ 7.2 RANDOM-ACCESS MEMORY

In this section, we look at the structure and function of **random-access memory** (RAM). In this context the term "random" means that any memory location can be accessed in the same amount of time, regardless of its position in the memory. This is a major improvement over the early days when access times depended on the position of a rotating drum or an acoustic delay. Actually, there still is some location dependence because nearby data can be retrieved more quickly on average in a **block access** than accessing a single word, but the time needed to access any particular word at random is pretty much the same.

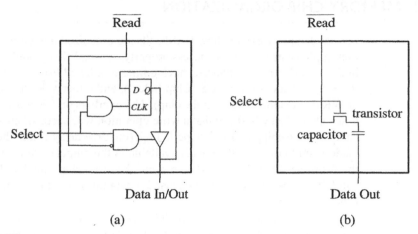

Figure 7-2
Functional behavior of a RAM cell: (a) static and (b) dynamic.

Figure 7-2a shows the functional behavior of a RAM cell that stores a single bit. The figure represents the memory element as a D flip-flop, with additional controls to allow the cell to be selected, read, and written. There is a (bidirectional) data line for data input and output. We will use cells similar to the one shown in Figure 7-2a when we discuss RAM chips. Note that this illustration does not necessarily represent the actual physical implementation, but only its functional behavior.

There are many ways to implement a memory cell. RAM chips that are based upon flip-flops, as in Figure 7-2a, are referred to as **static** RAM (SRAM), chips, because the contents of each location persist as long as power is applied to the chips. SRAMs are fast but are relatively large and consume a lot of power. They are typically used for memory applications that are small but fast.

Dynamic RAM chips, referred to as **DRAMs**, employ a **capacitor** that stores a minute amount of electric charge, in which the charge level represents a 1 or a 0, as shown in Figure 7-2b. A logical 1 can be stored in the capacitor by placing a 1 on both the Select and Read lines. Capacitors are much smaller than flip-flops, and so a capacitor based DRAM can hold much more information in the same area than an SRAM. Since the charges on the capacitors dissipate with time, the charge in the capacitor storage cells in DRAMs must be restored, or **refreshed,** frequently with special circuitry. DRAMs are smaller and slower than SRAMs, and are typically used for the main memory because they support low cost, low power, and high density.

DRAMs are susceptible to premature discharging as a result of interactions with naturally occurring gamma rays. This is a statistically rare event, and a system may run for days before an error occurs. For this reason, early personal computers (PCs) did not use error-detection circuitry. PCs would be turned off at the end of the day, and so undetected errors would not accumulate. This helped to keep the prices of PCs competitive. With the drastic reduction in DRAM prices and the increased uptimes of PCs operating in a myriad of important long-running applications such as automated teller machines (ATMs) and network file servers (NFSs), error detection circuitry is now commonplace in PCs. (See Chapter 9 for more on error detection and correction.)

■ 7.3 MEMORY CHIP ORGANIZATION

In this section we explore how RAM cells are organized into chips, and how this organization implements the random access property. A simplified pinout of a RAM chip is shown in Figure 7-3. An m-bit address, having lines numbered from 0 to $m - 1$, is applied to pins $A_0 - A_{m-1}$, while asserting $\overline{CS}$ (Chip Select), and either $\overline{WR}$ (for writing data to the chip) or WR (for reading data from the chip). The overbars on $\overline{CS}$ and $\overline{WR}$ indicate that the chip is selected when CS=0 and that a write operation will occur when WR = 0. When reading data from the chip, after a time period t_{AA} (the time delay from when the address lines are made valid to the time the data is available at the output), the w-bit data word appears on the data lines $D_0 - D_{w-1}$. When writing data to a chip, the data lines must also be held valid for a time period t_{AA}. Notice that the data lines are bidirectional in Figure 7-3, which is normally the case.

The address lines $A_0 - A_{m-1}$ in the RAM chip shown in Figure 7-3 contain an address, which is decoded from an m-bit address into one of 2^m locations within the chip, each of which has a w-bit word associated with it. The chip thus contains $2^m \times w$ bits.

Now consider the problem of creating a RAM that stores four four-bit words. A RAM can be thought of as a collection of registers. We can use four-bit registers to store the words, and then introduce an addressing mechanism that allows one of the words to be selected for reading or for writing. Figure 7-4 shows a design for the memory that is known as a two-dimensional (2D) organization, with words in one dimension and bits in another dimension. Two address lines A_0 and A_1 select a word for reading or writing via the 2-to-4 decoder. The outputs of the registers can be safely tied together without risking an electrical short because the 2-to-4 decoder ensures that at most one register is enabled at a time, and the disabled registers are electrically disconnected through the use of tri-state buffers. The Chip Select line in the decoder is not necessary, but will be used later in constructing larger RAMs. A simplified drawing of the RAM is shown in Figure 7-5.

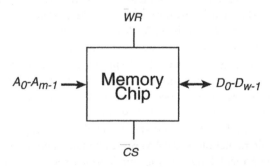

Figure 7-3
Simplified RAM chip pinout.

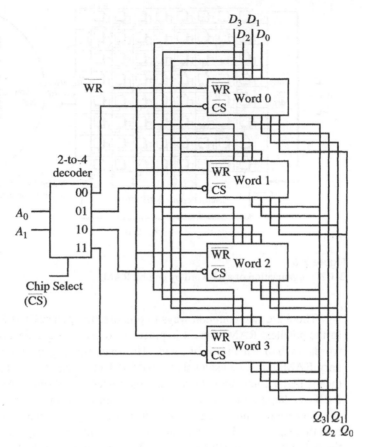

Figure 7-4
A four-word memory with four bits per word in a 2D organization.

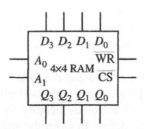

Figure 7-5
A simplified version of the four-word by four-bit RAM.

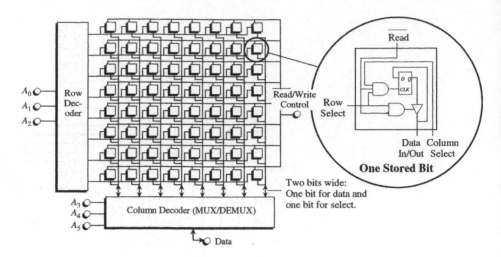

Figure 7-6
2-1/2D organization of a 64-word by one-bit RAM.

There are two common ways to organize the generalized RAM shown in Figure 7-3. In the smallest RAM chips it is practical to use a single decoder to select one out of 2^m words, each of which is w bits wide. However, this organization is not economical in ordinary RAM chips. Consider that a 64M $\times$ 1 chip has 26 address lines (64M $= 2^{26}$). This means that a conventional decoder would need 2^{26} 26-input AND gates, which manifests itself as a large cost in terms of chip area—and this is just for the decoder.

Since most integrated circuits (ICs) are roughly square, an alternate decoding structure that significantly reduces the decoder complexity decodes the rows separately from the columns. This is referred to as a **2-1/2D organization**. The 2-1/2D organization is by far the most prevalent organization for RAM ICs. Figure 7-6 shows a 2^6-word $\times$1-bit RAM with a 2-1/2D organization. The six address lines are evenly split between a row decoder and a column decoder (the column decoder is actually a MUX/DEMUX combination). A single bidirectional data line is used for input and output.

During a read operation, an entire row is selected and fed into the column MUX, which selects a single bit for output. During a write operation, the single bit to be written is distributed by the DEMUX to the target column, while the row decoder selects the proper row to be written.

In practice, to reduce pin count, there are generally only $m/2$ address pins on the chip, and the row and column addresses are time-multiplexed on these $m/2$ address lines. First, the $m/2$-bit row address is applied along with a row address strobe, $\overline{\text{RAS}}$, signal. The row address is latched and decoded by the chip. Then the $m/2$-bit column address is applied, along with a column address strobe, $\overline{\text{CAS}}$. There may be additional pins to control the chip refresh and other memory functions. The use of a CAS signal also reduces the relatively large access time for the first byte transfer, because the row decoding has already been accomplished and only the column decoding needs to be done to access successive locations.

Even with this 2-1/2D organization and splitting the address into row and column components, there is still a great fan-in/fan-out demand on the decoder logic gates, and the (still) large number of address pins forces memory chips into large footprints on printed circuit boards (PCBs). In order to reduce the fanin/fanout constraints, **tree decoders** may be used, which are discussed on the companion Web-site. A memory architecture that serializes the address lines onto a single input pin is discussed in Section 7.4.

Although DRAMs are very economical, SRAMs offer greater speed. The refresh cycles, error-detection circuitry, and low operating powers of DRAMs create a speed difference that places DRAM speed at roughly 1/4 of SRAM speed, but SRAMs also incur a significant cost.

The performance of both types of memory (SRAM and DRAM) can be improved by accessing a number of words in succession, constituting a **block**. In this situation, memory accesses can be **interleaved** so that while one memory is accessing address A_m, other memories are accessing $A_{m+1}, A_{m+2}, A_{m+3}$, etc. In this way the access time for each word can appear to be many times faster.

7.3.1 Constructing Large RAMS From Small RAMS

We can construct larger RAM modules from smaller RAM modules. Both the word size and the number of words per module can be increased. For example, eight 16M × 1-bit RAM modules can be combined to make a 16M × 8-bit RAM module, and 16 16M × 8-bit RAM modules can be combined to make a 256M × 8-bit RAM module.

As a simple example, consider using the four-word × four-bit RAM chip shown in Figure 7-5 as a building block to first make a four-word × eight-bit module, and then an eight-word × four-bit module. We would like to increase the width of the four-bit words and also increase the number of words. Consider first the problem of increasing the word width from four bits to eight. We can accomplish this by simply using two chips, tying their CS (chip select) lines together so they are both selected together, and juxtaposing their data lines, as shown in Figure 7-7.

Consider now the problem of increasing the number of words from four to eight. Figure 7-8 shows a configuration that accomplishes this. The eight words are distributed

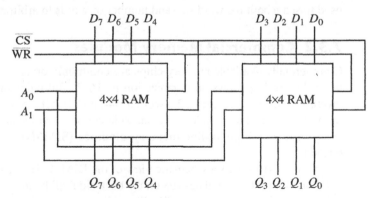

Figure 7-7

Two four-word by four-bit RAMs are used in creating a four-word by eight-bit RAM.

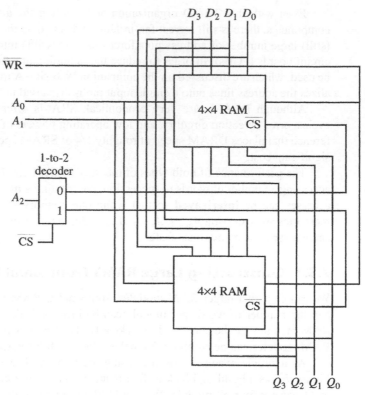

Figure 7-8
Two four-word by four-bit RAMs are used in creating an eight-word by four-bit RAM.

over the two four-word RAMs. Address line A_2 is needed because there are now eight words to be addressed. A decoder for A_2 enables either the upper or lower memory module by using the $\overline{CS}$ lines, and then the remaining address lines (A_0 and A_1) are decoded within the enabled module. A combination of these two approaches can be used to scale both the word size and number of words to arbitrary RAM sizes.

7.3.2 Commercial Memory Modules

Commercially available memory chips are commonly organized into standard configurations. Figure 7-9 shows an organization of 16 2^{27}-bit chips on a **dual in-line memory module (DIMM)** that form a 2^{25} word × 64-bit (256 MB) module. The memory chips are on both sides of the module (only one side can be seen in this view), thus the "dual" in "dual in-line." **Single in-line memory modules (SIMMs)** have memory chips on only one side.

Figure 7-10 shows a schematic view of the DIMM. The electrical contacts (numbered 1–84 on the front side and 85–168 on the back side) all lie in a single line on each side. For 2^{28} memory locations we need 28 address lines, but only 14 address lines (A0–A13) are provided. The 14-bit addresses for the row and column are loaded separately, and the CAS and RAS signals are applied after the corresponding portion of the address is made

Figure 7-9
256 MB dual in-line memory module organized for a 64-bit word with 16 16M × 8-bit RAM chips (eight chips on each side of the DIMM).

available. Although this organization appears to double the time it takes to access any particular memory location, on average, the access time is much better since only the row or column address needs to be updated.

The 64 data bits on lines DQ1–DQ64 form eight bytes that are read or written in parallel. In order to form a 64-bit word with 16 memory chips, eight bits (a byte) are accessed in parallel for each chip, with two sets of 64 bits that can be organized into two banks, allowing accesses to be interleaved. As with the other "active low" signals, the Write Enable lines have a bar over the corresponding symbol ($\overline{W}$), which means that a write takes place when a 0 is placed on this line. A read takes place otherwise. The RAS lines also causes a refresh operation, which must be performed at least every 8 ms to restore the charges on the capacitors. Refresh cycles consume only 1%—2% of the active DRAM cycles. The **serial presence detect** (SPD) is contained in a separate nonvolatile memory on the module. The SPD contains configuration data that can be queried by the processor, such as the DRAM organization, the module configuration, and timing parameters. **Parity bits** are used for error detection (sometimes memories return incorrect data and we need to recognize when that happens). Chapter 9 covers error correction in detail.

Pin assignments for the DIMM are shown in Figure 7-11. Notice the large number of power pins, labeled V_{SS} for "voltage from source to source" (for the ground), and V_{DD} for "voltage from drain to drain" (the positive side of the power supply), which are needed to distribute the power load.

7.3.3 Read-Only Memory

When a computer program is loaded into memory, it remains in the memory until it is overwritten or until the power is turned off. For some applications, the program never changes, and so it is hardwired into a **read-only memory** (ROM). ROMs are used to store programs in videogames, calculators, microwave ovens, and automobile fuel-injection controllers, among many other applications.

A ROM is a simple device. All that is needed is a decoder, some output lines, and a few logic gates. There is no need for flip-flops or capacitors. Figure 7-12 shows a four-word ROM that stores four four-bit words (0101, 1011, 1110, and 0000). Each address input (00, 01, 10, or 11) corresponds to a different stored word.

For high-volume applications, ROMs are factory-programmed. As an alternative, for low-volume or prototyping applications, programmable ROMs (PROMs) are often used, which allow their contents to be written by a user with a relatively inexpensive device

**MH32EN64KPU EXTENDED-DATA-OUT
DYNAMIC RAM MODULE**

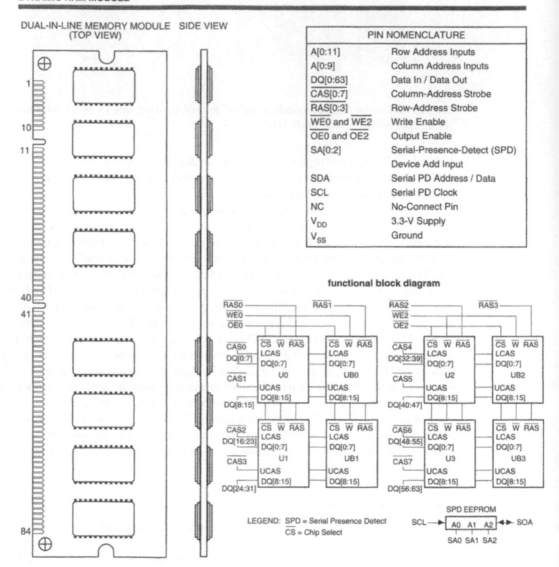

Figure 7-10
Schematic diagram of 256 MB dual in-line memory module.
(Source: adapted from http://www-s.ti.com/sc/ds/tm4en64kpu.pdf.)

called a **PROM burner**. Unfortunately for the early videogame industry, these PROM burners are also capable of reading the contents of a PROM, which can then be duplicated onto another PROM; worse still, the contents can be deciphered through reverse engineering and then modified and written to a new, contraband game cartridge.

PIN NO.	NAME	PIN NO.	NAME	PIN NO.	NAME	PIN NO.	NAME
1	V_{SS}	43	V_{SS}	85	V_{SS}	127	V_{SS}
2	DQ0	44	$\overline{OE2}$	86	DQ32	128	NC
3	DQ1	45	$\overline{RAS2}$	87	DQ33	129	$\overline{RAS3}$
4	DQ2	46	$\overline{CAS2}$	88	DQ34	130	$\overline{CAS6}$
5	DQ3	47	$\overline{CAS3}$	89	DQ35	131	$\overline{CAS7}$
6	V_{DD}	48	$\overline{WE2}$	90	V_{DD}	132	NC
7	DQ4	49	V_{DD}	91	DQ36	133	V_{DD}
8	DQ5	50	NC	92	DQ37	134	NC
9	DQ6	51	NC	93	DQ38	135	NC
10	DQ7	52	NC	94	DQ39	136	NC
11	DQ8	53	NC	95	DQ40	137	NC
12	V_{SS}	54	V_{SS}	96	V_{SS}	138	V_{SS}
13	DQ9	55	DQ16	97	DQ41	139	DQ48
14	DQ10	56	DQ17	98	DQ42	140	DQ49
15	DQ11	57	DQ18	99	DQ43	141	DQ50
16	DQ12	58	DQ19	100	DQ44	142	DQ51
17	DQ13	59	V_{DD}	101	DQ45	143	V_{DD}
18	V_{DD}	60	DQ20	102	V_{DD}	144	DQ52
19	DQ14	61	NC	103	DQ46	145	NC
20	DQ15	62	NC	104	DQ47	146	NC
21	NC	63	NC	105	NC	147	NC
22	NC	64	V_{SS}	106	NC	148	V_{SS}
23	V_{SS}	65	DQ21	107	V_{SS}	149	DQ53
24	NC	66	DQ22	108	NC	150	DQ54
25	NC	67	DQ23	109	NC	151	DQ55
26	V_{DD}	68	V_{SS}	110	V_{DD}	152	V_{SS}
27	$\overline{WE0}$	69	DQ24	111	NC	153	DQ56
28	$\overline{CAS0}$	70	DQ25	112	$\overline{CAS4}$	154	DQ57
29	$\overline{CAS1}$	71	DQ26	113	$\overline{CAS5}$	155	DQ58
30	$\overline{RAS0}$	72	DQ27	114	$\overline{RAS1}$	156	DQ59
31	$\overline{OE0}$	73	V_{DD}	115	NC	157	V_{DD}
32	V_{SS}	74	DQ28	116	V_{SS}	158	DQ60
33	A0	75	DQ29	117	A1	159	DQ61
34	A2	76	DQ30	118	A3	160	DQ62
35	A4	77	DQ31	119	A5	161	DQ63
36	A6	78	V_{SS}	120	A7	162	V_{SS}
37	A8	79	NC	121	A9	163	NC
38	A10	80	NC	122	A11	164	NC
39	A12	81	NC	123	NC	165	SA0
40	V_{DD}	82	SDA	124	V_{DD}	166	SA1
41	NC	83	SCL	125	NC	167	SA2
42	NC	84	V_{DD}	126	NC	168	V_{DD}

Figure 7-11
Pin assignment for 168-pin DIMM.

Although the PROM allows the designer to delay decisions about what information is stored, it can only be written once, or can be rewritten only if the existing pattern is a subset of the new pattern. Early erasable PROMs (EPROMs) could be written several times, after being erased with ultraviolet light (for UVPROMs) through a window that is mounted on the integrated circuit package. Electrically erasable PROMs (EEPROMs) allow their contents to be rewritten electrically. **Flash** memories are a form of PROM that can be electrically rewritten, and are used extensively in digital video cameras, personal data assistants (PDAs), for control programs in set-top cable television decoders, and other devices (see Section 7.3.4 for more details on flash memory).

PROMs can be used for control units and for **arithmetic logic units** (ALUs). As an example of this type of application, consider creating an ALU that performs the four functions Add, Subtract, Multiply, and Divide on eight-bit operands. We can generate a truth table that enumerates all 2^{16} possible combinations of operands and all 2^2 combinations of functions, and send the truth table to a PROM burner, which loads it into the PROM.

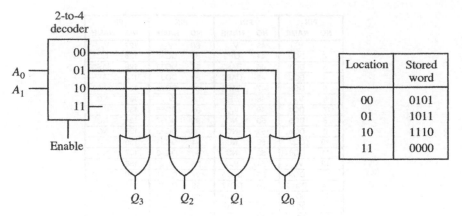

Figure 7-12
A ROM stores four four-bit words.

This brute-force **lookup table** (LUT) approach is not as impractical as it may seem, and is actually used in a number of situations. The PROM does not have to be very big: there are $2^8 \times 2^8$ combinations of the two input operands and there are 2^2 functions, so we need a total of $2^8 \times 2^8 \times 2^2 = 2^{18}$ words in the PROM, which is small by current standards.

The configuration for a PROM ALU is shown in Figure 7-13. The address lines are used for the operands and the function select inputs, and the outputs are produced by simply recalling the precomputed word stored at the addressed location. This approach is typically faster than using a hardware implementation for the functions, but it is not extensible to large word widths without applying some form of decomposition. 64-bit operands are becoming standard on computers today, and a corresponding PROM ALU would be prohibitively large if it were implemented with a single PROM. PROM LUTs are commonly used for portions of an ALU, however, such as the starting estimate in floating-point division based on Newton's iteration (see Section 3.4.3).

7.3.4 Flash Memory

Flash memory, which also goes by names like "flash RAM," **SD** (secure digital) disks and **jump drives** in various packaged forms, provides an electrically rewritable RAM type of memory that retains its contents after electrical power is removed, making it a **nonvolatile memory**. A section of memory cells can be erased in a single step, or "flash," thus the name. Flash memory is commonly used for fast, removable storage in digital cameras, PDAs, videogame consoles, laptop computers, and other devices.

Figure 7-14 shows an external view of an SD flash module that measures just 24 mm $\times$ 32 mm and stores 1 GB. The package consists of a plastic base card, a memory chip with bonding wires to the external contacts, and a resin layer that holds it all together.

Each flash storage cell stores a single bit in a **floating gate** as a negative charge, which can later be erased through a process knows as **Fowler-Nordheim tunneling**. A control gate determines the setting of the floating gate. The configuration of a flash storage cell is shown in Figure 7-15. A charge is applied to the floating gate through the bit

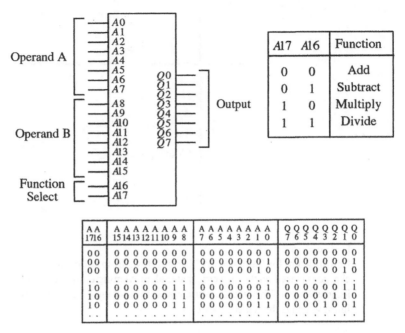

A17	A16	Function
0	0	Add
0	1	Subtract
1	0	Multiply
1	1	Divide

A A 17 16	A A A A A A A A 15 14 13 12 11 10 9 8	A A A A A A A A 7 6 5 4 3 2 1 0	Q Q Q Q Q Q Q Q 7 6 5 4 3 2 1 0
0 0	0 0 0 0 0 0 0 0	0 0 0 0 0 0 0 0	0 0 0 0 0 0 0 0
0 0	0 0 0 0 0 0 0 0	0 0 0 0 0 0 0 1	0 0 0 0 0 0 0 1
0 0	0 0 0 0 0 0 0 0	0 0 0 0 0 0 1 0	0 0 0 0 0 0 1 0
. .	. . . .	. . . .	. . . .
1 0	0 0 0 0 0 0 1 1	0 0 0 0 0 0 0 1	0 0 0 0 0 0 1 1
1 0	0 0 0 0 0 0 1 1	0 0 0 0 0 0 1 0	0 0 0 0 0 1 1 0
1 0	0 0 0 0 0 0 1 1	0 0 0 0 0 0 1 1	0 0 0 0 1 0 0 1
. .	. . . .	. . . .	. . . .

Figure 7-13
A lookup table (LUT) implements an eight-bit ALU.

line, which places a negative charge (logical 0) on the control gate that remains after power is removed. A logical 1 has no charge (less than a threshold, actually, as a pure chargeless state is not practical). Before new data can be written, the stored charge must first be cleared by applying a higher voltage than used in writing. Again, this clearing

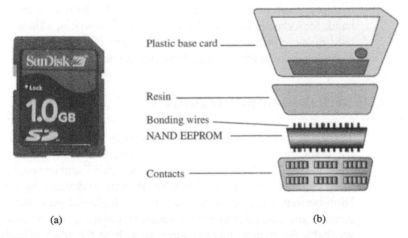

(a)   (b)

Figure 7-14
(a) External view of flash memory module and (b) flash module internals.
(Source: adapted from HowStuffWorks.com.)

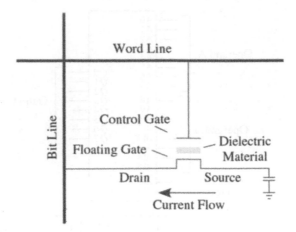

Figure 7-15
Cell structure for flash memory. Current flows from source to drain when a sufficient negative charge is placed on the dielectric material, preventing current flow through the word line. This is the logical 0 state. When the dielectric material is not charged, current flows between the bit and word lines, which is the logical 1 state.

step can be done in a single "flash" operation. The dielectric material is the key to storing data: dielectrics are poor conductors of electricity but are good at supporting electrostatic fields. Read and write speeds are on the order of 13 MB/s and 19 MB/s respectively, placing the devices closer to hard disk drives in terms of function rather than as main memory.

One disadvantage of flash memory is that it can only endure about 100,000 program/ erase cycles. This limits the lifetime if we want to replace a hard magnetic disk with flash memory; swap areas for virtual memory get hit hard with frequent writes. On the other hand, for some applications that have infrequent writes, a flash memory replacement for a hard disk can work well. Apple's iPod Nano departs from a tradition of miniature hard magnetic disks in iPods, using flash memory and no disks.

■ 7.4 CASE STUDY: RAMBUS MEMORY

There was a time when computer technology would be pushed from the laboratory into the marketplace. As the consumer marketplace for computing devices exploded, the "technology push" was replaced by "market pull," and consumer demand then dominated the preferences of technologists when it came to developing a new memory technology. High-performance, expensive memory for high-end processors was displaced by high-density, low-cost memory for consumer electronics, such as videogames. It became more profitable for memory manufacturers to address the needs of high-volume consumer markets, rather than devote costly chip fabrication facilities to a comparatively small high-end market.

The consumer electronics industry now dominates the memory market, and even high-end non-consumer processors make heavy use of consumer electronics technology, exploiting architectural enhancements instead of riskier one-of-a-kind hardware approaches, or exploiting innovations in supporting technologies (such as high-speed interconnects) to compensate for the performance shortcomings of what we might call "videogame memory."

Videogame memory is not all that low-end, however, and in fact, makes use of extraordinary technology enhancements that squeeze the most performance out of ever denser, low-cost devices. A leading memory technology that was introduced into Intel-based personal computers in 1999 was developed by Rambus, Inc. The Rambus DRAM (RDRAM) retrieves a block of eight bytes internal to the DRAM chip on every access, and multiplexes the eight bytes onto a narrow eight-bit or 16-bit channel, operating at a rate of 800 MHz when it was introduced and now at twice that rate.

A typical DRAM core (that is, the storage portion of an ordinary DRAM) can store or retrieve a line of eight bytes with a 200 MHz cycle. This is internal to the DRAM chip: most DRAMs only deliver one byte per cycle, but the RDRAM technology can multiplex that up to eight bytes per 200 MHz cycle using a higher external clock of 1.6 GHz. That higher rate is fed to a memory controller (the "chipset" on an Intel machine) that demuxes it into a 32-bit wide or 64-bit wide data stream at a lower rate, such as 400 MHz, going into a Pentium (or other processor chip). See Figure 7-16 for a comparison of the "slow wide" conventional RAM approach and the "fast narrow" Rambus approach.

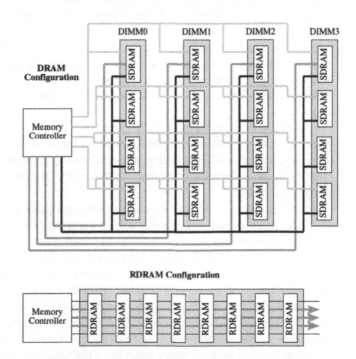

Figure 7-16
Comparison of DRAM and RDRAM configurations.

The Rambus RIMM modules (Rambus Inline Memory Modules) look similar to ordinary SIMMs and DIMMs, but they operate differently. The Rambus memory uses **microstrip technology** (also known as **transmission lines**) on the motherboard, which implements a crude shield that reduces **radio frequency** (RF) effects that interfere with data traveling through wires on the motherboard, called **traces**. In designing a printed circuit board (PCB) for Rambus technology, the critical parameters are (1) dielectric thickness of the PCB, (2) separation of the memory modules, and (3) trace width. There must be a ground plane (an electrical return path) beneath every signal line, with no **vias** (connections between board layers) along the path. All signals go on the top layer of the PCB. (A PCB can have a number of layers, typically no more than eight). The memory controller and memory modules must all be equally spaced, such as .5 inches from the memory controller to the first RIMM, then .5 inches to the next, etc.

The "Rambus Channel" is made up of transmission line traces. The trace widths end up being about twice as wide as ordinary traces, on the order of 12 mils (300 microns). Although 300 microns is relatively small for a board trace, if we want to send 128 signals over a PCB, using a 600-micron **pitch** (center-to-center spacing) with 300 microns between 300 micron traces, this corresponds to a footprint of 128×600 microns = 76 mm. This is a large footprint compared with lower-speed solutions that allow a much closer packing density.

In reality, the eight-bit version of the Rambus Channel only has 13 high-speed signals (the address is serialized onto a single line, there are eight data lines, one parity line, two clock lines, and one command line), and so the seemingly large footprint is not a near-term problem. With a 16-bit version of the Rambus Channel available at 1.6 GHz and 512 MB per module, the bandwidth problem appears to be in hand for a number of years using this technology. Extensibility to large word widths such as 64 bits or 128 bits will pose a significant challenge down the road, however, because the **chipset**, which controls access between the processor and the main memory, will need to support that same word width— a formidable task with current packaging methods that already have over 500 pins on the chipset.

Although Rambus memory of this type became available in 1998, the RIMM modules were not widely available until 1999, timed for the availability of a new memory controller (chipset) for the RIMMs. The memory controller is an important aspect of this type of memory because the view of memory that the CPU perceives is different from the actual physical memory.

Rambus memory is more expensive than conventional DRAM memory, but overall system cost can be reduced, which makes it attractive in low-cost, high-performance consumer electronics such as the Nintendo 64 video game console, which was a milestone adoption of this technology. The Nintendo 64 (see Figure 7-17) has four primary chips: a 64-bit MIPS RS4300i CPU; a Reality coprocessor that integrates all graphics, audio and memory-management functions; and two Rambus memory chips.

The Rambus technology provides the Nintendo 64 with a bandwidth of 562.5 MB/s using a 31-pin interface to the memory controller (an impressive rate at the time). By comparison, a system using typical 64-bit-wide synchronous DRAMs (SDRAMs) requires a 110-pin interface to the memory controller. This reduction in pin count allows the memory-controller to fit on the same **die** (the silicon chip) as the graphics and sound functions, in a relatively low-cost, 160-pin packaged chip.

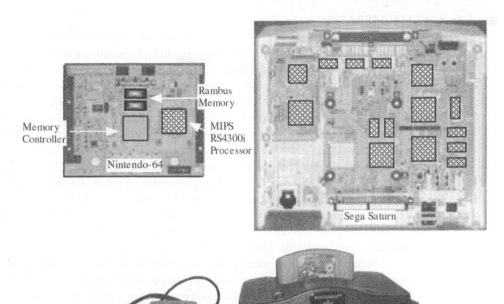

Figure 7-17
Rambus technology on the Nintendo 64 motherboard (top left) makes possible cost savings over the conventional Sega Saturn motherboard design (top right). The Nintendo 64 uses costlier plug-in cartridges (bottom), as opposed to inexpensive CD-ROMs used by the Sega Saturn.

The Rambus memory subsystem is made up of two memory chips that occupy 1.5 square inches of board space. An equivalent SDRAM design would require six square inches of board space. The space savings of using the Rambus approach enabled Nintendo to fit all of its components on a board measuring five by six inches, which is one quarter the size of the system board used in the competing Sega Saturn. In addition, Nintendo was able to use only a two-layer board instead of the four layers used in the Sega Saturn.

The cost savings Nintendo realized by choosing the Rambus solution over the 64-bit SDRAM approach are significant. The ability to use a two-layer implementation saved Nintendo $5 per unit in manufacturing costs. Taken altogether, Nintendo estimates the total bill of materials cost savings over an equivalent SDRAM-based design was about 20 percent.

These cost savings need to be placed in perspective with the marketplace, however. The competing Sega Saturn and Sony Playstation use CD-ROMs for game storage, which cost under $2 each to mass produce. The Nintendo 64 uses a plug-in ROM cartridge that costs close to $10 each to mass produce, and can only store 1% of what can be stored on a CD-ROM. This choice of media may have a great impact on the overall system architecture, and so the Rambus approach may not benefit all systems to the same degree. Details matter a great deal when it comes to evaluating the impact of a new technology on a particular market, or even a segment of a market.

■ 7.5 CACHE MEMORY

Most of the memory references in an executing program are made to a small number of locations. Typically, 90% of the execution time of a program is spent in just 10% of the code. This property is known as the **locality principle**. When a program references a memory location, it is likely to reference that same memory location again soon, which is known as **temporal locality**. Similarly, there is **spatial locality**, by which a memory location that is near a recently referenced location is more likely to be referenced than a memory location that is farther away. Temporal locality arises because programs spend much of their time in iteration or in commonly used subroutines, and thus the same section of code is visited a disproportionately large number of times. Spatial locality arises because data and program code tend to be stored in contiguous locations. Although 10% of the code accounts for the bulk of memory references, accesses within the 10% tend to be clustered. Thus, for a given interval of time, most of memory accesses come from an even smaller set of locations than 10% of a program's size.

Memory access is generally slow when compared with the speed of the central processing unit (CPU), and so the memory poses a significant bottleneck in computer performance. Since most memory references come from a small set of locations, the locality principle can be exploited in order to improve performance. A small but fast **cache memory**, in which the contents of the most commonly accessed locations are maintained, can be placed between the main memory and the CPU. When a program executes, the cache memory is searched first, and the referenced word is accessed in the cache if the word is present. If the referenced word is not in the cache, then a free location is created in the cache and the referenced word is brought into the cache from the main memory. The word is then accessed in the cache. Although this process takes longer than accessing main memory directly, the overall performance can be improved if a high proportion of memory accesses are satisfied by the cache, as is normally the case.

In principle, a large cache memory is desirable so that a large number of memory references can be satisfied by the cache. Unfortunately, a large cache is slower and more expensive than a small cache. A compromise that works well in practice is to first make a cache memory that is close to the CPU as fast as it can be within a given size constraint, and then to compensate for not being large enough, add another cache that is closer to the main memory. In fact, modern memory systems may have several levels of cache, referred to as Level 1 (L1), Level 2 (L2), and even, in some cases, Level 3 (L3), with the L1 cache being closest to the CPU and organized for speed, and the L3 cache being the farthest from the CPU (and closest to the main memory) and being organized primarily to satisfy memory references missed by the L1 and L2 caches. In most instances the L1 cache is implemented right on the CPU chip. The UltraSPARC IV+ has L1, L2, and L3 caches all on the same chip (see Section 1.1).

A cache memory is faster than main memory for a number of reasons. Faster electronics can be used, which also results in a greater expense in terms of money, size, and power requirements. Since the cache is small, however, this increase in cost is relatively small. A cache memory has fewer locations than a main memory, and as a result it has a shallower decoding tree, which reduces the access time. The cache is placed both physically closer and logically closer to the CPU than the main memory, and this placement avoids communication delays.

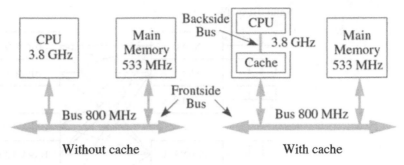

Figure 7-18
Placement of cache memory in a computer system.

A situation that highlights the placement of the cache is shown in Figure 7-18. A simple computer without a cache memory is shown in the left side of the figure. This cacheless computer contains a CPU that has a clock speed of 3.8 GHz, but communicates over a slower 800 MHz system bus to a main memory that supports a lower clock speed of 533 MHz. The system bus is commonly referred to as the **frontside bus**. A few bus cycles are normally needed to synchronize the CPU with the bus, and thus the difference in speed between main memory and the CPU can be as large as a factor of ten or more. A cache memory can be positioned closer to the CPU, as shown in the right side of Figure 7-18, so that the CPU sees fast accesses over a 3.8 GHz direct path (known as the **backside bus**) to the cache.

A number of hardware schemes have been developed for translating main memory addresses to cache memory addresses. The user does not need to know about the address translation, which has the advantage that cache memory enhancements can be introduced into a computer without a corresponding need for modifying application software. The choice of cache mapping scheme affects cost and performance, and there is no single best method that is appropriate for all situations. We will study three commonly used methods next.

7.5.1 Associative Mapped Cache

In this section, an **associative** mapping scheme is studied, which has the most flexibility (and greatest cost) for accessing a cache memory. Figure 7-19 shows an associative mapping scheme for a 2^{32}-word memory space that is divided into 2^{27} **blocks** of $2^5 = 32$ words per block. The main memory is not physically partitioned in this way, but this is the view of main memory that the cache sees. **Cache blocks**, or **cache lines**, as they are commonly known, typically range in size from eight to 64 bytes. Data is moved in and out of the cache a line at a time using memory interleaving (discussed in Section 7.3).

The cache for this example consists of 2^{14} **slots** into which main memory blocks are placed. The line size is 64 bits (eight bytes). There are more main memory blocks than there are cache slots, and any one of the 2^{27} main memory blocks can be mapped into each cache slot (with only one block placed in a slot at a time). To keep track of which one of the 2^{27} possible blocks is in each slot, a 27-bit **tag** field is added to each slot that holds an identifier in the range from 0 to $2^{27} - 1$. The tag field is the most significant 27 bits of the

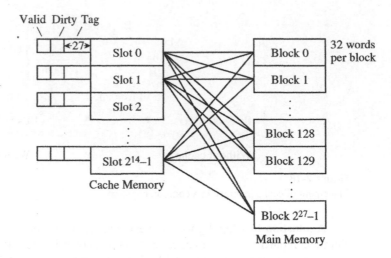

Valid Dirty Tag

Cache Memory

32 words per block

Main Memory

Figure 7-19
An associative mapping scheme for a cache memory.

32-bit memory address presented to the cache. All the tags are stored in a special tag memory where they can be searched in parallel. Whenever a new block is stored in the cache, its tag is stored in the corresponding tag memory location.

When a program is first loaded into main memory, the cache is cleared, and so while a program is executing, a **valid** bit is needed to indicate whether or not the slot holds a line that belongs to the program being executed. There is also a **dirty** bit that keeps track of whether or not a line has been modified while it is in the cache. A slot that is modified must be written back to the main memory before the slot is reused for another line.

A referenced location that is found in the cache results in a **hit**; otherwise, the result is a **miss**. When a program is initially loaded into memory, the valid bits are all set to 0. The first instruction that is executed in the program will therefore cause a miss, since none of the program is in the cache at that point. The block that causes the miss is located in the main memory and is loaded into the cache.

In an associative mapped cache, each main memory block can be mapped to any cache slot. The mapping from main memory blocks to cache slots is performed by partitioning an address into fields for the tag and the word (also known as the "byte" field) as shown below:

Tag	Word
27 bits	5 bits

When a reference is made to a main memory address, the cache hardware intercepts the reference and searches the cache tag memory to see if the requested line is in the cache. For each slot, if the valid bit is 1, then the tag field of the referenced address is compared with the tag field of the slot. All of the tags are searched in parallel, using an **associative memory.** See Section 7.7.1 for more on associative memories. If any tag in the cache tag memory matches the tag field of the memory reference, then the word is taken from the position in the slot specified by the word field. If the referenced word is not found in the cache, then the main memory block that contains the word is brought into the cache and the referenced word is then taken from the cache. The tag, valid, and dirty fields are updated, and the program resumes execution.

Consider how an access to memory location $(A035F014)_{16}$ is mapped to the cache. The leftmost 27 bits of the address form the tag field, and the remaining five bits form the word field, as shown below:

Tag	Word
1 0 1 0 0 0 0 0 0 0 1 1 0 1 0 1 1 1 1 0 0 0 0 0 0 0	1 0 1 0 0

If the addressed word is in the cache, it will be found in word $(14)_{16}$ of a slot that has a tag of $(501AF80)_{16}$, which is made up of the 27 most significant bits of the address. If the addressed word is not in the cache, then the block corresponding to the tag field $(501AF80)_{16}$ will be brought into an available slot in the cache from the main memory, and the memory reference that caused the miss will then be satisfied from the cache.

Although this mapping scheme is powerful enough to satisfy a wide range of memory access situations, there are two implementation problems that limit performance. First, the process of deciding which slot should be freed when a new block is brought into the cache can be complex. This process requires a significant amount of hardware and introduces delays in memory accesses. A second problem is that when the cache is searched, the tag field of the referenced address must be compared with all 2^{14} tag fields in the cache. (Alternative methods that limit the number of comparisons are described in Sections 7.5.2 and 7.5.3.)

In terms of chip area, Figure 7-20 shows an estimate of chip space based on the amount of storage needed. There are 2^{14} cache slots that each hold 256 bits for the cache line (32 bytes $\times$ 8 bits/byte), plus 27 tag bits, a valid bit, and a dirty bit, for a total of 2^{14} slots $\times$ (256 line + 27 tag + 1 valid + 1 dirty) bits/slot = 4,669,440 bits. This is the dominant space cost; the cache control logic is typically a small fraction in size by comparison.

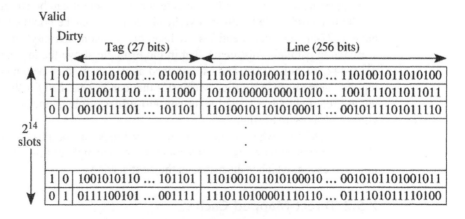

Figure 7-20
Area allocation for associative mapping scheme based on bits stored.

Replacement Policies in Associative Mapped Caches

When a new line needs to be placed in an associative mapped cache, an available slot must be identified. If there are unused slots, such as when a program begins execution, then the first slot with a valid bit of 0 can simply be used. When all of the valid bits for all cache slots are 1, however, then one of the active slots must be freed for the new line. Four common replacement policies are: **least recently used** (LRU), **least frequently used** (LFU), **first-in first-out** (FIFO), and **random**. A fifth policy, used for analysis purposes only, is **optimal**.

For the LRU policy, a time stamp is added to each slot, which is updated when any slot is accessed. When a slot must be freed for a new block, the contents of the least recently used slot, as identified by the age of the corresponding time stamp, are discarded and the new block is written to that slot. The LFU policy works similarly, except that only one slot is updated at a time by incrementing a frequency counter that is attached to each slot. When a slot is needed for a new block, the least frequently used slot is freed. The FIFO policy replaces slots in round-robin fashion, one after the next in the order of their physical locations in the cache. The random replacement policy simply chooses a slot at random.

The optimal replacement policy is not practical, but is used for comparison purposes to determine how effective other replacement policies are compared to the best possible. That is, the optimal replacement policy is determined only after a program has already executed, and so it is of little help for a running program, but can conceivably be useful if the same program will run on the same data set again.

Studies have shown that the LFU policy is only slightly better than the random policy. The LRU policy can be implemented efficiently, and is sometimes preferred over the others for that reason. A simple implementation of the LRU policy is covered in Section 7.5.7.

Advantages and Disadvantages of the Associative Mapped Cache

The associative mapped cache has the advantage that any main memory block can be placed into any cache slot. This means that regardless of how irregular the data and program references are, if a slot is available for the block, it can be stored in the cache. This results in considerable hardware overhead needed for cache bookkeeping. Each slot must have a 27-bit tag that identifies its location in main memory, and each tag must be searched in parallel. This means that in the example above the tag memory must be $27 \times 2^{14} = 442,368$ bits in size, and as described above, there must be a mechanism for searching the tag memory in parallel. Memories that can be searched for their contents, in parallel, are referred to as associative, or **content-addressable** memories. We will discuss this kind of memory in Section 7.7.

By restricting where each main memory block can be placed in the cache, we can eliminate the need for an associative memory. An example of this kind of cache is a **direct mapped cache**, which is discussed in the next section.

7.5.2 Direct-Mapped Cache

Figure 7-21 shows a direct mapping scheme for a 2^{32} word memory. As before, the memory is divided into 2^{27} blocks of $2^5 = 32$ words per block, and the cache consists of 2^{14} slots.

Valid Dirty Tag

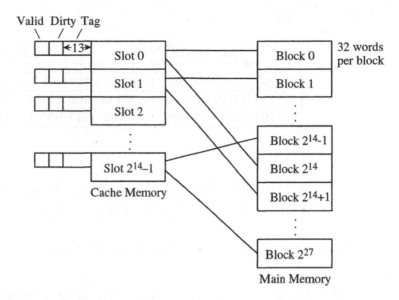

Figure 7-21
A direct mapping scheme for cache memory.

There are more main memory blocks than there are cache slots, and a total of $2^{27}/2^{14} = 2^{13}$ main memory blocks can be mapped onto each cache slot. In order to keep track of which of the 2^{13} possible blocks is in each slot, a 13-bit tag field is added to each slot which holds an identifier in the range from 0 to $2^{13} - 1$.

This scheme is called "direct mapping" because each cache slot corresponds to an explicit set of main memory blocks. For a direct mapped cache, each main memory block can be mapped to only one slot, but each slot can receive more than one block. The mapping from main memory blocks to cache slots is performed by partitioning an address into fields for the tag, the slot, and the word as shown below:

Tag	Slot	Word
13 bits	14 bits	5 bits

The 32-bit main memory address is partitioned into a 13-bit tag field, followed by a 14-bit slot field, followed by a five-bit word field. When a reference is made to a main memory address, the slot field identifies in which of the 2^{14} slots the block will be found if it is in the cache. If the valid bit is 1, then the tag field of the referenced address is compared with the tag field of the slot. If the tag fields are the same, then the word is taken from the position in the slot specified by the word field. If the valid bit is 1 but the tag fields are not the same, then the slot is written back to main memory if the dirty bit is set, and the corresponding main memory block is then read into the slot. For a program that has just started execution, the valid bit will be 0, and so the block is simply written to the slot. The valid bit for the block is then set to 1, and the program resumes execution.

Consider how an access to memory location $(A035F014)_{16}$ is mapped to the cache. The bit pattern is partitioned according to the word format shown above. The leftmost

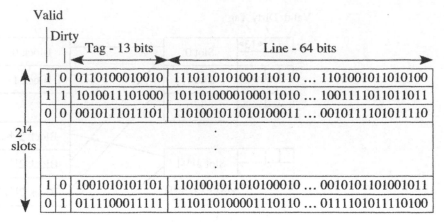

Figure 7-22
Area allocation for direct mapping scheme based on bits stored.

13 bits form the tag field, the next 14 bits form the slot field, and the remaining five bits form the word field as shown below:

Tag	Slot	Word
1 0 1 0 0 0 0 0 0 0 1 1 0	1 0 1 1 1 1 1 0 0 0 0 0 0 0	1 0 1 0 0

If the addressed word is in the cache, it will be found in word $(14)_{16}$ of slot $(2F80)_{16}$, which will have a tag of $(1406)_{16}$.

Advantages and Disadvantages of the Direct-Mapped Cache

The direct-mapped cache is a relatively simple scheme to implement. The tag memory in the example above is only $13 \times 2^{14} = 212{,}992$ bits in size, less than half of the associative mapped cache. Furthermore, there is no need for an associative search, since the slot field of the main memory address from the CPU is used to "direct" the comparison to the single slot where the block will be if it is indeed in the cache. See Figure 7-22 for the area allocation, which is 2^{14} slots $\times$ (256 line + 13 tag + 1 valid + 1 dirty) bits/slot = 4,440,064 stored bits, which is 229,376 bits fewer than the associative scheme.

This simplicity comes at a cost. Consider what happens when a program references locations that are 2^{19} words apart, which is the size of the cache. This pattern can arise naturally if a matrix is stored in memory by rows and is accessed by columns. Every memory reference will result in a miss, which will cause an entire block to be read into the cache even though only a single word is used. Worse still, only a small fraction of the available cache memory will actually be used.

Now it may seem that any programmer who writes a program this way deserves the resulting poor performance, but in fact, fast matrix calculations use power-of-two dimensions (which allows shift operations to replace costly multiplications and divisions for array indexing), and so the worst-case scenario of accessing memory locations that are 2^{19} addresses apart is not all that unlikely. To avoid this situation without paying the high implementation price of a fully associative cache memory, the **set-associative mapping** scheme can be used, which combines aspects of both direct mapping and associative mapping. Set-associative mapping, which is also known as **set-direct mapping**, is described in the next section.

7.5.3 Set-Associative Mapped Cache

The set-associative mapping scheme combines the simplicity of direct mapping with the flexibility of associative mapping. Set-associative mapping is more practical than fully associative mapping because the associative portion is limited to just a few slots that make up a set, as illustrated in Figure 7-23. For this example, two blocks make up a set, and so it is a **two-way** set associative cache. If there are four blocks per set, then it is a four-way set associative cache.

Since there are 2^{14} slots in the cache, there are $2^{14}/2 = 2^{13}$ sets. When an address is mapped to a set, the direct mapping scheme is used, and then associative mapping is used within a set. The format for an address has 13 bits in the set field, which identifies the set in which the addressed word will be found if it is in the cache. There are five bits for the word field as before and there is a 14-bit tag field that together make up the remaining 32 bits of the address, as shown below:

Tag	Set	Word
14 bits	13 bits	5 bits

As an example of how the set associative cache views a main memory address, consider again the address $(A035F014)_{16}$. The leftmost 14 bits form the tag field, followed by 13 bits for the set field, followed by five bits for the word field, as shown below:

Tag	Set	Word
1 0 1 0 0 0 0 0 0 0 1 1 0 1	0 1 1 1 1 1 0 0 0 0 0 0 0	1 0 1 0 0

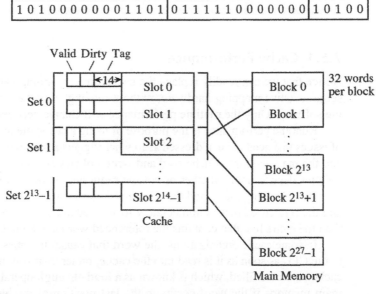

Figure 7-23
A set-associative mapping scheme for a cache memory.

As before, the partitioning of the address field is known only to the cache, and the rest of the computer is oblivious to any address translation.

Advantages and Disadvantages of the Set-Associative Mapped Cache

In the example above, the tag memory increases only slightly from the direct mapping example, to $14 \times 2^{14} = 229, 376$ bits, and only two tags need to be searched for each memory reference. The set-associative cache is widely used in today's microprocessors. See Figure 7-24 for the area calculation, which is 2^{14} slots $\times$ (256 line + 14 tag + 1 valid + 1 dirty) bits/slot = 4,456,448 stored bits, which is much less than associative mapping and only a little more than direct mapping.

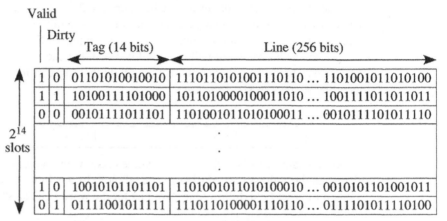

Figure 7-24
Area allocation for set-associative mapping scheme based on bits stored.

7.5.4 Cache Performance

Notice that we can readily replace the cache direct mapping hardware with associative or set-associative mapping hardware, without making any other changes to the computer or the software. Only the runtime performance will change between methods.

Runtime performance is the purpose of using a cache memory, and there are a number of issues that need to be addressed as to what triggers a line to be moved between the cache and the main memory. Cache read and write policies are summarized in Figure 7-25. The policies depend upon whether or not the requested word is in the cache. If a cache read operation is taking place, and the referenced word is in the cache, then there is a cache **hit** and the referenced data is immediately forwarded to the CPU. When a cache **miss** occurs, then the entire line that contains the referenced word is read into the cache.

In some cache organizations, the word that causes the miss is immediately forwarded to the CPU as soon as it is read into the cache, rather than waiting for the remainder of the cache slot to be filled, which is known as a **load-through** operation. For a non-interleaved main memory, if the word occurs in the last position of the block, then no performance gain is realized since the entire line is brought in before load-through can take place.

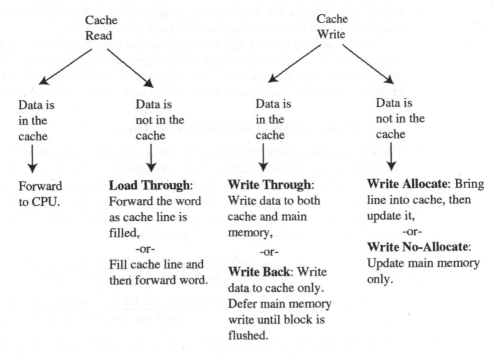

Figure 7-25
Cache read and write policies.

For an interleaved main memory, the order of accesses can be organized so that a load-through operation will always result in a performance gain.

For write operations, there may be two different copies of the word, one in the cache, and one in main memory. If both are updated simultaneously, this is referred to as **write-through**. If the write is deferred until the cache line is flushed from the cache, this is referred to as **write-back**. The use of a dirty bit is only needed for a write-back policy. Even if the data item is not in the cache when the write occurs, there is the choice of bringing the block containing the word into the cache and then updating it, known as **write-allocate**, or updating it in main memory without involving the cache, known as **write-no-allocate**.

Some computers have separate caches for instructions and data, which is a variation of a configuration known as the **Harvard architecture** (also known as a **split cache**) in which instructions and data are stored in separate sections of memory. Since instruction slots can never be dirty (unless we write self-modifying code, which is rare these days), an instruction cache is simpler than a data cache. In support of this configuration, observations have shown that most of the memory traffic moves away from main memory rather than toward it. Statistically, there is only one write to memory for every four read operations from memory. One reason for this is that instructions are only read from the main memory, and are never written to the memory except by the system loader. Another reason is that operations on data typically involve reading two operands and storing a single result, which means there are two read operations for every write operation. A cache that only handles reads, while sending writes directly to main memory can thus also be effective, although not necessarily as effective as a read/write cache.

As to which cache read and write policies are best, there is no simple answer. The organization of a cache is optimized for each computer architecture and the mix of programs that the computer executes. Cache organization and cache sizes are normally determined by the results of simulation runs that expose the nature of memory traffic.

7.5.5 Hit Ratios and Effective Access Times

Two measures that characterize the performance of a cache memory are the **hit ratio** and the **effective access time**. The hit ratio is computed by dividing the number of times referenced words are found in the cache by the total number of memory references. The effective access time is computed by dividing the total time spent accessing memory (summing the main memory and cache access times) by the total number of memory references. The corresponding equations are given below:

$$Hit\ ratio\ =\ \frac{No.\ times\ referenced\ words\ are\ in\ cache}{Total\ number\ of\ memory\ accesses}$$

$$Effective\ access\ time\ =\ \frac{(\#\ hits)(time\ per\ hit)\ +\ (\#\ misses)(time\ per\ miss)}{Total\ number\ of\ memory\ access}$$

Consider computing the hit ratio and the effective access time for a program running on a computer that has a direct mapped cache with four 16-word slots. The layout of the cache and the main memory is shown in Figure 7-26. The cache access time is 80 ns, and the time for transferring a main memory block to the cache is 2500 ns. Assume that load-through is used in this architecture and that the cache is initially empty. A sample program executes from memory locations 48–95, and then loops 10 times from 15–31 before halting.

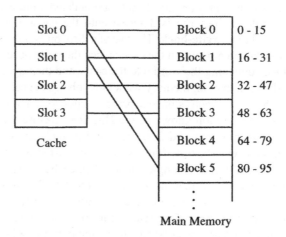

Figure 7-26
An example of a direct mapped cache memory.

Event	Location	Time	Comment
1 miss	48	2500ns	Memory block 3 to cache slot 3
15 hits	49-63	80ns×15=1200ns	
1 miss	64	2500ns	Memory block 4 to cache slot 0
15 hits	65-79	80ns×15=1200ns	
1 miss	80	2500ns	Memory block 5 to cache slot 1
15 hits	81-95	80ns×15=1200ns	
1 miss	15	2500ns	Memory block 0 to cache slot 0
1 miss	16	2500ns	Memory block 1 to cache slot 1
15 hits	17-31	80ns×15=1200ns	
9 hits	15	80ns×9=720ns	Last nine iterations of loop
144 hits	16-31	80ns×144=11,520ns	Last nine iterations of loop

Total hits = 213   Total misses = 5

Figure 7-27
A table of events for a program executing on an architecture with a small direct mapped cache memory.

We record the events as the program executes as shown in Figure 7-27. Since the memory is initially empty, the first instruction that executes causes a miss. A miss thus occurs at location 48, which causes main memory block 3 to be read into cache slot 3. This first memory access takes 2500 ns to complete. Load-through is used for this example, and so the word that causes the miss at location 48 is passed directly to the CPU while the rest of the block is loaded into the cache slot. The next event consists of 15 hits for locations 49 through 63. The events that follow are recorded in a similar manner, and the result is a total of 213 hits and five misses. The total number of accesses is 213 + 5 = 218. The hit ratio and effective access time are computed as shown below:

$$Hit\ ratio\ =\ \frac{213}{218}\ =\ 97.7\%$$

$$Effective\ Access\ Time\ =\ \frac{(213)(8\text{ns}) + (5)(2500(\text{ns}))}{218}\ =\ 136\text{ns}$$

Although the hit ratio is 97.7%, the effective access time for this example is almost 75% longer than the cache access time. This is due to the large amount of time spent in accessing a block from main memory.

7.5.6 Multilevel Caches

As the sizes of silicon ICs have increased and the packing density of components on ICs has increased, it has become possible to include portions or all of the cache memory on the same IC as the processor. With the increasing capacity of silicon chips, **multilevel caches** have been developed in which the fastest level of the cache, L1, is on the same chip as the processor and keeps up with the speed of the processor[1], and the remaining caches are

---

[1] The L1 cache access time may actually be a few CPU cycles; in fact, the L1 cache on the Pentium 4 (Northwood) has an access time of two CPU cycles. The processor is engineered so that the CPU is rarely starved for data (for example, the L1 cache is not accessed on every cycle).

placed farther away than the L1 cache but typically on the same silicon die as the processor, or at least in the same integrated circuit package if not on the same die. Data and instruction caches are commonly separately maintained in the L1 cache (referred to as a **split cache**), while the L2 cache and L3 cache are usually **unified**, which means that the same cache holds both data and instructions.

In order to compute the hit ratio and effective access time for a multilevel cache, the hits and misses must be recorded among all caches. Relationships for the overall hit ratio and the overall effective access time for a two-level cache are shown below. H_1 is the hit ratio for the L1 cache, H_2 is the hit ratio for the L2 cache (which is the same as the L1 miss ratio), and T_{EFF} is the overall effective access time. The method can be extended to any number of levels.

$$H_1 = \frac{No.\ times\ accessed\ word\ is\ in\ L1\ cache}{Total\ number\ of\ memory\ accesses}$$

$$H_2 = \frac{No.\ times\ accessed\ word\ is\ in\ L2\ cache}{No.\ times\ accessed\ word\ is\ not\ in\ L2\ cache}$$

$$T_{EFF} = (No.\ L1\ cache\ hits)(L1\ cache\ hit\ time) +$$
$$(No.\ L2\ cache\ hits)(L2\ cache\ hit\ time) +$$
$$(No.\ L2\ cache\ misses)(L2\ cache\ miss\ time)$$
$$/Total\ number\ of\ memory\ accesses$$

As an example, consider a two-level cache in which the L1 hit time is 5 ns, the L2 hit time is 20 ns, and the L2 miss time is 100 ns. There are 10,000 memory references of which 10 cause L2 misses and 90 cause L1 misses. Compute the hit ratios of the L1 and L2 caches and the overall effective access time.

H_1 is the ratio of the number of times the accessed word is in the L1 cache to the total number of memory accesses. There is a total of 85 (L1) and 15 (L2) misses, and so:

$$H_1 = \frac{(10,000 - 10 - 90)hits}{10,000\ accesses} = 99\%$$

H_2 is the ratio of the number of times the accessed word is in the L2 cache to the number of times the L2 cache is accessed, and so:

$$H_2 = \frac{(100 - 10)hits}{100\ accesses} = 90\%$$

The effective access time is then:

$$T_{EFF} = (10,000 - 10 - 90\ L1\ hits)(5\ ns\ per\ L1\ hit) +$$
$$(100 - 10\ L2\ hits)(20\ ns\ per\ L2\ hit) +$$
$$(10\ L2\ cache\ misses)(100\ ns\ per\ L2\ cache\ miss)$$
$$/10,000\ accesses.$$
$$= 523\ ns\ per\ access$$

7.5.7 Cache management

The management of a cache memory presents a complex problem to a system programmer. If a given memory location represents an I/O port, as it may in memory-mapped systems, then it probably should not appear in the cache at all. If it is cached, the value in the I/O port may change, and this change will not be reflected in the value of the data stored in the cache. This is known as "stale" data: the copy that is in the cache is "stale" compared with the value in main memory. Likewise, in **shared-memory multiprocessor** environments (see Chapter 10), where more than one processor may access the same main memory, either the cached value or the value in main memory may become stale due to the activity of one or more of the CPUs. At a minimum, the cache in a multiprocessor environment should implement a write-through policy for those cache lines that map to shared memory locations.

For these reasons and others, most modern processor architectures allow the system programmer to have some measure of control over the cache. For example, the Motorola PPC processor's cache, which normally enforces a write-back policy, can be set to a write-through policy on a per-line basis. Other instructions allow individual lines to be specified as noncacheable or to be marked as invalid, loaded, or flushed.

Internal to the cache, replacement policies (for associative and set-associative caches) need to be implemented efficiently. An efficient implementation of the LRU replacement policy can be achieved with the **Neat Little LRU Algorithm** (origin unknown). Continuing with the cache example used in Section 7.5.5, we construct a matrix in which there is a row and a column for every slot in the cache, as shown in Figure 7-28. Initially, all of the cells are set to 0. Each time that a slot is accessed, 1s are written into each cell in the row of the table that corresponds to that slot. 0s are then written into each cell in the column that corresponds to that slot. Whenever a slot is needed, the row that contains all 0s is the

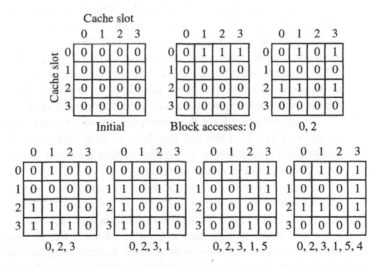

Figure 7-28

A sequence is shown for the Neat Little LRU Algorithm for a cache with four slots. Main memory blocks are accessed in the sequence 0, 2, 3, 1, 5, 4.

oldest and is used next. At the beginning of the process, more than one row will contain all 0s, and so a tie-breaking mechanism is needed. The first row with all 0s is one method that will work, which we use here.

The example shown in Figure 7-28 shows the configuration of the matrix as blocks are accessed in the order: 0, 2, 3, 1, 5, 4. Initially, the matrix is filled with 0s. After a reference is made to block 0, the row corresponding to block 0 is filled with 1s and the column corresponding to block 0 is filled with 0s. For this example, block 0 happens to be placed in slot 0, but for other situations, block 0 can be placed in any slot. The process continues until all cache slots are in use at the end of the sequence 0, 2, 3, 1. In order to bring the next block (5) into the cache, a slot must be freed. The row for slot 0 contains 0s, and so it is the least recently used slot. Block 5 is then brought into slot 0. Similarly, when block 4 is brought into the cache, slot 2 is overwritten.

7.5.8 Cache Coherency

The use of a cache memory is fairly straightforward in principle: all memory requests are intercepted and an attempt is made to satisfy them via the cache (which may have more than one level). If that is not possible, then main memory is accessed for the missed reference and the cache is updated with a new line that contains the reference.

The operation is not so straightforward when more than one processor shares the same main memory, which is a common configuration. Each processor "core" may have its own thread of execution with its own private storage, but there are storage areas that are shared among multiple processes, like system buffers. When there are multiple processors, there are multiple caches too, and there is a danger that one processor updates its cached copy of a variable without the other processor knowing about it. This problem, known as **cache coherency**, has a few solutions.

The primary goal of cache coherence is to ensure that every cache sees the same value for a referenced location, and that means making sure that any shared operand that is changed in one processor is updated throughout the system. In a **directory-based** approach, shared data is placed in a common directory that maintains cache coherence. When a cache needs to load a line from main memory, it goes through the directory. The directory can either update any outdated caches or simply invalidate outdated entries, forcing the other caches to reload a line when they need it again.

An alternative approach is **snooping**, in which each cache watches the memory bus for any requests for a line that they have, in which case a cache memory for one processor would satisfy the memory request for another on reading, and all caches would update or invalidate their own entries on writing.

This brings us to the issue of **false sharing**, which reduces cache performance when two operands that are not shared between processes share the same cache line. The situation is shown in Figure 7-29. The problem is that each process will invalidate the other's cache line when writing data without a real need; the unshared operands would get correctly flushed to main memory at their natural pace without having to invalidate and update cache lines. A solution to this problem is to avoid it by ensuring that operands are assigned to memory locations so that false sharing does not arise. (See [Hewlett Packard, 2005] for an example.)

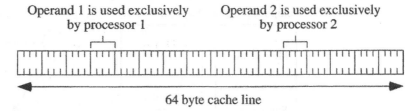

Figure 7-29
A false sharing situation arises when two processors read and write different locations in the same cache line.

7.6 VIRTUAL MEMORY

Despite the enormous advancements in creating ever larger memories in smaller areas, computer memory is still like closet space in the sense that there is never enough of it. An economical method of extending the apparent size of the main memory is to augment it with disk space, which is one aspect of **virtual memory** that we cover in this section. Disk storage appears near the bottom of the memory hierarchy, with a lower cost per bit than main memory, and so it makes sense to use disk storage to hold the portions of a program or data sets that do not entirely fit into the main memory. In a different aspect of virtual memory, complex address mapping schemes are supported, which give greater flexibility in how the memory is used. We explore these aspects of virtual memory next.

7.6.1 Overlays

An early approach to using disk storage to augment the main memory made use of overlays, in which an executing program overwrites its own code with other code as needed. In this scenario, the programmer has the responsibility of managing memory usage. Figure 7-30 shows an overlay example in which a program contains a main routine and three subroutines A, B, and C. The physical memory is smaller than the size of the program, but is larger than any single routine. A strategy for managing memory using overlays is to modify the program so that it keeps track of which subroutines are in memory, and reads in subroutine code as needed. Typically, the main routine serves as the **driver** and manages the bulk of the bookkeeping. The driver stays in memory while other routines are brought in and out.

Figure 7-30 shows a **partition graph** that is created for the example program. The partition graph identifies which routines can overlay others based on which subroutines call others. For this example, the main routine is always present, and supervises which subset of subroutines are in memory. Subroutines B and C are kept in the same partition in this example because B calls C, but subroutine A is in its own partition because only the main routine calls A. Partition #0 can thus overlay partition #1, and partition #1 can overlay partition #0.

Although this method can work well in a variety of situations, a cleaner solution would be to let the operating system manage the overlays, which can be effective with a single program running. When more than one program is loaded into memory, however, then the application routines that manage the overlays cannot operate without interacting with the operating system in order to find out which portions of memory are available. This scenario

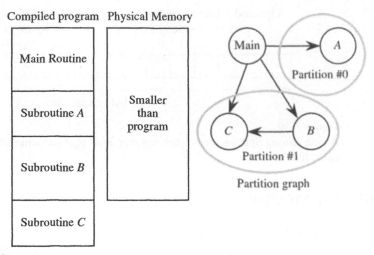

Figure 7-30
A partition graph for a program with a main routine and three subroutines.

introduces a great deal of complexity into managing the overlay process since there is a heavy interaction between the operating system and each program. The process is also very susceptible to programming errors. An alternative method that can be managed by the operating system alone is called **paging**, which is described in the next section.

7.6.2 Paging

Paging is a form of automatic overlaying that is managed by the operating system. The address space is partitioned into equal sized blocks, called **pages**. Pages are normally an integral power of two in size, such as $2^{13} = 8192$ bytes. Paging makes the physical memory appear larger than it truly is by mapping the physical memory address space to some portion of the virtual memory address space, which is stored on a disk. An illustration of a small virtual memory mapping scheme is shown in Figure 7-31. Eight virtual pages of 1024 bytes each (which is small by current standards but manageable for an example) are mapped to four physical **page frames**.

An implementation of virtual memory must handle references that are made outside of the portion of virtual space that is mapped to physical space. The following sequence of events is typical when a referenced virtual location is not in physical memory, which is referred to as a **page fault**:

1. A page frame is identified to be overwritten. The contents of the page frame are written to secondary memory (a disk) if changes were made to it, so that the changes are recorded before the page frame is overwritten. The associative mapping scheme is preferred for virtual memory because it offers the most flexibility, and the computation cost is small compared to the millions of cycles needed to transfer a page between a cache and the main memory.

2. The virtual page that we want to access is located in secondary memory and is written into physical memory, in the page frame located in step (1) above.

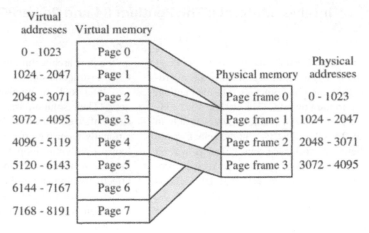

Figure 7-31
A mapping between a virtual and a physical memory.

3. The page table is updated to map the new section of virtual memory onto the physical memory (see below).

4. Execution continues.

For the virtual memory shown in Figure 7-31, there are $2^{13} = 8192$ virtual locations in the entire virtual space and so an executing program must generate 13-bit addresses, which are interpreted as a three-bit page number and a 10-bit offset within the page. Given the three-bit page number, we need to find out where the page is: it is either in one of the four page frames, or it is in secondary memory. In order to keep track of which pages are in physical memory, a **page table** is maintained, as illustrated in Figure 7-32, which corresponds to the mapping shown in Figure 7-31.

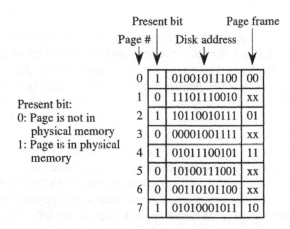

Figure 7-32
A page table for a virtual memory.

Intel vs. Motorola: The Pentium P4 and PowerPC G4e L1 Caches

The release of the Intel Pentium and the Motorola PowerPC in the early 1990s ushered in a new age for microprocessors. By 2001 Intel had progressed to the Pentium P4 and Motorola to the PowerPC G4e. By late 2002 PPC clock speeds were in the 1 GHz range; Intel was able to clock the P4 at 2.8 GHz. The P4's higher clock speed translates to better performance, but it brings with it increased demand on the memory system to keep the processor fed with instructions and data. The L1 cache is critical to effective performance at these clock speeds, since only the L1 cache has an access time of one to two clock cycles vs. six or more for the L2 cache.

Both Intel and Motorola chose to use "split L1 caches," the I-cache for instructions and the D-cache for data. Motorola used their L1 I-cache in the conventional way: to cache their RISC-style instructions on their way to execution. Intel could not use this approach without some modification. Their 1980s-style CISC instruction set, kept around for the sake of upward binary compatibility, does not map well to pipelined and superscalar architectures, for all the reasons discussed in Chapter 6. Intel's solution was to decode or "crack" each CISC instruction into a sequence of RISC-like fragments known as μops or uops, which could then be scheduled into the execution units in a way similar to the way RISC instructions are scheduled. There is a hidden advantage to this approach—as architectures evolve, Intel can change the "uop instruction set" in order to optimize execution on the new architecture without changing the underlying CISC instruction set.

Intel took an innovative approach to caching the uops. Their solution was to retain the uops in the L1 cache after execution for later reuse. Since most computationally intensive programs spend most of their time in loops, if an entire loop can be held in the L1 cache, the loop's instructions need to be decoded to uops only once, effectively eliminating the instruction fetch! When the I-cache is used to keep instructions or uops around after execution, it is called a **trace cache.** When the L1 cache is filled for the first time after a miss, the cache goes into "trace segment build" mode. In this mode the processor fetches instructions from the L2 cache, translates them into uops, builds a "trace segment" with them, loads the trace cache with the trace segment, and enters "trace execute" mode.

Motorola does not use a trace cache, but they do use some instruction cracking to even out instruction execution times. The G4e L1 I-cache can hold 8K 32-bit instructions. Intel quotes their L1 cache as having a capacity of 12K uops. The two processors are roughly equivalent in benchmark performance, though Intel does pay a penalty for this: heat dissipation. The P4 dissipates 68 watts, whereas the G4e dissipates only 30 watts. This paid off for Apple: they were able to capture a sizeable portion of the laptop market because their PowerBooks had a longer battery lifetime.

The page table has as many entries as there are virtual pages. (Practical cases are much larger than this example, and can use 64-bit or even larger addresses.) The Present bit indicates whether or not the corresponding page is in physical memory. The Disk address field is a pointer to the location where the corresponding page can be found on a disk unit. The operating system normally manages the disk accesses, and so the page table only needs to maintain the disk addresses that the operating system assigns to blocks when the system starts up. The disk addresses normally do not change during the course of computation. The Page frame field indicates which physical page frame holds a virtual page, if the page is in physical memory. For pages that are not in physical memory, the page frame fields are invalid, and so they are marked with "xx" in Figure 7-32.

In order to translate a virtual address to a physical address, we take two page frame bits from the page table and append them to the left of the 10-bit offset, which produces the physical address for the referenced word. Consider the situation shown in Figure 7-33, in which a reference is made to virtual address 1001101000101. The three leftmost bits of the

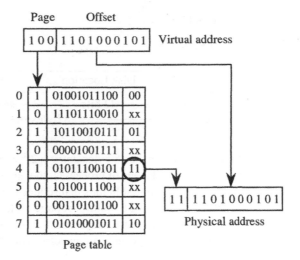

Figure 7-33
A virtual address is translated into a physical address.

virtual address (100) identify the page. The bit pattern that appears in the page frame field (11) is appended to the left of the 10-bit offset (1101000101), and the resulting address (111101000101) indicates which physical memory address holds the referenced word.

It may take a relatively long period of time for a program to be loaded into memory. The entire program may never be executed, and so the time required to load the program from a disk into the memory can be reduced by loading only the portion of the program that is needed for a given interval of time. The **demand paging** scheme does not load a page into memory until there is a page fault. After a program has been running for a while, only the pages being used will be in physical memory (this is referred to as the **working set**), so demand paging does not have a significant negative impact on long-running programs.

Consider again the memory mapping shown in Figure 7-31. The size of the virtual address space is 2^{13} words and the physical address space is 2^{12} words. There are eight pages that each contain 2^{10} words. Assume that the memory is initially empty, and that demand paging is used for a program that executes from memory locations 1030 to 5300. The execution sequence will make accesses to pages 1, 2, 3, 4, and 5, in that order. The page replacement policy is FIFO. Figure 7-34 shows the configuration of the page table as execution proceeds. The first access to memory will cause a page fault on virtual address 1030, which is in page #1. The page is brought into physical memory, and the valid bit and page frame field are updated in the page table. Execution continues, until page #5 must be brought in, which forces out page #1 due to the FIFO page replacement policy. The final configuration of the page table in Figure 7-34 is shown after location 5300 is accessed.

This is a small example that exposes the concept of paging with simple parameters, but a practical example might have a page table with 2^{20} entries and a page size of 16 KB. Adding to the storage needed for the page table, we would need to introduce a dirty bit to keep track of which pages have been changed and need to be written back to the disk. A page table entry might then occupy eight bytes as shown below:

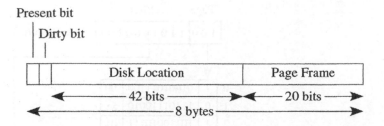

Present bit

Dirty bit

| | | Disk Location | Page Frame |

←——— 42 bits ———→←—— 20 bits ——→

←————————— 8 bytes —————————→

The size of the page table is then 8 bytes/entry $\times 2^{20}$ entries = 8 MB. Every process gets its own page table, and with dozens of processes, the page table alone can consume all of the main memory. There are a few solutions that reduce the amount of main memory allocated to the page table, such as using a multilevel page table or actually allowing the page table to be swapped out. This may seem dangerous, but is workable as long as certain key pages that control the rest of the page table are never swapped out.

7.6.3 Segmentation

Virtual memory as we have discussed it up to this point is one-dimensional in the sense that addresses grow either up or down. **Segmentation** divides the address space into **segments**, which may be of arbitrary size. Each segment is its own one-dimensional address space. This allows tables, stacks, and other data structures to be maintained as logical enti-

0	0	01001011100	xx	
1	1	11101110010	00	
2	0	10110010111	xx	
3	0	00001001111	xx	After fault on page #1
4	0	01011100101	xx	
5	0	10100111001	xx	
6	0	00110101100	xx	
7	0	01010001011	xx	

0	0	01001011100	xx	
1	1	11101110010	00	
2	1	10110010111	01	
3	0	00001001111	xx	After fault on page #2
4	0	01011100101	xx	
5	0	10100111001	xx	
6	0	00110101100	xx	
7	0	01010001011	xx	

0	0	01001011100	xx	
1	1	11101110010	00	
2	1	10110010111	01	
3	1	00001001111	10	After fault on page #3
4	0	01011100101	xx	
5	0	10100111001	xx	
6	0	00110101100	xx	
7	0	01010001011	xx	

0	0	01001011100	xx	
1	0	11101110010	xx	
2	1	10110010111	01	
3	1	00001001111	10	Final
4	1	01011100101	11	
5	1	10100111001	00	
6	0	00110101100	xx	
7	0	01010001011	xx	

Figure 7-34
The configuration of a page table changes as a program executes. Initially, the page table is empty. In the final configuration, four pages are in physical memory.

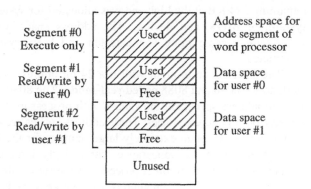

Figure 7-35
A segmented memory allows two users to share the same word processor.

ties that grow without bumping into each other. Segmentation allows for **protection**, so that a segment may be specified as "read only" to prevent changes or "execute only" to prevent unauthorized copying. This also protects users from trying to write data into instruction areas. (Paging can also support protection; see Section 7.6.4 for more on protection.)

When segmentation is used with virtual memory, the size of each segment's address space can be very large, and so the physical memory devoted to each segment is not committed until it is needed.

Figure 7-35 illustrates a segmented memory. The executable code for a word processing program is loaded into Segment #0. This segment is marked as "execute only" and is thus protected from writing. Segment #1 is used for the data space for user #0 and is marked as "read/write" for user #0 so that no other user can have access to this area. Segment #2 is used for the data space for user #1 and is marked as "read/write" for user #1. The same word processor can be used by both user #0 and user #1, in which case the code in segment #0 is shared but each user has a separate data segment.

Segmentation is not the same thing as paging. With paging, the user does not see the automatic overlaying. With segmentation, the user (or more likely, the programmer) is aware of where segment boundaries are. The operating system manages both protection and mapping, and so an ordinary user does not normally need to deal with bookkeeping, but a more sophisticated user such as a computer programmer may see the segmentation frequently when array pointers are pushed past segment boundaries in errant programs.

In order to specify an address in a segmented memory, the user's program must specify a segment number and an address within the segment. The operating system then translates the user's segmented address to a physical address.

To summarize the differences between segmentation and paging, segmentation extends the logical size of memory by supporting multiple address spaces. Paging, on the other hand, allows a large address space to be accessible to a single program. The differences may seem subtle but are important, and may best be described with a historical perspective on how these aspects of virtual memory were developed. When Intel came out with the 8086 and 8088 processors in the late 1970s, the address space went up to 1 MB (a large size at the time), of which the first 640 KB was used for physical RAM, and the remaining 384 KB at the high end was allocated for system code (the **basic input/output system**, or **BIOS**) and devices. The address space was quickly exhausted, however, as software became more sophisticated and memory-hungry, and as memory prices plummeted.

The Intel 80286 brought with it a 24-bit address space and a backward-compatible mode to the 8086 and 8088 called **real-mode**. The 80386 came out shortly after that with a 32-bit address space, and nowadays with processors such as the Intel IA-64 (Itanium), we have 64-bit address spaces. These address spaces are not filled with contiguous physical memory — 2^{64} is an extremely large number for the IA-64. However, a running program should have the appearance that a fairly large chunk of that address space is available to it and that no other process can interfere with its use of that space.

An advantage of segmentation is that a process can be loaded into any area of memory and execute as if it were located at memory address 0 (or any other convenient address) without the need to "patch up" references that need to change as a result of relocation. A special segment mapping register (known as a **segment descriptor** in Intel architectures) contains the offset of the segment within the overall address space, and is added in to every reference for that segment. As long as segments are arranged so as not to overlap, bounds can be checked to ensure that a process does not access memory space assigned to another process. A disadvantage of segmentation is that memory addresses must be handled in two parts: a base address for a segment, and an offset within a segment.

7.6.4 Protection

Memory protection prevents one process from corrupting the memory of another process by enforcing memory bounds that are allocated to each process through the use of hardware registers. Segmentation is one approach to implementing protection. All access to the main memory is limited to the address range specified by the segment registers assigned to each process. If a process attempts to access memory outside of its assigned space, then a **general protection fault** is generated and the operating system handles the fault, typically by terminating the program and informing the user, and also possibly entering a debug mode.

Paging is another approach to protection. Each process has its own page table, which defines disk blocks that make up pages that are knit together into a linear address space. The same page can appear in different page tables, thus giving the view to each process that it has the exclusive use of the memory when in fact large portions may be shared among processes. Protection is handled by ensuring that memory references appear within the page table space. Since a page fault is generated when a reference is made to an address outside of the pages that are present in the page table, the memory bounds can be checked at that point via software with little added time penalty considering the long time (millions of cycles) needed to satisfy a page fault. Pages that are read-only would not be flushed back to the disk, which helps prevent corruption of the shared copy.

7.6.5 Fragmentation

When a computer is "booted up," it goes through an initialization sequence that loads the operating system into memory. A portion of the address space may be reserved for I/O

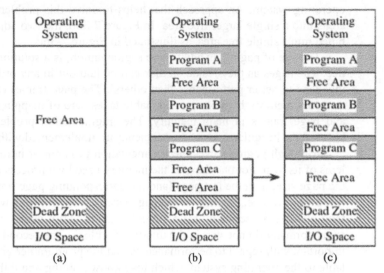

Figure 7-36
Free area of memory (a) after initialization; (b) after fragmentation; (c) after coalescing.

devices, and the remainder of the address space is then available for use by the operating system. This remaining portion of the address space may be only partially filled with physical memory: the rest comprises a "dead zone" that must never be accessed since there is no hardware that responds to the dead zone addresses.

Figure 7-36a shows the state of a memory just after the initialization sequence. The "free area" is a section of memory that is available to the operating system for loading and executing programs. During the course of operation, programs of various sizes will be loaded into memory and executed. When a program finishes execution, the memory space that is assigned to that program is released to the operating system. As programs are loaded and executed, the free area becomes subdivided into a collection of small areas, none of which may be large enough to hold a program that would fit unless some or all of the free areas are combined into a single large area. This is a problem known as **fragmentation**, and is encountered with segmentation (without paging) because the segments, which differ in size, must ultimately be mapped within a single linear address space.

Figure 7-36b illustrates the fragmentation problem. When the operating system needs to find a free area that is large enough to hold a program, it will rarely find an exact match. The free area will generally be larger than the program, which has the effect of subdividing the free areas more finely as programs are mismatched with free areas. One method of assigning programs to free areas is called **first fit**, in which the free areas are scanned until a large enough area is found that will satisfy the program. Another method is called **best fit**, in which the free area is used that wastes the least amount of space. While best fit makes better use of memory than first fit, it requires more time because all of the free areas must be scanned.

Regardless of which algorithm is used, the process of assigning programs or data to free areas tends to produce smaller free areas (Knuth, 1974). This makes it more difficult to find a single contiguous free area that is large enough to satisfy the needs of the operating system. An approach that helps to solve this problem coalesces adjacent free areas into a single larger free area. In Figure 7-36b, the two adjacent free areas are combined into a single free area, as illustrated in Figure 7-36c.

The use of paging, in addition to segmentation, is a solution that works well in practice. The pages as they reside on disk can be laid out in any order (although some orderings lead to better performance than others). The page frames can appear in any order in the main memory because the page table takes care of mappings between pages on disk and page frames in main memory. The fragmentation problem has now been solved because the irregular sizes of the segments are implemented with fixed-size pages.

Although paging solves the fragmentation problem, it introduces performance problems of its own. For one thing, if the memory used by a process does not map exactly into the page size, then the last page (and the corresponding page frame) will only be partially filled. On average, one half of the page size is wasted in this way per data/program area (and a single process may have multiple data/program areas) because data and program areas normally do not start in the middle of a block. The second issue, and probably more important with regard to performance, is that the programmer gives up control of the page table to the operating system, which may know nothing about the best way to map pages to page frames. Overall though, the problems introduced by paging are outweighed by the benefits.

7.6.6 The Translation Lookaside Buffer

The virtual memory mechanism, while being an elegant solution to the problem of accessing large programs and data files, has a significant problem associated with it. At least two memory references are needed to access a value in memory: one reference is to the page table to find the physical page frame, and another reference is for the actual data. The **translation lookaside buffer** (TLB) is a solution to this problem.

The TLB is a small associative memory typically placed on the CPU die that stores the most recent translations from virtual to physical address, and is in effect a cache for the page table. The first time that a given virtual address is translated into a physical address, this translation is stored in the TLB. Each time the CPU issues a virtual address, the TLB is searched for that virtual address. If the virtual page number exists in the TLB, then the TLB returns the physical page number, which can be immediately sent to the main memory (but normally, the cache memory would intercept the reference to main memory and satisfy the reference out of the cache).

An example TLB is shown in Figure 7-37. The TLB holds eight entries for a system that has 32 pages and 16 page frames. The virtual page field is five bits wide because there are $2^5 = 32$ pages. Likewise, the physical page field is four bits wide because there are $2^4 = 16$ page frames.

TLB misses are handled in much the same way as other memory misses. Upon a TLB miss the virtual address is applied to the memory system, where it is looked up in the page table. If it is found in the page table, then the TLB is updated, and the next reference to that page will thus result in a TLB hit.

Valid	Virtual page number	Physical page number
1	0 1 0 0 1	1 1 0 0
1	1 0 1 1 1	1 0 0 1
0	- - - - -	- - - -
0	- - - - -	- - - -
1	0 1 1 1 0	0 0 0 0
0	- - - - -	- - - -
1	0 0 1 1 0	0 1 1 1
0	- - - - -	- - - -

Figure 7-37
An example TLB that holds eight entries for a system with 32 virtual pages and 16 page frames.

7.6.7 Putting it All Together

Virtual memory is divided into pages that are relatively large when compared with cache memory blocks, which tend to be only a few words in size. Copies of the most heavily used blocks are kept in cache memory as well as in main memory, and also in the virtual memory image that is stored on a hard disk. When a memory reference is made on a computer that contains both cache and virtual memories, the TLB sees the reference first, and then the cache hardware sees the reference and satisfies the reference if the word is in the cache. If the referenced word is not in the cache, then the block that contains the word is read into the cache from the main memory, and the referenced word is then taken from the cache. If the page that contains the word is not in the main memory, then the page is brought into the main memory from a disk unit, and the block is then loaded into the cache so that the reference can be satisfied.

The use of virtual memory causes some intricate interactions with the cache. For example, since more than one program may be using the cache and the virtual memory, the timing statistics for two runs of a program executing on the same set of data may be different. Also, when a dirty block needs to be written back to main memory, it is possible that the page frame that contains the corresponding virtual page has been overwritten. This would cause the page to be loaded back to main memory from secondary memory in order to flush the dirty block from the cache memory to the main memory. In practice, however, this situation would not arise because the memory hierarchy is inclusive: if a block at a lower level is removed, then the corresponding blocks at the higher levels are removed at the same time. Thus, when a page is flushed, all of the corresponding cache and TLB entries are also flushed.

Figure 7-38 relates the interactions among cache memory, TLB, and paging. The memory hierarchy comes into play only when an instruction is executed that references a memory location, such as `ld` or `st`. The address is first checked against the TLB to see if a translation has already been made from the virtual page to a physical page frame. If the translation has been made and is still valid in the TLB, then the translated address is read from the TLB and is used to access the L1 cache. If it is not in the TLB, then the transla-

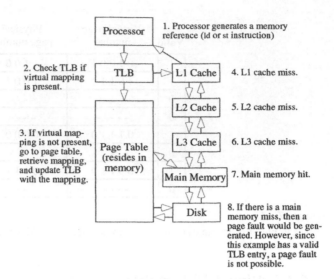

Figure 7-38

Interaction among cache memory, TLB, and page table, for a reference that is in the main memory but is not in the multi-level cache.

tion is made via the page table and the translated entry is placed in the TLB. This may not be as slow as it seems, because the page table is cached, and the reference can be sent to the TLB and the cache simultaneously, in the hope that the TLB search is successful. If the TLB search is unsuccessful then the cache access is ignored before it gets to the processor. There are misses in each of the L1, L2, and L3 caches as they are visited in order. Finally, the reference is satisfied by the main memory and an entire cache line is brought into each of the missed caches. Notice that the memory reference has to be satisfied by the time it gets to main memory. A page fault would not be possible because the TLB entry for the page is valid.

■ 7.7 ADVANCED TOPICS

This section covers two topics that are of practical importance in specialized memory systems: content-addressable (associative) memories, and dual-port memories. The first are required for associative caches, such as a TLB, or in other situations when data must be looked up at high speed based on its value, rather than on the address of where it is stored. The latter are used in some graphics processors in which one port is used for processing and the other is used for refreshing the screen. An example of a dual-port memory is covered at the end of this section.

7.7.1 Content-Addressable (Associative) Memories

In an ordinary RAM, an address is applied to the memory, and the contents of the given location are either read or written. In a **content-addressable memory** (CAM), also known

Address	Value
0000A000	0F0F0000
0000A004	186734F1
0000A008	0F000000
0000A00C	FE681022
0000A010	3152467C
0000A014	C3450917
0000A018	00392B11
0000A01C	10034561

←—32 bits—→ ←—32 bits—→

Random access memory

Field1	Field2	Field3
000	A	9E
011	0	F0
149	7	01
091	4	00
000	E	FE
749	C	6E
000	0	50
575	1	84

←12 bits→ ←4 bits→ ←8 bits→

Content addressable memory

Figure 7-39
Relationships between random-access memory and content-addressable memory.

as an **associative memory**, a word composed of **fields** is applied to the memory and the resulting address (or index) is returned if the word or field is present in the memory. If the word or field is not present then an error condition is raised. The physical location of a CAM word is generally not as significant as the values contained in the fields of the word. Relationships among addresses, values, and fields for RAM and CAM are shown for a small example in Figure 7-39.

Values are stored in sequential locations in a RAM, with an address acting as the key to locate a word. Four-byte address increments are used in this example, in which the word size is four bytes. Values are stored in fields in the CAM, and in principle any field of a word can be used to key on the rest of the word. If the CAM words are reordered, then the contents of the CAM are virtually unchanged since physical location has no bearing on the interpretation of the fields. On the other hand, reordering of the RAM may change the meanings of its values entirely. This comparison suggests that CAM may be a preferred means for storing information when there is a significant cost in maintaining data in sorted order.

When a search is made through a RAM for a particular value, the entire memory may need to be searched, one word at a time, when the memory is not sorted. When the RAM is maintained in sorted order, a number of accesses may still be required to either find the value being searched or to determine the value is not stored in the memory. In a CAM, the value being searched is broadcast to all of the words simultaneously; logic at each word makes a field comparison for membership, and in just a few steps the answer is known. A few additional steps may be needed to collect the results but in general the time required to search a CAM is less than for a RAM in the same technology, for a number of applications.

Except for maintaining tags in cache memories and in translating among network addresses for routing applications (see Chapter 8), CAMs are not in common use largely due to the difficulty of implementing an efficient design with conventional technology. Consider the block diagram of a CAM shown in Figure 7-40. A Central Control unit sends a comparand to each of 4096 cells, where comparisons are made. The result is put in the Tag bits T_i that are collected by a Data Gathering Device and sent to the Central Control unit (note that "Tag" is used differently here than in cache memory). When the Central Control unit loads the value to be searched into the comparand register, it sets up a mask to block out fields that are not part of the value. A small local processor in each cell makes a

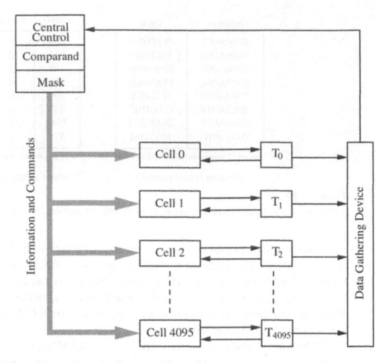

Figure 7-40
Overview of CAM. (Source: Foster, 1976.)

comparison between its local word and the broadcast value and reports the result of the comparison to the Data Gathering Device.

A number of problems arise when an attempt is made to implement this CAM architecture in a conventional technology such as **very large scale integration** (VLSI). The broadcast function that sends the comparand to the cells can be implemented with low latency if a tree structure is used. An H-tree (Mead and Conway, 1980) can be used for the tree layout if it will fit on a single IC. If the tree cannot be contained on a single chip, then connections must be made among a number of chips, which quickly limits chip density. For example, a node of a tree that has a single four-bit input and two four-bit outputs needs 12 input/output (I/O) pins and three control pins if only one node is placed on a chip. A three node subtree needs 25 pins and a seven node subtree needs 45 pins, as illustrated in Figure 7-41. A 63-node subtree requires 325 pins, excluding power and control pins; this is getting close to the limit of most present-day packaging technologies which do not go much higher than 1000 pins per package. A useful CAM would contain thousands of such nodes with wider data paths, so the I/O bandwidth limit is realized early in the design of the CAM. Compromises can be made by multiplexing data onto the limited number of I/O connections but this reduces effective speed, which is a major reason for using a CAM in the first place.

Although implementations of CAMs are difficult, they do find practical uses, such as in TLBs and in network devices. In the case of a network router, data packets are received from several processors and are then distributed back to the processors or to other network routers. (See the next section for details on how CAM is used in a network router.) Each

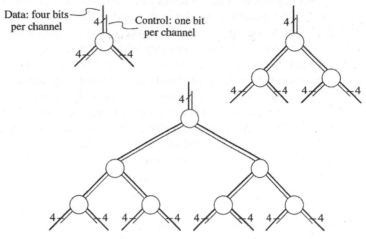

Figure 7-41
Addressing subtrees for a CAM.

processor has a unique address which the CAM keys on to determine if the target processor for each packet is in its own network or if it must be forwarded to another network.

▓ 7.8 CASE STUDY: ASSOCIATIVE MEMORY IN ROUTERS

A router by definition has more than one interface and forwards traffic among its interfaces. The placement of routers in a small network is shown in Figure 7-42. Each router has three interfaces and needs to choose the best path over which to forward packets based on parameters such as the destination addresses of the packets, the bandwidth capabilities of the links, the traffic loads of the links, and the number of router "hops" to the destination.

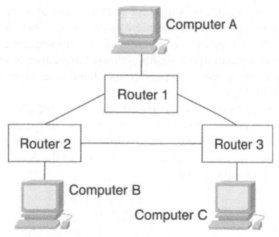

Figure 7-42
A simple network with three routers.

A key aspect of how a router does its job is through the use of an associative memory, similar in concept but simpler in design than the content-addressable memory described in the previous section. Every packet that enters a router has a destination address that the router uses to index into a **routing table** that determines the best interface over which to forward the packet. Small home routers may contain only a few entries in their routing tables, but routers along the **Internet backbone** may contain 60,000 or more entries.

The use of associative memories in these high-end routers reduces the lookup time by allowing a search to be performed in a single operation. The search is based on the destination address, rather than the physical memory address. The access methods for this type of memory have been standardized into an interface interoperability agreement produced by the **Network Processing Forum**.

Despite the development of standardized methods for CAM, economies of scale are once again leaning in the direction of a brute-force approach to table lookups. The entire IPv4 address space for network packets is $2^{32} = 4,294,967,296$ in size, which seems like a very large number. Although the IPv6 address space is much larger, with 2^{128} entries, migration to IPv6 has been slow and IPv4 is still used pervasively. A routing table with over four billion entries, while large, is not out of the question, and may soon become a practical approach for these high-end routers.

EXAMPLE 7-1 Memory Design Example: A Dual-Port RAM

A **dual-read** or **dual-port** RAM allows any two words to be simultaneously read from the same memory. As an example, we will design a 2^{20}-word by eight-bit dual-read RAM. For our design, any two words can be read at a time, but only one word can be written at a time. Our approach is to create two separate 2^{20} word memories. When writing into the dual-read RAM, the address lines of both single-read RAMs are set identically and the same data is written to both single-read memories. During a read operation, the address lines of each single-read RAM are set independently, so that two different words can be simultaneously read.

Figure 7-43 shows a block diagram for the dual-read RAM. During a write operation, the A address is used for both single-read RAMs. Tri-state buffers at the B RAM address inputs are controlled by the $\overline{\text{WR}}$ line. When WR = 0, the A address is used at the B address input; otherwise, the B address is used at the B address input. The numbers that appear adjacent to the slashes indicate the number of individual lines that are represented by the single line: an 8 next to a slash indicates eight lines and a 20 next to a slash indicates 20 lines.

Each tri-state buffer has 20 input lines and 20 output lines, but Figure 7-43 uses a notation in which a single buffer represents 20 separate tri-state buffers that share the same control input. A buffer delay is inserted on the WR line in order to compensate for the delay on the complemented WR line, so that the A and B addresses are not unintentionally simultaneously enabled.

■

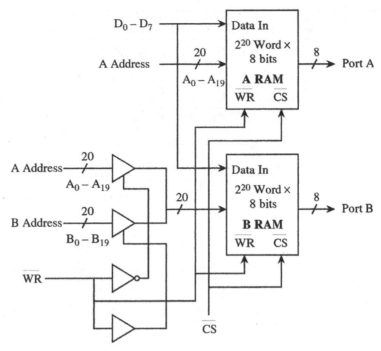

Figure 7-43
Block diagram of dual-read RAM.

■ 7.9 CASE STUDY: THE INTEL PENTIUM 4 MEMORY SYSTEM

The Intel Pentium processor is typical of modern processors in its memory configurations, with some unique features. Figure 7-44 shows a simplified diagram of the memory elements and data paths. There are two L1 caches—a 16 KB four-way set associative data, or D-cache, and an instruction, or I-cache, which holds up to 12K decoded instructions. This is also known as the **trace cache** and removes decoder latency from main execution loops. The L2 cache, which is known as the Advance Transfer Cache, is eight-way set associative, unified for data and instructions, and can be as large as 2 MB. The optional L3 cache, if present, is 2 MB in size. All caches (L1 data, trace, L2, and L3) reside on the same die as the processor.

The L1 line size is 64 bytes and the L2 line size is 128 bytes. The L2 cache is inclusive of the L1 cache, which means that the L1 cache is mirrored at all times. It thus takes two cycles (64 bytes/line × eight bits/byte / 256 bits/cycle = two cycles/line) to transfer a line into the L1 cache.

One of the amazing technological advances is that all of the caches are now resident on the same die, which was not practical just a few years ago. The Pentium Pro, released in the mid-1990s got as close as it could, with an on-die L1 cache (8 KB D-cache, 8 KB I-cache), and a 512 KB L2 cache on a separate die but mounted in the same package, with no L3 cache. (See the companion Web site for details on the Pentium II memory system.)

There is a separate TLB for the instruction and data caches, 128 entries in size and four-way set associative for the instruction TLB, and 64 entries in size and fully associative for the data TLB.

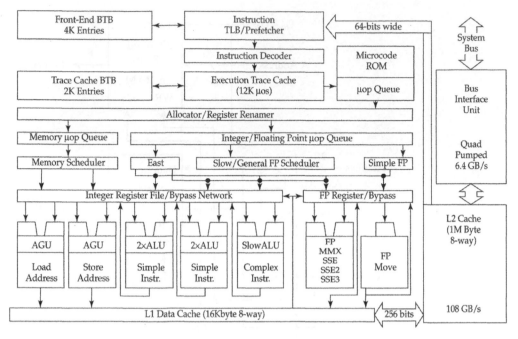

Figure 7-44

The Intel 4 Pentium memory system, based on the Intel NetBurst microarchitecture (Source: adapted from http://www.intel.com/technology/itj/2004/volume08issue01/ art01_microarchitecture/p03_netburst.htm.)

Summary

Memory is organized in a hierarchy in which the densest memory offers the least performance and least cost, whereas the greatest performance is realized with the memory that has the least density. In order to bridge the gap between the two, the principle of locality is exploited in cache and virtual memories.

A cache memory maintains the most frequently used blocks in a small, fast memory that is local to the CPU. A paged virtual memory augments a main memory with disk storage. The physical memory serves as a window on the paged virtual memory, which is maintained in its entirety on a hard magnetic disk.

Cache and paged virtual memories are used together, but for different reasons. A cache memory improves the average access time to the main memory, whereas a paged virtual memory extends the size of the main memory.

In an example memory architecture, the Intel Pentium 4 has a split L1 cache composed of a data cache and an Advance Transfer Cache (for decoded instructions) and a TLB that reside on the Pentium core, a unified L2 cache that resides on the same die as the Pentium, and an optional L3 cache that is also resident on the processor die. When paging is implemented, the page table is located in memory, with the TLB reducing the number of times that the page table is referenced. The L1, L2, and L3 cache memories then reduce the number of times main memory is accessed. The Pentium also supports segmentation, which has its own set of mapping registers and control hardware that resides on the Pentium.

Problems

7.1 A ROM lookup table and two D flip-flops implement a state machine as shown in the diagram below. Construct a state table that describes the machine.

ROM contents

Location	Value
A_0 A_1 A_2	R_0 R_1 R_2
0 0 0	0 0 1
0 0 1	1 1 0
0 1 0	1 0 0
0 1 1	0 0 0
1 0 0	1 0 1
1 0 1	1 1 1
1 1 0	0 0 1
1 1 1	0 0 0

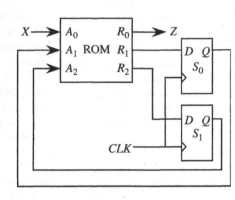

7.2 Fill in four memory locations for the lookup table shown in Figure 7-13 in which each of the four operations add, subtract, multiply, and divide are performed on $A = 16$ and $B = 4$. Show the address and the value for each case.

7.3 Design an eight-word, 32-bit RAM using 8×8 RAMs.

7.4 Design a 16-word, four-bit RAM using 4×4 RAMs and a single external decoder.

7.5 Given a number of n-word by p-bit RAM chips:
(a) Show how to construct an n-word $\times 4p$-bit RAM using these chips. Use any other logic components you have seen in the text you need.
(b) Show how to construct a $4n$-word $\times$ p-bit RAM using these chips.

7.6 A direct-mapped cache consists of 128 slots. Main memory contains 16K blocks of 16 words each. Access time of the cache is 10 ns, and the time required to fill a cache slot is 200 ns. Load-through is not used; that is, when an accessed word is not found in the cache, the entire block is brought into the cache and the word is then accessed through the cache. Initially, the cache is empty. Note: When referring to memory, 1K = 1024.
(a) Show the format of the memory address.
(b) Compute the hit ratio for a program that loops 10 times from locations 15–200. Note that although the memory is accessed twice during a miss (once for the miss and once again to satisfy the reference), a hit does not occur for this case. To a running program, only a single memory reference is observed.

(c) Compute the effective access time for this program.

7.7 A fully associative mapped cache has 16 blocks, with eight words per block. The size of main memory is 2^{16} words and the cache is initially empty. Access time of the cache is 40 ns, and the time required to transfer eight words between main memory and the cache is 1 µs.
(a) Compute the sizes of the tag and word fields.
(b) Compute the hit ratio for a program that executes from memory locations 20–45, then loops four times from memory locations 28–45 before halting. Assume that when there is a miss, the entire cache slot is filled in 1 µs, and the first word is not seen by the CPU until the entire slot is filled. That is, assume load-through is not used. Initially, the cache is empty.
(c) Compute the effective access time for the program described in part (b) above.

7.8 A two-way set-associative mapped cache has 16 blocks, with eight words per block. The size of main memory is 2^{16} words, and the cache is initially empty. Access time of the cache is 40 ns, and the time required to transfer eight words between main memory and the cache is 1 µs.
(a) Compute the sizes of the tag, set, and word fields.
(b) Compute the hit ratio for a program that executes from memory locations 20–45, then loops four times from memory locations 28–45 before halting. Assume that when there is a miss, the entire cache slot is filled in 1 µs, and the first word is not seen by the CPU until the entire slot is filled. That is, assume load-through is not used. Initially, the cache is empty.

(c) Compute the effective access time for the program described in part (b) above.

7.9 Compute the total number of bits of storage needed for the associative mapped cache shown in Figure 7-19 and the direct mapped cache shown in Figure 7-21. Include valid, dirty, and tag bits in your count. Assume that the word size is eight bits.

7.10 (a) How far apart do memory references need to be spaced to cause a miss on every cache access using the direct mapping parameters shown in Figure 7-21?
(b) Using your solution for part (a) above, compute the hit ratio and effective access time for that program with $T_{Miss} = 1000$ ns, and $T_{Hit} = 10$ ns. Assume that load-through is used.

7.11 True or false: A dirty bit is needed for write-back and write-through policies.

7.12 A computer has 16 pages of virtual address space but only four physical page frames. Initially the physical memory is empty. A program references the virtual pages in the order: 0 2 4 5 2 4 3 11 2 10.
(a) Which references cause a page fault with the LRU page replacement policy?
(b) Which references cause a page fault with the FIFO page replacement policy?

7.13 On some computers, the page table is stored in memory. What would happen if the page table is swapped out to disk? Since the page table is used for every memory reference, is there a page replacement policy that guarantees that the page table will not get swapped out? Assume that the page table is small enough to fit into a single page (although in practice it is not).

7.14 A virtual memory system has a page size of 1024 words, eight virtual pages, four physical page frames, and uses the LRU page replacement policy. The page table is as follows:

Page #	Present bit	Disk address / Page frame field	
0	0	01001011100	xx
1	0	11101110010	xx
2	1	10110010111	00
3	0	00001001111	xx
4	1	01011100101	01
5	0	10100111001	xx
6	1	00110101100	11
7	0	01010001011	xx

(a) What is the main memory address for virtual address 4096?
(b) What is the main memory address for virtual address 1024?
(c) A fault occurs on page 0. Which page frame will be used for virtual page 0?

7.15 When running a particular program with N memory accesses, a computer with a cache and paged virtual memory generates a total of M cache misses and F page faults. T_1 is the time for a cache hit; T_2 is the time for a main memory hit; and T_3 is the time to load a page into main memory from the disk.
(a) What is the cache hit ratio?
(b) What is the main memory hit ratio? That is, what percentage of main memory accesses do not generate a page fault?
(c) What is the overall effective access time for the system?

7.16 A computer contains both cache and paged virtual memories. The cache can hold either physical or virtual addresses, but not both. What are the issues involved in choosing between caching virtual or physical addresses? How can these problems be solved by using a single unit that manages all memory mapping functions?

7.17 How much storage is needed for the page table for a virtual memory that has 2^{32} bytes, with 2^{12} bytes per page and eight bytes per page table entry?

7.18 Compute the gate input count for the decoder(s) of a 64×1-bit RAM for both the 2D and the 2-1/2D cases. Assume that an unlimited fan-in/fan-out is allowed. For both cases, use ordinary two-level decoders. For the 2-1/2D case, treat the column decoder as an ordinary MUX. That is, ignore its behavior as a DEMUX during a write operation.

7.19 A video game cartridge needs to store 2^{20} bytes in a ROM.
(a) If a 2D organization is used, how many leaves will be at the deepest level of the decoder tree?
(b) How many leaves will there be at the deepest level of the decoder tree for a 2-1/2D organization?

7.20 The contents of a CAM are shown below. Which set of words will respond if a key of 00A00020 is used on fields 1 and 3? Fields 1 and 3 of the key must match the corresponding fields of a CAM word in order for that word to respond. The remaining fields are ignored during the matching process but are included in the retrieved words.

Field →	4	3	2	1	0
F 1	A 0	0 0	2	8
0 4	2 9	D 1	F	0
3 2	A 1	1 0	3	E
D F	A 0	5 0	2	D
0 0	5 3	7 F	2	4

Further Reading

(Stallings, 1993) and (Mano, 1991) give readable explanations of RAM. A number of memory databooks ((Micron, 1992) and (Texas Instruments, 1991)) give practical examples of memory organization. (Foster, 1976) is the seminal reference on CAM. (Mead and Conway, 1980) describe the H-tree structure in the context of VLSI design. (Franklin et al. 1982) explores issues in partitioning chips, which arise in splitting an H-tree for a CAM. (Sedra and Smith, 1997) discuss the implementation of several kinds of static and dynamic RAM.

(Hamacher et al. 1990) gives a classic treatment of cache memory. (Tanenbaum, 1990) gives a readable explanation of virtual memory. (Hennessy and Patterson, 1995) and (Przybylski, 1990) cover issues relating to cache performance. Segmentation on the Intel Pentium processor is covered in (Intel, 1993). Kingston Technology gives a broad tutorial on memory technologies at http://www.kingston.com/king/mg0.htm. (Hewlett- Packard, 2005) covers a coding example that deconflicts false sharing. (Rambus, 2001) describes advantages of the RDRAM approach to memory organization. (Rotenberg, 1996) covers the basis for a trace cache, and (Canton and Hill, 2003) covers measurements of cache performance using the SPEC CPU2000 benchmark suite.

Canton, J.F., and Hill, M. D., "Cache performance for SPEC CPU2000 benchmarks," v3.0, http://www.cs.wisc.edu/multifacet/misc/spec2000cachedata (May 2003).

Foster, C. C., *Content Addressable Parallel Processors*, Van Nostrand Reinhold Company (1976).

Franklin, M. A., Wann, D. F., and Thomas, W. J., "Pin limitations and partitioning of VLSI interconnection networks," *IEEE Trans Comp.*, C-31, 1109 (Nov. 1982).

Hamacher, V. C., Vranesic, Z. G., and Zaky, S. G., *Computer Organization*, 3/e, McGraw Hill (1990).

Hennessy, J. L. and Patterson, D. A., *Computer Architecture: A Quantitative Approach*, 2/e, Morgan Kaufmann Publishers, (1995).

Hewlett Packard Corporation, "False cache line sharing," in *Parallel Programming Guide for HP-UX Systems*, Chapter 13: "Troubleshooting," http://docs.hp.com/en/B3909-90003/ch13s02. html.

Intel Corporation, *Pentium Processor User's Manual*, Volume 3: *Architecture and Programming Manual* (1993).

Knuth, D., *The Art of Computer Programming: Fundamental Algorithms*, vol. 1, 2/e, Addison-Wesley (1974).

Mano, M., *Digital Design*, 2/e, Prentice Hall (1991).

Mead, C. and Conway, L., *Introduction to VLSI Systems*, Addison Wesley (1980).

Micron, *DRAM Data Book*, Micron Technologies, Inc., 2805 East Columbia Road, Boise, Idaho (1992).

Przybylski, S. A., *Cache and Memory Hierarchy Design*, Morgan Kaufmann Publishers (1990).

Rambus, *RDRAM: Maximizing the Value of PCs and Workstations*, Document WP0003-R Version 1.0, http://www.rambus.com/downloads/MaxVal4DT_WP0003_V100.pdf, Rambus Inc., (August 2001).

Rotenberg, E., Bennett, S., and Smith, J., "Trace Cache: A Low Latency Approach to High Bandwidth Instruction Fetching," *Proceedings of the International Symposium on Microarchitecture* (1996).

Sedra, A., and Smith, K., *Microelectronic Circuits*, 4/e, Oxford University Press, (1997).

Stallings, W., *Computer Organization and Architecture*, 3/e, MacMillan Publishing (1993).

Tanenbaum, A., *Structured Computer Organization*, 3/e, Prentice Hall (1990).

Texas Instruments, *MOS Memory: Commercial and Military Specifications Data Book*, Texas Instruments, Literature Response Center, P.O. Box 172228, Denver, Colorado (1991).

7.21 When the TLB shown in Figure 7-37 has a miss, it accesses the page table to resolve the reference. How many entries are in that page table?

7.22 The cache examples we have used in this chapter place the tag field on the far left and the word (or byte) field on the far right. Would it make any difference if we swapped the positions and placed the tag field on the right and the word/byte field on the left?

CHAPTER 8

BUSES AND PERIPHERALS

In the earlier chapters, we considered how the CPU interacts with data that is accessed internal to the CPU or is accessed within the main memory, which may be extended to a hard magnetic disk for virtual memory. While the access speeds at the different levels of the memory hierarchy vary dramatically, for the most part, the CPU sees the same response rate from one access to the next. The situation when accessing input/output (I/O) devices is very different.

- The speeds of I/O data transfers can range from extremely slow, such as reading data entered from a keyboard, to so fast that the CPU may not be able to keep up, as may be the case with data streaming from a fast disk drive or real-time graphics being written to a video monitor.

- I/O activities are **asynchronous**, that is, not synchronized to the CPU clock, as are memory data transfers. Additional signals, called handshaking signals, may need to be incorporated on a separate I/O bus to coordinate when the device is ready to have data read from it or written to it.

- The quality of the data may be suspect. For example, line noise during data transfers using the public switched telephone network, or errors caused by media defects on disk drives, mean that error detection and correction strategies may be needed to ensure data integrity.

- Many I/O devices are mechanical, and are in general more prone to failure than the CPU and main memory. A data transfer may be interrupted due to mechanical failure, or to special conditions such as a printer being out of paper, for example.

I/O software modules, referred to as device drivers, must be written in such a way as to address the issues mentioned above.

In this chapter we discuss the nature of communicating using buses, starting first with simple bus fundamentals and then exploring multiple-bus architectures. We then take a look at some of the more common I/O devices that are connected to these buses. We will focus primarily on "part of the computer" communication in this chapter, and will defer "part of the network" communication to the next chapter.

In the next sections we discuss communications from the viewpoints of communications at the CPU and motherboard level, and then branch out to peripheral devices.

8.1 PARALLEL BUS ARCHITECTURES

A computer system may contain many components that need to communicate with each other. In a worst-case (but unlikely) scenario, all N components may need to simultaneously communicate with every other component, in which $N \times (N-1)/2$ links are needed for N components. Imagine just $N = 10$ components (CPU, graphics processor, a few memory modules, a few network interface cards, CD-ROM, a few hard magnetic disks) with a 64-bit datapath. The number of wires needed to support this is $\frac{10 \times 9}{2} \times 64 = 2880$, which is an enormous degree of complexity. The number of links becomes prohibitively large for even small values of N, but fortunately not all devices need to communicate simultaneously.

A **bus** is a common pathway that connects a number of devices. An example of a bus can be found on the **motherboard** (the main circuit board that contains the central processing unit) of a personal computer, as illustrated in simplified form in Figure 8-1. (For a look at a real motherboard, see Figure 1-17.) A typical motherboard contains **integrated circuits** (ICs) such as the CPU chip and memory chips, board **traces** (wires) that connect the chips, a number of buses for chips or devices that need to communicate with each other, and **bridges** that connect the buses. In Figure 8-1, an I/O bus is used for a number of cards that plug into the connectors, perpendicular to the motherboard in this example configuration. We will cover bridges in detail later in the chapter.

8.1.1 Bus Structure, Protocol, and Control

A bus consists of the physical parts, like connectors and wires, and a **bus protocol**. The wires can be partitioned into separate groups for control, address, data, and power, as illustrated in Figure 8-2. A single bus may have a few different power lines, and the example

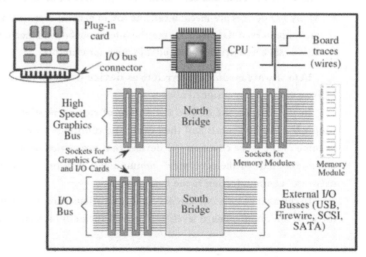

Figure 8-1
A simplified motherboard of a personal computer (top view).

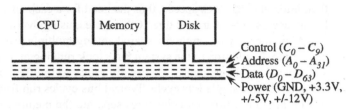

Figure 8-2
Simplified illustration of a bus.

shown in Figure 8-2 has lines for ground (GND) at 0 V, a positive voltage at +3.3 V, positive and negative voltages at +5 V, and −5 V, respectively, and positive and negative voltages at +12 V and −12 V, respectively.

The devices share a common set of wires, and only one device may send data at any one time. All devices simultaneously listen, but normally only one device receives. Only one device can be a **bus master**, and the remaining devices are then considered to be **slaves**. The master controls the bus, and can be either a sender or a receiver.

An advantage of using a bus is to eliminate the need for connecting every device with every other device, which avoids the wiring complexity that would quickly dominate the cost of a system. Disadvantages of using a bus include the slowdown introduced by the master/slave configuration, the time involved in implementing a protocol (see below), and the lack of scalability to large sizes due to fanout and timing constraints.

A bus can be classified as one of two types: **synchronous** or **asynchronous**. For a synchronous bus, one of the devices that is connected to the bus contains an oscillator (a clock) that sends out a sequence of 1s and 0s at timed intervals, as illustrated in Figure 8-3. The illustration shows a train of pulses that repeat at 2 ns intervals, which corresponds to a clock rate of 500 MHz. Ideally, the clock would be a perfect square wave (instantaneous rise and fall times) as shown in the figure. In practice, the rise and fall times are closer to a trapezoid shape, which limits the clock speed because the edges are not as sharp.

8.1.2 Bus Clocking

For a synchronous bus, discussed below, a clock signal is used to synchronize bus operations. This bus clock is generally derived from the master system clock, but it may be slower than the master clock, especially in higher-speed CPUs. For example, one model of the Apple iMac G5 computer has a CPU speed of 2000 MHz, with a frontside bus speed of 667 MHz and a memory speed of 400 MHz, thus having a factor of 5 between the speeds of the CPU and the memory. This translates to memory access times that are much longer

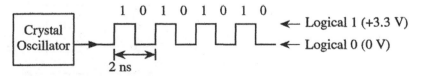

Figure 8-3
A 500 MHz bus clock.

than internal CPU clock speeds, thus the need for a cache memory. Typical cache memory has an access time of around three CPU cycles, using overlapped accesses.

Main memory is commonly shared among multiple processor **cores**, and this sharing takes time. In addition to the system bus clock running at a slower speed than the processor, several bus clock cycles are usually required to effect a bus transaction, referred to collectively as a single **bus cycle**. Typical bus cycles run from two to five bus clock periods in duration. Current architectures separate the memory and CPU so that they do not share the same bus, as discussed in Section 8.2. However, buses are still used through the machine, and in fact multiple processors commonly share the same path to the main memory.

8.1.3 The Synchronous Bus

As an example of how communication takes place over a synchronous bus, consider the timing diagram shown in Figure 8-4 for a synchronous read of a word of memory by a CPU. At some point early in time interval T_1, while the clock is high, the CPU places the address of the location it wants to read onto the address lines of the bus. At some later time during T_1, after the voltages on the address lines have become stable or "settled," the $\overline{MREQ}$ and $\overline{RD}$ lines are asserted by the CPU. $\overline{MREQ}$ informs the memory that it is selected for the transfer (as opposed to another device, like a disk). The $\overline{RD}$ line informs the selected device to perform a read operation. The overbars on $\overline{MREQ}$ and $\overline{RD}$ indicate that a 0 must be placed on these lines in order to assert these signals.

The read time of memory is typically slower than the bus speed, and so all of time interval T_2 is spent performing the read, as well as part of T_3. The CPU assumes a fixed read time of three bus cycles, and so the data is taken from the bus by the CPU during the third cycle. The CPU then releases the bus by de-asserting $\overline{MREQ}$ and $\overline{RD}$ in T_3. The

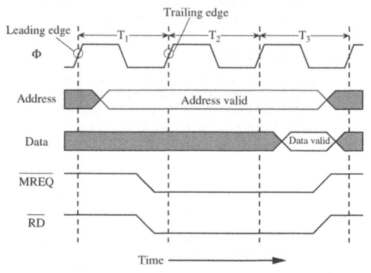

Figure 8-4
Timing diagram for a synchronous memory read. (Source: adapted from [Tanenbaum, 1999].)

shaded areas of the data and address portions of the timing diagram indicate that these signals are either invalid or unimportant at those times. The open areas, such as for the data lines during T_3, indicate valid signals. Open and shaded areas are used with crossed lines at either end to indicate that the levels of the individual lines may be different. Notice that the shape of the clock Φ is closer to a trapezoid than a square wave, which is a closer representation of the actual clock signal.

8.1.4 The Asynchronous Bus

If we replace the memory on a synchronous bus with a faster memory, then the memory access time will not improve because the bus clock is unchanged. If we increase the speed of the bus clock to match the faster speed of the memory, then slower devices that use the bus clock may not work properly.

An asynchronous bus solves this problem, but is more complex, because there is no bus clock. A master on an asynchronous bus puts everything that it needs on the bus (address, data, control), and then asserts $\overline{MSYN}$ (master synchronization). The slave then performs its job as quickly as it can, and then asserts $\overline{SSYN}$ (slave synchronization) when it is finished. The master then de-asserts $\overline{MSYN}$, which signals the slave to de-assert $\overline{SSYN}$. In this way, a fast master/slave combination responds more quickly than a slow master/slave combination.

As an example of how communication takes place over an asynchronous bus, consider the timing diagram shown in Figure 8-5. In order for a CPU to read a word from memory, it places an address on the bus, followed by asserting $\overline{MREQ}$ and $\overline{RD}$. After these lines settle, the CPU asserts $\overline{MSYN}$. This event triggers the memory to perform a read operation, which results in $\overline{SSYN}$ eventually being asserted by the memory. This is indicated by the **cause-and-effect** arrow between $\overline{MSYN}$ and $\overline{SSYN}$ shown in Figure 8-5. This method of synchronization is referred to as a "full handshake." In this particular

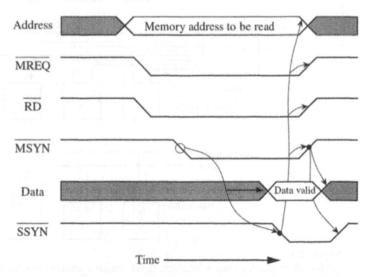

Figure 8-5
Timing diagram for asynchronous memory read. (Source: adapted from [Tanenbaum, 1999].)

implementation of a full handshake, asserting $\overline{MSYN}$ initiates the transfer, followed by the slave asserting $\overline{SSYN}$, followed by the CPU de-asserting $\overline{MSYN}$, followed by the memory de-asserting $\overline{SSYN}$. Notice the absence of a bus clock signal.

Asynchronous busses can be more difficult to debug than synchronous busses when there is a problem, and interfaces for asynchronous busses can be more difficult to make. For these reasons, synchronous busses are very common, particularly in personal computers.

8.1.5 Bus Arbitration—Masters and Slaves

Suppose now that more than one device wants to be a bus master at the same time. How is a decision made as to who will be the bus master? This is the **bus arbitration** problem, and there are two basic schemes: **centralized** and **decentralized** (distributed). Figure 8-6 illustrates four organizations for these two schemes. In Figure 8-6a, a centralized arbitra-

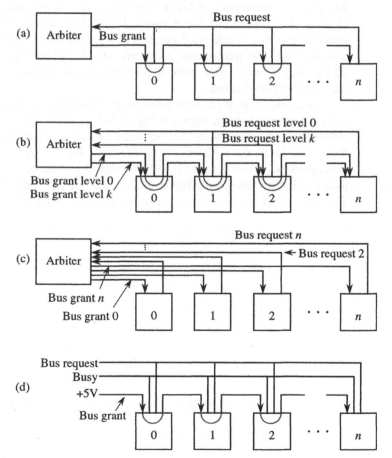

Figure 8-6
(a) Simple centralized bus arbitration; (b) centralized arbitration with priority levels;
(c) fully centralized bus arbitration; (d) decentralized bus arbitration. (Source: adapted from [Tanenbaum, 1999].)

tion scheme is used. Devices 0 through n are all attached to the same bus (not shown), and they also share a **bus request** line that goes into an **arbiter**. When a device wants to be a bus master, it asserts the bus request line. When the arbiter sees the bus request, it determines if a **bus grant** can be issued (it may be the case that the current bus master will not allow itself to be interrupted). If a bus grant can be issued, then the arbiter asserts the bus grant line. The bus grant line is **daisy chained** from one device to the next. The first device that sees the asserted bus grant and also wants to be the bus master takes control of the bus and does not propagate the bus grant to higher numbered devices. If a device does not want the bus, then it simply passes the bus grant to the next device. In this way, devices that are electrically closer to the arbiter have higher priorities than devices that are farther away.

Sometimes an absolute priority ordering is not appropriate and a number of bus request/bus grant lines are used, as shown in Figure 8-6(b). Lower-numbered bus request lines have higher priorities than higher-numbered bus request lines. In order to raise the priority of a device that is far from the arbiter, it can be assigned to a lower-numbered bus request line. Priorities are assigned within a group on the same bus request level by electrical proximity to the arbiter.

Taking this to an extreme, each device can have its own bus request/bus grant line, as shown in Figure 8-6(c). This fully centralized approach is the most powerful from a logical standpoint, but from a practical standpoint, it is the least scalable of all of the approaches. A significant cost is the need for additional lines (a precious commodity) on the bus. Nevertheless, current architectures use a number of small buses rather than one large bus and so this approach is practical after all.

In a fourth approach, a decentralized bus arbitration scheme is used, as illustrated in Figure 8-6(d). Notice the lack of a central arbiter. A device that wants to become a bus master first asserts the bus request line, and then it checks if the bus is busy. If the busy line is not asserted, then the device sends a 0 to the next higher-numbered device on the daisy chain, asserts the busy line, and de-asserts the bus request line. If the bus is busy, or if a device does not want the bus, then it simply propagates the bus grant to the next device.

Arbitration needs to be a fast operation, and for that reason, a centralized scheme will only work well for a small number of devices (up to about eight). For a large number of devices, a decentralized scheme is more appropriate.

Given a system that makes use of one of these arbitration schemes, imagine a situation in which n card slots are used, and then card m is removed, where $m < n$. What happens? On older systems, because each bus request line is directly connected to all devices in a group, and the bus grant line is passed through each device in a group, a bus request from a device with an index greater than m will never see an asserted bus grant line, which can result in a system crash. This can be a frustrating problem to identify, because a system can run indefinitely with no problems, until the higher-numbered device is accessed.

When a card is removed, higher cards would have to be repositioned to fill in the missing slot, or a dummy card that continues the bus grant line should be inserted in place of the removed card. Fast devices (like disk controllers) would be given higher priority than slow devices (like terminals), and would thus be placed close to the arbiter in a centralized scheme, or close to the beginning of the bus grant line in a decentralized scheme.

This is an imperfect solution given the opportunities for leaving gaps in the bus and getting the device ordering wrong. These days, it is more common for each device to have a separate path to the arbiter, as we will see in the next section.

■ 8.2 BRIDGE-BASED BUS ARCHITECTURES

From a logical viewpoint, all of the system components are connected directly to the system bus. From an operational viewpoint, this approach is overly burdensome on the system bus because simultaneous transfers cannot take place among the various components. For example, a graphics component may be repainting a video screen at the same time that a cache line is being retrieved from main memory, while an I/O transfer is taking place over a network.

These different transfers are typically segregated onto separate buses through the use of **bridges**. Figure 8-7 illustrates bridging for a typical Intel architecture. At the top of the diagram are two CPU cores arranged in a **symmetric multiprocessor** (SMP) configura-

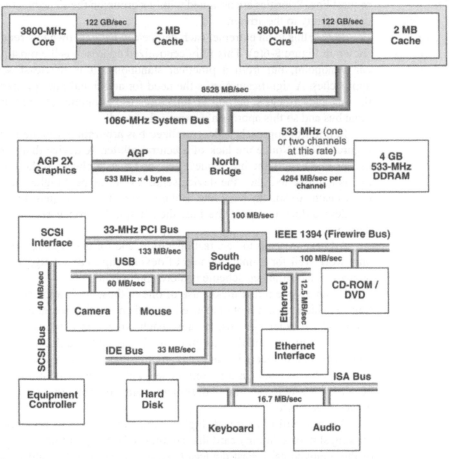

Figure 8-7
Bridging with dual Pentium processors. (Source: http://www.intel.com.)

tion. The operating system performs load balancing by selecting one processor over another when assigning tasks (this is different from parallel processing, discussed in Chapter 10, in which multiple processors work on a common problem). Each processor has a "backside bus" to its own cache of 122 GB/sec (32 bytes wide × 3800 MHz), thus segregating cache traffic from other bus traffic.

Working down from the top of the diagram, the two processors converge on the System Bus (sometimes called the "frontside bus"). The System Bus is eight bytes wide and makes four transfers per 266 MHz clock period (**quad-pumping**), thus achieving an effective bus clock speed of 4 × 266 MHz = 1066 MHz. The total available bandwidth is then 8 bytes × 1066 MHz = 8528 MB/sec that is shared between the processors.

At the center of the diagram is the "North Bridge," which connects the System Bus to the remaining buses. The North Bridge acts as a go-between among the System Bus, the main memory, the graphics processor, and a hierarchy of other busses. To the right of the North Bridge is the main memory (double data rate RAM, or DDRAM), connected to the North Bridge by a 4264 MB/sec per-channel bus, of which there may be two.

In this particular example, a separate bus known as the Advanced Graphics Port (AGP) is provided from the North Bridge to the graphics processor over a 533 MHz × 4 bytes = 2132 MB/sec bus. Graphics rendering (that is, filling an object with color) commonly needs texture information that is too large to place economically on a graphics card. The AGP allows a high-speed path between the graphics processor and the main memory, where texture maps can be stored.

Below the North Bridge is the South Bridge, which connects the remaining busses to the North Bridge. The 33 MHz Peripheral Component Interconnect (PCI) bus has a number of components connected to it, such as the Small Computer System Interface (SCSI) controller, which is yet another bus that in this illustration accepts an equipment controller. Prior to the introduction of the AGP, graphics cards were placed on the PCI bus, which created a bottleneck for other bus traffic.

Attached to the South Bridge is a 60 MB/sec Universal Serial Bus (USB), a 33 MB/sec integrated Drive Electronics (IDE) bus, a 16.7 MB/sec Industry Standard Architecture (ISA) bus, an Ethernet network interface card (NIC), and a 100 MB/sec IEEE 1394 (Firewire) bus. The IDE bus is generally used for older disk drives, the ISA bus is generally used for moderate-rate devices like printers and voice-band modems, and the USB buses are used for low-bit-rate devices like mice and snapshot digital cameras. The Firewire bus is used for real-time peripheral devices like a DVD-ROM. The USB and Firewire buses are discussed in detail in Section 8.5.

■ 8.3 INTERNAL COMMUNICATION METHODOLOGIES

Computer systems have a wide range of communication tasks. The CPU must communicate with memory and with a wide range of I/O devices, from extremely slow devices such as keyboards to high-speed devices like disk drives and network interfaces. There may be multiple CPUs that communicate with one another either directly or through a shared memory, as described in the previous section for the dual-processor configuration.

Three methods for managing input and output are **programmed I/O** (also known as **polling**), **interrupt-driven I/O**, and **direct memory access** (DMA).

8.3.1 Programmed I/O

Consider reading a block of data from a disk. In programmed I/O, the CPU polls each device to see if it needs servicing. In a restaurant analogy, the waiter approaches the patron and asks if the patron is ready to order.

The operations that take place for programmed I/O are shown in the flowchart in Figure 8-8. The CPU first checks the status of the disk by reading a special register that can be accessed in the memory space, or by issuing a special I/O instruction if this is how the architecture implements I/O. If the disk is not ready to be read or written, then the process loops back and checks the status continuously until the disk is ready. This is referred to as a **busy-wait**, and is the method used for the network interface card programming example in Chapter 6. When the disk is finally ready, then a transfer of data is made between the disk and the CPU.

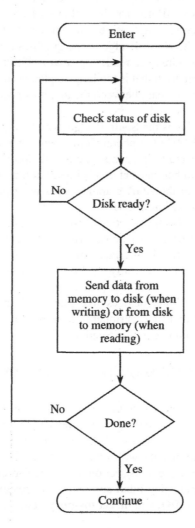

Figure 8-8
Programmed I/O flowchart
for a disk transfer.

After the transfer is completed, the CPU checks to see if there is another communication request for the disk. If there is, then the process repeats; otherwise the CPU continues with another task.

In programmed I/O the CPU wastes time polling devices. Another problem is that high-priority devices are not checked until the CPU is finished with its current I/O task, which may have a low priority. Programmed I/O is simple to implement, however, and so it has advantages in some applications.

8.3.2 Interrupt-Driven I/O

With interrupt-driven I/O, the CPU does not access a device until it needs servicing, and so it does not get caught up in busy-waits. In interrupt-driven I/O, the device requests service through a special interrupt request line that goes directly to the CPU. The restaurant analogy would have the patron politely tapping silverware on a water glass, thus interrupting the waiter, when service is required.

A flowchart for interrupt-driven I/O is shown in Figure 8-9. The CPU issues a request to the disk for reading or for writing, and then immediately resumes execution of another

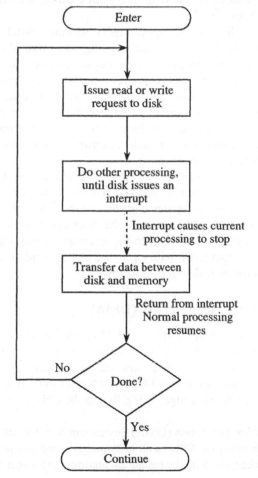

Figure 8-9
Interrupt-driven I/O flowchart
for a disk transfer.

process. At some later time, when the disk is ready, it interrupts the CPU. The CPU then invokes an **interrupt service routine** (ISR) for the disk and returns to normal execution when the interrupt service routine completes its task. The ISR is similar in structure to the trap procedure presented in Chapter 4, except that traps occur asynchronously with respect to the process being executed by the CPU: an interrupt can occur at any time during program execution.

There are times when a process being executed by the CPU should not be interrupted because some critical operation is taking place. For this reason, instruction sets include instructions to disable and enable interrupts under programmed control. (The waiter can ignore the patron at times.) Whether or not interrupts are accepted is generally determined by the state of the Interrupt Flag (IF) which is part of the Processor Status Register. Furthermore, in most systems priorities are assigned to the interrupts, enforced either by the processor or by a **peripheral interrupt controller** (PIC). (The waiter may attend to the head table first.) At the top priority level in many systems, there is a **non-maskable interrupt** (NMI) that, as the name implies, cannot be disabled. (The waiter will in all cases pay attention to the fire alarm!) The NMI is used for handling potentially catastrophic events such as power failures, and more ordinary but crucially uninterruptible operations such as file system updates.

At the time when an interrupt occurs (sometimes loosely referred to as a **trap**, even though traps usually have a different meaning, as explained in Chapter 5), the Processor Status Register and the Program Counter (%psr and %pc for the ARC) are automatically pushed onto the stack, and the Program Counter is loaded with the address of the appropriate interrupt service routine. The Processor Status Register is pushed onto the stack because it contains the interrupt flag (IF), and the processor must disable interrupts for at least the duration of the first instruction of the ISR. (See Problem 8.2.) Execution of the interrupt routine then begins. When the interrupt service routine finishes, execution of the interrupted program then resumes.

The ARC jmpl instruction (see Chapter 4) will not work properly for resuming execution of the interrupted routine, because in addition to restoring the program counter contents, the processor status register must be restored. Instead, the rett (return from trap) instruction is invoked, which reverses the interrupt process and restores the %psr and %pc registers to their values prior to the interrupt. In the ARC architecture, rett is an arithmetic format instruction with op3 = 111001, and an unused rd field (all zeros). (See Chapter 4 for more details on rett.)

8.3.3 Direct Memory Access (DMA)

Although interrupt-driven I/O frees the CPU until the device requires service, the CPU is still responsible for making the actual data transfer. Figure 8-10 highlights the issue. In order to transfer a block of data between the memory and the disk using either programmed I/O or interrupt driven I/O, every word travels over the system bus (or equivalently, through the North Bridge) twice: first to the CPU, then again over the system bus to its destination.

A **direct memory access** (DMA) device can transfer data directly to and from memory, rather than using the CPU as an intermediary, and can thus relieve congestion on the system bus. In keeping with the restaurant analogy, the waiter serves everyone at one table

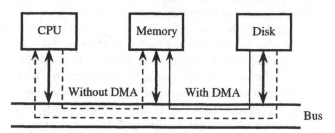

Figure 8-10
DMA transfer from disk to memory bypasses the CPU.

before serving anyone at another table. DMA services are usually provided by a DMA controller, which is itself a specialized processor whose specialty is transferring data directly to or from I/O devices and memory. Most DMA controllers can also be programmed to make memory-to-memory block moves. A DMA device thus takes over the job of the CPU during a transfer. In setting up the transfer, the CPU programs the DMA device with the starting address in main memory, the starting address in the device, and the length of the block to be transferred.

Figure 8-11 illustrates the DMA process for a disk transfer. The CPU sets up the DMA device and then signals the device to start the transfer. While the transfer is taking place, the CPU continues execution of another process. When the DMA transfer is

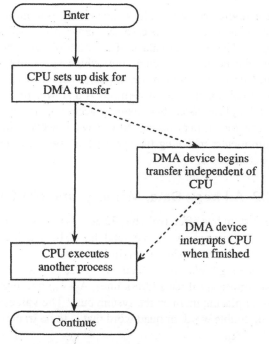

Figure 8-11
DMA flowchart for a disk transfer.

completed, the device informs the CPU through an interrupt. A system that implements DMA thus also implements interrupts as well.

If the DMA device transfers a large block of data without relinquishing the bus, the CPU may become starved for instructions or data, and thus its work is halted until the DMA transfer has completed. In order to alleviate this problem, DMA controllers usually have a "cycle-stealing" mode. In **cycle-stealing DMA** the controller acquires the bus, transfers a single byte or word, and then relinquishes the bus. This allows other devices, and in particular the CPU, to share the bus during DMA transfers. In the restaurant analogy, a patron can request a check while the waiter is serving another table.

■ 8.4 CASE STUDY: COMMUNICATION ON THE INTEL PENTIUM ARCHITECTURE

The Intel Pentium processor family is Intel's current state-of-the art implementation of their venerable x86 family, which began with the Intel 8086, released in 1978. The Pentium is itself a processor family, with versions that emphasize high speed, multiprocessor environments, graphics, low power, etc. In this section we examine the common features that underlie the Pentium System Bus, which connects the Pentium to the North Bridge (Section 8.2).

8.4.1 System Clock, Bus Clock, and Bus Speeds

Interestingly, the system clock speed is set as a multiple of the bus clock. The value of the multiple is set by the processor whenever it is reset, according to the values on several of its pins. The possible values of the multiple vary across family members. For example, when the Pentium Pro came out, which is a family member adapted for multiple CPU applications, it could have multipliers ranging from 2 to 3-1/2. We mention here that the reason for clocking the system bus at a slower rate than the CPU is that CPU operations can take place faster than memory access operations. For older versions of the Pentium, this was the primary reason. Nowadays, however, there is also a focus on reducing power requirements; matching the system bus speed to the applications can have a significant impact on power.

8.4.2 Address, Data, Memory, and I/O Capabilities

The system bus effectively has 32 address lines, and can thus address up to 4 GB of main memory (there are ways to extend this). The data bus is 64 bits wide; thus the processor is capable of transferring an eight-byte quadword in one bus cycle. (Intel x86 words are 16 bits long.) We say "effectively" because in fact the Pentium processor decodes the least significant three address lines, A_2–A_0, into eight "byte enable" lines, BE0#–BE7#, prior to placing them on the system bus.[1] The values on these eight lines specify the byte, word, double word, or quad word that is to be transferred from the base address specified by A_{31}–A_3.

---

[1] The "#" symbol is Intel's notation for a bus line that is active low.

8.4.3 Data Words have Soft Alignment

Data values have so-called **soft alignment**, meaning that words, double words, and quad words should be aligned on even word, double word, and quad word boundaries for maximum efficiency, but the processor can tolerate misaligned data items. The penalty for accessing misaligned words may be two bus cycles, which are required to access both halves of the datum.[2]

As a bow to the small address spaces of early family members, all Intel processors have separate address spaces for memory and I/O accesses. The address space to be selected is specified by the M/IO# bus line. A high value on this line selects the four GB memory address space, and low specifies the I/O address space. Separate opcodes, IN and OUT, are used to access this space. It is the responsibility of all devices on the bus to sample the M/IO# line at the beginning of each bus cycle to determine the address space to which the bus cycle is referring—memory or I/O. Figure 8-12 shows these address spaces graphically. I/O addresses in the x86 family are limited to 16 bits, allowing up to 64K I/O locations.

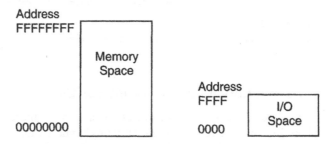

Figure 8-12
Intel memory and I/O address spaces.

8.4.4 Bus Cycles in the Pentium Family

The Pentium processor has a total of 18 different bus cycles to serve different needs. These include the standard memory read and write bus cycles, the bus hold cycle, (used to allow other devices to become the bus master), an interrupt acknowledge cycle, various "burst" cache access cycles, and a number of other special-purpose bus cycles. In this case study we examine the read and write bus cycles, the "burst read" cycle, in which a burst of data can be transferred, and the bus hold/hold acknowledge cycle, which is used by devices that wish to become the bus master.

---

[2] Many systems require so-called hard alignment. Misaligned words are not allowed, and their detection causes a processor exception to be raised.

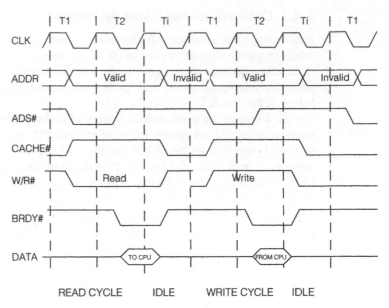

Figure 8-13
The standard Intel Pentium read and write bus cycles.

8.4.5 Memory Read and Write Bus Cycles

The "standard" read and write cycles are shown in Figure 8-13. By convention, the states of the Intel bus are referred to as "T states," where each T state is one clock cycle. There are three T states shown in the figure: T1, T2, and Ti, where Ti is the "idle" state, the state that occurs when the bus is not engaged in any specific activity and when no requests to use the bus are pending. Recall that a "#" following a signal name indicates that a signal is active low, in keeping with Intel conventions.

Both read and write cycles require a minimum of two bus clocks, T1 and T2:

- The CPU signals the start of all new bus cycles by asserting the Address Status signal, ADS#. This signal both defines the start of a new bus cycle and signals to memory that a valid address is available on the address bus, ADDR. Note the transition of ADDR from invalid to valid as ADS# is asserted.

- The de-assertion of the cache load signal, CACHE#, indicates that the cycle will be composed of a single read or write, as opposed to a burst read or write, covered later in this section.

- During a read cycle the CPU asserts read, W/R#, simultaneously with the assertion of ADS#. This signals the memory module that it should latch the address and read a value at that address.

- Upon a read, the memory module asserts the Burst Ready, BRDY#, signal as it places the data, DATA, on the bus, indicating that there is valid data on the data pins. The CPU uses BRDY# as a signal to latch the data values.

- Since CACHE# is deasserted, the assertion of a single BRDY# signifies the end of the bus cycle.

- In the write cycle, the memory module asserts BRDY# when it is ready to accept the data placed on the bus by the CPU. Thus BRDY# acts as a handshake between memory and the CPU.

- If memory is too slow to accept or drive data within the limits of two clock cycles, it can insert "wait" states by not asserting BRDY# until it is ready to respond.

8.4.6 The Burst Read Bus Cycle

Because of the critical need to supply the CPU with instructions and data from memory that is inherently slower than the CPU, Intel designed the burst read and write cycles. These cycles read and write four eight-byte quad words in a burst, from consecutive addresses. Figure 8-14 shows the Pentium burst read cycle.

The burst read cycle is initiated by the processor placing an address on the address lines and asserting ADS# as before, but now, by asserting the CACHE# line the processor signals the beginning of a burst read cycle. In response the memory asserts BRDY# and places a sequence of four eight-byte quad words on the data bus, one quad word per clock, keeping BRDY# asserted until the entire transfer is complete.

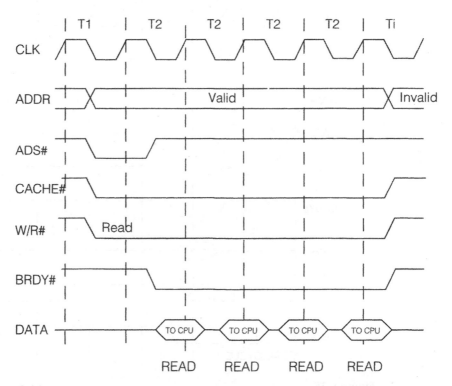

Figure 8-14
The Intel Pentium burst read bus cycle.

There is an analogous cycle for burst writes. There is also a mechanism for coping with slower memory by slowing the burst transfer rate from one per clock to one per two clocks.

8.4.7 Bus Hold for Request by Bus Master

There are two bus signals for use by devices requesting to become bus master: hold (HOLD) and hold acknowledge (HLDA). Figure 8-15 shows how the transactions work. The figure assumes that the processor is in the midst of a read cycle when the HOLD request signal arrives. The processor completes the current (read) cycle, and inserts two idle cycles, Ti. During the falling edge of the second Ti cycle the processor floats all of its lines and asserts HLDA. It keeps HLDA asserted for two clocks. At the end of the second clock cycle the device asserting HLDA "owns" the bus, and it may begin a new bus operation at the following cycle, as shown at the far right end of the figure. In systems of any complexity there will be a separate bus controller chip to mediate among the several devices that may wish to become the bus master.

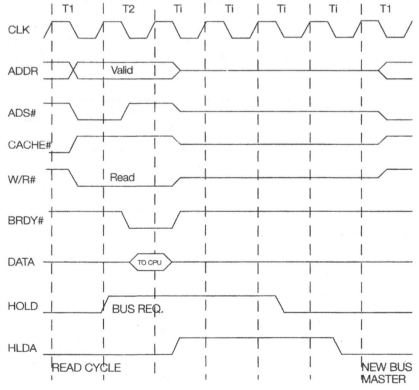

Figure 8-15
The Intel Pentium Hold–Hold Acknowledge bus cycle.

8.4.8 Data Transfer Rates

Let us compute the data transfer rates for the read and burst read bus cycles. In the first case, eight bytes are transferred in two clock cycles. If the bus clock speed is 133 MHz, this is a maximum transfer rate of

$$\frac{8}{2} \times 133 \times 10^6$$

or 532 million bytes per second. In burst mode this rate increases to four eight-byte bursts in five clock cycles, for a transfer rate of

$$\frac{32}{5} \times 133 \times 10^6$$

or 851 million bytes per second. (Intel literature uses four cycles rather than five as the denominator, thus arriving at a burst rate of 1064 million bytes per second. Take your pick.)

At the 851 million byte rate, with a bus clock multiplier of 3-1/2, the data transfer rate to the CPU is

$$\frac{851 \times 10^6}{3.5 \times 133 \times 10^6}$$

or about two bytes per clock cycle. Thus under optimum, or ideal conditions, the CPU is probably just barely kept supplied with bytes. In the event of a branch instruction or other interruption in memory activity, the CPU will become starved for instructions and data.

The Intel Pentium is typical of modern processors. It has a number of specialized bus cycles that support multiprocessors, cache memory transfers, and other special situations. Refer to the Intel literature (see Further Reading at the end of the chapter) for more details.

■ 8.5 SERIAL BUS ARCHITECTURES

Somewhat counterintuitively, serial (bit-by-bit) communication turns out to have significant advantages over parallel communication. There is a "break-even" distance at which serial communication is more economical, which is on the order of a few feet depending on the bit rate, the allowable footprint for the communication method, and the cost budgeted for the interconnect. Serial interconnects require higher bit rates to compensate for the lack of parallelism. On the other hand, serial interconnects use smaller cables, which are a big advantage, consume less power, less space, have more manageable timing issues, and cost less money. In general, parallel interconnects are used within a computer and serial interconnects are used outside of a computer, with some exceptions.

We explore three serial interconnection approaches below.

Figure 8-16
RS-232 connector types. [Sheila Terry/Photo Researchers, Inc.]

8.5.1 RS-232

The first serial interconnection method is not a bus at all, but a simple point-to-point interconnect known as **recommended standard-232C**, or simply RS-232. The RS-232 standard commonly uses 9-pin and 25-pin connectors, but uses others as well (see Figure 8-16). Pin 7 of the 25-pin connector is for signal ground, pin 2 sends data, and pin 3 receives data. Other pins are for handshaking and other functions. Two communicating systems need to see the transmit signal from one side appear on the receive pin of the other, and so the transmit and receive lines are crossed in a connecting cable.

RS-232 is used for slow-bit-rate devices such as mice, keyboards, and non-graphics terminals.

8.5.2 Universal Serial Bus (USB)

Universal Serial Bus (USB) and IEEE 1394 (**Firewire**) are two groups of standards for interconnecting peripheral devices. USB initially supported data transfer rates of 12 Mbps, with as many as 127 devices connected to a single host controller through special hub devices in a tree-like manner (Figure 8-17a). The standard has evolved to USB 2.0, which supports data rates up to 480 Mbps. USB is typically used for mice, keyboards, modems, disk drives, and other devices.

(a)   (b)   (c)

Figure 8-17
(a) USB hub; (b) USB cable; (c) Firewire cable.

USB provides electrical power to the devices, so that there is no need for additional power supplies for the devices.

8.5.3 Firewire

Firewire (Figure 8-17b), initially developed by Apple Computer in the 1990s, is similar to USB in many respects but has traditionally been faster, providing data transfer rates of 100 Mbps, 200 Mbps, 400 Mbps, or 800 Mbps. Also known as IEEE 1394, a key advantage of Firewire is support for **isochronous** data transfer, in which a continuous, guaranteed data transfer is supported at a predetermined rate. This makes Firewire attractive for applications such as digital video and digital audio. Like USB, Firewire also provides electrical power to the devices.

USB and Firewire both support hot pluggability (cables can be connected and disconnected while in use) and plug-and-play—the connection is automatic once the cable is plugged in. Firewire supports peer-to-peer connections—similar devices can be connected and either daisy-chained or branched as in the USB tree configuration, whereas USB only allows end devices to be connected to a host computer, though possibly with intervening hubs.

■ 8.6 MASS STORAGE

In Chapter 7, we saw that computer memory is organized as a hierarchy, in which the fastest method of storing information (registers) is expensive and not very dense, and the slowest methods of storing information (tapes, disks, etc.) are inexpensive and are very dense. Registers and random-access memories require continuous power to retain their stored data, whereas **media** such as magnetic tapes and magnetic disks retain information indefinitely after the power is removed, which is known as **indefinite persistence**. This type of storage is said to be **nonvolatile**. There are many kinds of nonvolatile storage, and only a few of the more common methods are described below. We start with one of the most prevalent forms: the **magnetic disk**.

8.6.1 Magnetic Disks

A magnetic disk is a device for storing information that supports a large storage density and a relatively fast access time. A **moving-head** magnetic disk is composed of a stack of one or more **platters** that are spaced close together and are connected via a **spindle**, as shown in Figure 8-18. The most common size for desktop personal computer disks is 3.5″ diameter by name, but the platters are actually 3.74″ in diameter. Laptop hard disk drives use 2.5″ diameters or smaller. Each platter has two **surfaces** made of aluminum, glass or ceramic material (which expands less than aluminum as it heats up) that are coated with small particles of a magnetic material such as iron oxide, which is the essence of rust. This is why disk platters, floppy diskettes, audio tapes, and other magnetic media are brown. Binary 1s and 0s are stored by magnetizing small areas of the material.

A single **head** is dedicated to each surface. Six heads are used in the example shown in Figure 8-18, for the six surfaces. The top surface of the top platter and the bottom

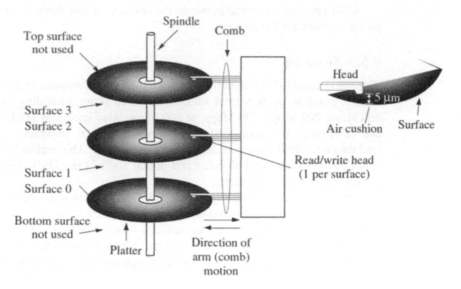

Figure 8-18
A multiplatter hard magnetic disk.

surface of the bottom platter were sometimes not used on multi-platter disks because they were more susceptible to contamination than the inner surfaces (before air filters became standard in sealed drives). The heads are attached to a common **arm** (also known as a **comb**) that moves in and out to reach different portions of the surfaces. Desktop computer hard drives typically have from one to five platters at 20 GB per surface.

In a hard disk drive, the platters rotate at a constant speed of typically 5400 to 15,000 revolutions per minute (RPM). The heads read or write data by magnetizing the magnetic material as it passes under the heads when writing, or by sensing the magnetic fields when reading. Only a single head is used for reading or writing at any time, so data is stored in serial fashion even though the heads can in principle be used to read or write several bits in parallel. One reason that the parallel mode of operation is not normally used is that heads can become misaligned, which corrupts the way that data is read or written. A single surface is relatively insensitive to the alignment of the corresponding head because the head position is always accurately known with respect to reference markings on the disk.

Data Encoding

Only the transitions between magnetized areas are sensed when reading a disk, and so runs of 1s or 0s may not be accurately detected unless a method of encoding is used that embeds timing information into the data to identify the breaks between bits. **Manchester encoding** is one method that addresses this problem, and another method is **modified frequency modulation** (MFM). For comparison, Figure 8-19a shows an ASCII 'F' character encoded as it would be inside of a CPU. Figure 8-19b shows the same character encoded in the Manchester code. In Manchester encoding there is a transition between high and low signals on every bit, resulting in a transition within every bit period. A transition from

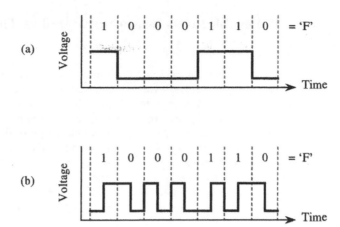

Figure 8-19
(a) Straight amplitude encoding of ASCII 'F'; (b) Manchester encoding of ASCII 'F'.

low to high indicates a 1, whereas a transition from high to low indicates a 0. These transitions are used to recover the timing information.

A single surface contains several thousand concentric **tracks**, which in turn are composed of **sectors** of typically 512 bytes in size, stored serially, as shown in Figure 8-20. The sectors are spaced apart by **inter-sector gaps**, and the tracks are spaced apart by **inter-track gaps**, which simplify positioning of the head. A set of corresponding tracks on all of the surfaces forms a **cylinder**. For instance, track 0 on each of surfaces 0, 1, 2, 3, 4, and 5 in Figure 8-18 collectively form cylinder 0. The number of bytes per sector is generally invariant across the entire platter.

In modern disk drives the number of tracks per sector may vary in **zones**, where a zone is a group of tracks having the same number of sectors per track. Zones near the

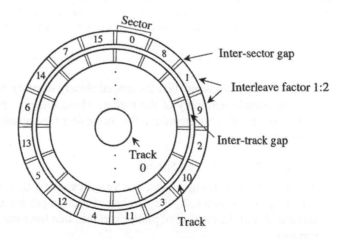

Figure 8-20
Organization of a disk platter with a 1:2 interleave factor.

Intel (PC) vs. Motorola (Macintosh): USB vs. FireWire

PCs and Macintoshes have an assortment of external buses for both slow and fast devices. Manufacturers have used slow, inexpensive serial interfaces for devices such as keyboards and mice. There is a natural impulse on the part of manufacturers continually to improve their offerings, including the external buses. Ironically, however, competition in the PC world prevented this from happening. In 1983 IBM faced competition in the form of the Compaq PC, the first "IBM—compatible" PC. Within the next few years literally dozens of manufacturers were selling IBM—compatible PCs, and IBM's share of the market was minimal. This concept of IBM-compatibility without IBM influence impeded the introduction of new, innovative external buses because of the lack of agreement or consensus among the many vendors. No vendor had sufficient market share to impose a new external bus architecture on the others unless all agreed, except perhaps for Intel.

Since only Apple Computer sold the Macintosh, their designers were free to innovate without these constraints. In 1987, for example, Apple introduced the Apple Desktop Bus (ADB) for slow devices such as keyboards, mice, and graphic tablets. The ADB had the advantage that devices could be daisy-chained: several devices could be connected serially to the same ADB port. Apple also incorporated the 230 Kbps IEEE 422 serial bus, which was considerably faster and more reliable than the slower RS-232 serial ports in use on PCs of the time, and the SCSI bus, which was superior for disk I/O. Apple's advantage was at the same time their disadvantage, however. None of these buses survived for long on the back panel of the Mac. No PC manufacturer used these technologies; few peripheral vendors would trouble to produce compatible peripheral devices because of the low volume, and when they did, the devices were usually significantly more expensive. By the late 1980s, both the PC and Macintosh camps were working on next-generation serial buses. Buses that were hot-pluggable and self-configuring could support dozens of devices in daisy-chain fashion, and could even supply a small amount of power, "bus powered," to devices. USB was developed by a consortium of seven companies, with considerable influence by Intel, with low cost as a major driving force. It was incorporated into both PCs and Macs in 1998. While the consortium of seven was developing the USB, Apple, stung no doubt by their lack of success in setting bus standards, was designing FireWire with a consortium of consumer electronics firms such as Sony and Canon as major influences—Apple was aiming at a high-speed, consumer-oriented bus, but with less emphasis on low cost. Think of a camcorder that talks to a VCR over FireWire, at 10x the bandwidth of USB. Apple introduced FireWire at almost the same time as USB was seen on PCs. USB lost and continues to lose to FireWire on almost all benchmarks. Perhaps by emphasizing the wider consumer applications, Apple can break their losing bus streak.

Ironically, in 2005 Apple removed FireWire from the iPod and replaced it with USB.

center of the platter where bits are spaced closely together have fewer sectors, while zones near the outside periphery of the platter, where bits are spaced farther apart, have more sectors per track. This technique for increasing the capacity of a disk drive is known as **zone-bit recording**.

Disk drive Capacities and Speeds

If a disk has only a single zone, its storage capacity, C, can be computed from the number of bytes per sector, N, the number of sectors per track, S, the number of tracks per surface, T, and the number of platter surfaces that have data encoded in them, P, with the formula:

$$C = N \times S \times T \times P$$

A high-capacity disk drive may have N = 512 bytes, S = 1,000 sectors per track, T = 30,000 tracks per surface, and P = 8 platter surfaces. The total capacity of this drive is C = 512 bytes/sector × 1000 sectors/track × 30,000 tracks/surface × 8 platter surfaces = 123 GB.

Maximum data transfer speed is governed by three factors: the time to move the head to the desired track, referred to as the head **seek time**, the time for the desired sector to appear under the read/write head, known as the **rotational latency**, and the time to transfer the sector from the disk platter once the sector is positioned under the head, known as the **transfer time**. Transfers to and from a disk are always carried out in complete sectors. Partial sectors are never read or written.

Head seek time is the largest contributor to overall access time of a disk. Manufacturers usually specify an average seek time, which is roughly the time required for the head to travel half the distance across the disk. The rationale for this definition is that it is difficult to know, *a priori*, which track the data is on, or where the head is positioned when the disk access request is made. Thus it is assumed that the head will, on average, be required to travel over half the surface before arriving at the correct track. On modern disk drives average seek time is approximately 5 ms.

Once the head is positioned at the correct track, it is again difficult to know ahead of time how long it will take for the desired sector to appear under the head. Therefore the average rotational latency is taken to be 1/2 the time of one complete revolution, which is on the order of 2–4 ms. The sector transfer time is just the time for one complete revolution divided by the number of sectors per track. If large amounts of data are to be transferred, then after a complete track is transferred, the head must move to the next track. The parameter of interest here is the track-to-track access time, which is approximately 1 ms (notice that the time for the head to travel past multiple tracks is much less than 1 ms per track). An important parameter related to the sector transfer time is the **burst rate**, the rate at which data streams on or off the disk once the read/write operation has started. The burst rate equals the disk speed in revolutions per second times the capacity per track. This is not necessarily the same as the transfer rate, because there is a setup time needed to position the head and synchronize timing for each sector.

The maximum transfer rate computed from the factors above may not be realized in practice. The limiting factor may be the speed of the bus interconnecting the disk drive and its interface, or it may be the time required by the CPU to transfer the data between the disk and main memory. For example, disks that operate with the **Small Computer Systems Interface** (SCSI) standards have a transfer rate between the disk and a host computer of from 5 to 40 MB/second, which may be slower than the transfer rate between the head and the internal buffer on the disk (faster external buses like USB and Firewire have all but replaced SCSI). Disk drives contain internal buffers that help match the speed of the disk with the speed of transfer from the disk unit to the host computer.

Disk Drives are Delicate Mechanisms

The strength of a magnetic field drops off as the square of the distance from the source of the field, and for this reason, it is important for the head of the disk to travel as close to the surface as possible. The distance between the head and the platter can be as small as 5 μm. The engineering and assembly of a disk do not have to adhere to such a tight tolerance—

the head assembly is aerodynamically designed so that the spinning motion of the disk creates a cushion of air that maintains a distance between the heads and the platters. Particles in the air contained within the disk unit that are larger than 5 μm can come between the head assembly and the platter, which results in a **head crash**.

Smoke particles from cigarette ash are 10 μm or larger, and so smoking should not take place when disks are exposed to the environment. Disks are usually assembled into sealed units in **clean rooms**, so that virtually no large particles are introduced during assembly. Unfortunately, materials used in manufacturing (such as glue) that are internal to the unit can deteriorate over time and can generate particles large enough to cause a head crash. For this reason, sealed disks (formerly called **Winchester** disks) contain filters that remove particles generated within the unit and prevent particulate matter from entering the drive from the external environment.

Floppy Disks

A **floppy disk**, or **diskette**, contains a flexible plastic platter coated with a magnetic material like iron oxide. Although only a single side is used on one surface of a floppy disk in many systems, both sides of the disks are coated with the same material in order to prevent warping. Access time is slower than a hard disk because a flexible disk cannot spin as quickly as a hard disk. The rotational speed of a typical floppy disk mechanism is only 300 RPM, and may be varied as the head moves from track to track to optimize data transfer rates. Such slow rotational speeds mean that access times of floppy drives are 250–300 ms, roughly 500 times slower than hard drives. Capacities vary, but range up to 1.44 MB.

Floppies are inexpensive because they can be removed from the drive mechanism and because of their small size. The head comes in physical contact with the floppy disk but this does not result in a head crash. It does, however, place wear on the head and on the media. For this reason, floppies spin only when they are being accessed.

When floppies were first introduced, they were encased in flexible, thin plastic enclosures, which gave rise to their name. The flexible platters were later encased in rigid plastic and have since been referred to as "diskettes."

Several high-capacity floppy-like removable disk drives have made their appearance in recent years. The Iomega REV drive, as one example, has a capacity of 35 GB and access times that are about twice those of hard drives. These technologies are not considered floppy, however, because they use hard magnetic disks.

Disk File Systems

A **file** is a collection of sectors that are linked together to form a single logical entity. A file that is stored on a disk can be organized in a number of ways. The most efficient method is to store a file in consecutive sectors so that the seek time and the rotational latency are minimized. A disk normally stores more than one file, and it is generally difficult to predict the maximum file size. Fixed file sizes are appropriate for some applications, though. For instance, satellite images may all have the same size in any one sampling.

An alternative method for organizing files is to assign sectors to a file on demand, as needed. With this method, files can grow to arbitrary sizes, but there may be many head movements involved in reading or writing a file. After a disk system has been in use for a period of time, the files on it may become **fragmented**, that is, the sectors that make up the files are scattered over the disk surfaces. Several vendors produce optimizers that will defragment a disk, reorganizing it so that each file is again stored in contiguous sectors and tracks.

A related facet in disk organization is **interleaving**. If the CPU and interface circuitry between the disk unit and the CPU all keep pace with the internal rate of the disk, then there may still be a hidden performance problem. After a sector is read and buffered, it is transferred to the CPU. If the CPU then requests the next contiguous sector, it may be too late to read the sector without waiting for another revolution. If the sectors are interleaved, for example if a file is stored on alternate sectors, say 2, 4, 6, etc., then the time required for the intermediate sectors to pass under the head may be enough to set up the next transfer. In this scenario, two or more revolutions of the disk are required to read an entire track, but this is less than the revolution per sector that would otherwise be needed. If a single sector time is not long enough to set up the next read, a greater interleave factor can be used, such as 1:3 or 1:4. In Figure 8-20, an interleave factor of 1:2 is used.

An operating system has the responsibility for allocating blocks (sectors) to a growing file, and for reading the blocks that make up a file, and so it needs to know where to find the blocks. The **master control block** (MCB) is a reserved section of a disk that keeps track of the makeup of the rest of the disk. The MCB is normally stored in the same place on every disk for a particular type of computer system, such as the innermost track. In this way, an operating system does not have to guess at the size of a disk; it only needs to read the MCB in the innermost track.

Figure 8-21 shows one version of an MCB. Not all systems keep all of this information in the MCB, but it has to be kept *somewhere*, and some of it may even be kept in parts of the files. There are four major components to the MCB. The Preamble section specifies information relating to the physical layout of the disk, such as the number of surfaces, number of sectors per surface, etc. The Files section cross-references file names with the list of sectors of which they are composed, and file attributes such as the file creation date, last modification date, the identification of the owner, and protections. Only the starting sector is needed for a fixed file size disk; otherwise, a list of all of the sectors that make up a file is maintained.

The Free blocks section lists the positions of blocks that are free to be used for new or growing files. The Bad blocks section lists positions of blocks that are free but produce **checksums** (see Section 9.3.3) that indicate errors. The bad blocks are thus unused.

As a file grows in size, the operating system reads the MCB to find a free block and then updates the MCB accordingly. Unfortunately, this generates a great deal of head movement, since the MCB and free blocks are rarely (if ever) on the same track. For every block that is accessed, an additional access is needed to reference the MCB, thus doubling the work load on the disk. A solution used in practice is to copy the MCB into main memory and make updates there, and then periodically update the MCB on the disk, which is known as **syncing** the disk.

A problem with having two copies of the MCB, one on the disk and one in main memory, is that if a computer is shut down before the main-memory version of the MCB is synced to the disk, then the integrity of the disk is destroyed. The normal shutdown procedure for personal computers and other machines syncs the disks, so it is important to shut

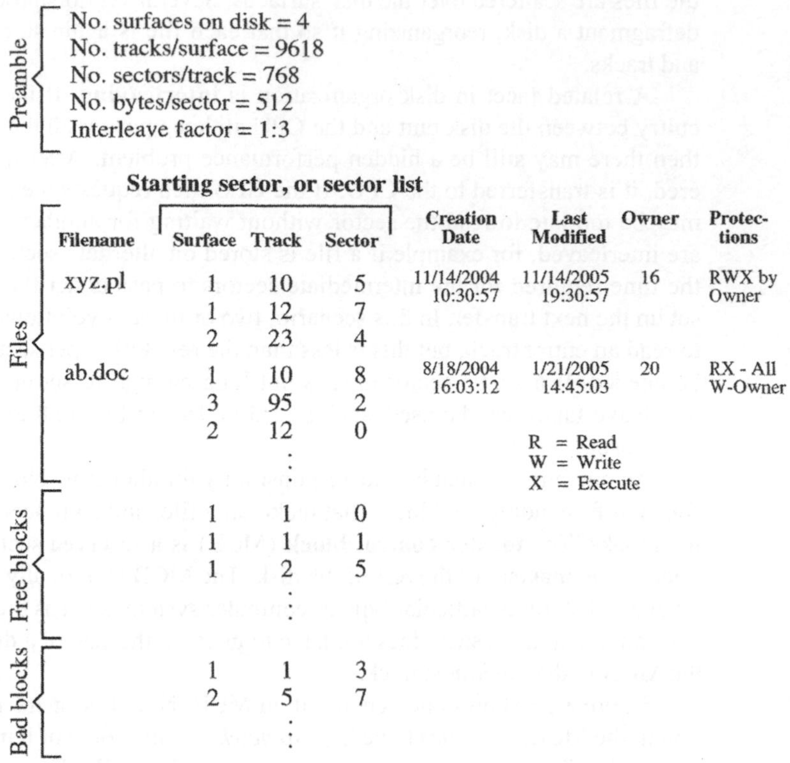

Preamble
No. surfaces on disk = 4
No. tracks/surface = 9618
No. sectors/track = 768
No. bytes/sector = 512
Interleave factor = 1:3

Starting sector, or sector list

Filename	Surface	Track	Sector	Creation Date	Last Modified	Owner	Protections
Files							
xyz.pl	1	10	5	11/14/2004 10:30:57	11/14/2005 19:30:57	16	RWX by Owner
	1	12	7				
	2	23	4				
ab.doc	1	10	8	8/18/2004 16:03:12	1/21/2005 14:45:03	20	RX - All W-Owner
	3	95	2				
	2	12	0				
	⋮						

R = Read
W = Write
X = Execute

Free blocks

1	1	0
1	1	1
1	2	5
⋮		

Bad blocks

1	1	3
2	5	7
⋮		

Figure 8-21
Simplified example of an MCB.

down a computer this way rather than by simply shutting off the power. In the event that a disk is not properly synced, there is usually enough redundant information for a disk-recovery program to restore the integrity of the disk, but sometimes this cannot be done perfectly—thus the importance of maintaining backup copies of hard disk data. (See Problem 8.12 for an alternative MCB organization that makes recovery easier.)

8.6.2 Magnetic Tape

A magnetic tape unit typically has a single read/write head, but may have separate heads for reading and writing. A spool of plastic (Mylar) tape with a magnetic coating passes the head, which magnetizes the tape when writing or senses stored data when reading. Magnetic tape is an inexpensive means for storing large amounts of data, but access to any particular portion is slow because all of the prior sections of the tape must pass the head before the target section can be accessed.

In its simplest form, information is stored on a tape in two-dimensional fashion, as shown in Figure 8-22. Bits are stored along the length of the tape in **segments** organized along up to 32 **tracks**. Each segment is made up of blocks of 512 or 1024 bytes, in bit serial fashion. A file is made up of a collection of (typically contiguous) segments. A seg-

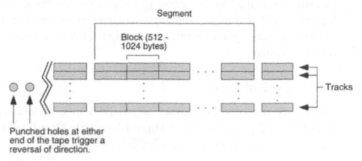

Figure 8-22
A portion of a magnetic tape.

ment is the smallest amount of data that can be read from or written to a tape. The reason for this is physical rather than logical. A tape is normally motionless. When we want to write a segment to the tape, then a motor starts the tape moving, which takes a finite amount of time. Once the tape is up to speed, the segment is written, and the motion of the tape is then stopped, which again takes a finite amount of time. The starting and stopping times consume unusable sections of the tape that are known as **inter-record gaps**.

Digital audio tape (DAT) formatting supports higher densities, on the order of 72 GB for a small 73 mm × 54 mm profile. The read/write head is placed at an angle to the tape as shown in Figure 8-23, allowing data to be crisscrossed over the same area using opposite polarities, which maintains separation of the bits.

A tape is suitable for storing large amounts of data, such as backups of disks or scanned images, but is not suitable for random-access reading and writing. There are two reasons for this. First, the sequential access can require a great deal of time if the head is not positioned near the target section of tape. The second reason arises when records are overwritten in the middle of the tape, which is not generally an operation that is allowed in tape systems. Although individual records are the same size, the inter-record gaps eventually creep into the records (this is called **jitter**) because starting and stopping is not precise.

A **physical record** (essentially, a segment) may be subdivided into an integral number of **logical records**. For example, a physical record that is 16,384 bytes in length may be composed of four logical records that are each 4096 bytes in length. Access to logical

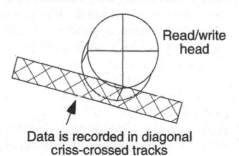

Figure 8-23
Digital audio tape (DAT) crisscrossed storage pattern.

records is managed by an operating system, so that the user has the perspective that the logical record size relates directly to a physical record size, when in fact, only physical records are read from or written to the tape. There are thus no inter-record gaps between logical records.

8.6.3 Optical Disks

Several technologies take advantage of optics to store and retrieve data. Both the **Compact Disc** (CD) and the newer **Digital Versatile Disc** (DVD), discussed below, employ light to read data encoded on a reflective surface.

The Compact Disc

The CD was introduced in 1983 as a medium for playback of music. CDs have the capacity to store 74 minutes of audio, in digital stereo (two-channel) format. The audio is sampled at $2 \times 44,000$ 16-bit samples per second, which translates to nearly 700 MB in capacity. Since the introduction of the CD in 1983, CD technology has improved in terms of price, density, and reliability, leading to the development of **CD ROMs** (CD read-only memories) for computers, which also have the same 700-MB capacity. Their low cost, only a few cents each when produced in volume, coupled with good reliability and high capacity, have made CD ROMs the medium of choice for distributing commercial software, replacing floppy disks (although even this high-density storage medium is being replaced with DVDs, which are discussed in the next section).

CD ROMs are "read only" because they are stamped from a master disk similarly to the way that audio CDs are created. A CD ROM disk consists of aluminum coated plastic, which reflects light differently for **lands** or **pits**, which are smooth or pitted areas, respectively, that are created in the stamping process. The master is created with high accuracy using a high-power laser. The pressed (stamped) disks are less accurate, and so a complex error-correction scheme is used known as a **crossinterleaved Reed–Solomon** error-correcting code. Errors are also reduced by assigning 1s to pit-land and land-pit transitions, with runs of 0s assigned to smooth areas, rather than assigning 0s and 1s to lands and pits, similar to Manchester encoding.

Unlike a magnetic disk in which all of the sectors on concentric tracks are lined up like a sliced pie (where the disk rotation uses **constant angular velocity**), a CD is arranged in a spiral format (using **constant linear velocity**), as shown in Figure 8-24. The pits are laid down on this spiral with equal spacing from one end of the disk to the other. The speed of rotation, originally 350 RPM on the outer tracks and 500 RPM on the inner tracks but now up to 48 times faster, is adjusted so that the disk moves more slowly when the head is at the edge than when it is at the center. Thus CD ROMs suffer from the same long access time as floppy disks because of the high rotational latency, but they are suitable for applications in which data is accessed in contiguous segments, such as for multimedia.

CD ROM technology is appropriate for distributing large amounts of data inexpensively when there are many copies to be made, because the cost of creating a master and pressing the copies is distributed over the cost of each copy. If only a few copies are made, then the cost of each disk is high because CDs cannot be as economically pressed in small quantities. CDs also cannot be written after they are pressed. (They can be economically

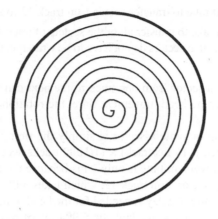

Figure 8-24
Spiral storage format for a CD.

burned and reburned in small quantities with inexpensive CD ROM makers but expensive rewritable disks, which is a different process that produces much less durable disks.) A later technology that addressed this problem is the **write once read many** (WORM) optical disk, in which a low-intensity laser in the CD controller writes onto the optical disk (but only once for each bit location). The writing process is normally slower than the reading process, and the controller and media are more expensive than for CD ROMs. WORM drives worked well for backup and archiving applications but have since been replaced with DVDs and other media technologies.

The Digital Versatile Disc

A newer version of optical disk storage is the **Digital Versatile Disc**, also known as **Digital Video Disk** or just DVD. There are industry standards for DVD-Audio, DVD-Video, and DVD-ROM and DVD-RAM data storage. When a single side of the DVD is used with a single layer, its storage capacity can be up to 4.7 GB. The DVD standards also include the capability of storing data on both sides in two layers on each side by varying the focal length of the optical read/write mechanism, for a total capacity of 17 GB. Double-sided DVDs only have printing on the nonreadable areas. The DVD technology is an evolutionary step up from the CD, rather than being an entirely new technology, and in fact the DVD player is backwardly compatible—it can be used to play CDs and CD ROMs as well as DVDs.

EXAMPLE 8-1 TRANSFER TIME FOR A HARD DISK

Consider calculating the transfer time for a hard magnetic disk. For this example, assume that a disk rotates once every 6 ms. The seek time to move the head between adjacent tracks is 1 ms. There are 1000 sectors per track that are stored in linear order (non-interleaved), from sector 0 to sector 999. The head sees the sectors in that order.

Assume the read/write head is positioned at the start of sector 1 on track 12. There is a memory buffer that is large enough to hold an entire track. Data is transferred between disk locations by reading the source data into memory, positioning the read/write head over the destination location, and writing the data to the destination.

- How long will it take to transfer sector 1 on track 12 to sector 1 on track 13?

- How long will it take to transfer all of the sectors of track 12 to the corresponding sectors on track 13? Note that sectors do not have to be written in the same order they are read.

Solution

The time to transfer a sector from one track to the next can be decomposed into its parts: the sector read time, the head movement time, the rotational delay, and the sector write time.

The time to read or write a sector is simply the time it takes for the sector to pass under the head, which is (6 ms/track) × (1/1000 tracks/sector) = .006 ms/sector. For this example, the head movement time is only 1 ms because the head moves between adjacent tracks. After reading sector 1 on track 12, which takes .006 ms, an additional 6 ms − .006 ms = 5.994 ms of rotational delay is needed for the head to line up with sector 1 again. The head movement time of 1 ms overlaps the 5.994 ms of rotational delay, and so only the greater of the two times (5.994 ms) is used.

We sum the individual times and obtain: .006 ms + 5.994 ms + .006 ms = 6.006 ms to transfer sector 1 on track 12 to sector 1 on track 13.

The time to transfer all of track 12 to track 13 is computed in a similar manner. The memory buffer can hold an entire track, and so the time to read or write an entire track is simply the rotational delay for a track, which is 6 ms. The head movement time is 1 ms, which is also the time for 167 sectors to pass under the head (at .006 ms per sector). Thus, after reading a track and repositioning the head, the head is now on track 13, at 168 sectors past the initial sector that was read on track 12.

Sectors can be written in a different order than they are read. Track 13 can thus be written starting with sector 168. The time to write track 13 is 6 ms, and the time for the entire transfer then is: 6 ms + 1 ms + 6 ms = 13 ms. Notice that the rotational delay is zero for this example because the head lands at the beginning of the first sector to be written. ∎

■ 8.7 RAID—REDUNDANT ARRAYS OF INEXPENSIVE DISKS

The storage density of hard magnetic disks has experienced similar improvements to circuit density following Moore's Law, approximately doubling every 18 months. As storage density progressed, earlier lower-density disks were left behind with a lot of capability at low prices. Researchers at the University of California at Berkeley investigated ways to combine these lower-priced disks to behave as one large disk with faster access times and fault tolerance. They coined the term "RAID" in 1987, for **Redundant Arrays of Inexpensive Disks**, which has since taken an alternative meaning of **Redundant Arrays of Independent Disks**.

There are several levels of RAID technology, each with its own features and tradeoffs. Figure 8-25 shows RAID level 0, which is known as "striped disk array without fault tolerance." The idea is to spread successive blocks (A–P in the figure) over multiple disks, with the expectation that those blocks will be accessed in order as a group. Disk requests are sent for all of the blocks, which are accessed whenever they become available. This

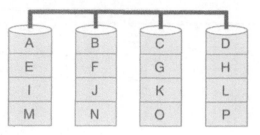

Figure 8-25
RAID level 0. (Source: ACNC, 2005.)

has the effect of speeding accesses because multiple disk heads and platters are working simultaneously.

RAID 0 access time improvement is constrained by the number of disk controllers: each disk needs to be on its own controller. There is no fault tolerance with RAID level 0—a single disk failure causes the entire RAID to fail, but the speedup is important for some applications like video production and editing.

RAID level 1, known as "Mirroring and Duplexing," is shown in Figure 8-26. RAID level 1 provides fault tolerance by duplicating data, and supports faster reads because two read requests can be satisfied at a time, one per drive within a pair. Both disks within a pair need to be written and so access times for writes are no better than without RAID, but since read requests occur more often than write requests, an overall performance improvement is realized. Should a disk fail, then the other drive within a pair takes over. This approach supports 100% redundancy and is simple, but there are more efficient approaches that require less redundancy.

RAID level 2, known as "bit-level striping with Hamming Code ECC," is shown in Figure 8-27. RAID level 2 spreads data at the bit level over multiple disks, and adds a few additional disks for error correction in a technique known as a **Hamming error correcting code (ECC),** which is covered in detail in Section 9.3. The idea is to add redundant information—a few additional "check" bits summed over each group of data bits – which allows the entire group to be reconstructed if a portion is missing. This approach performs on-the-fly error correction—if any disk fails, there is enough information in the remaining bits to recover the lost information.

RAID level 2 is fast, but it never caught on in a big way, largely due to cost: several disks are needed for error correction, which makes the initial investment steep.

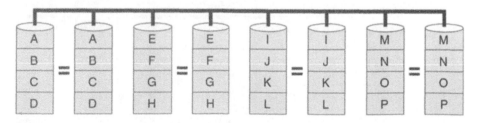

Figure 8-26
RAID level 1. (Source: ACNC, 2001.)

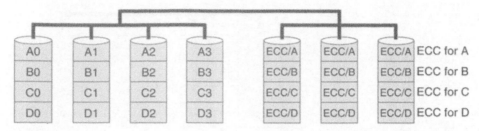

Figure 8-27
RAID level 2. (Source: ACNC, 2001.)

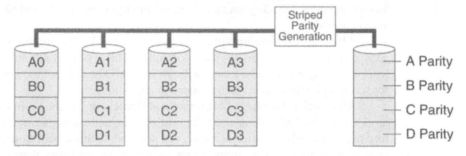

Figure 8-28
RAID level 3. (Source: ACNC, 2005.)

RAID level 3, known as "parallel transfer with parity" is shown in Figure 8-28. Data blocks are "striped" over the data disks, and a single stripe (essentially a checksum) is stored on a parity disk. If a single disk fails, all of its contents can be reconstructed from the remaining disks. The low entry cost of having a single-parity disk makes this approach more attractive than RAID level 2.

RAID level 4, known as "independent data disks with shared parity disk," is illustrated in Figure 8-29. This is similar to RAID level 3 except that data is accessed as independent blocks instead of as stripes. The independent aspect of RAID level 4 makes the hardware less expensive than RAID level 3, in which the disks are synchronized, but the process of rebuilding a disk in the event of a failure is difficult and inefficient.

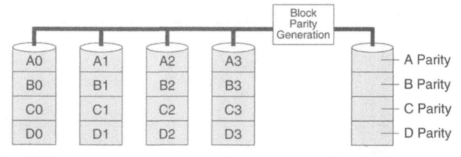

Figure 8-29
RAID level 4. (Source: ACNC, 2005.)

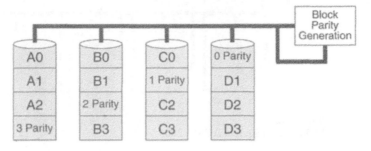

Figure 8-30
RAID level 5. (Source: ACNC, 2005.)

RAID level 5, known as "independent data disks with distributed parity blocks," is illustrated in Figure 8-30. RAID 5 is one of the most effective RAID approaches. Each entire data block is written onto a data disk. Parity for blocks in the same rank is generated on writes, recorded in a distributed location, and checked on reads. The data rate for read operations is high due to the distribution of data over several disks, and write operations are also faster than RAID 4 because the bottleneck for the parity drive has been removed. The overhead in processing parity limits the speed of write operations, but overall, RAID 5 has been widely adopted. As an application note, in general, RAID 1 protects operating system volumes, whereas RAID 5 protects data.

RAID level 6, known as "independent data disks with two independent distributed parity schemes," is illustrated in Figure 8-31. RAID 6 is essentially an extension of RAID 5 that allows additional fault tolerance by increasing the amount of error correction (parity). RAID 6 can sustain multiple disk failures.

RAID level 7, which is known as "asynchronous cached striping with dedicated parity," is a proprietary solution by Storage Computer Corporation. Although it is not an open standard like the lower-numbered RAID levels, it is used in the marketplace. An illustration of RAID 7 is shown in Figure 8-32. A high-speed internal cache transfer bus known as the **X-bus** (not shown) improves performance. All I/O transfers are asynchronous, independently controlled, and cached. Small reads in a multiuser environment have a very high cache hit rate.

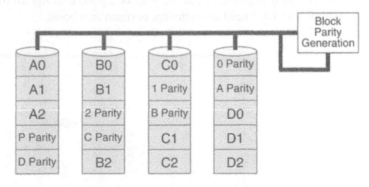

Figure 8-31
RAID level 6. (Source: ACNC, 2005.)

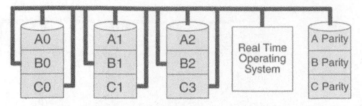

Figure 8-32
RAID level 7. (Source: ACNC, 2005.)

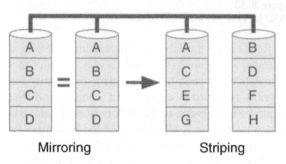

Figure 8-33
RAID level 10. (Source: ACNC, 2005.)

RAID level 10 is known as "very high reliability combined with high performance." An illustration of RAID 10 is shown in Figure 8-33. The name "RAID 10" comes from the fact that mirroring from RAID 1 is combined with striping from RAID 0, resulting in very good access times and reliability. The cost is high, however: notice that each block has three copies and that a minimum of four disks is needed.

Finally, RAID level 53, known as "high I/O rates and data transfer performance" is illustrated in Figure 8-34. RAID 53 is implemented as a striped (RAID level 0) array whose segments are RAID 3 arrays. (In a sense, RAID 53 should really be named RAID 0–3.) High I/O rates are achieved for small requests due to the RAID 0 striping and the RAID 3 array segments. RAID 53 may be a good solution for those who would have gone with RAID 3 but need an additional performance boost.

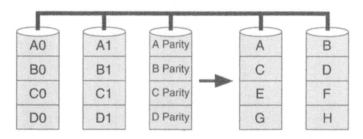

Figure 8-34
RAID level 53. (Source: ACNC, 2005.)

■ 8.8 INPUT DEVICES

In this section, we look at a few devices that are used exclusively for input of data. We start with one of the most prevalent devices, the **keyboard**.

8.8.1 Keyboards

Keyboards are used for manual input to a computer. A keyboard layout using the ECMA-23 Standard (2nd ed.) is shown in Figure 8-35. The "QWERTY" layout (for the upper left row of letters D01–D06) conforms to the traditional layout used in typewriters. Frequently used letters are placed far apart so that the typist is slowed and jams in mechanical typewriters are reduced. Although jams are not a problem with electronic keyboards, the traditional, purposely inefficient layout prevails.

When a character is typed, a bit pattern is created that is transmitted to a host computer. For seven-bit ASCII characters, only 128 bit patterns can be used, but many keyboards that expand on the basic ECMA-23 standard use additional modifier keys (shift, escape, and control) and so a seven-bit pattern is no longer large enough. A number of alternatives are possible, but one method that has gained acceptance is to provide one bit pattern for each modifier key and other bit patterns for the remaining keys.

Other modifications to the ECMA-23 keyboard include the addition of function keys (in row F, for example), and the addition of special keys such as tab, delete, and carriage return. Of historical interest, a modification that places frequently used keys together was developed for the **Dvorak keyboard** as shown in Figure 8-36. Despite the performance advantage of the Dvorak keyboard, it has not gained wide acceptance.

8.8.2 Tablets

A **digitizing tablet** is an input device that consists of a flat surface and either a pen-based **stylus** or **puck,** as illustrated in Figure 8-37. The tablet has an embedded two-dimensional mesh of wires that detects an induced current created by the puck as it is moved about the tablet. The tablet transmits X–Y (horizontal-vertical) positions and the state of the buttons

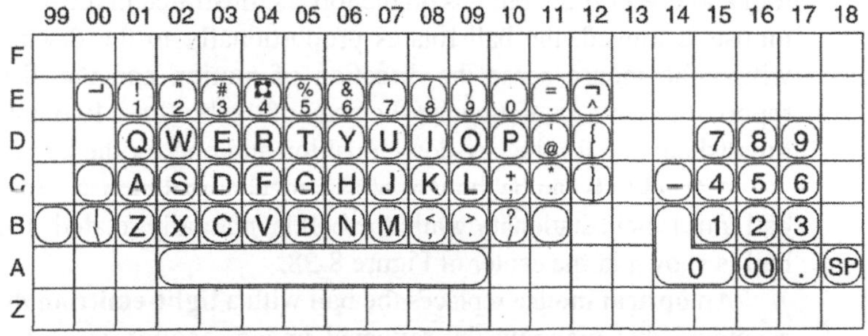

Figure 8-35
Keyboard layout for the ECMA-23 Standard (2nd ed.). Shift keys are frequently placed in the B row.

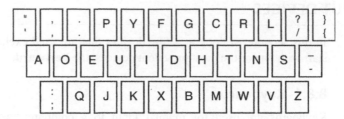

Figure 8-36
The Dvorak keyboard layout.

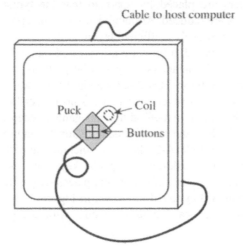

Figure 8-37
A tablet with a puck.

on the puck (or stylus) either continuously, or for an event such as a key click or a movement, depending on the control method. Tablets are commonly used for entering data from maps, photographs, charts, or graphs, or capturing handwriting.

8.8.3 Mice and Trackballs

A mechanical **mouse** is a hand-held input device that consists of a rubber ball on the bottom and one or more buttons on the top, as illustrated in the left side of Figure 8-38. As the mouse is moved, the ball rotates proportionally to the distance moved. Potentiometers within the mouse sense the direction of motion and the distance traveled, which are reported to the host along with the state of the buttons. Two button events are usually distinguished: one for the key-down position and one for the key-up position.

A **trackball** can be thought of as a mechanical mouse turned upside down. The trackball unit is held stationary while the ball is manually rotated. The configuration of a trackball is shown in the center of Figure 8-38.

An **optical mouse** replaces the ball with a **light-emitting diode** (LED) or a laser, with a camera that picks up the reflected image. Motion is sensed through changes in the reflected image. The optical mouse does not accumulate dirt as readily as the ball mouse, and can be used in a vertical position, in a weightless environment, or on just about any

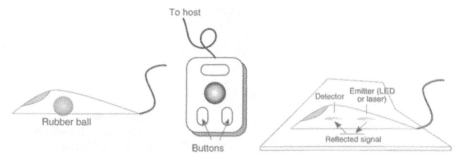

Figure 8-38
A mechanical mouse (left), a three-button trackball (center), and an optical mouse (right).

surface that has distinguishable features (meaning that a mirror would not be a good choice of surface).

8.8.4 Touch-Sensitive Pen-Based Display

Unlike a tablet, which uses an **active matrix** that senses an electromagnetic field induced by a stylus or puck, pen-based personal digital assistants (PDAs) use a **passive matrix** in which the pen can be anything that induces pressure on the screen (see Figure 8-39). Two transparent conducting layers are placed on the screen, separated by spacer dots. When the user applies pressure to the top layer, as with a stylus or simply a finger, the top and bottom layers make contact. The induced voltage at the edges varies according to the position of the stylus. If pressure is applied to two or more points, then the position is electrically

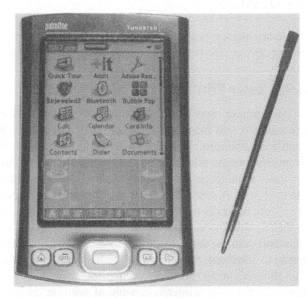

Figure 8-39
Personal digital assistant with passive matrix display and stylus.

Figure 8-40
A joystick with a selection button
and a rotatable rod.

averaged by the conducting layers since the PDA has no way to know that more than one location is simultaneously touched, but in normal use the stylus works well.

8.8.5 Joysticks

A **joystick** indicates horizontal and vertical position by the distance a rod that protrudes from the base is moved (see Figure 8-40). Joysticks are commonly used in video games and for indicating position in graphics systems. Potentiometers within the base of the joystick translate X–Y position information into voltages, which are then encoded in binary for input to a digital system. In a spring-loaded joystick, the rod returns to the center position when released. If the rod can be rotated, then an additional dimension can be indicated, such as height.

■ 8.9 OUTPUT DEVICES

There are many types of output devices. In the sections below, we explore three common output devices: the **laser printer,** the **video display**, and the **LCD panel**.

8.9.1 Laser Printers

A laser printer consists of a charged drum in which a laser discharges selected areas according to a bit-mapped representation of a page to be printed. As the drum advances for each scan line, the charged areas pick up electrostatically sensitive toner powder. The drum continues to advance and the toner is transferred to the paper, which is heated to fix the toner on the page. The drum is cleaned of any residual toner and the process repeats for the next page. A schematic diagram of the process is shown in Figure 8-41.

Since the toner is a form of plastic, rather than ink, it is not absorbed into the page but is melted onto the surface. For this reason, a folded sheet of laser printed paper will display cracks in the toner along the fold, and the toner is sometimes unintentionally transferred to other materials if exposed to heat or pressure (as from a stack of books).

Whereas older printers could print only ASCII characters or occasionally crude graphics, the laser printer is capable of printing arbitrary graphical information. Several languages have been developed for communicating information from computer to printer. One of the most common is the **Adobe PostScript** language. PostScript is a stack-based

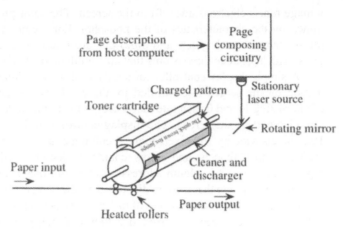

Figure 8-41

Schematic of a laser printer. (Source: adapted from [Tanenbaum, 1999].)

language that is capable of describing objects as diverse as ASCII characters, high-level shapes such as circles and rectangles, and low-level bit maps. It can be used to describe foreground and background colors and colors with which to fill objects.

8.9.2 Video Displays

A video display, or **monitor**, consists of a luminescent display device such as a cathode ray tube (CRT) or a liquid crystal display panel (described in the next section) and controlling circuitry. In a CRT, vertical and horizontal deflection plates steer an electron beam that sweeps the display screen in **raster** fashion (one line at a time, from left to right, starting at the top).

A configuration for a CRT is shown in Figure 8-42. An electron gun generates a stream of electrons that is imaged onto a phosphor-coated screen at positions controlled by voltages on the vertical and horizontal deflection plates. Electrons are negatively charged, and so a positive voltage on the grid accelerates electrons toward the screen and a negative

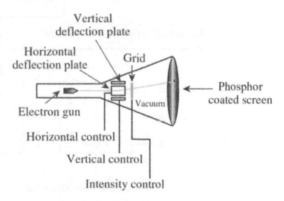

Figure 8-42

A CRT with a single electron gun.

voltage repels electrons away from the screen. The color produced on the screen is determined by the characteristics of the phosphor. For a color CRT, there are three different phosphor types (red, green, and blue) that are interleaved in a regular pattern, and three guns, which produce three beams that are simultaneously deflected on the screen.

A simple display controller for a CRT is shown in Figure 8-43. The writing of information on the screen is controlled by the clock, which generates a continuous stream of alternating 1s and 0s at a rate that corresponds to the update time for a single **pixel** (picture element) on the screen. The display controller in Figure 8-43 is for a screen that is 1024 pixels wide by 768 pixels high. A column counter is incremented from 0 to 1023 for each row, then repeats, and a row counter is incremented from 0 to 767, which then repeats. The row and column addresses index into the **frame buffer**, or "display RAM" that holds the image that is to be displayed on the screen. The contents of the frame buffer are transferred to the screen from 30 to 100 times per second. This technique of mapping a RAM area to the screen is referred to as **memory-mapped video**. Each pixel on the screen may be represented by from 1 to 24 or more bits in the frame buffer. When there is only a single bit per pixel, the pixel can only be on or off, black or white; multiple bits per pixel allow a pixel to have varying colors, or shades of gray.

Each pixel in the display controller of Figure 8-43 is represented by eight bits in the frame buffer, which means that one out of $2^8 = 256$ different values can be used for each pixel. In a simple configuration, the eight bits can be partitioned for the red, green, and blue (R, G, and B) inputs to the CRT as three bits for red, three bits for green, and two bits for blue. An alternative is to pass the eight-bit pixel value to a color lookup table (LUT) in which the eight-bit value is translated into 256 different 24-bit colors. Eight bits of the 24-bit output are then used for each of the red, green, and blue guns. A total of 2^{24} differ-

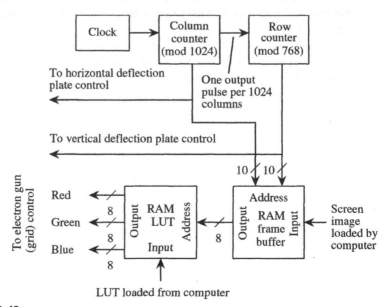

Figure 8-43
Display controller for a 1024 × 768 color monitor. (Source: adapted from [Hamacher et al., 1990].)

ent colors can be displayed, but only 2^8 of the 2^{24} can be displayed at any one time because the LUT has only 2^8 entries. The LUT can be reloaded as necessary to select different subsets of the 2^{24} colors. For example, in order to display a gray-scale image (no color), we must have R = G = B and so a ramp from 0 to 255 is stored for each of the red, green, and blue guns.

The human eye is relatively slow compared with the speed of an electronic device, and cannot perceive a break in motion that happens at a rate of about 25 Hz or greater. Thus a computer screen needs to be updated only 25 or 30 times a second in order for an observer to perceive a continuous image. Whereas video monitors for computer applications can have any scan rate that the designer wishes, in television applications the scan rate must be standardized. In Europe, a rate of 25 Hz is used for standard television, and a rate of 30 Hz is used in North America. The phosphor types used in the screens do not have a long persistence, and so scan lines are updated alternately in order to reduce flicker. The screen is thus updated at a 50 Hz rate in Europe and at a 60 Hz rate in North America, but only alternating lines are updated on each sweep. For high-resolution graphics, the entire screen may be updated at a 50 Hz or 60 Hz rate, rather than just the alternating lines.

The data rates between computer and video monitor can be quite high. Consider that a 24-bit per pixel monitor with 1024×768 pixel resolution and a refresh rate of 60 Hz requires a **bandwidth** of 3 bytes/pixel $\times$ (1024×768) pixels $\times$ 60 Hz, or roughly 140 MB per second. Fortunately, the hardware described above maps the frame buffer onto the screen without CPU intervention, but it is still up to the CPU to output pixels to the frame buffer when the image on the screen changes.

8.9.3 Liquid Crystal Displays (LCDs)

Liquid crystal displays (LCDs) have emerged as a prevalent choice for computer monitors. LCDs are small and lightweight when compared with tube monitors, consume less power and dissipate less heat, and are more shock resistant. On the downside, LCDs are less visible in bright light than tube monitors, they have a narrower viewing angle, and are less responsive to rapid motion (which creates a ghosting effect), and commonly suffer manufacturing defects of a few pixels per display. On balance, however, the advantages of LCDs outweigh the disadvantages for many applications.

Figure 8-44 shows the layout of an **active matrix** LCD display. A fluorescent panel emits white light, which is oriented in all directions. After passing through a horizontal polarizing filter, only horizontally polarized light passes on to the liquid crystals. A transistor in each location twists the liquid crystal molecules, which has the effect of rotating the polarization between 0° to 90° depending on how the transistor is set. This is known as an **active matrix** LCD, in which every element is actively refreshed by a transistor. A **passive matrix** LCD only has electrical controls at the edges of the columns and rows, and each element must maintain its state as they are refreshed in sequence. Active matrix displays are thus more brilliant than passive matrix displays and have more vivid colors.

After the light is rotated by the liquid crystals, red, green, and blue filters separate the light into its respective colors. In the final step, the light passes through a vertical polarizing filter, in which only light that has been rotated 90° is fully transmitted, while light that is only partially rotated is partially transmitted.

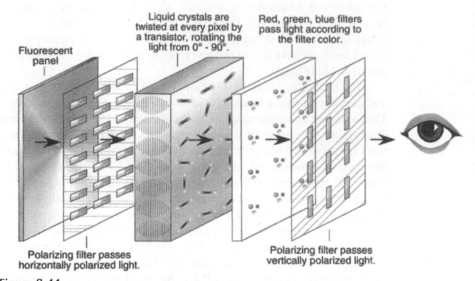

Figure 8-44
Active matrix color liquid crystal display (LCD).

Notice that what we think of as a single pixel is actually made up of three subpixels: one each for red, green, and blue.

■ 8.10 CASE STUDY: GRAPHICS PROCESSING UNIT

A computer-generated scene can be constructed with three-sided polygons (triangles) in which three vertices and a single color or texture map are specified. A high-quality scene may require hundreds of thousands of polygons, processed in a given order to create a pixellated image. There is too much processing overhead to generate scenes in real time without the help of a **graphics processing unit** (GPU), which is typically integrated into desktop computers but can also be added on separately.

A GPU manages four main tasks in a graphics pipeline:

1. **geometry processing**, which creates the vertices of the triangle. This step is commonly done by the host processor/operating system.

2. **vertex processing**, which converts vertices to pixels.

3. **texture application**, which applies textures to pixels.

4. **rasterization**, which applies lighting and other effects to the textured pixels.

As an example, in Figure 8-45, the Matrox Parhelia-512 GPU takes a 256-bit-wide input and fills a 512-bit-wide Memory Controller Array. The word width of this GPU is 512 bits, with a color depth of 10 bits per RGB (red, green, blue) color per pixel. The geometry processing is done by a mix of Microsoft's DirectX 9 application programming interface (API) and specialized hardware that encodes high-resolution geometric detail into **displacement maps**, which represent height displacements from a low-resolution object mesh.

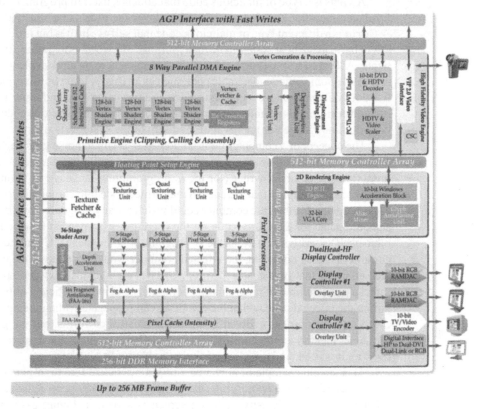

Figure 8-45
Matrox Parhelia-512 graphics processing unit.

Vertex processing is handled by the Quad Vertex Shader Array, which can operate on four 128-bit vertices in parallel. Texture application is handled by the Quad Texturing Unit, which continues the four pipelines from the Quad Vertex Shader Array. Rasterization is handled by the five-Stage Pixel Shader. Notice the deep pipelining, starting from the Quad Vertex Shader Array, through the 36-Stage Shader Array (with varying depths depending on the application), and finally to the Pixel Cache. Unlike ordinary computer applications that suffer pipeline stalls on branches every four or five instructions, for graphics applications, deep pipelines can be kept filled for long runs of polygon processing, and so this is a good architectural approach.

■ 8.11 CASE STUDY: HOW A VIRUS INFECTS A MACHINE

As the explosive growth of personal computers has permeated every aspect of society, people and machines have become more greatly interconnected. This pervasive exposure amplifies both the good and bad things that people contribute to the world, and one of the bad things is a destructive form of programming referred to loosely as "viruses," although there is a taxonomy of purposely malformed software of which a virus is only one type.

A **virus** is a type of malicious code that attaches itself to program or data files and performs an undesirable action, such as taking over the user's machine and replicating itself. A **worm** is a different type of malicious code that self-replicates but is not intended to cause direct harm to the host system. The main purpose of a worm is to gather information and replicate. A **Trojan horse** is malicious code that appears to be a benevolent program but actually masks some other undesirable code such as a virus. A **logic bomb** is malicious code that lies dormant until some event occurs, such as a particular date and time, and then springs to life and performs some undesirable action. In all cases, the malicious code operates without the prior knowledge nor approval of the users of the systems it affects.

The concept of a computer virus embodied in a Trojan horse goes back several decades, exemplified in a classic paper by Ken Thompson outlining a mechanism by which an untrustworthy compiler-writer (for the C programming language in Thompson's example) could create a compiler that introduced malformed code into compiled programs, such as the login program. Further, the compiler could watch for any programs named "cc.c", which is a standard name for the source code for the C compiler (somewhat enigmatically, the C compiler itself is written mostly in the C programming language). Upon recognizing that a C compiler is being compiled, the infected compiler would introduce code into the newly created compiler that perpetuates the process. Thus a maliciously written program can quietly infect a great number of programs and computers and, with sufficient obfuscation applied to hiding the infected code within the compiler, can propagate without being detected.

Virus creation has evolved into more sophisticated forms, but the general concept is the same: identify a vulnerability, which could be in the way that a program is written or in the way it is used, and quietly exploit that vulnerability.

As a simple example of how a user might be tricked into divulging confidential information, consider a password-protected computer that many people share, such as in a computer center in a university. A logon screen is shown in Figure 8-46. What if someone wrote a program that displays this same logon screen and walked away with this fake logon screen displayed? The program could steal the user name and password of an unsuspecting user.

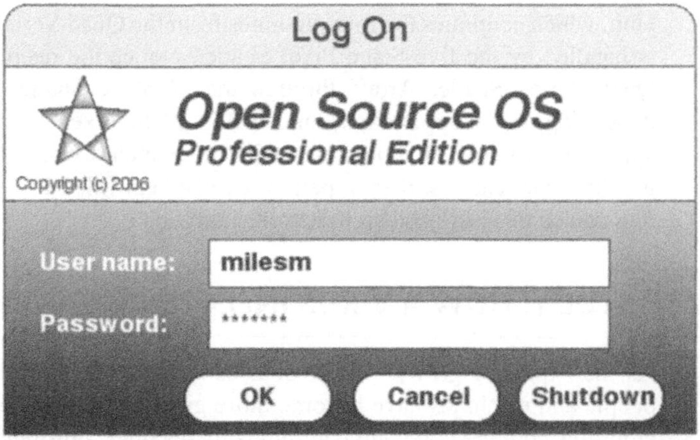

Figure 8-46
A logon screen.

This vulnerability exploits the way that people use computers, but there are countless vulnerabilities that leave a system open to an attack just in the way that programs are written. One infamous example is the "Slammer" worm that quickly infected thousands of Windows server machines running Microsoft SQL. Within 15 minutes of its release on Saturday, January 25, 2003, huge sections of the Internet fell out of existence.

The way that Slammer works is by exploiting a vulnerability called a **buffer overflow**. The Slammer worm masquerades as an ordinary user datagram protocol (UDP) network packet that would normally be sent to a Microsoft SQL database server, requesting a service. The first byte in the payload is 04, which tells the SQL server that the name of the target database follows, which must be no longer than 16 bytes and must end in 00.

In the Slammer packet, there is no terminating 00 byte, and the code has been constructed such that when the SQL server reads the packet, it ends up overwriting the 128 bytes of memory reserved for the request and spilling the additional bytes into the stack located nearby. The server continues by unknowingly executing the overwritten code, which instructs the server to find and attack other Microsoft SQL servers.

Needless to say, Microsoft responded quickly with a bug fix. The underlying vulnerability to a buffer overflow attack is not unique to Microsoft SQL Server, however, and the lesson for us is to be very careful about writing code that accepts data from potentially untrustworthy, or just plain unreliable, sources. Ken Thompson concluded that you can only trust code that you write yourself, but actually, you can only trust code that you write and only you use. For practical purposes, this is rarely the case. The answer is to protect yourself and your data the best that you can, and to be on the constant lookout for vulnerabilities in your code, your data, and how your computers are used.

Summary

Input, output, and communication involve the transfer of information between transmitters and receivers. The transmitters, receivers, and methods of communication are often mismatched in terms of speed and in how information is represented, and so an important consideration is how to match input and output devices with a system using a particular method of communication.

A bus provides a fixed bandwidth that is shared among a number of devices. A hierarchy of buses can be interconnected with bridges, so that independent transfers can take place simultaneously. From a programmer's perspective, communication is handled via programmed I/O, interrupt-driven I/O, or DMA.

Mass storage devices come in a variety of forms. Examples of mass storage devices are hard magnetic disks and magnetic tape drives. Optical storage provides greater density per unit area than magnetic storage, but is more expensive and does not offer the same degree of user writability. Examples of optical storage devices are CD ROMs and DVDs.

There is a wide range of other input/output devices. A few that we studied in this chapter that are not mass storage devices can be grouped into input devices and output devices. Examples of input devices are keyboards, tablets, mice, trackballs, and joysticks. Examples of output devices are laser printers, video displays, and LCD panels.

Problems

8.1 What is the minimum time needed to transfer 100 MB from the audio device to a processor core, using the bridge architecture and parameters shown in Figure 8-7?

8.2 Why must the CPU ensure that interrupts are disabled before handing control over to the interrupt service routine?

8.3 Show the Manchester encoding for the bit sequence 10011101.

8.4 A disk that has 16 sectors per track uses an interleave factor of 1:4. What is the smallest number of revolutions of the disk required to read all of the sectors of a track in sequence?

8.5 A hard magnetic disk has two surfaces. The storage area on each surface has an inner radius of 1 cm and an outer radius of 5 cm. Each track holds the same number of bits, even though each track differs in size from every other. The maximum storage density of the media is 10,000 bits/cm. The spacing between corresponding points on adjacent tracks is .1 mm, which includes the inter-track gap. Assume that the inter-sector gaps are negligible and that a track exists on each edge of the storage area.
(a) What is the maximum number of bits that can be stored on the disk?
(b) What is the data transfer rate from the disk to the head in bits per second at a rotational speed of 3600 RPM?

8.6 A disk has 128 tracks of 32 sectors each, on each surface of eight platters. The disk spins at 3600 RPM and takes 15 ms to move between adjacent tracks. What is the longest time needed to read an arbitrary sector located anywhere on the disk?

8.7 A 300 Mbyte (300×2^{20} bytes) disk has 815 cylinders, with 19 heads, a track-to-track speed of 7.5 m/s (that is, 7.5 meters per second), and a rotation rate of 3600 RPM. The fact that there are 19 heads means that there are 10 platters, and only 19 surfaces are used for storing data. Each sector holds the same amount of data, and each track has the same number of sectors. The transfer time between the disk and the CPU is 300 Kbytes/sec. The track-to-track spacing is .25 mm.
(a) Compute the time to read a track (*not* the time to transmit the track to a host). Assume that interleaving is not used.
(b) What is the minimum time required to read the entire disk pack to a CPU, given the best of all possible circumstances? Assume that the head of the first surface to be read is positioned at the beginning of the first sector of the first track and that an entire cylinder is read before the

arm is moved. Also assume that the disk unit can buffer an entire cylinder, but no more. During operation, the disk unit first fills its buffer, then empties it to the CPU, and only then does it read more of the disk.

8.8 A fixed head disk has one head per track. The heads do not move, and thus there is no head-movement component in calculating the access time. For this problem, calculate the time that it takes to copy one surface to another surface. This is an internal operation to the disk and does not involve any communication with the host. There are 1000 cylinders, each track holds 10 sectors, and the rotation rate of the disk is 3000 RPM. The sectors all line up with each other. That is, within a cylinder, sector 0 on each track lines up with sector 0 on every other track, and within a surface, sector 0 on each track begins on the same line drawn from the center of the surface to the edge.

An internal buffer holds a single sector. When a sector is read from one track, it is held in the buffer until it is written onto another track. Only then can another sector be read. It is not possible to simultaneously read and write the buffer, and the buffer must be entirely loaded or entirely emptied—partial reads or writes are not allowed. Calculate the minimum time required to copy one surface to another, given the best starting conditions. The surfaces must be direct images of each other. That is, sector *i* in the source surface must be directly above or below sector *i* in the destination surface.

8.9 Compute the storage capacity of a 6250 byte per inch (BPI) tape that is 600 ft long and has a record size of 2048 bytes. The size of an inter-record gap is .5 in.

8.10 A bit-mapped display is 1024 pixels wide by 1024 pixels high. The refresh rate is 60 Hz, which means that every pixel is rewritten to the screen 60 times a second, but only one pixel is written at any time. What is the maximum time allowed to write a single pixel?

8.11 How many bits need to be stored in the LUT in Figure 8-43? If the LUT is removed and the RAM is changed to provide the 24-bit R, G, and B output directly, how many additional bits need to be stored in the RAM? Assume that the initial size of the RAM is $2^{10} \times 2^{10} = 2^{20}$ words × 8 bits/word.

8.12 The MCB as presented in Section 8.2.1 keeps track of every sector on the disk. An alternative organization, which significantly reduces the size of the MCB, is to store blocks in **chains**. The idea is to store only the first block of a file in the MCB, and then store a pointer to the succeeding block at the end of the first block. Each succeeding block is linked in a similar manner.

(a) How does this approach affect the time to access the middle of a file?

(b) After a system crash, would a disk recovery be easier if only the first sector of a file is stored in the MCB and the remaining list of sectors is stored in a header at the beginning of each file? How does this approach affect storage?

Further Reading

Intel data sheets and other literature, including the Pentium family of hardware and programmer's manuals, can be ordered from Intel Literature Sales, PO Box 7641, Mt. Prospect IL 60056-7641, or, in the U. S. and Canada, by calling (800) 548-4725.

Advanced Computer & Network Corporation (ACNC, 2005) provides a concise description of RAID.

(Hamacher et al., 1996) provides explanations of communication devices and a number of peripherals such as an alphanumeric CRT controller. (Tanenbaum, 1999) and (Stallings, 1996) also give readable explanations of peripheral devices. The material on synchronous and asynchronous buses and bus arbitration is influenced by a treatment in (Tanenbaum, 1999). (Thompson, 1984) is a classic reference on how a trusted but malformed piece of code like a compiler can spread viruses.

ACNC, http:/ /www.acnc.com/raid.html (Aug. 2005).

Hamacher, V. C., Vranesic, Z. G., and Zaky, S. G., *Computer Organization*, 4/e, McGraw Hill (1996).

Stallings, W., *Computer Organization and Architecture: Designing for Performance*, 5/e, Prentice Hall (2000).

Tanenbaum, A., *Structured Computer Organization*, 4/e, Prentice Hall (1999).

Thompson, K., "Reflections on trusting trust," *Communications of the ACM*, 27, No. 8, pp. 761–763, (Aug. 1984).

CHAPTER 9

NETWORKING AND COMMUNICATION

Communication is the process of transferring information from a source to a destination. In the context of computer architecture, communication systems for the most part cover distances between computers and may involve the public telephone system, radio, and television. Wide-area communication systems have become very complex, with all combinations of voice, data, and video being transferred by wire, optical fiber, radio, and microwaves. Communication routes may traverse distances over land, under water, through local radio cells, reflected by the troposphere, and via satellite. Data that originates as analog voice signals may be converted to digital data streams for efficient routing over long distances, and then converted back to an analog signal, without the awareness of those communicating.

In this chapter we focus on communication between entities located at distances ranging within a kilometer for a local area network (LAN), and across much larger distances for wide area networks (WANs) as typified by the Internet. As we make our way through the various networks, we will explore the architectures of the components that handle the network data. We start by discussing a few principles of communication.

■ 9.1 A FEW MODULATION SCHEMES

People communicate over telephone lines by forming audible sounds that are converted to electrical signals, which are transmitted to a receiver where they are converted back to audible sounds. This does not mean that people always need to speak and hear in order to communicate over a telephone line: this audible medium of communication is also used to transmit digitally encoded information.

Figure 9-1 shows a configuration in which two computers communicate over a telephone line through the use of **modems** (a contraction of "modulator/demodulator"). A telephone modem transforms an electrical signal from a computer into an audible form for transmission, and performs the reverse operation when receiving. Modems are not only used for telephone communication: they are also used in other communication systems as well, such as data-over-cable TV networks and digital subscriber loop, also known as DSL, over standard copper telephone wiring.

Modem communication over a telephone line is normally performed in serial fashion, a single digit (not necessarily bit) at a time, in which the digits have an encoding that is

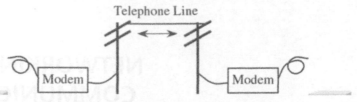

Figure 9-1

Communication over a telephone line with modems.

appropriate for the transmission medium. There are a number of **modulation** schemes used in communication, which are encodings of data into the medium. Figure 9-2 illustrates three common forms of modulation.

Amplitude modulation (AM) uses the strength of the signal to encode 1s and 0s. AM lends itself to simple implementations that are inexpensive to build. However, since there is information in the amplitude of the signal, anything that changes the amplitude affects the signal. For an AM radio, a number of situations affect the amplitude of the signal (such as driving under a bridge or proximity to electrical lines, lightning, etc.).

Frequency modulation (FM) is not nearly as sensitive to amplitude-related problems because information is encoded in the frequency of the signal rather than in the amplitude. The FM signal on a radio is relatively static-free and does not diminish as the receiver passes under a bridge.

Phase modulation (PM) is most typically used in modems, where four phases (90 degrees apart) double the data bandwidth by transmitting two bits at a time (referred to as **dibits**). The use of phase offers a degree of freedom in addition to frequency, and is appropriate when the number of available frequencies is restricted.

In **pulse code modulation** (PCM) an analog signal is sampled and converted into binary. Figure 9-3 shows the process of converting an analog signal into a PCM binary

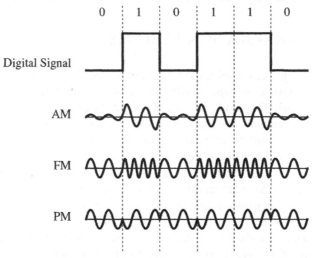

Figure 9-2

Three common forms of modulation.

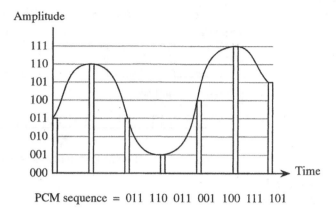

PCM sequence = 011 110 011 001 100 111 101

Figure 9-3
Conversion of an analog signal into a PCM binary sequence.

sequence. The original signal is sampled at twice the rate of the highest significant frequency, producing values at discrete intervals. The samples are encoded in binary and catenated to produce the PCM sequence.

PCM is a digital approach and has all of the advantages of digital information systems. By using repeaters at regular intervals, the signal can be perfectly restored. By decreasing the distance between repeaters, the effective bandwidth of a channel can be significantly increased. Analog signals, however, can at best be guessed and can only be approximately restored. There is no good way to make analog signals perfect in a noisy environment.

Shannon's result about the data rate of a noisy channel applies here:

$$\text{data rate} = \text{bandwidth} \times \log(1 + S/N)$$

where S is the signal and N is the noise. Since a digital signal can be made to use arbitrarily noisy channels (in which S/N is large) because of its noise immunity, higher data rates can be achieved over the same channel. This is one of the driving forces in the move to all-digital technology in the telecommunications industry. The transition to all-digital has also been driven by the rapid drop in the cost of digital circuitry.

■ 9.2 TRANSMISSION MEDIA

In a geographically close environment, computers can be connected with private cables in a number of configurations. For geographically distant systems, the **public switched telephone network** (PSTN) can be used. Users connect to the PSTN with modems that convert logical bits into audible sounds. People can hear at frequencies up to about 20 KHz, but only speak at frequencies up to about 4 KHz, which is approximately the bandwidth that traditional telephony will pass on a voice-grade line. An analog signal (such as voice) that is approximated with a digital signal needs to be sampled at least twice per cycle (to capture the high and low values), and so a sampling rate of 8 KHz is needed to digitize a

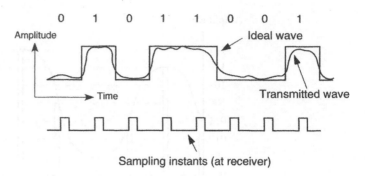

Figure 9-4
Ideal vs. actual transmitted waves.

voice-grade line. At eight bits per sample, that gives a bit rate of 8 bits/cycle × 8 KHz = 64 Kbits/sec, which is what is available on an ordinary telephone line in North America. One sample out of every eight is used by the telephone company to administer the line, and so the maximum bit rate possible on an ordinary voice-grade line is 56 Kbits/sec.

A transmitted binary sequence is converted into high/low values, but the waveform gets attenuated and distorted, more so at high frequencies and long distances. Figure 9-4 illustrates the sampling problem. The binary pattern 01011001 is represented by an ideal wave, which is only approximated by a transmitted wave. The ideal wave contains discontinuities that are difficult to produce with a real wave. In terms of analysis, we can think of the ideal wave as being approximated by a superposition of sinusoidal waves, with sharper edges achieved at higher frequencies.

Unfortunately, high frequencies are attenuated more than low frequencies in most media, and different frequencies propagate at different rates, which leads to distortions of the wave as it propagates. The degree of distortion varies with the transmission medium, a few of which are described here.

9.2.1 Two-Wire Open Lines

In one of the simplest scenarios, a pair of wires, open to free space, carries a signal and a return (the "ground"). The two-wire open line configuration is shown in Figure 9-5a. The lines emit electromagnetic radiation, and they also pick up noise, not necessarily the same amount of noise for each line, that distorts the difference signal. The lines are also vulnerable to "capacitive coupling," which means they pick up unwanted signals from neighboring wires. The speed and distance for reliable transmission is limited to about 19.2 Kbps and 50 m.

9.2.2 Twisted-Pair Lines

If we twist the pair of lines in the two-wire open line configuration, then any spurious external noise that is introduced to the line affects both the signal and ground (reference) wires in the same way. Figure 9-5b shows the twisted-wire configuration. The difference signal is thus unaffected, and reliable transmission can go up to 1 Mbps over 100 m.

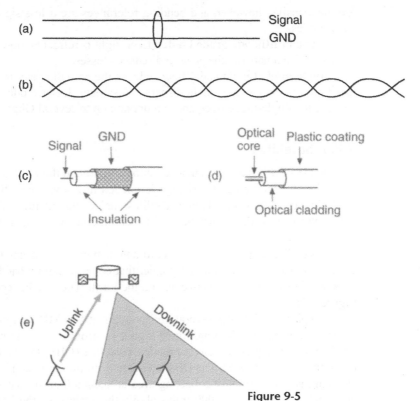

Figure 9-5

Transmission media. (a) Two-wire open lines; (b) twisted-pair lines; (c) coaxial cable; (d) optical fiber (e) satellite.

9.2.3 Coaxial Cable

For higher speeds (10 Mbps) and longer distances (hundreds of meters), the signal wire is placed inside the reference conductor (coaxially) with an insulator between the two, as shown in Figure 9-5c. (The braiding of the outer conductor makes the cable more flexible.) The idea is that the center conductor is effectively shielded from external interference and is also shielded from losses from electromagnetic radiation.

9.2.4 Optical Fiber

Optical communication is immune to electromagnetic interference and crosstalk, and supports a much wider bandwidth. There is a need for optoelectronic conversions on each end, which is commercially available up to a few Gbps (using laser diodes.) Optical fiber consists of the optical core, optical cladding, and a plastic coating, as shown in Figure 9-5d.

A light-emitting diode (LED) is a less expensive light source than a laser diode, but it emits light at various angles, and so a **multimode stepped index** fiber is used that reflects light less than the "critical angle" back into the core. Because the path lengths differ, the received pulse is wider and only modest bit rates can be supported. The LEDs are inexpensive, however, and bending tolerances are a less significant issue than with laser diodes.

With a **multimode graded index** fiber, light is refracted more as it moves away from the core, which narrows the pulse and reduces losses.

Single-mode (monomode) fiber reduces the core diameter to a single wavelength so that light travels along a single dispersionless path. Laser diodes are commonly used as sources for single-mode fiber, and can operate up to several Gbps over tens of kilometers.

9.2.5 Satellites

Man-made satellites that are launched into orbit around the Earth are used for communication when a broad area of coverage is needed at a lower cost than a wireline network (including optical fibers). Natural satellites, inside and outside of Earth orbits (such as the Moon and asteroids), can also be used for communication, but are not generally in use for such purposes.

In satellite communication, a collimated microwave beam is transmitted from the ground to a satellite, where a transponder that covers a certain band of frequencies retransmits the signal to an area of coverage on the Earth. The satellite configuration is shown in Figure 9-5e.

A typical satellite has several transponders at 500 MHz per channel. A small area of coverage means that the transmitted signal is stronger and the receiving dishes can be smaller. This is typical for direct-broadcast satellite (DBS) television, in which very small receiving dishes are used. The DBS satellites orbit the Earth at a low orbit, approximately 700 Km, and so a smaller collecting area is needed than for satellites that are placed in geosynchronous orbit (23,000 miles above the surface of the Earth), where the Earth's attractive gravitational force and the repelling centrifugal force are balanced, so that the satellite appears stationary over the ground when the orbit collocates with the Equator. This is why large satellite dishes are aimed in the direction of the Equator.

For two-way satellite network communication, the delay between the end-user and the satellite needs to be tolerable. The uplink to the satellite is generally slower than the downlink. This matches the typical mode of operation for an end user on the Internet, since less than 10% of the network traffic goes from the end user to the Internet, and over 90% of the network traffic goes from the Internet to the end user. The speed of communication is limited by c (the speed of light in a vacuum), which is approximately 1 ns per foot or 5 µs per mile (5280 feet per mile). Over a distance of 23,000 miles, the free-space delay is more than 100 ms to the satellite and another 100 ms back to the Earth, plus a processing delay. This is more than the acceptable average delay of 100 ms needed for a keystroke response. Low Earth orbit (LEO) is only 700 Km and introduces a much smaller delay, on the order of spanning the distance of a few states in the United States; it is therefore better suited for interactive networking.

9.2.6 Terrestrial Microwave

Ground based line-of-sight links are effective up to 30 miles, particularly for crossing difficult terrain, although they are prone to atmospheric disturbances, flocks of geese, etc. Longer distances, up to 150 miles, can be covered in a tropospheric scatter (TROPO) con-

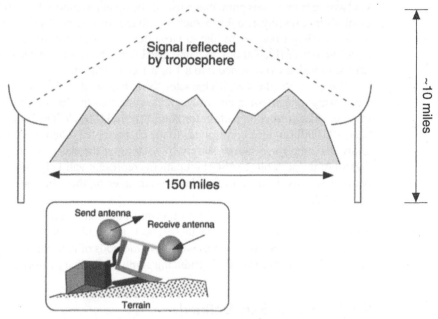

Figure 9-6
Tropospheric scatter configuration.

figuration, as shown in Figure 9-6. The troposphere starts at the earth's surface and extends six miles in altitude over polar regions and 10 miles over tropical regions. A transmitted beam is bounced one time through the troposphere to a receiving TROPO terminal up to 150 miles away.

9.2.7 Radio

In cellular radio communication, a radio base station is placed in the middle of a **cell**, which is generally less than 20 Km in diameter. A restricted band of frequencies is used within a cell for communication between roaming cellular devices and the base station. Neighboring cells use a different band of frequencies, so that there is no confusion at the cell boundary where a **handoff** is made as a roaming end-user transits from one cell to another, which normally involves a frequency change.

Total available bandwidth in a cell is small, on the order of 2 MB/s, which is subdivided over the number of channels in use. In congested areas, cell sizes are smaller than in less densely populated areas, sometimes extending no farther than a single building.

■ 9.3 ERROR DETECTION AND CORRECTION

In situations involving communications between computers, and even inside a computer system such as a hard disk drive, there is a finite chance that the data is received or has been stored in error due to noise in the communication channel. The data representations we have seen up to this point make use of the binary symbols 1 and 0. In reality, the binary symbols take on physical forms such as voltages or phases. The physical form is subject to noise that is introduced by the environment, such as atmospheric phenomena, gamma rays, and power fluctuations, to name just a few. The noise can cause errors, also known as **faults**, in which a 0 is turned into a 1 or a 1 is turned into a 0.

Suppose that the ASCII character 'b' is transmitted from a sender to a receiver and that during transmission, an error occurs, such that the least significant bit is incorrectly inverted. The correct bit pattern for ASCII 'b' is 1100010. The bit pattern that the receiver sees is 1100011, which corresponds to the character 'c.' There is no way for the receiver to know that an error occurred simply by looking at the received character. The problem is that all of the possible 2^7 ASCII bit patterns represent valid characters, and if any of the bit patterns is transformed into another through an error, then the resulting bit pattern appears to be valid.

It is possible for the sender to transmit additional "check bits" along with the data bits. The receiver can examine these check bits and under certain conditions not only detect errors, but correct them as well. Two methods of computing these additional bits are described below. We start by introducing some preliminary information and definitions.

9.3.1 Bit Error Rate Defined

There are many different ways that errors can be introduced into a system, and those errors can take many different forms. For the moment, we will assume that the probability that a given bit is received in error is independent of the probability that other bits near it are received in error. In this case, we can define the **bit error rate** (BER) as the probability that a given bit is erroneous. This must be a small number, and is usually less than 10^{-12} errors per bit examined for fiber networks. That means, loosely speaking, that as bits are examined, only one in every 10^{12} bits will be erroneous (in radio networks, as many as 1 in every 100 packets may contain an error).

As an example, if we are receiving a bit stream from a serial communications line at, say, 10 million bits per second, and the BER is 10^{-10}, then the number of errors per second will be $10 \times 10^{6} \times 10^{-10}$ or 10^{-3} errors per second, approximately 1 error every 15 minutes.

9.3.2 Hamming Codes

One of the simplest and oldest methods of error detection was used to detect errors in transmitting and receiving characters in telegraphy. A **parity bit**, 1 or 0, was added to each character to make the total number of 1s in the character even or odd, as agreed upon by sender and receiver. In our example of transmitting the ASCII character 'b,' 1100010, assuming even parity, a 1 would be attached as a parity bit to make the total number of 1s even, resulting in the bit pattern 11000101 being transmitted. The receiver could then examine the bit pattern, and if there was an even number of 1s, the receiver could assume that the character was received without error. (This method fails if there is a significant probability of two or more bits being received in error. In this case, other methods must be used, as discussed later in this section.) The principles behind this approach are explored below.

If additional bits are added to the data then it is possible to not only detect errors, but to correct them as well. Some of the most popular error-correcting codes are based on the work of Richard Hamming while at Bell Telephone Laboratories (now Lucent Technologies).

We can detect single-bit errors in the ASCII code by adding a redundant bit to each **codeword** (character). The **Hamming distance** defines the logical distance between two valid codewords, as measured by the number of digits (bits) that differ between the code-words. If a single bit changes in an ASCII character, then the resulting bit pattern represents a different ASCII character. The corresponding Hamming distance for this code is 1. If we recode the ASCII table so that there is a Hamming distance of 2 between valid code-words, then two bits must change in order to convert one character into another. We can then detect a single-bit error because the corrupted word will lie in the forbidden zone between valid codewords.

One way to recode ASCII for a Hamming distance of two is to assign a parity bit, which takes on a value of 0 or 1, to make the total number of 1s in a codeword odd or even. If we use **even parity**, then the parity bit for the character 'a' is 1, since there are three 1s in the bit pattern for 'a': 1100001 and assigning a parity bit of 1 (to the left of the codeword in this example) makes the total number of 1s in the recoded 'a' even: 11100001. This is illustrated in Figure 9-7. Similarly, the parity bit for 'c' is 0, which results in the recoded bit pattern: 01100011. If we use **odd parity** instead, then the parity bits take on the opposite values: 0 for 'a' and 1 for 'c,' which results in the recoded bit pat-terns 01100001 and 11100011, respectively. It does not matter whether we use even parity or odd parity, as long as the sender and receiver use the same method.

The recoded ASCII table now has $2^8 = 256$ entries, of which half of the entries (the ones with an odd number of 1s) represent invalid codewords. If an invalid codeword is received, then the receiver knows that an error occurred and can request a retransmission. There is not enough information, however, to determine the exact location of the error.

A retransmission may not always be practical, and for these cases it would be helpful to both detect and correct an error. The use of a parity bit will detect an error, but will not

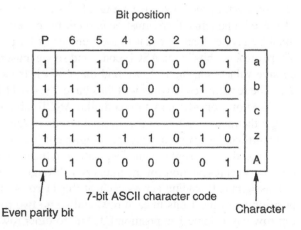

Figure 9-7
Even parity bits are assigned to a few ASCII characters.

locate the position of an error. If the bit pattern 11100011 is received in a system that uses even parity, then the presence of an error is known because the parity of the received word is odd. There is not enough information from the parity bit alone to determine if the original pattern was 'a', 'b', or any of five other characters in the ASCII table. In fact, the original character might even be 'c' if the error is in the parity bit.

In order to construct an error-correcting code that is capable of detecting and correcting single-bit errors, we must add more redundancy than a single parity bit to the ASCII code by further extending the number of bits in each codeword. For instance, consider the bit pattern for 'a': 1100001. If we wish to detect and correct a single-bit error in any position of the word, then we need to assign seven additional bit patterns to 'a' in which exactly one bit changes in the original 'a' codeword: 0100001, 1000001, 1110001, 1101001, 1100101, 1100011, and 1100000. We can do the same for 'b' and the remaining characters, but we must construct the code in such a way that no bit pattern is common to more than one ASCII character; otherwise we will have no means to determine the original bit pattern unambiguously.

A problem with using redundancy in this way is that we assign eight bit patterns to every character: one for the original bit pattern and seven for the neighboring error patterns. Since there are 2^7 characters in the ASCII code, and since we need 2^3 bit patterns for every character, then we can only recode $2^7/2^3 = 2^4$ characters if we use only the original seven bits in the representation.

In order to recode all of the characters, we must add additional **redundant bits** (also referred to as **check bits**) to the codewords. Let us now determine how many bits we need. If we start with a k-bit word that we would like to recode and use r check bits, then the following relationship must hold:

$$2^k \times (k + r + 1) \leq 2^{k+r} \equiv k + r + 1 \leq 2^r \tag{9.1}$$

The reasoning behind this relationship is that for each of the 2^k original words, there are k bit patterns in which a single bit is corrupted in the original word, plus r bit patterns in which one of the check bits is in error, plus the original uncorrupted bit pattern. Thus, our error-correcting code will have a total of $2^k \times (k + r + 1)$ bit patterns. In order to support all of these bit patterns, there must be enough bit patterns generated by $k + r$ bits; thus 2^{k+r} must be greater than or equal to the number of bit patterns in the error correcting code. There are $k = 7$ bits in the ASCII code, and so we must now solve for r. If we try a few successive values, starting at 1, we find that $r = 4$ is the smallest value that satisfies relation 9.1. The resulting codewords will thus have $7 + 4 = 11$ bits.

We now consider how to recode the ASCII table into the 11-bit code. Our goal is to assign the redundant bits to the original words in such a way that any single-bit error can be identified. One way to make the assignment is shown in Figure 9-8. Each of the 11 bits in the recoded word are assigned a position in the table indexed from 1 to 11, and the four-bit binary representations of the integers 1 through 11 are shown next to each index. With this assignment, reading across each of the 11 rows of four check bits, there is a unique positioning of the 1 bits in each row, and so no two rows are the same. For example, the top row has a single 1 in position C1, but no other row has only a single 1 in position C1 (other rows have a 1 in position C1, but they also have 1s in the other check bit positions).

Check bits C8 C4 C2 C1	Bit position checked
0 0 0 1	1
0 0 1 0	2
0 0 1 1	3
0 1 0 0	4
0 1 0 1	5
0 1 1 0	6
0 1 1 1	7
1 0 0 0	8
1 0 0 1	9
1 0 1 0	10
1 0 1 1	11

Figure 9-8
Check bits for a single-error-correcting
ASCII code.

Now, reading down each of the four check-bit columns, the positions of the 1 bits tell us which bits, listed in the rightmost 'Bit position checked' column, are included in a group that must form even parity. For example, check bit C8 covers a group of four bits in positions 8, 9, 10, and 11 that collectively must form even parity. If this property is satisfied when the 11-bit word is transmitted, but an error in transmission causes this group of bits to have odd parity at the receiver, then the receiver will know that there must be an error in position 8, 9, 10, or 11. The exact position can be determined by observing the remaining check bits, as we will see.

In more detail, each bit in the 11-bit encoded word, which includes the check bits, is assigned to a unique combination of the four check bits C1, C2, C4, and C8. The combinations are computed as the binary representation of the position of the bit being checked, starting at position 1. C1 is thus in bit position 1, C2 is in position 2, C4 is in position 4, etc. The check bits can appear anywhere in the word, but normally appear in positions that correspond to powers of 2 in order to simplify the process of locating an error. This particular code is known as a **single-error-correcting (SEC)** code.

Since the positions of the 1s in each of the check bit combinations is unique, we can locate an error by simply observing which of the check bits are in error. Consider the format shown in Figure 9-9 for the ASCII character 'a'. The values of the check bits are determined according to the table shown in Figure 9-8. Check bit C1 = 0 creates even parity for the bit group {1, 3, 5, 7, 9, 11}. The members in this group are taken from the positions that have 1s in the C1 column in Figure 9-8. Check bit C2 = 1 creates even parity for the bit group {2, 3, 6, 7, 10, 11}. Similarly, check bit C4 = 0 creates even parity for the bit group {4, 5, 6, 7}. Finally, check bit C8 = 0 creates even parity for the bit group {8, 9, 10, 11}.

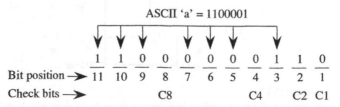

Figure 9-9
Format for a single-error-correcting ASCII code.

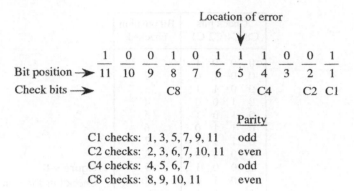

Figure 9-10
Parity computation for an ASCII character in an SEC code.

As an alternative to looking up members of a parity group in a table, in general, bit n of the coded word is checked by those check bits in positions $b_1, b_2, \ldots, b_j$ such that $b_1 + b_2 + \cdots + b_j = n$. For example, bit 7 is checked by bits in positions 1, 2, and 4 because $1 + 2 + 4 = 7$.

Now suppose that a receiver sees the bit pattern 10010111001. Assuming that the SEC code for ASCII characters described above is used, what character was sent? We start by computing the parity for each of the check bits as shown in Figure 9-10. As shown in the figure, check bits C1 and C4 have odd parity. In order to locate the error, we simply add up the positions of the odd check bits. The error then, is in position $1 + 4 = 5$. The word that was sent is 10010101001. If we strip away the check bits, then we end up with the bit pattern 1000100, which corresponds to the ASCII character 'D'.

One way to think about an SEC code is that valid codewords are spaced far enough apart so that a single error places a corrupted codeword closer to one particular valid codeword than to any other valid codeword. For example, consider an SEC code for a set of just two symbols: {000, 111}. The Hamming distance relationships for all three-bit patterns are shown for this code in the cube in Figure 9-11. The cube has correspondingly higher dimensions for larger word sizes, resulting in what is called a **hypercube**. The two

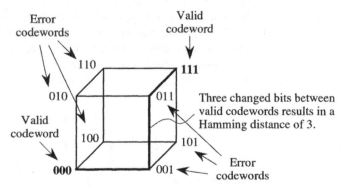

Figure 9-11
Hamming distance relationships among three-bit codewords. Valid codewords are 000 and 111. The remaining codewords represent errors.

valid codewords are shown on opposing vertices. Any single bit error will locate an invalid codeword at a different vertex on the cube. Every error codeword has a closest valid codeword, which makes single error correction possible.

SECDED Encoding

If we now consider the case in which there are two errors, then we can see that the SEC code works for **double error detection (DED)**, but not for **double error correction (DEC)**. This is sometimes referred to as **SECDED** encoding. Since valid codewords are spaced at a Hamming distance of 3, two errors will locate an error codeword on the cube, and thus two errors can be detected. The original codeword cannot be determined unambiguously, however, since vertices that correspond to two errors from one codeword overlap vertices that correspond to a single error from another codeword. Thus, every SEC code is also a DED code, but every DED code is not necessarily a DEC code. In order to correct two errors, a Hamming distance of five must be maintained. In general, a Hamming distance of $p + 1$ must be maintained in order to detect p errors, and a Hamming distance of $2p + 1$ must be maintained to correct p errors.

9.3.3 Vertical Redundancy Checking

The SEC code is used for detecting and correcting single bit errors in individual data words. Redundant bits are added to each data word, and each resulting codeword is treated independently. This recoding scheme is sometimes referred to as **horizontal** or **longitudinal redundancy checking** (LRC) because the width of the codeword is extended for the redundant bits.

An alternative approach is to use a **vertical redundancy checking** (VRC) code, in which a **checksum** word is added at the end of a group of words that are transmitted. In this case, parity is computed on a column-by-column basis, forming a checksum word that is appended to the message. This allows a run of a few contiguous errors to be detected and corrected. The checksum word is computed and transmitted by the sender, and is recomputed and compared to the transmitted checksum word by the receiver. If an error is detected, then the receiver must request a retransmission, since there is not enough redundancy to identify the position of an error. The VRC and LRC codes can be combined to improve error checking, as shown for the ASCII characters 'A' through 'H' in Figure 9-12.

P	Code	Character
0	1000001	A
0	1000010	B
1	1000011	C
0	1000100	D
1	1000101	E
1	1000110	F
0	1000111	G
0	1001000	H
1	0001000	Checksum

Figure 9-12
Combined LRC and VRC checking. Checksum bits form even parity for each column.

In some situations, errors are bursty, and may corrupt several contiguous bits both horizontally and vertically. A more powerful scheme such as **cyclic redundancy checking** (CRC) is more appropriate for this situation, which is a variation of VRC checking in which the bits are grouped in a special way, as described in the next section.

9.3.4 Cyclic Redundancy Checking

Cyclic redundancy checking is a more powerful error detection and correction scheme that operates in the presence of **burst errors**, which each begin and end with a bit error, with zero or more intervening corrupted bits. The two endpoint corrupted bits are included in the burst error. If the length of a burst error is B, then there must be B or more uncorrupted bits between burst errors.

CRCs use **polynomial codes**, in which a frame to be transmitted is divided by a polynomial and the remainder is appended to the frame as a **frame-check sequence** (FCS), commonly known as the **CRC digits**. The frame is transmitted (or stored on a disk) along with the CRC digits. After receiving the frame, the receiver then goes through the same computation, using the same polynomial, and if the remainders agree then there are no detectable errors. There can be undetectable errors, and the goal in creating a CRC code is to select a polynomial that covers the statistically likely errors for a given fault model.

The basic approach starts with a k-bit message to be transmitted, $M(x)$, which is appended with n 0s in which n is the degree of the **generator polynomial**, $G(x)$, with $k > n$. This extended form of $M(x)$ is divided by $G(x)$ using modulo-2 arithmetic (in which carries and borrows are discarded), and then the remainder, $R(x)$, which is no more than n bits wide, forms the CRC digits for $M(x)$.

As an example, consider a frame to be transmitted:

$$M(x) = 1\ 1\ 0\ 1\ 0\ 1\ 1\ 0\ 1\ 1$$

and a generator polynomial $G(x) = x^4 + x + 1$. The **degree** of $G(x)$ (the highest exponent) is 4, and so we append four zeros to $M(x)$ to form the dividend of the computation.

The divisor is 10011, which corresponds to the coefficients in $G(x)$ written as:

$$G(x) = 1 \times x^4 + 0 \times x^3 + 0 \times x^2 + 1 \times x^1 + 1 \times x^0.$$

Notice that $G(x)$ has a degree of $n = 4$ and that there are $n + 1 = 5$ coefficients. The CRC digits are then computed as shown in Figure 9-13. The divisor (10011) is divided into the dividend, but the magnitudes of the divisor and dividend do not play a role in determining whether the divisor "goes into" the dividend at the location of a particular digit. All that matters is that the number of bits in the divisor (which has no leading zeros) matches the same number of bits in the dividend (which also must not have leading zeros at the position being checked.) Note that there are no borrows in modulo-2 subtraction, and that a bit-by-bit exclusive-OR (XOR) operation between the divisor and the dividend achieves the same result.

Now suppose that the transmitted frame $T(x) = M(x) + R(x)$ gets corrupted during transmission. The receiver needs to detect that this has happened. The receiver divides the received frame by $G(x)$, and all burst errors that do not include $G(x)$ as a factor will be caught because there will be a nonzero remainder for these cases. That is, as long as the 1s in 10011 do not coincide with the positions of errors in the received frame, all errors will be caught. In general, a polynomial code of degree n will catch all burst errors of length $\leq n$.

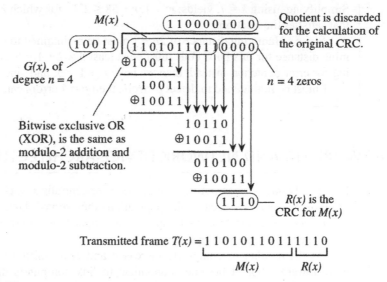

Figure 9-13
Calculation of the CRC digits.

Common polynomials that give good error coverage include:

$$CRC\text{-}16 = x^{16} + x^{15} + x^2 + 1$$

$$CRC\text{-}CCITT = x^{16} + x^{12} + x^5 + 1$$

$$CRC\text{-}32 = x^{32} + x^{26} + x^{23} + x^{16} + x^{12} + x^{11} + x^{10} + x^8 + x^7 + x^5 + x^4$$
$$+ x^2 + x + 1$$

A deeper analysis of CRC codes is beyond the scope of this book, and the reader is referred to (Hamming, 1986) for further details.

EXAMPLE 9-1   Double Error Correction

Consider how many check bits are needed for a double-error correcting ASCII code. There are $k = 7$ bits for each ASCII character, and we need to add r check bits to each codeword. For each of the 2^k ASCII characters there are $k + r$ possible one-bit error patterns, there are $\dfrac{(k+r)(k+r-1)}{2}$ possible two-bit error patterns, and there is one bit pattern for the uncorrupted codeword. There are 2^{k+r} possible bit patterns, and so the following relation must hold:

$$2^k \times \left[(k+r) + \frac{(k+r)(k+r-1)}{2} + 1 \right] \le 2^{k+r}$$

| Number of original codewords | Number of one-bit errors | Number of two-bit errors | Uncorrupted codeword | Number of possible bit patterns |

Simplifying, using $k = 7$, yields: $r^2 + 15r + 58 \leq 2^{r+1}$ for which $r = 7$ is the smallest value that satisfies the relation.

Since a Hamming distance of $2p + 1$ must be maintained to correct p errors, the Hamming distance for this DEC code must be at least $2 \times 2 + 1 = 5$. If we use the same encoding for error detection instead, then we have $p + 1 = 5$, and since a Hamming distance of $p + 1$ must be maintained to detect p errors, then $p = 4$ errors can be detected.

■

■ 9.4 NETWORKING AND NETWORK DEVICE ARCHITECTURES

In the early days of computing, computers were centralized facilities that contained most or all of the resources used by the populations they served. Data was transferred between computers via media (punched paper cards, paper tapes, magnetic tapes, and magnetic disks), hand-carried by an operator.

As the number of computers increased and costs shifted away from hardware and more toward labor, it became economical to link computers directly so that resources could be shared. This is what networking is about.

A **local area network** (LAN) is a communication medium that interconnects computers over a limited geographical distance of a few kilometers at most. A LAN allows a set of closely grouped computers and other devices to share common resources such as data, software applications, printers, and mass storage.

A LAN consists of hardware, software, and protocols. The hardware may take the form of cables and interface circuitry. The software is typically embedded in an operating system and is responsible for connecting a user to the network. The protocols are sets of rules that govern format, timing, sequencing, and error control. Protocols are important for ensuring that data is packaged for injection into the network and is extracted from the network properly. The data to be transmitted is decomposed into pieces, each of which is prepended with a **header** that contains information about parameters such as the destination, the source, error protection bits, and a time stamp. The data, which is often referred to as the **payload**, is combined with the header to form a **packet** that is injected into the network. A receiver goes through the reverse process of extracting the data from the packet.

The process of communicating over a network is normally carried out in a hierarchy of steps, each of which has its own protocol. The steps must be followed in sequence for transmission, and in the reverse sequence when receiving. This leads to the notion of a **protocol stack** that isolates each protocol being used within the hierarchy.

9.4.1 The OSI Model

The **Open System Interconnection** (OSI) model is a set of protocols established by the International Standards Organization (ISO) in an attempt to define and standardize data communications. In the OSI model the communication process is divided into seven layers: **application, presentation, session, transport, network, data link**, and **physical,** as summarized in Figure 9-14. As an aid in remembering the layers, a mnemonic is sometimes used: **P**lease **D**o **N**ot **T**hrow **S**ausage **P**izza **A**way.

The OSI model does not give a single definition of how data communications actually take place. Instead, the OSI model serves as a reference for how the process should be divided and what protocols should be used at each layer. The concept is that equipment providers can select a protocol for each layer while ensuring compatibility with equipment from other providers that may use different protocols.

The highest level in the OSI model is the application layer, which provides an interface to allow applications to communicate with each other over the network. It offers high-level support for applications that interact over the network, such as database services for network database programs, message handling for electronic mail (e-mail) programs, and file handling for file transfer programs.

The presentation layer ensures that information is presented to communication applications in a common format. This is necessary because different systems may use different internal data formats. For instance, some systems use a big-endian internal format while others use a little-endian internal format. The function of the presentation layer is to insulate the applications from these differences.

The session layer establishes and terminates communication sessions between host processes. The session layer is responsible for maintaining the integrity of communication even if the layers below it lose data. It also synchronizes the exchange, and establishes reference points for continuing an interrupted communication.

The transport layer ensures reliable transmission from source to destination. It allocates communication resources so that data is transferred both quickly and cost effectively. The session layer makes requests to the transport layer, which prioritizes the

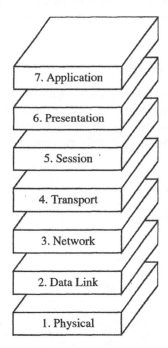

Figure 9-14
The seven layers of the OSI model.

requests and makes trade-offs among speed, cost, and capacity. For example, a transmission may be split into several packets that are transmitted over a number of networks in order to obtain a faster communication time. Packets may thus arrive at the destination out of order, and it is the responsibility of the transport layer to ensure that the session layer receives data in the same order in which it is sent. The transport layer provides error recovery from source to destination, and also provides flow control (that is, it ensures that the speeds of the sender and receiver are matched).

The network layer routes data through intermediate systems and subnetworks. Unlike the upper layers, the network layer is aware of the network **topology**, which is the connectivity among the network components. The network layer informs the transport layer of the status of potential and existing connections in the network in terms of speed, reliability, and availability. The network layer is typically implemented with **routers**, which connect different networks that use the same transport protocol.

The data-link layer manages the direct connections between components on a network. This layer is divided into the **logical link control** (LLC), which is independent of the network topology, and the **media access control** (MAC), which is specific to the topology. In some networks the physical connections between devices are not permanent, and it is the responsibility of the data link layer to tell the physical layer when to make connections. This layer deals in units of **frames** (single packets, or collections of packets that may be interleaved) that contain addresses, data, and control information.

The physical layer ensures that raw data is transmitted from a source to a destination over the physical medium. It transmits and repeats signals across network boundaries. The physical layer does *not* include the hardware itself, but includes methods of accessing the hardware.

9.4.2 Topologies

There are three primary LAN organizations, as illustrated in Figure 9-15. The **bus** topology is the simplest of the three. Components are connected to a bus system by simply plugging them into the single cable that runs through the network or, in the case of a wireless network, by simply emitting signals into a common medium. Advantages of

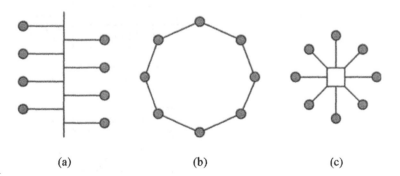

    (a)   (b)   (c)

Figure 9-15
(a) Bus; (b) ring; and (c) star network topologies.

this type of topology are that each component can communicate directly with any other component on the bus and that it is relatively simple to add another component to the network. Control is distributed among the components, and so there is no single network component that serves as an intermediary, which reduces the initial cost of this type of network. Disadvantages of this topology include a limit on the length of the cable from the bus to each network component (for a wireline network) and that a break in the cable may be needed in order to add another component to the network, which disrupts the rest of the network.

The **ring** topology uses a single cable, in which the ends are joined. Packets are passed around the ring through each network component until they reach their destinations. At the destinations, the packets are extracted from the network and are not passed farther along the ring. If a packet makes its way back to the originating system, then the transmission is unsuccessful, and so the packet is stopped and a new transmission can be attempted.

In a **star** topology, each component is connected to a central **hub** that serves as an intermediary for all communication over the network. In a simple configuration, the hub receives data from one component and forwards it to all of the other components, leaving it to the individual components to determine whether or not they are the intended target. In a more sophisticated configuration, the hub receives data and forwards it to a specific network component.

An advantage of a star topology is that most of the network service, troubleshooting, and wiring changes take place at the central hub. A disadvantage is that a problem with the hub affects the entire network. Another disadvantage is that geometrically, the star topology requires more cable than a bus or a ring because a separate cable connects each network component to the hub. Even so, the star topology is very common for LANs.

9.4.3 Ethernet

Ethernet is one of the most prevalent bus-based networks (Figure 9-16), although in its current form it more closely resembles a star topology. Ethernet uses **carrier sense multiple access** with **collision detection** (CSMA/CD) for transmission. With CSMA/CD, when a network component wants to transmit data, it first listens for a carrier. If there is a carrier

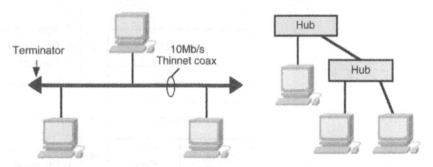

Figure 9-16
Coax-based Ethernet local area network—bus topology (left), and unshielded twisted pair (UTP)-based Ethernet local area network—star topology (right).

present on the line, which is placed there by a transmitting device, then it transmits nothing and listens again after a random waiting period. The random waiting period is important in order to avoid a **deadlock** in which components that are trying to access the bus perpetually listen and wait in synchrony.

If there is no traffic on the line, then transmission can begin by placing a carrier on the line with the data. The source also listens for **collisions** in which two or more components simultaneously transmit. A collision is detected by the presence of more than one carrier. Collisions can occur in a fully operational network as a result of the finite time it takes for a signal to travel the length of the bus. The propagation of signals on the bus is bounded by the speed of light over the length of the bus, which can be up to 500 meters in some Ethernet installations. When a collision occurs, the transmitting components wait for a random interval before retransmitting.

Transmitted data moves in both directions over the bus. Every component sees every packet of data, but extracts only those packets with corresponding destination addresses. After a packet is successfully delivered, the destination can generate an acknowledgment to the sender, typically at the transport layer. If the sender does not receive an acknowledgment after a fixed period of time (which must be greater than the round-trip delay through the network), then it retransmits the message.

Collisions should occur infrequently in practice, and so the overhead of recovering from a collision is not very significant. A serious degradation in Ethernet performance does not occur until traffic increases to about 35% of network capacity.

An internet is a collection of interconnected networks. The Internet is probably the most well-known internet, using the **TCP/IP protocol** and **IP addresses** in what is known as the **TCP/IP protocol** suite described below. The seven-layer OSI model has been simplified in the Internet model, which can be thought of as having only four layers, as illustrated by the protocol stack shown in Figure 9-17. At the bottom of the protocol stack is the Link layer, which is made up of the medium access control (MAC) and physical (PHY) sublayers. The Link layer resolves contention for the medium when more than one device wants to transmit, manages the logical grouping of bits into frames, and implements error protection.

The Link layer is responsible for simply getting a frame of bits from one machine to a directly connected machine. This is fine for point-to-point communication between two cooperating processes on different machines. In order for multiple processes to share the

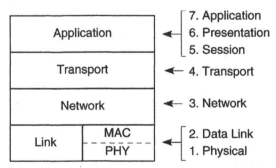

Figure 9-17
Internet protocol stack.

same link, however, a protocol is needed to coordinate which data goes to what process. This is the responsibility of the Network layer, which is implemented with the **Internet Protocol** (IP) for the Internet.

The network layer deals only with hop-by-hop communication. The Transport layer deals with end-to-end communication, in which there may be a number of intervening systems between the sender and receiver. The Transport layer deals with retransmission (for errors or packets dropped due to congestion), sequencing (packets may arrive out of order), flow control (applying back-pressure to the source to relieve congestion) and error protection (the Link layer does not do enough error protection on its own). For the Internet, the Transport layer is implemented with the **Transmission Control Protocol** (TCP). The TCP/IP combination at the Network and Transport layers is the predominant Internet protocol suite. Any other appropriate protocols can be used at the Link and Application layers, and there are also other protocols used within the Network and Transport layers.

At the Application layer, a process can exchange data with another process anywhere on the Internet and treat the connection as if it were a file on the local system. It reads and writes bytes with ordinary read and write system calls, frequently implemented with **sockets**, which are pathways to the network through the operating system.

Internet Addresses

Every interface on the Internet has a unique IP address. Version 4 of the IP protocol, known as IPv4, is widely used but is gradually being replaced by IPv6, which uses addresses that are four times wider and has several enhancements and simplifications of IPv4. We will use IPv4 for this discussion.

An example of an IPv4 address "dotted decimal notation" is shown below:

$$165.230.140.67$$

Each number that is delimited by a dot is an unsigned byte in the range from 0 through 255. The equivalent bit pattern for the IPv4 address shown above is then:

$$10100101.11100110.10001100.10000011$$

The leftmost bits determine the class of the address. Figure 9-18 shows the five IPv4 classes. Class A has seven bits for the network identification (ID), known as the netid, and 24 bits for the host ID (hostid). There can thus be at most 2^7 class A networks and 2^{24} hosts on each class A network. A number of these addresses are reserved, and so the number of addresses that can be assigned to hosts is fewer than the number of possible addresses.

Class B addresses use 14 bits for the netid and 16 bits for the hostid. Class C addresses use 21 bits for the netid and eight bits for the hostid. Class D addresses are used for **multicast** groups, to which an end system that has a class A, B, or C address subscribes and thereby receives all network traffic intended for that group. This is an efficient mechanism for sending the same packets to multiple subscribers, without flooding the network with broadcasts and without the sender needing to keep track of all of the current subscribers. Class E addresses are unused.

The available supply of IPv4 addresses was expected to run out soon after the year 2000, and so it was imperative that IPv6 be quickly adopted. New life has been breathed into the IPv4 address space, however, by reusing IP addresses that are simultaneously in

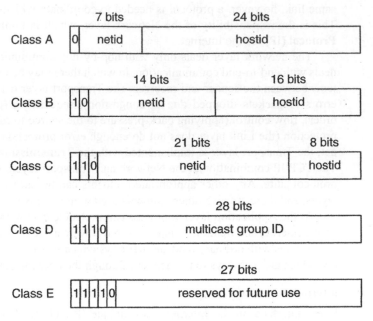

Figure 9-18
Five classes of IPv4 addresses.

use elsewhere (using a protocol that allows sharing of IP addresses on private networks). IP addresses are also temporarily assigned from a pool for the duration of a session, such as for a dialup line through a modem, providing further relief to the limited supply of IPv4 addresses.

Ports

Loosely speaking, a **port** is how a process is known to the world. A port number identifies the source process, and a port number also identifies the destination process. Strictly speaking, the port identifies a network entry point for a process. Ports 0-1023 are **well-known ports** for server processes. For example, the `http` (Web server) port is 80. On a Unix, Windows, or MacOS command line, the following command:

```
telnet yahoo.com 80
```

will connect the user directly to the HTTP server. (What to type to the Web server after connecting is another topic.) If the 80 is not present on the command line, then 23 is assumed, which is for a telnet connection; most systems will refuse this from outside users for security reasons.

Encapsulation

Network data is **encapsulated** as it passes through the network layers, as illustrated in Figure 9-19. The user data is sent to the network using read and write system calls similar to those that would be used for reading and writing files. The application layer sends user data to the Transport layer, where the operating system adds a TCP header that identifies

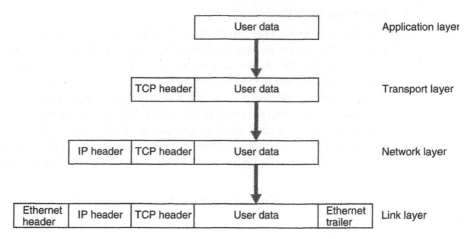

Figure 9-19
Encapsulation in the TCP/IP protocol suite.

the source and destination ports, forming a TCP segment. The TCP segment is passed down to the network layer, where the TCP segment is repackaged into IP datagrams, each with an IP header identifying the source and destination systems. The IP datagrams are sent to the Link layer, where the datagrams are encapsulated into Ethernet frames (for this example). The reverse process takes place on the receiving system.

A single TCP segment may be decomposed into a number of IP datagrams that are independently routed through the Internet. Each IP datagram contains the source and destination IP addresses (in the IP header), the source and destination ports (in the TCP header), and the protocol at the next layer of encapsulation (in the IP header—TCP is only one of the transport layer protocols used in the Internet.) Collectively, these five parameters uniquely identify each IP datagram as it traverses the Internet, which helps ensure that the datagrams arrive at the correct receiving process.

The Domain Name System

The Domain Name System (DNS) is a distributed database that maps between hostnames and IP addresses and provides mail routing information. For example, `aramis.rutgers.edu` maps to `128.6.4.2` (and vice versa). The DNS is responsible for interacting with programs that need to map between names and addresses.

Each domain (like `rutgers.edu`) maintains its own database of information and runs a name server that other systems across the Internet can query. Access to the DNS is provided through a **resolver** embodied in library routines that are silently linked into high-level programs that access the network.

The Internet Corporation for Assigned Names and Numbers (ICANN, formerly known as the InterNIC) manages the top-level domains and delegates authority for second-level domains. Within a **zone**, a local administrator maintains the name server database. There must be a primary name server, which loads its database from a file, and secondary name servers, which get their information from the primary name server. Caching is used, so that a query that causes other servers to be contacted does not cause future queries to cause additional contacts to other servers.

The World Wide Web

The World Wide Web (or, simply, "the Web") is made up of client processes (Web browsers) and Web servers running the HyperText Transport Protocol (HTTP), at the Application layer of the Internet. As distinctions become blurred in everyday usage, it is important to keep in mind that the Web is built on top of the Internet—the Web is not the Internet itself.

In 1989, Tim Berners-Lee at CERN (the European high-energy physics facility) developed a text-based Web for exchanging technical documents among colleagues. In February 1993, the National Center for Supercomputing Applications (NCSA) at the University of Illinois at Urbana-Champaign released a graphical version of the Mosaic Web browser, as well as an HTTP server, both free of charge, and the Web exploded to where it is today.

9.4.4 Hubs, Bridges, Switches, Routers, and Gateways

As networks grow in size, they can be subdivided into smaller networks that are interconnected. The smaller **subnetworks** operate almost entirely independently of one another and can use different protocols and topologies.

If the subnetworks all use the same topology and the same protocols, then it may be the case that all that is needed to extend the network are **repeaters**. A repeater amplifies the signals on the network, which become attenuated according to the distance traveled. The subnetworks are not entirely independent because every subnetwork sees all of the traffic that occurs on the other subnetworks. A network with simple repeaters is not extensible to large sizes. Since noise is amplified as well as the signal, the noise will eventually dominate the signal if too many repeaters are used in succession.

An Ethernet **hub** (Figure 9-20) receives frames on one interface, regenerates the signal, and copies the frame to all of its other interfaces. A hub does not sense the bits in each frame; it simply regenerates the signal. Electrically, each hub segment is distinct from the others and so any noise on one segment does not affect another. However, the segments are all logically the same, and if there is traffic on a segment where a frame is being copied, then a frame collision will occur. That collision may even propagate to the other segments depending on how much protection circuitry is in the hub. The bandwidth of a single segment is shared among all of the segments.

An Ethernet **switch** senses the bits in each frame and records the source and destination headers for each frame. In this way, the switch learns which hosts are on which segments, and can limit traffic to travel only between the sending and receiving segments. Separate send and receive wire-pairs are supported, which eliminates collisions if each host has its own port on the switch. Switches buffer frames in queues, so that collisions can be prevented in situations when another frame is already being copied to a segment. The queuing also allows each segment of a switch to operate at a different speed (10 Mbps, 100 Mbps, or 1000 Mbps). Unlike a hub, each segment of a switch has its own bandwidth that is not shared with the other segments, which means that a switch can support much greater throughput.

A hub is a central connection point for end systems. A hub simply copies packets from one network interface to all of the others, as illustrated in the configuration shown in Figure 9-20. Hubs have modest intelligence these days, by isolating collisions on single network links (that is, if two packets collide on a span of the network, which is a normal

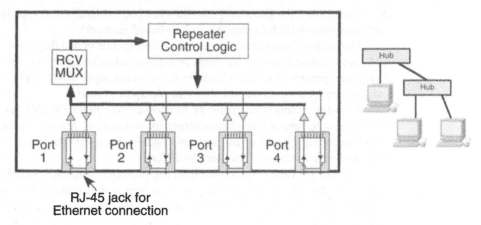

Figure 9-20
Architecture of an Ethernet hub.

but unwanted condition, the collision signal is not propagated to the other network links) and by limiting certain types of traffic from being sent to all other interfaces.

A switch, formerly referred to as a **bridge** (different from the bus bridge introduced in Chapter 8), does more than simply amplify signal levels. A hub only restores the individual signal levels to logical 1 or 0, which prevents noise from accumulating. Switches have some level of intelligence, and can typically interpret the destination address of a packet and route it to the appropriate subnetwork (Figure 9-21). In this way, network traffic can

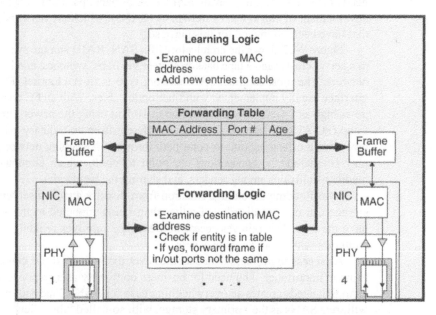

Figure 9-21
Architecture of an Ethernet switch.

be reduced, since the alternative method would be to blindly send each incoming packet to each subnetwork (as for a repeater-or hub-based network).

Although switches have some level of intelligence in that they sense the incoming bits and make routing decisions based on destination addresses, they are unaware of protocols. A **router** operates at a higher level, in the network layer. Routers typically connect logically separate networks that use the same transport protocol.

A **router** connects one network to another (see Figure 9-23b) and makes decisions with respect to forwarding packets across its boundaries. A router by definition has more than one network interface and forwards packets between interfaces. The network protocols used on either side of a router can differ.

A router forwards packets based on the protocol, whereas a switch forwards packets based only on the destination address. A switch is in a sense a high-speed hub with no shared bandwidth. A switch eliminates media access conflicts because there is no contention for the media.

A **gateway** translates packets up through the application layer of the OSI model (layers 4 through 7). Gateways connect dissimilar networks by performing protocol conversions, message format conversions, and other high-level functions.

■ 9.5 STORAGE AREA NETWORKS

With the explosion of data created by businesses, the importance of data has grown far beyond the capabilities of hard magnetic disks attached to single computers. The driving needs for fast access, high availability, ease of backups, and remote access have led to the development of **storage area networks** (SANs), which are networks of storage resources that have been optimized for this purpose.

Figure 9-22 shows the architecture of a SAN. RAID storage systems are interconnected to a server cluster and a tape backup system via hubs, switches, and bridges over a dedicated network. The most common SAN network type is **fiber channel** (FC), which uses a serial interface usually implemented with fiber optic cables. With an FC connection, data rates can go as high as 1 Gbps over distances up to 10 Km using the newer Fibre Channel-Arbitrated Loop (FC-AL). What makes a channel different from an ordinary network is that a channel provides an effective point-to-point path through a switching network. Although the fabric may be shared, the connections are point to point, which eliminates contention for the medium, collisions among senders, and sharing the bandwidth.

By offloading the storage function from directly attached servers to a SAN, access to storage can now be distributed rather than being funneled to the server that happens to have the data. This relieves access bottlenecks, improves reliability, and supports backup strategies that do not degrade access.

As access to business data becomes ever more criticial, we can expect that SANs will grow in importance. The need for business continuity as a response to disasters or rapidly changing needs creates an overwhelming case for SANs. Futurists speculate that end users will treat SANs as their primary storage, with so-called "thin clients" attached to SANs via high-speed networks. However SAN usage evolves, it is a demonstrated architectural approach that is expected to rise in importance.

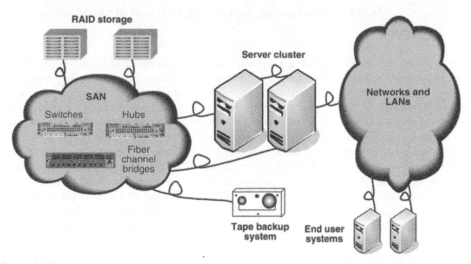

Figure 9-22
A storage area network (SAN) is made up of storage devices, backup devices, access servers, and a specialized network that connects the devices.

■ 9.6 CASE STUDY: CISCO ROUTER ARCHITECTURE

A router by definition has two or more network interfaces (such as for Ethernet) and forwards packets among its interfaces. Each interface handles a network segment, identified by a unique network address. For example, a router with three interfaces that have interface addresses of 192.168.1.1, 192.168.2.1, and 192.168.3.1 have network addresses of 192.168.1.0, 192.168.2.0, and 192.168.3.0, respectively, as shown in Figure 9-23. The rightmost eight bits of the network address are allocated for host computers and router interfaces on the network, supporting address ranges [192.168.1.1–192.168.1.254], [192.168.2.1–192.168.2.254], and [192.168.3.1–192.168.3.254]. Notice that the lowest

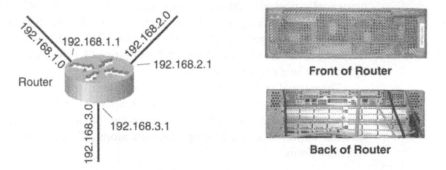

Figure 9-23
A router that supports three network segments.

Intel vs. Motorola: Networks in the Automobile

Automotive electronics have come a long way since 1978, when the Cadillac Seville incorporated the first microprocessor, a Motorola 6802. Today's mid-sized car will have in the range of 50 embedded microprocessors— the current 7-series BMW has over 100 microprocessors. It has been estimated that by 2015 these microprocessors will be running 100 million lines of code. New cars frequently carry over 200 pounds of electronics and more than a mile of wiring. Networking these microprocessors is not a simple task. The many subsystems in the vehicle have widely differing communications requirements. The seat reclining system obviously has lower priority and speed requirements than the air bag control system. As a result there are several serial buses for different requirements, and a number of bus protocols have been developed specifically for use in vehicle applications, from the 20 Kbps local interconnect network, (lin) to the 15-year-old 1-Mbps Car (now controller) area network, (Can) bus.

The Can bus is now seen in machine tools, railway signaling, and operating elevators. The Can and the newer Can2 bus are capable of handling past and some present automobile networking tasks, but are inadequate to handle the new "X-by-wire" applications. "X-by-wire" describes control systems where electronics replace or enhance mechanical or hydraulic systems. Drive-by-wire, steer-by-wire, brake-by-wire, etc., have reliability, speed, and latency requirements that are exhausting the capabilities of the Can system. Another attribute that was not a factor when Can was developed

is detecting and isolating the "jabbering sensor", where a sensor failure causes it to monopolize the bus, rendering it unusable.

Motorola (now Freescale Semiconductor) has had a close association with the car and its Electronics since their introduction of one of the first car radios in 1930. Thus it is not surprising that the Cadillac mentioned above used a Motorola microprocessor. Motorola and Freescale Semiconductor have been active in the development of advanced automotive network protocols such as Byteflight and Flexray, competitive technologies that were designed from the ground up to support by-wire applications. They take alternative approaches but both incorporate a 10 Mbps collisionless protocol with maximum latency guarantees and fiber optic cable instead of wire. Motorola sits on both standards committees and has developed device interfaces and compatible microcontrollers for both.

When Intel began operations in the late 1960s automotive electronics was an insignificant market. Thus Intel's expertise in the automotive electronics area has been focused on microprocessors, microcontrollers and peripheral devices for the car. In the automotive networking area Intel has been at the forefront of Can and Can2 IC development and implementation as opposed to more advanced network controllers. New Can protocols continue to emerge; it would not be surprising if these advanced Can protocols kept Can and Intel competitive for many years.

numerically possible address in each range (192.168.1.0, 192.168.2.0, 192.168.3.0) is reserved for identifying the network segment[1] and that the highest numerically possible address in each range (192.168.1.255, 192.168.2.255, 192.168.3.255) is reserved for what is known as the broadcast address: packets destined for the broadcast address are received by all hosts on a network segment.

The internal architecture of a router is very similar to that of an ordinary computer. In fact, for years, many routers were simply computers that had multiple network interfaces and routing application software. Present-day routers are specialized to handle the network traffic loads and routing functions more efficiently, but still take the basic von Neumann form.

---

[1] While not strictly permissible in the past, the network address can be assigned to a host with newer routers. This is important for recovering wasted addresses for segments that are allocated only a few addresses.

A block diagram of a Cisco 3600 series router is shown in Figure 9-24. The input and output for the router is handled among the "Network Modules", which are for Ethernet and WAN connections, and also the Dual **UART** (Universal Asynchronous Receiver/ Transmitter), which provides two serial ports for administrative console and modem interfaces. The CPU for a 3660 model is a 225 MHz IDT RISC processor (R5271) with 2 MB of Level-2 cache memory.

There are four types of memory other than the cache memory. The Boot ROM stores the startup code that locates and loads the **internetwork operating system** (IOS). The nonvolatile RAM (NVRAM) stores user configurations that remain after the router is powered off. The flash memory stores the IOS. The DRAM is used as the working memory and is divided into two parts: processor memory and packet memory with the proportion (initially 75% and 25%, respectively) configured by the user.

The CPU and network modules on the Cisco 3660 are interconnected via a 25-MHz, 32-bit PCI bus. During operation, packets arrive on interfaces and are buffered in queues until the processor can look at the destination address in the packet header. It then compares the destination address with its routing table and sends the packet out on the interface specified by the routing table. If the packet ends up going out on the same interface that it arrived on, then the router sends it out and also generates a message to the sender telling it to update its routing table for a better path. This is one way that routing tables are dynamically maintained. Other methods involve monitoring the time that it takes for test packets to be sent and received, and listening for update information from other routers regarding their traffic loads.

Although a router performs a specialized function as an autonomous system, it behaves very much as an ordinary computer with an operating system. In general, this is also the case for many other network devices and embedded systems. The basic principles of a stored-program computer are at the foundation of all of these systems.

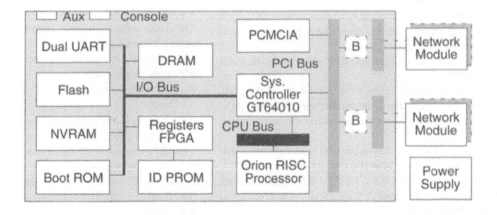

Figure 9-24
Block diagram of the Cisco 3600 series router architecture.

Summary

Communication involves the transfer of information between systems. As a rule, data is transferred in bit-serial fashion because the time-of-flight delays dominate the transfer time for high-speed networks. However, modulation schemes allow many bits to be encoded in a single sample, such as for a dibit. The choice of modulation scheme impacts the introduction of errors into the transmission of information. Error detection and correction are made possible through redundancy, in which there are more bit patterns possible than the number of valid bit patterns. If the error bit patterns do not have a single closest valid codeword, then error detection is possible but error correction is not possible. If every error bit pattern is reachable from only one valid bit pattern, then error correction is also possible.

Local area networks (LANs) manage complexity by using layering that is based on the OSI model. These days, LANs are typically connected to wide area networks (WANs), most notably the Internet. The Internet is based on the TCP/IP protocol suite. User data is encapsulated at the Application, Transport, Network, and Link layers, and is sent through the Internet and de-encapsulated (de-muxed) on the receiving system. As it is passed through the Internet, the data traverses various devices (like hubs, switches, and routers) and transmission media that vary in bandwidth and distance capabilities. The devices that carry this network traffic have specialized architectures, with the higher-level devices (routers) looking remarkably similar to general-purpose computers.

Problems

9.1 What is the Hamming distance for the ASCII SEC code discussed in Section 9.3.2?

9.2 Construct the SEC code for the ASCII character 'Q' using even parity.

9.3 For parts (a) through (d) below, use a SEC code with even parity, with the same check bit positions that we used in the chapter.

(a) How many check bits should be added to encode a six-bit word?

(b) Construct the SEC code for the six-bit word 1 0 1 1 0 0. When constructing the code, number the bits from right to left starting with 1, as in the method described in Section 9.3.2.

(c) A receiver sees a two-bit SEC encoded word that looks like 1 1 1 0 0. What is the initial two-bit pattern?

(d) The 12-bit word 1 0 1 1 1 0 0 1 1 0 0 1 complete with an SEC code (even parity) is received. What 12-bit word was actually sent?

9.4 How many check bits are needed for a SEC code for an initial word size of 1024?

9.5 Construct a checksum word for EBCDIC characters 'V' through 'Z' using vertical redundancy checking with even parity. *Do not* use longitudinal redundancy checking.

9.6 Compare the number of bits used for parity in the SEC code with the simple parity VRC code, for 1024 eight-bit characters.

(a) Compute the number of check bits generated using SEC only (horizontally).

(b) Compute the number of checksum bits using VRC only.

9.7 The SEC code discussed in Section 9.3.2 can be turned into a double error detecting/SEC (DED/SEC) code by adding one more bit that creates even parity over the SEC code (which includes the parity bit being added.) Explain how double error detection works while also maintaining single error correction with this approach.

9.8 Compute the CRC for a message to be transmitted $M(x) = 101100110$ and a generator polynomial $G(x) = x^3 + x^2 + 1$.

9.9 What is the longest burst error that CRC-32 is sure to catch?

9.10 To which IPv4 class does address 165.230.140.67 belong?

9.11 How many networks (not hosts) can the IPv4 class A, B, and C addresses support? That is, how many distinct class A, B, and C network addresses are numerically possible? Assume for this problem that no addresses are reserved for special purposes (although by convention there are reserved addresses).

9.12 Network media always carry data in bit-serial fashion, and essentially never in parallel. That is not to say that data could not be carried over a network in byte-parallel or word-parallel fashion; there simply is no advantage to doing it this way. To see why this is the case, calculate the time required to transmit a 32-bit word

between two computers over a 32-foot network. The network speed is 1 Gbps per channel. The time-of-flight delay imposed by the distance is 1 ns per foot. Calculate the time to transmit the 32-bit word using a single channel (bit-serial fashion) and using 32 channels (word-parallel fashion).

9.13 How many bytes per second will the Cisco 3660 router PCI bus support?

9.14 When we looked at Hamming codes in this chapter, we learned that adding a single parity bit will find the existence of a single-bit error, but will not identify the location of the error. All of the RAID levels higher than RAID level 0 covered in Chapter 8 can actually detect *and* locate a single-bit error, making error correction possible. How do you think this can be done with only a single parity bit?

Further Reading

(Tanenbaum, 2002) gives a thorough treatment of local area networks according to the OSI model, and is a good reference on network communication in general. (Halsall, 1996) gives a thorough and readable treatment of network media types. (Hamming, 1986) and (Peterson and Weldon, 1972) give detailed treatments of error-correcting codes. There are several Web-related resources covering networks in the automobile, notably (Marsh, 2003) and (Goldberg, 2002).

Marsh, D. "Network Protocols Compete for Highway Supremacy," Electronic Design News (EDN), www.edn.com/article/CA303304.html pp. 26–38, (June 2003).

Goldberg, L.H., "Motorola Maps Out Its Future at Smart Networks Developer's Form," analog ZONE, www.analogzone.com/nete0729.htm (July 23, 2003).

Cisco, "Cisco 3600 series router architecture", Document ID: 7442, http://www.cisco.com/en/US/prodcts/hw/routers/ps274/products_tech_note09186a00801e1155.shtml, as referenced (Oct. 23, 2005).

Halsall, F., *Data Communications, Computer Networks, and Open Systems*, 4/e, Addison-Wesley (1996).

Hamming, R. W., *Coding and Information Theory*, 2/e, Prentice-Hall (1986).

Peterson, W. Wesley and Weldon, E. J., Jr., *Error-Correcting Codes*, 2/e, The MIT Press (1972).

Tanenbaum, A., *Computer Networks*, 4/e, Prentice Hall, (2002).

CHAPTER 10

ADVANCED COMPUTER ARCHITECTURE

In earlier chapters, the fetch-execute cycle takes the form "fetch an instruction, execute that instruction, fetch the next instruction, etc." This gives the impression of a straight-line linear progression of program execution. In fact, the processor architectures of today have many advanced features that go beyond this simple paradigm. We saw an enhancement of this paradigm in Chapter 6 with pipelining, in which several instructions sharing the same hardware can simultaneously be in various phases of execution.

Pipelining can lead to an increase in the number of cycles needed to execute any one instruction, but more importantly, it leads to overall improvements in performance. This is because short pipeline stages support higher clock rates and allow multiple instructions to be in various stages of execution. This approach cannot be extended indefinitely: there are diminishing returns as we try to increase clock rates and keep pipelines filled. We can turn to parallel processing, in which multiple processors are coordinated to work on a single problem. We start the chapter with the topic of parallel processing, touching both on parallel architectures and program decomposition.

With the concepts of parallel processing in mind, we then take a look at parallel processing enhancements that have made their way into mainstream processors. We introduce superscalar execution, in which several instructions are executed simultaneously using different portions of the hardware, although with possibly only some of the results contributing to the overall computation. We then introduce very long instruction word (VLIW) architectures, in which each instruction word specifies multiple instructions (of smaller widths) that are executed simultaneously.

Exploring a different aspect of advanced architecture, we look at a class of programmable logic devices (PLDs) that bridges the gap between pure software programmability and special-purpose hardware. These devices support rapid time to market and relatively low development costs. We explore a number of these devices and their impact on special-purpose systems.

The chapter concludes with a look at a few forward-looking, unconventional architectural approaches.

■ 10.1 PARALLEL ARCHITECTURE

One method of improving the performance of a processor is to increase the clock rate. This will work up to a point where the power budget becomes unmanageable (higher clock rates consume more power). With proper cooling (e.g. using a heat sink and a fan), a

6 cm^2 processor such as the Itanium Montecito can dissipate up to 130 watts. Thermal loads cannot be practically increased a great deal more, because the circuitry will not tolerate higher temperatures, and exotic cooling methods are needed.

An alternative approach to increasing the clock rate is to increase the number of processors, and decompose and distribute a single program onto the processors. This approach is known as **parallel processing**, in which a number of processors work collectively, in parallel, on a common problem. In the discussion below, we explore performance metrics for parallel processing, and then look at specific types of parallel architectures.

10.1.1 Measuring Performance

A parallel architecture can be characterized in terms of three parameters: (1) the number of **processing elements** (PEs); (2) the interconnection network among the PEs; and (3) the organization of the memory. As a simple example, in the four-stage instruction pipeline that we saw in Figure 6-14, there are four PEs. The interconnection network among the PEs is a simple **ring**. The memory is an ordinary RAM that is external to the pipeline.

Characterizing the architecture of a parallel processor is a relatively easy task, but measuring the performance is not nearly so simple. Although we can easily measure the increased speed that a simple enhancement like a pipeline offers, the overall speedup is data dependent: not all programs and data sets map well onto a pipelined architecture. Other performance considerations of pipelined architectures that are also data dependent are the cost of flushing a pipeline, the increased area cost, the latency (input to output delay) of the pipeline, etc.

A few common measures of performance are **parallel time**, **speedup**, **efficiency**, and **throughput**. The parallel time is simply the absolute time needed for a program to execute on a parallel processor. The speedup is the ratio of the time for a program to execute on a sequential (nonparallel, that is) processor to the time for that same program to execute on a parallel processor. In a simple form, we can represent speedup (S, now in the context of parallel processing) as:

$$S = \frac{T_{Sequential}}{T_{Parallel}}$$

Since a sequential algorithm and a parallel version of the same algorithm may be programmed very differently for each machine, we need to qualify $T_{Sequential}$ and $T_{Parallel}$ so that they apply to the best implementation for each machine.

There is more to the story. If we want to achieve a speedup of 100, it is not enough to simply distribute a single program over 100 processors. The problem is that not many computations are easily decomposed in a way that fully utilizes the available PEs. If there are even a small number of sequential operations in a parallel program, then the speedup can be significantly limited. This is summarized by **Amdahl's law**, in which speedup is expressed in terms of the number of processors p and the fraction f of operations that must be performed sequentially:

$$S = \frac{1}{f + \frac{1-f}{p}}$$

For example, if $f = 10\%$ of the operations must be performed sequentially, then speedup can be no greater than 10 regardless of how many processors are used:

$$S = \frac{1}{0.1 + \dfrac{0.9}{10}} \cong 5.3 \qquad\qquad S = \frac{1}{0.1 + \dfrac{0.9}{\infty}} = 10$$

$$p = 10 \; processors \qquad\qquad p = \infty \; processors$$

This brings us to measurements of **efficiency**. Efficiency is the ratio of speedup to the number of processors used. For a speedup of 5.3 with 10 processors, the efficiency is:

$$\frac{5.3}{10} = .53, \text{ or } 53\%$$

If we double the number of processors to 20, then the speedup increases to 6.9 but the efficiency reduces to 34%. Thus, parallelizing an algorithm can improve performance to a limit that is determined by the amount of sequential operations. Efficiency is drastically reduced as speedup approaches its limit, and so it does not make sense to simply use more processors in a computation in the hope that a corresponding gain in performance will be achieved.

Throughput is a measure of how much computation is achieved over time, and is of special concern for I/O-bound and pipelined applications. For the case of a four-stage pipeline that remains filled, in which each pipeline stage completes its task in 1 ns, the average time to complete an operation is 1 ns even though it takes 4 ns to execute any one operation. The overall throughput for this situation is then:

$$1.0 \; \frac{operation}{ns} = 10^9 \text{ operations per second}$$

10.1.2 The Flynn Taxonomy

Computer architectures can be classified in terms of their **instruction streams** and their **data streams**, using a taxonomy developed by M. J. Flynn (Flynn, 1972). A conventional sequential processor fits into the **single instruction stream, single data stream** (SISD) category, as illustrated in Figure 10-1a. Only a single instruction is executed at a time in a SISD processor, although pipelining may allow several instructions to be in different phases of execution at any given time.

In a **single instruction stream, multiple data stream** (SIMD) processor, several identical processors perform the same sequence of operations on different data sets, as illustrated in Figure 10-1b. A SIMD system can be thought of as a room filled with mail sorters, all sorting different pieces of mail into the same set of bins.

In a **multiple instruction stream, multiple data stream** (MIMD) processor, several processors perform different operations on different data sets, but are all coordinated to execute a single parallel program, as illustrated in Figure 10-1c.

In a **multiple instruction stream, single data stream** (MISD) processor, a single data stream is operated on by several functional units, as illustrated in Figure 10-1d. The

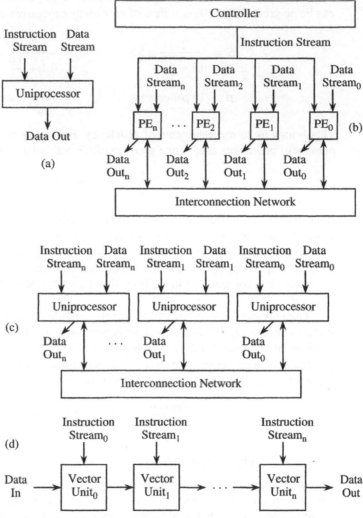

Figure 10-1
Classification of architectures according to the Flynn taxonomy: (a) SISD; (b) SIMD; (c) MIMD; (d) MISD.

data stream is typically a vector of several related streams. This configuration is known as a **systolic array**, which we saw in Chapter 3 in the form of an array multiplier.

10.1.3 Interconnection Networks

When a computation is distributed over a number of PEs, the PEs need to communicate with each other through an **interconnection network**. There is a host of topologies for interconnection networks, each with their own characteristics in terms of **crosspoint complexity** (an asymptotic measure of area), **diameter** (the length of the worst-case path through the network), and **blocking** (whether or not a new connection can be established

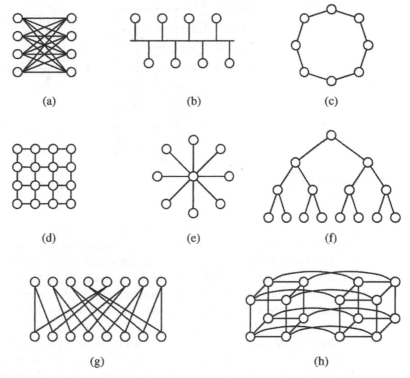

Figure 10-2
Network topologies: (a) crossbar; (b) bus; (c) ring; (d) mesh; (e) star; (f) tree; (g) perfect shuffle; (h) hypercube.

in the presence of other connections). A few representative topologies and control strategies for configuring networks are described below.

One of the most powerful network topologies is the **crossbar**, in which every PE is directly connected to every other PE. An abstract view of a crossbar is illustrated in Figure 10-2a, in which four PEs are interconnected. In the close-up view in Figure 10-3, the crossbar contains **crosspoint switches**, which are configurable devices that either connect or disconnect the lines that go through it. In general, for N PEs, the crosspoint complexity (the number of crosspoint switches) is N^2. In Figure 10-2a, $N = 4$ (not 8) because the output ports of the PEs on the left and the input ports of the PEs on the right belong to the same PEs. The crosspoint complexity is thus $4^2 = 16$. The network diameter is 1 since every PE can directly communicate with every other PE, with no intervening PEs. The number of crosspoint switches that are traversed is not normally considered in evaluating the network diameter. The crossbar is **strictly nonblocking**, which means that there is always an available path between every input and output regardless of the configuration of existing paths.

At the other extreme of complexity is the bus topology, which is illustrated in Figure 10-2b. With the bus topology, a fixed amount of bus bandwidth is shared among the PEs. The crosspoint complexity is N for N PEs, and the network diameter is 1, so the bus grows

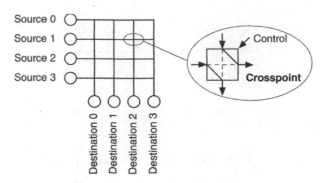

Figure 10-3
Internal organization of a crossbar.

more gracefully than the crossbar. There can only be one source at a time, and there is normally only one receiver, so blocking is a frequent situation for a bus.

In a ring topology, there are N crosspoints for N PEs, as shown in Figure 10-2c. As for the crossbar, each crosspoint is contained within a PE. The network diameter is $N/2$, but the collective bandwidth is N times greater than for the case of the bus. This is because adjacent PEs can communicate directly with each other over their common link without affecting the rest of the network.

In the mesh topology, there are N crosspoints for N PEs but the diameter is only $2\sqrt{N}$, as shown in Figure 10-2d. All PEs can simultaneously communicate in just $3\sqrt{N}$ steps, as discussed in (Leighton, 1992) using an **off-line routing algorithm** (in which the crosspoint settings are determined external to the PEs).

In the star topology, there is a central hub through which all PEs communicate, as shown in Figure 10-2e. Since all of the connection complexity is centralized, the star can only grow to sizes that are bounded by the technology, which is normally less than for decentralized topologies like the mesh. The crosspoint complexity within the hub varies according to the implementation, which can be anything from a bus to a crossbar.

In the tree topology, there are N crosspoints for N PEs and the diameter is $2\log_2 N - 1$, as shown in Figure 10-2f. The tree is effective for applications in which there is a great deal of distributing and collecting of data.

In the perfect shuffle topology, there are N crosspoints for N PEs, as shown in Figure 10-2g. The diameter is $\log_2 N$ since it takes $\log_2 N$ passes through the network to connect any PE with any other in the worst case. The perfect shuffle name comes from the property that if a deck of 2^N cards, in which N is an integer, is cut in half and interleaved N times, then the original configuration of the deck is restored. All N PEs can simultaneously communicate in $3\log_2 N - 1$ passes through the network, as presented in (Wu and Feng, 1981).

Finally, the hypercube has N crosspoints for N PEs, with a diameter of $\log_2 N - 1$, as shown in Figure 10-2h. The smaller number of crosspoints with respect to the perfect shuffle topology is balanced by a greater connection complexity in the PEs.

Let us now consider the behavior of blocking in interconnection networks. Figure 10-4a shows a configuration in which four processors are interconnected with a two-stage perfect shuffle network in which each crosspoint either passes both inputs straight through to

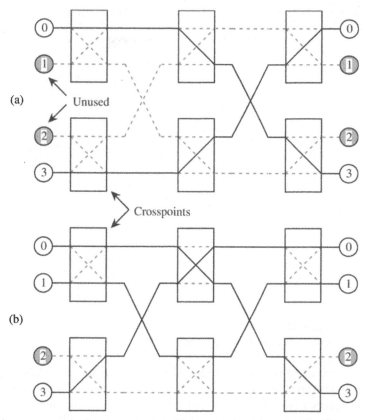

Figure 10-4
(a) Crosspoint settings for connections $0 \rightarrow 3$ and $3 \rightarrow 0$; (b) adjusted settings to accommodate
connection $1 \rightarrow 1$.

the outputs, or exchanges the inputs to the outputs. A path is enabled from processor 0 to
processor 3, and another path is enabled from processor 3 to processor 0. Neither processor 1 nor processor 2 needs to communicate, but they participate in some arbitrary connections as a side effect of the crosspoint settings that are already specified.

Suppose that we want to add another connection, from processor 1 to processor 1.
There is no way to adjust the unused crosspoints to accommodate this new connection
because all of the crosspoints are already set, and the needed connection does not occur as
a side effect of the current settings. Thus, connection $1 \rightarrow 1$ is now blocked.

If we are allowed to disturb the settings of the crosspoints that are currently in use,
then we can accommodate all three connections, as illustrated in Figure 10-4b. An interconnection network that operates in this manner is referred to as a **rearrangeably
nonblocking network**.

The three-stage **Clos network** is **strictly nonblocking**. That is, there is no need to
disturb the existing settings of the crosspoints in order to add another connection. An
example of a three-stage Clos network is shown in Figure 10-5 for four PEs. In the input
stage, each crosspoint is actually a crossbar that can make any connection of the two

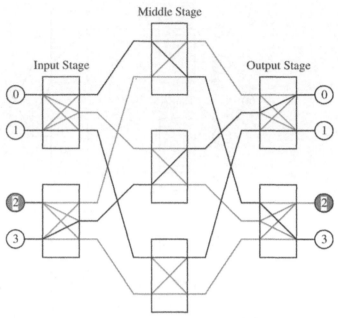

Middle Stage

Input Stage

Output Stage

Figure 10-5
A three-stage Clos network for four PEs.

inputs to the three outputs. The crosspoints in the middle stage and the output stage are also small crossbars. The number of inputs to each input crosspoint and the number of outputs from each output crosspoint is selected according to the desired complexity of the crosspoints and the desired complexity of the middle stage.

The middle stage has three crosspoints in this example, and in general, there are $(n-1) + (p-1) + 1 = n + p - 1$ crosspoints in the middle stage, in which n is the number of inputs to each-input crosspoint and p is the number of outputs from each output crosspoint. This is how the three-stage Clos network maintains a strictly nonblocking property. There are $n-1$ ways that an input can be blocked at the output of an input-stage crosspoint as a result of existing connections. Similarly, there are $p-1$ ways that existing connections can block a desired connection into an output crosspoint. In order to ensure that every desired connection can be made between available input and output ports, there must be one more path available.

For this case, $n = 2$ and $p = 2$, and so we need $n + p - 1 = 2 + 2 - 1 = 3$ paths from every input crosspoint to every output crosspoint. Architecturally, this relationship is satisfied with three crosspoints in the middle stage that each connect every input crosspoint to every output crosspoint.

EXAMPLE 10-1   Strictly Nonblocking Network

For this example, we want to design a strictly nonblocking (three-stage Clos) network for 12 channels (12 inputs and 12 outputs to the network) while maintaining a low maximum complexity of any crosspoint in the network.

There are a number of ways that we can organize the network. For the input stage, we can have two input nodes with six inputs per node, or six input nodes with two inputs per node, to list just two possibilities. We have similar choices for the output stage Let us start by looking at a configuration that has two nodes in the input stage and two nodes in the output stage, with six inputs for each node in the input stage and six outputs for each node in the output stage. For this case, $n = p = 6$, which means that $n + p - 1 = 11$ nodes are needed in the middle stage, as shown in Figure 10-6. The maximum complexity of any node for this case is $6 \times 11 = 66$, for each of the input and output nodes.

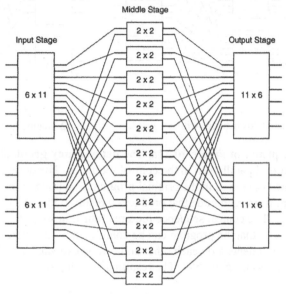

Figure 10-6
A 12-channel three-stage Clos network with $n = p = 6$.

Now let us try using six input nodes and six output nodes, with two inputs for each input node and two outputs for each output node. For this case, $n = p = 2$, which means that $n + p - 1 = 3$ nodes are needed in the middle stage, as shown in Figure 10-7. The maximum node complexity for this case is $6 \times 6 = 36$ for each of the middle-stage nodes, which is better than the maximum node complexity of 66 for the previous case.

Similarly, networks for $n = p = 4$ and $n = p = 3$ are shown in Figures 10-8 and 10-9, respectively. The maximum node complexity for each of these networks is $4 \times 7 = 28$ and $4 \times 4 = 16$, respectively. Among the four configurations studied here, $n = p = 3$ gives the lowest maximum node complexity.

∎

10.1.4 Mapping an Algorithm onto a Parallel Architecture

The process of mapping an algorithm onto a parallel architecture begins with a **dependency analysis** in which data dependencies among the operations in a program are identified. Consider the C code shown in Figure 10-10. In an ordinary SISD processor, the four numbered statements require four time steps to complete, as illustrated in the control

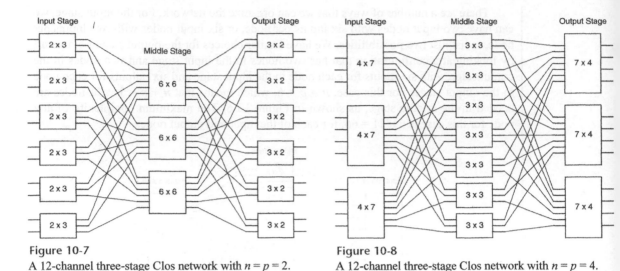

Figure 10-7
A 12-channel three-stage Clos network with $n = p = 2$.

Figure 10-8
A 12-channel three-stage Clos network with $n = p = 4$.

sequence of Figure 10-11a. The **dependency graph** shown in Figure 10-11b exposes the natural parallelism in the control sequence. The dependency graph is created by assigning each operation in the original program to a node in the graph, and then drawing a directed arc from each node that produces a result to the node(s) that needs it.

The control sequence requires four time steps to complete, but the dependency graph shows that the program can be completed in just three time steps, since operations 0 and 1 do not depend on each other and can be executed simultaneously (as long as there are two processors available.) The resulting speedup of

$$\frac{T_{Sequential}}{T_{Parallel}} = \frac{4}{3} = 1.3$$

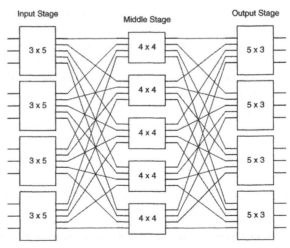

Figure 10-9
A 12-channel three-stage Clos network with $n = p = 3$.

```
                    func(x, y)   /* Compute (x² + y²) × y² */
                    int x, y;
Operation           {
numbers
                    int temp0, temp1, temp2, temp3;

          0    temp0 = x * x;
          1    temp1 = y * y;
          2    temp2 = temp0 + temp1;
          3    temp3 = temp1 * temp2;


                    return(temp3);
                    }
```

Figure 10-10
A C function computes $(x^2 + y^2) \times y^2$.

may not be very great, but for other programs, the opportunity for speedup can be substantial, as we will see.

Consider a matrix multiplication problem $A\mathbf{x} = \mathbf{b}$ in which A is a 4×4 matrix and $\mathbf{x}$ and $\mathbf{b}$ are both $4{\times}1$ matrices, as illustrated in Figure 10-12a. Our goal is to solve for the b_i, using the equations shown in Figure 10-12b. Every operation is assigned a number, starting from 0 and ending at 27. There are 28 operations, assuming that no operations can

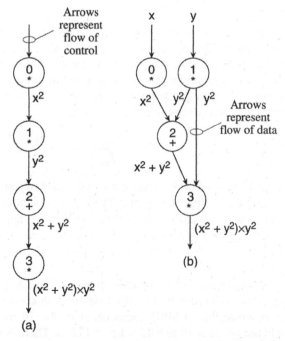

Figure 10-11
(a) Control sequence for C program; (b) dependency graph for C program.

(a)

$$\begin{bmatrix} a_{00} & a_{01} & a_{02} & a_{03} \\ a_{10} & a_{11} & a_{12} & a_{13} \\ a_{20} & a_{21} & a_{22} & a_{23} \\ a_{30} & a_{31} & a_{32} & a_{33} \end{bmatrix} \begin{bmatrix} x_0 \\ x_1 \\ x_2 \\ x_3 \end{bmatrix} = \begin{bmatrix} b_0 \\ b_1 \\ b_2 \\ b_3 \end{bmatrix}$$

(b)

$$b_0 = \overset{0}{\boxed{a_{00}x_0}} + \overset{4}{\boxed{a_{01}x_1}} + \overset{1}{\boxed{a_{02}x_2}} + \overset{6}{\quad} \overset{2}{\quad} \overset{5}{\quad} \overset{3}{\boxed{a_{03}x_3}}$$

$$b_1 = \overset{7}{\boxed{a_{10}x_0}} + \overset{11}{\boxed{a_{11}x_1}} + \overset{8}{\boxed{a_{12}x_2}} + \overset{13}{\quad}\overset{9}{\quad}\overset{12}{\quad}\overset{10}{\boxed{a_{13}x_3}}$$

$$b_2 = \overset{14}{\boxed{a_{20}x_0}} + \overset{18}{\boxed{a_{21}x_1}} + \overset{15}{\boxed{a_{22}x_2}} + \overset{20}{\quad}\overset{16}{\quad}\overset{19}{\quad}\overset{17}{\boxed{a_{23}x_3}}$$

$$b_3 = \overset{21}{\boxed{a_{30}x_0}} + \overset{25}{\boxed{a_{31}x_1}} + \overset{22}{\boxed{a_{32}x_2}} + \overset{27}{\quad}\overset{23}{\quad}\overset{26}{\quad}\overset{24}{\boxed{a_{33}x_3}}$$

Figure 10-12
(a) Problem setup for Ax = b; (b) equations for computing the b_i.

receive more than two operands. A program running on a SISD processor that computes the b_i requires 28 time steps to complete, if we make a simplifying assumption that additions and multiplications take the same amount of time.

A dependency graph for this problem is shown in Figure 10-13. The worst-case path from any input to any output traverses three nodes, and so the entire process can be completed in three time steps, resulting in a speedup of

$$\frac{T_{Sequential}}{T_{Parallel}} = \frac{28}{3} = 9.3$$

Now that we know the structure of the data dependencies, we can plan a mapping of the nodes of the dependency graph to PEs in a parallel processor. Figure 10-14a shows a mapping in which each node of the dependency graph for b_0 is assigned to a unique PE. The time required to complete each addition is 1 ns, the time to complete each multiplication is 10 ns, and the time to communicate between PEs is 100 ns. These numbers are for a fictitious processor, but the methods extend to real parallel processors.

As we can see from the parallel time of 212 ns to execute the program using the mapping shown in Figure 10-14a, the time spent in communication dominates performance. This is worse than a SISD approach, since the 16 multiplications and the 12 additions would require 16×10 ns $+ 12 \times 1$ ns $= 172$ ns. There is no processor-to-processor communication cost within a SISD processor, and so only the computation time is considered.

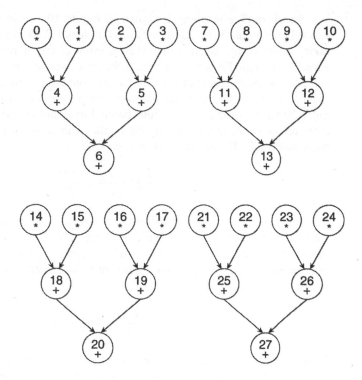

Figure 10-13
Dependency graph for matrix multiplication.

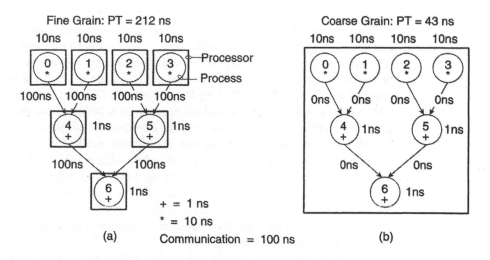

Figure 10-14
Mapping tasks to PEs: (a) one PE per operation; (b) one PE per b_i.

An alternative mapping is shown in Figure 10-14b in which all of the operations needed to compute b_0 are clustered onto the same PE. We have thus increased the **granularity** of the computation, which is a measure of the number of operations assigned to each PE. A single PE is a sequential, SISD processor, and so none of the operations within a cluster can be executed in parallel, but the communication time among the operations is reduced to 0. As shown in the diagram, the parallel time for b_0 is now 43 ns, which is much better than either the previous parallel mapping or a straight SISD mapping. Since there are no dependencies among the b_i, they can all be computed in parallel, using one processor per b_i. The actual speedup is now:

$$\frac{T_{Sequential}}{T_{Parallel}} = \frac{172}{43} = 4$$

Communication is always a bottleneck in parallel processing, and so it is important that we maintain a proper balance. We should not be led astray into thinking that adding processors to a problem will speed it up when in fact adding processors can increase execution time as a result of communication time. In general, we want to maintain a ratio in which:

$$\frac{T_{Communication}}{T_{Computation}} \leq 1$$

In this way, we can ensure that the bulk of the work goes into processing rather than just shuttling data between processors. We can think of this as a tradeoff between the "army of ants" (fine-grain) and "herd of elephants" (coarse-grain) approaches.

■ 10.2 SUPERSCALAR MACHINES AND THE POWERPC

In the pipelining discussion in Chapter 6, we saw how several instructions can be in various phases of execution at once. In this section, we look at superscalar architecture, which, with separate execution units, goes beyond pipelining by allowing several instructions to be executed simultaneously. In a superscalar architecture, there might be one or more separate **Integer Units** (IUs), **Floating-Point Units** (FPUs), and **Branch Processing Units** (BPUs). This implies that instructions need to be scheduled into the various execution units and, further, that instructions might be executed out of order.

Out-of-order execution means that instructions need to be examined prior to **dispatching** them to an execution unit, not only to determine which unit should execute them, but also to determine whether executing them out of order would result in an incorrect program, because of dependencies among the instructions. This in turn implies an **Instruction Unit**, IU, that can prefetch instructions into an instruction queue, determine the kinds of instructions and the dependence relations among them, and schedule them into the various execution units.

As an example of a modern superscalar architecture, let us examine the Motorola PowerPC™. The PowerPC (PPC) line of processors has made its mark on superscalar architecture, starting with the PPC 601 up through (as of this writing) the dual-core PA6T-

1682 running at 2 GHz. The main principles can be found in the original PPC 601, which serves to illustrate the important features of superscalar architectures.

10.2.1 Instruction Set Architecture of the PowerPC

The PowerPC is a 32-bit general-register RISC machine with an ISA that includes:

- 32 32-bit general-purpose integer registers (GPRs);
- 32 64-bit floating-point registers (FPRs);
- 8 4-bit condition code registers;
- nearly 50 special-purpose 32-bit registers that are used to control various aspects of memory management and the operating system;
- over 250 instructions (many of which are special-purpose).

10.2.2 Hardware Architecture of the PowerPC

Figure 10-15 shows the microarchitecture of the PowerPC. The flow of instructions and data proceeds via the System Interface, shown at the bottom of the figure, into the 32 KByte cache. From there, instructions are fetched eight at a time into the Instruction Unit, shown at the top of the fiture.The issue logic within the Instruction Unit examines the instructions in the queue for their kind and dependence and issues them into one of the three execution units IU, BPU, or FPU.

The IU is shown as containing the GPR file and an integer exception register, XER, which holds information about exceptions that arise within the IU. The IU can execute most integer instructions in a single clock cycle, thus obviating the need for any kind of pipelining of integer instructions.

The FPU contains the FPRs and the floating-point status and control register (FPSCR). The FPSCR contains information about floating-point exceptions and the type of result produced by the FPR. The FPU is pipelined, and most FP instructions can be issued at a rate of one per clock.

As mentioned above in the section on pipelining, branch instructions, especially conditional branch instructions, pose a bottleneck when trying to overlap instruction execution. This is because the branch condition must first be ascertained to be true; for example, "branch on plus" must test the N flag to ascertain that it is cleared. The branch address must then be computed, which often involves address arithmetic. Only then can the PC be loaded with the branch address.

The PowerPC attacks this problem in several ways. First, as mentioned above, there are eight four-bit condition code registers instead of the usual one. This allows up to eight instructions to have separate condition code bits, and therefore not interfere with one another's ability to set condition codes. The BPU looks in the instruction queue; if it finds a conditional branch instruction, it proceeds to compute the branch target address ahead of time and fetches instructions at the branch target. If the branch is taken, this results in effectively a zero-cycle branch, since the instruction at the branch target has already been fetched in anticipation of the branch condition being satisfied. The BPU also has a link register (LR) in which it can store subroutine return addresses, thus saving one GPR as well as several other registers used for special purposes. Note that the BPU can issue its

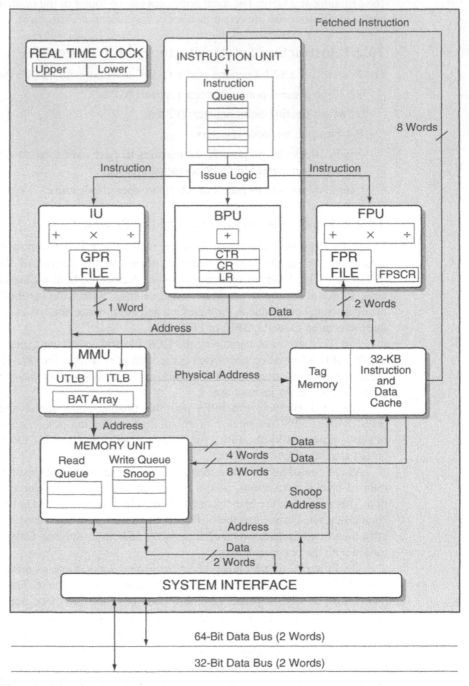

Figure 10-15
The PowerPC architecture (Source: adapted from the Motorola PowerPC 601 user manual).

addresses over a separate bus directly to the MME and Memory unit for prefetching instructions.

The RTC unit shown in the figure is a real time clock which has a calendar range of 137 years, with an accuracy of 1 ns.

The MMU and Memory Unit assist in fetching both instructions and data. Note the separate path for data items that goes from the cache directly to the GPR and FPR register files.

The PowerPC is typical of the modern general-purpose microprocessor. Current microprocessor families are superscalar in design, often having several of each kind of execution unit.

10.3 VLIW MACHINES, AND THE ITANIUM

An important architectural variation that in a sense competes with superscalar architectures is the **VLIW** (very long instruction word) architecture. In VLIW machines, multiple operations are packed into a single instruction word that may be 128 or more bits wide. A VLIW machine has multiple execution units, similar in that respect to a superscalar machine.

For a superscalar machine, the number of execution units has no impact on the ISA. In general, a single instruction encodes a single operation, and there can be multiple instructions executing simultaneously. The choice of how to issue instructions to execution units is made by the hardware at run time. For a VLIW processor, however, the ISA is designed with the multiple execution units in mind. A single instruction encodes multiple operations, and it is up to the compiler to determine how to package operations into instructions. This relieves the CPU of the need to examine instructions for dependencies, or to order or reorder instructions.

A disadvantage of this approach is that the compiler must out of necessity be pessimistic in its estimates of dependencies. If it cannot find enough instructions to fill the instruction word, it must fill the blank spots with NOP instructions. Furthermore, VLIW architectures require software to be recompiled to take advantage of the enhancements.

Despite these disadvantages, a supporting development has thrust VLIW architecture to the forefront. Simultaneous multithreading (SMT) transforms independent-thread parallelism into instruction-level parallelism (ILP). (Intel's Hyper-Threading is essentially SMT.) SMT makes a single processor appear to be several processors by providing multiple execution units with their own state while sharing other resources such as the memory. The idea is to identify independent threads of execution at compile time, and then schedule them on multiple cores in a VLIW style of architecture. This differs from ordinary single-threaded instruction-level parallelism, which relies on speculative execution and a runtime analysis that avoids or removes single-thread dependencies.

In order to support multiple cores on a single IC, the cores are simpler but are clocked at a lower rate. This may seem counterintuitive at first, but the improvement in the number of operations executed per cycle is greater than the reduction in clock rate. Further, this approach consumes less power than increasing the clock rate and putting more resources into speculative execution—the power budget is a significant limiting factor.

SMT fits naturally with applications that have inherent thread parallelism: database processing, scientific programs, and graphics applications. However, SMT has not yet fully made its way into everyday processing, at least in part because of the software development needed to support multiple threads. Applications need to be engineered to take advantage of SMT and for the moment, SMT is used primarily in high-end processors such as the Itanium, which is discussed next.

10.3.1 Case Study: The Intel IA-64 (Itanium) Architecture

In this section, we take a look at a microprocessor family developed by an alliance between Intel and Hewlett-Packard. We first look into the background that led to the decision to develop a new architecture, and then we look at the current state of the architecture.

10.3.2 Background—the 80x86 Cisc Architecture

In the late 1990s, the Intel 80x86 architecture, which was running on some 80% of desktop computers at the time, had its roots in the 8086 microprocessor that was designed in the late 1970s. The architectural roots of the family go back to the original Intel 8080, designed in the early 1970s. Being a persistent advocate of upward compatibility, Intel in the 1990s had been in a sense hobbled by a CISC architecture that was over 20 years old. Other vendors such as Motorola abandoned hardware compatibility for modernization, relying upon emulators to ease the transition to a new ISA.

In any case, Intel and Hewlett-Packard decided that the x86 architecture would soon reach the end of its useful life, and they began joint research on a new architecture. Intel and Hewlett-Packard have been quoted as saying that RISC architectures had "run out of gas," so to speak, so their search led in other directions. The result of their research led to the IA-64, which stands for "Intel Architecture-64." The first of the IA-64 family was known by the code name **Merced**, after the Merced River, near San Jose, California, but has since taken on the name **Itanium**.

10.3.3 The Itanium: an Epic Architecture

Intel refers to the Itanium architecture as Explicitly Parallel Instruction Computing, or **EPIC**. Intel takes pains to point out that it is *not* a VLIW nor even an LIW machine, perhaps out of sensitivity to the previous bad reputation that VLIW machines had received; however, some industry analysts refer to it as "the VLIW-like EPIC architecture."

Features

The Itanium has the following characteristics:

- 128 64-bit general-purpose registers (GPRs) and 128 80-bit floating-point registers (FPRs);
- 64 one-bit predicate registers (explained below);
- Instruction words contain three instructions packed into one 128-bit parcel;
- Execution units, roughly equivalent to IU, FPU, and BPU, appear in multiples of three, and the IA-64 instructions are scheduled into these multiples;

- It is the burden of the compiler to schedule the instructions to take advantage of the multiple execution units;
- Most of the instructions seem to be RISC-like, although the processor (still!) executes 80x86 binary codes, in a dedicated execution unit known as the DXU;
- Speculative loads: The processor loads values from memory well in advance of when they are needed. Exceptions caused by the loads are postponed until execution has proceeded to the place where the loads would normally have occurred;
- Predication (*not* prediction), where both sides of a conditional branch instruction are executed and the results from the side not taken are discarded.

These latter two features are discussed in more detail in the following two sections.

The Instruction Word

The 128-bit instruction word, shown in Figure 10-16, has three 41-bit instructions and a five-bit template. The template is placed by the compiler to tell the CPU which instructions in and near that instruction word can execute in parallel, hence the term "Explicit." The CPU need not analyze the code at run time to expose instructions that can be executed in parallel because the compiler determines that ahead of time. Compilers for most VLIW machines must place NOP instructions in slots where instructions cannot be executed in parallel. In the IA-64 scheme, the presence of the template identifies those instructions in the word that can and cannot be executed in parallel, so the compiler is free to schedule instructions into all three slots, regardless of whether they can be executed in parallel.

The six-bit predicate field in each instruction represents a tag placed there by the compiler to identify which leg of a conditional branch the instruction is a part of, and is used in branch predication.

Branch Predication

Rather than using branch prediction, the IA-64 architecture uses *branch predication* to remove penalties due to mis-predicted branches. When the compiler encounters a conditional branch instruction that is a candidate for predication, it selects two unique labels and labels the instructions in each leg of the branch instruction with one of the two labels, identifying which leg they belong to. Both legs can then be executed in parallel. There are 64 one-bit predicate registers, one corresponding to each of the 64 possible predicate identifiers.

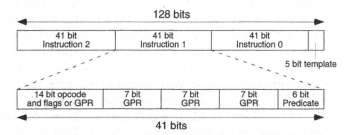

Figure 10-16
The 128-bit IA-64 instruction word.

When the actual branch outcome is known, the corresponding one-bit predicate register is set if the branch outcome is TRUE, and the one-bit predicate register corresponding to the FALSE label is cleared. Then the results from instructions having the correct predicate label are kept, and results from instructions having the incorrect (mis-predicted) label are discarded.

Speculative Loads

The Itanium architecture also employs **speculative loads**; that is, it examines the instruction stream for upcoming load instructions and loads the value ahead of time, *speculating* that the value will actually be needed and will not have been altered by intervening operations. If successful, this eliminates the normal latency inherent in memory accesses. The compiler examines the instruction stream for candidate load operations that it can "hoist" to a location earlier in the instruction sequence. It inserts a *check* instruction at the point where the load instruction was originally located. The data value is thus available in the CPU when the check instruction is encountered.

The problem that is normally faced by speculative loads is that the load operation may generate an exception, for example because the address is invalid. However, the exception may not be genuine, because the load may be beyond a branch instruction that is not taken, and thus would never actually be executed. The IA-64 architecture postpones processing the exception until the check instruction is encountered. If the branch is not taken then the check instruction will not be executed, and thus the exception will not be processed.

All of this complexity places a heavy burden on the compiler, which must be clever about how it schedules operations into the instruction words.

80x86 Compatibility

Intel was granted a patent for a method of supporting two instruction sets, one of which is the x86 instruction set. The patent describes instructions that allow switching between the two execution modes and sharing data between them. Roughly 10–15 mm^2 of the 432 mm^2 Itanium Madison design is devoted to the x86 instruction set, and so the legacy x86 lives on even at the expense of valuable die area.

Instruction Bundles

The IA-64 instruction stream is logically organized into instruction groups, which are collections of instructions that have no dependencies that would prevent them from being executed in parallel. The compiler determines instruction groups by applying rules, such as ensuring that no instruction in a group writes to a general-purpose register that is needed as an input to a later instruction in the group. The instruction groups are then assigned to instruction bundles, with three instructions per bundle. Instruction groups may span more than one instruction bundle, and one bundle may contain instructions from two groups.

There are six basic Itanium instruction types that must be arranged into bundles according to the resources they use. Figure 10-17 shows the six instruction types. The A instructions are for simple ALU operations like adds, subtracts, and bit-wise logical operations. The I instructions are non-ALU operations that need special resources like a multiplier or barrel shifter. M, F, and B instructions are for operations involving memory, floating point, and branches, respectively. The L+X instruction type allows two adjacent 41-bit instructions within a bundle to be combined into an instruction with a 64-bit immediate value, or can be used for long branches and calls.

Type	Description	Execution Unit Type
A	Integer (ALU)	I-unit or M-unit
I	Integer (non-ALU)	I-unit
M	Memory	M-unit
F	Floating point	F-unit
B	Branch	B-unit
L+X	Extended (64 bit immediate)	I-unit

Figure 10-17
Itanium instruction types.

The five-bit Template field tells the processor which types of instructions are in each slot, and also locates the position of a **stop** within a bundle, which indicates a transition between two instruction groups. Figure 10-18 shows the assignment of template values to instruction mixes.

Template	Instruction Slot 0	Instruction Slot 1	Instruction Slot 2	
0	M	I	I	
1	M	I	I	
2	M	I	I	
3	M	I	I	
4	M	L	X	
5	M	L	X	
8	M	M	I	
9	M	M	I	
10	M	M	I	
11	M	M	I	
12	M	F	I	
13	M	F	I	
14	M	M	F	
15	M	M	F	
16	M	I	B	
17	M	I	B	
18	M	B	B	
19	M	B	B	
22	B	B	B	
23	B	B	B	
24	M	M	B	
25	M	M	B	
28	M	F	B	
29	M	F	B	

Figure 10-18
Allowable combinations of instruction types assigned to instruction slots.

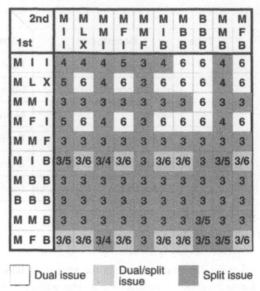

Figure 10-19

Maximum number of IA-64 instructions that can be executed for each pairing of bundles.

The original Merced implementation of the Itanium has two M units, two I units, two F units, and three B units. The Merced is a "two-banger" machine, so named for the up-and-down positions of a piston in an automobile engine. The Merced can execute two bundles at a time. A four-banger can execute four bundles at a time, in theory anyway: there need to be enough available execution units to make use of all of this capability.

Figure 10-19 shows the maximum number of instructions that can actually be executed at the same time in the two-banger, which has two M units, two I units, two F units, and three B units. The rows in the matrix correspond to the first of a pair of bundles, and the columns correspond to the second bundle in the pair. Templates 0, 1, 2, and 3 are all M-I-I bundles. If two of these bundles form a pair, then at most only four of the potential six instructions can be executed, because four I units are needed but only two are available. This is indicated by the 4 entry where the M-I-I row and the M-I-I column meet in the matrix. The two unused slots would be filled with NOPs.

As we can see in the matrix, the Merced implementation is starved for execution units in most bundle combinations, resulting in a "split issue" that allows less than a full issue of six instructions. Subsequent implementations, however, contain more processing units, which relieves the starvation problem.

■ 10.4 CASE STUDY: EXTENSIONS TO THE INSTRUCTION SET—THE INTEL MMX/SSEX AND MOTOROLA ALTIVEC SIMD INSTRUCTIONS

As integrated circuit technology provides ever-increasing capacity within the processor, processor vendors search for new ways to use that capacity. One way that both Intel and Motorola capitalized on the additional capacity was to extend their ISAs with new registers and instructions that are specialized for processing streams or blocks of data. In the late 1990s, Intel provided the multimedia extensions (MMX) to their Pentium processors and Motorola provided the AltiVec extension to their PowerPC processors. The MMX extensions led to the SSE, SSE2, and SSE3 extensions in the Intel line and have now been adopted by Apple in its new Intel-based Macintosh operating system, which has traditionally used Motorola processors with the Motorola-based AltiVec extensions. In this section we discuss why the extensions are useful and how Intel and Motorola implemented them.

10.4.1 Background

The processing of graphics, audio, and communication streams requires that the same repetitive operations be performed on large blocks of data. For example, a graphic image may be several megabytes in size, with repetitive operations required on the entire image for filtering, image enhancement, or other processing. So-called streaming audio (audio that is transmitted over a network in real time) may require continuous operation on the stream as it arrives. Likewise three-dimensional (3-D) image generation, virtual-reality environments, and even computer games require extraordinary amounts of processing power. In the past the solution adopted by many computer system manufacturers was to include special-purpose processors explicitly for handling these kinds of operations.

Although Intel and Motorola took slightly different approaches, the results are quite similar. Both instruction sets are extended with SIMD instructions and data types. The SIMD approach applies the same instruction to a **vector** of data items simultaneously. The term "vector" refers to a collection of data items, usually bytes or words.

Vector processors and processor extensions are by no means a new concept. The earliest CRAY and IBM 370 series computers had vector operations or extensions. In fact these machines had much more powerful vector-processing capabilities than these first microprocessor-based offerings from Intel and Motorola. Nevertheless, the Intel and Motorola extensions provide a considerable speedup in the localized, recurring operations for which they were designed. These extensions are covered in more detail below, but Figure 10-20 gives an introduction to the process for the MMX extensions (the SSE enhancements are similar, with a 128-bit word width starting with the SSE2). The figure shows the Intel PADDB (Packed Add Bytes) instruction, which performs eight-bit addition on the vector of eight bytes in register MM0 with the vector of eight bytes in register MM1, storing the results in register MM0. The SSE2 and SSE3 implementations are similar, but with 16 bytes in parallel.

10.4.2 The Base Architectures

Before we cover the SIMD extensions to the two processors, we will take a look at the base architectures of the two machines. Surprisingly, the two processors could hardly be more different in their ISAs.

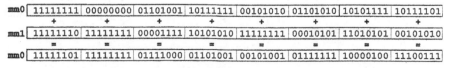

Figure 10-20
The vector addition of eight bytes by the Intel PADDB mm0, mm1 instruction.

The Intel Pentium

Aside from special-purpose registers that are used in operating-system-related matters, the Pentium ISA contains eight 32-bit integer registers, with each register having its own "personality." For example, the Pentium ISA contains a single accumulator (EAX) that holds arithmetic operands and results. The processor also includes eight 80-bit floating-point registers, that, as we will see, also serve as vector registers for the MMX instructions. The Pentium instruction set would be characterized as **CISC** (Complicated Instruction Set Computer). As discussed in the context of CISC vs. RISC in Chapter 6, the Pentium instructions vary in size from a single byte to nine bytes in length, and many Pentium instructions accomplish very complicated actions. The Pentium has many addressing modes, and most of its arithmetic instructions allow one operand or the result to be in either memory or a register. Much of the Intel ISA was shaped by the decision to make it binary-compatible with the earliest member of the family, the 8086/8088, introduced in 1978. (The 8086 ISA was itself shaped by Intel's decision to make it assembly-language compatible with the venerable eight-bit 8080, introduced in 1973.)

The Motorola PowerPC

The PowerPC, in contrast, was developed by a consortium of IBM, Motorola and Apple, "from the ground up," forsaking backward compatibility for the ability to incorporate the latest in RISC technology. The result was an ISA with fewer, simpler instructions, all instructions exactly one 32-bit word wide, 32 32-bit general-purpose integer registers and 32 64-bit floating-point registers. The ISA employs the "load/store" approach to memory access: memory operands have to be loaded into registers by load and store instructions before they can be used. All other instructions must access their operands and results in registers.

As we shall see below, the primary influence that the core ISAs described above have on the vector operations is in the way they access memory.

10.4.3 VECTOR Registers

Both architectures provide an additional set of dedicated registers in which vector operands and results are stored. Figure 10-21 shows the vector register sets for the two processors. Intel, perhaps for reasons of space, "aliased" their floating-point registers as MMX registers. This means that the Pentium's eight 64-bit floating-point registers also do double duty as MMX registers. This approach has the disadvantage that the registers can be used for only one kind of operation at a time. The register set must be "flushed" with a special instruction, EMMS (Empty MMX State), after executing MMX instructions and before executing floating-point instructions. The SSE, SSE2, and SSE3 implementations have their own register file and therefore have since eliminated the aliasing penalty.

Motorola, perhaps because their PowerPC processor occupies less silicon, implemented 32 128-bit vector registers as a new set, separate and distinct from their floating-point registers.

Vector Operands

Both Intel and Motorola's vector operations can operate on 8-, 16-, 32-, 64-, and in Motorola's case, 128-bit integers. Unlike Intel, which only supported integer vectors in the

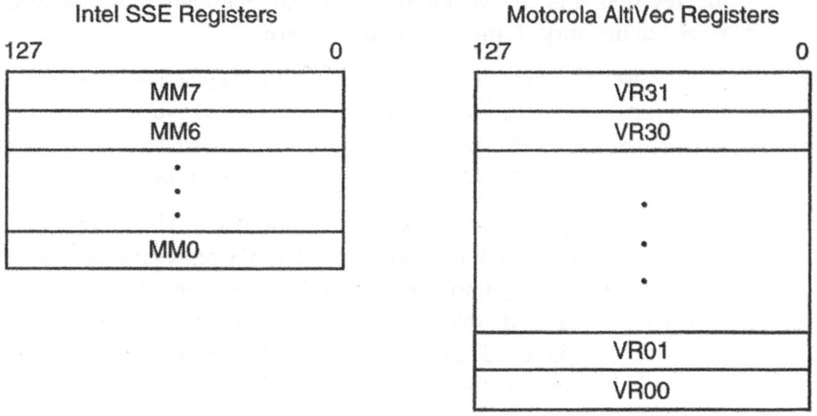

Intel SSE Registers

127   0

| MM7 |
| MM6 |
| •
•
• |
| MM0 |

Motorola AltiVec Registers

127   0

| VR31 |
| VR30 |
| •
•
• |
| VR01 |
| VR00 |

Figure 10-21
Intel and Motorola vector registers.

MMX, Motorola also supported 32-bit floating-point numbers and operations. The Intel SSE and later versions all support floating-point operations.

Both Intel and Motorola's vector registers can be filled, or packed, with 8-, 16-, 32-, 64-, and 128-bit data values. For byte operands, this results in eight or 16-way parallelism, as eight or 16 bytes are operated on simultaneously. This is how the SIMD nature of the vector operation is expressed: the same operation is performed on all of the objects in a given vector register.

Loading to and Storing from the Vector Registers

Intel continued their CISC approach in the way they load operands into their vector registers. There are two instructions for loading and storing values to and from the vector registers, MOVD and MOVQ, which move 32-bit doublewords and 64-bit quadwords, respectively. (The Intel word is 16 bits in size.) The syntax is:

```
MOVD       mm, mm/m32             ;move doubleword to a vector reg.
MOVD       mm/m32, mm             ;move doubleword from a vector reg.
MOVQ       mm, mm/m64             ;move quadword to a vector reg.
MOVQ       mm/m64, mm             ;move quadword from a vector reg.
```

- *mm* stands for one of the 8 MM vector registers;
- *mm/mm32* stands for one of the integer registers, an MM register, or a memory location;
- *mm/m64* stands for either an MM register or a memory location.

In addition, in the Intel vector arithmetic operations one of the operands can be in memory, as we will see below.

Motorola likewise remained true to their professed RISC philosophy in their load and store operations. The only way to access an operand in memory is through the vector load and store operations. There is no way to move an operand between any of the other internal registers and the vector registers. All operands must be loaded from memory and stored to memory. Typical load opcodes are:

```
lvebx      vD, rA|0, rB      ;load byte to vector reg vD, indexed.
lvehx      vD, rA|0, rB      ;move halfword to vector reg vD indexed.
lvewx      vD, rA|0, rB      ;move word to vector reg vD indexed.
lvx        vD, rA|0, rB      ;move doubleword to vector reg vD.
```

where vD stands for one of the 32 vector registers. The memory address of the operand is computed from (rA|0 + rB), where rA and rB represent any two of the integer registers r0-r32 and the "|0" symbol means that the value zero may be substituted for rA. The byte, half word, word, or doubleword is fetched from that address.

The term "indexed" in the list above refers to the location where the byte, halfword or word will be stored in the vector register. The least significant bits of the memory address specify the index into the vector register. For example, LSBs 011 would specify that the byte should be loaded into the third byte of the register. Other bytes in the vector register are undefined.

The store operations work exactly as the load instructions above except that the value from one of the vector registers is stored in memory.

10.4.4 Vector Arithmetic Operations

The vector arithmetic operations form the heart of the SIMD process. We will see that there is a new form of arithmetic, **saturation arithmetic**, and several new and exotic operations.

Saturation Arithmetic

Both vector processors provide the option of doing **saturation arithmetic** instead of the more familiar modulo wraparound kind discussed in Chapters 2 and 3. Saturation arithmetic works just like two's complement arithmetic as long as the results do not overflow or underflow. When results do overflow or underflow, in saturation arithmetic the result is held at the maximum or minimum allowable value, respectively, rather than being allowed to wrap around. For example, two's complement bytes are saturated at the high end at +127 and at the low end at −128. Unsigned bytes are saturated at 255 and 0. If an arithmetic result overflows or underflows these bounds the result is clipped, or "saturated," at the boundary.

The need for saturation arithmetic is encountered in the processing of color information. If color is represented by a byte in which 0 represents black and 255 represents white, then saturation allows the color to remain pure black or pure white after an operation rather than inverting upon overflow or underflow.

Instruction Formats

As the two architectures have different approaches to addressing modes, so their SIMD instruction formats also differ. Intel continues using two-address instructions, where the first source operand can be in an MM register, an integer register, or memory, and the second operand and destination is an MM register:

OP mm, mm32or64   ;mm ← mm OP mm/mm32/64

Motorola requires all operands to be in vector registers and employs three-operand instructions:

OP Vd, Va, Vb [,Vc];   Vd ← Va OP Vb [OP Vc]

This approach has the advantage that no vector register need be overwritten. In addition, some instructions can employ a third operand, Vc.

Arithmetic Operations

Perhaps not too surprisingly, the MMX and AltiVec instructions are quite similar. Both provide operations on 8-, 16-, 32-, 64-, and in the AltiVec case, 128-bit operands. In Table 10.1 below we see examples of the variety of operations provided by the two technologies. The primary driving forces for providing these particular operations is a combination of wanting to provide potential users of the technology with operations that they will find needed and useful in their particular application, the amount of silicon available for the extension, and the base ISA.

Table 10.1   **MMX and AltiVec arithmetic instructions**

Operation	Operands (bits)	Arithmetic
Integer Add, Subtract, signed and unsigned (B)	8, 16, 32, 64, 128	Modulo, saturated
Integer Add, Subtract, store carry-out in vector register (M)	32	Modulo
Integer Multiply, store high- or low-order half (I)	16←16×16	—
Integer multiply add: Vd = Va *Vb + Vc (B)	16←8×8 32←16×16	Modulo, saturated
Shift Left, Right, Arithmetic Right (B)	8, 16, 32, 64(I)	—
Rotate Left, Right (M)	8, 16, 32	—
AND, AND NOT, OR, NOR, XOR (B)	64(I), 128(M)	—
Integer Multiply every other operand, store entire result, signed and unsigned (M)	16←8×8 32←16×16	Modulo, saturated
Maximum, minimum. Vd←Max,Min(Va, Vb) (M)	8, 16, 32	Signed, unsigned
Vector sum across word. Add objects in vector, add this sum to object in second vector, place result in third vector register (M)	Various	Modulo, saturated
Vector floating point operations, add, subtract, multiply-add, etc. (M)	32	IEEE floating point

10.4.5 Vector Compare Operations

The ordinary paradigm for conditional operations, compare and branch on condition, will not work for vector operations, because each operand undergoing the comparison can yield different results. For example, comparing two word vectors for equality could yield TRUE, FALSE, FALSE, TRUE. There is no good way to employ branches to select different code blocks depending upon the truth or falsity of the comparisons. As a result, vector comparisons in both MMX and AltiVec technologies result in the explicit generation of

mm0	11111111	00000000	00000000	10101010	00101010	01101010	10101111	10111101
	==	==	==	==	==	==	==	==
mm1	11111111	11111111	00000000	10101010	00101011	01101010	11010101	00101010
	↓	↓	↓	↓	↓	↓	↓	↓
mm0	11111111	00000000	11111111	11111111	00000000	11111111	00000000	00000000
	(T)	(F)	(T)	(T)	(F)	(T)	(F)	(F)

Figure 10-22
Comparing two MMX byte vectors for equality.

TRUE or FALSE. In both cases, TRUE is represented by all 1s, and FALSE by all 0s in the destination operand. For example, byte comparisons yield FFH or 00H, 16-bit comparisons yield FFFFH or 0000H, and so on for other operands. These values, all 1s or all 0s, can then be used as masks to update values.

Example: comparing two byte vectors for equality

Consider comparing two MMX byte vectors for equality. Figure 10-22 shows the results of the comparison: strings of 1s where the comparison succeeded and 0s where it failed. This comparison can be used in subsequent operations. Consider the high-level language conditional statement:

$$\text{if (mm0} == \text{mm1) mm2} = \text{mm2 else mm2} = 0;$$

The comparison in Figure 10-22 above yields the mask that can be used to control the bytewise assignment. Register mm2 is ANDed with the mask in mm0 and the result stored in mm2, as shown in Figure 10-23. By using various combinations of comparison operations and masks, a full range of conditional operations can be implemented.

Vector Permutation Operations

The AltiVec ISA also includes a useful instruction that allows the contents of one vector to be permuted, or rearranged, in an arbitrary fashion, with the permuted result stored in another vector register.

10.4.6 Case Study Summary

The SIMD extensions to the Pentium and PowerPC processors provide powerful operations that can be used for block data processing. At the time these SIMD extension appeared, there were no common compiler extensions for these instructions. As a result, programmers who wanted to use these extensions had to be willing to program in assem-

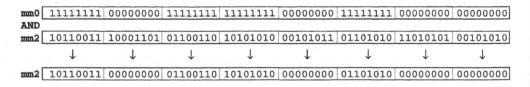

mm0 AND	11111111	00000000	11111111	11111111	00000000	11111111	00000000	00000000
mm2	10110011	10001101	01100110	10101010	00101011	01101010	11010101	00101010
	↓	↓	↓	↓	↓	↓	↓	↓
mm2	10110011	00000000	01100110	10101010	00000000	01101010	00000000	00000000

Figure 10-23
Conditional assignment of an MMX byte vector.

bly language. By now, compiler extensions are commonplace, such as with the Gnu gcc compiler.

An additional problem is that not all Pentium or PowerPC processors contain the extensions, only specialized versions. While the programmer can test for the presence of the extensions, in their absence the programmer must write a "manual" version of the algorithm. This means providing two sets of code, one that utilizes the extensions and one that utilizes the base ISA. This is still true to a degree: the SSE3 extensions are available only as an optional feature of machines supported by MacOS X for Intel.

■ 10.5 PROGRAMMABLE LOGIC DEVICES AND CUSTOM ICs

System architects and digital designers face many choices when embarking on a new design project. Given the overall project design requirements, what kind of performance must be achieved, what are the cost constraints, how many units are expected to be produced, and what is the development time frame? The digital logic designer can choose from a wide variety of IC solutions depending on the answers to these questions.

If the design requirements can be met by an off-the-shelf microprocessor, the designer may well take that route even though off-the-shelf microprocessors can cost several hundred dollars each. The microprocessors found in desktop and laptop computers comprise only about 5% of the total microprocessor market. The other 95% are embedded in items ranging from toys to microwave ovens, printers, and supercomputers.

There are many microprocessors that are developed specifically for embedded systems. These microprocessors, often called **microcontrollers** when used as part of an embedded system, range from four-bit and eight-bit processors, for use in applications such as small-appliance control and toys costing less than $.50 each, to 32-bit microprocessors for computationally intensive applications at correspondingly higher costs (but much less than off-the-shelf microprocessors). These devices differ from conventional microprocessors in that they have on-board RAM, ROM, and I/O. They often include integral clocks, counters, and other functional units to reduce the external part count. There are also many more variations on a given controller, such as the address space, the amount of RAM and ROM onboard, and the clock speed, to name just a few.

In many cases, off-the-shelf candidates do not have the specific processing capability required, or if they do, they are not cost effective for the particular application. This may be because they have too many unused features contributing to the cost or they require external parts that drive up total system cost. Many special-purpose applications require a large amount of processing power but cover a small problem domain. Examples include video and audio processors, graphics chips, and various medically related applications.

The designer must weigh the one-time development costs against the time-to-market constraints. With programmable logic devices the development costs are relatively small and the time to market is short. The per-item cost, however, will be high compared with a high-volume custom design. On the other end of the spectrum, a fully customized IC may cost over $200,000 in development costs alone and take weeks to months before parts are received, but once those costs have been incurred the per-item cost is low.

For quick development time and low development cost the designer turns to **programmable logic devices** (PLDs). These range from **programmable logic arrays**

(PLAs) and **programmable array logic** (PAL) devices to **complex programmable logic devices** (CPLDs) and **field-programmable gate arrays** (FPGAs). In the next section we discuss these devices, and we also discuss devices more suited to very high-volume uses: **application-specific integrated circuits** (ASICs) and fully customized ICs.

Designers often use the concept of **equivalent gates** in estimating the size of a logic device. Usually the equivalence is estimated relative to the two-input NAND gate. This method is only approximate because it does not take into account the size and complexity of interconnections. In the sections that follow, we describe the various PLDs, with some consideration of their size and typical usage. The reader should note that there are many different kinds of PLDs and a given PLD may contain fragments of smaller PLDs within it or may be a combination of several kinds of PLDs.

10.5.1 The Role of CAD Tools in PLD Design

Many of the devices described below may have hundreds of thousands of equivalent gates arranged in quite complex ways to suit the needs of a particular design. Computer-aided design (CAD) software is necessary to develop a design and program these devices, such as the Xilinx™ ISE tool suite. These integrated development environments allow the designer to develop the design using any combination of VHDL, Verilog, truth tables, and schematic capture. They have libraries of macro devices, such as ALUs, decoders and registers, that can be incorporated in the design by simply clicking and dragging the device from the device menu to the design screen. The design can be simulated with various input values and the behavior of the design can be verified prior to programming the devices. Some devices can be programmed repeatedly, others only once.

10.5.2 PLAs and PALs

Simple PLAs are described in Appendix A. PLAs and PALs are similar except that the OR gates in a PAL have a fixed number of inputs and the inputs are not programmable. PALs are more prevalent than PLAs because they are easier to manufacture and are less complex. Figure 10-24 shows a PAL device. Notice that each OR gate has a fan-in of two. In commercial devices, each OR gate output is usually connected to a **macrocell**, which is a small circuit containing a flip-flop, several multiplexers, and one or more tri-state drivers.

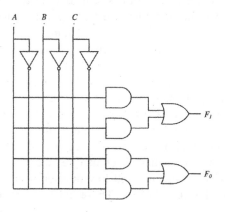

Figure 10-24
A PAL Device.

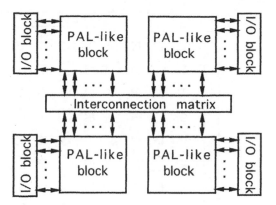

Figure 10-25
A complex programmable logic device.

This allows each OR gate output to be either directly output, stored, and/or fed back into the input AND plane, thus computing more complex functions. Commercial PALs may have 20 or more inputs and 10 or more pins that can be programmed as either inputs or outputs. These devices are most suitable for relatively small applications requiring a simple logic computation.

10.5.3 Complex Programmable Logic Devices

CPLDs are PAL-like or PLA-like blocks that can be combined with programmable interconnections as depicted in Figure 10-25. Commercial CPLDs may contain as many as 200,000 equivalent gates and have over 3,000 macrocells. Large CPLDs may have 200 or more I/O pins. They are programmed similarly to the way simple PLAs are programmed, by blowing fuses to break signal flow except where desired. CPLDs are generally employed in applications that require a controller and a significant amount of logic, such as might be found in modems, audio players, printers, flat panel displays and similar devices. When the application is more computationally intensive, FPGAs are usually employed.

10.5.4 Field-Programmable Gate Arrays

Unlike CPLDs, which employ large logic blocks and fewer interconnection options, FPGAs employ small logic blocks that can be programmably interconnected. Figure 10-26 depicts an FPGA. The white blocks are the logic blocks, each shaded block is a switch matrix, and the horizontal and vertical channels are wires. These logic blocks usually have from two to five inputs and a single output. They can be programmed to provide any logic function of the inputs. The logic blocks are programmed not by blowing fuses, but by storing the logic function in an array of flip-flops. These logic blocks are often referred to as lookup tables (LUTs). The outputs may be routed to flip-flops, and all LUTs are interconnected by arrays of switches and wires. Each switch is also programmed by setting or clearing a flip-flop that drives a transistor switch. Thus the FPGA functionality is programmed by RAM cells located within it. This has the significant advantage that the

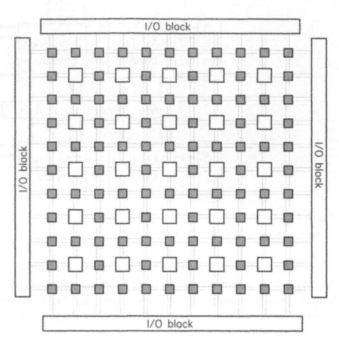

Figure 10-26
A Field-Programmable Gate Array.

FPGA can be reprogrammed many times. Because they use RAM cells, they lose their programming when power is removed. Thus the program is usually stored in a PROM, from which the FPGA is reprogrammed each time power is applied.

The Xilinx Virtex-4 FPGA has over 200,000 logic cells. These cells are not equivalent gates, but are actual logic cells with several switching components and connections. This, and similar high-capacity FPGAs can have **IP cores** embedded in them. The term "IP" in this context refers to Intellectual Property, meaning that the actual design of the core is owned by a third party and royalties are paid to the IP owner each time a device containing the core is sold. The term "core" usually refers to the core of a microprocessor. The Virtex-4 can contain two IBM PowerPC 405 32-bit processor cores that can be clocked at 500 MHz. Additional I/O cores can provide from 400 Mbps to 10 Gbps of I/O.

10.5.5 Application-Specific Integrated Circuits

PLDs are by definition programmable by the end user, whereas ASICs are designed by the programmer and fabricated at an IC fabrication facility, sometimes called a **silicon foundry**. The design cost depends on the particular kind of ASIC, with gate array ASICs being the lowest-cost alternative.

Gate Array ASICs The Gate Array ASIC is prefabricated with an originally unconnected "sea of gates," typically NANDs or NORs. The design process begins with the logic designer using CAD tools to design the final circuitry, much as in CPLD and FPGA design. When the design has been simulated and debugged, it is sent to the IC fabricator, where it may be "tweaked" by specialists in IC design. The gates are then interconnected by depositing patterns of metal wires that interconnect them. The finished ICs are tested and packaged at the fabrication facility and returned to the designer as finished products. Design costs will typically be in the $50,000 to $75,000 range by the time the project is complete, but once this high up-front cost is amortized, the per-part cost is considerably lower than it would be with the PLD approach.

Standard Cell ASICs   The **standard cell** approach is one step closer to a totally custom-designed, custom-made IC. In the standard cell approach, the logic designer once again uses the IC vendor's CAD tools to create a final design. However, the designer is limited to the standard cells that are in the vendor's library. Should the logic designer require a custom cell not in the library, the cost can rise significantly above the fully custom $200,000 cost, as it will require significant attention from the vendor's IC designers. Once again, this up-front development cost must be weighed against the lower per-unit cost of the finished product.

These new technologies put new processor design techniques in the hands of the designer that were unheard of just a few years ago, but with this capability comes the need to understand much more about low-level design tradeoffs.

■ 10.6 UNCONVENTIONAL ARCHITECTURES

The conventional stored program computer has reached a great deal of sophistication, but there are inherent limitations to what a conventional computer can do. For example, a conventional computer is incapable of flipping a coin in a truly random way, because the next state must be completely determined by the current state and input in a repeatable way for the same starting conditions. The best that a conventional computer can do is create pseudo-random numbers using some external random influence, such as the moment in time that a user pulls a lever.

A conventional computer is also incapable of reasoning about certain statements. In the seminal work of mathematician Kurt Gödel, no system of axioms and rules can be both complete and internally self-consistent. There is no way to prove (in the mathematical sense) the statement "This statement is false" in a system of logic that is both complete and self-consistent. In an extrapolation of Gödel's Law to digital logic, a computer cannot reason about itself the way that humans can.

The conventional stored-program paradigm is adequate for a wide array of applications, but there are unconventional paradigms that offer the potential for valuable new capabilities. Such paradigms might have to do with learning, self-organization, or some other computationally challenging application. In the sections below, we explore a few approaches to unconventional computing that have enjoyed a lot of attention.

10.6.1 DNA Computing

As traditional electronic computing approaches its physical limits, attention has turned to nontraditional approaches. One approach that surpasses electronic miniaturization is DNA computing, in which deoxyribonucleic acid (DNA) serves as a computer program and the

Intel vs. Motorola: Round and Round Again

In the end, the technology stories are always about people. The cult-like Mac community was overjoyed at Apple's decision in 2000 to move from the 16/32-bit MC68000 to the PowerPC. The PowerPC was developed by the AIM (Apple-IBM-Motorola) consortium, whose goal was to marry Apple's need for a 32-bit architecture with IBM's server-class RISC Power architecture and Motorola's ability to second-source the new offspring. Mac followers gloated over the low power consumption of the processor, and indeed it set the standard for the battery life/system performance benchmark. The PowerPC, given its RISC design, was capable of the most efficient instruction execution, almost by definition. At the introduction of the PowerPC, Apple CEO Steve Jobs said that Apple, with its new processor, would smash the "megahertz myth": the PowerPC could provide more performance at a lower clock frequency than the x86 architecture, because the PowerPC's RISC architecture was so much more efficient. The x86 architecture, on the other hand, ate up wattage trying to pound the square peg of a legacy ISA into the round hole of RISC-style pipelining, superscalar, out-of-order execution, and all of the other RISC features.

So when Steve Jobs stood up at the MacWorld Expo on Jan. 10, 2006, and told the world that the PowerPC architecture had been found wanting in the areas of heat dissipation, and that Apple would be moving to Intel and the x86 architecture with its superior ratio of processing power to heat dissipation, many were aghast. Looking back, there had been clues. For many years rumors had circulated that Apple maintained a secret lab where the Mac OS had been ported to the Intel x86 family, and that it was being kept current with the latest PowerPC version. IBM's PowerPC offerings were falling behind the x86 in the important measure of computing power per watt. Add to that, apparently IBM was ignoring Apple's need for a low-power version of the PowerPC in favor of work on the Cell microprocessor, a next-generation processor that was designed for the needs of the Microsoft X-Box rather than for the needs of Apple.

The outcome is that Apple abandoned IBM and its PowerPC architecture in favor of the microprocessor family used by the rival Microsoft, while IBM's head was turned by the large size of the X-box market. Shortly after the announcement anonymous sources were saying that IBM hadn't been informed until just days before the switch was announced publicly. The anonymous sources said that Steve Jobs had held animosity toward IBM since they had spurned his demands for more R & D to be expended in developing the next-generation low-power architecture.

Aside from this, it is interesting that Apple said they hadn't "done anything to particularly prohibit the running of Microsoft Windows on the same box." It does seem that Apple is going after Microsoft.

---

chemical processes that govern DNA recombination serve as the hardware. DNA is made up of a linear sequence of four nucleotides, adenine (A), guanine (G), cytosine (C), and thymine (T), which form an alphabet that determines characteristics of the living thing that carries it (and even nonliving things that carry it, such as viruses).

A strand of DNA is just 1–2 nm in width, with 3.4 nm between corresponding points in each turn of its helical structure. Human DNA has 80 million base pairs, and a typical human chromosome can be as long as 5 cm. DNA is coiled and packed so that it fits within the dimensions of a cell, and the packing ratio varies between 1000 and 10,000 depending on the state of the DNA structure. The 5 cm DNA length can thus be packed into a chromosome length of between 5–50 μm.

Researchers at USC made use of computing at these extraordinarily small dimensions in a landmark experiment in which the classical traveling salesman problem was cast in the form of a DNA computation. The traveling salesman problem involves finding the shortest overall path among N cities, visiting no city more than once, and given a starting and ending city.

In the USC experiment, led by Leonard Adleman and his team in 1994, each of seven cities is represented by a unique strand of DNA that is 20-nucleotides long. The path between two cities is represented by a 20-nucleotide strand in which two groups of 10 are designed to pair chemically with 10 nucleotides in the corresponding cities. When a strand representing the path between two cities comes into proximity with the two cities, it binds to those two cities. The process continues, culminating in a strand that starts and ends with the starting and ending cities.

Although this approach resulted in a molecule that represents the correct answer, it also resulted in trillions of molecules that represent wrong answers, and it takes a long time to sift through all of the potential solutions to find the correct solution. Still, this was an important step on the path toward practical DNA computing.

Later work at the Weizmann Institute of Science in Rehovot, Israel, resulted in the development of a programmable molecular machine. The Weizmann machine is capable of rudimentary operations such as determining whether a list has an even number of ones, but it is not capable of general computation.

While it remains to be seen whether DNA computing will ever rival conventional digital electronic computers, it may have special significance in an area of growing interest: DNA machines that monitor the health of our bodies from within, possibly even delivering drugs when needed.

10.6.2 Quantum Computing

Classical computing treats transistor switching as a macro-scale phenomenon. In order to switch reliably, a minimum of 1000 and in practice many more quanta (electrons or photons) must participate in the switching event. As the number of quanta are reduced and we approach the physical limits of switching, our reliance on classical physics breaks down and quantum physics takes over.

Consider the single-particle interference setup shown in Figure 10-27. At the macro scale, a stream of photons leaves the emitter and hits a half-silvered mirror (a 50%/50% beam splitter) that splits the incoming beam into two outgoing beams along the vertical and horizontal paths, each with 50% of the intensity of the incoming beam. Each of the beams hits a fully silvered mirror, which are recombined at a second beam splitter. At this second beam splitter, each beam is split again, so that each beam now has 25% of the original intensity. Each of the 25% beams is combined with a 25% beam from the other path, resulting in a 50% beam being passed to each detector.

Now, using the same setup, let us send a single photon (which cannot be split) to the first beam splitter. What will happen? If we place a detector on each of the paths leaving the first beam splitter, we will find that there is a 50% probability of the photon taking either path. When the photon is measured on one detector, it is not seen by the other detector, thus confirming that the photon is not actually split by the first beam splitter.

Something surprising happens at the second beam splitter, however. Measurement along each path leaving the first beam splitter shows that there is a 50% probability of the photon taking either path. Thus, when the photon arrives at either input to the second beam splitter (which also serves as a beam combiner), there should be an equal probability that the photon continues on to either the A or B detector. But this is not so in practice: 100% of the photons continue to detector A only! This is a characteristic of quantum phys-

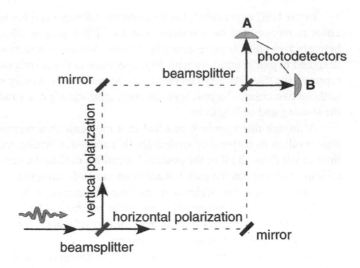

Figure 10-27
Single-particle interference experiment.

ics. Somehow, when a photon leaves the first beam splitter, a second complementary photon travels along the other path and interferes at the second beam splitter in such a way that only one final path is observed for 100% of the photons.

This property of quantum physics can be exploited to perform some difficult computations, and is the basis of quantum computing. The binary digit (bit) as we know it has two states, corresponding to a logical 1 or 0. The bit has a very different counterpart in quantum computing, known as the **quarternary bit**, or **qubit**, which can take on the logical state of 1 or 0, or the simultaneous superposition of states 1 or 0, with a coefficient corresponding to the mix of these two states.

Solving problems with quantum computing involves casting a problem in the form of qubits and applying a succession of transformations. The result is then observed. The transformations take place with the quantum equivalent of digital logic gates. While these quantum transformations can theoretically be modeled with ordinary digital logic, the mapping from quantum logic to digital logic is impractically inefficient.

Richard Feynman is credited as being among the first to recognize that quantum superposition has the potential to solve certain problems much faster than conventional computers, (Feynman, 1982). It would take until 1994 for a meaningful application to be identified, in which (Shor, 1994) outlined a method for factorization, which is an important problem in number theory that relates to cryptology.

There have been recent advancements in several quantum computing areas, but it remains to be seen whether or not a practical quantum computer can be developed.

10.6.3 Multi-Valued Logic

The primary reason that we use binary logic in computing is that transistors switch more reliably between saturated and non-saturated states, which can be thought of logically as

1s and 0s, than among the "in-between" states. With sufficient attention on design and operational tolerances, however, we can create multi-valued logic: a transistor can be made to switch reliably among three or more states. What is difficult is getting millions or billions of transistors to all switch reliably among three or more states. In smaller numbers, this has been done in practice for years, primarily for transmission, but generally not for computing itself.

If we could exploit multi-valued logic better, then what would we gain? Would we need less logic, and thereby reduce the transistor counts so that the reliability problem is also numerically reduced?

First, a little about what we know works well: transmission using multi-valued logic is more efficient than straight binary transmission. The idea is to reduce the number of channels needed for transmission over long distances, and thereby reduce the amount of copper used in wiring, or the number of frequencies consumed from the available spectrum. We saw a related principle in Chapter 9, in which information is carried in the phase of a signal. If we combine the phase and amplitude parameters, then a single bit period (that is, the time to transmit a single bit) can carry two bits. We can combine phase with amplitude and assign the bit patterns 00, 01, 10, and 11 to the combinations low-voltage in-phase, high-voltage in-phase, low-voltage out-of-phase, and high-voltage out-of-phase. The principle is known as quadrature amplitude modulation (QAM).

When it comes to logic functions, however, the tradeoff benefits are less clear. Intuitively, it seems like we can do a lot more with logic gates that operate in higher radices because there are more values possible with the same number of logic gates. Unfortunately, the truth tables grow larger because there are so many more combinations of inputs that must be enumerated, and the resulting logic can end up taking the same area as if a traditional binary approach is used.

There are some functions that can be implemented more economically in ternary (three-state) logic, however. As an example, consider a function that compares two two-bit inputs and produces an output that indicates less than, equal to, or greater than. We will create a truth table for the binary function and then a truth table for the ternary version of the same function, and will measure the complexity of each by counting the number of inputs and outputs in each table. For fairness in numerical values of the inputs, we will only allow the two-bit inputs to go from 00 to 10 in binary, which map to the ternary inputs 0, 1, and 2, consecutively.

Truth tables for binary and ternary comparison functions are shown in Figure 10-28. The first line in the binary table has an input pattern of $x_1x_0 = 00$ and $y_1y_0 = 00$. The output pattern is 01, which indicates that $x_1x_0 = y_1y_0$, as shown in the legend. There are four inputs for x_1x_0 and y_1y_0, and there are two outputs for $f_1f_0 = 00$. The first line in the binary table thus has a complexity of six. The next line for $x_1x_0 = 00$ and $y_1y_0 = 01$ also has a complexity of six, as well as the next line for $x_1x_0 = 00$ and $y_1y_0 = 10$. The next line, with $x_1x_0 = 00$ and $y_1y_0 = 11$, cannot arise in practice according to the problem description, and so the outputs are marked as $f_1f_0 = $ dd, which means "don't care". That is, it doesn't matter what values are chosen because the input pattern will not occur. The complexity of that line is thus 0.

Continuing in this manner, the complexity of the binary truth table is 6 per line × 9 non-don't care lines = 54. By comparison, each line of the ternary table has a complexity

x_1x_0 y_1y_0	f_1f_0
00 00	0 1
00 01	0 0
00 10	0 0
00 11	d d
01 00	1 0
01 01	0 0
01 10	0 0
01 11	d d
10 00	1 0
10 01	1 0
10 10	0 0
10 11	d d
11 00	d d
11 01	d d
11 10	d d
11 11	d d

$f_1f_0 = 00$ when $X < Y$
$f_1f_0 = 01$ when $X == Y$
$f_1f_0 = 10$ when $X > Y$
d = don't care

(a) Binary

x y	f
0 0	1
0 1	0
0 2	0
1 0	2
1 1	1
1 2	0
2 0	2
2 1	2
2 2	1

$f = 0$ when $x < y$
$f = 1$ when $x == y$
$f = 2$ when $x > y$

(b) Ternary

Figure 10-28
(a) Binary vs. (b) ternary truth tables for a comparison function.

of only three. There are nine lines in the ternary truth table, and so the ternary complexity is 3 per line × 9 lines = 27, which is half of the complexity for the binary example.

For this case, ternary logic reduces the circuit complexity, but would also increase the difficulty of a transistor-based realization of the circuit. The most compelling case for multi-valued logic remains in transmission, where the logic complexity is small and the cost of the communication medium is high.

10.6.4 Neural Networks

Some problems, such as human face recognition, do not lend themselves to easy algorithmic solutions. It is not that face recognition cannot be done with conventional computing means, in fact it is often done that way, but for many pattern-recognition problems, a solution based on **artificial neural networks** (ANNs) can offer significant improvements. An ANN is a computational paradigm that is based on animal neural networks, in which neurons receive signals through **synapses** located on either **dendrites** or the membrane of the neuron. If the received signals are strong enough to excite an **activation function** (surpassing a threshold in a simple case), then the neuron emits a signal through an **axon** that connects to the synapses of other neurons (see Figure 10-29).

In an ANN, the neuron is abstracted into a form in which input signals, modified by weights, feed into an activation function which produces an output, as shown in Figure 10-30. In a layered, feed-forward ANN, neurons are stratified into layers, and signals

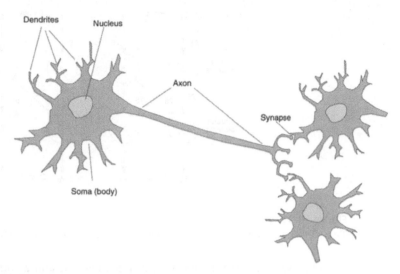

Figure 10-29
Model of a neuron.

flow in one direction from inputs through intermediate neurons to the outputs. If we modify the weights appropriately, then we can realize a complex behavior such as pattern recognition.

As an example, consider the ANN with four neurons shown in Figure 10-31a. Initially, all of the weights are set to .75, the activation function is a simple summation of the inputs multiplied by their respective weights, and the thresholds are set to .5. If the two inputs are set to $(-1, +2)$ what will the outputs be? Tracing through the network, we find that the weighted sum of the inputs (only one input for this case) to the neuron on the top left is $-1 \times .75 = -.75$. The threshold is .5, and so the output of the top left neuron is 0. Similarly, the weighted sum of the input to the top right neuron is $2 \times .75 = 1.5$. The threshold is .5, and so the output of the top right neuron is 1.5. Continuing, the weighted sum of the inputs to the bottom left neuron is $0 \times .75 + 1.5 \times .75 = 1.125$, and with a threshold of .5, the output produced at o_0 is 1.125. Likewise, the weighted sum of the inputs to the bottom right neuron is $0 \times .75 + 1.5 \times .75 = 1.125$, and with a threshold of .5, the output produced at o_1 is also 1.125.

Now look at Figure 10-31b. With the given weights, thresholds, and inputs, what will the outputs be? Using the same method as for Figure 10-31a, o_0 will be 1 and o_1 will be 0.

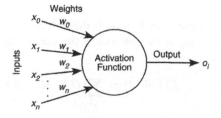

Figure 10-30
Model of an artificial neuron.

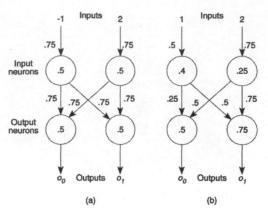

Figure 10-31
Two simple, feed-forward neural networks with inputs, weights, and thresholds as shown.

Suppose now that we have a set of input patterns and a corresponding set of output patterns. How can we assign the weights so that the network responds in a specific way to the input patterns? The **Back Propagation Algorithm** provides a method of training the network by assigning random weights, computing the error between the desired outputs and the actual outputs, and then successively refining the weights until the actual outputs are within an acceptable tolerance for a given input pattern. Once the ANN is trained, it will produce the trained outputs for the given inputs. The real power of an ANN comes in when input patterns do not exactly match the learned inputs: the ANN makes the closest match in accordance with the training.

The activation function for back propagation is the sum of the weighted inputs as in the previous example, which can be described by the equation:

$$A_j(\bar{x},\bar{w}) = \sum_{i=0}^{n} x_i w_{ji}$$

The **sigmoidal function** is generally used for the neuron output, because a simple linear threshold can otherwise introduce severe limitations:

$$O_j(\bar{x},\bar{w}) = \frac{1}{1 + e^{-A_i(\bar{x},\bar{w})}}$$

The goal of the training process is to minimize the error between the desired outputs and the actual outputs, for a given set of inputs. The error function for the output of each neuron is:

$$E_j(\bar{x}, \bar{w},d) = (O_j(\bar{x},\bar{w}) - d_j)^2$$

where O_j is the output of the neuron and d_j is the difference between the desired output and the actual output. The error in the network is the sum of the neuron output errors in the output layer:

$$E(\bar{x}, \bar{w}, \bar{d}) = \sum_{j}(O_j(\bar{x}, \bar{w}) - d_j)^2$$

Given the error of the network, we can compute more accurate weights using the method of **gradient descent**:

$$\Delta w_{ji} = -\eta \frac{\partial E}{\partial w_{ji}}$$

in which the change in the weight is Δw_{ij}, η is a constant, and the derivative of E is taken with respect to w_{ji}. We start by computing the derivative of E with respect to O_j, this is $2(O_j - d_j)$, which tells us how much the error depends on the output. We then need to calculate how much the activation function depends on the weights; this is the derivative of O_j with respect to w_{ji}, which is $O_j(1 - O_j)x_i$. We can then calculate $\frac{\partial E}{\partial w_{ji}}$ as shown below:

$$\frac{\partial E}{\partial w_{ji}} = \frac{\partial E}{\partial O_j}\frac{\partial O_j}{w_{ji}} = 2(O_j - d_j)O_j(1 - O_j)x_i$$

The adjustment on each weight is then, for a two-layer network:

$$\Delta w_{ji} = -2\eta(O_j - d_j)O_j(1 - O_j)x_i$$

For a multilayer network, the analysis is extended and the weights are adjusted accordingly for each neuron. The adjustment process is iterative, and in practice, deep networks should be avoided with back propagation because the time complexity of the learning process is exponential.

Neural networks have found important uses in a vast array of applications such as intrusion detection in networks, optical character recognition, DNA sequence analysis, terrain classification, and traffic control, to name just a few. Something that these applications share is a need for complex pattern recognition that cannot be easily satisfied with conventional approaches.

Summary

Parallel architectures can be classified as MISD, SIMD, or MIMD. The MISD approach is used for systolic array processing, and is the least general architecture of the three. In a SIMD architecture, all PEs carry out the same operations on different data sets, in an "army of ants" approach to parallel processing. The MIMD approach can be characterized as "herd of elephants," because there are a small number of powerful processors, each with their own data and instruction streams.

The current trend is moving away from the fine-grain parallelism that is exemplified by the MISD and SIMD approaches, and toward the MIMD approach, but in a different way than traditionally envisioned: as multiple functional units such as in the PowerPC and Itanium processors. This trend is due to the high time cost of communicating among PEs, and the economy of using interconnected functional units that share expensive resources (such as the memory).

A number of unconventional computing paradigms offer opportunities over conventional computing. These approaches include multivalued logic, quantum computing, DNA computing, and neural networks. Among these paradigms, neural networks have gained acceptance in certain classes of problems, such as pattern recognition, and multivalued logic has enjoyed penetration in communication. Quantum computing and DNA computing are still in the exploratory stages, and may offer new capabilities that have yet to be demonstrated.

Problems

10.1 Create a dependency graph for the following expression:

$$f(x, y) = x^2 + 2xy + y^2$$

10.2 Given 100 processors for a computation with 5% of the code that cannot be parallelized, compute speedup and efficiency.

10.3 What is the diameter of a 16-space hypercube?

10.4 For the strictly nonblocking network example at the end of Section 10.1.3, compute the total crosspoint complexity over all three stages.

10.5 Unlike a conventional digital computer that is based on binary logic, a DNA computer uses the four symbols A, G, C, and T, and is based on quarternary logic. Recode the comparison function truth table shown in Figure 10-28 using quarternary logic. Use the symbols 0, 1, 2, and 3.

10.6 Given the two-stage feed-forward neural network with the inputs, outputs, input weights, and threshold functions as shown below, compute the smallest possible weights for $b_0 - b_3$.

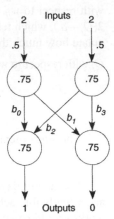

Further Reading

(Quinn, 1987) and (Hwang, 1993) survey the field of parallel processing in terms of architectures and algorithms. (Flynn, 1972) covers the Flynn taxonomy of architectures. (Yang and Gerasoulis, 1991) argue for maintaining a ratio of communication time to computation time of less than 1. (Hui, 1990) covers interconnection networks, and (Leighton, 1992) covers routing algorithms for a few types of interconnection networks. (Wu and Feng, 1981) cover routing on a shuffle-exchange network.

(Dulong, 1998) describes the IA-64. The PowerPC 601 architecture is described in (Motorola). (Eggers et al., 1997 and (Kihm et al., 2005) cover aspects of SMT. (Apple, 2006) covers a comparison between MMX and Altivec extensions.

(Feynman, 1982) proposes that quantum superposition has the potential to solve certain problems faster than conventional computers. (Shor, 1994) outlines a method for factorization using quantum computing. (Adleman, 1994) covers the landmark work that started the field of DNA computing. One of the earliest neural network models is reported in (McCulloch and Pitts, 1943). The back-propagation algorithm is reported in (Rumelhart and McClelland, 1986).

Adleman, L., "Molecular computation of solutions to combinatorial problems," *Science*, **266**, pp. 1021–1023, (11 November 1994).

Apple Computer, http://developer.apple.com/documentation/ Performance/Conceptual/Accelerate_sse_migration/ migration_sse_overview/chapter_2_section_4.html (January 2006).

Dulong, C., "The IA-64 architecture at work," *IEEE Computer*, **31**, pp. 24–32 (July 1998).

Eggers, S. J., Emer, J. S., H. Levy, M. Lo, J. L., Stamm, R. L. and D. M. Tullsen, "Simultaneous multithreading: A platform for next-generation processors," *IEEE Micro*, **17**, pp. 12–18 (September/October 1997).

Feynman, R. P., "Simulating physics with computers," *International Journal of Theoretical Physics*, **21**, pp. 467–488 (1982).

Flynn, M. J., "Some computer organizations and their Effectiveness," *IEEE Transactions on Computers*, **30**, no. 7, pp. 948–960 (1972).

Hennessy, J. L. and Patterson, D. A., *Computer Architecture: A Quantitative Approach*, 2/e, Morgan Kaufmann Publishers (1995).

Hui, J. Y., *Switching and Traffic Theory for Integrated Broadband Networks*, Kluwer Academic Publishers (1990).

Hwang, K., *Advanced Computer Architecture: Parallelism, Scalability, Programmability*, McGraw-Hill, (1993).

Kihm, Joshuan, Settle Alex, Janiszewski Andrew, Conners Dan, "Understanding the impact of inter-thread cache interference on ILP in modern SMT processors," *Journal of Instruction-Level Parallelism*, 7, pp. 1–28 (2005).

Leighton, F. T., *Introduction to Parallel Algorithms and Architectures: Arrays, Trees, Hypercubes*, Morgan Kaufmann (1992).

McCulloch, W. and Pitts. W., "A logical calculus of the ideas immanent in nervous activity, *Bulletin of Mathematical Biophysics*, **5**, pp. 115–133 (1943).

Motorola, Inc., *PowerPC 601 RISC Microprocessor User's Manual*, Motorola Literature Distribution, P. O. Box 20912, Phoenix, AZ, 85036.

Quinn, M. J., *Designing Efficient Algorithms for Parallel Computers*, McGraw-Hill (1987).

Rumelhart, D. and McClelland, J., Parallel Distributed Processing. MIT Press (1986).

Shor, P. W., "Algorithms for quantum computation: Discrete logarithms and factoring," in *Proceedings of the 35th Annual Symposium on Foundations of Computer Science*, IEEE Computer Society Press (1994).

Yang, T. and Gerasoulis, A., "A fast static scheduling algorithm for DAGs on an unbounded number of processors," *Proceedings of Supercomputing '91*, Albuquerque, New Mexico (Nov. 1991).

Wu, C.-L. and Feng, T.-Y., "The universality of the shuffle-exchange network," *IEEE Transactions on Computers*, **C-30**, no. 5, pp. 324–332 (1981).

DIGITAL LOGIC

■ A.1 INTRODUCTION

In this appendix, we take a look at a few basic principles of digital logic that we can apply in the design of a digital computer. We start by studying **combinational logic**, in which logical decisions are made based only on combinations of the inputs. We then look at **sequential logic**, in which decisions are made based on combinations of the current inputs as well as the past history of inputs. With an understanding of these underlying principles, we can design digital logic circuits from which an entire computer can be constructed. We begin with the fundamental building block of a digital computer, the **combinational logic unit** (CLU).

■ A.2 COMBINATIONAL LOGIC

A combinational logic unit translates a set of inputs into a set of outputs according to one or more mapping functions. The outputs of a CLU are strictly functions of the inputs, and the outputs are updated immediately after the inputs change. A basic model of a CLU is shown in Figure A-1. A set of inputs $i_0 - i_n$ is presented to the CLU, which produces a set of outputs according to mapping functions $f_0 - f_m$. There is no feedback from the outputs back to the inputs in a combinational logic circuit (we will study circuits with feedback in Section A.11).

Inputs and outputs for a CLU normally have two distinct values: high and low. When signals (values) are taken from a finite set, the circuits that use them are referred to as **digital**. A digital electronic circuit receives inputs and produces outputs in which 0 volts (0 V) is typically considered to be a low value and +3.3 V is considered to be a high value.

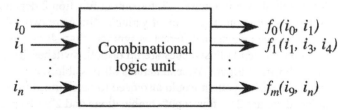

Figure A-1
External view of a combinational logic unit.

This convention is not used everywhere: high-speed circuits tend to use lower voltages; some computer circuits work in the **analog** domain, in which a continuum of values is allowed; and digital optical circuits might use phase or polarization in which high or low values are no longer meaningful. An application in which analog circuitry had traditionally been appropriate is in flight simulation, since the analog circuits more closely approximate the mechanics of an aircraft than do digital circuits.

Although the vast majority of digital computers are binary, **multi-valued** circuits also exist. A wire that is capable of carrying more than two values can be more efficient at transmitting information than a wire that carries only two values. A digital multi-valued circuit is different from an analog circuit in that a multi-valued circuit deals with signals that take on one of a finite number of values, whereas an analog signal can take on a continuum of values. The use of multi-valued circuits is theoretically valuable, but in practice it is difficult to create dense, reliable circuitry that distinguishes between more than two values. For this reason, multi-valued logic is currently in limited use.

In this text, we are primarily concerned with digital binary circuits, in which exactly two values are allowed for any input or output. Thus, we will consider only binary signals.

■ A.3 TRUTH TABLES

In 1854 George Boole published his seminal work on an algebra for representing logic. Boole was interested in capturing the mathematics of thought, and developed a representation for factual information such as "The door is open" or "The door is not open " Boole's algebra was further developed by Shannon into the form we use today. In Boolean algebra, we assume the existence of a basic postulate, that a binary variable takes on a single value of 0 or 1. This value corresponds to the 0 and $+5$ voltages mentioned in the previous section. The assignment can also be done in reverse order for 1 and 0, respectively. For purposes of understanding the behavior of digital circuits, we can abstract away the physical correspondence to voltages and consider only the symbolic values 0 and 1.

A key contribution of Boole is the development of the **truth table**, which captures logical relationships in a tabular form. Consider a room with two three-way switches A and B that control a light Z. Either switch can be up or down, or both switches can be up or down. When exactly one switch is up, the light is on. When both switches are up or down, the light is off. A truth table can be constructed that enumerates all possible settings of the switches, as shown in Figure A-2. In the table, a switch is assigned the value 0 if it is down, otherwise it is assigned the value 1. The light is on when $Z = 1$.

In a truth table, all possible input combinations of binary variables are enumerated and a corresponding output value of 0 or 1 is assigned for each input combination. For the truth table shown in Figure A-2, the output function Z depends upon input variables A and B. For each combination of input variables there are two values that can be assigned to Z: 0 or 1. We can choose a different assignment than shown in Figure A-2, in which the light is on only when both switches are up or both switches are down, in which case the truth table shown in Figure A-3 enumerates all possible states of the light for each switch setting. The wiring pattern would also need to be changed to correspond. For two input variables, there are $2^2 =$ four input combinations and $2^4 = 16$ possible assignments of outputs to input combinations. In general, since there are 2^n input combinations for n inputs, there are $2^{(2^n)}$ possible assignments of output values to input combinations.

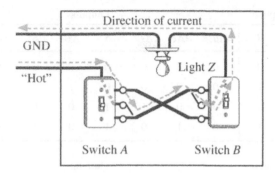

Inputs		Output
A	B	Z
0	0	0
0	1	1
1	0	1
1	1	0

Figure A-2
A truth table relates the states of three-way switches *A* and *B* to light *Z*.

Inputs		Output
A	B	Z
0	0	1
0	1	0
1	0	0
1	1	1

Figure A-3
Alternate assignments of
outputs to switch settings.

■ A.4 LOGIC GATES

If we enumerate all possible assignments of switch settings for two input variables, then we will obtain the 16 assignments shown in Figure A-4. We refer to these functions as **Boolean logic functions**. A number of assignments have special names. The *AND* function is true (produces a 1) only when *A* and *B* are 1, whereas the *OR* function is true when either *A* or *B* is 1 or when both *A* and *B* are 1. A function is false when its output is 0, and so the False function is always 0, whereas the True function is always 1. The plus signs '+' in the Boolean expressions denote logical *OR*, and do not imply arithmetic addition. The juxtaposition of two variables, as in *AB*, denotes logical *AND* among the variables.

The *A* and *B* functions simply repeat the *A* and *B* inputs, respectively, whereas the $\bar{A}$ and $\bar{B}$ functions **complement** *A* and *B* by producing a 0 where the uncomplemented function is a 1 and by producing a 1 where the uncomplemented function is a 0. In general, a bar over a term denotes the complement operation, and so the *NAND* and *NOR* functions are complements to *AND* and *OR*, respectively. The *XOR* function is true when either of its inputs, but not both, is true. The *XNOR* function is the complement to *XOR*. The remaining functions are interpreted similarly.

A **logic gate** is a physical device that implements a simple Boolean function. The functions that are listed in Figure A-4 have representations as logic gate symbols, a few of which are shown in Figure A-5 and Figure A-6. For each of the functions, *A* and *B* are binary inputs and *F* is the output.

Inputs		Outputs							
A	B	False	AND	$A\overline{B}$	A	$\overline{A}B$	B	XOR	OR
0	0	0	0	0	0	0	0	0	0
0	1	0	0	0	0	1	1	1	1
1	0	0	0	1	1	0	0	1	1
1	1	0	1	0	1	0	1	0	1

Inputs		Outputs							
A	B	NOR	XNOR	$\overline{B}$	$A + \overline{B}$	$\overline{A}$	$\overline{A} + B$	NAND	True
0	0	1	1	1	1	1	1	1	1
0	1	0	0	0	0	1	1	1	1
1	0	0	0	1	1	0	0	1	1
1	1	0	1	0	1	0	1	0	1

Figure A-4
Truth tables showing all possible functions of two binary variables.

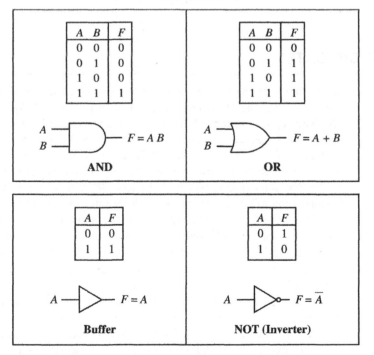

Figure A-5
Logic gate symbols for AND, OR, buffer, and NOT Boolean functions.

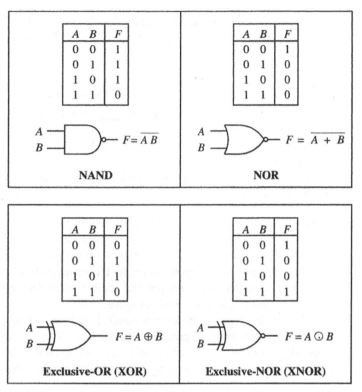

Figure A-6
Logic gate symbols for NAND, NOR, XOR, and XNOR Boolean functions.

In Figure A-5, the AND and OR gates behave as previously described. The output of the AND gate is true when both of its inputs are true and is false otherwise. The output of the OR gate is true when either or both of its inputs are true and is false otherwise. The buffer simply copies its input to its output. Although the buffer has no logical significance, it serves an important practical role as an amplifier, allowing a number of logic gates to be driven by a single signal. The NOT gate (also called an **inverter**) produces a 1 at its output for a 0 at its input, and produces a 0 at its output for a 1 at its input. Again, the inverted output signal is referred to as the complement of the input. The circle at the output of the NOT gate denotes the complement operation.

In Figure A-6, the NAND and NOR gates produce complementary outputs to the AND and OR gates, respectively. The exclusive-OR (XOR) gate produces a 1 when either of its inputs, but not both, is 1. In general, XOR produces a 1 at its output whenever the number of 1s at its inputs is odd. This generalization is important in understanding how an XOR gate with more than two inputs behaves. The exclusive-NOR (XNOR) gate produces a complementary output to the XOR gate.

The logic symbols shown in Figure A-5 and Figure A-6 are only the basic forms, and there are a number of variations that are often used. For example, there can be more

$$A \atop B \atop C \quad \rightarrow \quad F = ABC$$

(a)

$$A \atop B \quad \rightarrow \quad F = \overline{A + B}$$

(b)

$$A \atop B \quad \rightarrow \quad \overline{A + B} \atop A + B$$

(c)

Figure A-7
Variations of the basic logic gate symbols for (a) three inputs; (b) a negated output;
(c) complementary outputs.

inputs, as in the three-input AND gate shown in Figure A-7a. The circles at the outputs of
the NOT, NOR, and XNOR gates denote the complement operation, and can be placed at
the inputs of logic gates to indicate that the inputs are inverted upon entering the gate, as
shown in Figure A-7b. Depending on the technology used, some logic gates produce complementary outputs. The corresponding logic symbol for a complementary logic gate indicates both outputs, as illustrated in Figure A-7c.

Physically, logic gates are not magical, although it may seem that they are when a
device like an inverter can produce a logical 1 (+5 V in the next section, but generally lower
these days, around 3.3 V) at its output when a logical 0 (0 V) is provided at the input. The
next section covers the underlying mechanism that makes electronic logic gates work.

A.4.1 Electronic Implementation of Logic Gates

Electrically, logic gates have power terminals that are not normally shown. Figure A-8a
illustrates an inverter in which the +5 V and 0 V (GND) terminals are made visible. The +5
V signal is commonly referred to as V_{CC} for "voltage collector-collector." In a physical circuit, all of the V_{CC} and GND terminals are connected to the corresponding terminals of a
power supply.

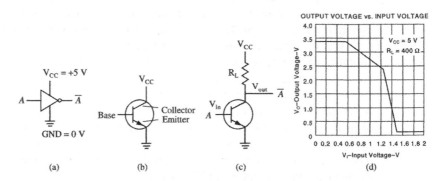

(a)   (b)   (c)   (d)

Figure A-8
(a) Power terminals for an inverter made visible; (b) schematic symbol for a transistor;
(c) transistor circuit for an inverter; (d) static transfer function for an inverter.

Logic gates are composed of electrical devices called **transistors**, which have a fundamental switching property that allows them to control a strong electrical signal with a weak signal. This supports the process of **amplification**, which is crucial for cascading logic gates. Without amplification, we would only be able to send a signal through a few logic gates before the signal deteriorated to the point that it was overcome by noise, which exists at every point in an electrical circuit to some degree.

The schematic symbol for a transistor is in Figure A-8b. When there is no positive voltage on the base, then a current will not flow from V_{CC} to GND. Thus, for an inverter, a logical 0 (0 V) on the base will produce a logical 1 (+5 V) at the collector terminal, as illustrated in Figure A-8c. If, however, a positive voltage is applied to V_{in}, then a current will flow from V_{CC} to GND, which prevents V_{out} from producing enough signal for the inverter output to be a logical 1. In effect, when +5 V is applied to V_{in}, a logical 0 appears at V_{out}. The input-output relationship of a logic gate follows the nonlinear curve shown in Figure A-8d for **transistor-transistor logic** (TTL). The nonlinearity is an important gain property that makes cascadable operation possible.

A useful paradigm is to think of current flowing through wires as water flowing through pipes. If we create a connection with a pipe from V_{CC} to GND, then the water flowing to V_{out} will be reduced to a great extent, although some water will still make it out. By choosing an appropriate value for the resistor R_L, the flow can be restricted in order to minimize this effect.

Since there will always be some current that flows even when we have a logical 0 at V_{out}, we need to assign logical 0 and 1 to voltages using safe margins. If we assign logical 0 to 0 V and logical 1 to +5 V, then our circuits may not work properly if .1 V appears at the output of an inverter instead of 0 V, which can happen in practice. For this reason, we design circuits in which assignments of logical 0 and 1 are made using **thresholds**. In Figure A-9a, logical 0 is assigned to the voltage range [0 V to 0.4 V] and logical 1 is assigned to the voltage range [2.4 V to +5 V]. The ranges shown in Figure A-9a are for the output of a logic gate. There may be some attenuation (a reduction in voltage) introduced in the connection between the output of one logic gate and the input to another, and for that reason, the thresholds are relaxed by 0.4 V at the input to a logic gate, as shown in Figure A-9b. These ranges can differ depending on the logic family. The output ranges

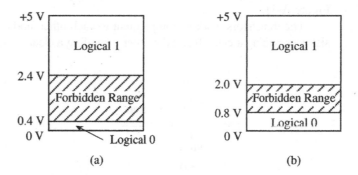

(a)   (b)

Figure A-9

Assignments of logical 0 and 1 to voltage ranges (a) at the output of a logic gates, (b) at the input to a logic gate.

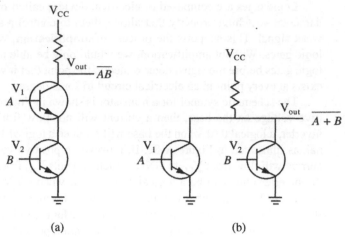

(a)   (b)

Figure A-10
Transistor circuits for (a) a two-input NAND gate and (b) a two-input NOR gate.

only make sense, however, if the gate inputs settle into the logical 0 or 1 ranges at the input. For this reason, inputs to a logic gate should never be left "floating"—disconnected from a gate output, V_{CC}, or GND.

Figure A-10 shows transistor circuits for two-input NAND and NOR gates. For the NAND case, both of the V_1 and V_2 inputs must be in the logical 1 region in order to produce a voltage in the logical 0 region at V_{out}. For the NOR case, if either or both of the V_1 and V_2 inputs are in the logical 1 region, then a voltage in the logical 0 region will be produced at V_{out}.

This form of logic (TTL) is relatively simple, but the most prevalent form of logic gates uses a different configuration of transistors known as **complementary metal oxide semiconductor (CMOS)** that supports high component densities at low powers. The basic idea is that there are n-type transistors that close a circuit (that is, a complete connection is made through the circuit) when a voltage is applied to the control terminal, and p-type transistors that open a circuit when a voltage is applied to the control terminal, as shown in Figure A-11.

The transistors work in complement to each other, and can be thought of as one transistor providing a clean 0 and the other providing a clean 1. While this is a bit of a simpli-

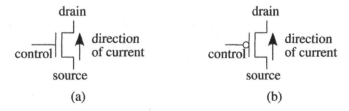

(a)   (b)

Figure A-11
Schematic symbols for (a) n-channel transistor and (b) p-channel transistor.

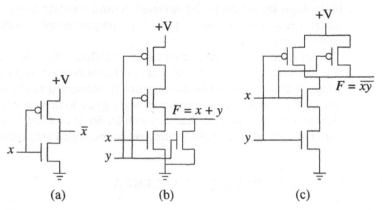

Figure A-12
CMOS configurations for (a) NOT, (b) NOR, and (c) NAND gates.

fication, it is helpful in understanding the CMOS configurations shown in Figure A-12 for NOT, NOR, and NAND gates. Compare A-12 with A-8 and A-10 and verify that the logical input/output relationships are the same.

A.4.2 Tri-State Buffers

A **tri-state buffer** behaves in a similar manner to the ordinary buffer that was introduced earlier, except that a control input is available to disable the buffer. Depending on the value of the control input, the output is either 0, 1, or *disabled*, thus providing three output states. In Figure A-13, when the control input C is 1, the tri-state buffer behaves like an ordinary buffer. When C is 0, then the output is electrically disconnected and no output is produced. The ϕs in the corresponding truth table entries mark the disabled (disconnected) states. The reader should note that the disabled state, ϕ, represents neither a 0 nor a 1, but rather the absence of a signal. In electrical circuit terms, the output is said to

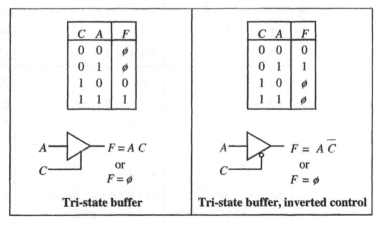

Figure A-13
Tri-state buffers.

be in **high impedance**. The inverted control tri-state buffer is similar to the tri-state buffer, except that the control input C is complemented as indicated by the bubble at the control input.

An electrically disconnected output is different from an output that produces a 0, in that an electrically disconnected output behaves as if no output connection exists whereas a logical 0 at the output is still electrically connected to the circuit. The tri-state buffer allows the outputs from a number of logic gates to drive a common line without risking electrical shorts, provided that only one buffer is enabled at a time. The use of tri-state buffers is important in implementing **registers**, which are described in Section A.14.

■ A.5 PROPERTIES OF BOOLEAN ALGEBRA

Table A.1 summarizes a few basic properties of Boolean algebra that can be applied to Boolean logic expressions. The postulates (known as **Huntington's postulates**) are basic axioms of Boolean algebra and therefore need no proofs. The theorems can be proven from the postulates. Each relationship shown in the table has both an AND and an OR form as a result of the **principle of duality**. The dual form is obtained by changing ANDs to ORs, and changing ORs to ANDs.

The **commutative** property states that the order that two variables appear in an AND or OR function is not significant. By the principle of duality, the commutative property has an AND form ($AB = BA$) and an OR form ($A + B = B + A$). The **distributive** property shows how a variable is distributed over an expression with which it is ANDed. By the principle of duality, the dual form of the distributive property is obtained as shown.

Table A.1 Basic properties of Boolean algebra

	Relationship	Dual	Property
Postulates	$A B = B A$	$A + B = B + A$	Commutative
	$A (B + C) = A B + A C$	$A + B C = (A + B)(A + C)$	Distributive
	$1 A = A$	$0 + A = A$	Identity
	$A \overline{A} = 0$	$A + \overline{A} = 1$	Complement
Theorems	$0 A = 0$	$1 + A = 1$	Zero and one theorems
	$A A = A$	$A + A = A$	Idempotence
	$A (B C) = (A B) C$	$A + (B + C) = (A + B) + C$	Associative
	$\overline{\overline{A}} = A$		Involution
	$\overline{A B} = \overline{A} + \overline{B}$	$\overline{A + B} = \overline{A}\, \overline{B}$	DeMorgan's Theorem
	$AB + \overline{A}C + BC$ $= AB + \overline{A}C$	$(A + B)(\overline{A} + C)(B + C)$ $= (A + B)(\overline{A} + C)$	Consensus Theorem
	$A (A + B) = A$	$A + A B = A$	Absorption Theorem

A B	$\overline{A\,B} = \overline{A} + \overline{B}$		$\overline{A + B} = \overline{A}\,\overline{B}$	
0 0	1	1	1	1
0 1	1	1	0	0
1 0	1	1	0	0
1 1	0	0	0	0

Figure A-14
DeMorgan's theorem is proven
for the two-variable case.

The **identity** property states that a variable that is ANDed with 1 or is ORed with 0 produces the original variable. The **complement** property states that a variable that is ANDed with its complement is logically false (produces a 0, since at least one input is 0), and a variable that is ORed with its complement is logically true (produces a 1, since at least one input is 1).

The **zero** and **one** theorems state that a variable that is ANDed with 0 produces a 0, and a variable that is ORed with 1 produces a 1. The **idempotence** theorem states that a variable that is ANDed or ORed with itself produces the original variable. For instance, if the inputs to an AND gate have the same value or the inputs to an OR gate have the same value, then the output for each gate is the same as the input. The **associative** theorem states that the order of ANDing or ORing is logically of no consequence. The **involution** theorem states that the complement of a complement leaves the original variable (or expression) unchanged.

DeMorgan's theorem, the **consensus theorem**, and the **absorption theorem** may not be obvious, and so we prove DeMorgan's theorem for the two-variable case using perfect induction (enumerating all cases), and leave algebraic proofs as exercises (See Problems A.23 and A.24). Figure A-14 shows a truth table for each expression that appears in either form of DeMorgan's theorem. The expressions that appear on the left and right sides of each form of DeMorgan's theorem produce equivalent outputs, which proves the theorem for two variables.

Not all of the logic gates discussed so far are necessary in order to achieve **computational completeness**, meaning that any digital logic circuit can be created from these gates. Three sets of logic gates that are computationally complete are: {AND, OR, NOT}, {NAND}, and {NOR} (there are others as well).

As an example of how a computationally complete set of logic gates can implement other logic gates that are not part of the set, consider implementing the OR function with the {NAND} set. DeMorgan's theorem can be used to map an OR gate onto a NAND gate, as shown in Figure A-15. The original OR function $(A + B)$ is complemented twice, which leaves the function unchanged by the involution property. DeMorgan's theorem then

DeMorgan's theorem: $\quad A + B = \overline{\overline{A + B}} = \overline{\overline{A}\,\overline{B}}$

Figure A-15
DeMorgan's theorem is used in mapping an OR gate onto a NAND gate.

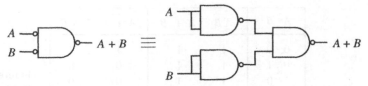

Figure A-16
Inverted inputs to a NAND gate implemented with NAND gates.

changes OR to AND and distributes the innermost overbar over the terms A and B. The inverted inputs can also be implemented with NAND gates by the property of idempotence, as shown in Figure A-16. The OR function is thus implemented with NANDs. Functional equivalence among logic gates is important for practical considerations, because one type of logic gate may have better operating characteristics than another for a given technology.

■ A.6 THE SUM-OF-PRODUCTS FORM AND LOGIC DIAGRAMS

Suppose now that we need to implement a more complex function than just a simple logic gate, such as the three-input **majority** function described by the truth table shown in Figure A-17. The majority function is true whenever more than half of its inputs are true, and can be thought of as a balance that tips to the left or right depending on whether there are more 0s or 1s at the input. This is a common operation used in fault recovery, in which the outputs of identical circuits operating on the same data are compared, and the greatest number of similar values determine the output (also referred to as "voting" or "odd one out").

Since no single logic gate discussed up to this point implements the majority function directly, we transform the function into a two-level AND-OR equation, and then implement the function with an arrangement of logic gates from the set {AND, OR, NOT} (for instance). The two levels come about because exactly one level of ANDed variables is followed by exactly one OR level. The Boolean equation that describes the majority function is true whenever F is true in the truth table. Thus, F is true when $A = 0$, $B = 1$, and $C = 1$, or when $A = 1$, $B = 0$, and $C = 1$, and so on for the remaining cases.

Minterm Index	A	B	C	F
0	0	0	0	0
1	0	0	1	0
2	0	1	0	0
3	0	1	1	1
4	1	0	0	0
5	1	0	1	1
6	1	1	0	1
7	1	1	1	1

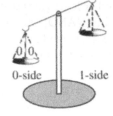

0-side   1-side

A balance tips to the left or right depending on whether there are more 0 s or 1s.

Figure A-17
Truth table for the majority function.

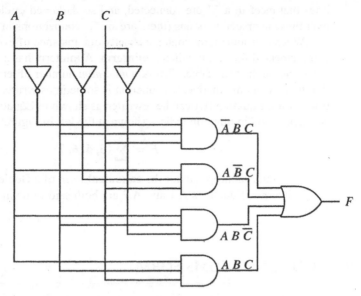

Figure A-18
A two-level AND-OR circuit implements the majority function. Inverters at the inputs are
not included in the two-level count.

One way to represent logic equations is to use the **sum-of-products (SOP)** form, in
which a collection of ANDed variables are ORed together. The Boolean logic equation
that describes the majority function is shown in SOP form in Equation A.1. Again, the '+'
signs denote logical OR and do not imply arithmetic addition.

$$F = \bar{A}BC + A\bar{B}C + AB\bar{C} + ABC \qquad (A.1)$$

By inspecting the equation, we can determine that four three-input AND gates will implement the four **product terms** $\bar{A}BC$, $A\bar{B}C$, $AB\bar{C}$, and ABC, and then the outputs of these
four AND gates can be connected to the inputs of a four-input OR gate as shown in Figure
A-18. This circuit performs the majority function, which we can verify by enumerating all
eight input combinations and observing the output for each case.

The circuit diagram shows a commonly used notation that indicates the presence or
absence of a connection, which is summarized in Figure A-19. Two lines that pass through
each other do not connect unless a darkened circle is placed at the intersection point. Two

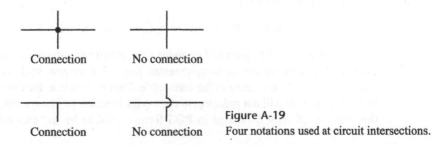

Figure A-19
Four notations used at circuit intersections.

lines that meet in a $\top$ are connected, and so darkened circles do not need to be placed over those intersection points (there are six $\top$ connections in Figure A-18).

When a product term contains exactly one instance of every variable, either in true or complemented form, it is called a **minterm**. A minterm has a value of 1 for exactly one of the entries in the truth table. That is, a *minimum* number of terms (one) will make the function true. As an alternative, the function is sometimes written as the logical sum over the true entries. Equation A.1 can be rewritten as shown in Equation A.2, in which the indices correspond to the minterm indices shown at the left in Figure A-17.

$$F = \sum \langle 3, 5, 6, 7 \rangle \tag{A.2}$$

This notation is appropriate for the **canonical** form of a Boolean equation, which contains only minterms. Equations A.1 and A.2 are both said to be in "canonical sum-of-products form."

■ A.7 THE PRODUCT-OF-SUMS FORM

As a dual to the sum-of-products form, a Boolean equation can be represented in the **product-of-sums (POS)** form. An equation that is in POS form contains a collection of ORed variables that are ANDed together. One method of obtaining the POS form is to start with the complement of the SOP form, and then apply DeMorgan's theorem. For example, referring again to the truth table for the majority function shown in Figure A-17, the complement is obtained by selecting input terms that produce 0s at the output, as shown in Equation A.3:

$$\overline{F} = \overline{A}\,\overline{B}\,\overline{C} + \overline{A}\,\overline{B}\,C + \overline{A}\,B\,\overline{C} + A\,\overline{B}\,\overline{C} \tag{A.3}$$

Complementing both sides yields Equation A.4:

$$F = \overline{\overline{A}\,\overline{B}\,\overline{C} + \overline{A}\,\overline{B}\,C + \overline{A}\,B\,\overline{C} + A\,\overline{B}\,\overline{C}} \tag{A.4}$$

Applying DeMorgan's theorem in the form $\overline{W + X + Y + Z} = \overline{W}\,\overline{X}\,\overline{Y}\,\overline{Z}$ at the outermost level produces Equation A.5:

$$F = (\overline{\overline{A}\,\overline{B}\,\overline{C}})(\overline{\overline{A}\,\overline{B}\,C})(\overline{\overline{A}\,B\,\overline{C}})(\overline{A\,\overline{B}\,\overline{C}}) \tag{A.5}$$

Applying DeMorgan's theorem in the form $\overline{WXYZ} = \overline{W} + \overline{X} + \overline{Y} + \overline{Z}$ to the parenthesized terms produces Equation A.6:

$$F = (A + B + C)(A + B + \overline{C})(A + \overline{B} + C)(\overline{A} + B + C) \tag{A.6}$$

Equation A.6 is in POS form and contains four **maxterms**, in which every variable appears exactly once in either true or complemented form. A maxterm, such as $(A + B + C)$, has a value of 0 for only one entry in the truth table. That is, it is true for the *maximum* number of truth table entries without reducing to the trivial function of always being true. An equation that consists of only maxterms in POS form is said to be in "canonical product-of-sums

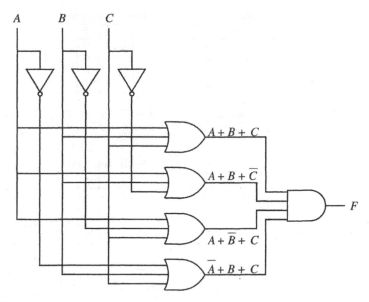

Figure A-20
A two-level OR-AND circuit that implements the majority function. Inverters are not included in the two-level count.

form." An OR-AND circuit that implements Equation A.6 is shown in Figure A-20. The OR-AND form is logically equivalent to the AND-OR form shown in Figure A-18.

One motivation for using the POS form over the SOP form is that it may result in a smaller Boolean equation. A smaller Boolean equation may yield in a simpler circuit, although this does not always hold true since there are a number of considerations that do not directly depend on the size of the Boolean equation, such as the complexity of the wiring topology.

The **gate count** is a measure of circuit complexity that is obtained by counting all of the logic gates. The **gate input count** is another measure of circuit complexity that is obtained by counting the number of inputs to all of the logic gates. For the circuits shown in Figures A-18 and A-20, a gate count of eight and a gate input count of 19 are obtained for both the SOP and POS forms. For this case, there is no difference in circuit complexity between the SOP and POS forms, but for other cases the differences can be significant. There is a variety of methods for reducing the complexity of digital circuits, a few of which are presented in Section A.17.

■ A.8 POSITIVE VS. NEGATIVE LOGIC

Up to this point we have assumed that high and low voltage levels correspond to logical 1 and 0, or TRUE and FALSE, respectively, which is known as **active high** or **positive logic**. We can make the reverse assignment instead: low voltage for logical 1 and high voltage for logical 0, which is known as **active low** or **negative logic**. The use of negative logic is sometimes preferred to positive logic for applications in which the logic inhibits an event rather than enabling an event.

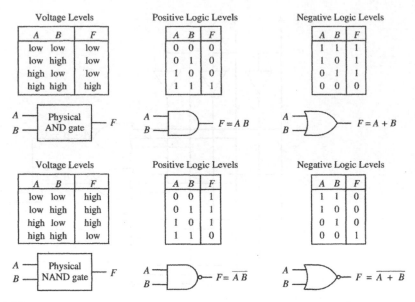

Figure A-21
Positive and negative logic assignments for AND-OR and NAND-NOR duals.

Figure A-21 illustrates the behavior of AND-OR and NAND-NOR gate pairs for both positive and negative logic. The positive logic AND gate behaves as a negative logic OR gate. The physical logic gate is the same regardless of the positive or negative sense of the logic—only the interpretation of the signals is changed.

The mixing of positive and negative logic in the same system should be avoided to prevent confusion, but sometimes it cannot be avoided. For these cases, a technique known as "bubble matching" helps keep the proper logic sense correct. The idea is to assume that all logic is asserted high (positive logic) and to place a bubble (denoting logical inversion) at the inputs or outputs of any negative logic circuits. Note that these bubbles are the same in function as the bubbles that appear at the complemented outputs of logic gates such as NOR and NAND. That is, the signal that leaves a bubble is the complement of the signal that enters it.

Consider the circuit shown in Figure A-22a, in which the outputs of two positive logic circuits are combined through an AND gate that is connected to a positive logic system. A logically equivalent system for negative logic is shown in Figure A-22b. In the process of bubble matching, a bubble is placed on each active low input or output as shown in Figure A-22c.

To simplify the process of analyzing the circuit, active low-input bubbles need to be matched with active low-output bubbles. In Figure A-22c there are bubble mismatches because there is only one bubble on each line. DeMorgan's theorem is used in converting the OR gate in Figure A-22c to the NAND gate with complemented inputs in Figure A-22d, in which the bubble mismatches have been fixed.

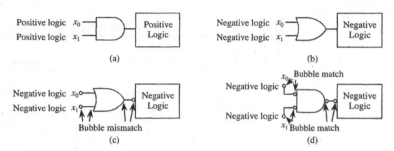

Figure A-22
The process of bubble matching.

A.9 THE DATA SHEET

Logic gates and other logic components have a great deal of technical specifications that are relevant to the design and analysis of digital circuits. The **data sheet**, or "spec sheet," lists technical characteristics of a logic component. An example of a data sheet is shown in Figure A-23. The data sheet starts with a title for the component, which for this case is the SN7400 NAND gate. The description gives a functional description of the component in textual form.

The package section shows the pin layout and the pin assignments. There can be several package types for the same component. The function table enumerates the input-output behavior of the component from a functional perspective. The symbols H and L stand for high and low voltages respectively, to avoid confusion with the sense of positive or negative logic. The symbol X indicates that the value at an input does not influence the output. The logic diagram describes the logical behavior of the component, using positive logic for this case. All four NAND gates are shown with their pin assignments.

The schematic shows the transistor level circuitry for each gate. Throughout the text, we treat this low-level circuitry as an abstraction that is embodied in the logic gate symbols.

The "absolute maximum ratings" section lists the range of environmental conditions in which the component will safely operate. The supply voltage can go as high as 7 V and the input voltage can go up to 5.5 V. The ambient temperature should be between 0° C and 70° C during operation, but can vary between –65° C and 150° C when the component is not being used.

Despite the absolute maximum rating specifications, the recommended operating conditions should be used during operation. The recommended operating conditions are characterized by minimum (MIN), normal (NOM), and maximum (MAX) ratings.

The electrical characteristics describe the behavior of the component under certain operating conditions. V_{OH} and V_{OL} are the minimum output high voltage and the maximum output low voltage, respectively. I_{IH} and I_{IL} are the maximum currents into an input pin when the input is high or low, respectively. I_{CCH} and I_{CCL} are the package's power supply currents when all outputs are high or low, respectively.

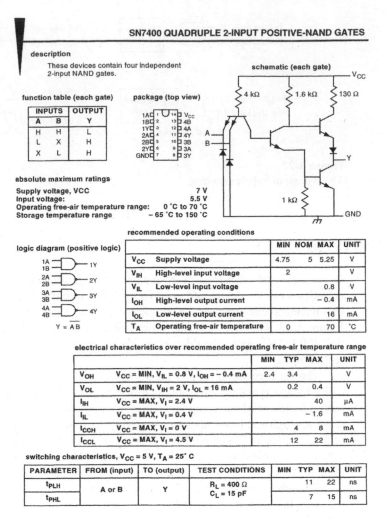

SN7400 QUADRUPLE 2-INPUT POSITIVE-NAND GATES

description

These devices contain four independent 2-input NAND gates.

function table (each gate)

INPUTS		OUTPUT
A	B	Y
H	H	L
L	X	H
X	L	H

package (top view)

```
1A  1  14  Vcc
1B  2  13  4B
1Y  3  12  4A
2A  4  11  4Y
2B  5  10  3B
2Y  6  9   3A
GND 7  8   3Y
```

schematic (each gate)

absolute maximum ratings

Supply voltage, VCC .... 7 V
Input voltage: .... 5.5 V
Operating free-air temperature range: 0 °C to 70 °C
Storage temperature range .... − 65 °C to 150 °C

logic diagram (positive logic)

```
1A ─┐
1B ─┘─ 1Y

2A ─┐
2B ─┘─ 2Y

3A ─┐
3B ─┘─ 3Y

4A ─┐
4B ─┘─ 4Y
```

$Y = \overline{AB}$

recommended operating conditions

		MIN	NOM	MAX	UNIT
V_{CC}	Supply voltage	4.75	5	5.25	V
V_{IH}	High-level input voltage	2			V
V_{IL}	Low-level input voltage			0.8	V
I_{OH}	High-level output current			− 0.4	mA
I_{OL}	Low-level output current			16	mA
T_A	Operating free-air temperature	0		70	°C

electrical characteristics over recommended operating free-air temperature range

		MIN	TYP	MAX	UNIT
V_{OH}	V_{CC} = MIN, V_{IL} = 0.8 V, I_{OH} = − 0.4 mA	2.4	3.4		V
V_{OL}	V_{CC} = MIN, V_{IH} = 2 V, I_{OL} = 16 mA		0.2	0.4	V
I_{IH}	V_{CC} = MAX, V_I = 2.4 V			40	µA
I_{IL}	V_{CC} = MAX, V_I = 0.4 V			− 1.6	mA
I_{CCH}	V_{CC} = MAX, V_I = 0 V		4	8	mA
I_{CCL}	V_{CC} = MAX, V_I = 4.5 V		12	22	mA

switching characteristics, V_{CC} = 5 V, T_A = 25° C

PARAMETER	FROM (input)	TO (output)	TEST CONDITIONS	MIN	TYP	MAX	UNIT
t_{PLH}	A or B	Y	R_L = 400 Ω C_L = 15 pF		11	22	ns
t_{PHL}					7	15	ns

Figure A-23
Simplified data sheet for 7400 NAND gate. (Source: adapted from [Texas Instruments, 1988]).

This data can be used in determining maximum **fan-outs** under the given conditions. Fan-out is a measure of the number of inputs that a single output can drive, for logic gates implemented in the same technology. That is, a logic gate with a fan-out of 10 can drive the inputs of 10 other logic gates of the same type. Similarly, **fan-in** is a measure of the number of inputs that a logic gate can accept (simply, the number of input lines to that gate). The absolute value of I_{OH} must be greater than or equal to the sum of all I_{IH} currents that are being driven, and I_{OL} must be greater than or equal to the sum of all I_{IL} currents (absolute values) that are being driven. The absolute value of I_{OH} for a 7400 gate is .4 mA (or 400 µA), and so a 7400 gate output can thus drive ten 7400 inputs (I_{IH} = 40 µA per input).

The switching characteristics show the propagation delay to switch the output from a low to a high voltage (t_{PLH}) and the propagation delay to switch the output from a high to a low voltage (t_{PHL}). The maximum ratings show the worst cases. A circuit can be safely designed using the typical case as the worst case, but only if a test-and-select-the-best approach is used. That is, since t_{PLH} varies between 11 ns and 22 ns and t_{PHL} varies between 7 ns and 15 ns from one packaged component to the next, components can be individually tested to determine their true characteristics. Not all components of the same type behave identically, even under the most stringent fabrication controls, and the differences can be reduced by testing and selecting the best components.

■ A.10 DIGITAL COMPONENTS

High-level digital circuit designs are normally made using collections of logic gates referred to as **components**, rather than individual logic gates. This allows a degree of circuit complexity to be abstracted away, and also simplifies the process of modeling the behavior of circuits and characterizing their performance. A few of the more common components are described in the sections that follow.

A.10.1 Levels of Integration

Up to this point, we have focused on the design of combinational logic units. Since we have been working with individual logic gates, we have been working at the level of **small scale integration** (SSI), in which there are 10–100 components per chip. ("Components" has a different meaning in this context, referring to transistors and other discrete elements.) Although we sometimes need to work at this low level in practice, typically for high-performance circuits, the advent of microelectronics allows us to work at higher levels of integration. In **medium-scale integration** (MSI), approximately 100–1000 components appear in a single chip. **Large-scale integration** (LSI) deals with circuits that contain 1000–10,000 components per chip, and **very-large-scale-integration** (VLSI) goes higher still. There are no sharp breaks between the classes of integration, but the distinctions are useful in comparing the relative complexity of circuits. In this section we deal primarily with MSI components.

A.10.2 Multiplexers

A **multiplexer** (MUX) is a component that connects a number of inputs to a single output. A block diagram and the corresponding truth table for a 4-to-1 MUX are shown in Figure A-24. The output F takes on the value of the data input that is selected by control lines A and B. For example, if $AB = 00$, then the value on line D_0 (a 0 or a 1) will appear at F. The corresponding AND-OR circuit is shown in Figure A-25.

When we design circuits with MUXes, we normally use the "black-box" form shown in Figure A-24, rather than the more detailed form shown in Figure A-25. In this way, we can abstract away detail when designing complex circuits.

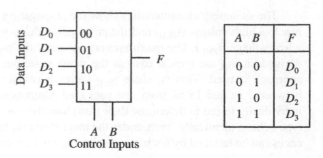

$$F = \overline{A}\,\overline{B}\,D_0 + \overline{A}\,B\,D_1 + A\,\overline{B}\,D_2 + A\,B\,D_3$$

Figure A-24
Block diagram and truth table for a 4-to-1 MUX.

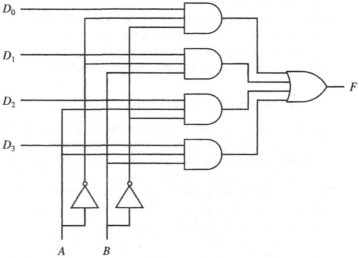

Figure A-25
An AND-OR circuit implements a 4-to-1 MUX.

Multiplexers can be used to implement Boolean functions. In Figure A-26, an 8-to-1 MUX implements the majority function. The data inputs are taken directly from the truth table for the majority function, and the control inputs are assigned to the variables A, B, and C. The MUX implements the function by passing a 1 from the input of each true minterm to the output. The 0 inputs mark portions of the MUX that are not needed in implementing the function, and as a result, a number of logic gates are underutilized. Although portions of MUXes are almost always unused in implementing Boolean functions, multiplexers are widely used because their generality simplifies the design process, and their modularity simplifies the implementation.

As another case, consider implementing a function of three variables using a 4-to-1 MUX. Figure A-27 shows a three-variable truth table and a 4-to-1 MUX that implements function F. We allow data inputs to be taken from the set $\{0, 1, C, \overline{C}\}$, and the groupings

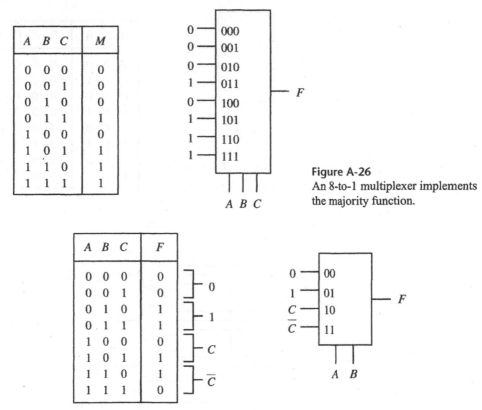

A	B	C	M
0	0	0	0
0	0	1	0
0	1	0	0
0	1	1	1
1	0	0	0
1	0	1	1
1	1	0	1
1	1	1	1

Figure A-26
An 8-to-1 multiplexer implements the majority function.

A	B	C	F
0	0	0	0
0	0	1	0
0	1	0	1
0	1	1	1
1	0	0	0
1	0	1	1
1	1	0	1
1	1	1	0

Figure A-27
A 4-to-1 MUX implements a three-variable function.

are obtained as shown in the truth table. When $AB = 00$, then $F = 0$ regardless of whether $C = 0$ or $C = 1$, and so a 0 is placed at the corresponding 00 data input line on the MUX. When $AB = 01$, then $F = 1$ regardless of whether $C = 0$ or $C = 1$, and so a 1 is placed at the 01 data input. When $AB = 10$, then $F = C$ since F is 0 when C is 0 and F is 1 when C is 1, and so C is placed at the 10 input. Finally, when $AB = 11$, then $F = \overline{C}$, and so $\overline{C}$ is placed at the 11 input. In this way, we can implement a three-variable function using a two-variable MUX.

A.10.3 Demultiplexers

A **demultiplexer** (DEMUX) is the converse of a MUX. A block diagram of a 1-to-4 DEMUX with control inputs A and B and the corresponding truth table are shown in Figure A-28. A DEMUX sends its single data input D to one of its outputs F_i according to the settings of the control inputs. A circuit for a 1-to-4 DEMUX is shown in Figure A-29. An application for a DEMUX is to send data from a single source to one of a number of destinations, such as from a call request button for an elevator to the closest elevator car. The DEMUX is not normally used in implementing ordinary Boolean functions, although there are ways to do this (see Problem A.16).

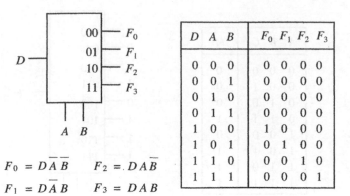

$$F_0 = D\bar{A}\bar{B} \qquad F_2 = D A \bar{B}$$

$$F_1 = D\bar{A}B \qquad F_3 = D A B$$

Figure A-28
Block diagram and truth table for a 1-to-4 DEMUX.

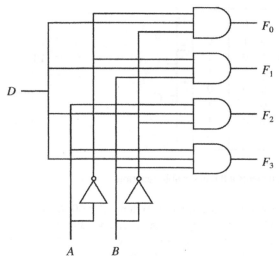

Figure A-29
A circuit for a 1-to-4 DEMUX.

A.10.4 Decoders

A **decoder** translates a logical encoding into a spatial location. Exactly one output of a decoder is high (logical 1) at any time, which is determined by the settings on the control inputs. A block diagram and a truth table for a 2-to-4 decoder with control inputs A and B are shown in Figure A-30. A corresponding logic diagram that implements the decoder is shown in Figure A-31. A decoder may be used to control other circuits, and at times it may be inappropriate to enable any of the other circuits. For that reason, we add an enable line to the decoder that forces all outputs to 0 if a 0 is applied at its input. (Notice the logical equivalence between the DEMUX with an input of 1 and the decoder.) One application for a decoder is in translating memory addresses into physical locations.

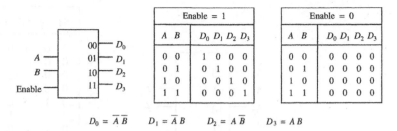

$$D_0 = \overline{A}\,\overline{B} \qquad D_1 = \overline{A}\,B \qquad D_2 = A\,\overline{B} \qquad D_3 = A\,B$$

Figure A-30
Block diagram and truth table for a 2-to-4 decoder.

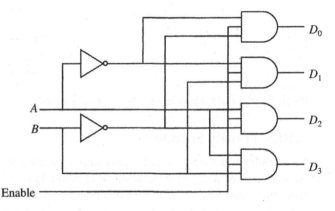

Figure A-31
An AND circuit for a 2-to-4 decoder.

Decoders can be used in implementing Boolean functions. Since each output line corresponds to a different minterm, a function can be implemented by logically ORing the outputs that correspond to the true minterms in the function. For example, in Figure A-32, a 3-to-8 decoder implements the majority function. Unused outputs remain disconnected.

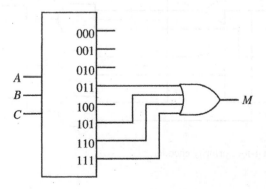

Figure A-32
A 3-to-8 decoder implements the majority function.

A_0	A_1	A_2	A_3	F_0	F_1
0	0	0	0	0	0
0	0	0	1	1	1
0	0	1	0	1	0
0	0	1	1	1	0
0	1	0	0	0	1
0	1	0	1	0	1
0	1	1	0	0	1
0	1	1	1	0	1
1	0	0	0	0	0
1	0	0	1	0	0
1	0	1	0	0	0
1	0	1	1	0	0
1	1	0	0	0	0
1	1	0	1	0	0
1	1	1	0	0	0
1	1	1	1	0	0

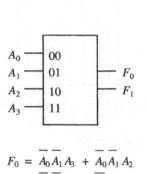

$$F_0 = \overline{A_0}\,\overline{A_1}\,A_3 + \overline{A_0}\,\overline{A_1}\,A_2$$

$$F_1 = \overline{A_0}\,A_2\,A_3 + \overline{A_0}\,A_1$$

Figure A-33
Block diagram and truth table for a 4-to-2 priority encoder.

A.10.5 Priority Encoders

An **encoder** translates a set of inputs into a binary encoding, and can be thought of as the converse of a decoder. A **priority encoder** is one type of an encoder in which an ordering is imposed on the inputs. A block diagram and a corresponding truth table for a 4-to-2 priority encoder are shown in Figure A-33. A priority scheme is imposed on the inputs in which A_i has higher priority than A_{i+1}. The two-bit output takes on the value 00, 01, 10, or 11 depending on which inputs are active (in the 1 state) and their relative priorities. When no inputs are active, then the output defaults to giving priority to A_0 ($F_0 F_1 = 00$).

Priority encoders are used for arbitrating among a number of devices that compete for the same resource. A circuit diagram for a 4-to-2 priority encoder is shown in Figure A-34.

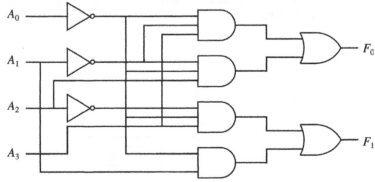

Figure A-34
Logic diagram for a 4-to-2 priority encoder.

(The circuit has been reduced using methods described in Section A.17. but the input/output behavior can be verified without needing to know the reduction method.)

A.10.6 Programmable Logic Arrays

A **programmable logic array** (PLA) is a component that consists of a customizable AND matrix followed by a customizable OR matrix. A PLA with three inputs and two outputs is shown in Figure A-35. The three inputs A, B, and C and their complements are available at the inputs of each of eight AND gates that generate eight product terms. The outputs of the AND gates are available at the inputs of each of the OR gates that generate functions F_0 and F_1. A programmable fuse is placed at each crosspoint in the AND and OR matrices. The matrices are customized for specific functions by disabling fuses. When a fuse is disabled at an input to an AND gate, then the AND gate behaves as if the input is tied to a 1. Similarly, a disabled input to an OR gate in a PLA behaves as if the input is tied to a 0.

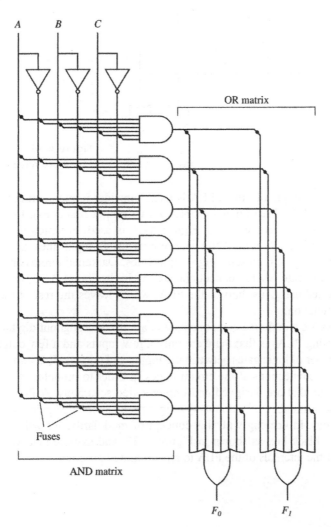

Figure A-35
A programmable logic array.

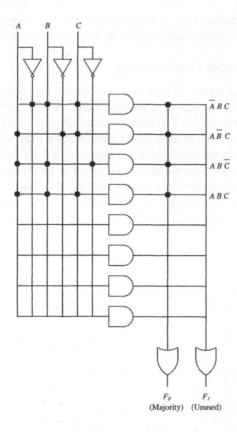

$\overline{A}\,B\,C$

$A\,\overline{B}\,C$

$A\,B\,\overline{C}$

$A\,B\,C$

F_0 F_1
(Majority)   (Unused)

Figure A-36
Simplified representation of a PLA.

As an example of how a PLA is used, consider implementing the majority function on a 3×2 PLA (three input variables $\times$ two output functions). In order to simplify the illustrations, the form shown in Figure A-36 is used, in which it is understood that the single input line into each AND gate represents six input lines, and the single input line into each OR gate represents eight input lines. Darkened circles are placed at the cross-points to indicate where connections are made. In Figure A-36, the majority function is implemented using just half of the PLA, which leaves the rest of the PLA available for another function.

PLAs are workhorse components that are used throughout digital circuits. An advantage of using PLAs is that there are only a few inputs and a few outputs, while there is a large number of logic gates between the inputs and outputs. It is important to minimize the number of connections at the circuit edges in order to modularize a system into discrete components that are designed and implemented separately. A PLA is ideal for this purpose, and a number of automated programs exist for designing PLAs from functional descriptions. In keeping with this concept of modularity, we will sometimes represent a PLA as a black box as shown in Figure A-37, and assume that we can safely leave the design of the internals of the PLA to an automated program.

$$A \longrightarrow$$
$$B \longrightarrow \boxed{\text{PLA}}$$
$$C \longrightarrow$$

$$F_0$$
$$F_1$$

Figure A-37
Black-box representation of a PLA.

EXAMPLE A-1 A Ripple-Carry Adder

As an example of how PLAs are used in the design of a digital circuit, consider designing a circuit that adds two binary numbers. Binary addition is performed similarly to the way we perform decimal addition by hand, as illustrated in Figure A-38. Two binary numbers A and B are added from right to left, creating a sum and a carry in each bit position. Two input bits and a carry-in must be summed at each bit position, so that a total of eight input combinations must be considered, as shown in the truth table in Figure A-39.

The truth table in Figure A-39 describes an element known as a **full adder**, which is shown schematically in the figure. A **half adder**, which could be used for the rightmost bit position, adds two bits and produces a sum and a carry, whereas a full adder adds two bits and a carry and produces a sum and a carry. The half adder is not used here in order to keep the number of different components to a minimum. Four full adders can be cascaded to form an adder large enough to add the four-bit numbers used in the example in Figure A-38, as shown in Figure A-40. The rightmost full adder has a carry-in (c_0) of 0.

Carry In $\longrightarrow$	0	0	0	0	1	1	1	1
Operand A $\longrightarrow$	0	0	1	1	0	0	1	1
Operand B $\longrightarrow$	+ 0	+ 1	+ 0	+ 1	+ 0	+ 1	+ 0	+ 1
	0 0	0 1	0 1	1 0	0 1	1 0	1 0	1 1

Carry Sum
Out

Example:

Carry	1 0 0 0
Operand A	0 1 0 0
Operand B	+ 0 1 1 0
Sum	1 0 1 0

Figure A-38
Example of addition for two unsigned binary numbers.

A_i B_i C_i	S_i	C_{i+1}
0 0 0	0	0
0 0 1	1	0
0 1 0	1	0
0 1 1	0	1
1 0 0	1	0
1 0 1	0	1
1 1 0	0	1
1 1 1	1	1

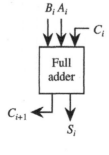

Figure A-39
Truth table for a full adder.

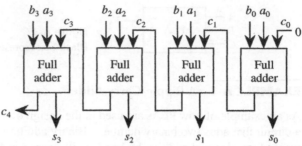

Figure A-40
A four-bit adder implemented with a cascade of full adders.

The reader should note that the value for a given sum bit cannot be computed until the carry-out from the previous full adder has been computed. The circuit is called a "ripple carry" adder because the correct values for the carry bits "ripple" through the circuit from right to left. The reader may also observe that even though the circuit looks "parallel," in reality the sum bits are computed serially from right to left. This is a major disadvantage to the circuit. We discussed ways of speeding up addition in Chapter 3.

An approach to designing a full adder is to use a PLA, as shown in Figure A-41. The PLA approach is very general, and computer-aided design (CAD) tools for VLSI typically favor the use of PLAs over random logic or MUXes because of their generality. CAD tools

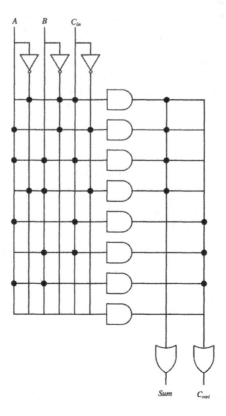

Figure A-41
PLA realization of a full adder.

typically reduce the sizes of the PLAs (we will see a few reduction techniques in Section A.17) and so the seemingly high gate count for the PLA is not actually so high in practice.

■

■ A.11 SEQUENTIAL LOGIC

In the earlier part of this appendix we explored combinational logic units, in which the outputs are completely determined by functions of the inputs. A sequential logic unit, commonly referred to as a **finite state machine** (FSM), takes an input and a current state and produces an output and a new state. An FSM is distinguished from a CLU in that the past history of the inputs to the FSM influences its state and output. This is important for implementing memory circuits as well as control units in a computer.

The classical model of a finite state machine is shown in Figure A-42. A CLU takes inputs from lines $i_0 - i_k$ that are external to the FSM, and also takes inputs from state bits $s_0 - s_n$ that are internal to the FSM. The CLU produces output bits $f_0 - f_m$ and new state bits. Delay elements maintain the current state of the FSM until a synchronization signal causes the D_i values to be loaded into the s_i, which appear at Q_i as the new state bits.

A.11.1 The S-R Flip-Flop

A **flip-flop** is an arrangement of logic gates that maintains a stable output even after the inputs are made inactive. The output of a flip-flop is determined by both the current inputs and the past history of inputs, and thus a combinational logic unit is not powerful enough to capture this behavior. A flip-flop can be used to store a single bit of information, and serves as a building block for computer memory.

If either or both inputs of a two-input NOR gate is 1, then the output of the NOR gate is 0, otherwise the output is 1. As we saw earlier in this appendix, the time that it takes for

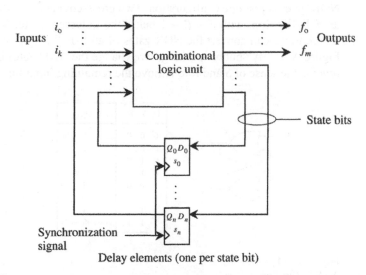

Figure A-42
Classical model of a finite state machine.

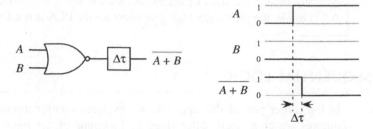

Timing Behavior

Figure A-43
A NOR gate with a lumped delay at its output.

a signal to propagate from the inputs of a logic gate to the output is not instantaneous, and there is some delay $\Delta\tau$ that represents the propagation delay through the gate. The delay is sometimes considered lumped at the output of the gate for purposes of analysis, as illustrated in Figure A-43. The lumped delay is not normally indicated in circuit diagrams but its presence is implied.

The propagation time through the NOR gate affects the operation of a flip-flop. Consider the **set-reset** (S-R) flip-flop shown in Figure A-44, which consists of two cross-coupled NOR gates. If we apply a 1 to S, then $\overline{Q}$ goes to 0 after a delay $\Delta\tau$, which causes Q to go to 1 (assuming R is initially 0) after a delay $2\Delta\tau$. As a result of the finite propagation time, there is a brief period of time $\Delta\tau$ when both the Q and $\overline{Q}$ outputs assume a value of 0; this is logically incorrect, but will be fixed when the **master-slave** configuration is discussed later. If we now apply a 0 to S, then Q retains its state until some later time when R goes to 1. The S-R flip-flop thus holds a single bit of information and serves as an elementary memory element.

There is more than one way to make an S-R flip-flop, and the use of cross-coupled NOR gates is just one configuration. Two cross-coupled NAND gates can also implement an S-R flip-flop, with $S = R = 1$ being the quiescent state. Making use of DeMorgan's theorem, we can convert the NOR gates of an S-R flip-flop into AND gates as shown in Figure A-45. By "bubble pushing," we change the AND gates into NAND gates, and then reverse the sense of S and R to remove the remaining input bubbles.

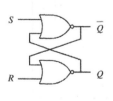

Q_i	S_i	R_i	Q_{i+1}
0	0	0	0
0	0	1	0
0	1	0	1
0	1	1	(disallowed)
1	0	0	1
1	0	1	0
1	1	0	1
1	1	1	(disallowed)

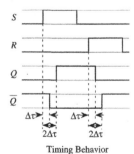

Timing Behavior

Figure A-44
An S-R flip-flop.

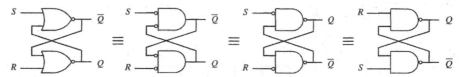

Figure A-45
A NOR implementation of an S-R flip-flop is converted into a NAND implementation.

A.11.2 The Clocked S-R Flip-Flop

Now consider that the inputs to the S-R flip-flop may originate from the outputs of some other circuits, whose inputs may originate from the outputs of other circuits, forming a cascade of logic circuits. This mirrors the form of conventional digital circuits. A problem with cascading circuits is that transitions may occur at times that are not desired.

Consider the circuit shown in Figure A-46. If signals *A*, *B*, and *C* all change from the 0 state to the 1 state, then signal *C* may reach the XOR gate before *A* and *B* propagate through the AND gate; this will momentarily produce a 1 output at *S*, which will revert to 0 when the output of the AND gate settles and is XORed with *C*. At this point it may be too late, however, since *S* may be in the 1 state long enough to set the flip-flop, destroying the integrity of the stored bit.

When the final state of a flip-flop is sensitive to the relative arrival times of signals, the result may be a **glitch**, which is an unwanted state or output. A circuit that can produce a glitch is said to have a **hazard**. The hazard may or may not manifest itself as a glitch, depending on the operating conditions of the circuit at a particular time.

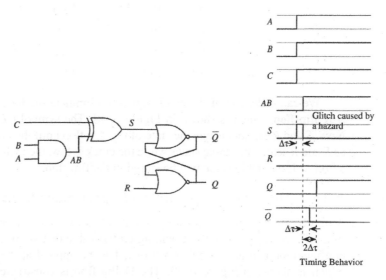

Figure A-46
A circuit with a hazard.

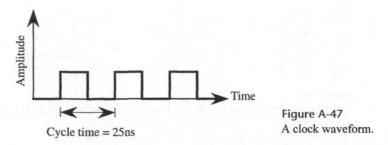

Figure A-47
A clock waveform.

Cycle time = 25ns

In order to achieve synchronization in a controlled fashion, a **clock** signal is provided, to which every state-dependent circuit (such as a flip-flop) synchronizes itself by accepting inputs only at discrete times. A clock circuit produces a continuous stream of 1s and 0s, as indicated by the waveform shown in Figure A-47. The time required for the clock to rise, then fall, then begin to rise again is called the **cycle time**. The square edges that are shown in the waveform represent an ideal square wave. In practice, the edges are rounded because instantaneous rise and fall times do not occur.

The **clock rate** is taken as the inverse of the cycle time. For a cycle time of 25 ns/cycle, the corresponding clock rate is 1/25 cycles/ns, which corresponds to 40,000,000 cycles per second, or 40 MHz (for 40 megahertz). A list of other abbreviations that are commonly used to specify cycle times and clock rates is shown in Table A.2.

Table A.2 **Standard scientific prefixes for cycle times and clock rates**

Prefix	Abbrev.	Quantity	Prefix	Abbrev.	Quantity
milli	m	10^{-3}	Kilo	K	10^{3}
micro	μ	10^{-6}	Mega	M	10^{6}
nano	n	10^{-9}	Giga	G	10^{9}
pico	p	10^{-12}	Tera	T	10^{12}
femto	f	10^{-15}	Peta	P	10^{15}
atto	a	10^{-18}	Exa	E	10^{18}

We can make use of the clock signal to eliminate the hazard by creating a **clocked S-R flip-flop**, which is shown in Figure A-48. The symbol *CLK* labels the clock input. Now, S and R cannot change the state of the flip-flop until the clock is high. Thus, as long as S and R settle into stable states while the clock is low, then when the clock makes a transition to 1, the stable value will be stored in the flip-flop.

A.11.3 The D Flip-Flop and the Master-Slave Configuration

A disadvantage of the S-R flip-flop is that in order to store a 1 or a 0, we need to apply a 1 to a different input (S or R) depending on the value that we want to store. An alternative configuration that allows either a 0 or a 1 to be applied at the input is the **D flip-flop**, which is shown in Figure A-49. The D flip-flop is constructed by placing an inverter across the S and R inputs of an S-R flip-flop. Now, when the clock goes high, the value on the D line is stored in the flip-flop.

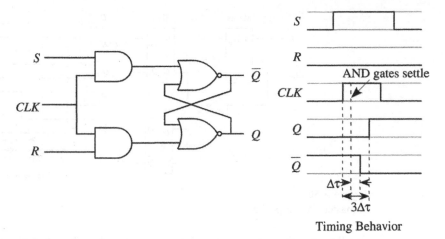

Figure A-48
A clocked S-R flip-flop.

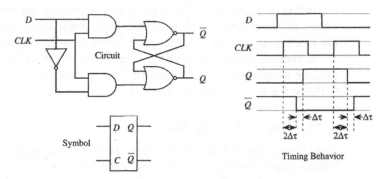

Figure A-49
A clocked D flip-flop. The letter C denotes the clock input in the symbol form. Note that if D and CLK change simultaneously enough, $3\Delta\tau$ are necessary for the clocked D flip-flop to become stable when D becomes 0, and $4\Delta\tau$ are necessary when D becomes 1.

The D flip-flop is commonly used in situations where there is feedback from the output back to the input through some other circuitry, and this feedback can sometimes cause the flip-flop to change states more than once per clock cycle. In order to ensure that the flip-flop changes state just once per clock, we break the feedback loop by constructing a **master-slave flip-flop,** as shown in Figure A-50. The master-slave flip-flop consists of two flip-flops arranged in tandem, with an inverted clock used for the second flip-flop. The master flip-flop changes when the clock is high, but the slave flip-flop does not change until the clock is low; thus the clock must first go high and then go low before the input at D in the master is clocked through to Q_S in the slave. The triangle shown in the symbol for the master-slave flip-flop indicates that transitions at the output occur only on a rising (0 to 1 transition) or falling (1 to 0 transition) edge of the clock. Transitions at the output do not occur continuously during a high level of the clock as for the clocked S-R

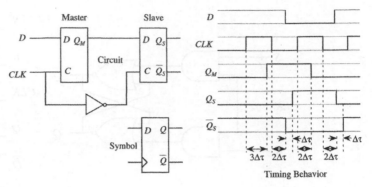

Figure A-50
A master-slave flip-flop.

flip-flop. For the configuration shown in Figure A-50, the transition at the output occurs on the falling edge of the clock.

A **level-triggered** flip-flop changes state continuously while the clock is high (or low, depending on how the flip-flop is designed). An **edge-triggered** flip-flop changes only on a high-to-low or low-to-high clock transition. Some textbooks do not place a triangle at the clock input in order to distinguish between level-triggered and edge-triggered flip-flops, and indicate one form or the other based on their usage or in some other way. In practice the notation is held somewhat loosely. Here, we will use the triangle symbol and will also make the flip-flop type clear from the way it is used.

A.11.4 J-K and T Flip-Flops

In addition to the S-R and D flip-flops, there are **J-K** and **T flip-flops**. The J-K flip-flop behaves similarly to an S-R flip-flop, except that it flips its state when both inputs are set to 1. The T flip-flop (for "toggle") alternates states, as when the inputs to a J-K flip-flop are set to 1. Logic diagrams and symbols for the clocked J-K and T flip-flops are shown in Figures A-51 and A-52, respectively. (The positions of the outputs in Figures A-51 and A-52 have been swapped as a notational convenience.)

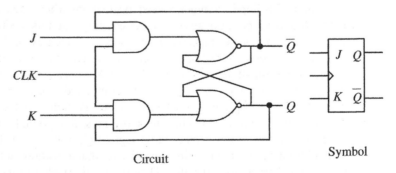

Figure A-51
Logic diagram and symbol for a basic J-K flip-flop.

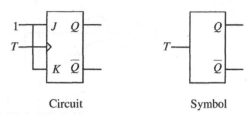

Circuit   Symbol

Figure A-52
Logic diagram and symbol for a T flip-flop.

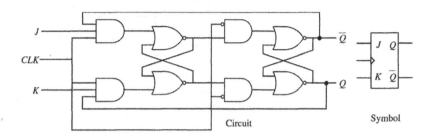

Circuit   Symbol

Figure A-53
Logic diagram and symbol for a master-slave J-K flip-flop.

A problem with the toggle mode of operation for the J-K flip-flop is that when *J* and *K* are both high when the clock is also high, the flip-flop may toggle more than once before the clock goes low. This is another situation in which a master-slave configuration is appropriate. A schematic diagram for a master-slave J-K flip-flop is shown in Figure A-53. The "endless toggle" problem is now fixed with this configuration, but there is a new problem of "one's catching." If an input is high for any time while the clock is high, and if the input is simply in a transition mode before settling, the flip-flop will "see" the 1 as if it were meant to be a valid input. The situation can be avoided if hazards are eliminated in the circuit that provides the inputs.

We can solve the one's catching problem by constructing edge-triggered flip-flops in which only the transition of the clock (low to high for positive-edge-triggered and high to low for negative-edge-triggered) causes the inputs to be sampled, at which point the inputs should be stable.

Figure A-54 shows a configuration for a negative-edge-triggered D flip-flop. When the clock is high, the top and bottom latches output 0s to the main (output) S-R latch. The D input can change an arbitrary number of times while the clock is high without affecting the state of the main latch. When the clock goes low, only the settled values of the top and bottom latches affect the state of the main latch. While the clock is low, if the D input changes, the main flip-flop is not affected.

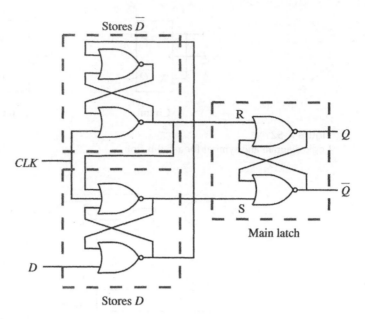

Figure A-54
Negative edge triggered D flip-flop.

■ A.12 DESIGN OF FINITE STATE MACHINES

Refer again to the classical model of an FSM shown in Figure A-42. The delay elements can be implemented with master-slave flip-flops, and the synchronization signal can be provided by the clock. In general, there should be a flip-flop on each feedback line. Notice that we can label the flip-flops in any convenient way as long as the meaning is clear: in Figure A-42, the positions of the inputs D_i and the outputs Q_i have been interchanged with respect to the flip-flop figures in the previous section.

Consider a modulo-4 synchronous counter FSM that counts from 00 to 11 and then repeats. A block diagram of a synchronous counter FSM is shown in Figure A-55. The RESET (positive logic) function operates synchronously with respect to the clock. The outputs appear as a sequence of values on lines q_0 and q_1 at time steps corresponding to the clock. As the outputs are generated, a new state s_1s_0 is generated that is fed back to the input.

We can consider designing the counter by enumerating all possible input conditions and then creating four functions for the output q_1q_0 and the state s_1s_0. The corresponding functions can then be used to create a combinational logic circuit that implements the counter. Two flip-flops are used for the two state bits.

How do we know that two state bits are needed on the feedback path? The fact is, we may not know in advance how many state bits are needed, and so we would like to have a more general approach to designing a finite state machine. For the counter, we can start by constructing a **state transition diagram** as shown in Figure A-56, in which each state rep-

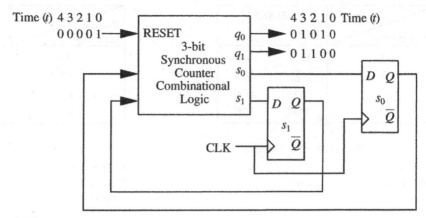

Figure A-55
A modulo-4 counter.

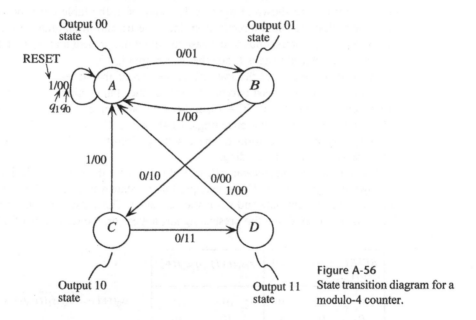

Figure A-56
State transition diagram for a
modulo-4 counter.

resents a count from 00 to 11 and the directed arcs represent transitions between states. State A represents the case in which the count is 00, and states B, C, and D represent counts 01, 10, and 11 respectively.

Assume the FSM is initially in state A. There are two possible input conditions: 0 or 1. If the input (RESET) line is 0, then the FSM advances to state B and outputs 01. If the RESET line is 1, then the FSM remains in state A and outputs 00. Similarly, when the FSM is in state B, the FSM advances to state C and outputs 10 if the RESET line is 0, otherwise the FSM returns to state A and outputs 00. Transitions from the remaining states are interpreted similarly.

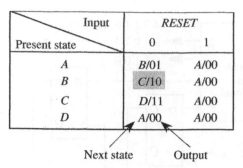

Input Present state	RESET 0	1
A	B/01	A/00
B	C/10	A/00
C	D/11	A/00
D	A/00	A/00

Next state   Output

Figure A-57
State table for a modulo-4 counter.

Input Present state (S_t)	RESET 0	1
A:00	01/01	00/00
B:01	10/10	00/00
C:10	11/11	00/00
D:11	00/00	00/00

Figure A-58
State table with state assignments for a modulo-4 counter.

Once we have created the state transition diagram, we can rewrite it in tabular form as a **state table,** as shown in Figure A-57. The present states are shown at the left, and the input conditions are shown at the top. The entries in the table correspond to next state/output pairs that are taken directly from the state transition diagram in Figure A-56. The highlighted entry corresponds to the case in which the present state is B and the input is 0. For this case, the next state is C and the next output is 10.

After we have created the state table, we encode the states in binary. Since there are four states, we need at least two bits to encode the states uniquely. We arbitrarily choose the encoding $A = 00$, $B = 01$, $C = 10$, and $D = 11$, and replace every occurrence of A, B, C, and D with their respective encodings, as shown in Figure A-58. In practice, the state encoding may affect the form of the resulting circuit, but the circuit will be logically correct regardless of the encoding.

From the state table, we can extract truth tables for the next state and output functions as shown in Figure A-59. The subscripts for the state variables indicate timing relationships. s_t is the present state and s_{t+1} is the next state. The subscripts are commonly omitted since it is understood that the present signals appear on the right side of the equation and

RESET $r(t)$	$s_1(t)$	$s_0(t)$	$s_1 s_0(t+1)$	$q_1 q_0(t+1)$
0	0	0	01	01
0	0	1	10	10
0	1	0	11	11
0	1	1	00	00
1	0	0	00	00
1	0	1	00	00
1	1	0	00	00
1	1	1	00	00

$$s_0(t+1) = \overline{r(t)s_1(t)s_0(t)} + \overline{r(t)}s_1(t)\overline{s_0(t)}$$

$$s_1(t+1) = \overline{r(t)}s_1(t)\overline{s_0(t)} + \overline{r(t)}s_1(t)\overline{s_0(t)}$$

$$q_0(t+1) = \overline{r(t)}\overline{s_1(t)}s_0(t) + \overline{r(t)}s_1(t)\overline{s_0(t)}$$

$$q_1(t+1) = \overline{r(t)}s_1(t)\overline{s_0(t)} + \overline{r(t)}s_1(t)\overline{s_0(t)}$$

Figure A-59
Truth table for the next state and output functions for a modulo-4 counter.

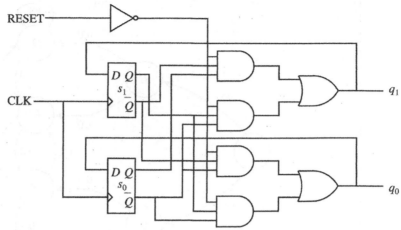

Figure A-60
Logic design for a modulo-4 counter.

the next signals appear on the left side of the equation. Notice that $s_0(t+1) = q_0(t+1)$ and $s_1(t+1) = q_1(t+1)$, so we only need to implement $s_0(t+1)$ and $s_1(t+1)$ and tap the outputs for $q_0(t+1)$ and $q_1(t+1)$.

Finally, we implement the next state and output functions using logic gates and master-slave D flip-flops for the state variables as shown in Figure A-60.

EXAMPLE A-2 A Sequence Detector

As another example, we would like to design a machine that outputs a 1 when exactly two of the last three inputs are 1. For example, an input sequence of 011011100 produces an output sequence of 001111010. There is a one-bit serial input line, and we can assume that initially no inputs have been seen. For this problem, we will use D flip-flops and 8-to-1 MUXes.

We start by constructing a state transition diagram, as shown in Figure A-61. There are eight possible three-bit sequences that our machine will observe: 000, 001, 010, 011, 100, 101, 110, and 111. State A is the initial state, in which we assume that no inputs have yet been seen. In states B and C, we have seen only one input, so we cannot output a 1 yet. In states D, E, F, and G we have only seen two inputs, so we cannot output a 1 yet, even though we have seen two 1s at the input when we enter state G. The machine makes all subsequent transitions among states D, E, F, and G. State D is visited when the last two inputs are 00. States E, F, and G are visited when the last two inputs are 01, 10, or 11, respectively.

The next step is to create a state table as shown in Figure A-62, which is taken directly from the state transition diagram. Next, we make a state assignment as shown in Figure A-63a. We then use the state assignment to create a truth table for the next state and output functions as shown in Figure A-63b. The last two entries in the table correspond to state 111, which cannot arise in practice, according to the state table in Figure A-63a. Therefore, the next state and output entries do not matter, and are labeled 'd' for **don't care**.

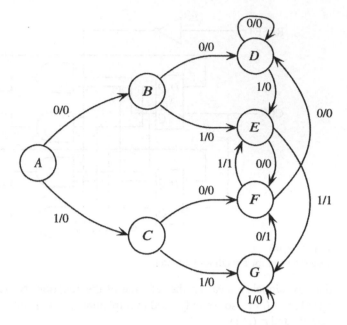

Figure A-61
State transition diagram for sequence detector.

Input Present state	X 0	1
A	B/0	C/0
B	D/0	E/0
C	F/0	G/0
D	D/0	E/0
E	F/0	G/1
F	D/0	E/1
G	F/1	G/0

Figure A-62
State table for sequence detector.

Finally, we create the circuit, which is shown in Figure A-64. There is one flip-flop for each state variable, so there are a total of three flip-flops. There are three next state functions and one output function, so there are four MUXes. Notice that the choice of s_2, s_1, and s_0 for the MUX control inputs is arbitrary. Any other grouping or ordering will also work.

	Input	X	
Present state		0	1
$S_2 S_1 S_0$		$S_2 S_1 S_0 Z$	$S_2 S_1 S_0 Z$
A: 000		001/0	010/0
B: 001		011/0	100/0
C: 010		101/0	110/0
D: 011		011/0	100/0
E: 100		101/0	110/1
F: 101		011/0	100/1
G: 110		101/1	110/0

(a)

Input and state at time t				Next state and output at time $t+1$			
S_2	S_1	S_0	X	S_2	S_1	S_0	Z
0	0	0	0	0	0	1	0
0	0	0	1	0	1	0	0
0	0	1	0	0	1	1	0
0	0	1	1	1	0	0	0
0	1	0	0	1	0	1	0
0	1	0	1	1	1	0	0
0	1	1	0	0	1	1	0
0	1	1	1	1	0	0	0
1	0	0	0	1	0	1	0
1	0	0	1	1	1	0	1
1	0	1	0	0	1	1	0
1	0	1	1	1	0	0	1
1	1	0	0	1	0	1	1
1	1	0	1	1	1	0	0
1	1	1	0	d	d	d	d
1	1	1	1	d	d	d	d

(b)

Figure A-63
State assignment and truth table for sequence detector.

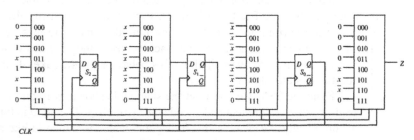

Figure A-64
Logic diagram for sequence detector.

EXAMPLE A-3   A Vending Machine Controller

For this example we will design a vending machine controller using D flip-flops and a black box representation of a PLA (as in Figure A-37). The vending machine accepts three U.S. coins: the nickel (5¢), the dime (10¢), and the quarter (25¢). When the value of the inserted coins equals or exceeds 20¢, then the machine dispenses the merchandise, returns any excess money, and waits for the next transaction.

We begin by constructing a state transition diagram, as shown in Figure A-65. In state A, no coins have yet been inserted, and so the money credited is 0¢. If a nickel or dime is inserted when the machine is in state A, then the FSM makes a transition to state B or state C, respectively. If a quarter is inserted, then the money credited to the customer is 25¢.

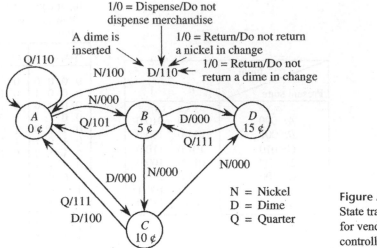

Figure A-65
State transition diagram for vending machine controller.

The controller dispenses the merchandise, returns a nickel in change, and remains in state A. This is indicated by the label Q/110 on the state A self-loop. States B and C are then expanded, producing state D, which is also expanded, resulting in the complete FSM for the vending machine controller.

Notice the behavior that is specified by the state transition diagram when a quarter is inserted when the FSM is in state D. Rather than dispensing the merchandise, returning 20¢, and returning to state A, the machine dispenses the merchandise, returns 15¢, and makes a transition to state B. The machine keeps the 5¢, and awaits the insertion of more money! In this case, we will allow this behavior for the sake of simplicity, as it keeps the number of states down.

From the FSM we construct the state table shown in Figure A-66a. We then make an arbitrary state assignment and encode the symbols N, D, and Q in binary as shown in Figure A-66b. Finally, we create a circuit diagram, which is shown in Figure A-67a. There are two state bits, so there are two D flip-flops. The PLA takes four inputs for the present-state bits and the x_1x_0 coin bits. The PLA produces five outputs for the next-state bits and the dispense and return nickel/return dime bits. (We can assume that the clock input is asserted only on an event such as an inserted coin.)

Input P.S.	N 00	D 01	Q 10
A	B/000	C/000	A/110
B	C/000	D/000	A/101
C	D/000	A/100	A/111
D	A/100	A/110	B/111

(a)

Input P.S. s_1s_0	N x_1x_0 00	D x_1x_0 01	Q x_1x_0 10
		$s_1s_0 / z_2z_1z_0$	
A:00	01/000	10/000	00/110
B:01	10/000	11/000	00/101
C:10	11/000	00/100	00/111
D:11	00/100	00/110	01/111

(b)

Figure A-66
(a) State table for vending machine controller; (b) state assignment for vending machine controller.

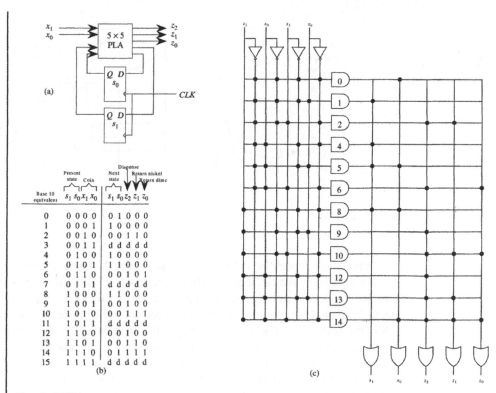

Figure A-67
(a) FSM circuit, (b) truth table, and (c) PLA realization for vending machine controller.

The truth table (b):

Base 10 equivalent	Present state $s_1 s_0$	Coin $x_1 x_0$	Next state $s_1 s_0$	Dispense z_2	Return nickel z_1	Return dime z_0
0	0 0	0 0	0 1	0	0	0
1	0 0	0 1	1 0	0	0	0
2	0 0	1 0	0 0	1	1	0
3	0 0	1 1	d d	d	d	d
4	0 1	0 0	1 0	0	0	0
5	0 1	0 1	1 1	0	0	0
6	0 1	1 0	0 0	1	0	1
7	0 1	1 1	d d	d	d	d
8	1 0	0 0	1 1	0	0	0
9	1 0	0 1	0 0	1	0	0
10	1 0	1 0	0 0	1	1	1
11	1 0	1 1	d d	d	d	d
12	1 1	0 0	0 0	1	0	0
13	1 1	0 1	0 0	1	1	0
14	1 1	1 0	0 1	1	1	1
15	1 1	1 1	d d	d	d	d

Notice that we have not explicitly specified the design of the PLA itself in obtaining the FSM circuit in Figure A-67a. At this level of complexity, it is common to use a computer program to generate a truth table and then feed the truth table to a PLA design program. We could generate the truth table and PLA design by hand, of course, as shown in Figures A-67b and A-67c.

■

■ A.13 MEALY *vs.* MOORE MACHINES

The outputs of the FSM circuits we have studied so far are determined by the present states and the inputs. The states are maintained in falling-edge-triggered flip-flops, and so a state change can only occur on the falling edge of the clock. Any changes that occur at the inputs have no effect on the state as long as the clock is low. The inputs are fed directly through the output circuits, however, with no intervening flip-flops. Thus a change to an input at any time can cause a change in the output, regardless of whether the clock is high or low. In Figure A-67, a change at either the x_1 or x_0 inputs will propagate through to the $z_2 z_1 z_0$ outputs independent of the level of the clock. This organization is referred to as the **Mealy** model of an FSM.

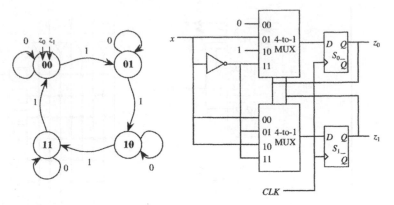

Figure A-68
A Moore binary counter FSM.

In the Mealy model, the outputs change as soon as the inputs change, and so there is no delay introduced by the clock. In the **Moore** model of an FSM, the outputs are embedded in the state bits, and so a change at the outputs occurs on the clock pulse *after* a change at the inputs. Both models are used by circuit designers, and either model may be encountered outside of this textbook. In this section we simply highlight the differences through an example.

An example of a Moore FSM is shown in Figure A-68. The FSM counts from 0 to 3 in binary and then repeats, similar to the modulo-4 counter shown in Figure A-60. The machine counts only when $x = 1$, otherwise the FSM maintains its current state. Notice that the outputs are embedded in the state variables, and so there is no direct path from the input to the outputs without an intervening flip-flop.

The Mealy model might be considered to be more powerful than the Moore model because in a single clock cycle, a change in the output of one FSM can ripple to the input of another FSM, whose output then changes and ripples to the next FSM, and so on. In the Moore model, lock-step synchronization is strictly maintained, and so this ripple scenario does not occur. Spurious changes in the output of an FSM thus have less influence on the rest of the circuit in the Moore model. This simplifies circuit analysis and hardware debugging, and for these situations, the Moore model may be preferred. In practice, both models are used.

■ A.14 REGISTERS

A single bit of information is stored in a D flip-flop. A group of N bits, making up an N-bit word, can be stored in N D flip-flops organized as shown in Figure A-69 for a four-bit word. We refer to such an arrangement of flip-flops as a "register." In this particular configuration, the data at inputs D_i are loaded into the register when the Write and Enable lines are high, synchronous with the clock. The contents of the register can be read at outputs Q_i only if the Enable line is high, since the tri-state buffers are in the electrically disconnected state when the Enable line is low. We can simplify the illustration by just marking the inputs and outputs, as shown in Figure A-70.

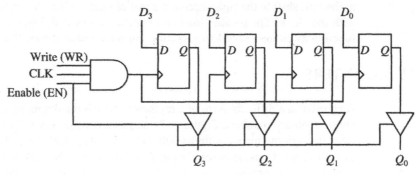

Figure A-69
A four-bit register.

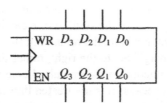

Figure A-70
Abstract representation of a
four-bit register.

A **shift register** copies the contents of each of its flip-flops to the next, while accepting a new input at one end and "spilling" the contents at the other end, which makes cascading possible. Consider the shift register shown in Figure A-71. The register can shift

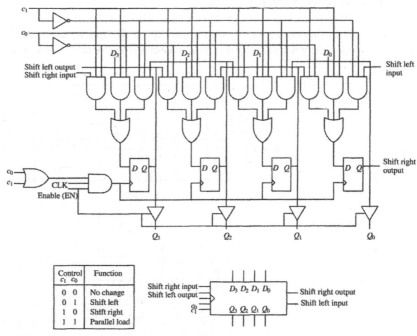

Control c_1 c_0	Function
0 0	No change
0 1	Shift left
1 0	Shift right
1 1	Parallel load

Figure A-71
Internal layout and block diagram for a left/right shifter with parallel read/write capabilities.

to the left, shift to the right, accept a parallel load, or remain unchanged, all synchronous with the clock. The parallel load and parallel read capabilities allow the shift register to function as either a **serial-to-parallel converter** or as a **parallel-to-serial converter**.

■ A.15 COUNTERS

A **counter** is a different form of a register in which the output pattern sequences through a range of binary numbers. Figure A-72 shows a configuration for a modulo-8 counter that steps through the binary patterns 000, 001, 010, 011, 100, 101, 110, 111 and then repeats. Three J-K flip-flops are placed in toggle mode, and each clock input is ANDed with the Q output from the previous stage, which successively halves the clock frequency. The result is a progression of toggle flip-flops operating at rates that differ in powers of two, corresponding to the sequence of binary patterns from 000 to 111.

Notice that we have added an active low asynchronous RESET line to the counter, which resets it to 000, independent of the states of the clock or enable lines. Except for the flip-flop in the least significant position, the remaining flip-flops change state according to changes in states from their neighbors to the right, rather than synchronously with respect to the clock. It is similar in function to the modulo-4 counter in Figure A-60, but is more easily extended to large sizes because it is not treated like an ordinary FSM for design purposes, in which all states are enumerated. It is, nevertheless, an FSM.

■ A.16 REDUCTION OF COMBINATIONAL LOGIC AND SEQUENTIAL LOGIC

Up to this point, we focused primarily on the functional correctness of digital logic circuits. Only a little consideration was given to the possibility that there may be more than

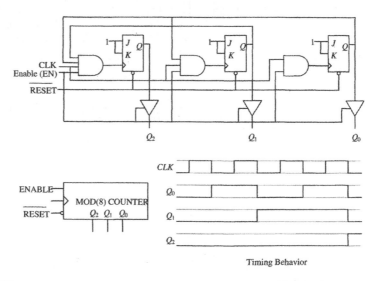

Figure A-72
A modulo-8 counter.

one way to design a circuit, with some designs being better than others in terms of component count (that is, the numbers and sizes of the logic gates).

In the remainder of this appendix, we take a systematic approach to reducing the numbers of components in a design. We first look at reducing the sizes of combinational logic expressions, which loosely correspond to the numbers and sizes of the logic gates in an implementation of a digital circuit. We then look at reducing the numbers of states in finite state machines (FSMs) and explore a few areas of FSM design that impact the numbers and sizes of logic gates in implementations of FSMs.

■ A.17 REDUCTION OF TWO-LEVEL EXPRESSIONS

In many cases the canonical **sum-of-products** (SOP) or **product-of-sums** (POS) forms are not minimal in terms of their number and size. Since a smaller Boolean equation translates to a lower gate input count in the target circuit, reduction of the equation is an important consideration when circuit complexity is an issue.

Three methods of reducing Boolean equations are described in the sections that follow: **algebraic reduction**, **Karnaugh map (K-map) reduction**, and **tabular reduction**. The algebraic method forms the basis for the other two methods. It is also the most abstract method, relying as it does only on the theorems of Boolean algebra.

The K-map and tabular methods are in fact pencil-and-paper implementations of the algebraic method. We discuss them because they allow the reader to visualize the reduction process, and thus to have a better intuition for how the process works. These manual processes can be used effectively to minimize functions that have about four or fewer variables. For larger functions, a computer-aided design (CAD) approach is generally more effective.

A.17.1 The Algebraic Method

The algebraic method applies the properties of Boolean algebra that were introduced earlier in a systematic manner to reduce expression size. Consider the Boolean equation for the majority function, which is repeated below:

$$F = \bar{A}BC + A\bar{B}C + AB\bar{C} + ABC \tag{A.7}$$

The properties of Boolean algebra can be applied to reduce the equation to a simpler form as shown in Equations A.8–A.10:

$$F = \bar{A}BC + A\bar{B}C + AB(\bar{C} + C) \qquad \text{Distributive property} \tag{A.8}$$

$$F = \bar{A}BC + A\bar{B}C + AB(1) \qquad \text{Complement property} \tag{A.9}$$

$$F = \bar{A}BC + A\bar{B}C + AB \qquad \text{Identity property} \tag{A.10}$$

The corresponding circuit for A.10 is shown in Figure A-73. In comparison with the majority circuit shown in Figure A-18, the gate count is reduced from eight to six and the gate input count is reduced from 19 to 13.

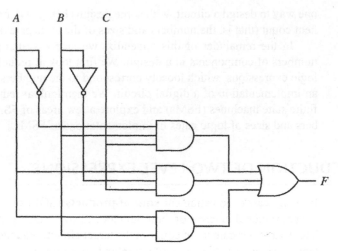

Figure A-73
Reduced circuit for the majority function.

We can reduce A.10 further. By applying the property of idempotence, we obtain A.11, in which we have reintroduced the minterm ABC;

$$F = \bar{A}BC + A\bar{B}C + AB + ABC \qquad \text{Idempotence property} \qquad \text{(A.11)}$$

We can then apply the distributive, complement, and identity properties again and obtain a simpler equation, as shown below:

$$F = \bar{A}BC + AC(\bar{B} + B) + AB \qquad \text{Distributive property} \qquad \text{(A.12)}$$

$$F = \bar{A}BC + AC(1) + AB \qquad \text{Complement property} \qquad \text{(A.13)}$$

$$F = \bar{A}BC + AC + AB \qquad \text{Identity property} \qquad \text{(A.14)}$$

Equation A.14 has a smaller gate input count of 11. We iterate this method one more time and reduce the equation further, as shown below:

$$F = \bar{A}BC + AC + AB + ABC \qquad \text{Idempotence property} \qquad \text{(A.15)}$$

$$F = BC(\bar{A} + A) + AC + AB \qquad \text{Distributive property} \qquad \text{(A.16)}$$

$$F = BC(1) + AC + AB \qquad \text{Complement property} \qquad \text{(A.17)}$$

$$F = BC + AC + AB \qquad \text{Identity property} \qquad \text{(A.18)}$$

Equation A.18 is now in its minimal two-level form, and can be reduced no further.

A.17.2 The K-Map Method

The K-map method is, in effect, a graphical technique that can be used to visualize the minterms in a function along with variables that are common to them. Variables that are

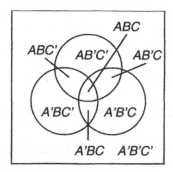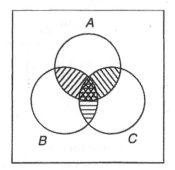

Figure A-74
A Venn diagram representation for three binary variables (left) and for the majority function (right).

common to more than one minterm are candidates for elimination, as discussed above. The basis of the K-map is the *Venn diagram*, which was originally devised to visualize concepts in set theory.

The Venn diagram for binary variables consists of a rectangle that represents the binary universe in SOP form. A Venn diagram for three variables A, B, and C is shown in Figure A-74. Within the universe is a circle for each variable. Within its circle a variable has the value 1, and outside of its circle a variable has the value 0. Intersections represent the minterms, as shown in the figure.

Adjacent shaded regions are candidates for reduction since they vary in exactly one variable. In the figure, region ABC can be combined with each of the three adjacent regions to produce a reduced form of the majority function. The *K-map is just a topological or relationship-preserving transformation of the Venn diagram*. As in the Venn diagram, in the K-map, minterms that differ in exactly one variable are placed next to each other.

A K-map for the majority function is shown in Figure A-75. Each cell in the K-map corresponds to an entry in the truth table for the function, and since there are eight entries in the truth table, there are eight cells in the corresponding K-map. A 1 is placed in each cell that corresponds to a true entry. A 0 is entered in each remaining cell, but can be omitted from the K-map for clarity as it is here. The labeling along the top and left sides is arranged in a **Gray code** in which exactly one variable changes between adjacent cells along each dimension.

Adjacent 1s in the K-map satisfy the condition needed to apply the complement property of Boolean algebra. Since there are adjacent 1s in the K-map shown in Figure A-75, a reduction is possible. Groupings of adjacent cells are made into rectangles in sizes that correspond to powers of 2, such as 1, 2, 4 and 8. These groups are referred to as **prime**

AB C	00	01	11	10
0			1	
1		1	1	1

Figure A-75
A K-map for the majority function.

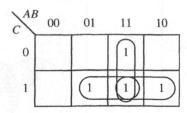

Figure A-76
Adjacency groupings for the majority function.

implicants. As groups increase in size above a 1-group (a group with one member), more variables are eliminated from a Boolean expression, and so the largest groups that can be obtained are used. In order to maintain the adjacency property, the shapes of groups must always be rectangular, and each group must contain a number of cells that corresponds to an integral power of two.

We start the reduction process by creating groups for 1s *that can be contained in no larger group*, and progress to larger groups until all cells with a 1 are covered at least once. The adjacency criterion is crucial, since we are looking for groups of minterms that differ in such a way that a reduction can be applied by using the complement and identity properties of Boolean algebra, as in:

$$ABC + AB\overline{C} = AB(C + \overline{C}) = AB(1) = AB \tag{A.19}$$

For the majority function, three groups of size two are made, as shown in Figure A-76. Every cell with a 1 has at least one neighboring cell with a 1, and so there are no 1-groups. We look next at 2-groups, and find that all of the 1-cells are covered by 2-groups. One of the cells is included in all three groups, which is allowed in the reduction process by the property of idempotence. The complement property eliminates the variable that differs between cells, and the resulting minimized equation is obtained:

$$M = BC + AC + AB \tag{A.20}$$

The BC term is derived from the 2-group $(ABC + \overline{A}BC)$, which reduces to $BC(A + \overline{A})$ and then to BC. The AC term is similarly derived from the 2-group $(ABC + A\overline{B}C)$, and the AB term is similarly derived from the 2-group $(ABC + AB\overline{C})$. The corresponding circuit is shown in Figure A-77. The gate count is reduced from eight to four as compared with the circuit shown in Figure A-18, and the gate input count is reduced from 19 to nine.

Looking more closely at the method of starting with 1-cells that can be included in no larger subgroups, consider what would happen if we started with the largest groups first. Figure A-78 shows both approaches applied to the same K-map. The reduction on the left is obtained by working with 1s that can be included in no larger subgroup, which is the method we have been using. Groupings are made in the order indicated by the numbers. A total of four groups are obtained, each of size two. The reduction on the right is obtained by starting with the largest groups first. Five groups are thus obtained, one of size four and four of size two. Thus, the minimal equation is not obtained if we start with the largest groups first. Both equations shown in Figure A-78 describe the same function, and a logically correct circuit will be obtained in either case; however, one circuit will not be produced from a minimized equation.

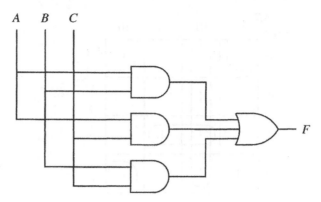

Figure A-77
Minimized AND-OR circuit for the majority function.

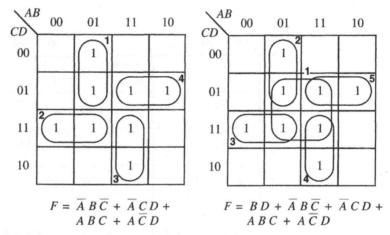

$$F = \overline{A}\,B\,\overline{C} + \overline{A}\,C\,D +$$
$$A\,B\,C + A\,\overline{C}\,D$$

$$F = B\,D + \overline{A}\,B\,\overline{C} + \overline{A}\,C\,D +$$
$$A\,B\,C + A\,\overline{C}\,D$$

Figure A-78
Minimal K-map grouping (left) and K-map grouping that is not minimal (right).

As another example, consider the K-map shown in Figure A-79. The edges of the K-map wrap around horizontally and vertically, and the four corners are logically adjacent. The corresponding minimized equation is shown in the figure.

Don't cares

Now consider the K-maps shown in Figure A-80. The d entries denote *don't cares*, which can be treated as 0s or as 1s at our convenience. A don't care represents a condition that cannot arise during operation. For example, if $X = 1$ represents the condition in which an elevator is on the ground floor and $Y=1$ represents the condition in which the elevator is on the top floor, then X and Y will not both be 1 at the same time, although they may both be 0 at the same time. Thus, a truth-table entry for an elevator function that corresponds to $X = Y = 1$ would be marked as a don't care.

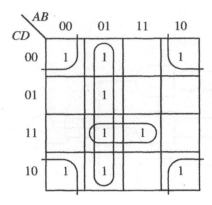

Figure A-79
The corners of a K-map are logically adjacent.

$$F = B\,C\,D + \overline{B}\,\overline{D} + \overline{A}\,B$$

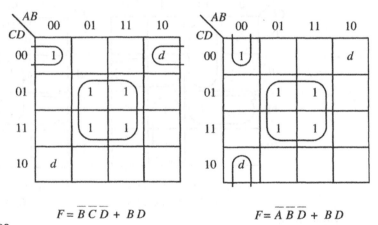

$$F = \overline{B}\,\overline{C}\,\overline{D} + B\,D$$

$$F = \overline{A}\,\overline{B}\,\overline{D} + B\,D$$

Figure A-80
Two different minimized equations are produced from the same K-map.

In Figure A-80, a more complex function is shown in which two different results are obtained from applying the same minimization process. The K-map on the left treats the top right don't care as a 1 and the bottom left don't care as a 0. The K-map on the right treats the top right don't care as a 0 and the bottom left don't care as a 1. Both K-maps result in minimized Boolean equations of the same size, and so it is possible to have more than one minimal expression for a Boolean function. In practice, one equation may be preferred over another, possibly in order to reduce the fan-out for one of the variables or to take advantage of sharing minterms with other functions.

Higher-dimensional maps are needed for more than four variables. While this is not covered here, the interested reader can find a detailed explanation of the method as well as a higher-level reduction technique known as **map-entered variables** on the companion Web site.

Multilevel circuits

It should be emphasized that a K-map reduces the size of a two-level expression, as measured by the number and sizes of the terms. This process does not necessarily produce a minimal form for multilevel circuits. For example, Equation A.18 is in its minimal two-level form, since only two levels of logic are used in its representation: three ANDed collections of variables (product terms) that are ORed together. The corresponding logic diagram that is shown in Figure A-77 has a gate-input count of nine. A three-level form can be created by factoring out one of the variables algebraically, such as A, as shown in Equation A.21:

$$M = BC + A(B + C) \tag{A.21}$$

The corresponding logic diagram that is shown in Figure A-81 has a gate input count of eight, and thus a less complex circuit is realized by using a multilevel approach. There is now a greater delay between the inputs and the outputs, however, and so we might create another measure of circuit complexity: the **gate delay**. A two-level circuit has a gate delay of two because there are two logic gates on the longest path from an input to an output. The circuit shown in Figure A-81 has a gate delay of three.

Although there are techniques that aid the circuit designer in discovering trade-offs between circuit depth and gate input count, the development of algorithms that cover the space of possible alternatives in reasonable time is only a partially solved problem.

A.17.3 The Tabular Method

An algorithmic approach to reducing Boolean expressions that lends itself to automation is commonly used for single- and multiple-output functions. The tabular method, also known as the **Quine-McCluskey** method, successively forms Boolean cross products among groups of terms that differ in one variable, and then uses the smallest set of reduced terms to cover the functions. This process is easier than the map method to implement on a computer, and an extension of the method allows terms to be shared among functions.

Reduction of single functions

The truth table shown in Figure A-82 describes a function F in four variables A, B, C, and D, and includes three don't cares. The tabular reduction process begins by grouping min-

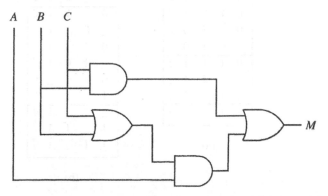

Figure A-81
A three-level circuit implements the majority function with a gate-input count of eight.

A	B	C	D	F
0	0	0	0	d
0	0	0	1	1
0	0	1	0	0
0	0	1	1	1
0	1	0	0	0
0	1	0	1	1
0	1	1	0	1
0	1	1	1	1
1	0	0	0	0
1	0	0	1	0
1	0	1	0	1
1	0	1	1	d
1	1	0	0	0
1	1	0	1	1
1	1	1	0	0
1	1	1	1	d

Figure A-82
A truth table representation of a
function with don't cares.

terms for which F is nonzero according to the number of 1s in each minterm. Don't care conditions are considered to be nonzero for this process. Minterm 0000 contains no 1s and is in its own group, as shown in Figure A-83a. Minterms 0001, 0010, 0100, and 1000 all contain a single 1, but only minterm 0001 has a nonzero entry and so it forms another group.

Initial setup

A	B	C	D	
0	0	0	0	√
0	0	0	1	√
0	0	1	1	√
0	1	0	1	√
0	1	1	0	√
1	0	1	0	√
0	1	1	1	√
1	0	1	1	√
1	1	0	1	√
1	1	1	1	√

(a)

After first
reduction

A	B	C	D	
0	0	0	_	*
0	0	_	1	√
0	_	0	1	√
0	_	1	1	√
_	0	1	1	√
0	1	_	1	√
_	1	0	1	√
0	1	1	_	*
1	0	1	_	*
_	1	1	1	√
1	_	1	1	√
1	1	_	1	√

(b)

After second
reduction

A	B	C	D	
0	_	_	1	*
_	_	1	1	*
_	1	_	1	*

(c)

Figure A-83
The tabular reduction process.

The next group has two 1s in each minterm, and there are six possible minterms that can belong to this group. Only minterms 0011, 0101, 0110, and 1010 have nonzero entries, and so they comprise this group. There are three nonzero entries in the next group, which has three 1s in each minterm. The nonzero minterms are 0111, 1011, and 1110. Finally, there is one nonzero entry that contains four 1s, and the corresponding minterm makes up the last group. For larger truth tables, the process continues until all nonzero entries are covered. The groups are organized so that adjacent groups differ in the number of 1s by one, as shown in Figure A-83a.

The next step in the reduction process is to form a **consensus** (the logical form of a cross product) between each pair of adjacent groups for all terms that differ in only one variable. The general form of the consensus theorem is restated below:

$$XY + \bar{X}Z + YZ = XY + \bar{X}Z \tag{A.22}$$

The term YZ is redundant since it is covered by the remaining terms, and so it can be eliminated. Algebraically, we can prove the theorem as shown below:

$$
\begin{aligned}
XY + \bar{X}Z + YZ &= XY + \bar{X}Z + YZ(X + \bar{X}) \\
&= XY + \bar{X}Z + XYZ + \bar{X}YZ \\
&= XY + XYZ + \bar{X}Z + \bar{X}YZ \\
&= XY(1 + Z) + \bar{X}Z(1 + Y) \\
&= XY + \bar{X}Z
\end{aligned}
$$

The consensus theorem also has a dual form:

$$(X + Y)(\bar{X} + Z)(Y + Z) = (X + Y)(\bar{X} + Z) \tag{A.23}$$

The idea of applying consensus in tabular reduction is to take advantage of the inverse property of Boolean algebra, similarly to the way we did for K-maps in the previous section. For example, 0000 and 0001 differ in variable D, so 000_ is listed at the top of the reduced table shown in Figure A-83b. The underscore marks the position of the variable that has been eliminated, which is D for this case. Minterms 0000 and 0001 in Figure A-83a are marked with checks to indicate that they are now covered in the reduced table.

After every term in the first group is crossed with every term in the second group, we then move on to form a consensus between terms in the second and third groups. Note that it is possible that some terms cannot be combined into a smaller term because they differ in more than one variable. For example, terms 0001 and 0011 combine into the smaller term 00_1 as shown in the top of the second group in Figure A-83b, but terms 0001 and 0110 cannot be combined because they differ in three variables.

Once a term is marked with a check, it can still be used in the reduction process by the property of idempotence. The objective in this step of the process is to discover all of the possible reduced terms, so that we can find the smallest set of terms that covers the function in a later step.

The process continues for the remaining groups. Any term that is not covered after all consensus groupings are made is marked with an asterisk to indicate that it is a prime implicant. After the first reduction is made for this example, all of the minterms shown in Figure A-83a are covered so there are no prime implicants at this point.

Now that the first reduction is made, we can start on the next reduction. In order for two reduced terms to be combined, they must again differ in exactly one variable. The underscores must line up, and only one of the remaining variables can differ. The first entry shown in Figure A-83b has an underscore in the rightmost field that does not coincide with any term in the next group, so an asterisk is placed next to it indicating that it can be reduced no further and is therefore a prime implicant. We continue by moving on to the second and third groups of Figure A-83b. Terms 00_1 and 01_1 combine to form the reduced term 0_ _1 in the table shown in Figure A-83c. The process continues until the second reduction is completed, which is shown in Figure A-83c.

In constructing the reduced table shown in Figure A-83c, the prime implicants from the previously constructed table (Figure A-83b) are not included. The process continues for additional reductions until only prime implicants remain. For this example, the process stops after the second reduction when the three terms become prime implicants, as shown in Figure A-83c.

Taken as a whole, the prime implicants form a set that completely covers the function, although not necessarily minimally. In order to obtain a minimal covering set, a **table of choice** is constructed as shown in Figure A-84. Each prime implicant has a row in the table of choice. The columns represent minterms in the original function that must be covered. Don't care conditions do not need to be covered, and are not listed.

A check is placed in each box that corresponds to a prime implicant that covers a minterm. For example, prime implicant 000_ covers minterm 0001, so a check is placed in the corresponding box. Some prime implicants cover several minterms, as for 0_ _1, which covers four minterms. After all boxes are considered, columns that contain a single check are identified. A single check in a column means that only one prime implicant covers the minterm, and the corresponding prime implicant that covers the minterm is marked with an asterisk to indicate that it is **essential**.

Essential prime implicants cannot be eliminated and must be included in the reduced equation for the function. For this example, prime implicants 011_, 101_, and _1_1 are essential. An essential prime implicant may cover more than one minterm, and so a

Prime Implicants	Minterms						
	0001	0011	0101	0110	0111	1010	1101
0 0 0 _	√						
*0 1 1 _				√	√		
*1 0 1 _						√	
0 _ _ 1	√	√	√		√		
_ _ 1 1		√			√		
* _ 1 _ 1			√		√		√

Figure A-84
Table of choice.

Eligible Set		Minterms	
		0001	0011
X	000_	√	
Y	0__1	√	√
Z	__11		√

Set 1	Set 2
0 0 0 _	0 _ _ 1
_ _ 1 1	

Figure A-85
Reduced table of choice.

reduced table of choice is created in which the essential prime implicants and the minterms they cover are removed, as shown in Figure A-85. The reduced table of choice may also have essential prime implicants, in which case a second reduced table of choice is created, and the process continues until the final reduced table of choice has only nonessential prime implicants.

The prime implicants that remain in the reduced table of choice form the **eligible set**, from which a minimal subset is obtained that covers the remaining minterms. As shown in Figure A-85, there are two sets of prime implicants that cover the two remaining minterms. Since Set 2 has the fewest terms, we choose that set and obtain a minimized equation for F that is made up of essential prime implicants and the eligible prime implicants in Set 2:

$$F = \bar{A}BC + A\bar{B}C + BD + \bar{A}D \tag{A.24}$$

Instead of using visual inspection to obtain a covering set from the eligible set, the process can be carried out algorithmically. The process starts by assigning a variable to each of the prime implicants in the eligible set, as shown in Figure A-85. A logical expression is written for each column in the reduced table of choice as shown below:

Column	Logical Sums
0001	$(X + Y)$
0011	$(Y + Z)$

In order to find a set that completely covers the function, prime implicants are grouped so that there is at least one check in each column. This means that the following relation must hold, in which G represents the terms in the reduced table of choice:

$$G = (X + Y)(Y + Z)$$

Applying the properties of Boolean algebra yields:

$$G = (X + Y)(Y + Z) = XY + XZ + Y + YZ = XZ + Y$$

Each of the product terms in this equation represents a set of prime implicants that covers the terms in the reduced table of choice. The smallest product term (Y) represents the smallest set of prime implicants (0_ _1) that covers the remaining terms. The same final equation is produced as before:

$$F = \bar{A}BC + A\bar{B}C + BD + \bar{A}D \tag{A.25}$$

Reduction of Multiple Functions

The tabular reduction method reduces a single Boolean function. When there is more than one function that use the same variables, then it may be possible to share terms, resulting in a smaller collective size of the equations. The method described here forms an intersection among all possible combinations of shared terms, and then selects the smallest set that covers all of the functions.

As an example, consider the truth table shown in Figure A-86, which represents three functions in three variables. The notation m_i denotes minterms according to the indexing shown in the table.

The canonical (unreduced) form of the Boolean equations is:

$$F_0(A,B,C) = m_0 + m_3 + m_7 \tag{A.26}$$

$$F_1(A,B,C) = m_1 + m_3 + m_4 + m_6 + m_7 \tag{A.27}$$

$$F_2(A,B,C) = m_2 + m_3 + m_6 + m_7 \tag{A.28}$$

An intersection is made for every combination of functions:

$$F_{0,1}(A,B,C) = m_3 + m_7 \tag{A.29}$$

$$F_{0,2}(A,B,C) = m_3 + m_7 \tag{A.30}$$

$$F_{1,2}(A,B,C) = m_3 + m_6 + m_7 \tag{A.31}$$

$$F_{0,1,2}(A,B,C) = m_3 + m_7 \tag{A.32}$$

Using the tabular reduction method described in the previous section, the following prime implicants are obtained:

Minterm	A	B	C	F_0	F_1	F_2
m_0	0	0	0	1	0	0
m_1	0	0	1	0	1	0
m_2	0	1	0	0	0	1
m_3	0	1	1	1	1	1
m_4	1	0	0	0	1	0
m_5	1	0	1	0	0	0
m_6	1	1	0	0	1	1
m_7	1	1	1	1	1	1

Figure A-86
A truth table for three functions in three variables.

Function	Prime implicant
F_0	000, _11
F_1	0_1, 1_0, _11, 11_
F_2	_1_
$F_{0,1}$	_11
$F_{0,2}$	_11
$F_{1,2}$	_11, 11_
$F_{0,1,2}$	_11

The list of prime implicants is reduced by eliminating those prime implicants in functions that are covered by higher-order functions. For example, _11 appears in $F_{0,1,2}$, and thus does not need to be included in the remaining functions. Similarly, 11_ appears in $F_{1,2}$ and does not need to appear in F_1 or in F_2 (for this case, it does not appear as a prime implicant in F_2 anyway). Continuing in this manner, a reduced set of prime implicants is obtained:

Function	Prime implicant
F_0	000
F_1	0_1, 1_0
F_2	_1_
$F_{0,1}$	none
$F_{0,2}$	none
$F_{1,2}$	11_
$F_{0,1,2}$	_11

A multiple output table of choice is then constructed as shown in Figure A-87. The rows correspond to the prime implicants, and the columns correspond to the minterms that must be covered for each function. Portions of rows are blocked out where prime implicants

Prime Implicants / Min-terms	$F_0(A,B,C)$			$F_1(A,B,C)$					$F_2(A,B,C)$			
	m_0	m_3	m_7	m_1	m_3	m_4	m_6	m_7	m_2	m_3	m_6	m_7
F_0 *000	√											
F_1 *0_1				√	√							
F_1 *1_0						√	√					
F_2 *_1_									√	√	√	√
$F_{1,2}$ 11_							√	√			√	√
$F_{0,1,2}$ *_11		√	√		√			√		√		√

Figure A-87
A multiple output table of choice.

from one function cannot be used to cover another. For example, prime implicant 000 was obtained from function F_0 and therefore cannot be used to cover a minterm in F_1 or F_2, and so these regions are blocked out. If, in fact, a prime implicant in F_0 can be used to cover a minterm in one of the remaining functions, then it will appear in a higher-order function such as $F_{0,1}$ or $F_{0,1,2}$.

The minimal form for the output equations is obtained in a manner similar to the tabular reduction process. We start by finding all of the essential prime implicants. For example, minterm m_0 in function F_0 is covered only by prime implicant 000, and thus 000 is essential. The row containing 000 is then removed from the table and all columns that contain a check mark in the row are also deleted. The process continues until either all functions are covered or only nonessential prime implicants remain, in which case the smallest set of nonessential prime implicants needed to cover the remaining functions is obtained using the method described in the previous section.

The essential prime implicants are marked with asterisks in Figure A-87. For this case, only one nonessential prime implicant (11_) remains, but since all minterms are covered by the essential prime implicants, there is no need to construct a reduced table. The corresponding reduced equations are:

$$F_0(A,B,C) = \overline{A}\,\overline{B}\,\overline{C} + BC \tag{A.33}$$

$$F_1(A,B,C) = \overline{A}C + A\overline{C} + BC \tag{A.34}$$

$$F_2(A,B,C) = B \tag{A.35}$$

A.17.4 Logic Reduction: Effect on Speed and Performance

Up to this point, we have largely ignored physical characteristics that affect performance and have focused entirely on organizational issues such as circuit depth and gate count. In this section, we explore a few practical considerations of digital logic.

Switching speed: The propagation delay (latency) between the inputs and output of a logic gate is a continuous effect, even though earlier we considered propagation delay to be negligible. A change at an input to a logic gate is also a continuous effect. In Figure A-88, an input to a NOT gate has a finite transition time, which is measured as the time between the 10% and 90% points on the waveform. This is referred to as the **rise time** for a rising signal and the **fall time** for a falling signal.

The propagation delay is the time between the 50% transitions on the input and output waveforms. The propagation delay is influenced by a number of parameters, and power is one parameter over which we have a good deal of control. As power consumption increases, propagation delay decreases, up to a limit. A rule of thumb is that the product of power consumption and the propagation delay for a logic gate stays roughly the same. Although we generally want fast logic, we do not want to operate with a high power dissipation because the consumed power manifests itself as heat that must be removed to maintain a safe and reliable operating condition.

In the CMOS logic family, power dissipation scales with speed. At a switching rate of 1 MHz, the power dissipation of a CMOS gate is about 1 mW. At this rate of power dissi-

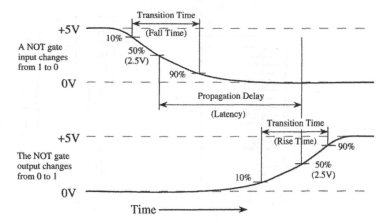

Figure A-88
Propagation delay for a NOT gate. (Source: adapted from [Hamacher *et al.*, 2001].)

pation, 10,000 CMOS logic gates dissipate 10,000 gates × 1 mW/gate = 10 W, which is at the limit of heat removal for a single integrated circuit using conventional approaches (for a 1 cm^2 chip).

Single CMOS chips can have on the order of 10^8 logic gates, however, and operate at rates in the GHz range. This gate count and speed are achieved partially by increasing the chip size, although this accounts for little more than a factor of 10. Voltages have dropped as well as transistor sizes, both of which have resulted in lower powers. However, the key to achieving such a high component count and switching speed while managing power dissipation is to switch only a fraction of the logic gates at any time, which luckily is the most typical operating mode for an integrated circuit.

Circuit depth: The latency between the inputs and outputs of a circuit is governed by the number of logic gates on the longest path from any input to any output. This is known as **circuit depth**. In general, a circuit with a small circuit depth operates more quickly than a circuit with a large circuit depth. There are a number of ways to reduce circuit depth that involve increasing the complexity of some other parameter. We look at one way of making this trade-off here.

Earlier in this appendix, we used a MUX to implement the majority function. Now consider using the four-variable MUX shown in Figure A-89 to implement Equation A.36. The equation is in two-level form, because only two levels of logic are used in its representation: six AND terms that are ORed together. A single MUX can implement this function, as shown in the left side of Figure A-89. The corresponding circuit depth is two (that is, the gate-level configuration of the inside of the MUX has two gate delays). If we factor out A and B then we obtain Equation A.37 and the corresponding four-level circuit shown in the right side of Figure A-89:

$$F(A, B, C, D) = \overline{A}\overline{B}\overline{C}\overline{D} + \overline{A}\overline{B}CD + \overline{A}B\overline{C}D + \overline{A}BC\overline{D} + A\overline{B}\overline{C}D + ABCD \qquad (A.36)$$

$$F(A, B, C, D) = \overline{A}\overline{B}(\overline{C}\overline{D} + CD) + \overline{A}B(\overline{C}D + C\overline{D}) + A\overline{B}(\overline{C}D) + AB(CD) \qquad (A.37)$$

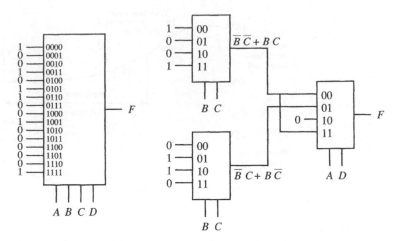

Figure A-89
A four-variable function implemented with a 16-to-1 MUX (left) and with 4-to-1 MUXes (right).

The gate input count of a 4-to-1 MUX is 18 as taken from Figure A-25 (including inverters), so the gate input count of the decomposed MUX circuit is $3 \times 18 = 54$. A single 16-to-1 MUX has a gate input count of 100. The 4-to-1 MUX implementation has a circuit depth of four (not including inverters) while the 16-to-1 MUX implementation has a circuit depth of two. We have thus reduced the overall circuit complexity at the expense of an increase in the circuit depth.

Although there are techniques that aid the circuit designer in discovering trade-offs between circuit complexity and circuit depth, the development of algorithms that cover the space of possible alternatives in reasonable time is only a partially solved problem.

Fan-in vs. circuit depth: Suppose that we need a four-input OR gate as used in Figure A-25, but only two-input OR gates are available. What should we do? This is a common practical problem that is encountered in a variety of design situations. The associative property of Boolean algebra can be used to decompose the OR gate that has a fan-in of four into a configuration of OR gates that each have a fan-in of two as shown in Figure A-90. In general, the decomposition of the four-input OR gate should be performed in balanced-tree fashion in order to reduce circuit depth. A **degenerate** tree can also be used as shown in Figure A-90, which produces a functionally equivalent circuit with the same number of logic gates as the balanced tree but results in a maximum circuit depth.

Although it is important to reduce circuit depth in order to decrease the latency between the inputs and the outputs, one reason for preferring the degenerate tree to the balanced tree is that the degenerate tree has a minimum cross-sectional diameter at each stage, which makes it easy to split the tree into pieces that are spread over a number of separate circuits. This mirrors a practical situation encountered in packaging digital circuits. The depth of the balanced tree is $\lceil \log_F(N) \rceil$ logic gates for an N-input gate mapped to logic gates with a fan-in of F, and the depth of the degenerate tree is $\left\lceil \dfrac{N-1}{F-1} \right\rceil$ logic gates for an N-input gate mapped to logic gates with a fan-in of F.

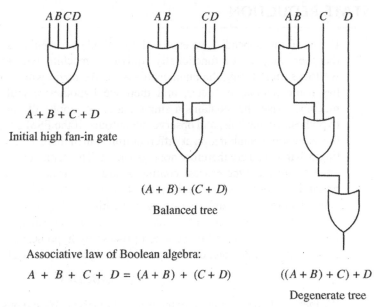

$A + B + C + D$

Initial high fan-in gate

$(A + B) + (C + D)$

Balanced tree

Associative law of Boolean algebra:

$$A + B + C + D = (A + B) + (C + D)$$

$((A + B) + C) + D$

Degenerate tree

Figure A-90
A logic gate with a fan-in of four is decomposed into logically equivalent configurations of logic gates with fan-ins of two.

In theory, any binary function can be realized in two levels of logic gates given an arbitrarily large stage of AND gates followed by an arbitrarily large stage of OR gates, both having arbitrarily large fan-in and fan-out. For example, an entire computer program can be compiled in just two gate levels if it is presented in parallel to a Boolean circuit that has an AND stage followed by an OR stage that is designed to implement this function. Such a circuit would be prohibitively large, however, since every possible combination of inputs must be considered.

Fan-outs larger than about 10 are too costly to implement in many logic families due to the sacrifice in performance, as it is similar to filling 10 or more leaky buckets from a single faucet. Boolean algebra for two-level expressions is still used to describe complex digital circuits with high fan-outs, however, and then the two-level Boolean expressions are transformed into multilevel expressions that conform to the fan-in and fan-out limitations of the technology. Optimal fan-in and fan-out are argued to be $e \cong 2.7$ (Mead and Conway, 1980) in terms of transistor stepping size for bringing a signal from an integrated circuit to a pin of the package. The derivation of that result is based on capacitance of bonding pads, signal rise times, and other considerations. The result cannot be applied to all aspects of computing since it does not take into account overall performance, which may create local variations that violate the e rule dramatically. Electronic digital circuits typically use fan-ins and fan-outs between 2 and 10.

■ A.18 STATE REDUCTION

Earlier in this appendix, we explored a method of designing an FSM without considering that there may exist a functionally equivalent machine with fewer states. In this section, we focus on reducing the number of states. We begin with a description of an FSM that has some number of states, and then we hypothesize that a functionally equivalent machine exists that contains a single state. We apply all combinations of inputs to the hypothesized machine, and observe the outputs. If the FSM produces a different output for the same input combination at different times, then there are at least two states that are distinguishable, and are therefore not equivalent. The distinguishable states are placed in separate groups, and the process continues until no further distinctions can be made. If any remaining groups have more than one state, then those states are equivalent and a smaller, equivalent machine can be constructed in which each group is collapsed into a single state.

As an example, consider state machine M_0 described by the state table shown in Figure A-91. We begin the reduction process by hypothesizing that all five states can be reduced to a single state, obtaining partition P_0 for a new machine M_1:

$$P_0 = (ABCDE)$$

We then apply a single input to the original machine M_0 and observe the outputs. When M_0 is in state A and an input of 0 is applied, then the output is 0. When the machine is in state A and an input of 1 is applied, then the output is 1. States B and E behave similarly, but states C and D produce outputs of 1 and 0 for inputs of 0 and 1, respectively. Thus, we know that states A, B, and E can be distinguished from states C and D, and we obtain a new partition P_1:

$$P_1 = (ABE)\,(CD)$$

After a single input is applied to M_0, we know that the machine will be in either the ABE group or the CD group. We now need to observe the behavior of the machine from its new state. One way to do this is to enumerate the set of possible next states in a tree, as shown in Figure A-92. The process of constructing the tree begins by listing all of the states in the same partition. For machine M_0, the initial partition $(ABCDE)$ is shown at the root of the tree. After a 0 is applied at the input to M_0, the next state will be one of C, D, C, C, or A for an initial state of A, B, C, D, or E, respectively. This is shown as the $(CDA)(CC)$ partition in the 0 side of the tree, down one **ply** (one level) from the root. The output produced by

Input Present state	X	
	0	1
A	C/0	E/1
B	D/0	E/1
C	C/1	B/0
D	C/1	A/0
E	A/0	C/1

Figure A-91
Description of state machine M_0 to be reduced.

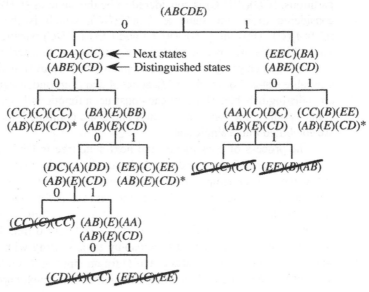

Figure A-92
A next state tree for M_0.

the (CDA) group is different from the output produced by the (CC) group, and so their corresponding initial states are distinguishable. The corresponding states that are distinguished are the groups (ABE) and (CD), which form the partition $(ABE)(CD)$ as shown.

Similarly, after a 1 is applied at the input to M_0, the next state will be one of E, E, B, A, or C for an initial state of A, B, C, D, or E, respectively. This is shown on the right side of the tree. To form the next ply, we look at the (CDA) and (CC) groups separately. When a 0 is applied at the input when M_0 is in any of states C, D, or A, then the outputs will be the same for states C and D (the output is a 1 and the next states are C and C) but will be different for state A (the output is a 0 and the next state is C). This is shown as $(CC)(C)$ on the 0,0 path from the root.

Similarly, when a 0 is applied at the input when M_0 is in either of states C or D, then the outputs are the same, and the set of target states is $(CC)(C)(CC)$ on the 0,0 path from the root as shown, which corresponds to a partition on the initial states of $(AB)(E)(CD)$ if we trace back to the root. Thus, at this point, A is indistinguishable from B, and C is indistinguishable from D, but each parenthesized group can be distinguished from each other if we apply the sequence 0,0 to M_0 and observe the outputs, regardless of the initial state.

Continuing in this manner, the tree is expanded until no finer partitions can be created. For example, when a partition contains a group of states that can no longer be distinguished, as for $(CC)(C)(CC)$, then an asterisk is placed adjacent to the partition for the corresponding initial states and the tree is not expanded further from that point. The tree shown in Figure A-92 is expanded beyond this point only to illustrate various situations that can arise.

If a partition is created that is visited elsewhere in the tree, then a slash is drawn through it and the tree is not expanded from that point. For purposes of comparing similar partitions, $(CD)(A)(CC)$ is considered to be the same as $(CD)(A)(C)$, and $(AA)(C)(DC)$ is considered to be the same as $(A)(C)(DC)$, which is the same as $(DC)(A)(C)$ and $(CD)(A)(C)$. Thus the $(CD)(A)(CC)$ and $(AA)(C)(DC)$ partitions are considered to be the same. After the tree is constructed, the partitions with asterisks expose the indistinguishable states. Each group of parentheses in an asterisk partition identifies a group of indistinguishable states. For machine M_0, states A and B are indistinguishable and states C and D are indistinguishable. Thus, we can construct a functionally equivalent machine to M_0 that contains only three states, in which A and B are combined into a single state and C and D are combined into a single state.

The process of constructing the next state tree is laborious because of its potential size, but we use it here in order to understand a simpler method. Rather than construct the entire tree, we can simply observe that once we have the first partition P_1, the next partition can be constructed by looking at the next states for each group and noting that if two states within a group have next states that are in different groups, then they are distinguishable since the resulting outputs will eventually differ. This can be shown by constructing the corresponding distinguishing tree. Starting with P_1 for M_0, we observe that states A and B have next states C and D for an input of 0 and have a next state of E for an input of 1, and so A and B are grouped together in the next partition. State E, however, has next states of A and C for inputs of 0 and 1, respectively, which differ from the next states for A and B, and thus state E is distinguishable from states A and B. Continuing for the (CD) group of P_1, the next partition is obtained as shown below:

$$P_2 = (AB)\,(CD)\,(E)$$

After applying the method for another iteration, the partition repeats, which is a condition for stopping the process:

$$P_3 = (AB)\,(CD)\,(E)\ \checkmark$$

No further distinctions can be made at this point, and the resulting machine M_1 has three states in its reduced form. If we make the assignment $A' = AB$, $B' = CD$, and $C' = E$, in which the prime symbols mark the states for machine M_1, then a reduced state table can be created as shown in Figure A-93.

Additional reductions can be made in the amount of logic needed to implement the FSM with a judicious choice of assigning binary codes to states. While this is not covered here, the interested reader can find a detailed explanation of the state assignment process on the companion Web site.

Input Current state	X	
	0	1
AB: A'	$B'/0$	$C'/1$
CD: B'	$B'/1$	$A'/0$
E: C'	$A'/0$	$B'/1$

Figure A-93
A reduced state table for machine M_1.

EXAMPLE A-4 REDUCTION EXAMPLE: A SEQUENCE DETECTOR

In this section, we tie together the reduction methods described in the previous sections. The machine we would like to design outputs a 1 when exactly two of the last three inputs are 1 (this machine appeared in the first example in Section A.12). An input sequence of 011011100 produces an output sequence of 001111010. There is one serial input line, and we can assume that initially no inputs have been seen.

We start by constructing a state transition diagram, as shown in Figure A-94. There are eight possible three-bit sequences that our machine will observe: 000, 001, 010, 011, 100, 101, 110, and 111. State A is the initial state, in which we assume that no inputs have yet been seen. In states B and C, we have seen only one input, so we cannot yet output a 1. In states D, E, F, and G we have only seen two inputs, so we cannot yet output a 1, even though we have seen two 1s at the input when we enter state G. The machine makes all subsequent transitions among states D, E, F, and G. State D is visited when the last two inputs are 00. States E, F, and G are visited when the last two inputs are 01, 10, or 11, respectively.

The next step is to create a state table and reduce the number of states. The state table shown in Figure A-95 is taken directly from the state transition diagram. We then apply the state reduction technique by hypothesizing that all states are equivalent, and then refining our hypothesis. The process is shown below:

$$P_0 = (ABCDEFG)$$
$$P_1 = (ABCD)\,(EF)\,(G)$$
$$P_2 = (A)\,(BD)\,(C)\,(E)\,(F)\,(G)$$
$$P_3 = (A)\,(BD)\,(C)\,(E)\,(F)\,(G)\ \checkmark$$

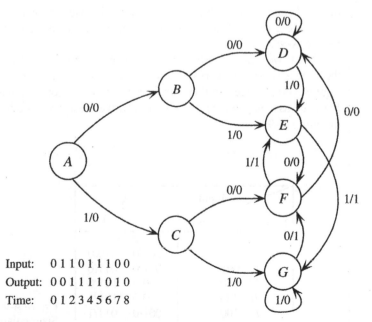

Input: 0 1 1 0 1 1 1 0 0
Output: 0 0 1 1 1 1 0 1 0
Time: 0 1 2 3 4 5 6 7 8

Figure A-94
State transition diagram for sequence detector.

Input ＼ Present state	X	
	0	1
A	B/0	C/0
B	D/0	E/0
C	F/0	G/0
D	D/0	E/0
E	F/0	G/1
F	D/0	E/1
G	F/1	G/0

Figure A-95
State table for sequence detector.

Input ＼ Present state	X	
	0	1
A: A'	B'/0	C'/0
BD: B'	B'/0	D'/0
C: C'	E'/0	F'/0
E: D'	E'/0	F'/1
F: E'	B'/0	D'/1
G: F'	E'/1	F'/0

Figure A-96
Reduced state table for sequence detector.

States B and D along the 0,0,0 path in the state transition diagram are equivalent. We create a reduced table, using primed letters to denote the new states as shown in Figure A-96.

Next, we make an arbitrary state assignment as shown in Figure A-97. We then use the state assignment to create K-maps for the next state and output functions as shown in Figure A-98. Notice that there are four don't care conditions that arise because the 110 and 111 state assignments are unused. Finally, we create the gate-level circuit, which is shown in Figure A-99.

Input ＼ Present state	X	
	0	1
$S_2 S_1 S_0$	$S_2 S_1 S_0 Z$	$S_2 S_1 S_0 Z$
A': 000	001/0	010/0
B': 001	001/0	011/0
C': 010	100/0	101/0
D': 011	100/0	101/1
E': 100	001/0	011/1
F': 101	100/1	101/0

Figure A-97
State assignment for sequence detector.

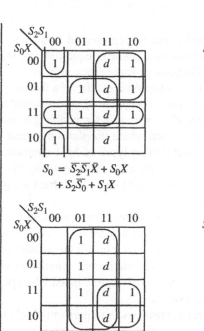

$$S_0 = \overline{S_2}\,\overline{S_1}\,\overline{X} + S_0 X$$
$$+ \, S_2 \overline{S_0} + S_1 X$$

$$S_1 = \overline{S_2}\,\overline{S_1}\,X + S_2 \overline{S_0}\,X$$

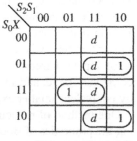

$$S_2 = S_2 S_0 + S_1$$

$$Z = S_2 \overline{S_0}\,X + S_1 S_0 X + S_2 S_0 \overline{X}$$

Figure A-98
K-map reduction of next
state and output functions
for sequence detector.

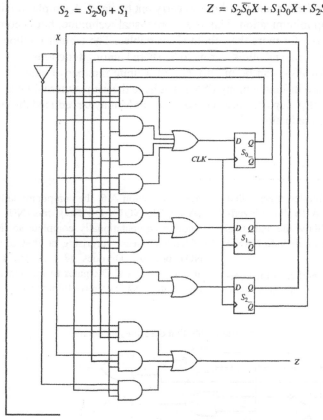

Figure A-99
Gate-level implementation
of sequence detector.

Summary

In theory, any Boolean function can be represented as a truth table, which can then be transformed into a two-level Boolean equation and implemented with logic gates. In practice, collections of logic gates may be grouped together to form MSI components, which contain on the order of a few to a few dozen logic gates. MUXes and PLAs are two types of MSI components that are used for implementing functions. Decoders are used for enabling a single output line based on the bit pattern at the input, which translates a logical encoding into a spatial location. There are several other types of MSI components as well. We find ourselves using MSI components in abstracting away the gate-level complexity of a digital circuit. LSI and VLSI circuits abstract away the underlying circuit complexity at higher levels still.

A finite state machine (FSM) differs from a combinational logic unit (CLU) in that the outputs of a CLU at any time are strictly a function of the inputs at that time whereas the outputs of an FSM are a function of its past history of inputs. Circuits that are generated from unreduced expressions may become very large, and so the expressions are reduced when possible into logically equivalent smaller expressions.

One method of reducing expressions is to perform algebraic manipulation using the properties of Boolean algebra. This approach is powerful but involves trial and error, and is tedious to carry out by hand. A simpler method is to apply K-map minimization. This is a more visual technique, but becomes difficult to carry out for more than about six variables. The tabular method lends itself to automation, and allows terms to be shared among functions.

An FSM can be in only one of a finite number of states at any time, but there are infinitely many FSMs that have the same external behavior. The number of flip-flops that are needed for an FSM may be reduced through the process of state reduction

Problems

A.1 Figure A-15 shows an OR gate implemented with a NAND gate and inverters, and Figure A-16 shows inverters implemented with NAND gates. Show the logic diagram for an AND gate implemented entirely with NAND gates.

A.2 Draw logic diagrams for each member of the computationally complete set {AND, OR, NOT} using only the computationally complete set {NOR}.

A.3 In Section A.5, the computationally complete sets {AND, OR, NOT}, {NAND}, and {NOR} are identified. Another computationally complete set is {AND, OR}, which may seem surprising at first because it lacks a NOT operator. Or does it? Can you devise a way to arrange AND and OR gates to implement NOT? (Note: this requires some creative thinking.)

A.4 Given the logic circuit shown below, construct a truth table that describes its behavior.

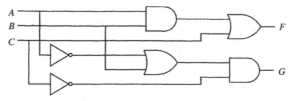

A.5 Construct a truth table for a three-input XOR gate.

A.6 Compute the gate input count of the 4-to-2 priority encoder shown in Figure A-34. Include the inverters in your count.

Design a circuit that implements function f using AND, OR, and NOT gates.

$$f(A, B, C) = \overline{A}BC + A\overline{\overline{C}}C + AB\overline{C}$$

Design a circuit that implements function g using AND, OR, and NOT gates. Do not attempt to change the form of the equation.

$$g(A, B, C, D, E) = A(BC + \overline{B}\overline{C}) + B(CD + E)$$

A.7 Are functions f and g shown below equivalent? Show how you arrive at your answer.

$$f(A, B, C) = ABC + \overline{A}B\overline{C}$$
$$g(A, B, C) = (A \oplus C)B$$

A.8 Write a Boolean equation that describes function F in the circuit shown below. Put your answer in SOP form (without parentheses).

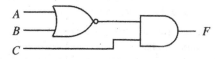

A.9 A four-bit **comparator** is a component that takes two four-bit words as inputs and produces a single bit of output. The output is a 0 if the words are identical, and is a 1 otherwise. Design a four-bit comparator with any of the logic gates you have seen in this appendix. Hint: Think of the four-bit comparator as four one-bit comparators combined in some fashion.

A.10 Redraw the circuit shown below so that the bubble matching is correct. The overbars on the variable and function names indicate active low logic.

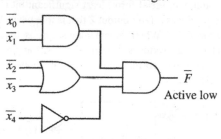
Active low

A.11 Use two 4-to-1 MUXes to implement the functions:

A	B	F_0	F_1
0	0	0	0
0	1	1	0
1	0	1	0
1	1	0	1

A.12 Use one 4-to-1 MUX to implement the majority function.

A.13 Use a 2-to-4 decoder and an OR gate to implement the XOR of two inputs A and B.

A.14 Draw a logic diagram that uses a decoder and two OR gates to implement functions F and G below. Be sure to label all lines in your diagram.

$$F(A, B, C) = \overline{A}B\overline{C} + \overline{A}\overline{B}C + A\overline{B}C + \overline{A}BC$$
$$G(A, B, C) = \overline{A}B\overline{C} + ABC$$

A.15 Design a circuit using only 2-to-1 multiplexers that implements the function of an 8-to-1 multiplexer. Show your design in the form of a logic diagram, and label all of the lines.

A.16 Since any combinational circuit can be constructed using only two-input NAND gates, the two-input NAND is called a universal logic gate. The two-input NOR is also a universal logic gate; however, AND and OR are not. Since a two-input NAND can be constructed using only 4-to-1 MUXes (it can be done with one 4-to-1 MUX), any combinational circuit can be constructed using only 4-to-1 MUXes. Consequently, the 4-to-1 MUX is also a universal device. Show that the 1-to-2 DEMUX is a universal device by constructing a two-input NAND using only 1-to-2 DEMUXes. Draw a logic diagram. Hint: Compose the NAND from an AND and an inverter each made from 1-to-2 DEMUXes.

A.17 A seven-segment display, such as you might find in a calculator, is shown below. The seven segments are labeled a through g. Design a circuit that takes as input a four-bit binary number and produces as output the control signal for just the b segment (not the letter 'b', which has the 1011 code). A 0 at the output turns the segment off, and a 1 turns the segment on. Show the truth table and an implementation using a single MUX and no other logic components. Label all of the lines of the MUX.

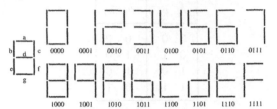

A.18 Implement function F shown in the truth table below using the 16-to-1 MUX shown. Label all of the lines, including the unmarked control line.

A	B	C	F
0	0	0	0
0	0	1	1
0	1	0	1
0	1	1	0
1	0	0	0
1	0	1	0
1	1	0	0
1	1	1	1

```
0000
0001
0010
0011
0100
0101
0110
0111         F
1000
1001
1010
1011
1100
1101
1110
1111

  A B C
```

A.19 A **strict encoder** takes 2^N binary inputs, of which exactly one input is 1 at any time and the remaining inputs are 0, and produces an N-bit coded binary output that indicates which of the N inputs is high. For this problem, create a truth table for a 4-to-2 strict encoder in which there are four inputs: A, B, C, and D, and two outputs: X and Y. A and X are the most significant bits.

A.20 Consider a combinational logic circuit with three inputs a, b, and c, and six outputs u, v, w, x, y, and z. The input is an unsigned number between 0 and 7, and the output is the square of the input. The most significant bit of the input is a, and the most significant bit of the output is u. Create a truth table for the six functions.

A.21 Consider the function $f(a, b, c, d)$ that takes on the value 1 if and only if the number of 1s in b and c is greater than or equal to the number of 1s in a and d.
(a) Write the truth table for function f.
(b) Use an 8-to-1 multiplexer to implement function f.

A.22 Create a truth table for a single digit ternary (base-3) comparator. The ternary inputs are A and B which are each a single ternary digit wide. The output Z is 0 for $A < B$, 1 for $A = B$, and 2 for $A > B$. Using this truth table as a guide, rewrite the truth table in binary using the assignment $(0)_3 \rightarrow (00)_2$, $(1)_3 \rightarrow (01)_2$, and $(2)_3 \rightarrow (10)_2$.

A.23 Prove the consensus theorem for three variables using perfect induction.

A.24 Use the properties of Boolean algebra to prove DeMorgan's theorem algebraically.

A.25 Can an S-R flip-flop be constructed with two cross-coupled XOR gates? Explain your answer.

A.26 Modify the state transition diagram in the vending machine example above to provide more realistic behavior (that is, it returns *all* excess money) when a quarter is inserted in state D.

A.27 Create a state transition diagram for an FSM that sorts two binary words A and B, most significant bit first, onto two binary outputs GE and LT. If A is greater than or equal to B, then A appears on the GE line and B appears on the LT line. If B is greater than A, then B appears on the GE line and A appears on the LT line.

A.28 Design a circuit that produces a 1 at the Z output when the input X changes from 0 to 1 or from 1 to 0, and produces a zero at all other times. For the initial state, assume a 0 was last seen at the input. For example, if the input sequence is 00110 (from left to right), then the output sequence is 00101. Show the state transition diagram, the state table, state assignment, and the final circuit using MUXes.

A.29 Design an FSM that outputs a 1 when the last three inputs are 011 or 110. Just show the state table. Do not draw a circuit.

A.30 Design a finite state machine that takes two binary words X and Y in serial form, least significant bit (LSB) first, and produces a 1-bit output Z that is true when $X > Y$ and is 0 for $X \le Y$. When the machine starts, assume that $X = Y$. That is, Z produces 0s until $X > Y$. A sample input sequence and the corresponding output sequence are shown below.

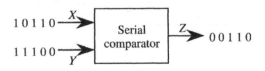

A.31 Create a state transition diagram for an FSM that sorts two ternary inputs, most significant digit first, onto two ternary outputs GE and LT. If A is greater than or equal to B, then A appears on the GE line and B appears on the LT line; otherwise B appears on the GE line and A appears on the LT line. A sample input/output sequence is shown below. Use the ternary symbols 0, 1, and 2 when you label the arcs.

Input A: 0 2 1 1 2 0 1 2
Input B: 0 2 1 2 0 2 1 1
Output GE: 0 2 1 2 0 2 1 1
Output LT: 0 2 1 1 2 0 1 2
Time: 0 1 2 3 4 5 6 7

A.32 Create a state transition diagram for a machine that computes an even parity bit z for its two-bit input x_1x_0. The machine outputs a 0 when all of the previous two-bit inputs collectively have an even number of 1s, and outputs a 1 otherwise. For the initial state, assume that the machine starts with even parity.

A.33 Given the state transition diagram shown below,
(a) Create a state table.
(b) Design a circuit for the state machine described by your state table using D flip-flop(s), a single decoder, and OR gates. For the state assignment, use the bit pattern that corresponds to the position of each letter in the alphabet, starting from 0. For example, A is at position 0, so the state assignment is 000; B is at position 1, so the state assignment is 001, and so on.

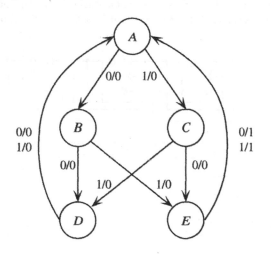

A.34 Redraw the circuit shown in Figure A-18 using AND and OR gates that have fan-in = 2.

A.35 Suppose that you need to implement an N-input AND gate using only three-input AND gates. What is the minimum number of gate delays required to implement the N-input AND gate? A single AND gate has a gate delay of 1; two cascaded AND gates have a combined gate delay of 2, etc.

A.36 Given the following functions, construct K-maps and find minimal sum-of-products expressions for f and g.

$f(A,B,C,D) = 1$ when two or more inputs are 1, otherwise $f(A,B,C,D) = 0$.

$g(A,B,C,D) = 1$ when the number of inputs that are 1 is even (including the case when no inputs are 1), otherwise

$$g(A,B,C,D) = \overline{f(A, B, C, D)}.$$

A.37 Use K-maps to simplify function f and its don't care condition below. Perform the reduction for (a) the sum-of-products form and (b) the product-of-sums form.

$$f(A, B, C, D) = \sum(2, 8, 10, 11) + \sum_{d}(0, 9)$$

A.38 Given a logic circuit, is it possible to generate a truth table that contains don't cares? Explain your answer.

A.39 The following K-map is formed incorrectly. Show the reduced equation that is produced by the incorrect map, and then form the K-map correctly and derive the reduced equation from the correct map. Note that both K-maps will produce functionally correct equations, but only the properly formed K-map will produce a minimized two-level equation.

D \ ABC	000	001	011	010	110	111	101	100
0	1			1	1			1
1	1			1	1			1

A.40 Use the tabular method to reduce the function:

$$f(A, B, C, D) =$$
$$\sum(3, 5, 7, 10, 13, 15) + \sum_{d}(2, 6)$$

A.41 Use the tabular method to reduce the following multiple-output truth table:

Minterm	A	B	C	D	F_0	F_1	F_2
m_0	0	0	0	0	0	0	1
m_1	0	0	0	1	0	0	0
m_2	0	0	1	0	0	0	0
m_3	0	0	1	1	1	0	0
m_4	0	1	0	0	0	0	1
m_5	0	1	0	1	1	1	0
m_6	0	1	1	0	0	0	0
m_7	0	1	1	1	1	1	0
m_8	1	0	0	0	0	0	0
m_9	1	0	0	1	0	0	0
m_{10}	1	0	1	0	0	1	1
m_{11}	1	0	1	1	0	0	0
m_{12}	1	1	0	0	0	0	0
m_{13}	1	1	0	1	1	1	0
m_{14}	1	1	1	0	1	1	1
m_{15}	1	1	1	1	1	1	1

A.42 Reduce the equation for F shown below to its minimal two-level form, and implement the function using a three-input, one-output PLA.

$$F(A, B, C) = ABC + \bar{A}BC + A\bar{B}\bar{C} + \bar{A}\bar{B}C$$

A.43 Use function decomposition to implement function F below with two 4-to-1 MUXes. Parenthesize the equation so that C and D are in the innermost level as in Equation A.22. Make sure that every input to each MUX is assigned to a value (0 or 1), to a variable, or to a function.

$$F(A, B, C, D) = ABCD + AB\bar{C}D + ABC\bar{D} + \bar{A}B$$

A.44 Reduce the following state table:

Input	X	
Present state	0	1
A	D/0	G/1
B	C/0	G/0
C	A/0	D/1
D	B/0	C/1
E	A/1	E/0
F	C/1	F/0
G	E/1	G/1

A.45 Reduce the following state table:

Input	XY			
Present state	00	01	10	11
A	A/0	B/0	C/0	D/0
B	A/0	B/1	D/0	D/1
C	E/1	B/0	B/0	E/1
D	A/0	D/1	D/0	B/1
E	C/1	D/0	D/0	E/1

A.46 The following ternary state table may or may not reduce. Show the reduction process (the partitions) and the reduced state table.

Input	x		
Present state	0	1	2
A	B/0	E/2	G/1
B	D/2	A/1	D/0
C	D/2	G/1	B/0
D	B/2	F/1	C/0
E	A/0	E/2	C/1
F	C/0	E/2	F/1
G	D/0	E/2	A/1

A.47 The following circuit has three master-slave J-K flip-flops. There is a single input CLK and three outputs Q_2, Q_1, and Q_0 that initially have the value 0. Complete the timing diagram by showing the values for Q_2, Q_1, and Q_0. Assume that there are no delays through the flip-flops.

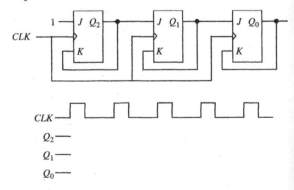

A.48 In the following reduced state table, the state assignments have already been made. Design the machine using D flip-flops, AND and OR gates. Use K-maps to reduce the expressions for the next state and output functions. Be careful to construct the K-maps correctly, since there are only three rows in the state table.

Present state \ Input	X	
	0	1
YZ		
A: 00	00/0	01/1
B: 01	10/1	00/1
C: 10	01/1	10/0

Further Reading

Shannon's contributions to switching algebra (Shannon, 1938; Shannon, 1949) are based on the work of (Boole, 1854), and form the basis of switching theory as we now know it. The vast number of contributions to Boolean algebra is too great to enumerate here. (Kohavi, 1978) is a good general reference for CLUs and FSMs, and provides a thorough treatment of combinational logic reduction and state reduction. A contribution by (Davidson, 1979) covers a method of decomposing NAND-based circuits, which is mostly of historical interest now because some computers were composed entirely of NAND gates.

Some texts distinguish between a flip-flop and a latch. (Tanenbaum, 1999) distinguishes between the two by defining a flip-flop as edge-triggered, whereas a latch is level-triggered. This may be the correct definition, but in practice, the terms are frequently interchanged and any distinction between the two is obscured.

(Booth, 1984) gives a good explanation of the Quine-McCluskey reduction process. (Agrawal and Cheng, 1990) cover design for testability based on state assignments.

Agrawal, V. D., and Cheng, K. T., "Finite state machine synthesis with embedded test function," *Journal of Electronic Testing: Theory and Applications*, **1**, pp. 221–228, (1990).

Boole, G., *An Investigation of the Laws of Thought*, Dover Publications, Inc., New York (1854).

Booth, T. L., *Introduction to Computer Engineering: Hardware and Software Design*, 3/e, John Wiley & Sons (1984).

Davidson, E. S., "An algorithm for NAND decomposition under network constraints," *IEEE Trans. Comp.*, **C-18** (12), 1098 (1979).

Kohavi, Z., *Switching and Finite Automata Theory*, 2/e, McGraw-Hill (1978).

Shannon, C. E., "A symbolic analysis of relay and switching circuits," *Trans. AIEE*, **57**, pp. 713–723 (1938).

Shannon, C. E., "The synthesis of two-terminal switching circuits," *Bell System Technical Journal*, **28**, pp. 59–98 (1949).

Tanenbaum, A., *Structured Computer Organization*, 4/e, Prentice Hall (1999).

USING ARCTools

B.1 INTRODUCTION

This appendix describes how to launch and use the ARCTools toolset. ARCTools is a Java application, and should run on all platforms on which Java runs, including Mac OS X, Windows, and Linux. The ARCTools toolset includes the following features:

- An integrated assembler and simulator for the ARC ISA as described in Chapter 4.
- Extensions to the ISA described in Chapter 4 with several additional actual and synthetic instructions.
- A trap mechanism.
- A simple macroprocessing facility.
- Ability to specify instruction timings.
- A multi-level cache memory simulator.
- A number of example programs showing the features of the toolset.

B.2 ACCESSING AND LAUNCHING ARCTOOLS

ARCTools is available as a zip file. Your instructor will indicate where the ARCTools zip file is located. As of this printing ARCToolsv2.x.y.zip (replace x and y with the current version numbers) is available at `ftp://ece.colorado.edu/pub/CAO/ARCTools` and at `http://iiusatech.com/~murdocca/CAO/Tools`.

Unzipping the file should produce the files shown in Figure B-1:
The README files provide the following information:

README-FIRST.txt–This file describes how to download and run ARCTools on your platform. For most modern operating systems ARCTools will launch when double-clicked.

README.txt–This file describes how to use the ARCTools program.

README-INSTRUCTIONS.txt–This file lists all of the instructions supported by ARCTools.

The examples directory contains a number of example programs.

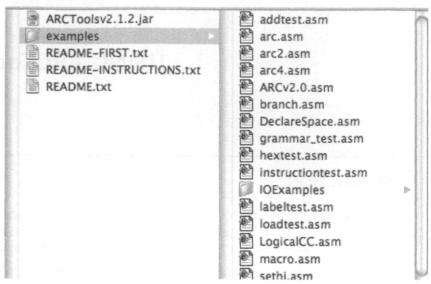

Figure B-1
Contents of the ARCTools directory after unzipping.

B.2.1 Launching ARCTools

The simulator and assembler are contained within the Java jar file ARCToolsv2.x.y.jar (replace x and y with the current version numbers). Launching the program will be dependent on the operating system being used. Windows and Mac OS X users can double-click the jar file. If your computer does not have the Java Runtime Environment (JRE) a copy can be downloaded from `http://java.sun.com/`

When first launched, the user is presented with the simulator window shown in Figure B-2. The operation of the simulator will be discussed later. First we cover the operation of the assembler. The ARC assembler is invoked by clicking on the Edit button in the simulator window.

■ B.3 THE ARC ASSEMBLER

Clicking on Edit brings up the text editor window as shown in Figure B-3. This places the user in the assembler's editor, where programs can be edited, assembled, and saved.

The buttons in the Edit window shown in Figure B-3 permit the user to assemble an ARC assembly language file, say, File.asm, and to display the results–the original asm file, and, if the file assembled successfully, the listing file, File.lst, and the "bin" file, File.bin. "Bin" is in quotation marks because the file is encoded not in binary, but for ease of reading the file, in the ASCII equivalent using the ASCII characters 0 through F.

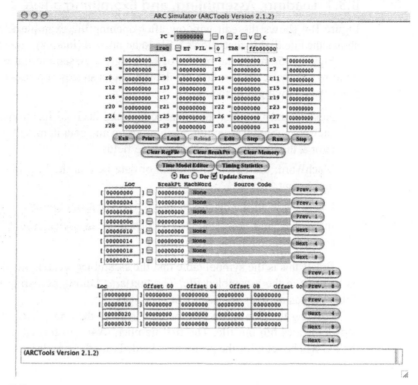

Figure B-2
The ARCTools simulator window.

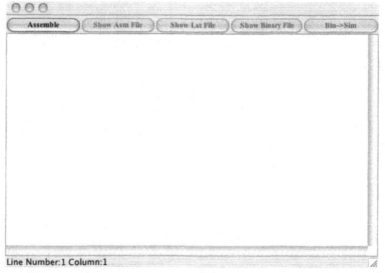

Figure B-3
The ARCTools edit window.

B.3.1 Loading, Assembling, and Examining a File

Figure B-4 shows the edit window after opening the example file arc4.asm. The figure shows the File dialog that allows a file to be opened (loaded), saved, and printed.

Figure B-5 shows the results of clicking the Assemble button. Notice that the Edit window automatically displays the .lst file after a successful assembly. The listing file displays the following information:

HexLoc and DecLoc: the hexadecimal and decimal locations of each data item and each assembled instruction. Each program and data item will be loaded into the simulator at the location specified by these fields.

MachWord: the 32-bit instruction or data item at the location specified, in hexadecimal format.

Label: the label if a label was inserted by the programmer

Instruction and comment: the reformatted assembly language instruction and any comment added by the programmer.

Below this is the symbol table that the assembler created, displaying each symbol and its location in the assembled file. The text area below the listing file displays the ARC-Tools version number and any error messages.

Pressing the Show Bin File button displays the "bin" file, as shown in Figure B-6, shows the arc4.bin bin file. The first number, 0x404 in this case, is the address at which the PC will be set after the program is loaded into the simulator.

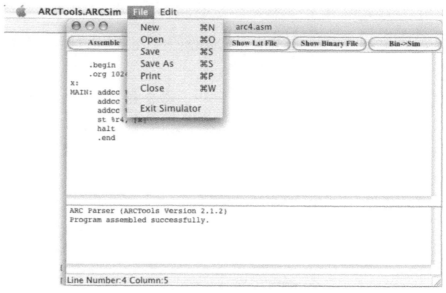

Figure B-4
The Edit window with an asm file and the file dialog

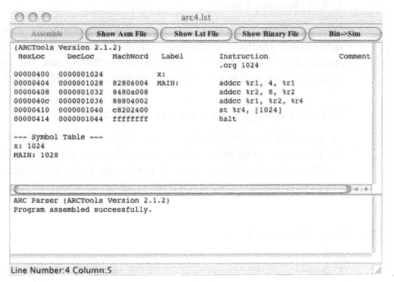

Figure B-5
The arc4 program after assembly, showing arc4.lst, the listing file

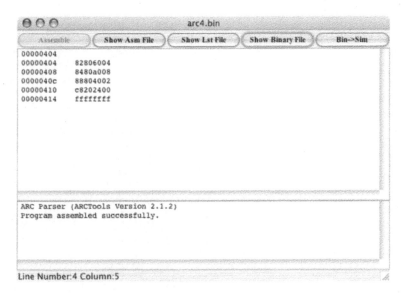

Figure B-6
The arc4 bin file, displayed after pressing the Show Binary File button

IMPORTANT NOTE: As is the case in the C programming language, the label Main: or main: is an instruction to the program loader to set the PC to that location.

B.3.2 Saving Files

When the Save or Save As file command is executed, ARCTools saves all three files with their proper extensions, arc4.asm, arc4.lst, and arc4.bin in the example, in the location specified. If Save or Save As is invoked when a .asm file has been modified and not assembled, the user is issued a warning that the .lst and .bin files are out of date.

B.3.3 Loading Files into the Simulator

As would be expected, the Bin -> Sim button loads the bin file into the simulator and sets the PC as described previously. Files need not be saved prior to this operation. Each time the Bin -> Sim button is pressed the simulator is cleared of any previous settings and values prior to loading the bin program.

■ B.4 THE ARC SIMULATOR

Figure B-7 shows the appearance of the simulator window after the Bin ->Sim button is pressed. Notice that the PC has been set to the starting address of the program, 0x404, and the flags, registers, and memory have been cleared, except for the actual program.

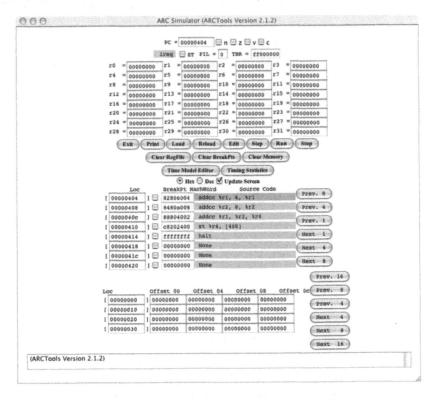

Figure B-7
The ARCTools simulator window after pressing Bin -> Sim.

All of the text fields in the simulator window are editable. The user may type in any valid value. Pressing the return key updates the field and the simulator with the new value. This allows the user to modify the contents of registers or memory. The simulator is updated after the user has entered the new value and pressed the return key.

The top of the simulator window shows the PC, and the N, Z, V, and C flag check-boxes, which may be set or cleared by the user. During a simulation the boxes will be checked or cleared according to the current values of the flags.

The ireq field will turn red when there is a pending exception request. The ET check-box enables and disables traps. PIL is the processor interrupt level, and TBR the contents of the Trap Base Register.

Below that are displayed the 32 general-purpose registers, and below them are the main simulator controls:

Exit quits the simulator application,

Print prints the simulator window. Due to a Java bug, the entire window may not be printed. If this occurs the user is advised to use a screen capture utility.

Load prompts the user for the name of an ARC .bin file to load. See the discussion following Figure B.3 for a description of the ARC file types.

Reload reloads the same file as specified with the LOAD button above. Using the RELOAD button allows the user to execute a fresh copy of the previously loaded file without having to specify a file name.

Edit as described previously, brings up the edit window.

Step executes the single instruction pointed to by the current value of the PC, and then stops. This is sometimes referred to as "single step."

Run starts execution beginning at the instruction pointed to by the current value of the PC. Execution will continue until a `halt` instruction is encountered, or until the STOP button is pressed.

Stop terminates execution of the running program. This function can be helpful when the programmer has neglected to put a `halt` instruction in the program, or when the program is stuck in a loop.

Clear Regfile, **Clear BreakPts**, and **Clear Memory** clear the contents of the register file, the breakpoints, and memory respectively.

Time Model Editor and **Timing Statistics** allow program execution times to be computed, and will be described later.

Hex and **Dec** radio buttons determine whether the values in registers and memory will be displayed in hexadecimal or decimal, respectively.

The **Update Screen** checkbox determines whether the values in the simulator window will be updated after each instruction, or only after the program has halted. Unchecking this box will speed up the execution time of the simulator considerably, since otherwise most of the simulation time is spent in updating the simulator window. This can be quite helpful in shortening the running time of long-running programs.

The middle area in the simulator window is devoted to the currently executing instructions: their locations, hexadecimal values, and the disassembled instructions themselves. The **Prev.** and **Next** 1, 4, and 8 buttons allow the programmer to step forward or backward in the program to examine values in those areas. Pressing these buttons has no effect on subsequent program execution. Since the disassembler does not have access to the symbols or labels in the original assembly language program, the actual hexadecimal values are inserted into the instructions.

When the **BreakPt** checkbox beside a given instruction is checked, execution of the program halts *prior to* executing the break-pointed instruction. This serves as a diagnostic tool by permitting the programmer to pause the program at any place during execution, and to examine the state of the running program at that point.

The next area in the simulator provides a window into memory contents. The window shows the contents of sixteen consecutive word addresses. The window location can be changed either by typing the desired location into one of the Loc windows, or by using the **Prev.** and **Next** buttons as before.

The message area at the bottom of the simulator window displays the ARCTools version number, and any messages. During I/O activities the message area also serves as a console window, or output device.

■ B.5 INSTRUCTIONS AND PSEUDO INSTRUCTIONS RECOGNIZED BY ARCTOOLS

B.5.1 Instructions–Actual, Synthetic, and Pseudo

Table B.1 shows the instructions recognized by ARCTools. The meaning and encoding of these instructions are described in Chapter 4, Section 4.2.

Table B.1   Instructions recognized by ARCTools

add	addcc	and	andcc	andn
andncc	ba	bcc	bcs	be
bg	bge	bgu	bl	ble
bleu	bn	bne	bneg	bpos
bvc	bvs	call	jmpl	ld
ldsb	ldsh	ldub	lduh	or
orcc	orn	orncc	rd	rett
sethi	sll	sra	srl	st
stb	sth	sub	subcc	ta
wr	xnor	xnorcc	xor	xorcc

Table B.2 shows the synthetic instructions that are recognized by the ARCTools assembler. Synthetic instructions are described in Section 4.4. Here we just note once more that synthetic instructions are only provided as a convenience to the programmer, and have no effect on the actual instruction set as recognized by the actual machine, or, in the case of ARCTools, the simulator.

Note to instructors: you may wish to disallow the use of synthetic instructions, at least in the early stages of the students' learning of assembly language, lest they be confused by the difference between actual and synthetic instructions.

Table B.2   Synthetic instructions recognized by ARCTools

Synthetic Instruction	Instruction Generated	Comment
not rs1, rd	xnor rs1, %r0, rd	1's complement
neg rs2, rd	sub %r0, rs2, rd	2's complement
inc rd	add rd, 1, rd	increment by 1
dec rd	sub rd, 1, rd	decrement by 1
clr rd	and rd, %r0, rd	clear a register
cmp rs1, reg_or_imm	subcc rs1, reg_or_imm, %r0	compare, set cc's
tst rs2	orcc %r0, rs2, %r0	test
mov reg_or_imm, rd	or %r0, reg_or_imm, rd	move a value

Table B.3 describes the pseudo-operations recognized by the ARCTools assembler. See Section 4.3 for more details on how pseudo-ops work. Note: the .align pseudo-op is not recognized by the ARCTools assembler. The programmer must assure that all words, including instruction words, are aligned on even-word boundaries. If the programmer is uncertain about whether this is true at some point in the program, the prudent action would be to use a .org pseudo-op to round the location counter up to the next address divisible by 4.

Table B.3   Pseudo-ops recognized by ARCTools

Pseudo-operations	Meaning
.equ value	Equate a symbol to a value
.begin	begin assembly
.end	end of assembly language text
.org value	move location counter to value
.dwb value	reserve space for value words
.macro Name [,params]*	begin definition of macro Name, with an optional, comma-separated parameter list
.if <cond>	assemble if <cond> is true (only used in macros)
.endif	end of .if construct (only used in macros)
.endmacro	end of macro definition

■ B.6 THE MACROPROCESSOR

The ARCTools macro processing facility allows the specification of macroinstructions. Macroinstructions, or macros, are similar to synthetic instructions, but they can contain multiple instructions within them, and parameters can be passed into the macro. The ARCTools macroprocessor allows macros to call other macros as long as there is no recursive loop. Macros can also contain assemble-time tests, in the form .if --- .endif. The macroprocessor does not allow access to external programming languages or scripts as some do, because of the requirement that ARCTools be platform-independent.

Below are some examples of the use of macros.

A Simple Macro - add4

Here is a very simple macro that adds 4 to its operand:

```
    .begin
    .macro add4 opnd, rslt      !Macro name is add4
    addcc opnd, 4, rslt         !Parameters are opnd and rslt
    .endmacro
Main:
    add4 %r1, %r2               !Invoke the macro
    halt
    .end
```

Another simple macro adds two memory operands and stores the result in memory:

```
.macro addMemOpnds Mem1, Mem2, Mem3
ld [Mem1], %r3
ld [Mem2], %r4
addcc %r3, %r4, %r5
st %r5, [Mem3]
.endmacro
```

It should be noted that this macro violates several principles; against RISC principles it allows arithmetic on memory operands, and worse, it destroys the contents of %r3, %r4, and %r5. In a program of any size the programmer is likely to forget this fact and wonder why the program fails to work properly. The proper thing would be for the macro to save the contents of the three registers to a stack or to dedicated memory locations, then perform the addition, and then restore the registers at the end of the macro.

There are a number of other features to the macro assembler, including macros invoking other macros. See the programs macro.asm, ARCv2.0.asm, and grammar_test.asm in the examples directory.

■ B.7 MEASURING PROGRAM PERFORMANCE

ARCTools incorporates a feature called TimeModel. TimeModel simulates the time it takes to fetch and execute instructions. It also has a cache simulator and simulates the time for memory operations to complete. TimeModel has two windows associated with it: a configuration window and a statistics window.

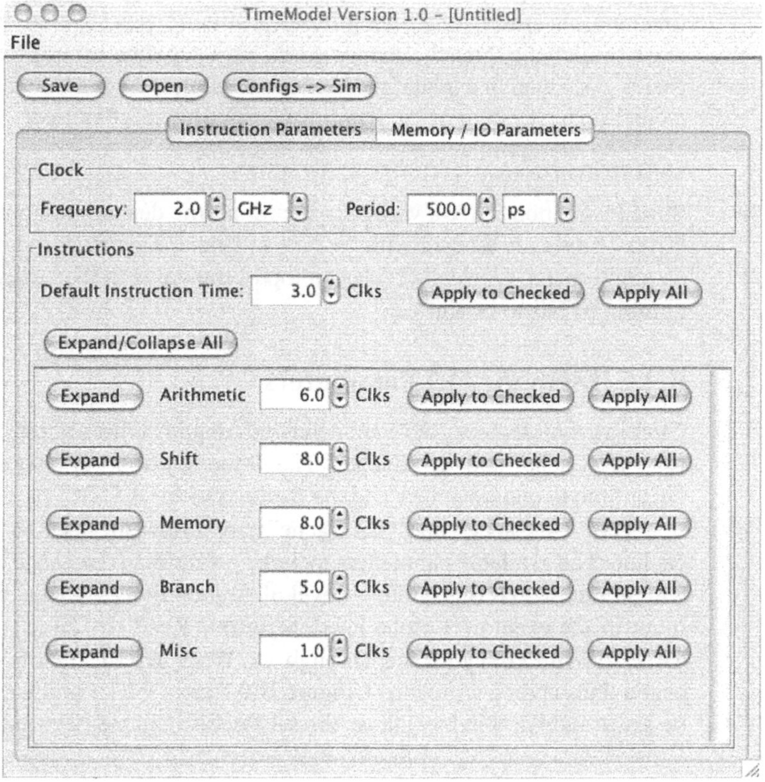

Figure B-8
Instruction Parameters Window.

B.7.1 The TimeModel configuration Editor

To launch TimeModel's configuration window press the "Time Model Editor" button. This window, shown in Figure B-8, allows the user to set the parameters supported in TimeModel. The three buttons at the top of the figure allow configurations to be saved, loaded from a file, and set to the simulator.

Setting the Clock Frequency / Period

Below the buttons in the figure are two tabs: "Instruction Parameters" and "Memory / IO Parameters." The panel under the Instruction Parameters tab allows the user to set the clock frequency or period of the ARCTools simulator. Setting the frequency displays the corresponding period, and *vice-versa*.

Configuring Instruction Timing

The Instructions panel allows the user to specify instruction timings in clock ticks. At the simplest level the user can click "Apply All" to give all instructions the same timing.

By clicking the various "Expand/Collapse" and "Apply to Checked/Apply to all" buttons one can specify one timing for all instructions, a separate timing for each instruction class, arithmetic, branch, memory, etc., or a separate timing for each instruction. This is easier to do than to explain; the user is encouraged to experiment with the buttons to reach a clear understanding of the flexibility of timing specification.

Shift Instructions

Shift Instructions have a variable execution time depending upon the shift count. The shift "Clks" boxes are labeled with "+ $(n - 1)$ Clks". This means shift instructions execute for an additional $n - 1$ clocks cycles on top of the value in the "Clks" box, where n equals the number of bits to be shifted.

B.7.2 Memory / IO Parameters

Clicking the Memory / IO Parameters tab displays three additional tabs: "Memory and I/O", "L1 Cache" and "L2 Cache." The "Memory and I/O" tab allows you to set the read/write time to main memory and the ready time for the CRT device.

The "L1 Cache" and "L2 Cache" tabs allow the user to configure the L1 and L2 caches. The available parameters include: – Enabling the cache – Cache Size – Block Size (cache line size) – Bus width – Level of Associativity – Replacement Algorithm (replacement in the event of a cache line eviction) – Read Hit Time – Read Miss Time – Write Time – Write Policy (Write Through vs. Write Back) – Write Allocation (Allocation of cache lines upon a write miss). Figure B-9 shows the L1 and L2 cache parameters that can be set. A similar window allows the setting of main memory and I/O timing.

B.7.3 TimeModel's Statistics Window

Once the clock, instruction timing, and memory access times are specified, the user can run a program and gather statistics on program performance.

Clicking on the "Timing Statistics" button in the main simulator window brings up the Statistics Window. The Statistics Window gathers statistics on the ARC program being simulated. It displays the statistics of the most recently executed instruction, a graphical view of the L1 and L2 caches, and a log history of instructions that have executed in the ARC program under test. See Figure B-10 at the end of this chapter for an example of how data is displayed in the window.

The "Execution Statistics" text area shows the statistics of the most recently executed instruction. It breaks the execution time of an instruction into its various parts (i.e. fetch time, execution time, memory operations etc.). The "L1 Statistics" and "L2 Statistics" show the statistics for the L1 and L2 caches, such as the number of read hits and misses, writes, line evictions, etc.

Below "Execution Statistics" is the "Time Trace Log." Each time an instruction is simulated, an entry is added to the Time Trace Log. Each entry is a concatenation of the statistics in "Execution Statistics," "L1 Statistics" and "L2 Statistics." Entries can only be added if the Statistics Window is open, and by default entries are not added to the Time Trace Log. You can activate logging with the "Don't log" check box. The reason for this

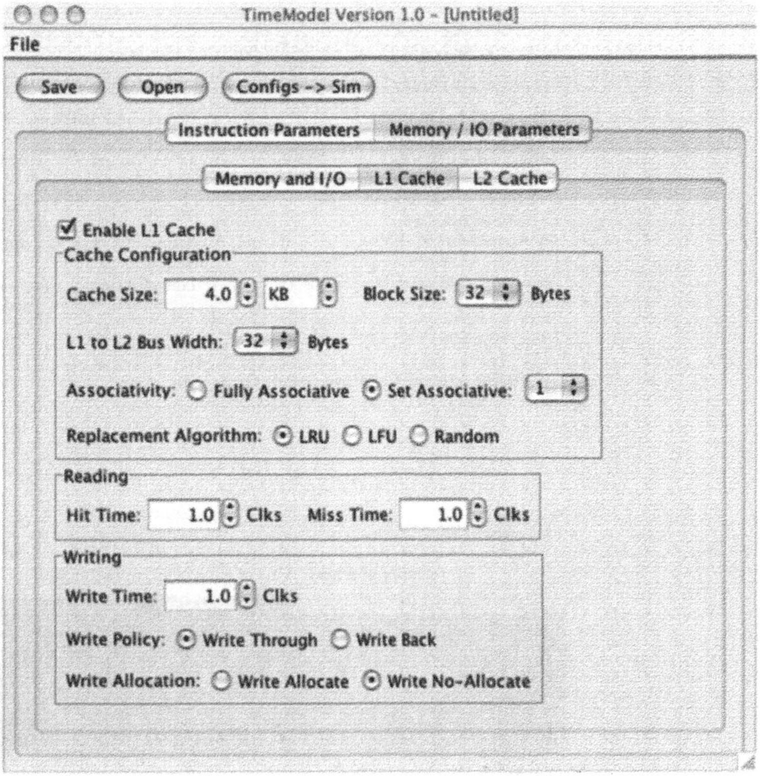

Figure B-9
Adjustable parameters in the L1 Cache window.

default is that if the log gets very large it will slow the progress of the simulator. You can also clear the log using the "Clear Log" button.

The Statistics Window has several "Update" checkboxes that enable/disable the updating of the statistics while ARCTools is actively simulating a program (when the "Run" button is pressed in the main simulator). If the simulator stops for any reason, all statistics items will update automatically to the freshest set of statistics.

B.7.4 The Cache Simulator View

Below the Time Trace Log is a view of the cache simulator. The L1 and L2 caches are represented graphically by large blue rectangles. The rectangles are divided into a number of rows (indicated by the "Number of Rows" box) and a number of columns, which are calculated by TimeModel. The rows and columns divide the larger rectangle into a number of smaller green or red rectangles (cache line rectangles); each smaller rectangle represents a cache line (or cache block). Cache line rectangles are not necessarily visible until simulation has begun. During simulation, unused cache lines remain blue, clean cache lines become green, and dirty cache lines turn red.

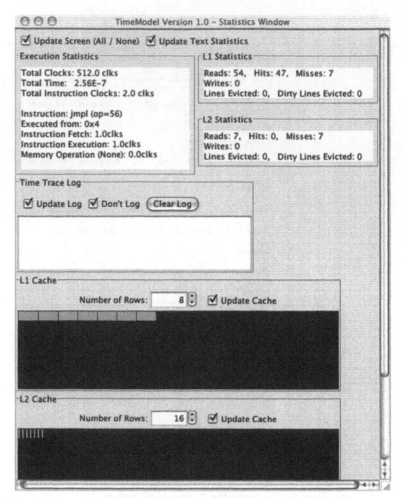

Figure B-10
The Timing Statistics window

The Cache lines in the graphic are arranged by row, and all cache lines of an associative set are considered contiguous. Therefore, the top left cache line rectangle represents the first line of the cache, and the next cache line rectangle (to the right of the first rectangle) represents the second line of the cache. For a 2-way set associative cache, the first and second cache lines are the first and second cache lines in the first associative set.

INDEX

Printed and bound by CPI Group (UK) Ltd, Croydon, CR0 4YY

20/07/2023

03238342-0001